THE DEVIL'S PANTIES

Volume
2
by Jennie Breeden

ARCHAIA STUDIOS PRESS

The Devil's Panties
Volume 2
Written & Illustrated
by Jennie Breeden

Published by
Archaia Studios Press
586 Devon Street, 3rd Floor
Kearny, NJ 07032
www.aspcomics.com

Mark Smylie & Aki Liao, *Publishers*
Joseph Illidge, *Comics Editor*
Pauline Beney, *Art Director*
Brian Petkash & Lys Fulda, *Marketing*

Write to:
editorial@aspcomics.com

The Devil's Panties Volume 2
July 2008
FIRST PRINTING
10 9 8 7 6 5 4 3 2 1

ISBN 1-932386-36-X
ISBN 13: 978-1-932386-36-3

Printed in Hong Kong.

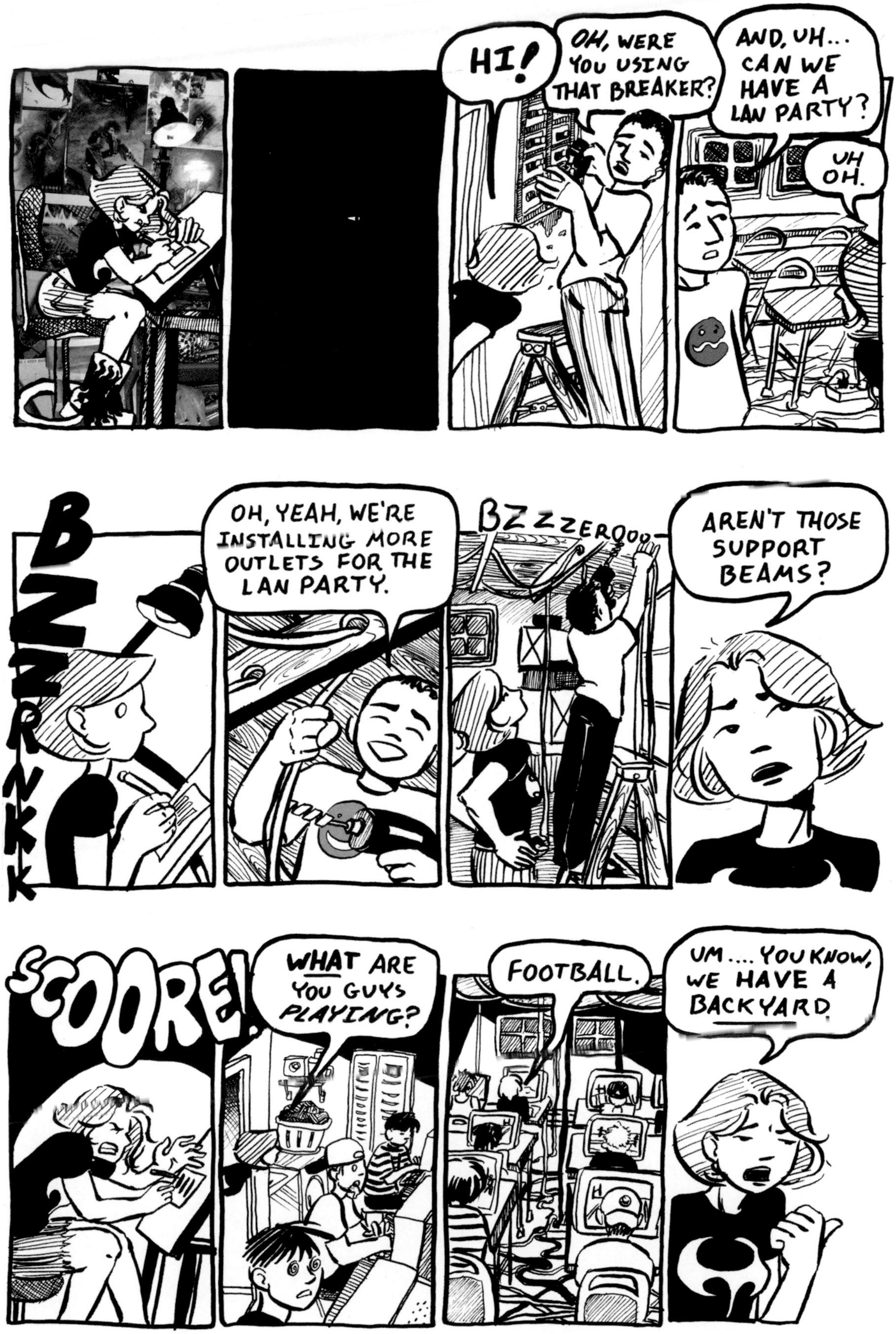
HI!
OH, WERE YOU USING THAT BREAKER?
AND, UH... CAN WE HAVE A LAN PARTY?
UH OH.
BZZZRRNKKK
OH, YEAH, WE'RE INSTALLING MORE OUTLETS FOR THE LAN PARTY.
BZZZEROOO
AREN'T THOSE SUPPORT BEAMS?
SCOORE!
WHAT ARE YOU GUYS PLAYING?
FOOTBALL.
UM.... YOU KNOW, WE HAVE A BACKYARD.

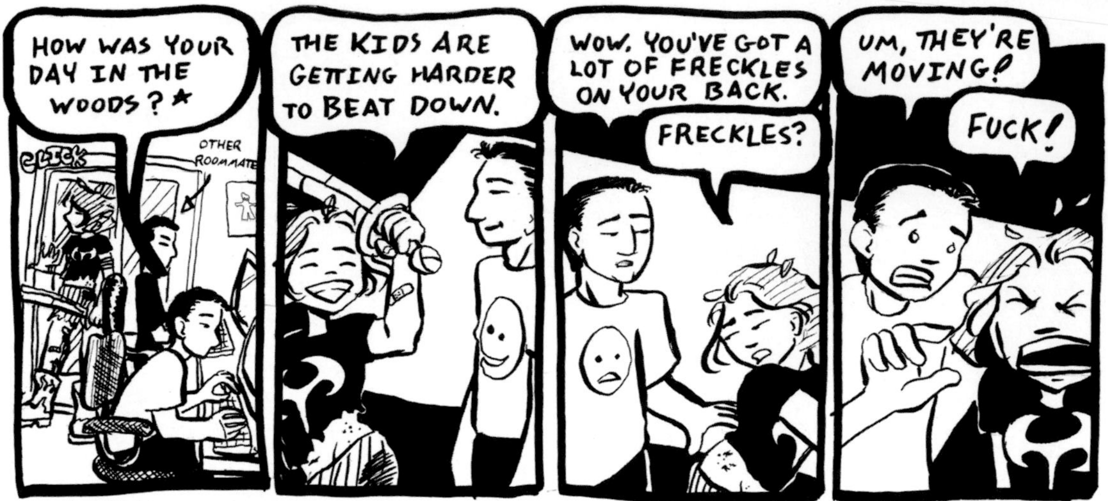
HOW WAS YOUR DAY IN THE WOODS? *
CLICK
OTHER ROOMMATE
THE KIDS ARE GETTING HARDER TO BEAT DOWN.
WOW, YOU'VE GOT A LOT OF FRECKLES ON YOUR BACK.
FRECKLES?
UM, THEY'RE MOVING!
FUCK!

WWW.GEEBASONPARADE.COM

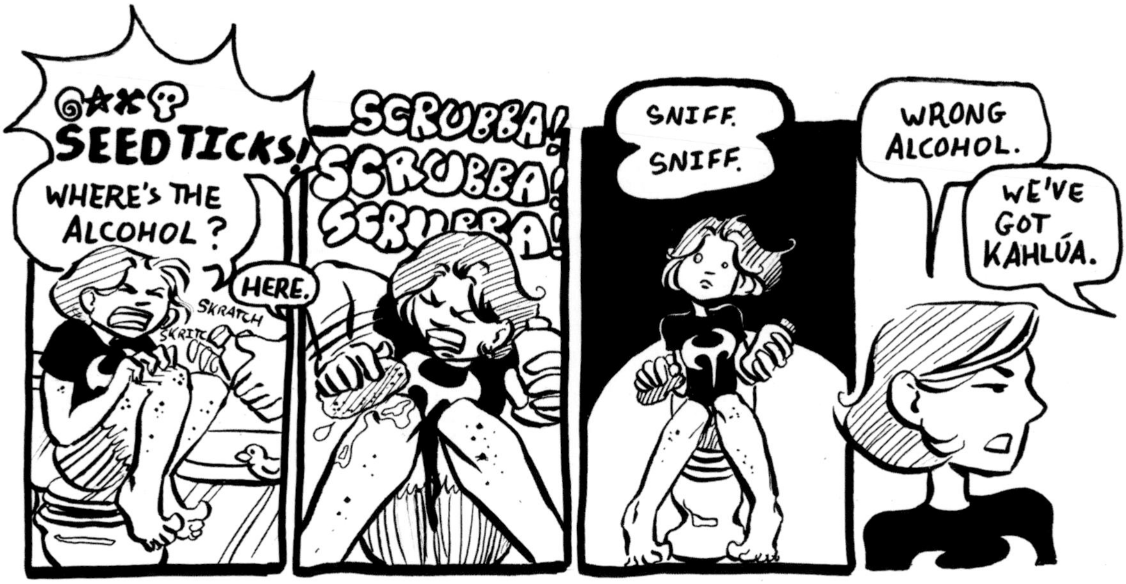
SEEDTICKS!
WHERE'S THE ALCOHOL?
HERE.
SKRATCH
SKRITCH
SCRUBBA! SCRUBBA! SCRUBBA!
SNIFF. SNIFF.
WRONG ALCOHOL.
WE'VE GOT KAHLÚA.

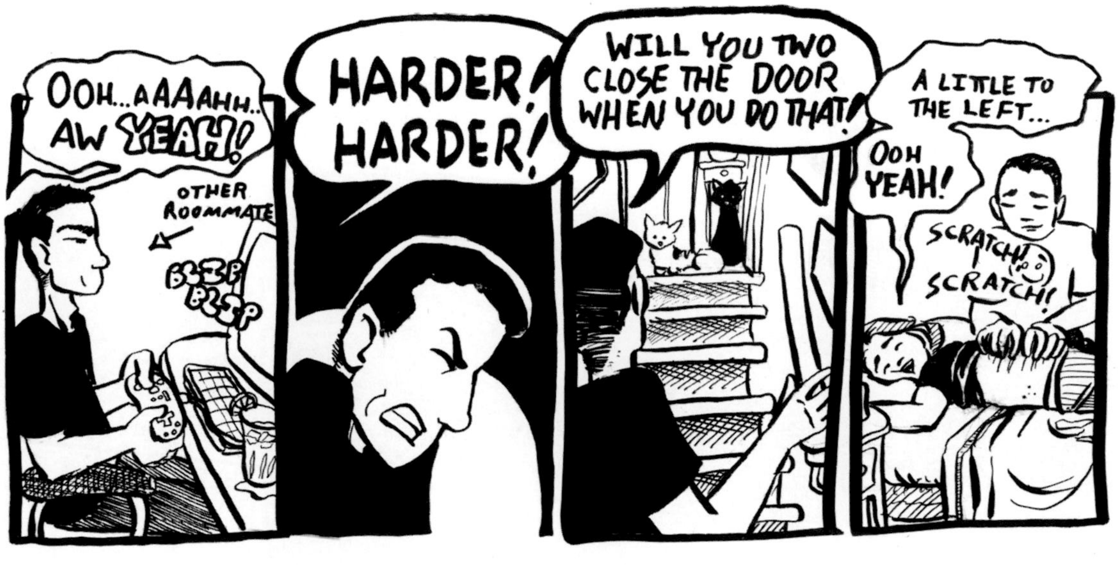
OOH...AAAAHH.. AW YEAH!
OTHER ROOMMATE
BLIP BLIP
HARDER! HARDER!
WILL YOU TWO CLOSE THE DOOR WHEN YOU DO THAT!
A LITTLE TO THE LEFT...
OOH YEAH!
SCRATCH! SCRATCH!

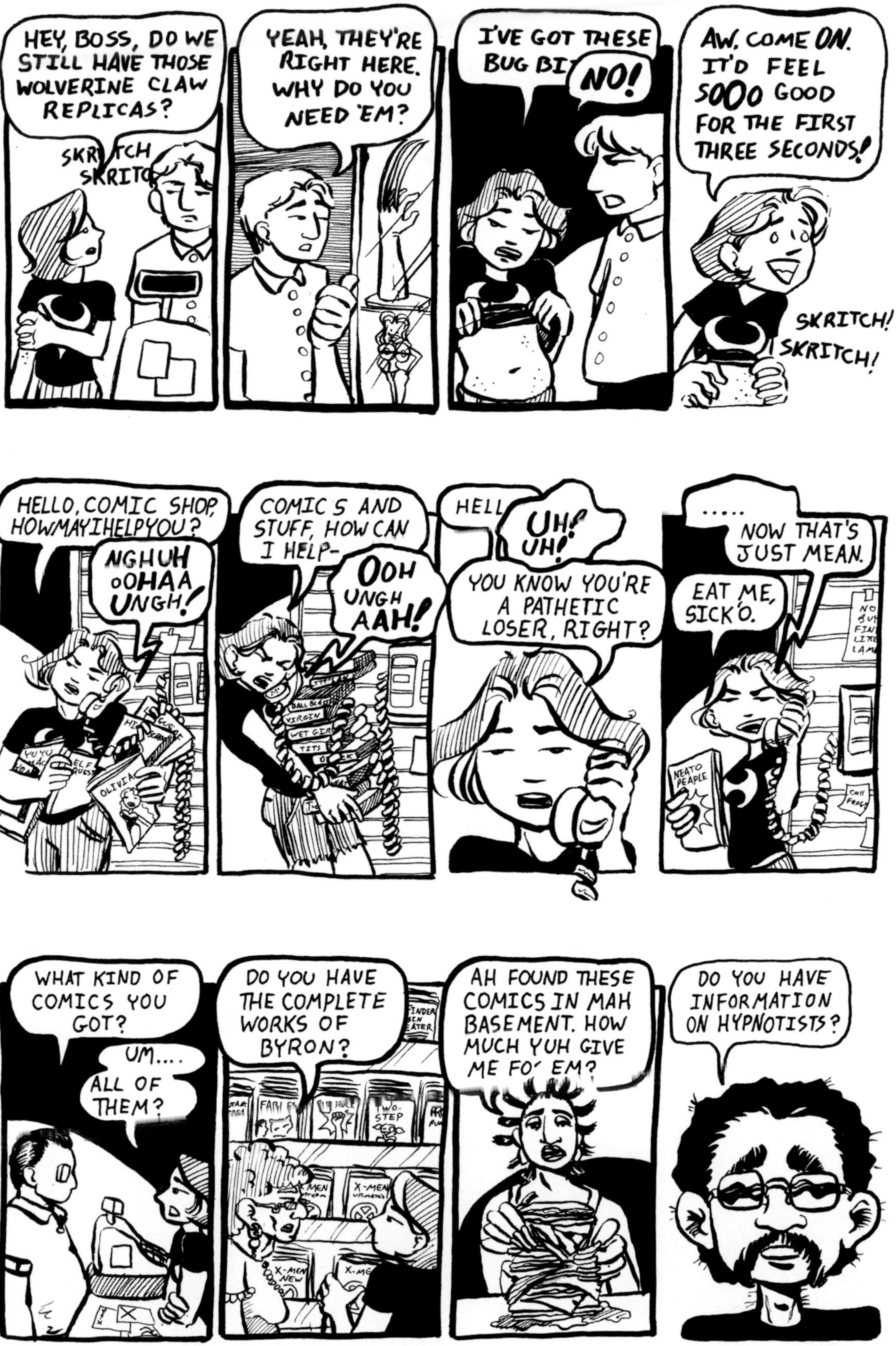
HEY, BOSS, DO WE STILL HAVE THOSE WOLVERINE CLAW REPLICAS?
SKRITCH SKRITCH
YEAH, THEY'RE RIGHT HERE. WHY DO YOU NEED 'EM?
I'VE GOT THESE BUG BI–
NO!
AW, COME ON. IT'D FEEL SOOO GOOD FOR THE FIRST THREE SECONDS!
SKRITCH! SKRITCH!
HELLO, COMIC SHOP, HOWMAYIHELPYOU?
NGHUH OOHAA UNGH!
COMICS AND STUFF, HOW CAN I HELP–
OOH UNGH AAH!
HELL–
UH! UH!
YOU KNOW YOU'RE A PATHETIC LOSER, RIGHT?
.....
NOW THAT'S JUST MEAN.
EAT ME, SICK'O.
NEATO PEAPLE
WHAT KIND OF COMICS YOU GOT?
UM....
ALL OF THEM?
DO YOU HAVE THE COMPLETE WORKS OF BYRON?
AH FOUND THESE COMICS IN MAH BASEMENT. HOW MUCH YUH GIVE ME FO' EM?
DO YOU HAVE INFORMATION ON HYPNOTISTS?

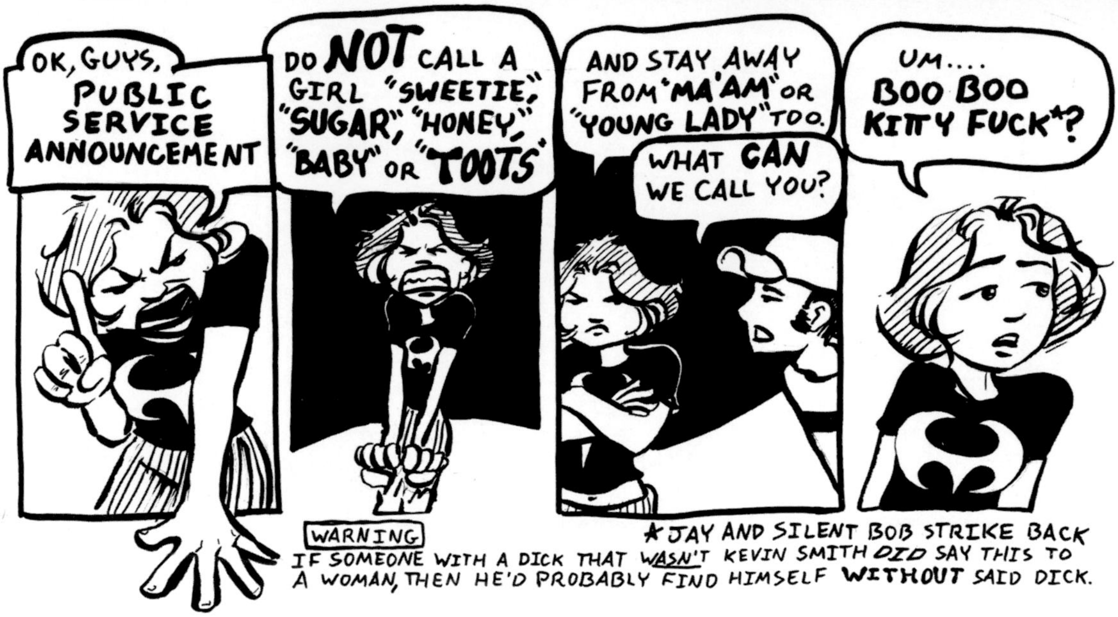
OK, GUYS, PUBLIC SERVICE ANNOUNCEMENT
DO NOT CALL A GIRL "SWEETIE", "SUGAR", "HONEY", "BABY" OR "TOOTS"
AND STAY AWAY FROM "MA'AM" OR "YOUNG LADY" TOO.
WHAT CAN WE CALL YOU?
UM.... BOO BOO KITTY FUCK*?
WARNING
IF SOMEONE WITH A DICK THAT WASN'T KEVIN SMITH DID SAY THIS TO A WOMAN, THEN HE'D PROBABLY FIND HIMSELF WITHOUT SAID DICK.
*JAY AND SILENT BOB STRIKE BACK

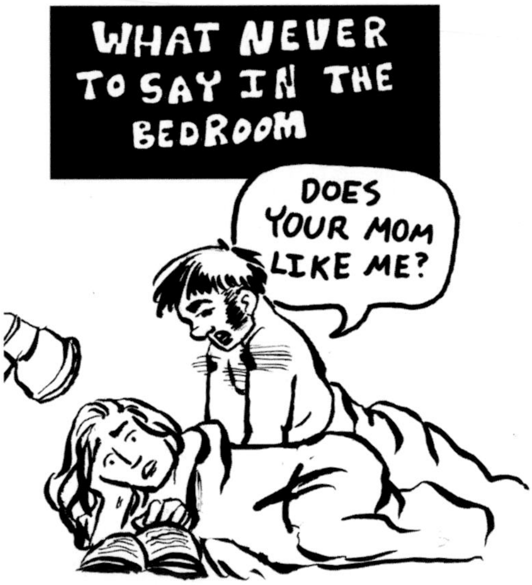
WHAT NEVER TO SAY IN THE BEDROOM
DOES YOUR MOM LIKE ME?

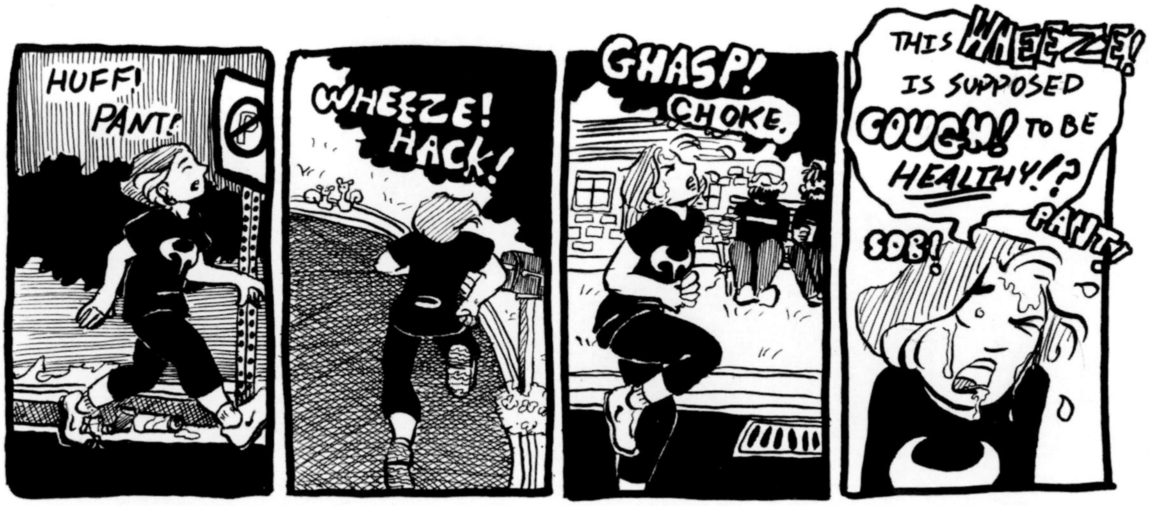
HUFF! PANT!
WHEEZE! HACK!
GHASP! CHOKE.
THIS WHEEZE! IS SUPPOSED COUGH! TO BE HEALTHY!?
PANT!
SOB!

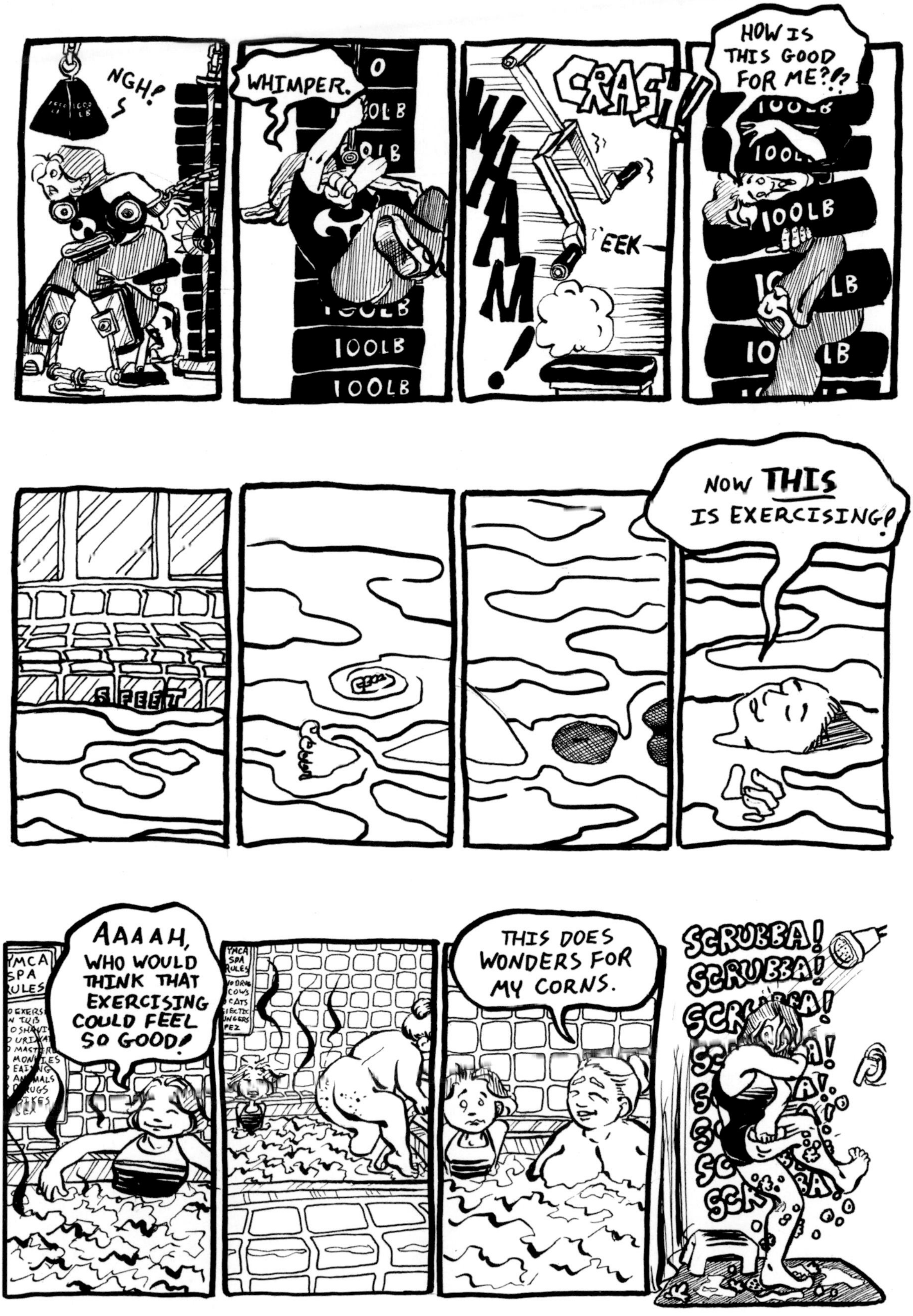
NGH!
WHIMPER.
100LB
CRASH!
WHAM!
EEK
HOW IS THIS GOOD FOR ME?!?
100LB
NOW THIS IS EXERCISING!
AAAAH, WHO WOULD THINK THAT EXERCISING COULD FEEL SO GOOD!
YMCA SPA RULES
THIS DOES WONDERS FOR MY CORNS.
SCRUBBA! SCRUBBA!

WHAT NEVER TO SAY IN THE BEDROOM
I'VE BEEN THINKING A LOT ABOUT GOD LATELY.
TIME

FAMOUS LAST WORDS

I NEVER REACTED TO IT BEFORE

NAH, WE'LL BE FINE!

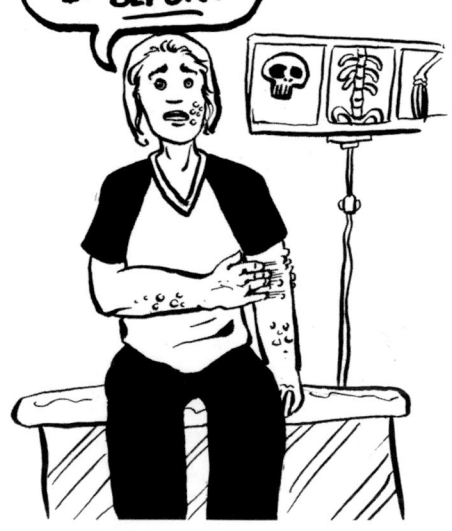

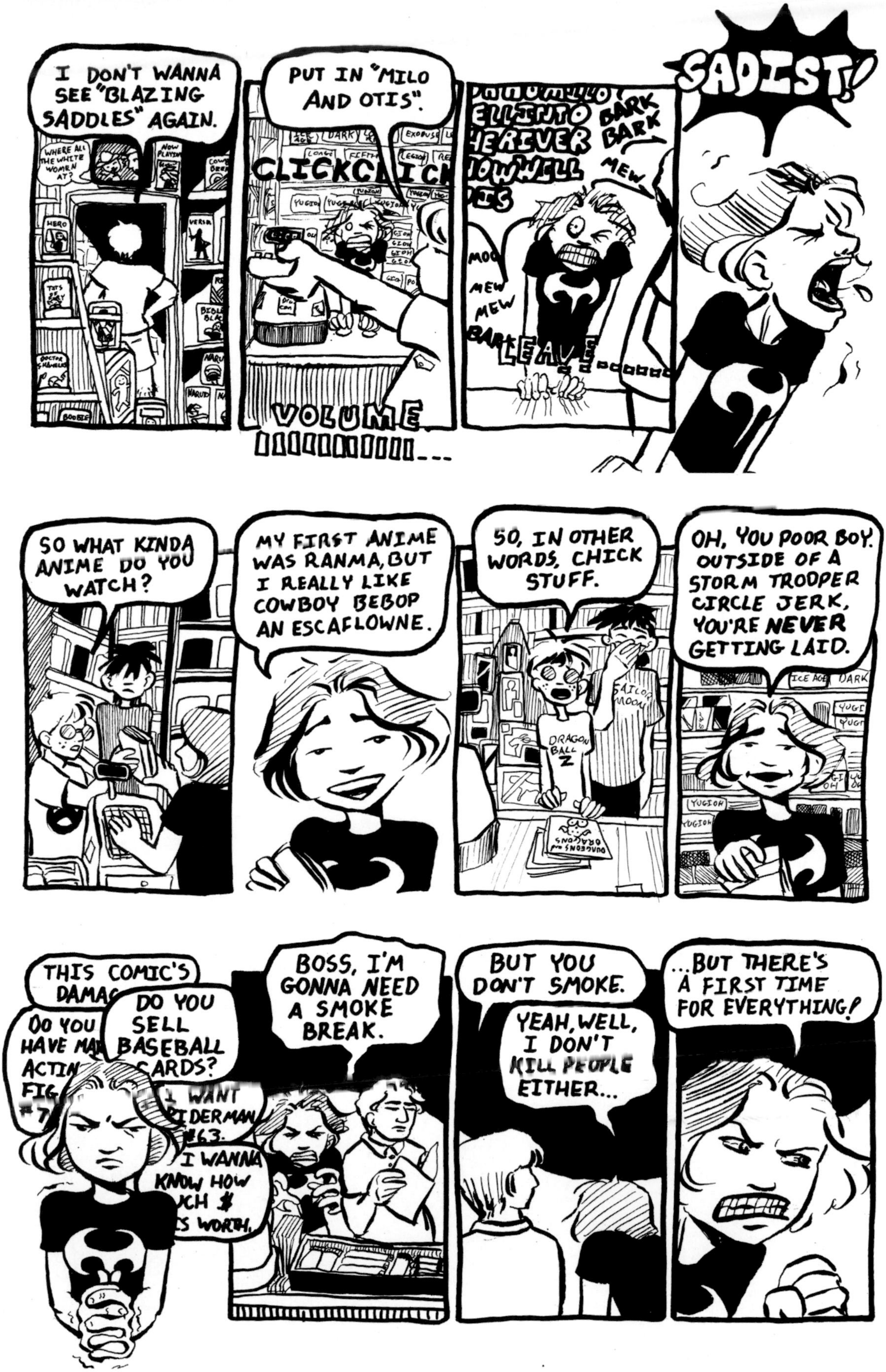
I DON'T WANNA SEE "BLAZING SADDLES" AGAIN.
WHERE ALL THE WHITE WOMEN AT?
PUT IN "MILO AND OTIS".
CLICKCLICK
VOLUME
BARK BARK
MEW
MOO
MEW MEW
LEAVE
SADIST!
SO WHAT KINDA ANIME DO YOU WATCH?
MY FIRST ANIME WAS RANMA, BUT I REALLY LIKE COWBOY BEBOP AN ESCAFLOWNE.
SO, IN OTHER WORDS, CHICK STUFF.
OH, YOU POOR BOY. OUTSIDE OF A STORM TROOPER CIRCLE JERK, YOU'RE NEVER GETTING LAID.
THIS COMIC'S DAMAG
DO YOU SELL BASEBALL CARDS?
DO YOU HAVE MA ACTIN FIG
I WANT IDERMAN #63.
I WANNA KNOW HOW UCH $ S WORTH.
BOSS, I'M GONNA NEED A SMOKE BREAK.
BUT YOU DON'T SMOKE.
YEAH, WELL, I DON'T KILL PEOPLE EITHER...
...BUT THERE'S A FIRST TIME FOR EVERYTHING!

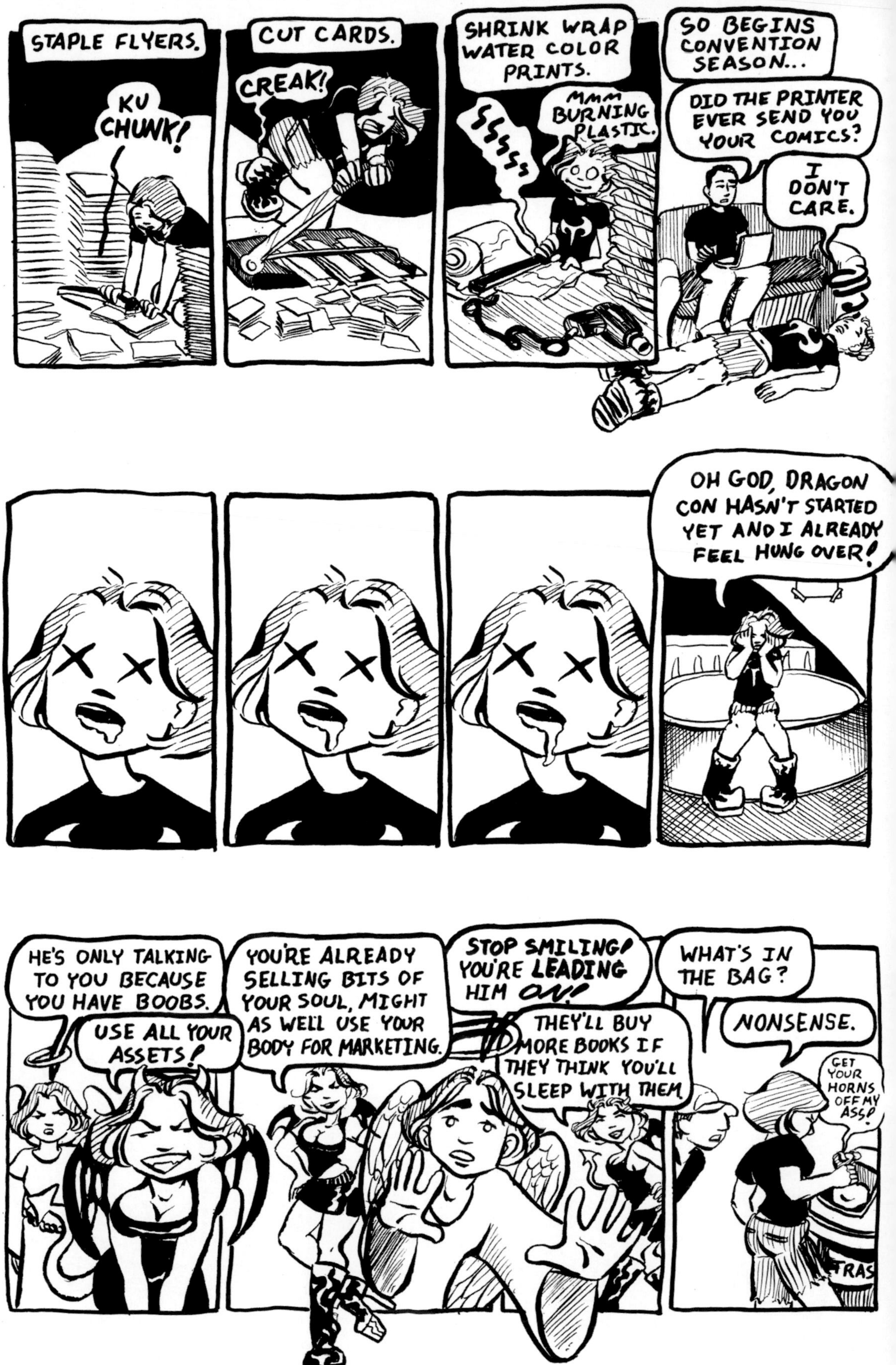
STAPLE FLYERS.
KU CHUNK!
CUT CARDS.
CREAK!
SHRINK WRAP WATER COLOR PRINTS.
SSSSSS
MMM BURNING PLASTIC.
SO BEGINS CONVENTION SEASON...
DID THE PRINTER EVER SEND YOU YOUR COMICS?
I DON'T CARE.
OH GOD, DRAGON CON HASN'T STARTED YET AND I ALREADY FEEL HUNG OVER!
HE'S ONLY TALKING TO YOU BECAUSE YOU HAVE BOOBS.
USE ALL YOUR ASSETS!
YOU'RE ALREADY SELLING BITS OF YOUR SOUL, MIGHT AS WELL USE YOUR BODY FOR MARKETING.
STOP SMILING! YOU'RE LEADING HIM ON!
THEY'LL BUY MORE BOOKS IF THEY THINK YOU'LL SLEEP WITH THEM.
WHAT'S IN THE BAG?
NONSENSE.
GET YOUR HORNS OFF MY ASS!

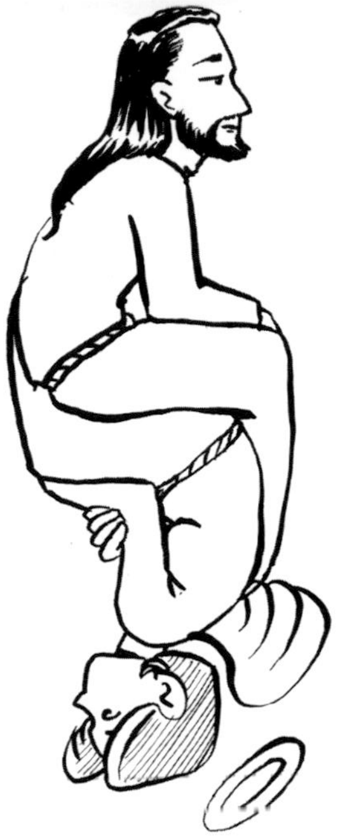

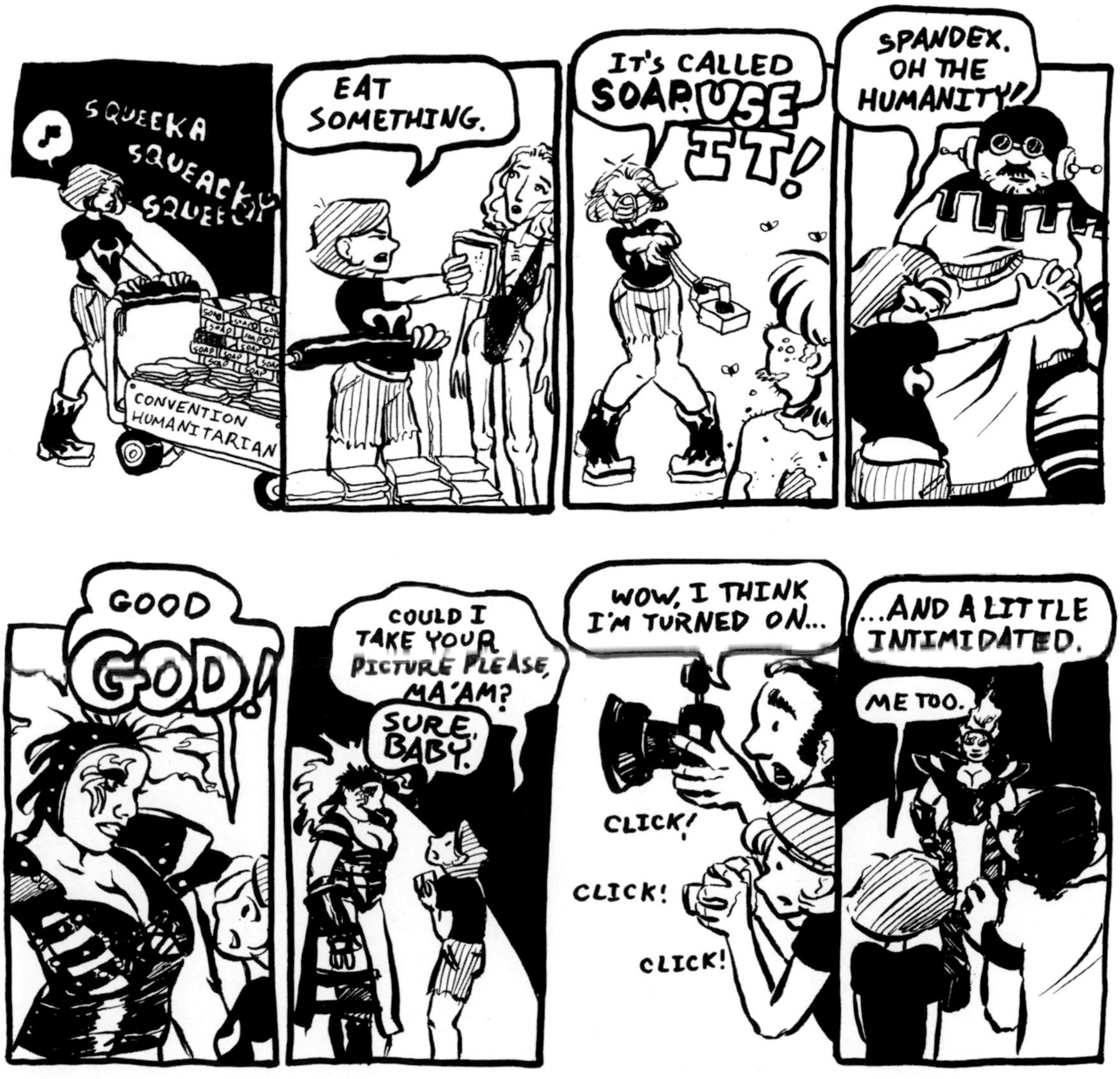
SQUEEKA
SQUEACKY
SQUEE
CONVENTION HUMANITARIAN
EAT SOMETHING.
IT'S CALLED SOAP. USE IT!
SPANDEX. OH THE HUMANITY!
GOOD GOD!
COULD I TAKE YOUR PICTURE PLEASE, MA'AM?
SURE, BABY.
WOW, I THINK I'M TURNED ON...
CLICK!
CLICK!
CLICK!
...AND A LITTLE INTIMIDATED.
ME TOO.

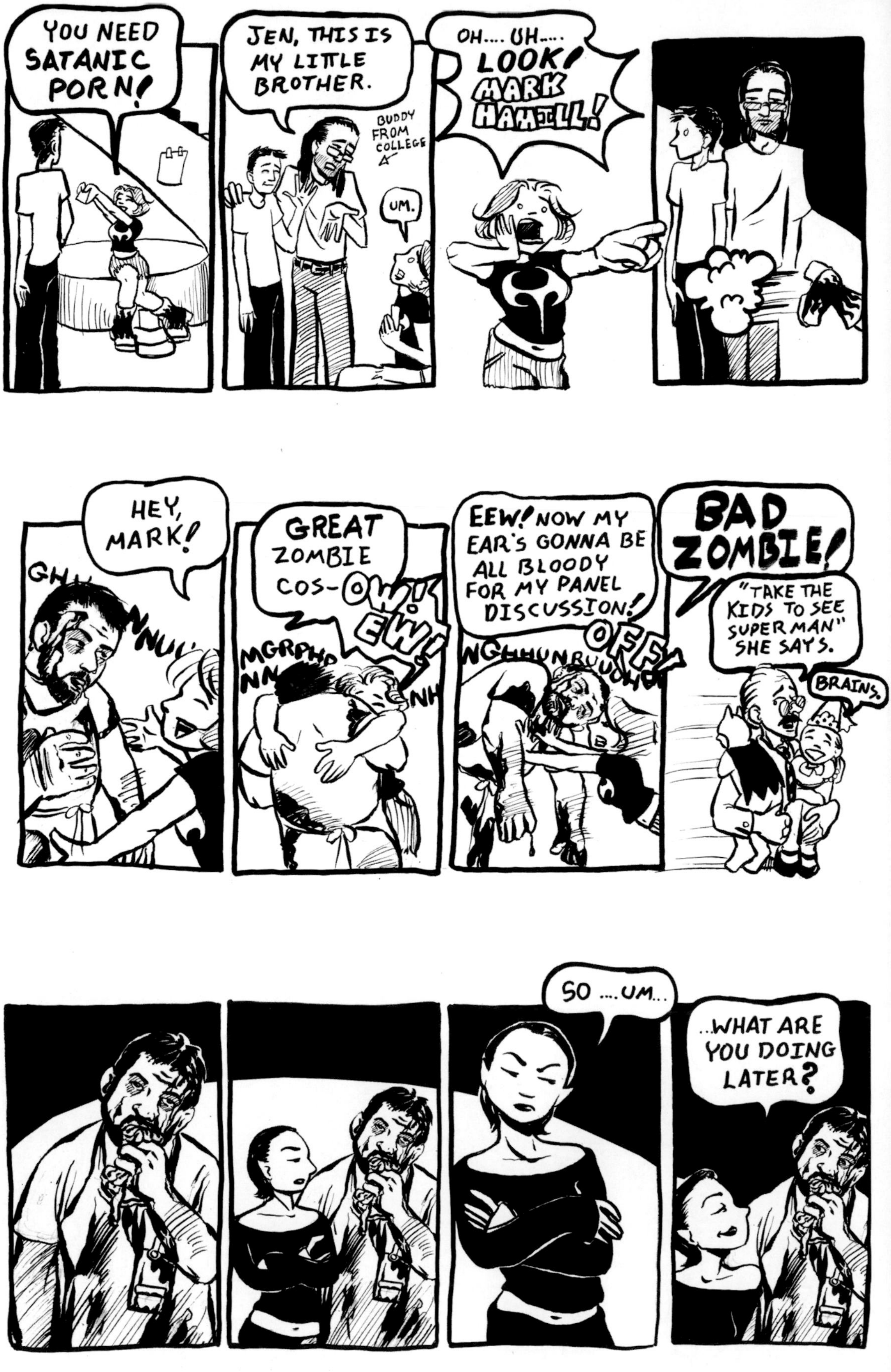

YOU NEED SATANIC PORN!
JEN, THIS IS MY LITTLE BROTHER.
BUDDY FROM COLLEGE
UM.
OH.... UH.... LOOK! MARK HAMILL!
HEY, MARK!
GHNNU
GREAT ZOMBIE COS- OW! EW!
MGRPHR NN
NH
EEW! NOW MY EAR'S GONNA BE ALL BLOODY FOR MY PANEL DISCUSSION!
OFF!
NGHHUNRUUOH
BAD ZOMBIE!
"TAKE THE KIDS TO SEE SUPERMAN" SHE SAYS.
BRAINS.
SO ....UM...
...WHAT ARE YOU DOING LATER?

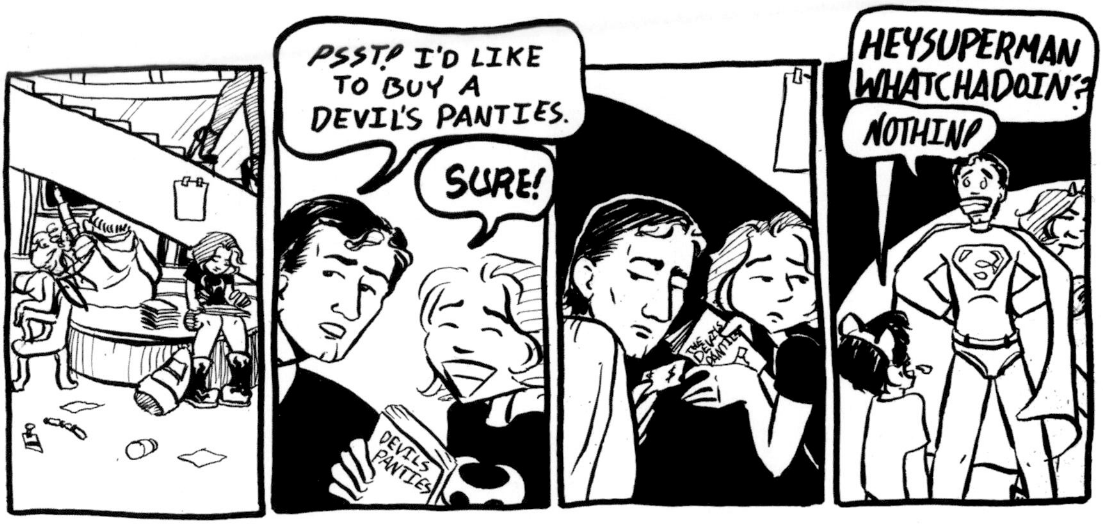
PSST! I'D LIKE TO BUY A DEVIL'S PANTIES.
SURE!
DEVILS PANTIES
HEYSUPERMAN WHATCHADOIN'?
NOTHIN!

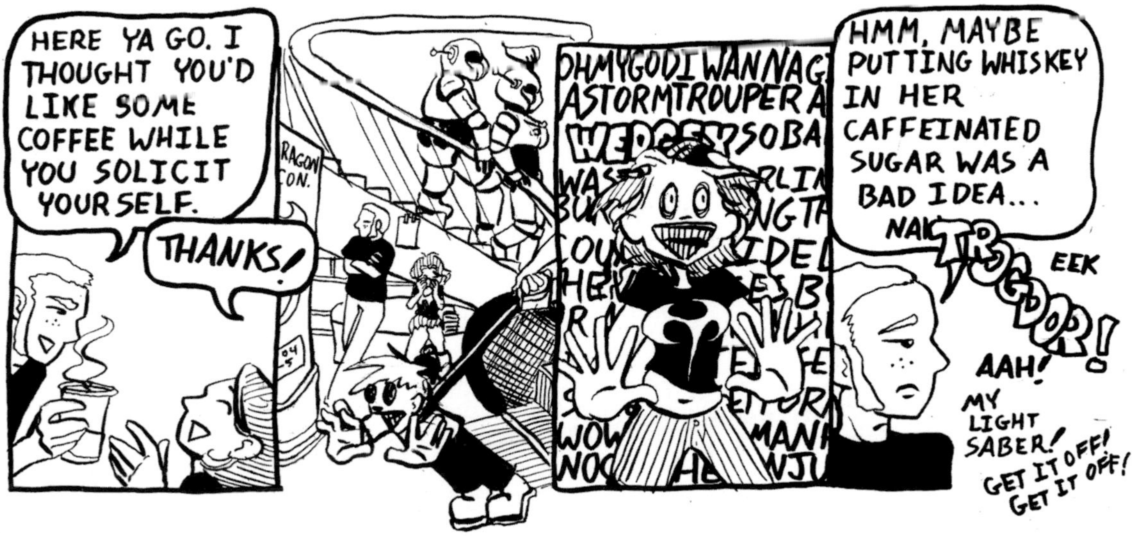
HERE YA GO. I THOUGHT YOU'D LIKE SOME COFFEE WHILE YOU SOLICIT YOURSELF.
THANKS!
DRAGON CON.
OHMYGODIWANNAGI
ASTORMTROUPERA
HMM, MAYBE PUTTING WHISKEY IN HER CAFFEINATED SUGAR WAS A BAD IDEA...
TROGDOR!
EEK
AAH!
MY LIGHT SABER!
GET IT OFF!
GET IT OFF!

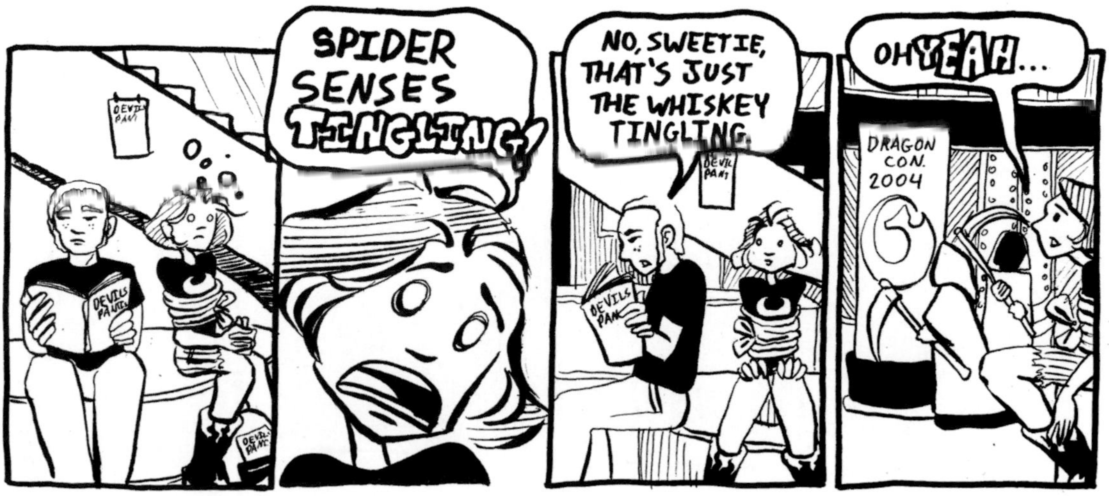
SPIDER SENSES TINGLING!
NO, SWEETIE, THAT'S JUST THE WHISKEY TINGLING.
DEVILS PANT
OH YEAH...
DRAGON CON. 2004

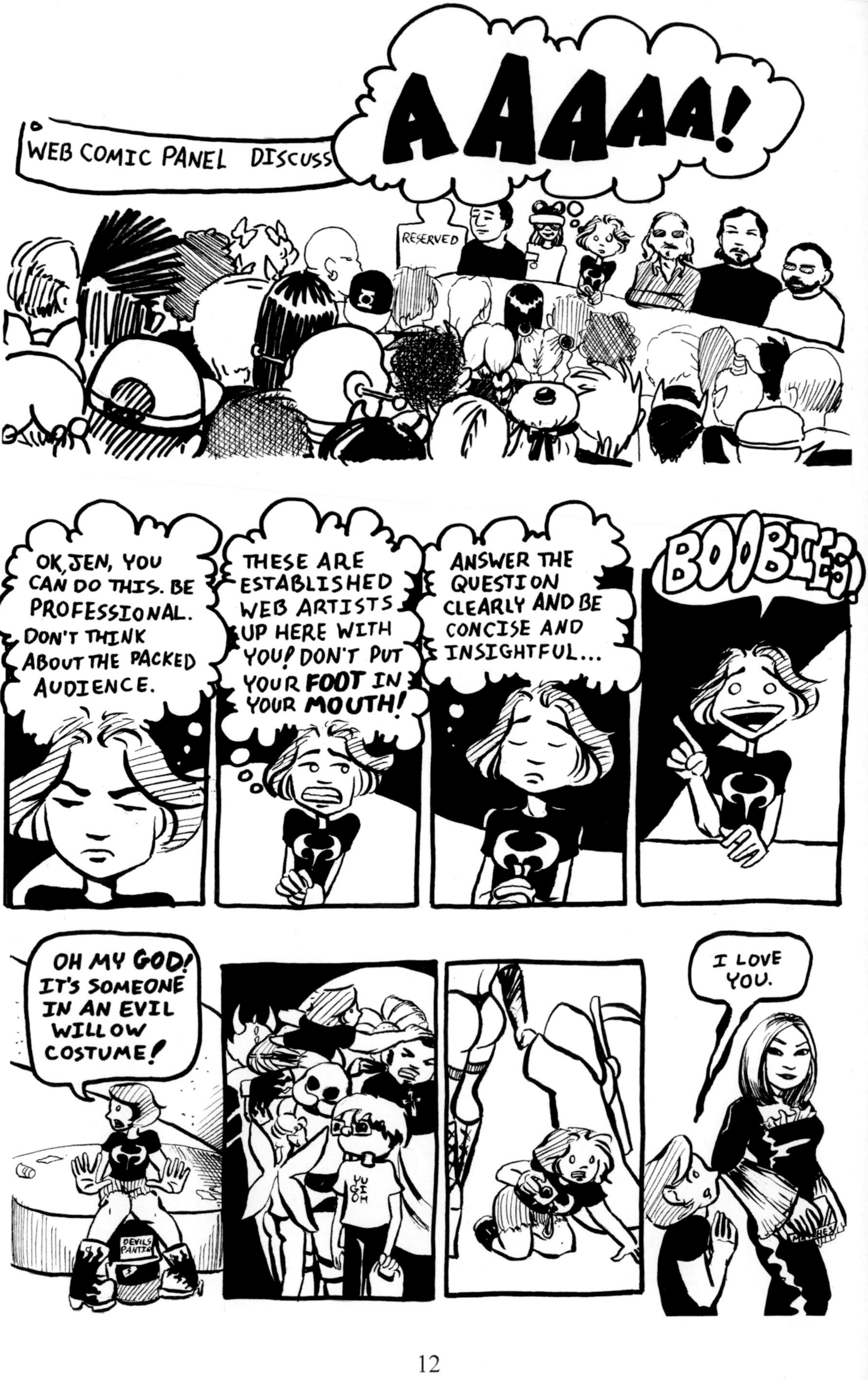
WEB COMIC PANEL DISCUSS
AAAAA!
RESERVED
OK, JEN, YOU CAN DO THIS. BE PROFESSIONAL. DON'T THINK ABOUT THE PACKED AUDIENCE.
THESE ARE ESTABLISHED WEB ARTISTS UP HERE WITH YOU! DON'T PUT YOUR FOOT IN YOUR MOUTH!
ANSWER THE QUESTION CLEARLY AND BE CONCISE AND INSIGHTFUL...
BOOBIES!
OH MY GOD! IT'S SOMEONE IN AN EVIL WILLOW COSTUME!
I LOVE YOU.

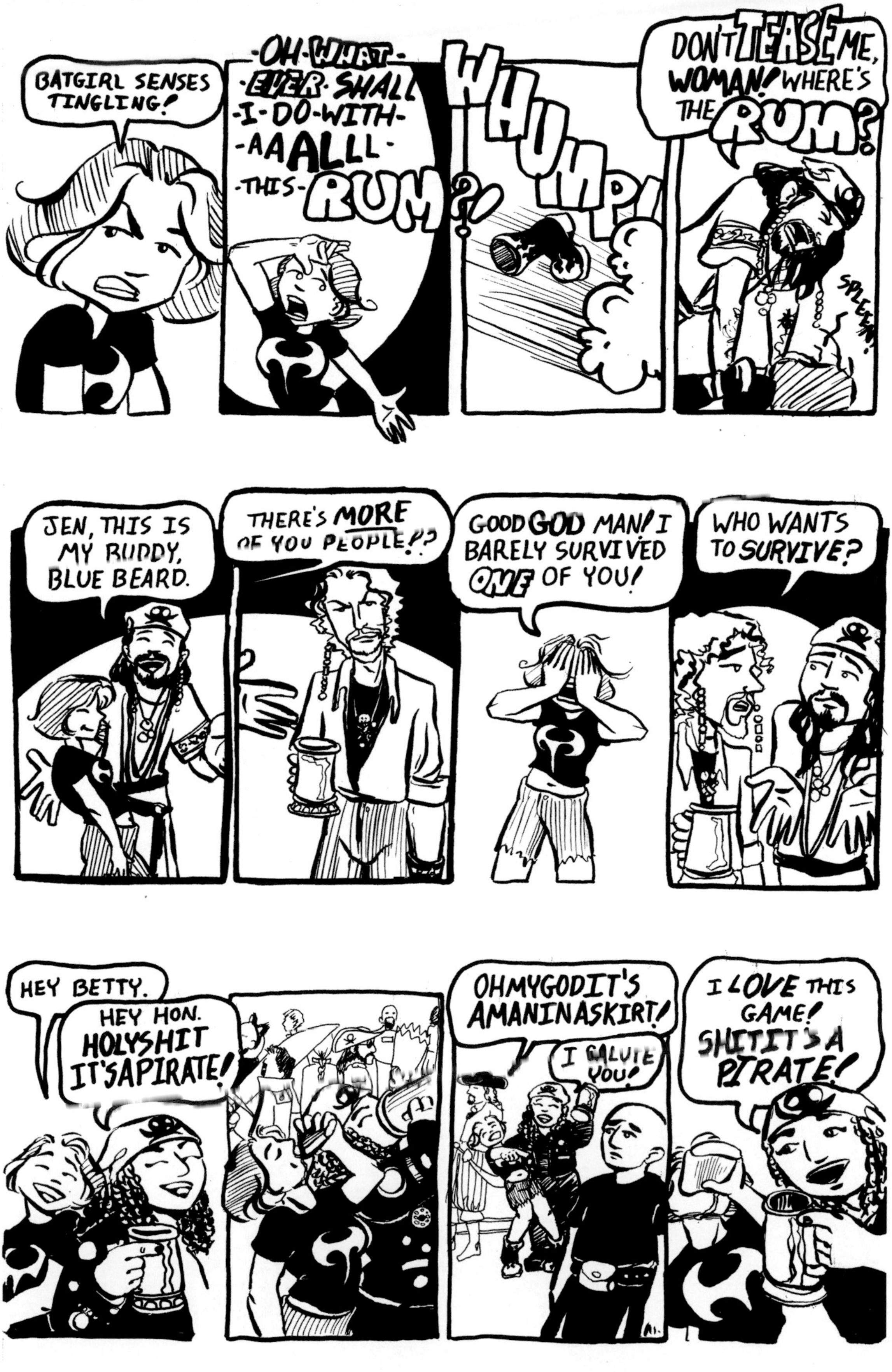
BATGIRL SENSES TINGLING!
-OH-WHAT-EVER-SHALL-I-DO-WITH-AAALLL-THIS-RUM?!
WHUMP!
DON'T TEASE ME, WOMAN! WHERE'S THE RUM?
SPLEESH!
JEN, THIS IS MY BUDDY, BLUE BEARD.
THERE'S MORE OF YOU PEOPLE!?
GOOD GOD MAN! I BARELY SURVIVED ONE OF YOU!
WHO WANTS TO SURVIVE?
HEY BETTY.
HEY HON. HOLYSHIT IT'SAPIRATE!
OHMYGODIT'S AMANINASKIRT!
I SALUTE YOU!
I LOVE THIS GAME! SHITIT'SA PIRATE!

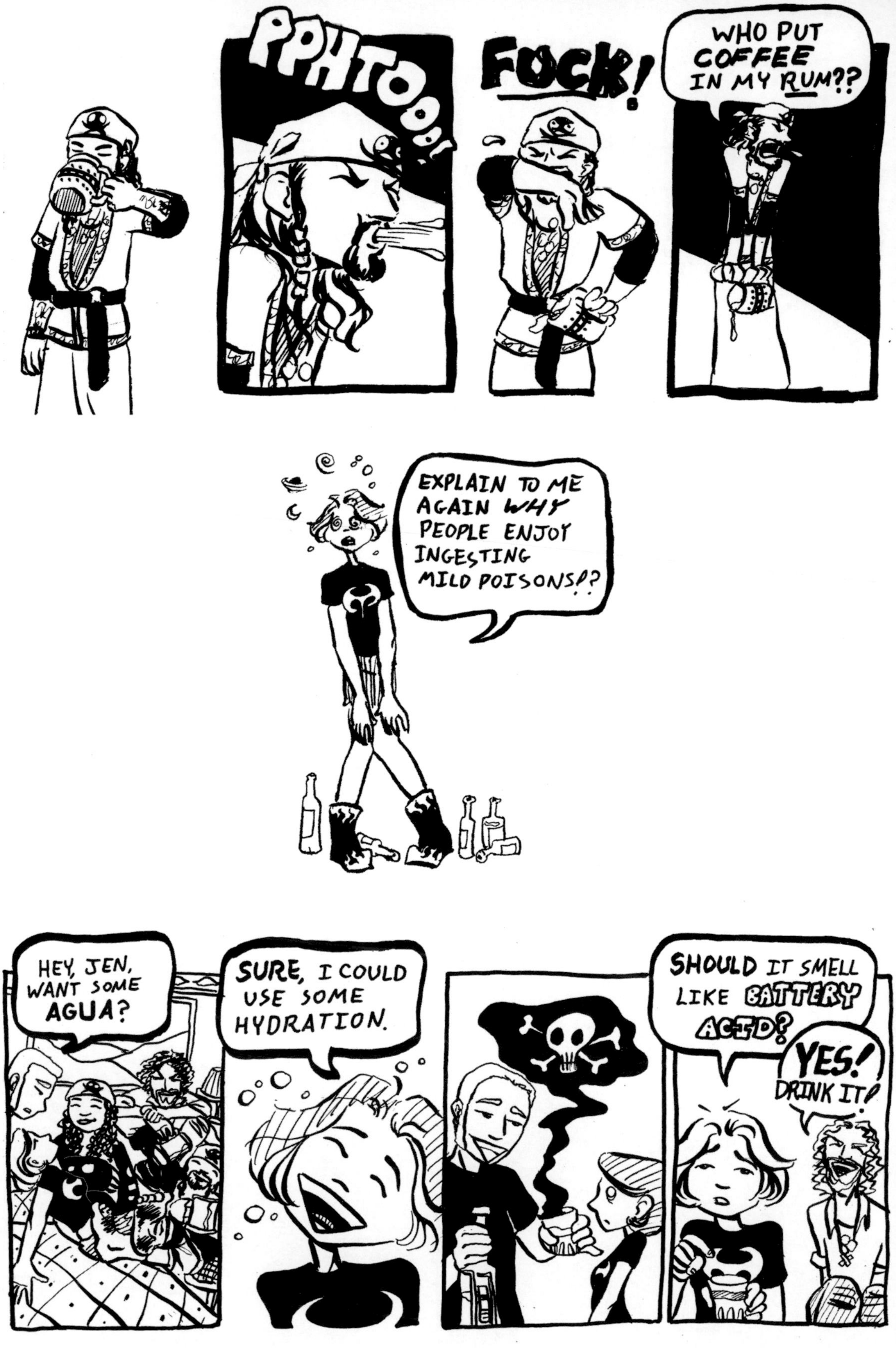
PPHTOO!!
FOCK!
WHO PUT COFFEE IN MY RUM??
EXPLAIN TO ME AGAIN WHY PEOPLE ENJOY INGESTING MILD POISONS!?
HEY, JEN, WANT SOME AGUA?
SURE, I COULD USE SOME HYDRATION.
SHOULD IT SMELL LIKE BATTERY ACID?
YES! DRINK IT!

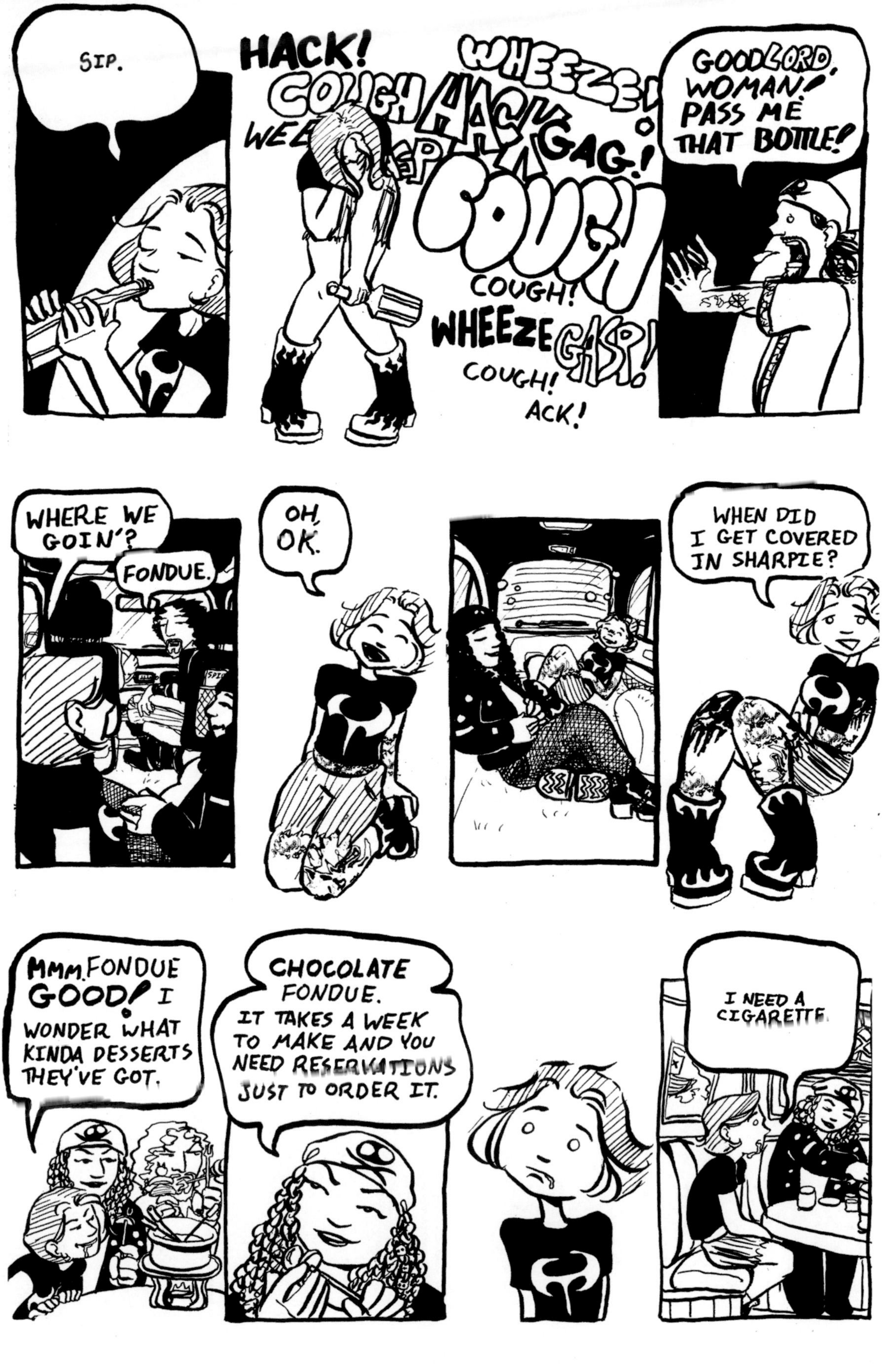

SIP.
HACK!
COUGH
WHEEZE!
HACK
GAG!
COUGH
COUGH!
WHEEZE
GASP!
COUGH!
ACK!
GOOD LORD, WOMAN! PASS ME THAT BOTTLE!
WHERE WE GOIN'?
FONDUE.
OH, OK.
WHEN DID I GET COVERED IN SHARPIE?
MMM. FONDUE GOOD! I WONDER WHAT KINDA DESSERTS THEY'VE GOT.
CHOCOLATE FONDUE. IT TAKES A WEEK TO MAKE AND YOU NEED RESERVATIONS JUST TO ORDER IT.
I NEED A CIGARETTE.

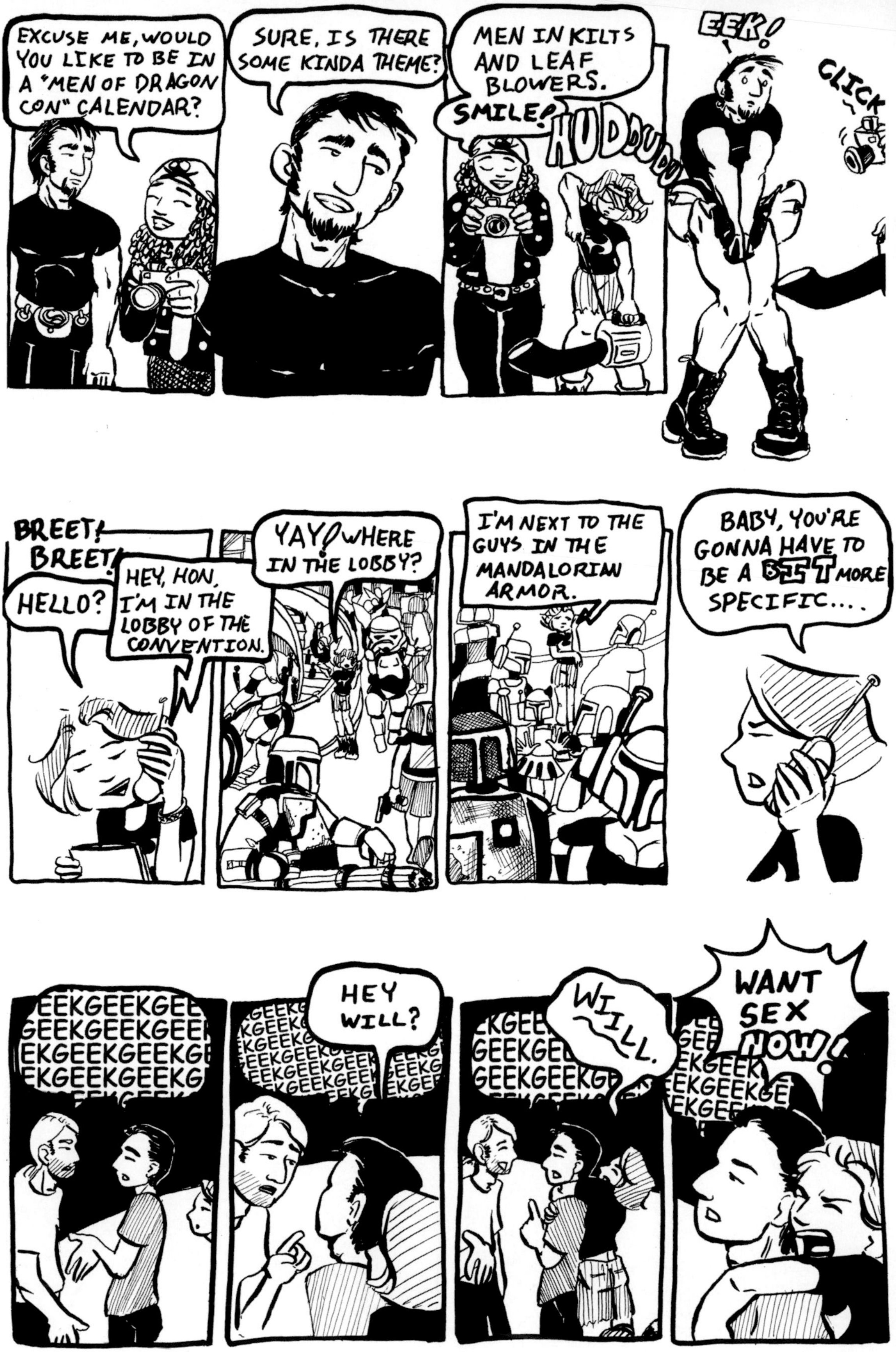
EXCUSE ME, WOULD YOU LIKE TO BE IN A "MEN OF DRAGON CON" CALENDAR?
SURE, IS THERE SOME KINDA THEME?
MEN IN KILTS AND LEAF BLOWERS.
SMILE!
HUDDUDUDU
EEK!
CLICK
BREET! BREET!
HELLO?
HEY, HON, I'M IN THE LOBBY OF THE CONVENTION.
YAY! WHERE IN THE LOBBY?
I'M NEXT TO THE GUYS IN THE MANDALORIAN ARMOR.
BABY, YOU'RE GONNA HAVE TO BE A BIT MORE SPECIFIC....
HEY WILL?
WIILL.
WANT SEX NOW!

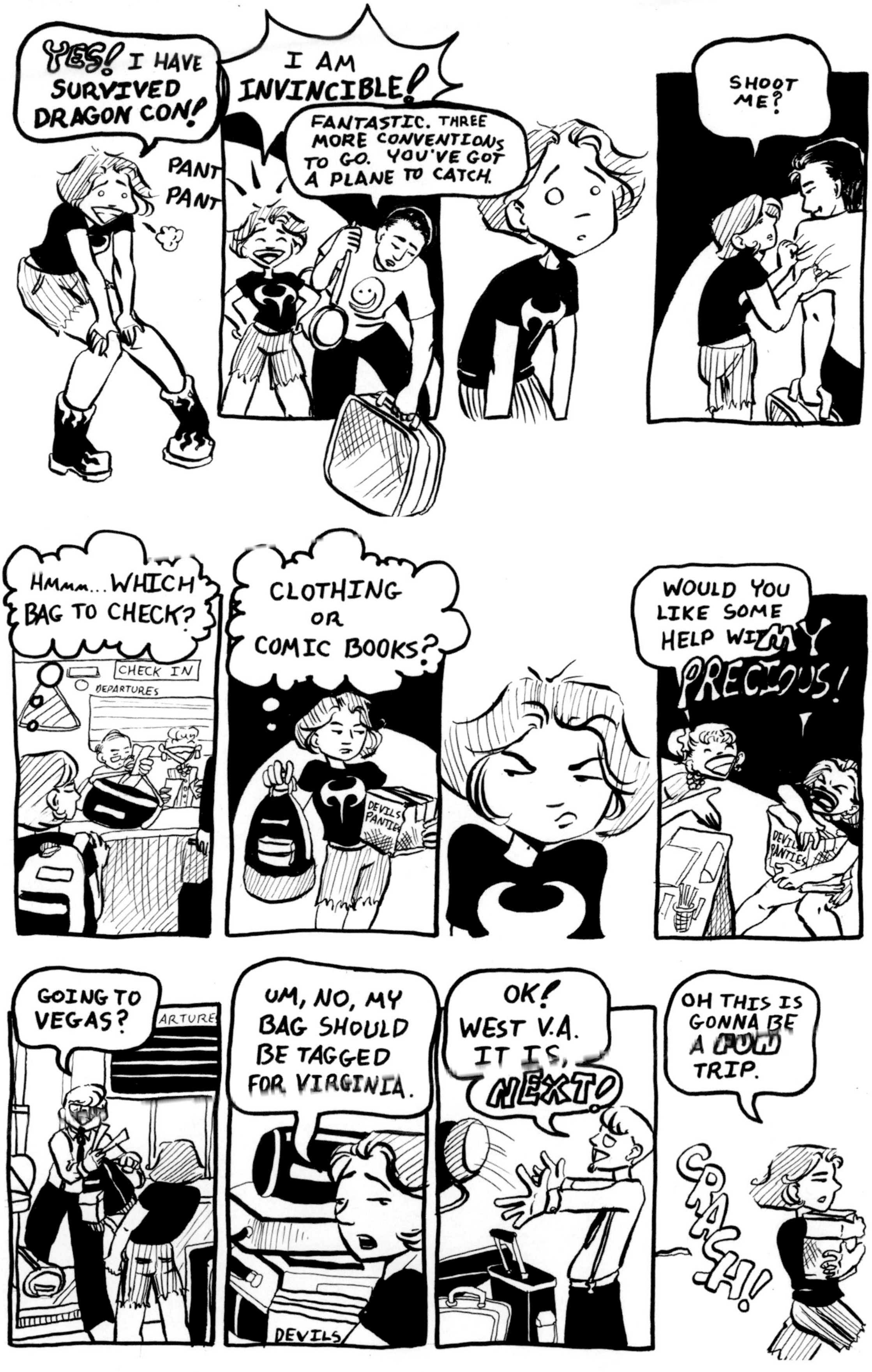
YES! I HAVE SURVIVED DRAGON CON!
PANT PANT
I AM INVINCIBLE!
FANTASTIC. THREE MORE CONVENTIONS TO GO. YOU'VE GOT A PLANE TO CATCH.
SHOOT ME?
HMMM... WHICH BAG TO CHECK?
CHECK IN
DEPARTURES
CLOTHING OR COMIC BOOKS?
DEVILS PANTIES
WOULD YOU LIKE SOME HELP WI
MY PRECIOUS!
DEVILS PANTIES
GOING TO VEGAS?
ARTURES
UM, NO, MY BAG SHOULD BE TAGGED FOR VIRGINIA.
DEVILS
OK! WEST V.A. IT IS,
NEXT!
OH THIS IS GONNA BE A FUN TRIP.
CRASH!

REMOVE LL METAL EMS AND N CRATE OCEDING UGH... ETE...

DEVIL... PAR...

REMOVE SHOES

BOOT BUCKLE, NECKLACE, STUDS ON BELT OH ME FUC IT

SUBDIVISIONS TAKING OVER THE BACK WOODS. STRIP MALLS AND ROADS EXPANDING...

...MY LITTLE HOME TOWN IS CHANGING SO MUCH.

WILL IT EVER BE THE SAME HOME THAT I REMEMBER?

SKYLER, STOP WATCHING TV AND DO YOUR CHORES! XIAN, WHERE'S MY DRILL!

HOME SWEET HOME!

YAY, SKYLER! IT'S SO GOOD TO SEE YOU SISTER, DARLING!

SO, JEN, YOU GAY YET?

DAMNIT, SKYLER! YOU'VE MET MY BOYFRIEND!

DENIAL ISN'T JUST A RIVER IN EGYPT, SISTER, DARLING!

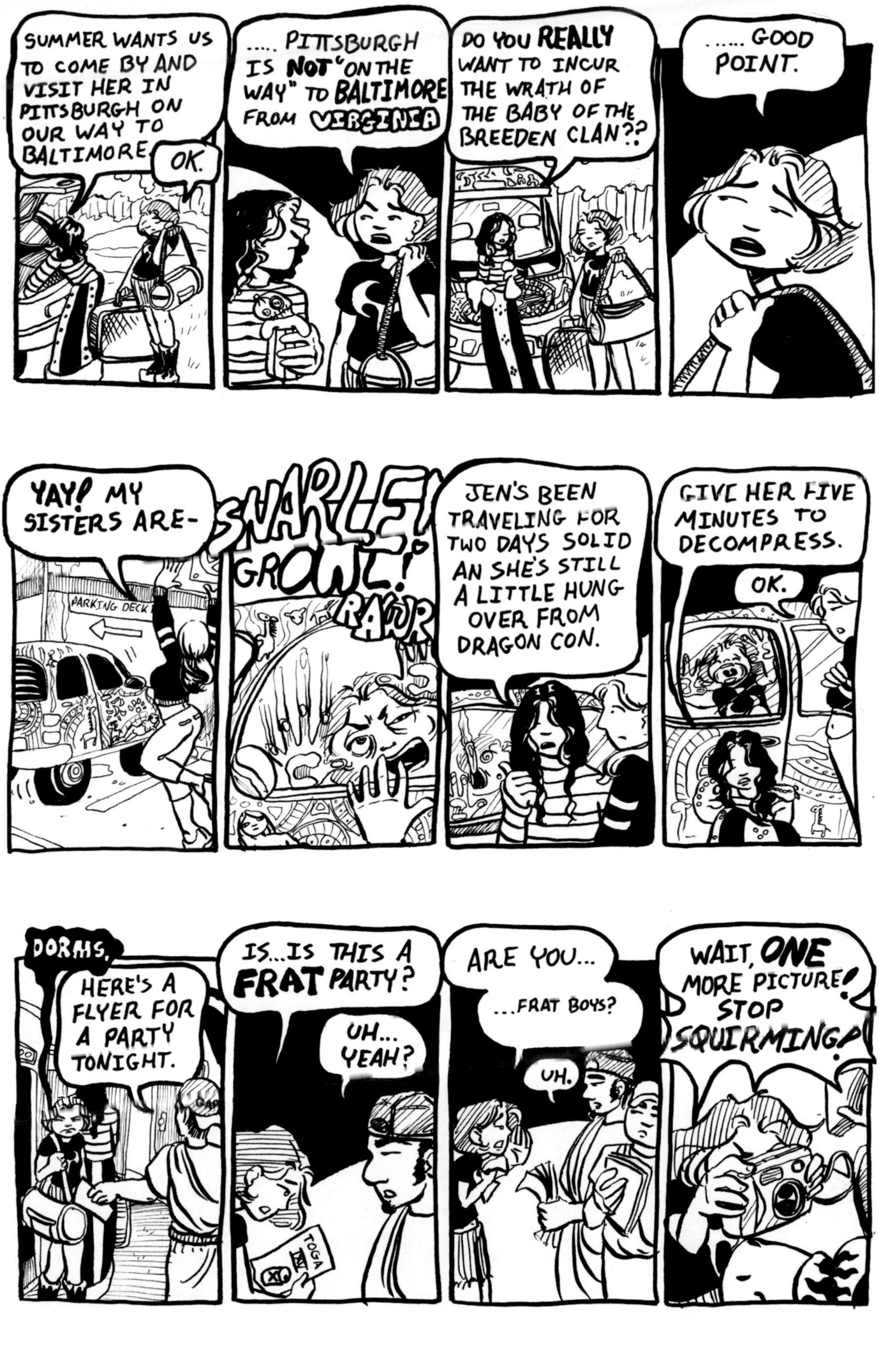
SUMMER WANTS US TO COME BY AND VISIT HER IN PITTSBURGH ON OUR WAY TO BALTIMORE.
OK.
..... PITTSBURGH IS NOT "ON THE WAY" TO BALTIMORE FROM VIRGINIA
DO YOU REALLY WANT TO INCUR THE WRATH OF THE BABY OF THE BREEDEN CLAN??
...... GOOD POINT.
YAY! MY SISTERS ARE-
SNARLE!
GROWL!
RAWR
PARKING DECK
JEN'S BEEN TRAVELING FOR TWO DAYS SOLID AN SHE'S STILL A LITTLE HUNG OVER FROM DRAGON CON.
GIVE HER FIVE MINUTES TO DECOMPRESS.
OK.
DORMS.
HERE'S A FLYER FOR A PARTY TONIGHT.
IS...IS THIS A FRAT PARTY?
UH... YEAH?
TOGA
ARE YOU...
...FRAT BOYS?
UH.
WAIT, ONE MORE PICTURE! STOP SQUIRMING!

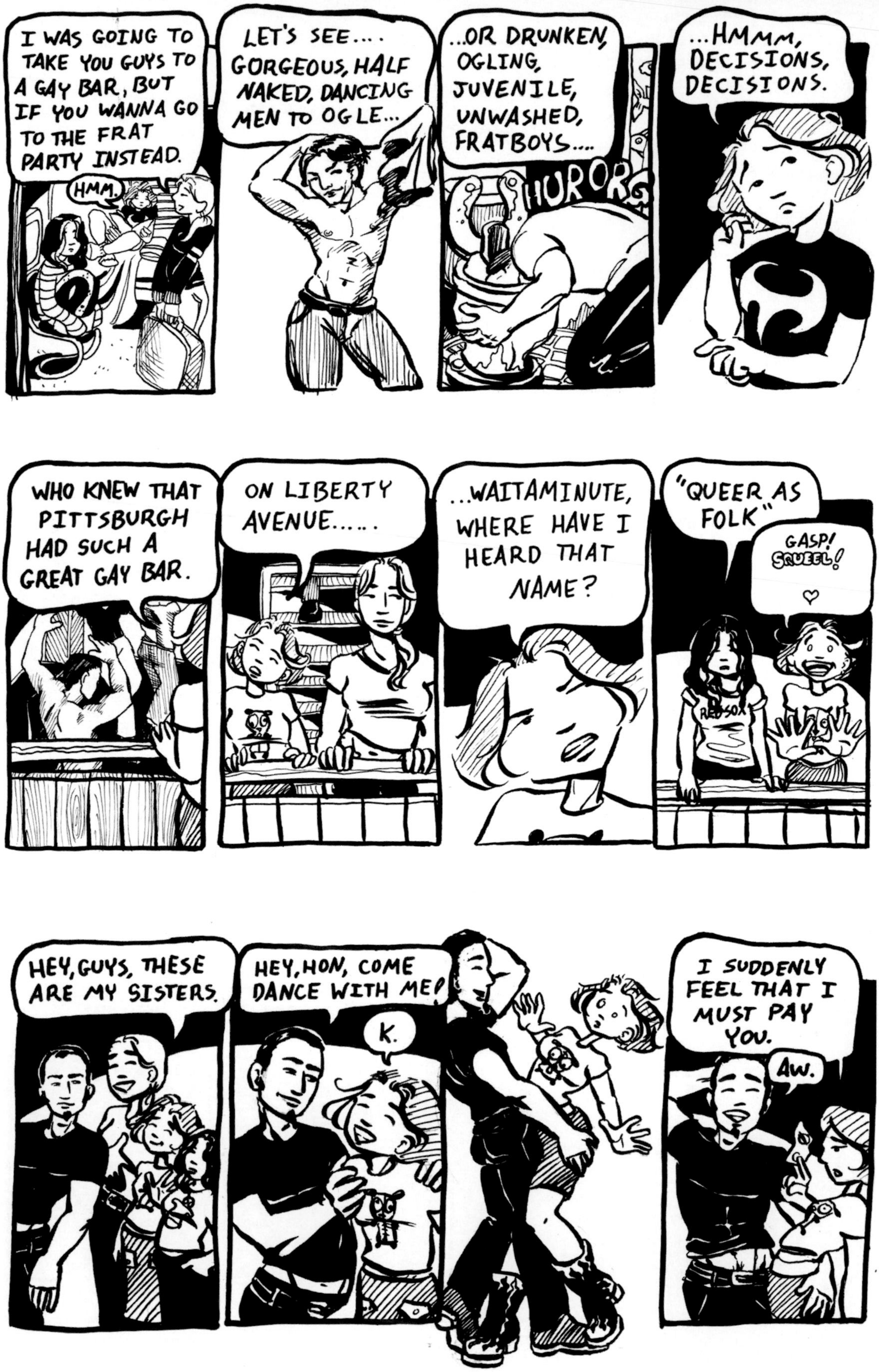
I WAS GOING TO TAKE YOU GUYS TO A GAY BAR, BUT IF YOU WANNA GO TO THE FRAT PARTY INSTEAD.
HMM.
LET'S SEE.... GORGEOUS, HALF NAKED, DANCING MEN TO OGLE...
...OR DRUNKEN, OGLING, JUVENILE, UNWASHED, FRATBOYS....
HURORG
...HMMM, DECISIONS, DECISIONS.
WHO KNEW THAT PITTSBURGH HAD SUCH A GREAT GAY BAR.
ON LIBERTY AVENUE......
...WAITAMINUTE, WHERE HAVE I HEARD THAT NAME?
"QUEER AS FOLK"
GASP! SQUEEL!
HEY, GUYS, THESE ARE MY SISTERS.
HEY, HON, COME DANCE WITH ME?
K.
I SUDDENLY FEEL THAT I MUST PAY YOU.
AW.

EXCUSE ME, COULD I—

DO YOU HAVE ANY—

HEEYY...

GOOD GOD, MY BOOBS HAVE NO POWER HERE.

I'M GLAD SUMMER BROUGHT US TO THIS CLUB, IT'S GREAT! WHERE'S OUR BABY SIS, ANYWAY?

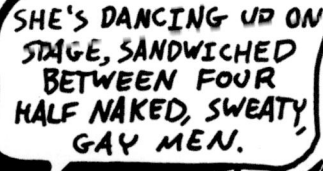

SHE'S DANCING UP ON STAGE, SANDWICHED BETWEEN FOUR HALF NAKED, SWEATY, GAY MEN.

AAH! IT BURNS!

HEY, SUMMER, CAN I COME WITH YOU TO YOUR MORNING CLASS?

SURE.

WELCOME TO POP CULTURE 101

TODAY WE'LL BE TALKING ABOUT REALITY TV.

AND PEOPLE THINK COMIC BOOKS* IS A FLUFF MAJOR?

*SEQUENTIAL ART
YES, I MAJORED IN IT.

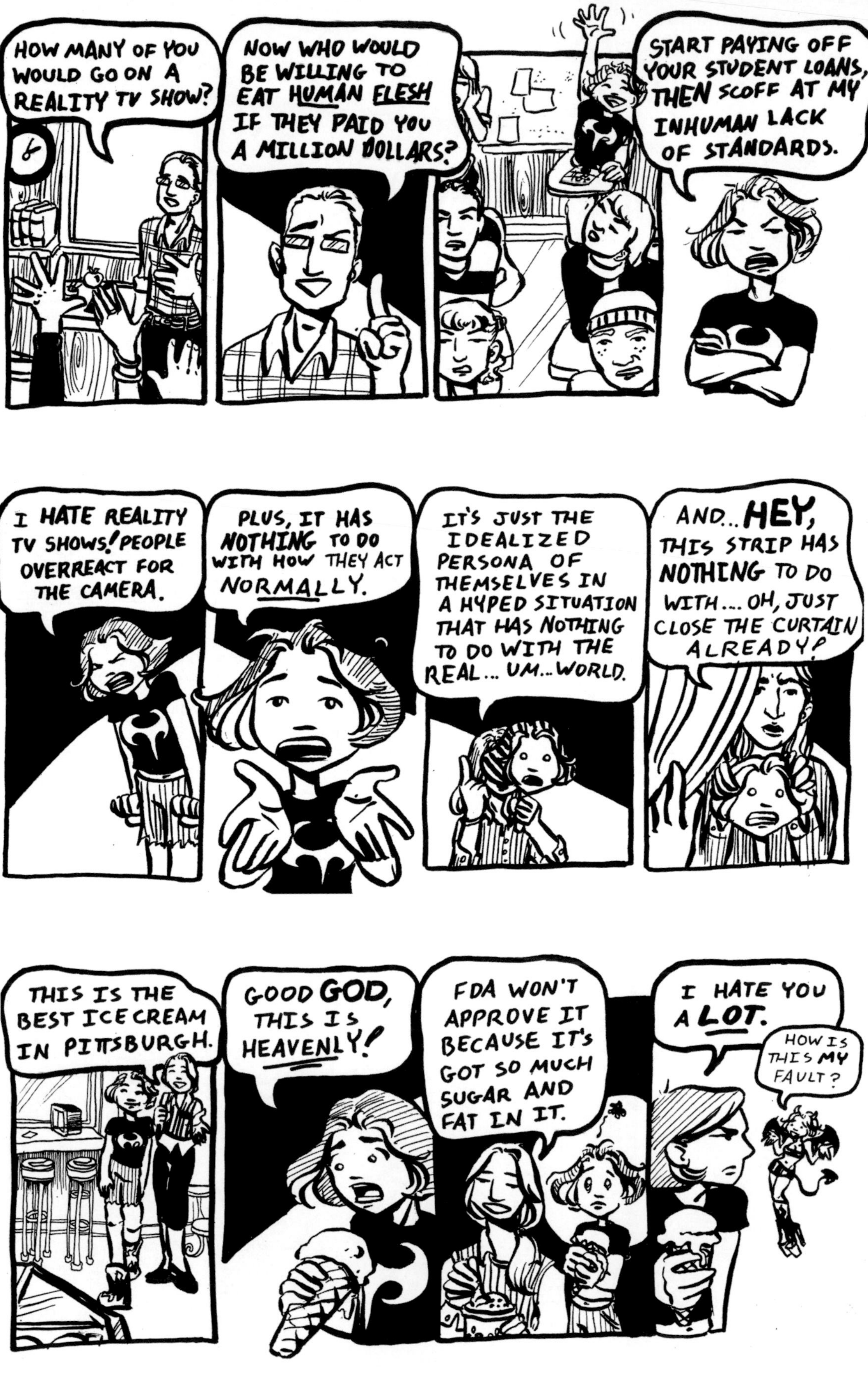

HOW MANY OF YOU WOULD GO ON A REALITY TV SHOW?
NOW WHO WOULD BE WILLING TO EAT HUMAN FLESH IF THEY PAID YOU A MILLION DOLLARS?
START PAYING OFF YOUR STUDENT LOANS, THEN SCOFF AT MY INHUMAN LACK OF STANDARDS.
I HATE REALITY TV SHOWS! PEOPLE OVERREACT FOR THE CAMERA.
PLUS, IT HAS NOTHING TO DO WITH HOW THEY ACT NORMALLY.
IT'S JUST THE IDEALIZED PERSONA OF THEMSELVES IN A HYPED SITUATION THAT HAS NOTHING TO DO WITH THE REAL... UM... WORLD.
AND... HEY, THIS STRIP HAS NOTHING TO DO WITH.... OH, JUST CLOSE THE CURTAIN ALREADY!
THIS IS THE BEST ICE CREAM IN PITTSBURGH.
GOOD GOD, THIS IS HEAVENLY!
FDA WON'T APPROVE IT BECAUSE IT'S GOT SO MUCH SUGAR AND FAT IN IT.
I HATE YOU A LOT.
HOW IS THIS MY FAULT?

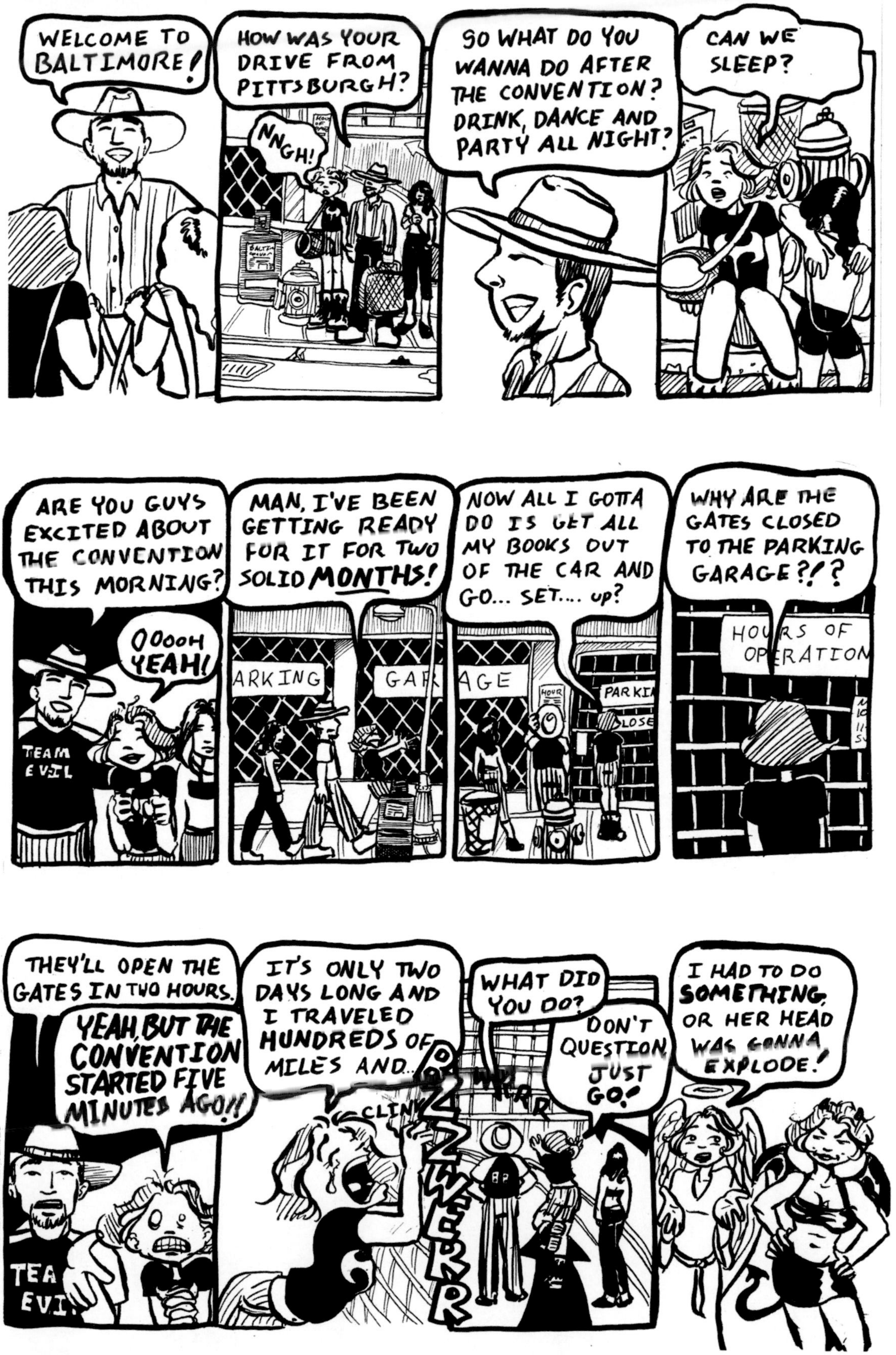
WELCOME TO BALTIMORE!
HOW WAS YOUR DRIVE FROM PITTSBURGH?
NNGH!
SO WHAT DO YOU WANNA DO AFTER THE CONVENTION? DRINK, DANCE AND PARTY ALL NIGHT?
CAN WE SLEEP?
ARE YOU GUYS EXCITED ABOUT THE CONVENTION THIS MORNING?
OOOOH YEAH!
TEAM EVIL
MAN, I'VE BEEN GETTING READY FOR IT FOR TWO SOLID MONTHS!
PARKING GARAGE
NOW ALL I GOTTA DO IS GET ALL MY BOOKS OUT OF THE CAR AND GO... SET.... up?
WHY ARE THE GATES CLOSED TO THE PARKING GARAGE?!?
HOURS OF OPERATION
THEY'LL OPEN THE GATES IN TWO HOURS.
YEAH, BUT THE CONVENTION STARTED FIVE MINUTES AGO!!
IT'S ONLY TWO DAYS LONG AND I TRAVELED HUNDREDS OF MILES AND...
CLINK
ZZWEERRR
WHAT DID YOU DO?
DON'T QUESTION, JUST GO!
I HAD TO DO SOMETHING, OR HER HEAD WAS GONNA EXPLODE!

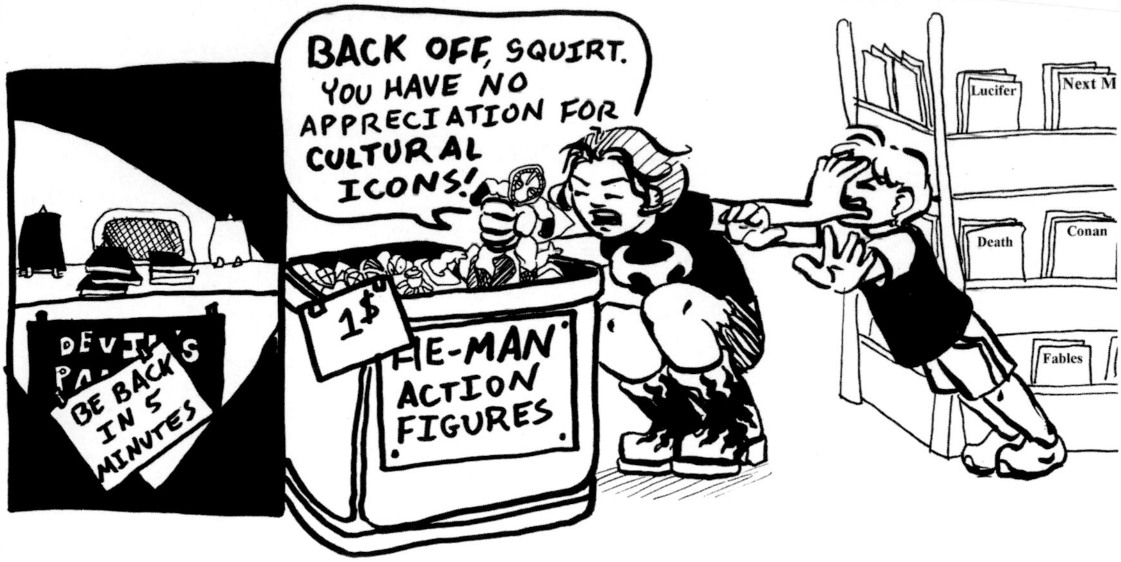
DEVI
BE BACK IN 5 MINUTES
BACK OFF, SQUIRT. YOU HAVE NO APPRECIATION FOR CULTURAL ICONS!
1$
HE-MAN ACTION FIGURES
Lucifer
Next M
Death
Conan
Fables

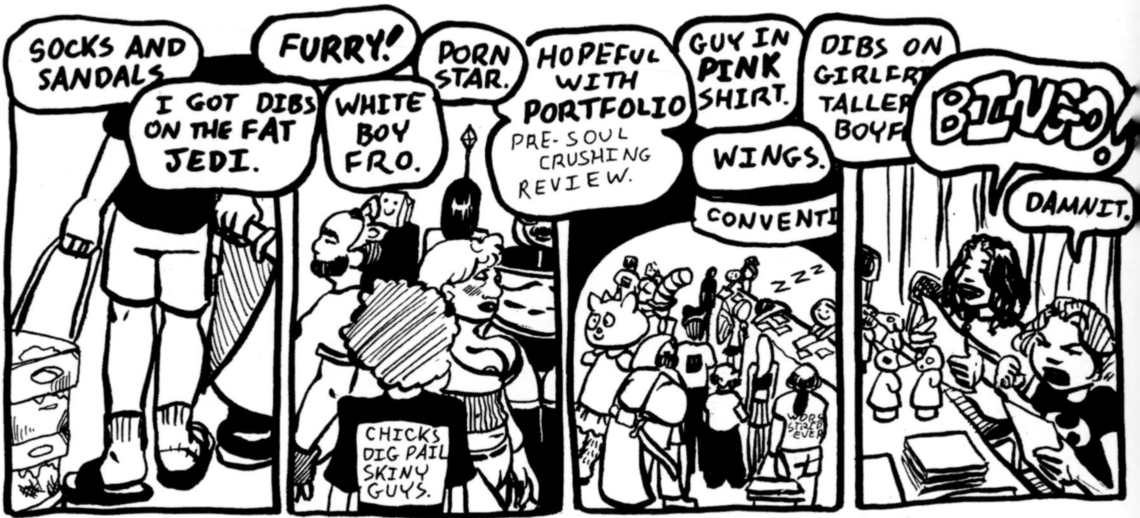
SOCKS AND SANDALS
I GOT DIBS ON THE FAT JEDI.
FURRY!
WHITE BOY FRO.
PORN STAR.
CHICKS DIG PAIL SKINY GUYS.
HOPEFUL WITH PORTFOLIO
PRE-SOUL CRUSHING REVIEW.
GUY IN PINK SHIRT.
WINGS.
CONVENTI
ZZZ
DIBS ON GIRLFR TALLER BOYF
BINGO!
DAMNIT.

COMIC CON BINGO PROVIDED BY WWW.YOUNGAMERICANCOMICS.COM

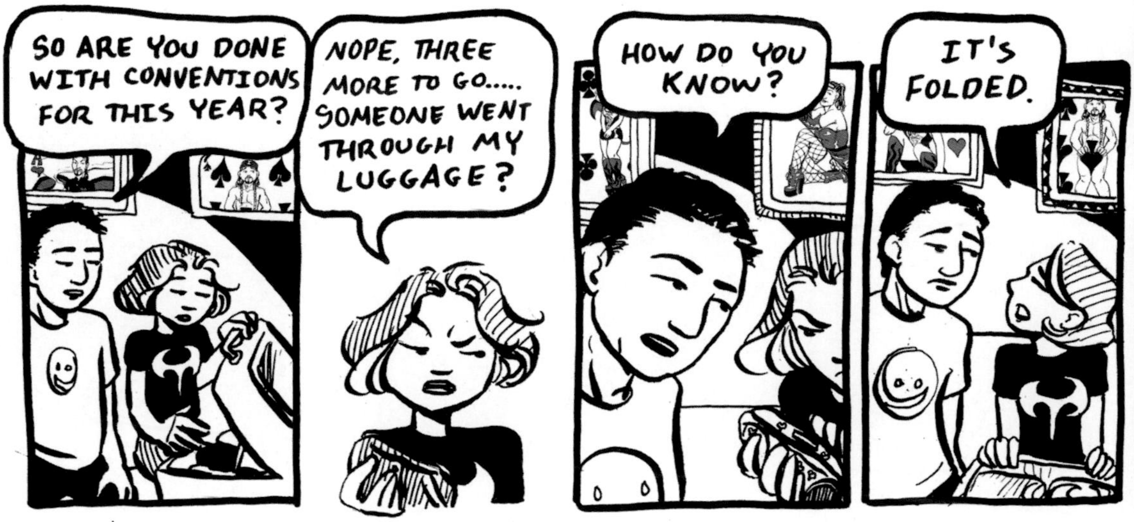
SO ARE YOU DONE WITH CONVENTIONS FOR THIS YEAR?
NOPE, THREE MORE TO GO..... SOMEONE WENT THROUGH MY LUGGAGE?
HOW DO YOU KNOW?
IT'S FOLDED.

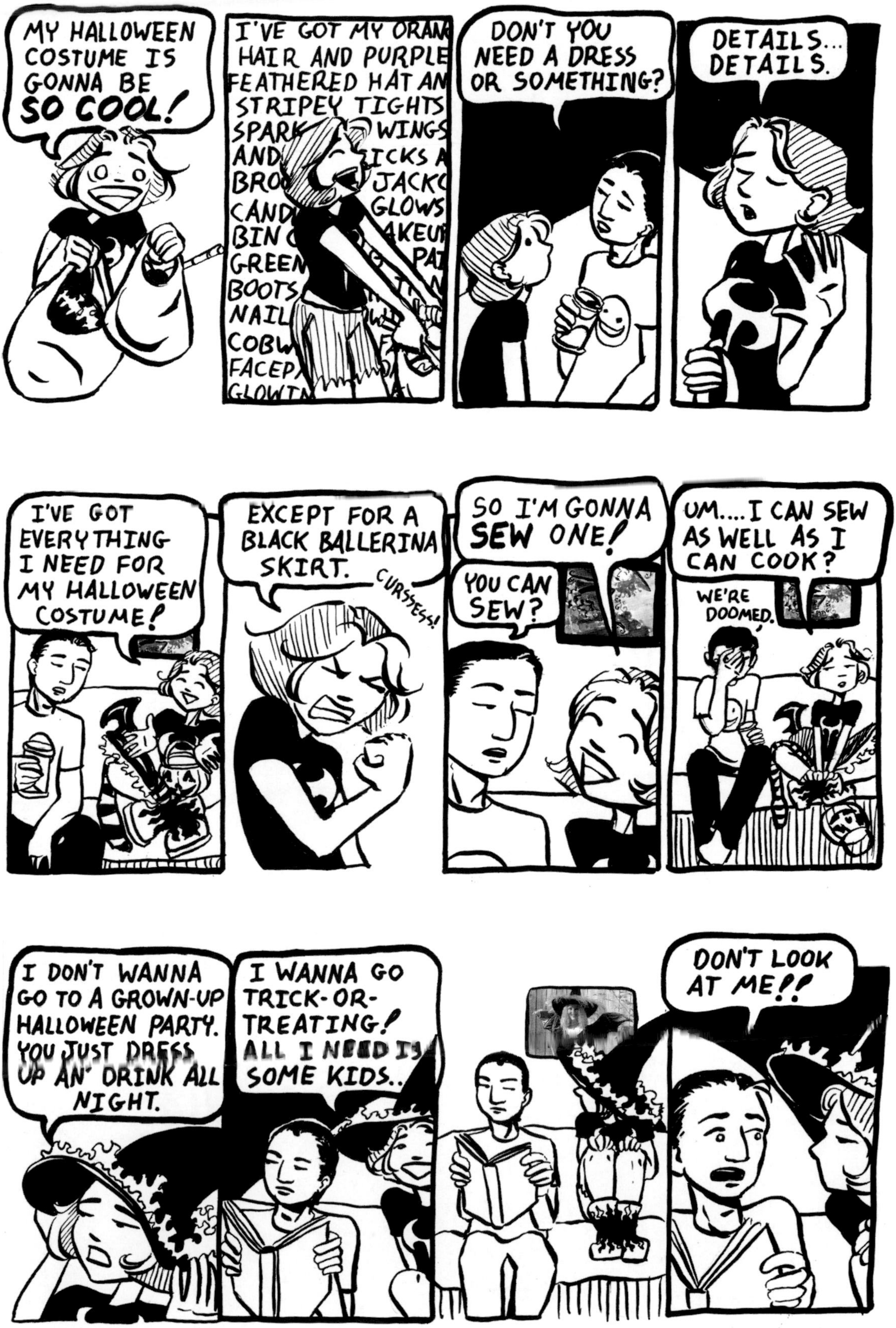
MY HALLOWEEN COSTUME IS GONNA BE SO COOL!
I'VE GOT MY ORAN HAIR AND PURPLE FEATHERED HAT AN STRIPEY TIGHTS SPARK WINGS AND ICKS A BRO JACK CAND GLOWS BIN AKEU GREEN PA BOOTS NAIL COBW FACEP GLOWT
DON'T YOU NEED A DRESS OR SOMETHING?
DETAILS... DETAILS.
I'VE GOT EVERYTHING I NEED FOR MY HALLOWEEN COSTUME!
EXCEPT FOR A BLACK BALLERINA SKIRT.
CURSSESS!
SO I'M GONNA SEW ONE!
YOU CAN SEW?
UM.... I CAN SEW AS WELL AS I CAN COOK?
WE'RE DOOMED.
I DON'T WANNA GO TO A GROWN-UP HALLOWEEN PARTY. YOU JUST DRESS UP AN' DRINK ALL NIGHT.
I WANNA GO TRICK-OR-TREATING! ALL I NEED IS SOME KIDS..
DON'T LOOK AT ME!!

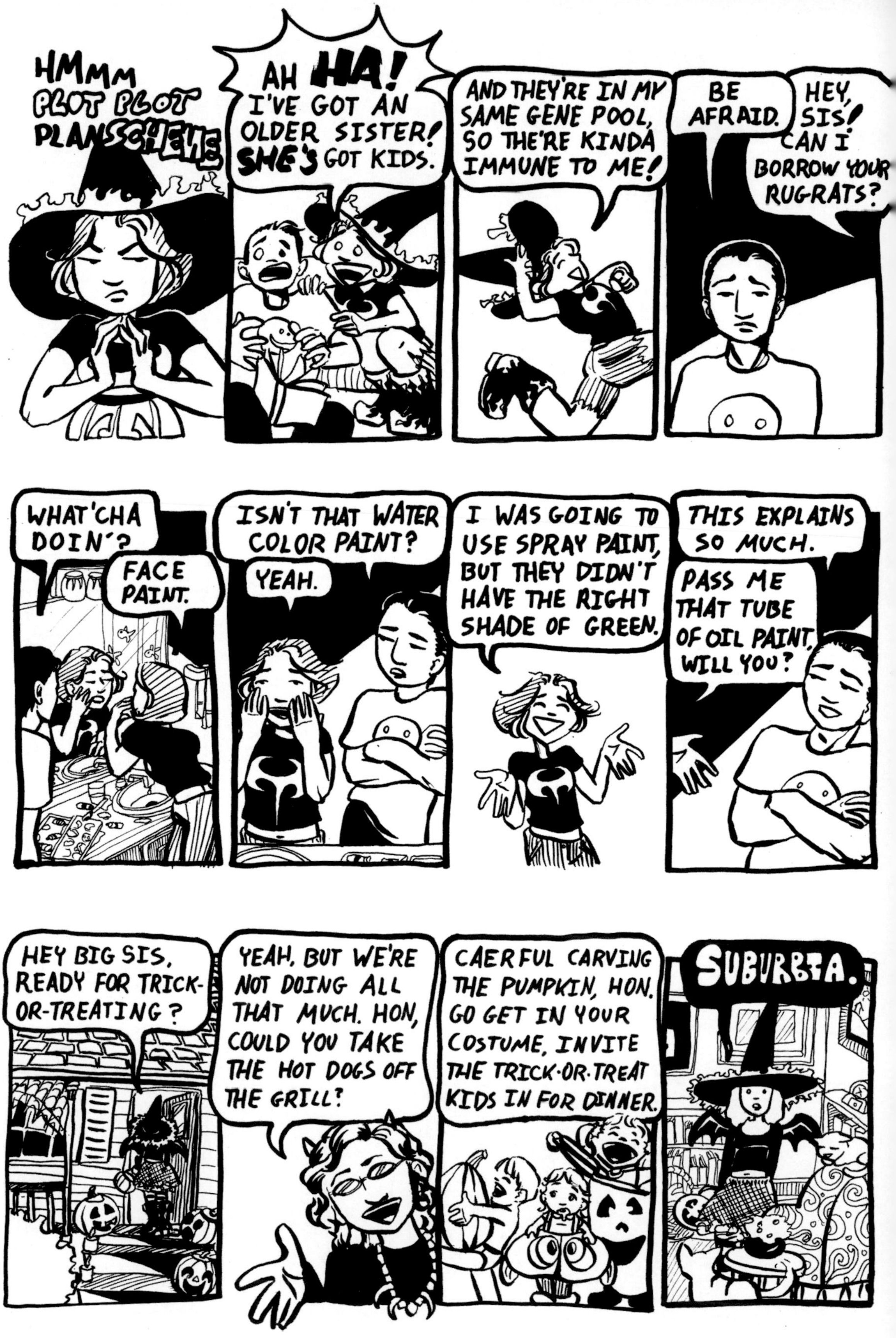
HMMM
PLOT PLOT
PLANSCHEME
AH HA!
I'VE GOT AN OLDER SISTER! SHE'S GOT KIDS.
AND THEY'RE IN MY SAME GENE POOL, SO THE'RE KINDA IMMUNE TO ME!
BE AFRAID.
HEY, SIS! CAN I BORROW YOUR RUGRATS?
WHAT'CHA DOIN'?
FACE PAINT.
ISN'T THAT WATER COLOR PAINT?
YEAH.
I WAS GOING TO USE SPRAY PAINT, BUT THEY DIDN'T HAVE THE RIGHT SHADE OF GREEN.
THIS EXPLAINS SO MUCH.
PASS ME THAT TUBE OF OIL PAINT, WILL YOU?
HEY BIG SIS, READY FOR TRICK-OR-TREATING?
YEAH, BUT WE'RE NOT DOING ALL THAT MUCH. HON, COULD YOU TAKE THE HOT DOGS OFF THE GRILL?
CAERFUL CARVING THE PUMPKIN, HON. GO GET IN YOUR COSTUME, INVITE THE TRICK-OR-TREAT KIDS IN FOR DINNER.
SUBURBIA.

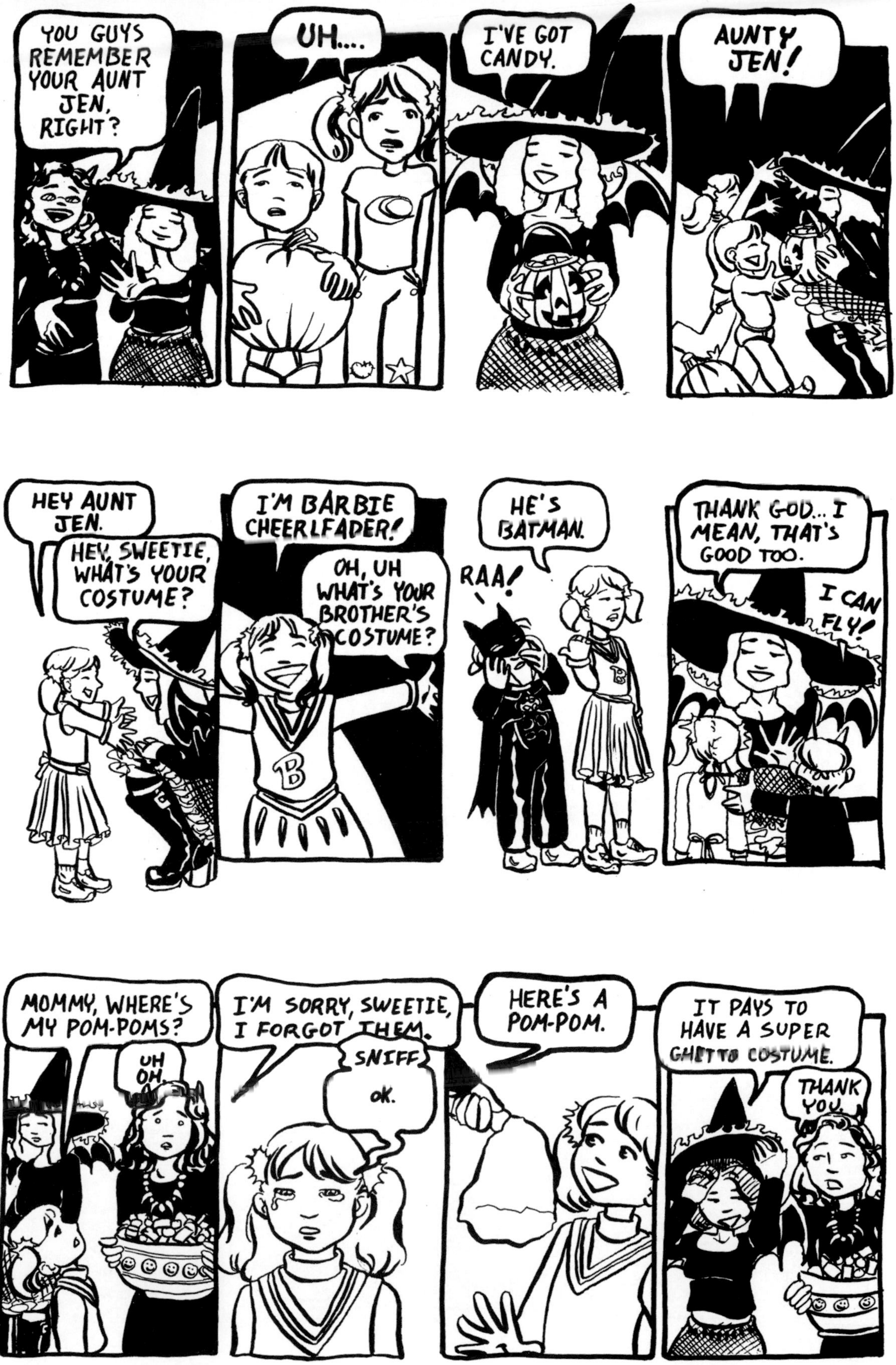
YOU GUYS REMEMBER YOUR AUNT JEN, RIGHT?
UH....
I'VE GOT CANDY.
AUNTY JEN!
HEY AUNT JEN.
HEY, SWEETIE, WHAT'S YOUR COSTUME?
I'M BARBIE CHEERLEADER!
OH, UH WHAT'S YOUR BROTHER'S COSTUME?
HE'S BATMAN.
RAA!
THANK GOD... I MEAN, THAT'S GOOD TOO.
I CAN FLY!
MOMMY, WHERE'S MY POM-POMS?
UH OH.
I'M SORRY, SWEETIE, I FORGOT THEM.
SNIFF
OK.
HERE'S A POM-POM.
IT PAYS TO HAVE A SUPER GHETTO COSTUME.
THANK YOU.

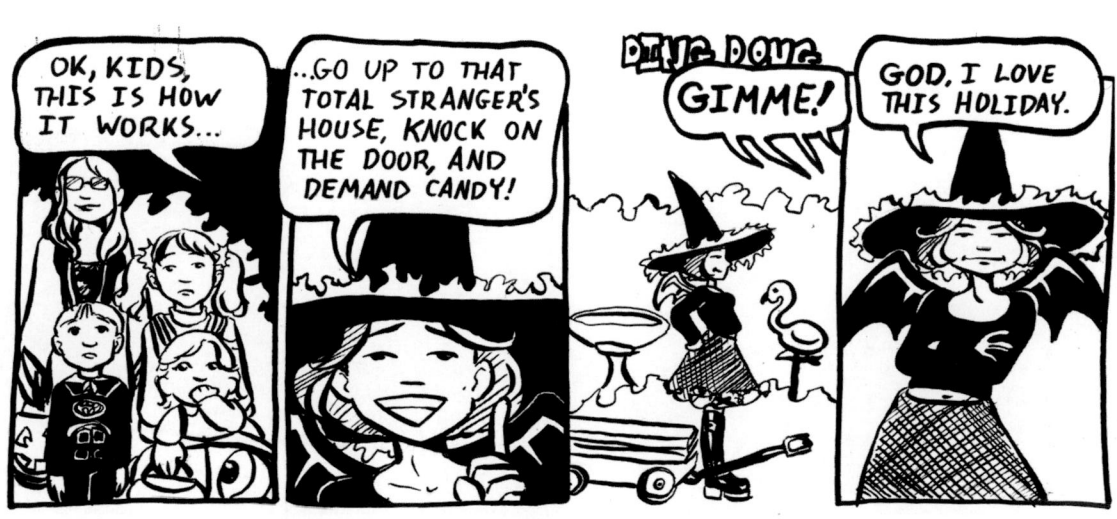

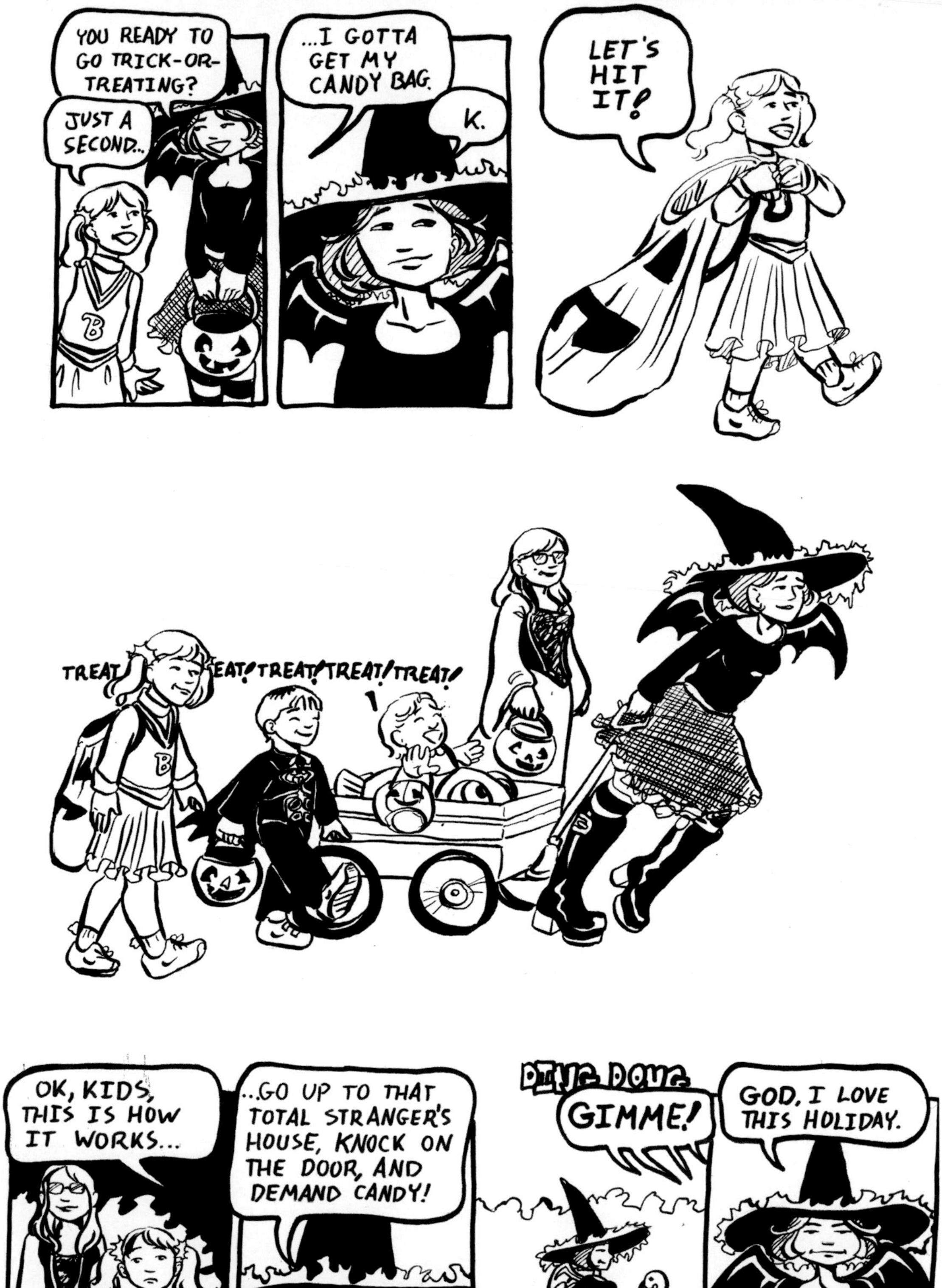
YOU READY TO GO TRICK-OR-TREATING?
JUST A SECOND..
...I GOTTA GET MY CANDY BAG.
K.
LET'S HIT IT!
TREAT
EAT! TREAT! TREAT! TREAT!
OK, KIDS, THIS IS HOW IT WORKS...
...GO UP TO THAT TOTAL STRANGER'S HOUSE, KNOCK ON THE DOOR, AND DEMAND CANDY!
DING DONG
GIMME!
GOD, I LOVE THIS HOLIDAY.

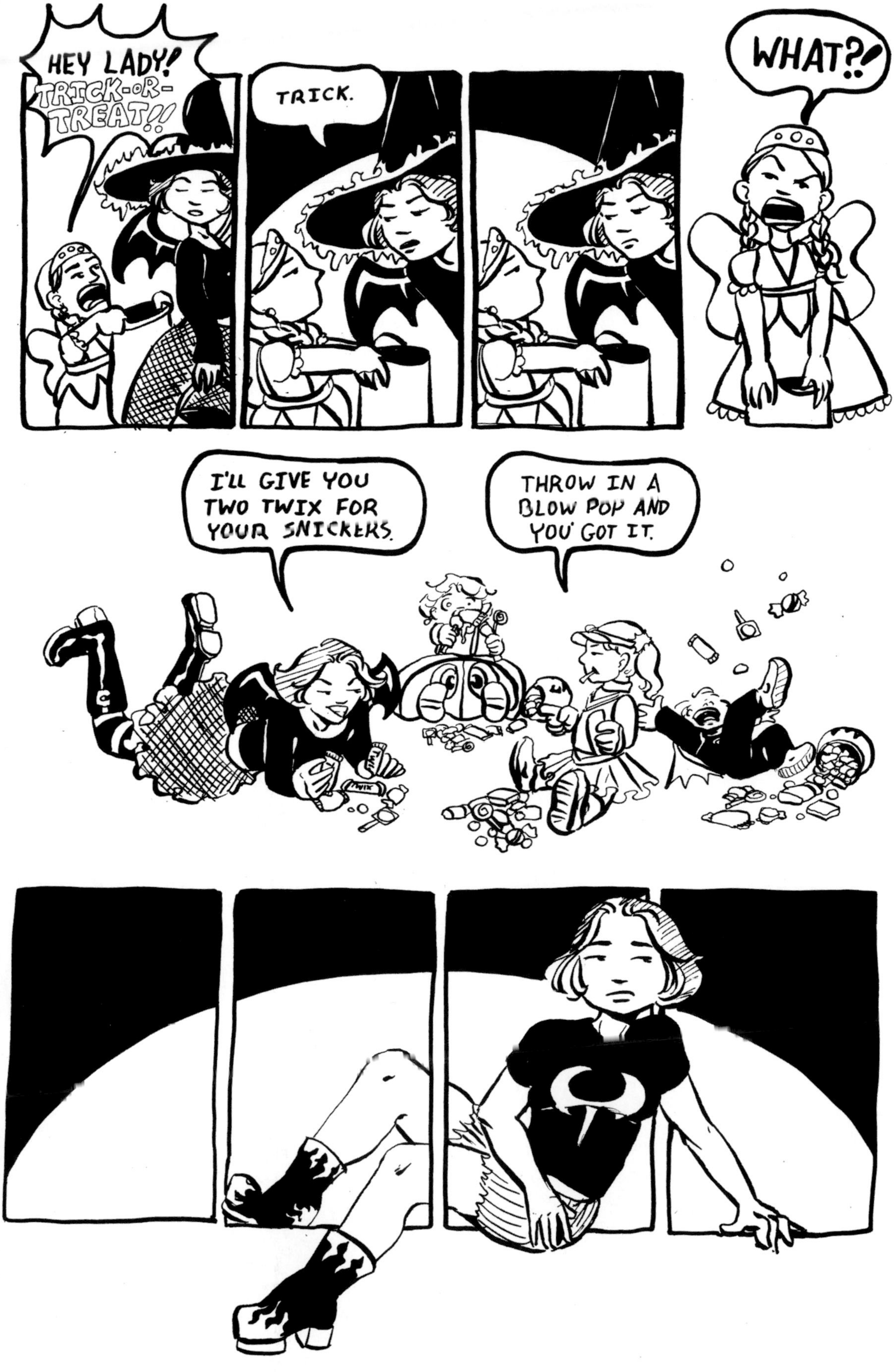
HEY LADY! TRICK-OR-TREAT!!
TRICK.
WHAT?!
I'LL GIVE YOU TWO TWIX FOR YOUR SNICKERS.
THROW IN A BLOW POP AND YOU GOT IT.
TWIX

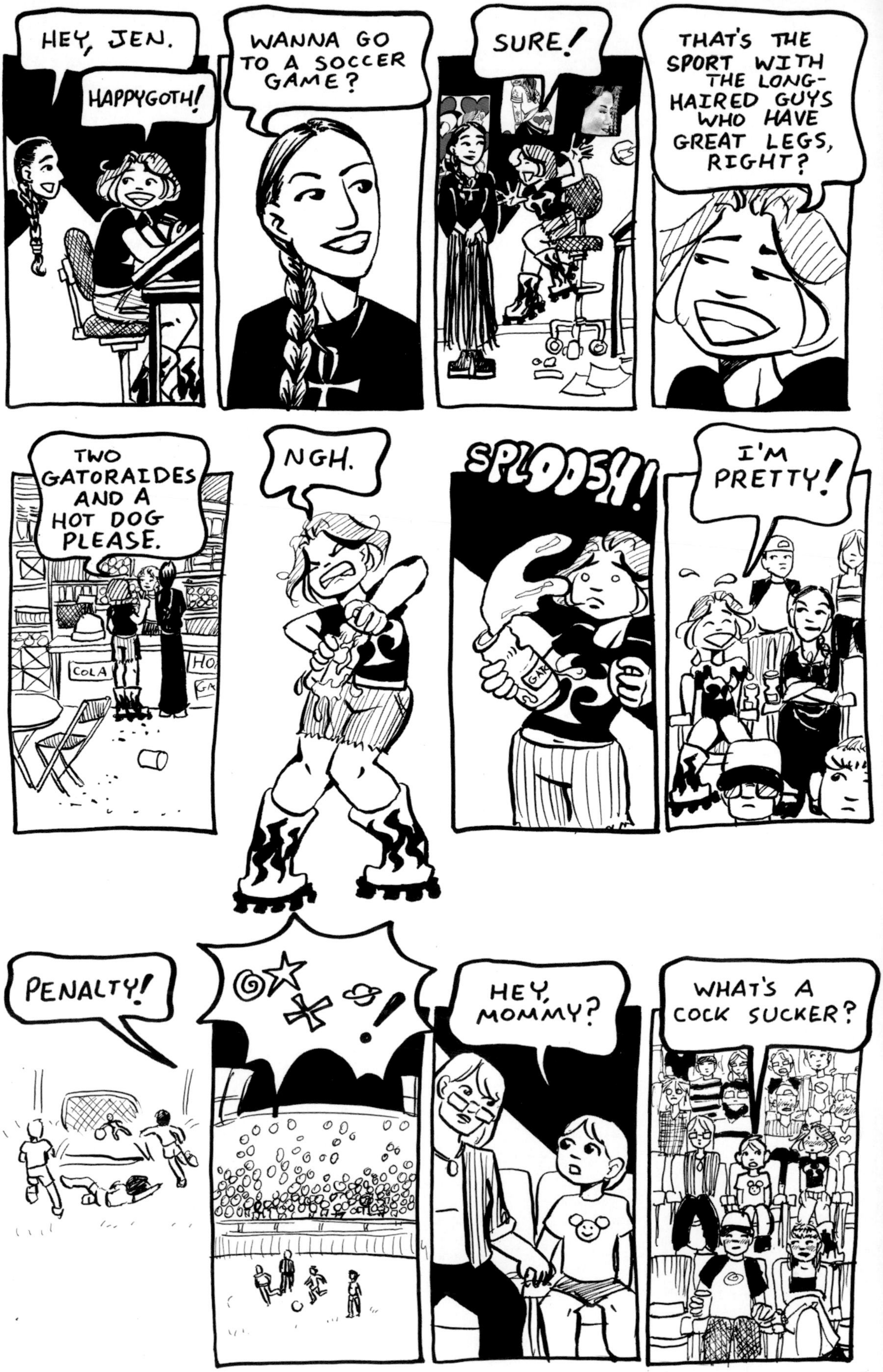
HEY, JEN.
HAPPYGOTH!
WANNA GO TO A SOCCER GAME?
SURE!
THAT'S THE SPORT WITH THE LONG-HAIRED GUYS WHO HAVE GREAT LEGS, RIGHT?
TWO GATORAIDES AND A HOT DOG PLEASE.
COLA
NGH.
SPLOOSH!
I'M PRETTY!
PENALTY!
HEY, MOMMY?
WHAT'S A COCK SUCKER?

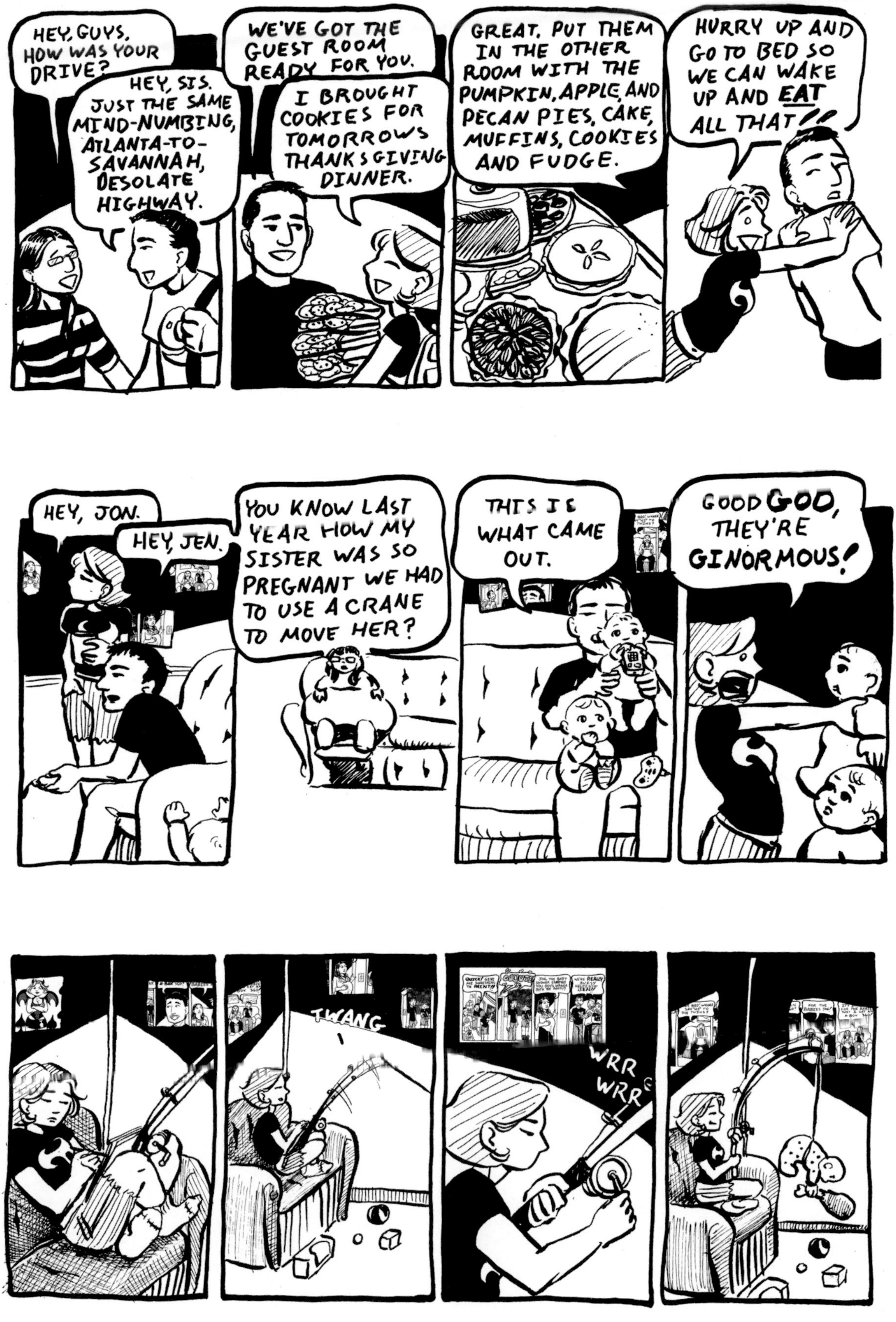
HEY, GUYS. HOW WAS YOUR DRIVE?
HEY, SIS. JUST THE SAME MIND-NUMBING, ATLANTA-TO-SAVANNAH, DESOLATE HIGHWAY.
WE'VE GOT THE GUEST ROOM READY FOR YOU.
I BROUGHT COOKIES FOR TOMORROWS THANKSGIVING DINNER.
GREAT. PUT THEM IN THE OTHER ROOM WITH THE PUMPKIN, APPLE, AND PECAN PIES, CAKE, MUFFINS, COOKIES AND FUDGE.
HURRY UP AND GO TO BED SO WE CAN WAKE UP AND EAT ALL THAT!!!
HEY, JON.
HEY, JEN.
YOU KNOW LAST YEAR HOW MY SISTER WAS SO PREGNANT WE HAD TO USE A CRANE TO MOVE HER?
THIS IS WHAT CAME OUT.
GOOD GOD, THEY'RE GINORMOUS!
TWANG
WRR WRR

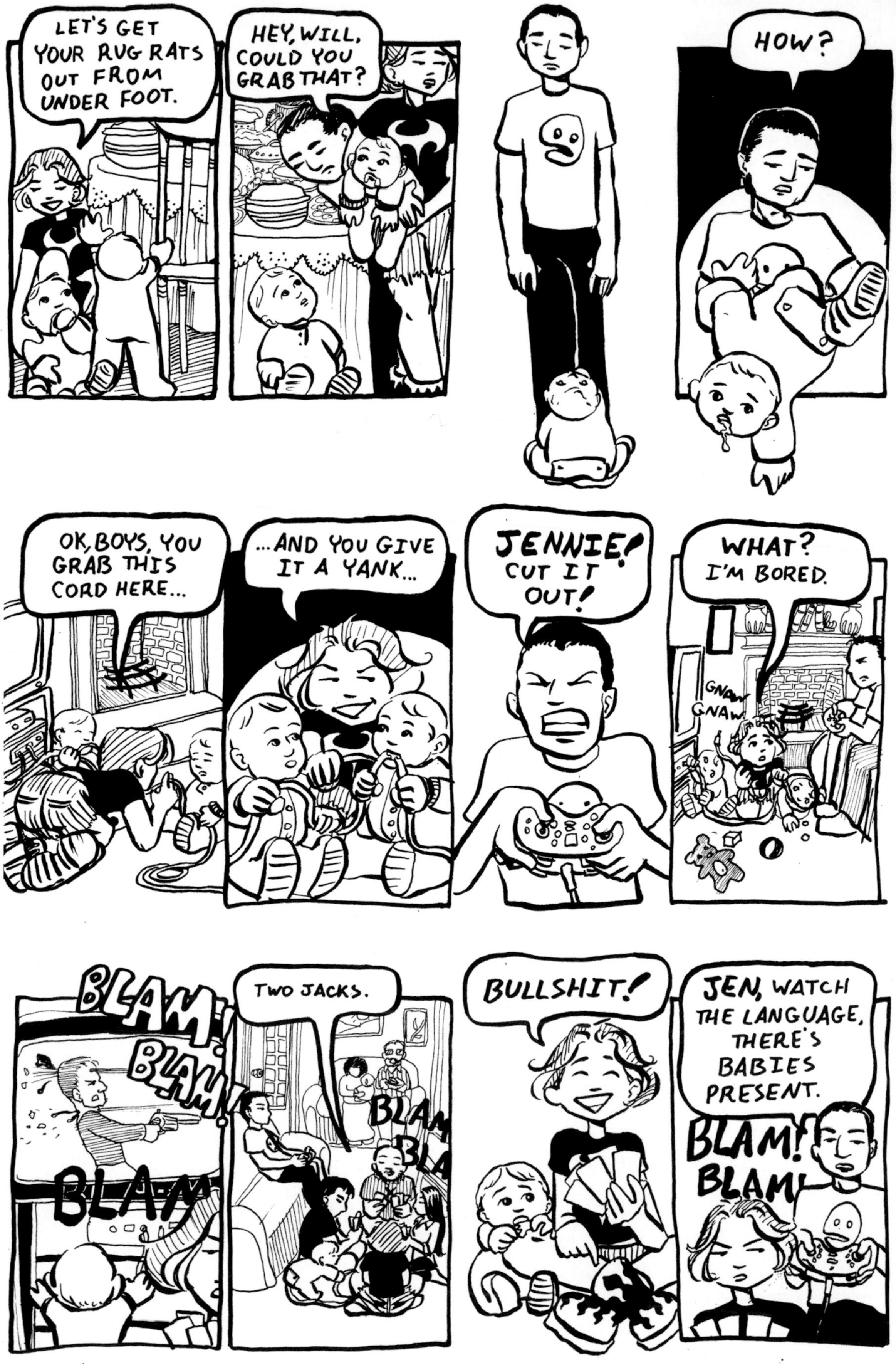
LET'S GET YOUR RUG RATS OUT FROM UNDER FOOT.
HEY, WILL, COULD YOU GRAB THAT?
HOW?
OK, BOYS, YOU GRAB THIS CORD HERE...
...AND YOU GIVE IT A YANK...
JENNIE! CUT IT OUT!
WHAT? I'M BORED.
GNAW GNAW
BLAM! BLAM! BLAM
TWO JACKS.
BLAM BLA
BULLSHIT!
JEN, WATCH THE LANGUAGE, THERE'S BABIES PRESENT.
BLAM! BLAM!

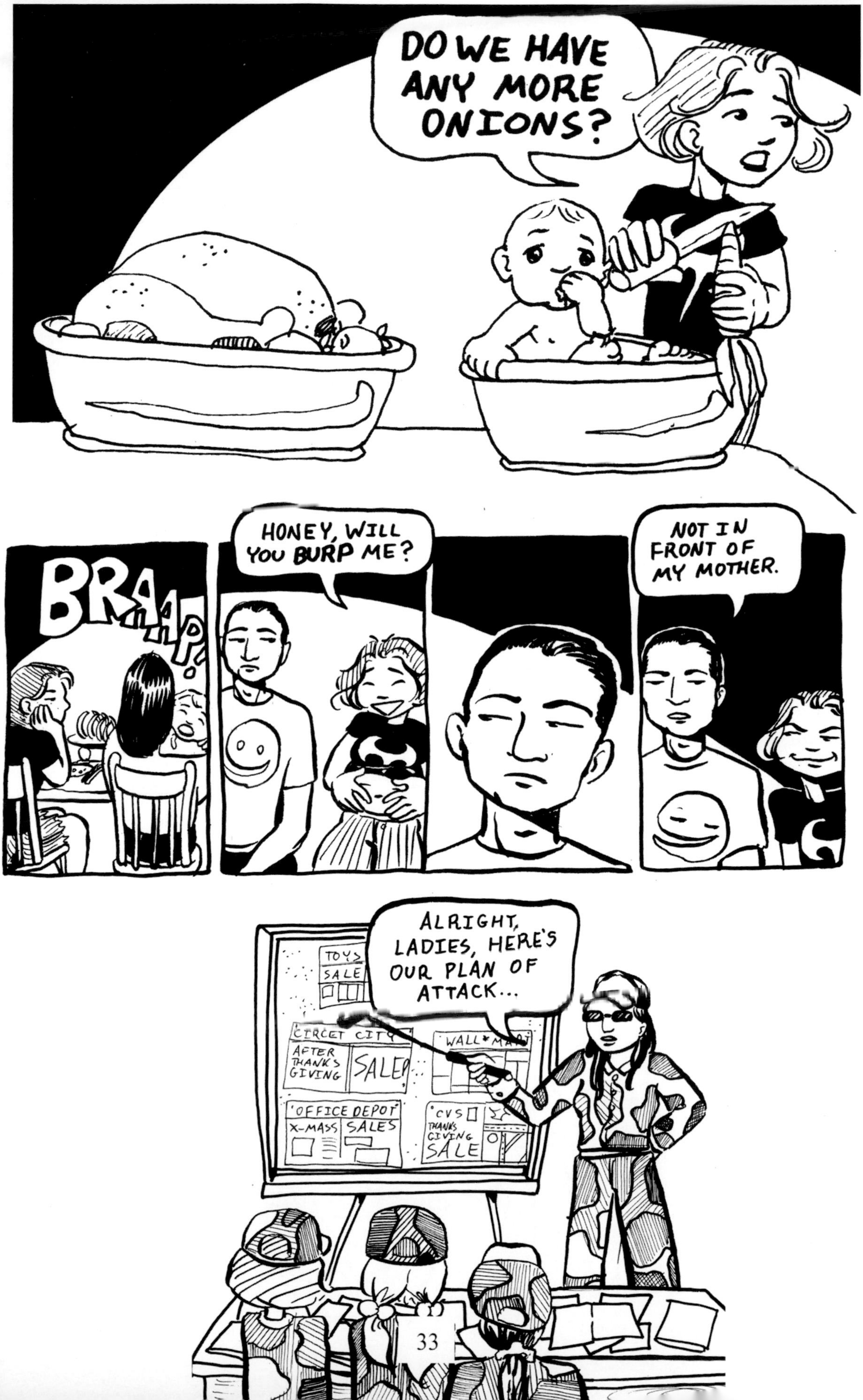
DO WE HAVE ANY MORE ONIONS?
BRAAAP!
HONEY, WILL YOU BURP ME?
NOT IN FRONT OF MY MOTHER.
ALRIGHT, LADIES, HERE'S OUR PLAN OF ATTACK...
TOYS SALE
CIRCET CITY
AFTER THANKS GIVING
SALE!
OFFICE DEPOT
X-MASS
SALES
CVS
THANKS GIVING SALE

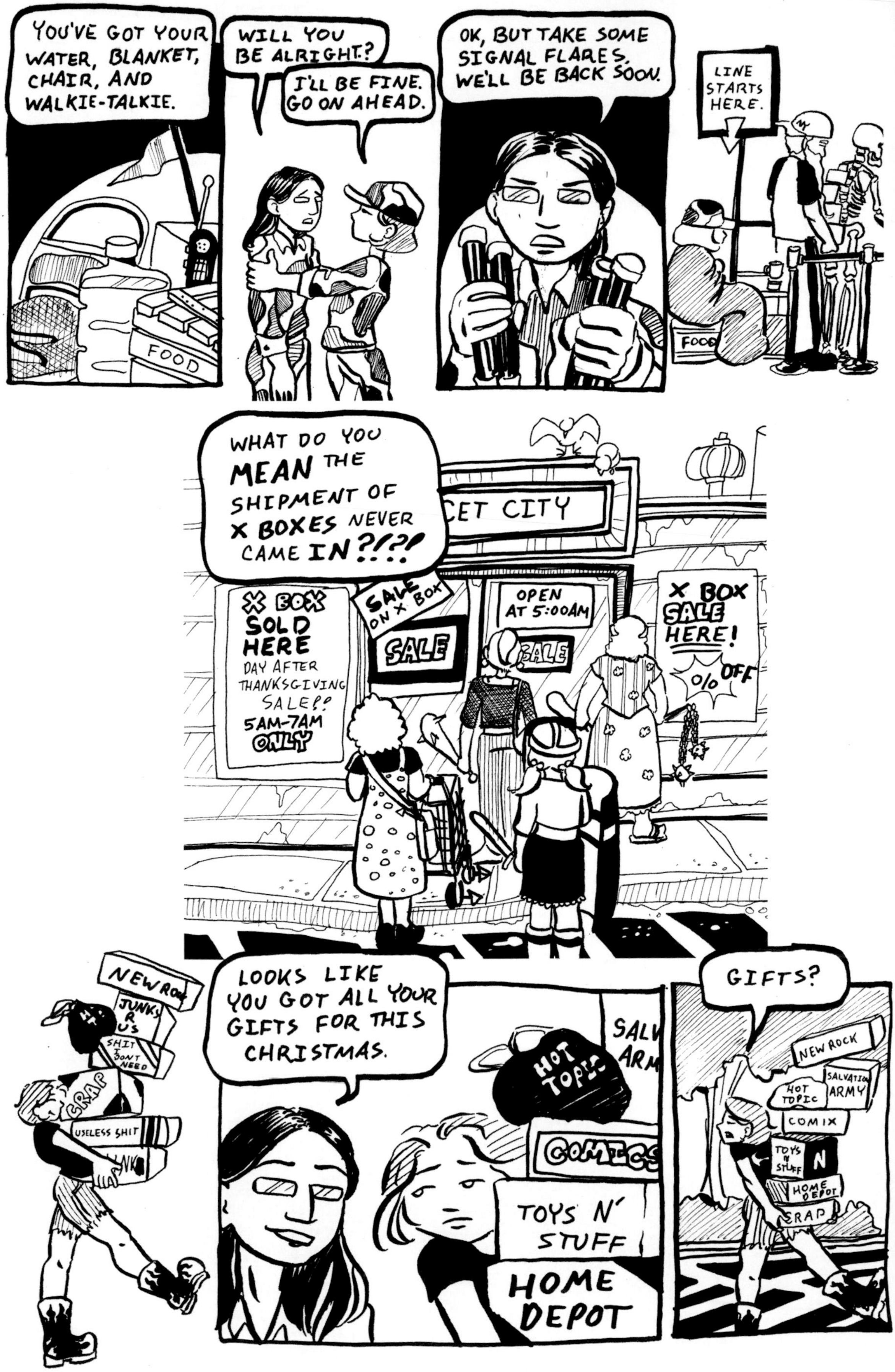
YOU'VE GOT YOUR WATER, BLANKET, CHAIR, AND WALKIE-TALKIE.
FOOD
WILL YOU BE ALRIGHT?
I'LL BE FINE. GO ON AHEAD.
OK, BUT TAKE SOME SIGNAL FLARES. WE'LL BE BACK SOON.
LINE STARTS HERE.
FOOD
WHAT DO YOU MEAN THE SHIPMENT OF X BOXES NEVER CAME IN?!?!
CET CITY
X BOX SOLD HERE DAY AFTER THANKSGIVING SALE!! 5AM-7AM ONLY
SALE ON X BOX
SALE
OPEN AT 5:00AM
SALE
X BOX SALE HERE!
% OFF
NEW ROCK
JUNKS R US
SHIT I DONT NEED
CRAP
USELESS SHIT
JUNK
LOOKS LIKE YOU GOT ALL YOUR GIFTS FOR THIS CHRISTMAS.
HOT TOPIC
SALV ARM
COMICS
TOYS N' STUFF
HOME DEPOT
GIFTS?
NEW ROCK
HOT TOPIC
SALVATION ARMY
COMIX
TOYS N STUFF
N
HOME DEPOT
CRAP

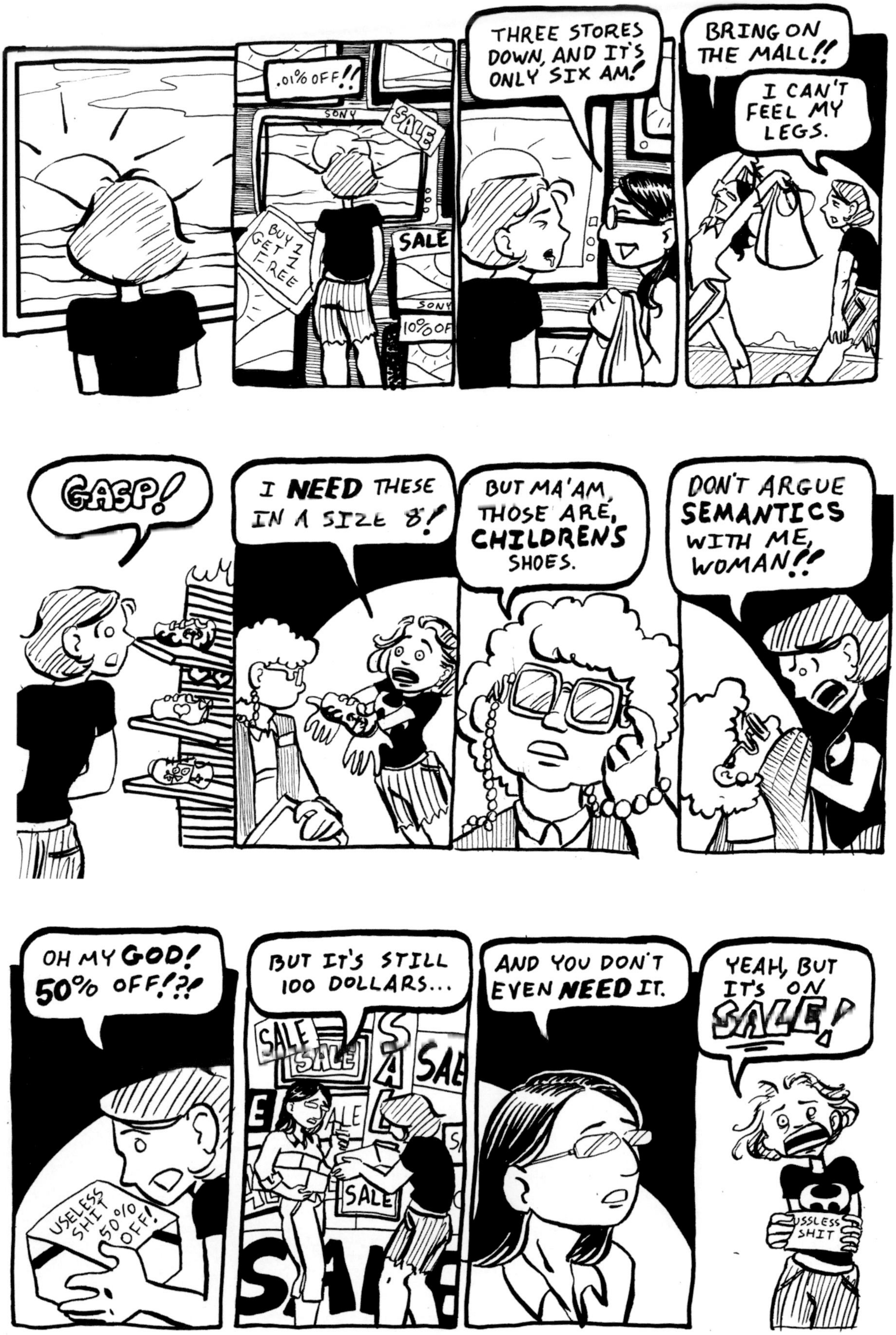

.01% OFF!!
SONY
SALE
BUY 1 GET 1 FREE
SALE
SONY
10% OFF
THREE STORES DOWN, AND IT'S ONLY SIX AM!
BRING ON THE MALL!!
I CAN'T FEEL MY LEGS.
GASP!
I NEED THESE IN A SIZE 8!
BUT MA'AM, THOSE ARE CHILDREN'S SHOES.
DON'T ARGUE SEMANTICS WITH ME, WOMAN!!
OH MY GOD! 50% OFF!?!
USELESS SHIT 50% OFF!
BUT IT'S STILL 100 DOLLARS...
SALE
AND YOU DON'T EVEN NEED IT.
YEAH, BUT IT'S ON SALE!
USSLESS SHIT

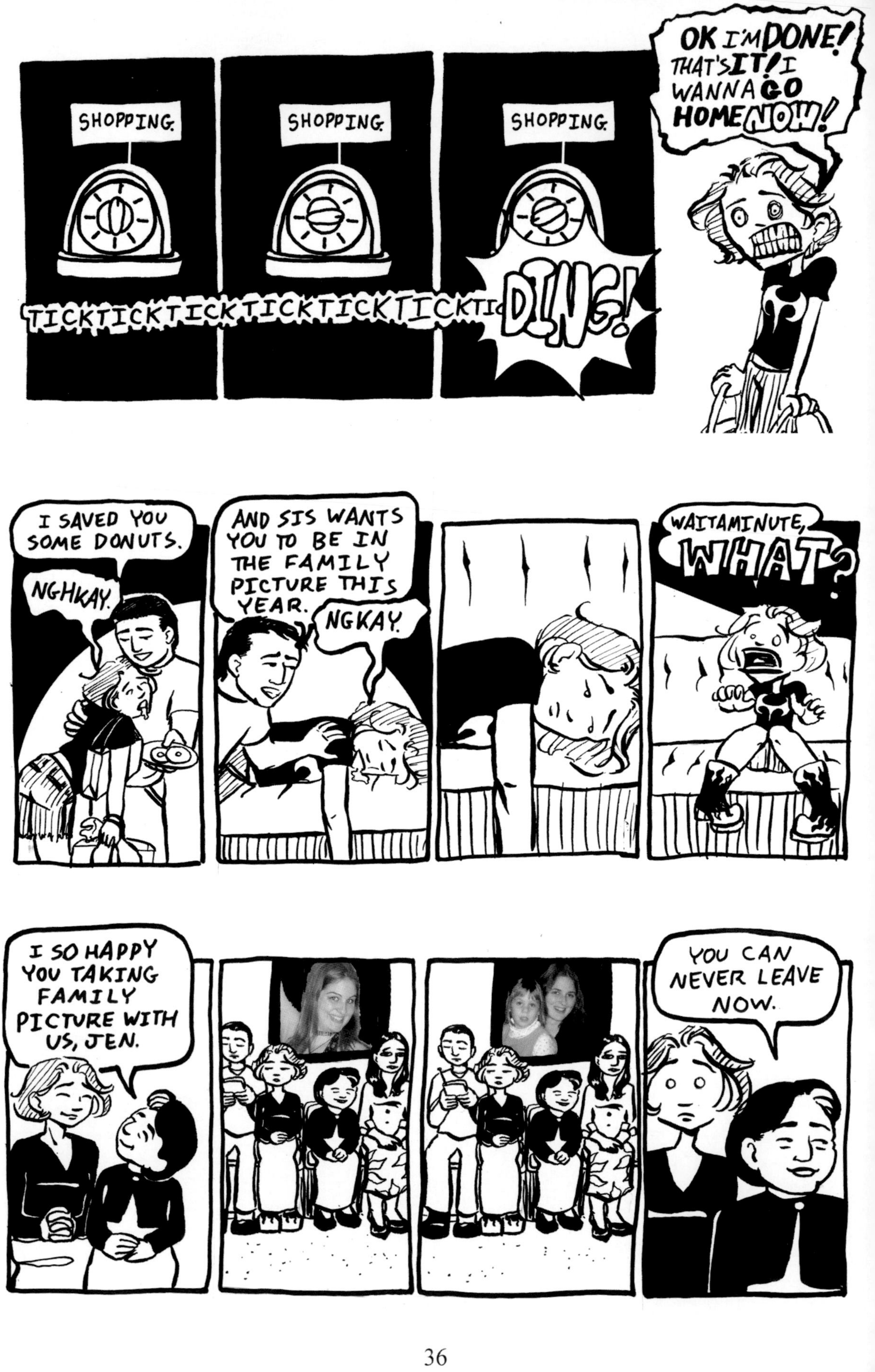
SHOPPING.
SHOPPING.
SHOPPING.
TICKTICKTICKTICKTICKTICKTI
DING!
OK I'M DONE! THAT'S IT! I WANNA GO HOME NOW!
I SAVED YOU SOME DONUTS.
NGHKAY.
AND SIS WANTS YOU TO BE IN THE FAMILY PICTURE THIS YEAR.
NGKAY.
WAITAMINUTE, WHAT?
I SO HAPPY YOU TAKING FAMILY PICTURE WITH US, JEN.
YOU CAN NEVER LEAVE NOW.

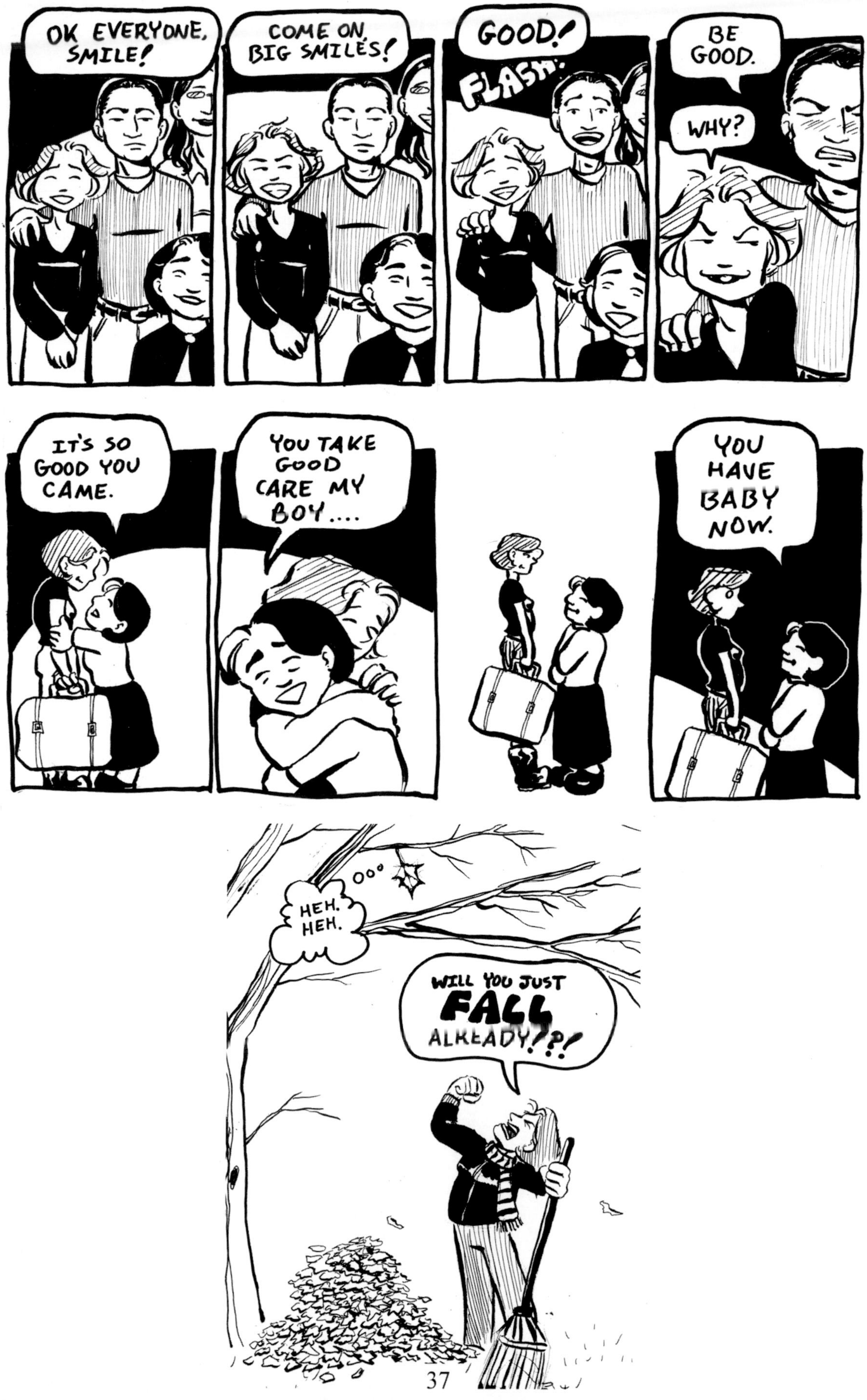
OK EVERYONE, SMILE!
COME ON, BIG SMILES!
GOOD!
FLASH!
BE GOOD.
WHY?
IT'S SO GOOD YOU CAME.
YOU TAKE GOOD CARE MY BOY....
YOU HAVE BABY NOW.
OOO
HEH. HEH.
WILL YOU JUST FALL ALREADY?!?!

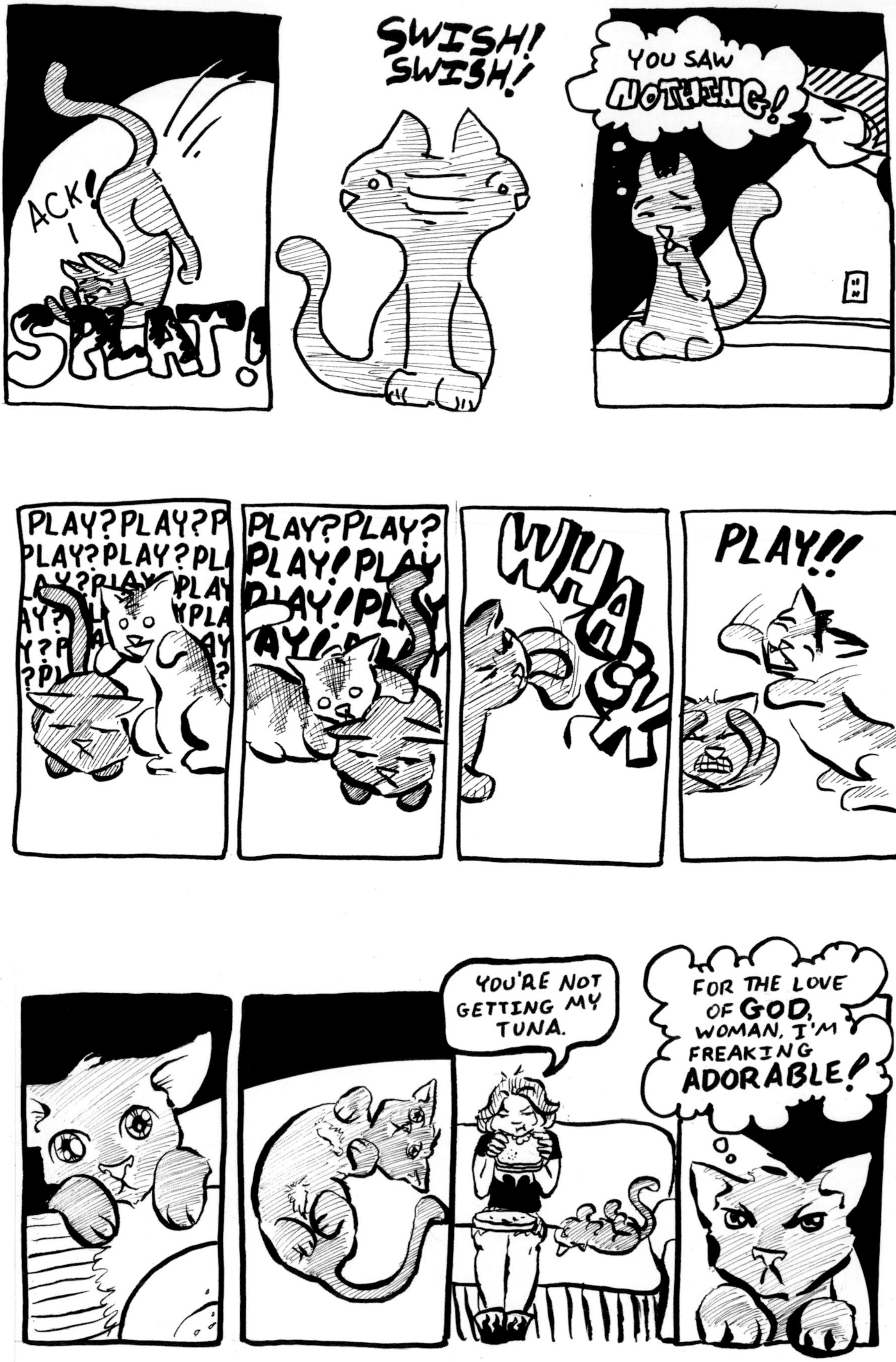
ACK!
SPLAT!
SWISH! SWISH!
YOU SAW NOTHING!
PLAY? PLAY? PLAY? PLAY?
PLAY? PLAY? PLAY! PLAY!
WHACK
PLAY!!
YOU'RE NOT GETTING MY TUNA.
FOR THE LOVE OF GOD, WOMAN, I'M FREAKING ADORABLE!

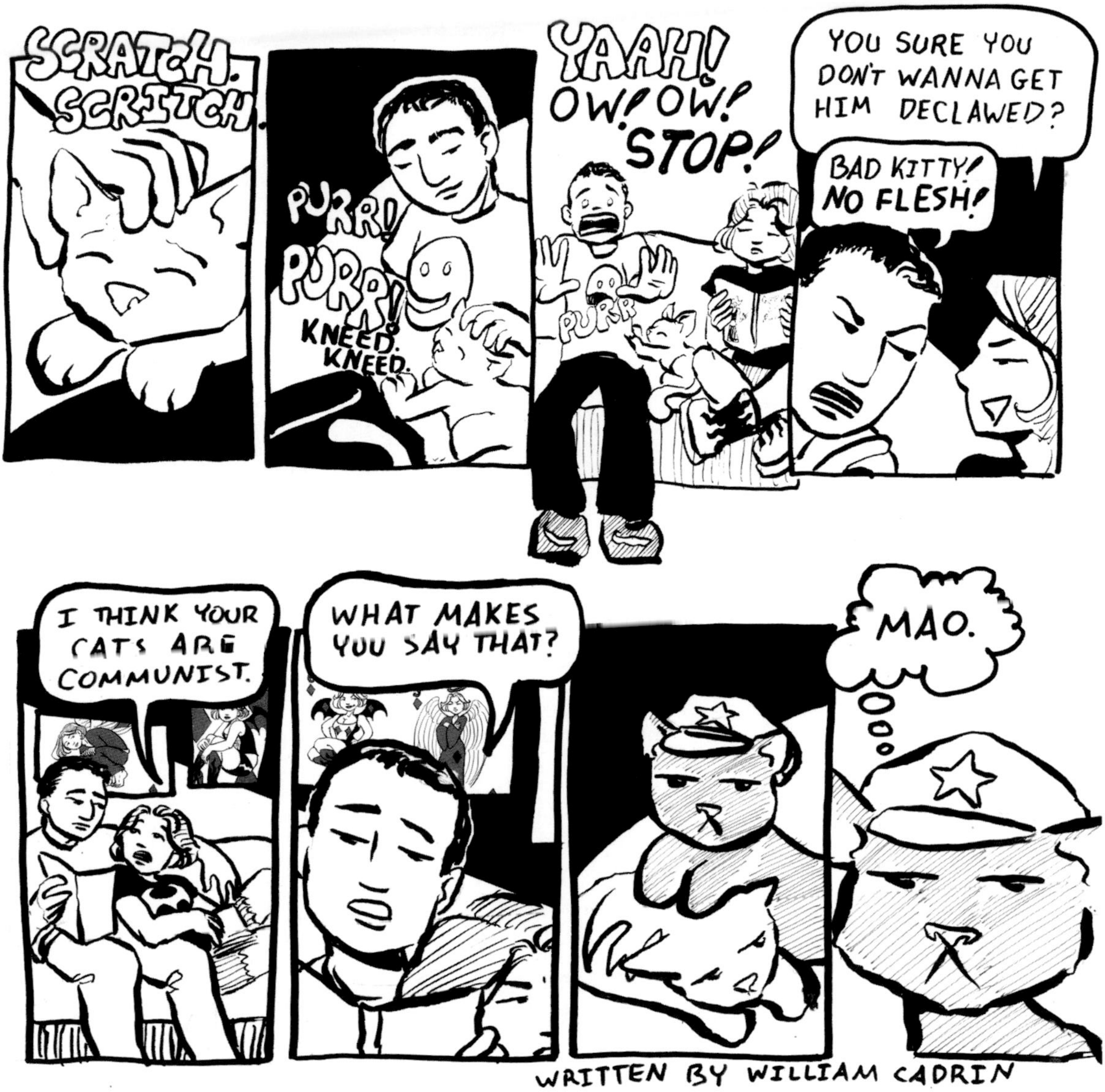
SCRATCH. SCRITCH.
PURR! PURR!
KNEED. KNEED.
YAAH! OW! OW! STOP!
PURR
YOU SURE YOU DON'T WANNA GET HIM DECLAWED?
BAD KITTY! NO FLESH!
I THINK YOUR CATS ARE COMMUNIST.
WHAT MAKES YOU SAY THAT?
MAO.
WRITTEN BY WILLIAM CADRIN

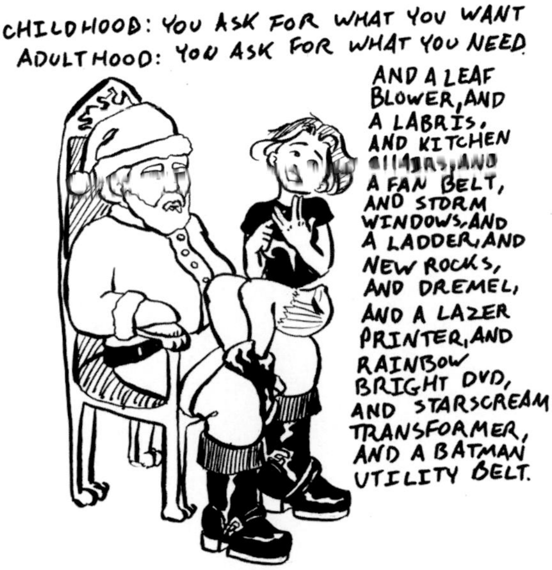
CHILDHOOD: YOU ASK FOR WHAT YOU WANT
ADULTHOOD: YOU ASK FOR WHAT YOU NEED.
AND A LEAF BLOWER, AND A LABRIS, AND KITCHEN
A FAN BELT, AND STORM WINDOWS, AND A LADDER, AND NEW ROCKS, AND DREMEL, AND A LAZER PRINTER, AND RAINBOW BRIGHT DVD, AND STARSCREAM TRANSFORMER, AND A BATMAN UTILITY BELT.

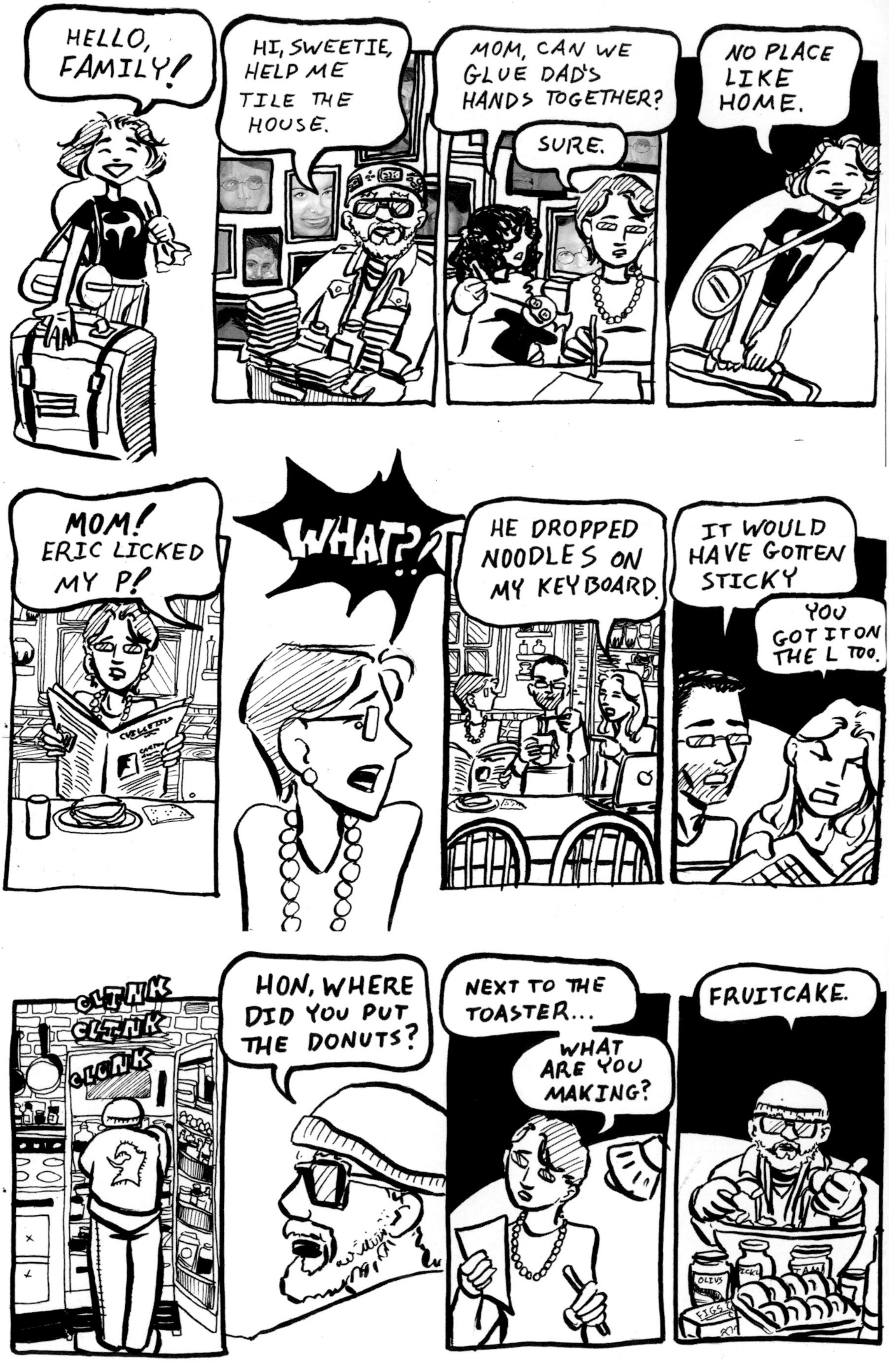
HELLO, FAMILY!
HI, SWEETIE, HELP ME TILE THE HOUSE.
MOM, CAN WE GLUE DAD'S HANDS TOGETHER?
SURE.
NO PLACE LIKE HOME.
MOM! ERIC LICKED MY P!
WHAT?!
HE DROPPED NOODLES ON MY KEYBOARD.
IT WOULD HAVE GOTTEN STICKY
YOU GOT IT ON THE L TOO.
CLINK CLINK CLONK
HON, WHERE DID YOU PUT THE DONUTS?
NEXT TO THE TOASTER...
WHAT ARE YOU MAKING?
FRUITCAKE.

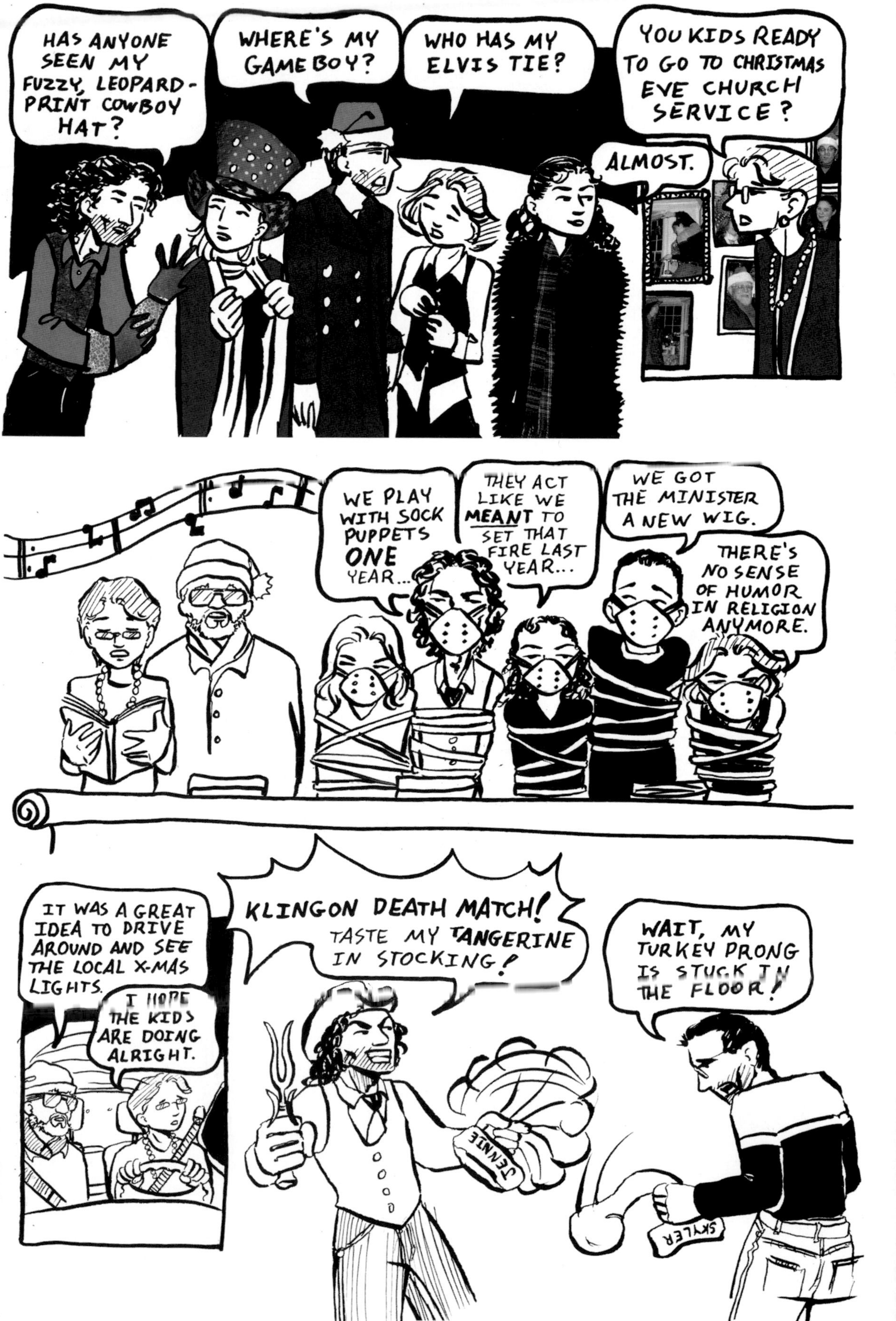

HAS ANYONE SEEN MY FUZZY, LEOPARD-PRINT COWBOY HAT?
WHERE'S MY GAMEBOY?
WHO HAS MY ELVIS TIE?
YOU KIDS READY TO GO TO CHRISTMAS EVE CHURCH SERVICE?
ALMOST.
WE PLAY WITH SOCK PUPPETS ONE YEAR...
THEY ACT LIKE WE MEANT TO SET THAT FIRE LAST YEAR...
WE GOT THE MINISTER A NEW WIG.
THERE'S NO SENSE OF HUMOR IN RELIGION ANYMORE.
IT WAS A GREAT IDEA TO DRIVE AROUND AND SEE THE LOCAL X-MAS LIGHTS.
I HOPE THE KIDS ARE DOING ALRIGHT.
KLINGON DEATH MATCH! TASTE MY TANGERINE IN STOCKING!
JENNIE
WAIT, MY TURKEY PRONG IS STUCK IN THE FLOOR!
SKYLER

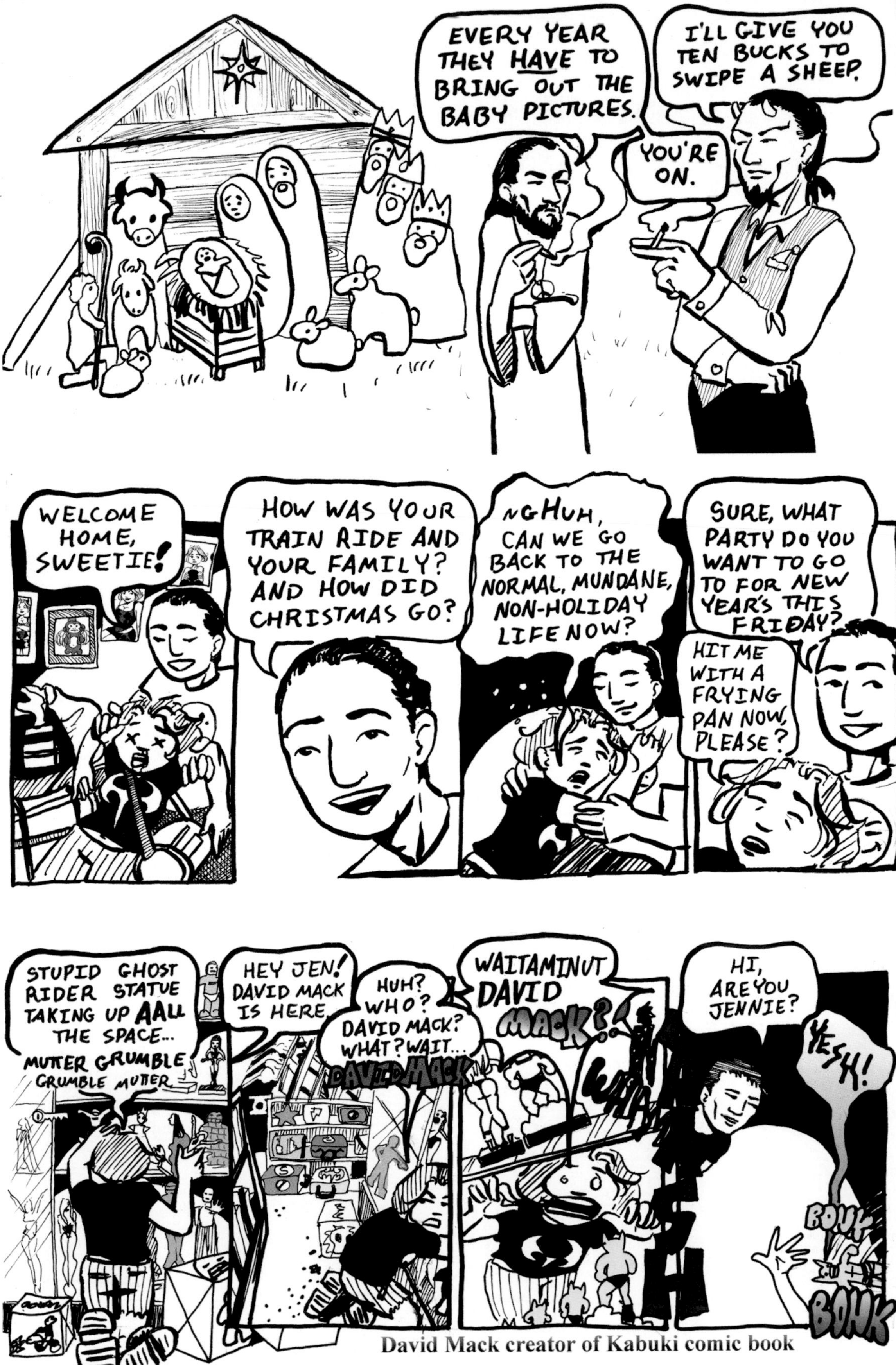
EVERY YEAR THEY HAVE TO BRING OUT THE BABY PICTURES.
I'LL GIVE YOU TEN BUCKS TO SWIPE A SHEEP.
YOU'RE ON.
WELCOME HOME, SWEETIE!
HOW WAS YOUR TRAIN RIDE AND YOUR FAMILY? AND HOW DID CHRISTMAS GO?
NGHUH, CAN WE GO BACK TO THE NORMAL, MUNDANE, NON-HOLIDAY LIFE NOW?
SURE, WHAT PARTY DO YOU WANT TO GO TO FOR NEW YEAR'S THIS FRIDAY?
HIT ME WITH A FRYING PAN NOW, PLEASE?
STUPID GHOST RIDER STATUE TAKING UP AALL THE SPACE...
MUTTER GRUMBLE GRUMBLE MUTTER
HEY JEN! DAVID MACK IS HERE.
HUH? WHO? DAVID MACK? WHAT? WAIT...
DAVID MACK
WAITAMINUT DAVID MACK?!
HI, ARE YOU JENNIE?
YESH!
BONK
BONK
David Mack creator of Kabuki comic book

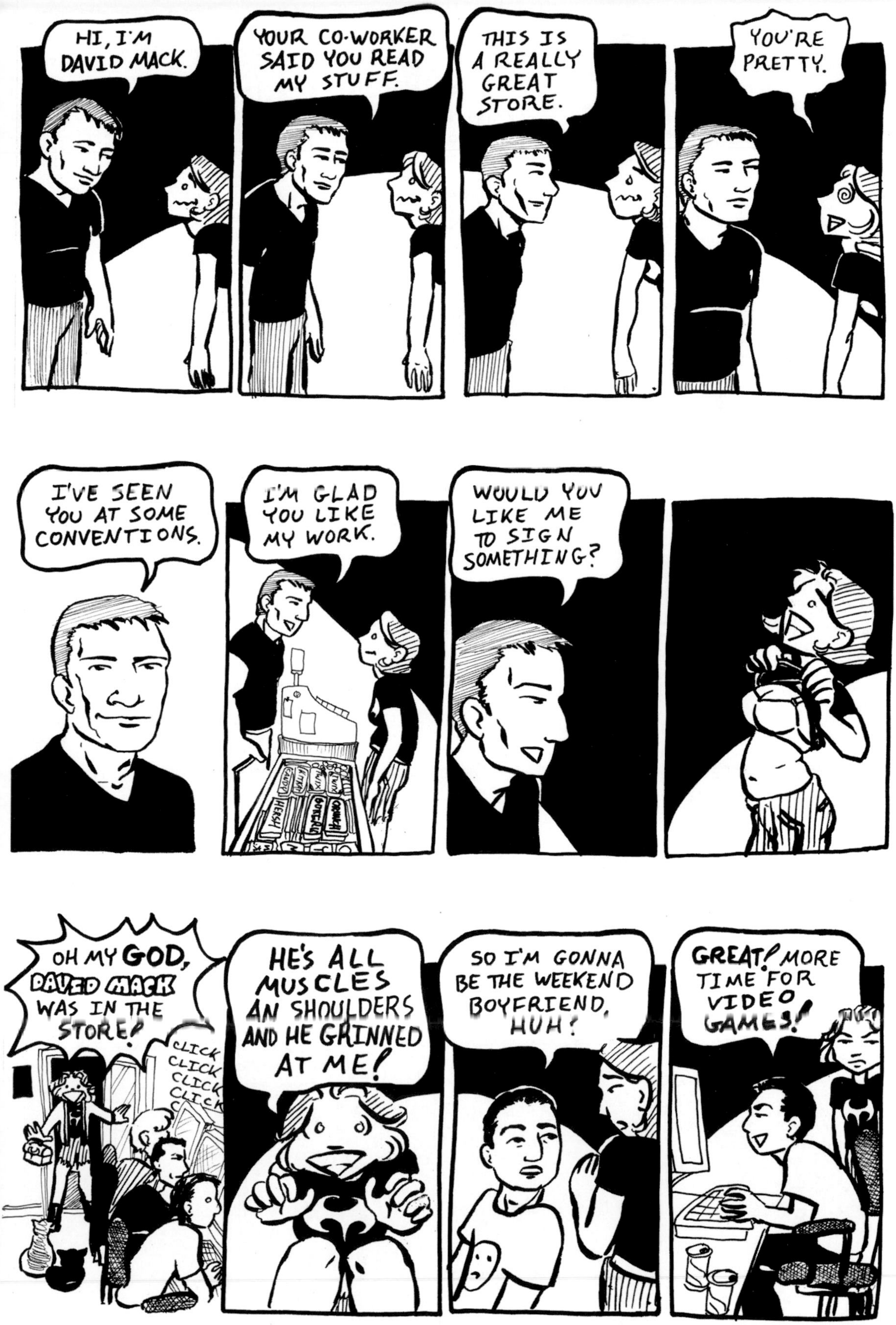
HI, I'M DAVID MACK.
YOUR CO-WORKER SAID YOU READ MY STUFF.
THIS IS A REALLY GREAT STORE.
YOU'RE PRETTY.
I'VE SEEN YOU AT SOME CONVENTIONS.
I'M GLAD YOU LIKE MY WORK.
WOULD YOU LIKE ME TO SIGN SOMETHING?
OH MY GOD, DAVID MACK WAS IN THE STORE!
CLICK CLICK CLICK CLICK
HE'S ALL MUSCLES AN SHOULDERS AND HE GRINNED AT ME!
SO I'M GONNA BE THE WEEKEND BOYFRIEND, HUH?
GREAT! MORE TIME FOR VIDEO GAMES!

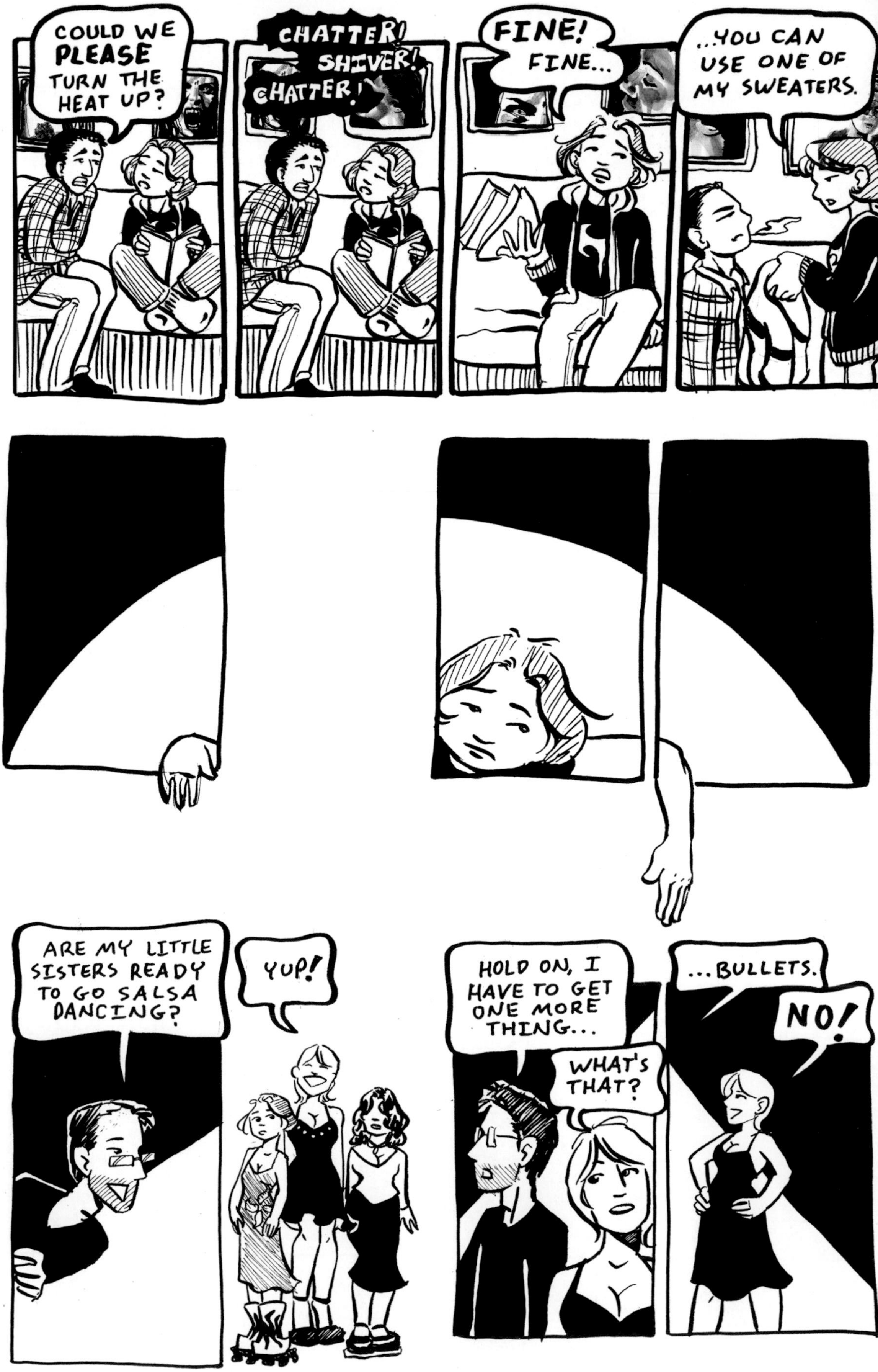
COULD WE PLEASE TURN THE HEAT UP?
CHATTER! SHIVER! CHATTER!
FINE! FINE...
...YOU CAN USE ONE OF MY SWEATERS.
ARE MY LITTLE SISTERS READY TO GO SALSA DANCING?
YUP!
HOLD ON, I HAVE TO GET ONE MORE THING...
WHAT'S THAT?
...BULLETS.
NO!

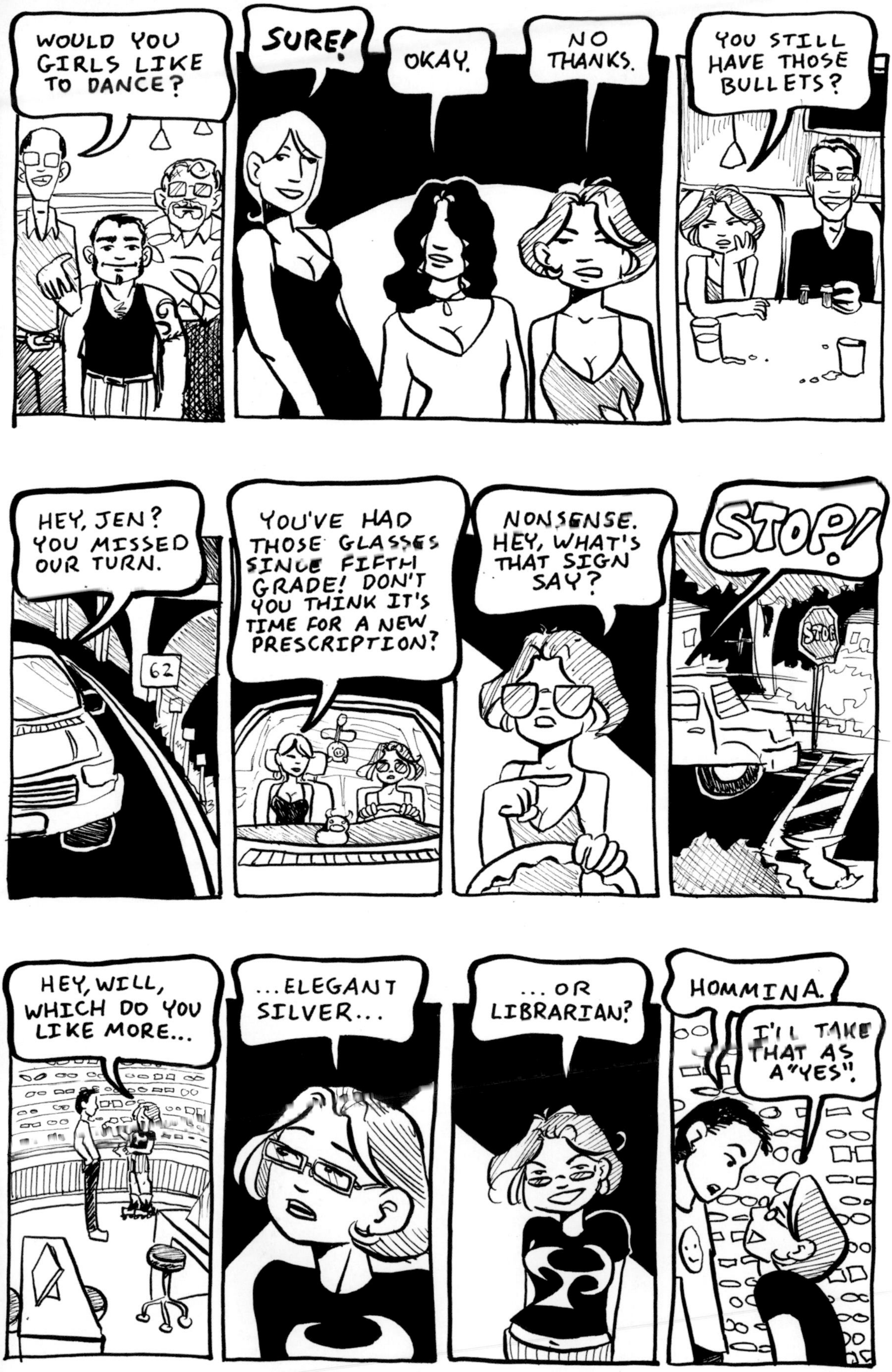
WOULD YOU GIRLS LIKE TO DANCE?
SURE!
OKAY.
NO THANKS.
YOU STILL HAVE THOSE BULLETS?
HEY, JEN? YOU MISSED OUR TURN.
62
YOU'VE HAD THOSE GLASSES SINCE FIFTH GRADE! DON'T YOU THINK IT'S TIME FOR A NEW PRESCRIPTION?
NONSENSE. HEY, WHAT'S THAT SIGN SAY?
STOP!
STOP
HEY, WILL, WHICH DO YOU LIKE MORE...
...ELEGANT SILVER...
...OR LIBRARIAN?
HOMMINA.
I'LL TAKE THAT AS A "YES".

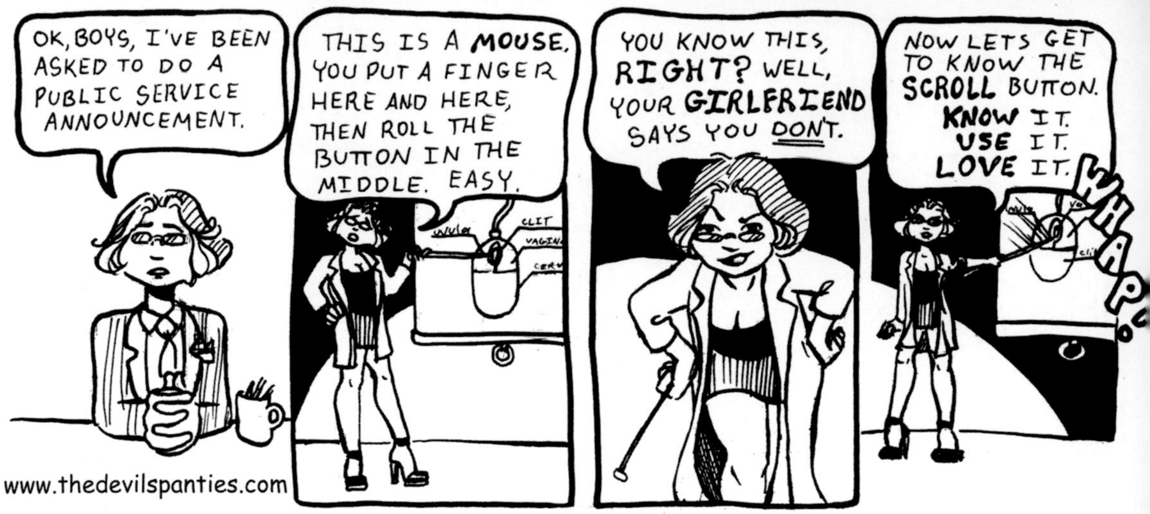
OK, BOYS, I'VE BEEN ASKED TO DO A PUBLIC SERVICE ANNOUNCEMENT.
www.thedevilspanties.com
THIS IS A MOUSE. YOU PUT A FINGER HERE AND HERE, THEN ROLL THE BUTTON IN THE MIDDLE. EASY.
CLIT
YOU KNOW THIS, RIGHT? WELL, YOUR GIRLFRIEND SAYS YOU DON'T.
NOW LETS GET TO KNOW THE SCROLL BUTTON. KNOW IT. USE IT. LOVE IT.
WHAP!

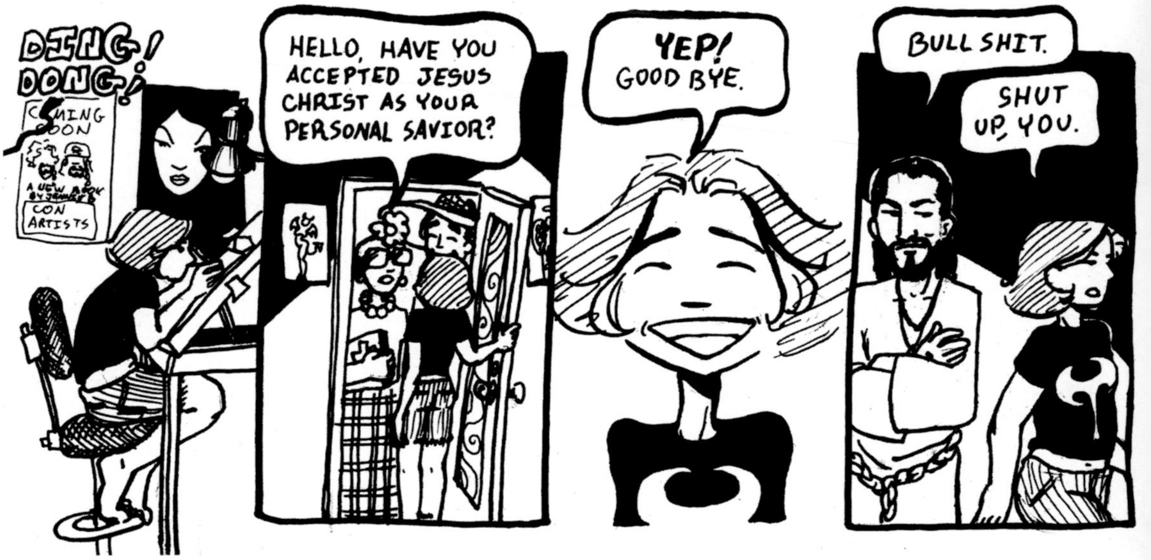
DING! DONG!
CON ARTISTS
HELLO, HAVE YOU ACCEPTED JESUS CHRIST AS YOUR PERSONAL SAVIOR?
YEP! GOOD BYE.
BULL SHIT.
SHUT UP, YOU.

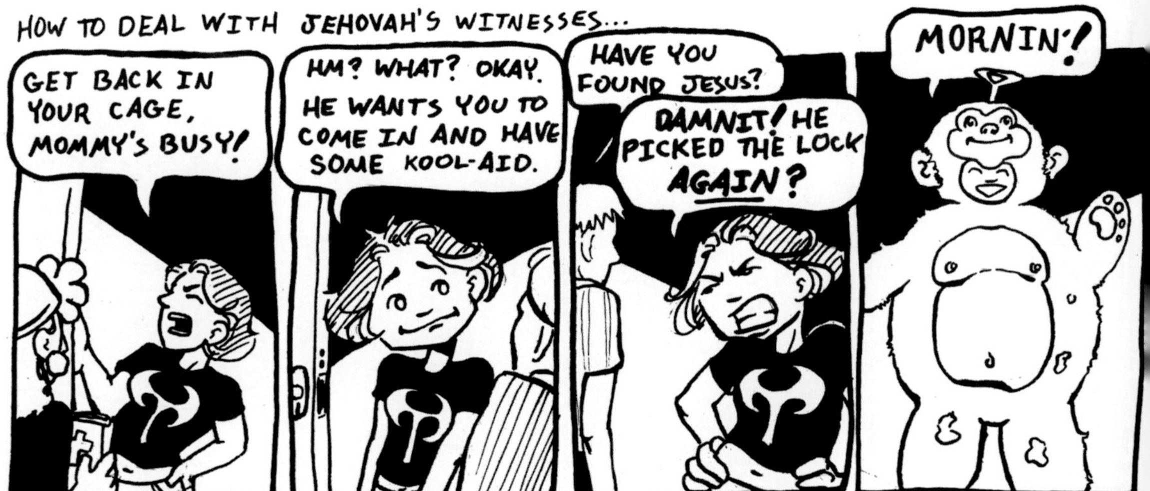
HOW TO DEAL WITH JEHOVAH'S WITNESSES...
GET BACK IN YOUR CAGE, MOMMY'S BUSY!
HM? WHAT? OKAY. HE WANTS YOU TO COME IN AND HAVE SOME KOOL-AID.
HAVE YOU FOUND JESUS?
DAMNIT! HE PICKED THE LOCK AGAIN?
MORNIN'!

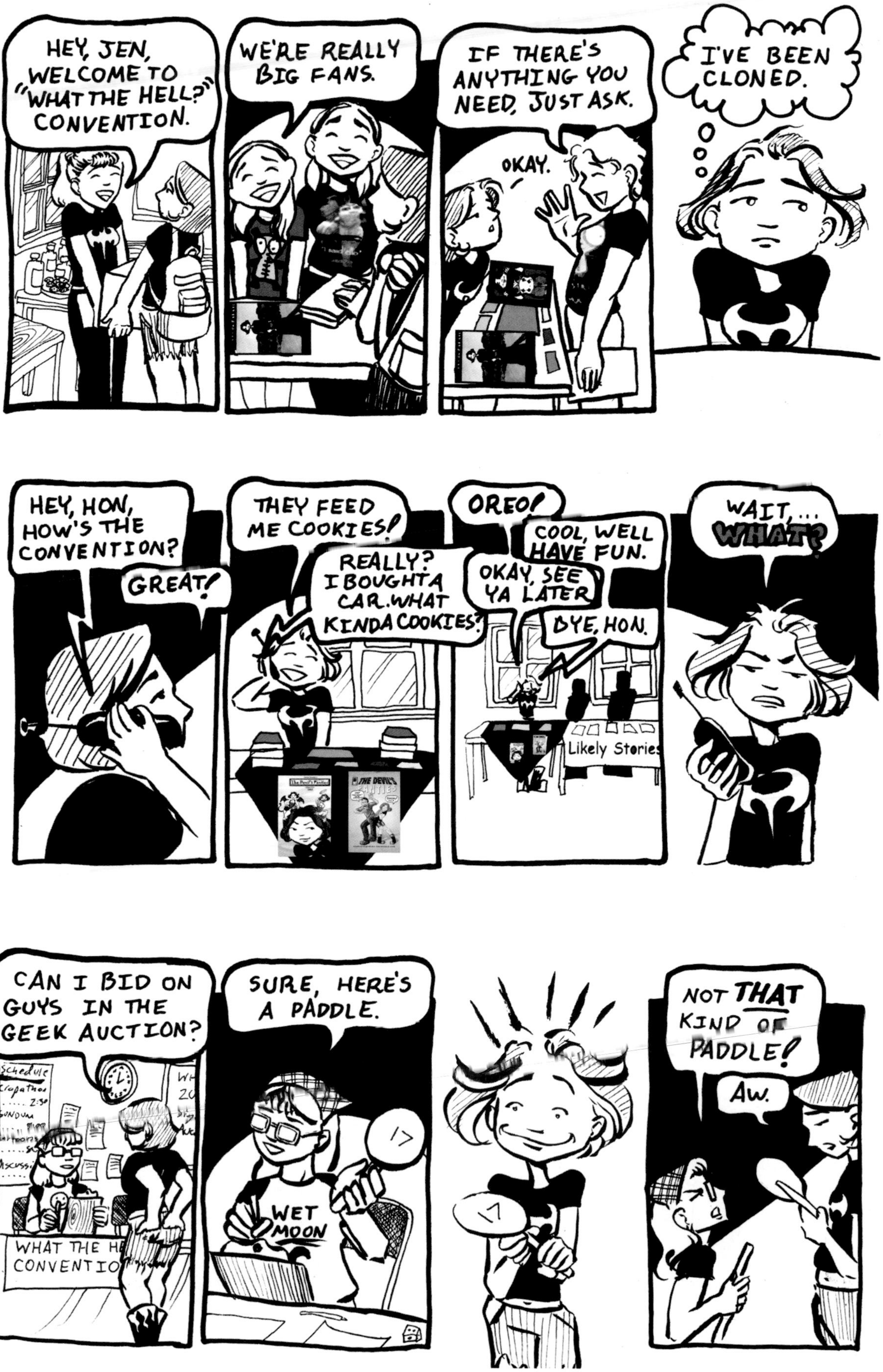
HEY, JEN, WELCOME TO "WHAT THE HELL?" CONVENTION.
WE'RE REALLY BIG FANS.
IF THERE'S ANYTHING YOU NEED, JUST ASK.
OKAY.
I'VE BEEN CLONED.
HEY, HON, HOW'S THE CONVENTION?
GREAT!
THEY FEED ME COOKIES!
REALLY? I BOUGHT A CAR. WHAT KINDA COOKIES?
OREO!
COOL, WELL HAVE FUN.
OKAY, SEE YA LATER
BYE, HON.
Likely Stories
WAIT, ... WHAT?
CAN I BID ON GUYS IN THE GEEK AUCTION?
Schedule
WHAT THE HE
CONVENTIO
SURE, HERE'S A PADDLE.
WET MOON
NOT THAT KIND OF PADDLE!
AW.

 I'M STEALING YOUR GIRLFRIEND AND TAKING HER TO FLORIDA!

 GREAT! JUST DON'T FEED HER AFTER MIDNIGHT.

 YEAH, AND DON'T GET HER WET.

ER- I MEAN....

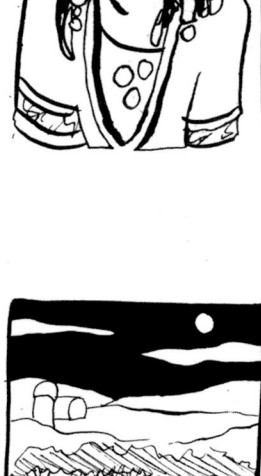

 EVERYTHING IS FINE!

SKREECH!

 IT'LL BE FINE. WE'LL JUST SLEEP AFTER WE SET UP AND BEFORE THE CON OPENS.

 I'M SORRY, ARTISTS' ALLEY DOESN'T SET UP UNTIL AFTER THE SHOW OPENS.

INFORMATION

 WELCOME TO F©^ED UP CON!

Z Z Z Z

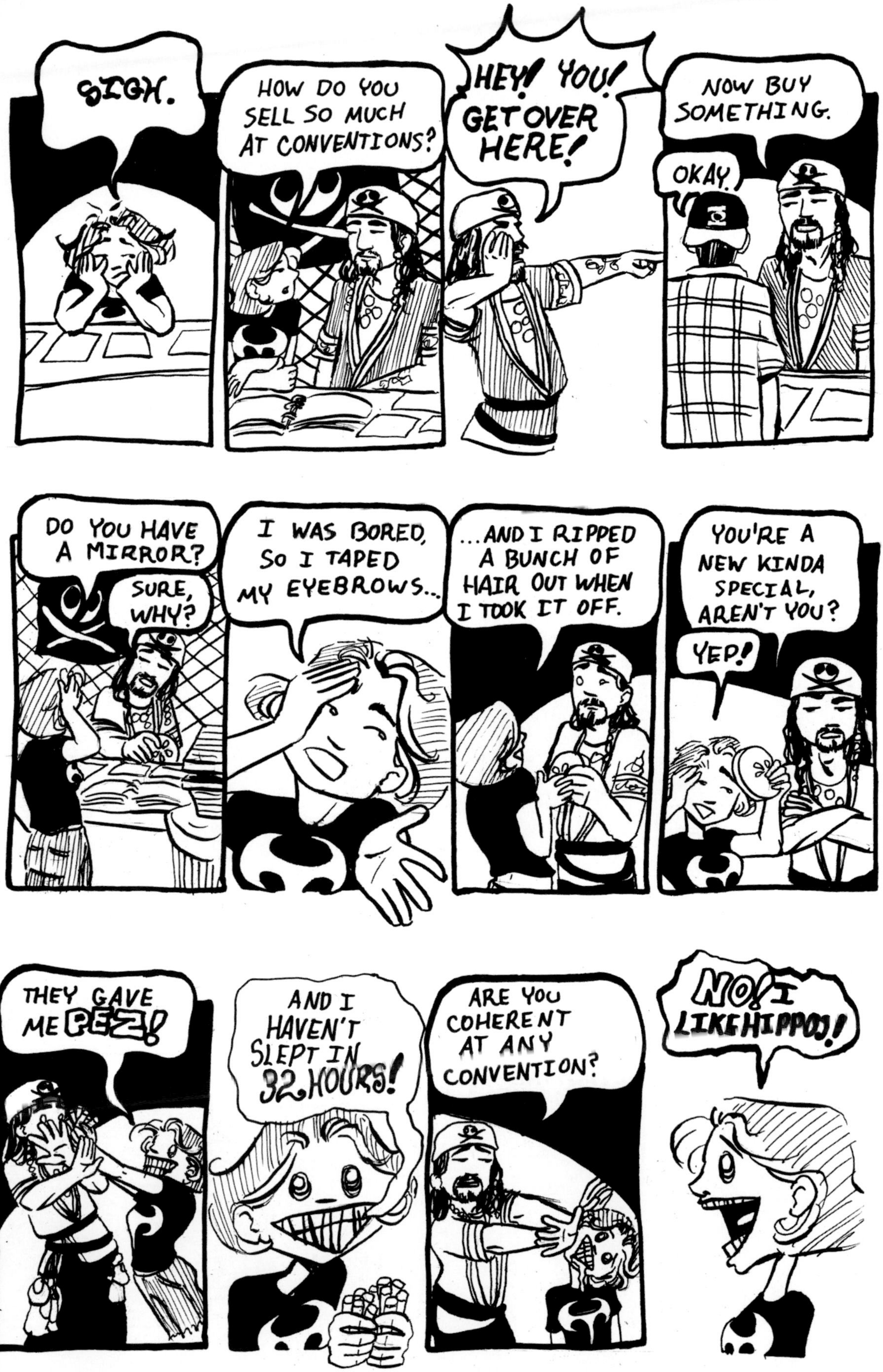
SIGH.
HOW DO YOU SELL SO MUCH AT CONVENTIONS?
HEY! YOU! GET OVER HERE!
NOW BUY SOMETHING.
OKAY.
DO YOU HAVE A MIRROR?
SURE, WHY?
I WAS BORED, SO I TAPED MY EYEBROWS...
...AND I RIPPED A BUNCH OF HAIR OUT WHEN I TOOK IT OFF.
YOU'RE A NEW KINDA SPECIAL, AREN'T YOU?
YEP!
THEY GAVE ME PEZ!
AND I HAVEN'T SLEPT IN 32 HOURS!
ARE YOU COHERENT AT ANY CONVENTION?
NO! I LIKE HIPPOS!

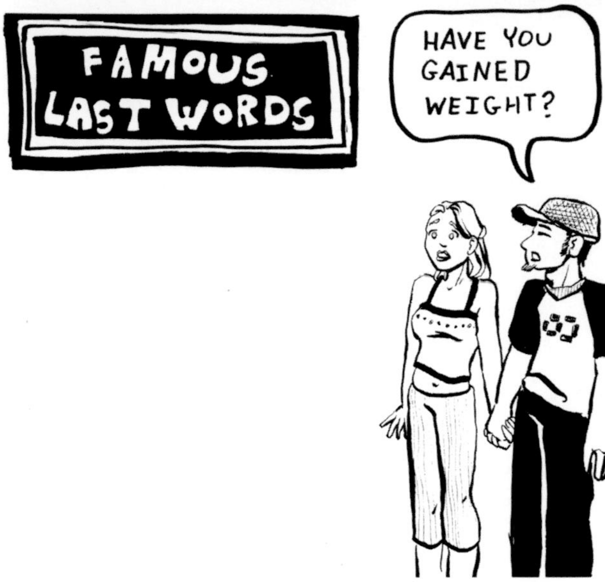
FAMOUS LAST WORDS
HAVE YOU GAINED WEIGHT?

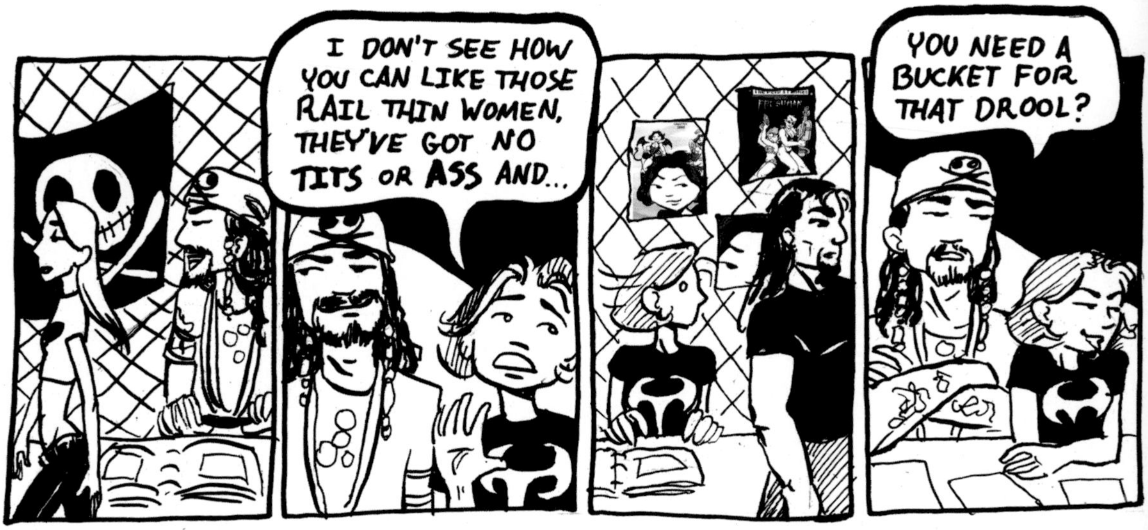
I DON'T SEE HOW YOU CAN LIKE THOSE RAIL THIN WOMEN, THEY'VE GOT NO TITS OR ASS AND...
YOU NEED A BUCKET FOR THAT DROOL?

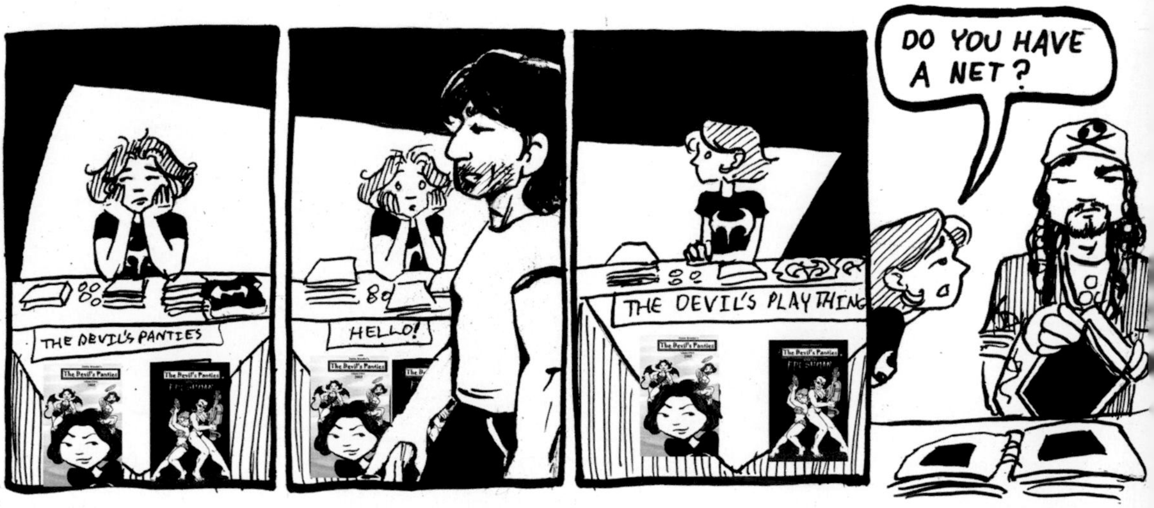
THE DEVIL'S PANTIES
HELLO!
THE DEVIL'S PLAYTHING
DO YOU HAVE A NET?

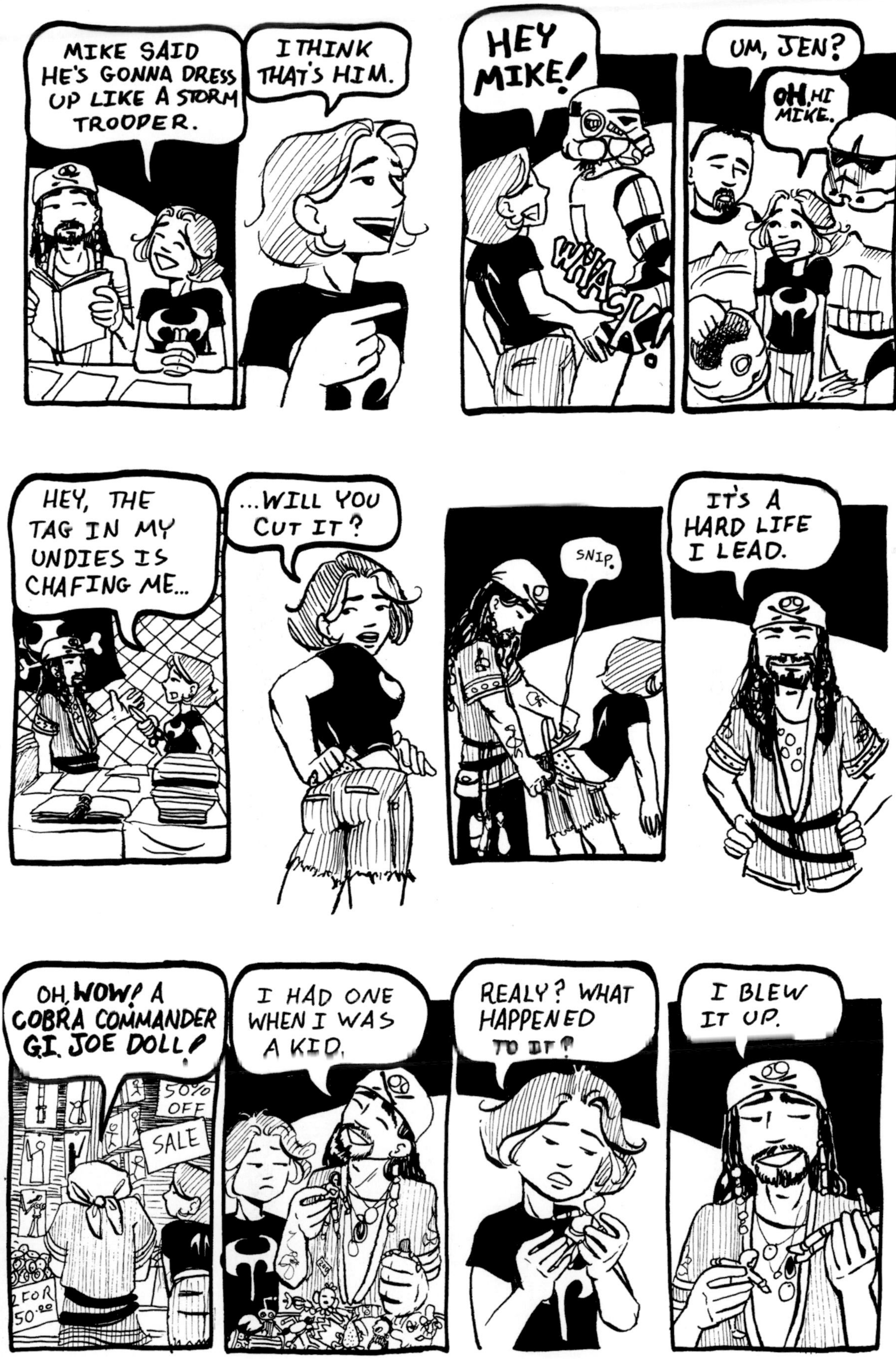
MIKE SAID HE'S GONNA DRESS UP LIKE A STORM TROOPER.
I THINK THAT'S HIM.
HEY MIKE!
WHACK!
UM, JEN?
OH, HI MIKE.
HEY, THE TAG IN MY UNDIES IS CHAFING ME...
...WILL YOU CUT IT?
SNIP.
IT'S A HARD LIFE I LEAD.
OH, WOW! A COBRA COMMANDER G.I. JOE DOLL!
50% OFF
SALE
2 FOR 50.00
I HAD ONE WHEN I WAS A KID.
REALY? WHAT HAPPENED TO IT?
I BLEW IT UP.

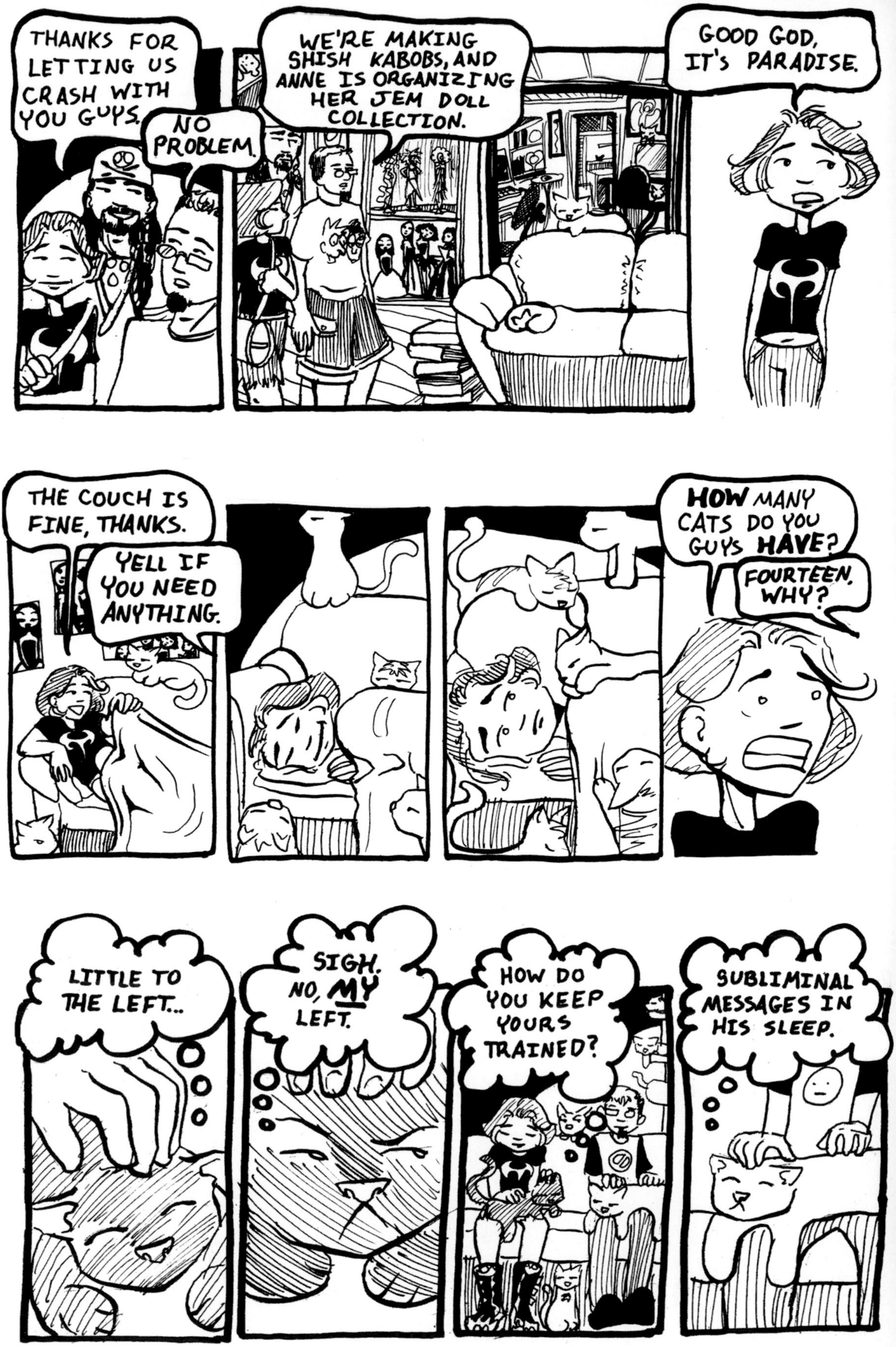
THANKS FOR LETTING US CRASH WITH YOU GUYS.
NO PROBLEM.
WE'RE MAKING SHISH KABOBS, AND ANNE IS ORGANIZING HER JEM DOLL COLLECTION.
GOOD GOD, IT'S PARADISE.
THE COUCH IS FINE, THANKS.
YELL IF YOU NEED ANYTHING.
HOW MANY CATS DO YOU GUYS HAVE?
FOURTEEN, WHY?
LITTLE TO THE LEFT...
SIGH. NO, MY LEFT.
HOW DO YOU KEEP YOURS TRAINED?
SUBLIMINAL MESSAGES IN HIS SLEEP.

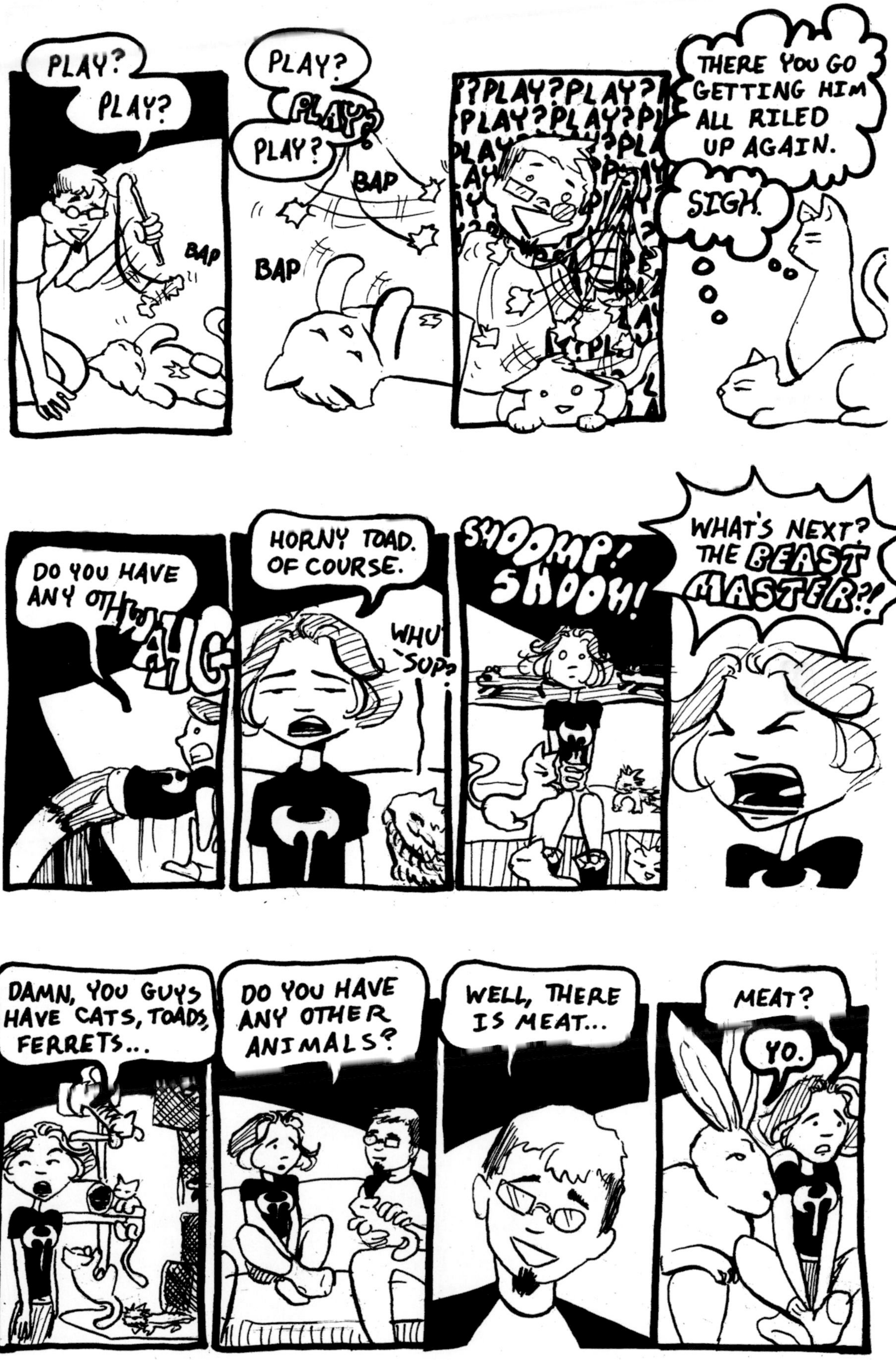
PLAY?
PLAY?
BAP
PLAY?
PLAY?
PLAY?
BAP
BAP
?PLAY?PLAY?
PLAY?PLAY?P
THERE YOU GO GETTING HIM ALL RILED UP AGAIN.
SIGH.
DO YOU HAVE ANY OTH
HORNY TOAD. OF COURSE.
WHU' SUP?
SHOOMP! SHOOH!
WHAT'S NEXT? THE BEAST MASTER?!
DAMN, YOU GUYS HAVE CATS, TOADS, FERRETS...
DO YOU HAVE ANY OTHER ANIMALS?
WELL, THERE IS MEAT...
MEAT?
YO.

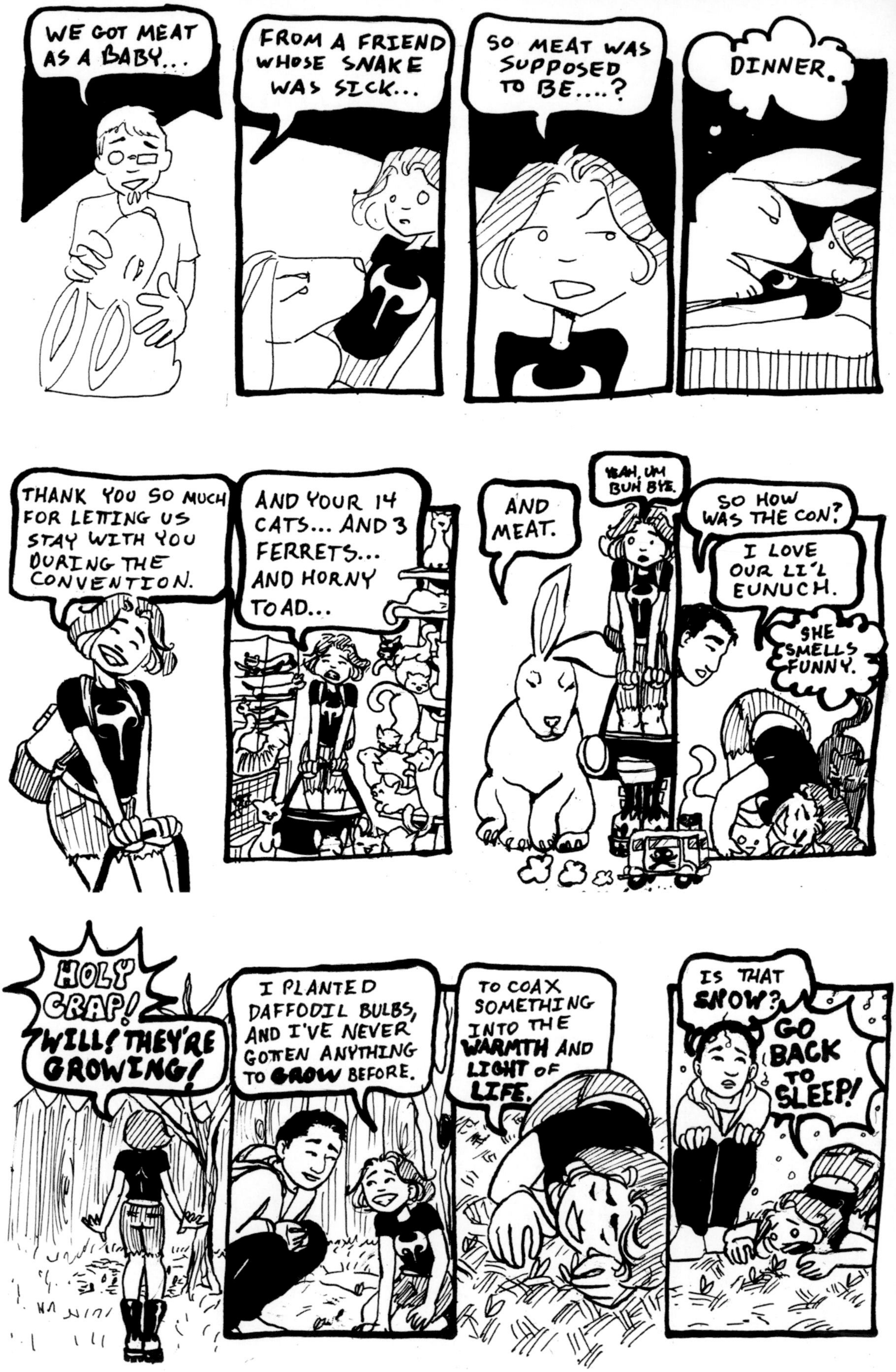
WE GOT MEAT AS A BABY...
FROM A FRIEND WHOSE SNAKE WAS SICK...
SO MEAT WAS SUPPOSED TO BE....?
DINNER.
THANK YOU SO MUCH FOR LETTING US STAY WITH YOU DURING THE CONVENTION.
AND YOUR 14 CATS... AND 3 FERRETS... AND HORNY TOAD...
AND MEAT.
YEAH, UM BUH BYE.
SO HOW WAS THE CON?
I LOVE OUR LI'L EUNUCH.
SHE SMELLS FUNNY.
HOLY CRAP! WILL! THEY'RE GROWING!
I PLANTED DAFFODIL BULBS, AND I'VE NEVER GOTTEN ANYTHING TO GROW BEFORE.
TO COAX SOMETHING INTO THE WARMTH AND LIGHT OF LIFE.
IS THAT SNOW?
GO BACK TO SLEEP!

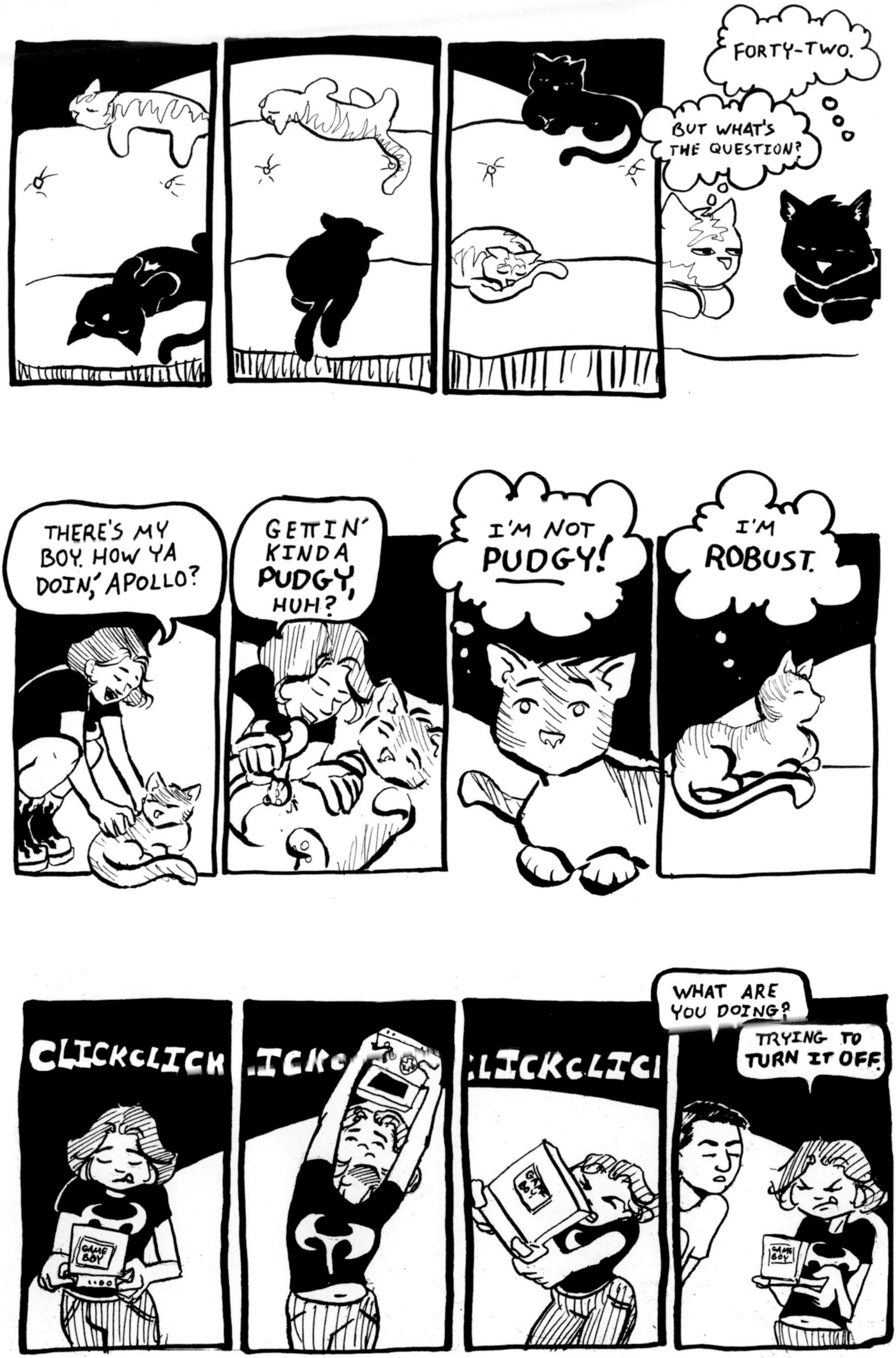
FORTY-TWO.
BUT WHAT'S THE QUESTION?
THERE'S MY BOY. HOW YA DOIN,' APOLLO?
GETTIN' KINDA PUDGY, HUH?
I'M NOT PUDGY!
I'M ROBUST.
CLICKCLICK
CLICKCLICK
CLICKCLICK
WHAT ARE YOU DOING?
TRYING TO TURN IT OFF.

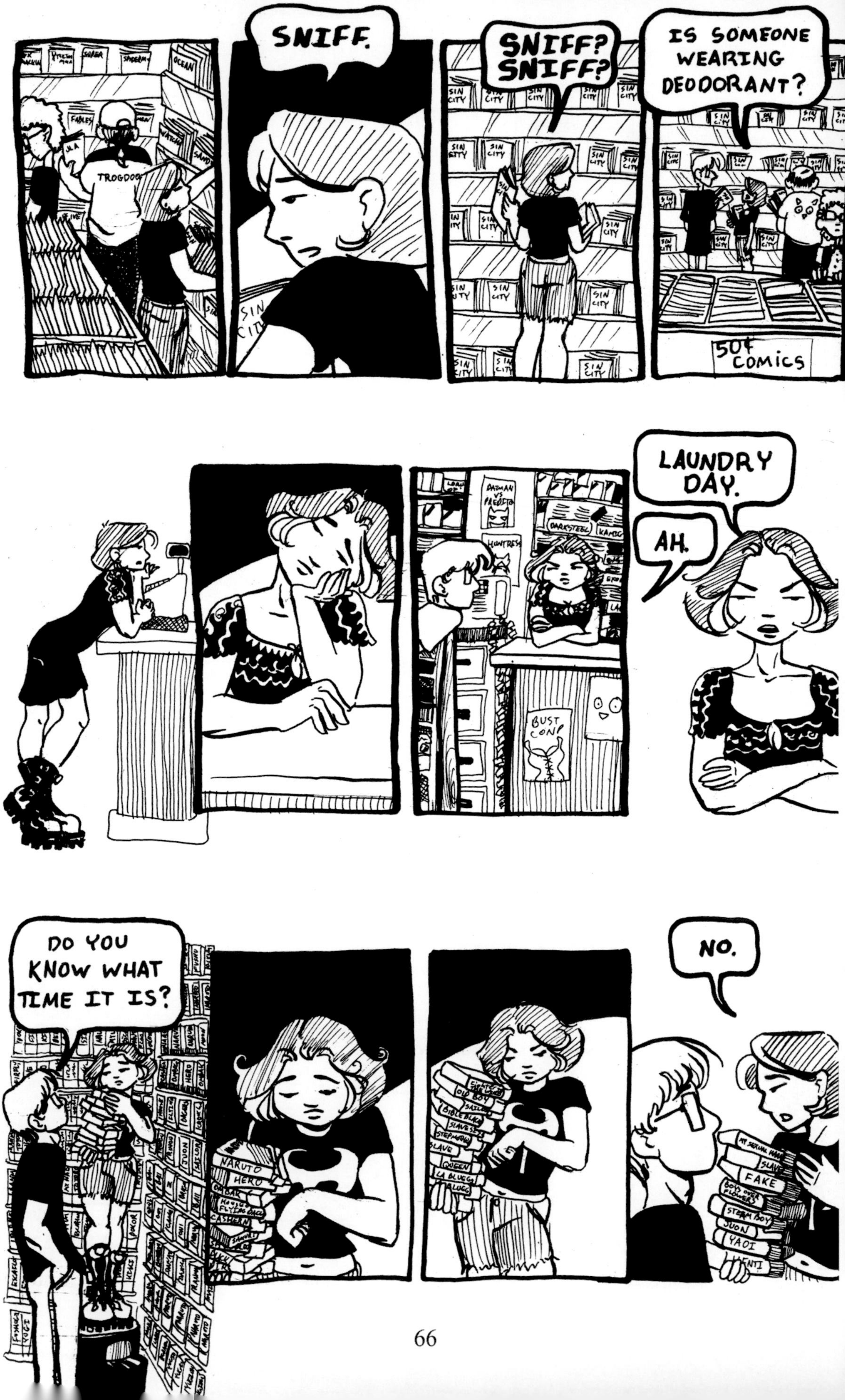
SNIFF.
SNIFF? SNIFF?
IS SOMEONE WEARING DEODORANT?
LAUNDRY DAY.
AH.
DO YOU KNOW WHAT TIME IT IS?
NO.

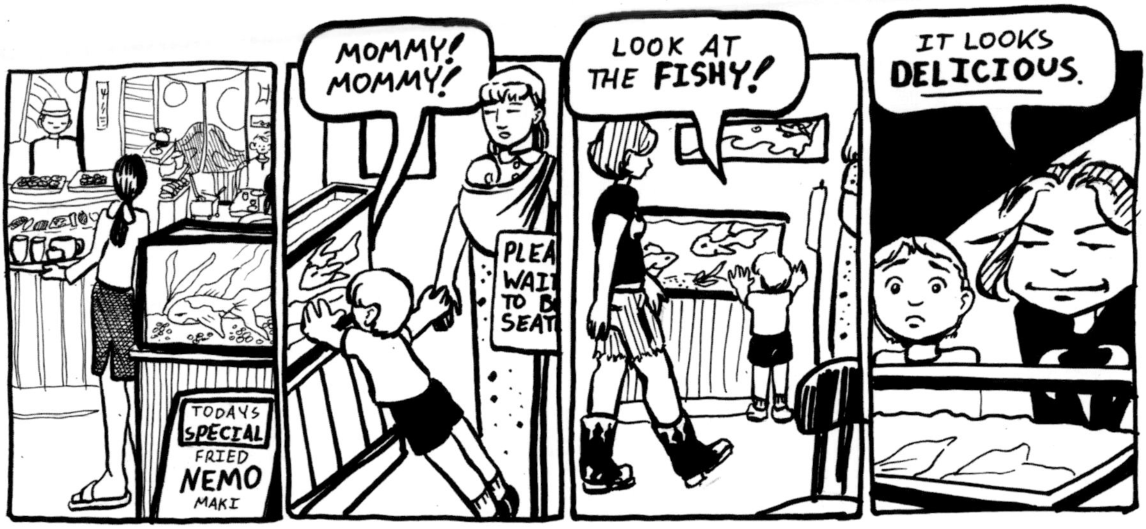
TODAYS SPECIAL FRIED NEMO MAKI
MOMMY! MOMMY!
LOOK AT THE FISHY!
IT LOOKS DELICIOUS.

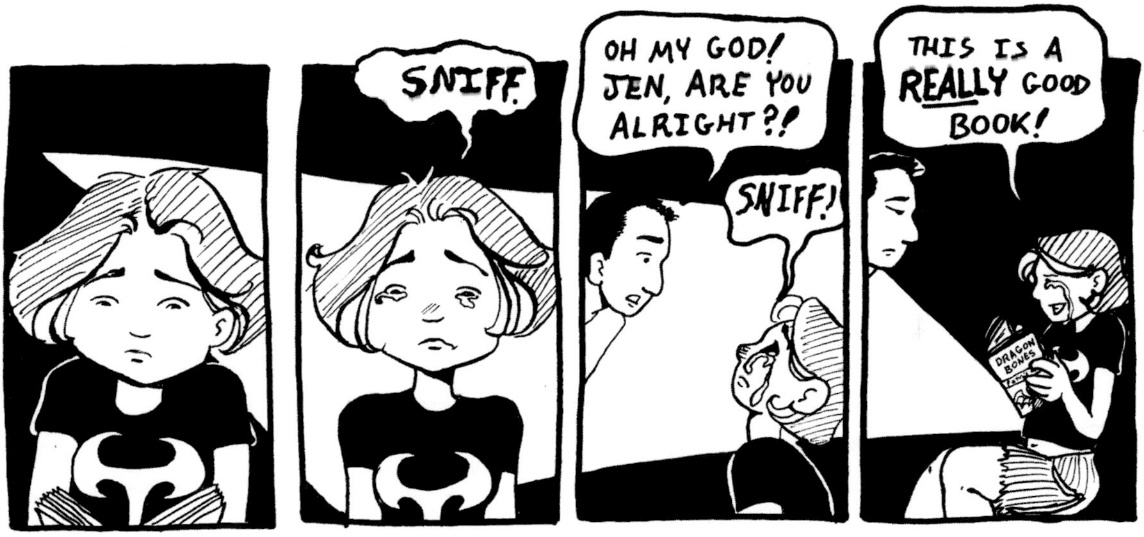
SNIFF.
OH MY GOD! JEN, ARE YOU ALRIGHT?!
SNIFF!
THIS IS A REALLY GOOD BOOK!
DRAGON BONES

I MET PATRICIA BRIGGS AT CONBUST AND HER BOOK
"DRAGON BONES" MADE ME BAWL AND IT'S JUST THE ASSHOLE WHO DIES!

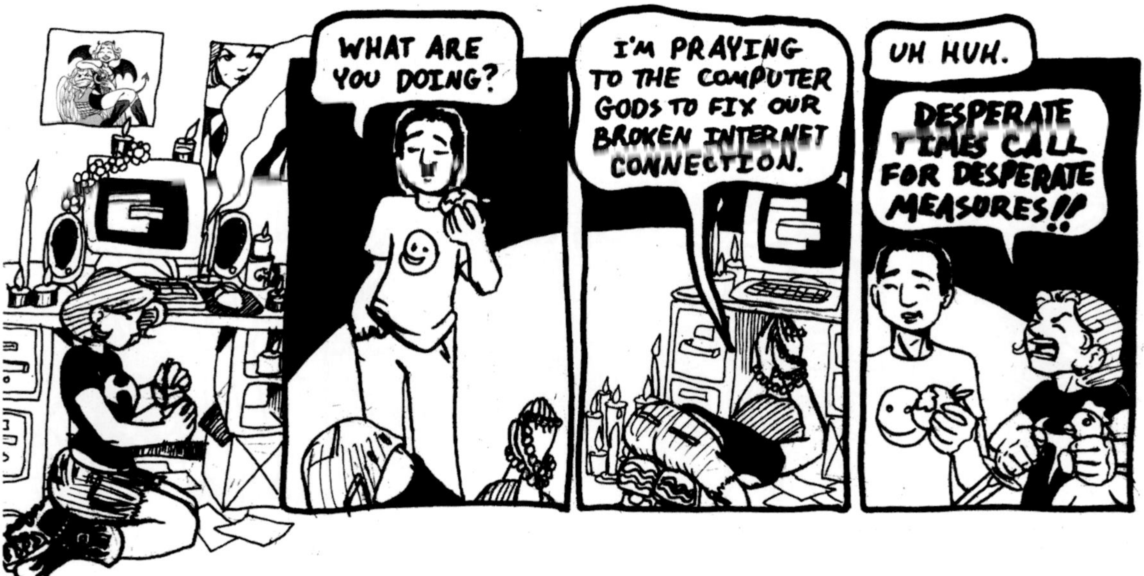
WHAT ARE YOU DOING?
I'M PRAYING TO THE COMPUTER GODS TO FIX OUR BROKEN INTERNET CONNECTION.
UH HUH.
DESPERATE TIMES CALL FOR DESPERATE MEASURES!!

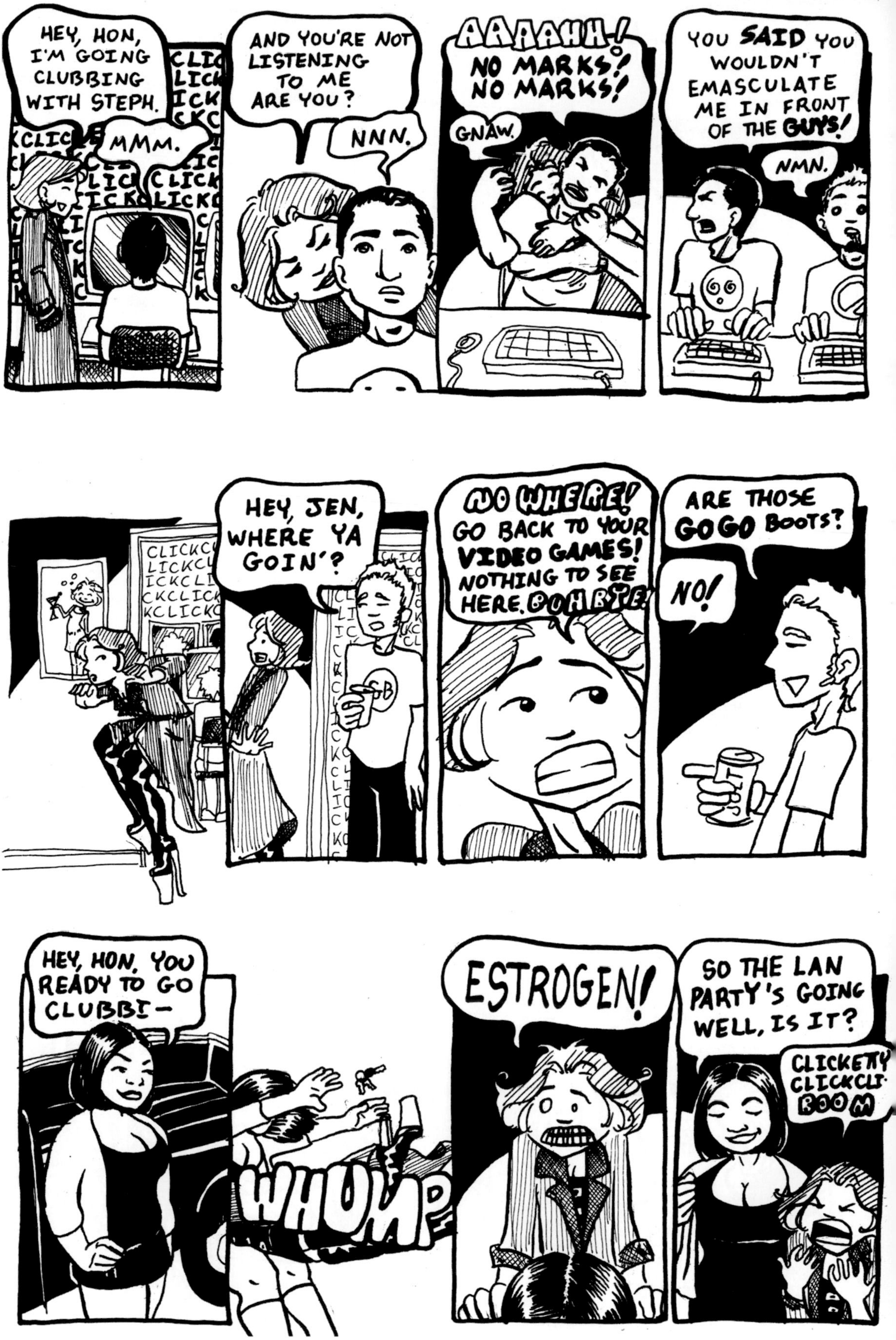
HEY, HON, I'M GOING CLUBBING WITH STEPH.
MMM.
AND YOU'RE NOT LISTENING TO ME ARE YOU?
NNN.
AAAAHH! NO MARKS! NO MARKS!
GNAW.
YOU SAID YOU WOULDN'T EMASCULATE ME IN FRONT OF THE GUYS!
NMN.
HEY, JEN, WHERE YA GOIN'?
NO WHERE! GO BACK TO YOUR VIDEO GAMES! NOTHING TO SEE HERE. BOH BYE!
ARE THOSE GOGO BOOTS?
NO!
HEY, HON, YOU READY TO GO CLUBBI-
WHUMP
ESTROGEN!
SO THE LAN PARTY'S GOING WELL, IS IT?
CLICKETTY CLICKCLI-BOOM

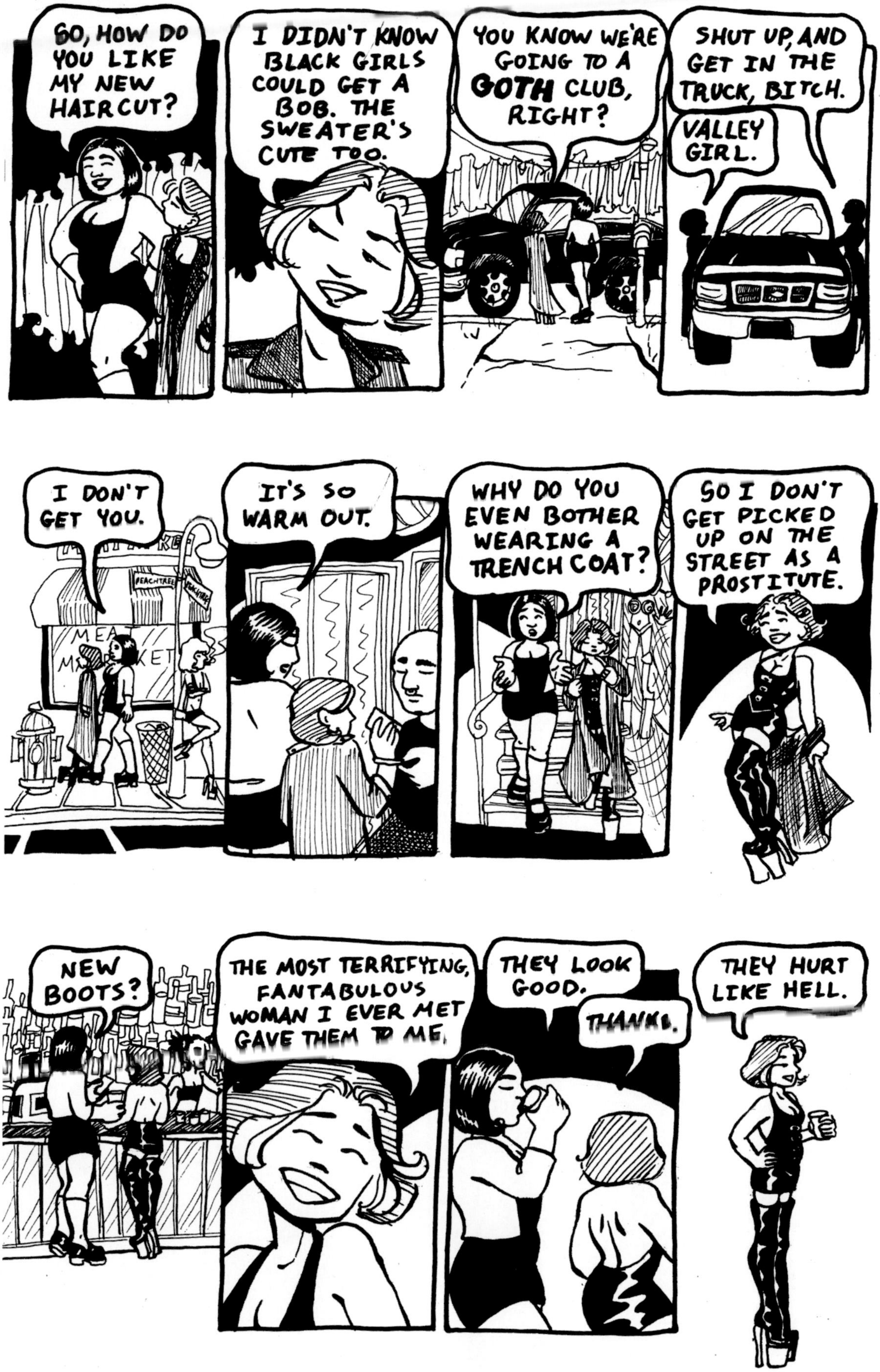
SO, HOW DO YOU LIKE MY NEW HAIRCUT?
I DIDN'T KNOW BLACK GIRLS COULD GET A BOB. THE SWEATER'S CUTE TOO.
YOU KNOW WE'RE GOING TO A GOTH CLUB, RIGHT?
SHUT UP, AND GET IN THE TRUCK, BITCH.
VALLEY GIRL.
I DON'T GET YOU.
MEAT MARKET
PEACHTREE
IT'S SO WARM OUT.
WHY DO YOU EVEN BOTHER WEARING A TRENCH COAT?
SO I DON'T GET PICKED UP ON THE STREET AS A PROSTITUTE.
NEW BOOTS?
THE MOST TERRIFYING, FANTABULOUS WOMAN I EVER MET GAVE THEM TO ME.
THEY LOOK GOOD.
THANKS.
THEY HURT LIKE HELL.

Panel 1-3 (wordless dancing figure)

FUNKY DANCING.

I'M TRYING NOT TO FALL OVER!

HEY, BABY, YOU REALLY KNOW HOW TO SHAKE IT!

WANNA GET OUT OF HERE?

HEY!

YOU MESSIN' WITH **MY** WOMAN?!

OH GOD, I'M NOT GOING TO MAKE IT TO THE CAR.

STEPH, TAKE THESE BOOTS AWAY FROM ME! THEY'RE TOO PAINFUL, I C—

WOOHOO HOT STUFF!

NEVER MIND I'M KEEPING THEM.

EGO FEELS NO PAIN?

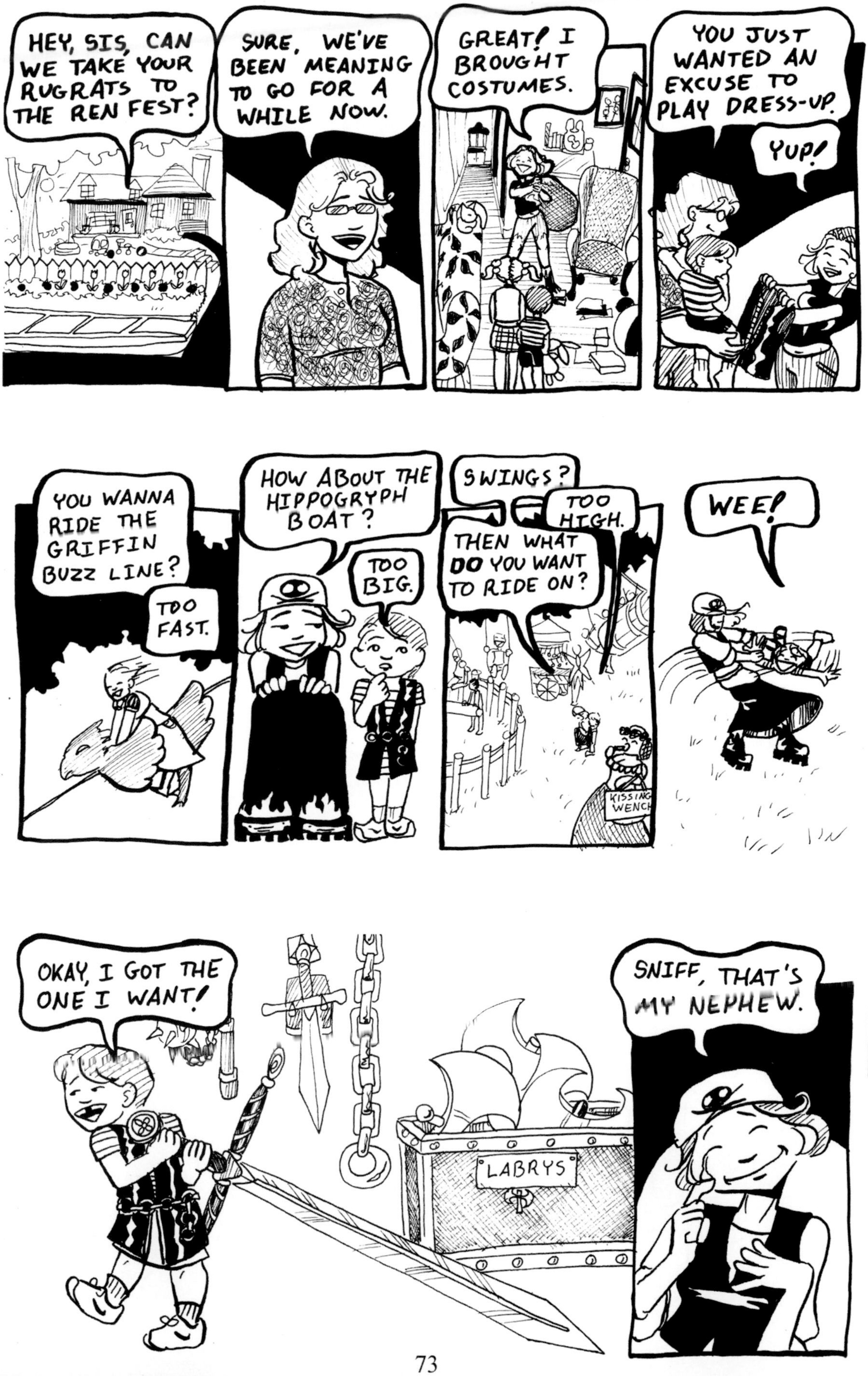
HEY, SIS, CAN WE TAKE YOUR RUGRATS TO THE REN FEST?
SURE, WE'VE BEEN MEANING TO GO FOR A WHILE NOW.
GREAT! I BROUGHT COSTUMES.
YOU JUST WANTED AN EXCUSE TO PLAY DRESS-UP.
YUP!
YOU WANNA RIDE THE GRIFFIN BUZZ LINE?
TOO FAST.
HOW ABOUT THE HIPPOGRYPH BOAT?
TOO BIG.
SWINGS?
TOO HIGH.
THEN WHAT **DO** YOU WANT TO RIDE ON?
KISSING WENCH
WEE!
OKAY, I GOT THE ONE I WANT!
LABRYS
SNIFF, THAT'S MY NEPHEW.

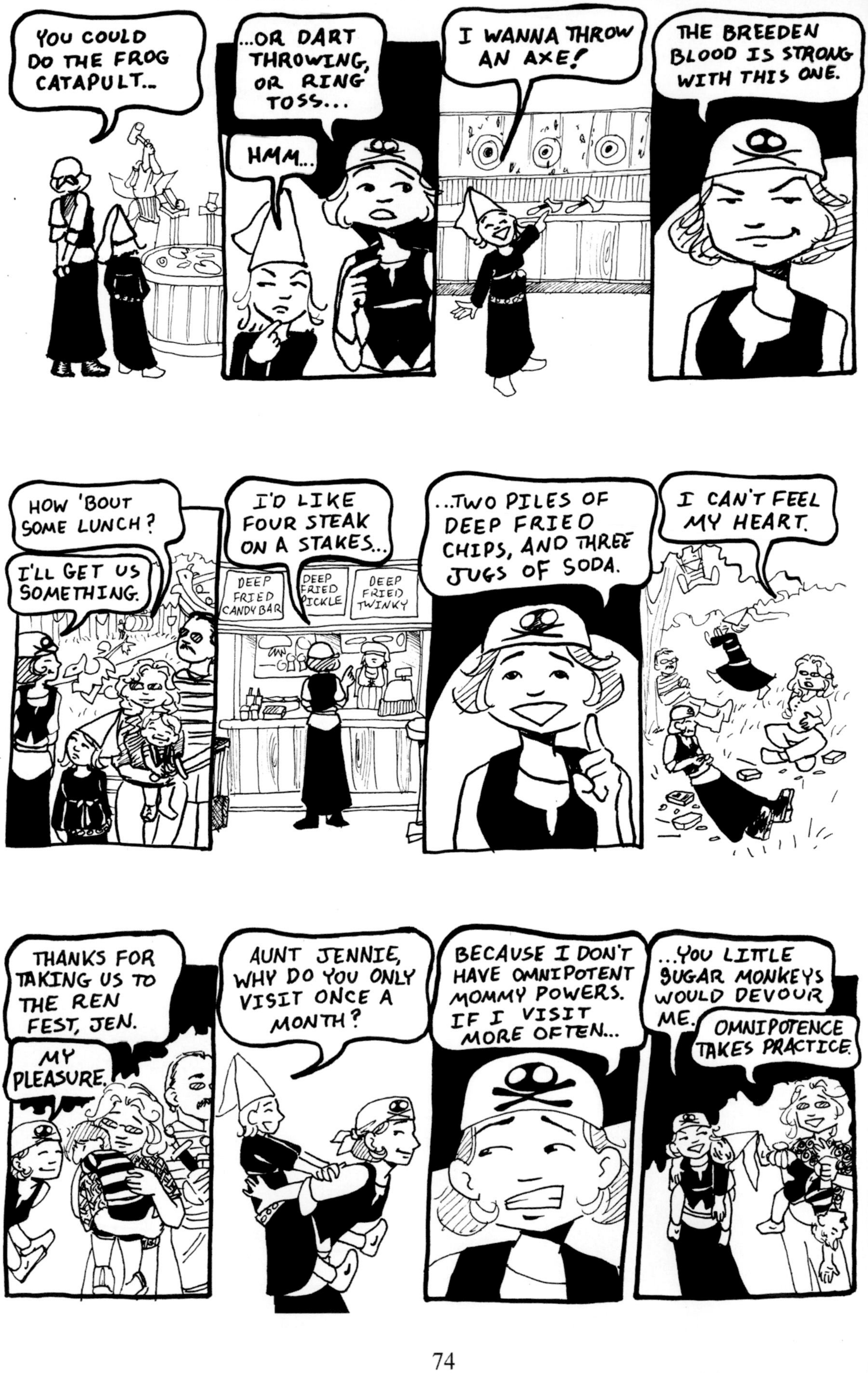
YOU COULD DO THE FROG CATAPULT...
...OR DART THROWING, OR RING TOSS...
HMM...
I WANNA THROW AN AXE!
THE BREEDEN BLOOD IS STRONG WITH THIS ONE.
HOW 'BOUT SOME LUNCH?
I'LL GET US SOMETHING.
I'D LIKE FOUR STEAK ON A STAKES...
DEEP FRIED CANDY BAR
DEEP FRIED PICKLE
DEEP FRIED TWINKY
...TWO PILES OF DEEP FRIED CHIPS, AND THREE JUGS OF SODA.
I CAN'T FEEL MY HEART.
THANKS FOR TAKING US TO THE REN FEST, JEN.
MY PLEASURE.
AUNT JENNIE, WHY DO YOU ONLY VISIT ONCE A MONTH?
BECAUSE I DON'T HAVE OMNIPOTENT MOMMY POWERS. IF I VISIT MORE OFTEN...
...YOU LITTLE SUGAR MONKEYS WOULD DEVOUR ME.
OMNIPOTENCE TAKES PRACTICE.

FAMOUS LAST WORDS.

YOU NEVER KNOW. YOU MIGHT LIKE IT.

WHEN WAS YOUR LAST VISIT?

1998.

GRACIOUS! WHY HAVE YOU WAITED SO LONG?

UM...

FEAR?

WHAT NOT TO SAY IN THE BEDROOM.

WHAT DO YOU MEAN THE BATTERY'S DEAD?!

-GILMORE

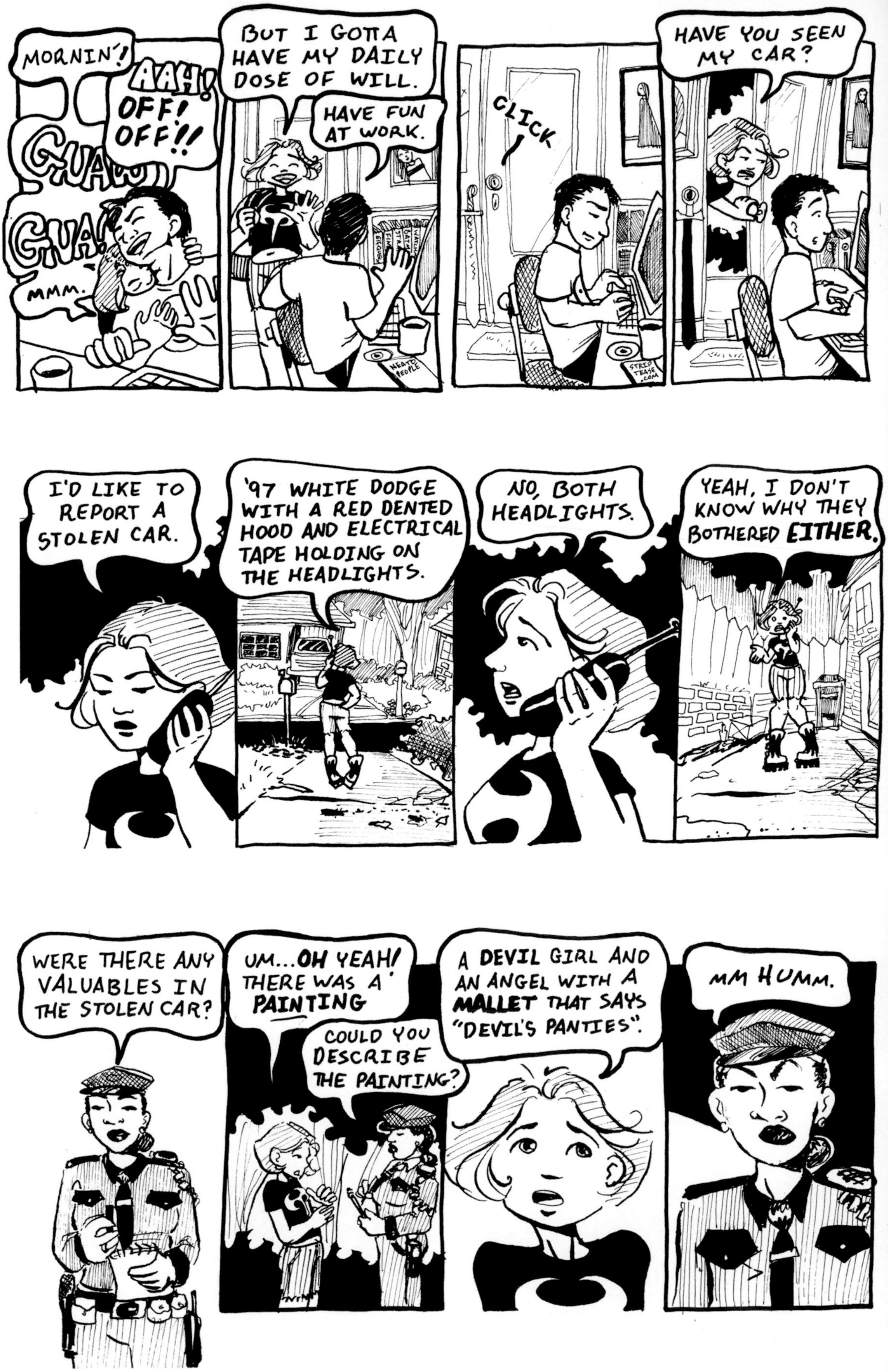
MORNIN'!
AAH! OFF! OFF!!
GUAW
GUA!
MMM.
BUT I GOTTA HAVE MY DAILY DOSE OF WILL.
HAVE FUN AT WORK.
CLICK
HAVE YOU SEEN MY CAR?
I'D LIKE TO REPORT A STOLEN CAR.
'97 WHITE DODGE WITH A RED DENTED HOOD AND ELECTRICAL TAPE HOLDING ON THE HEADLIGHTS.
NO, BOTH HEADLIGHTS.
YEAH, I DON'T KNOW WHY THEY BOTHERED EITHER.
WERE THERE ANY VALUABLES IN THE STOLEN CAR?
UM...OH YEAH! THERE WAS A PAINTING
COULD YOU DESCRIBE THE PAINTING?
A DEVIL GIRL AND AN ANGEL WITH A MALLET THAT SAYS "DEVIL'S PANTIES".
MM HUMM.

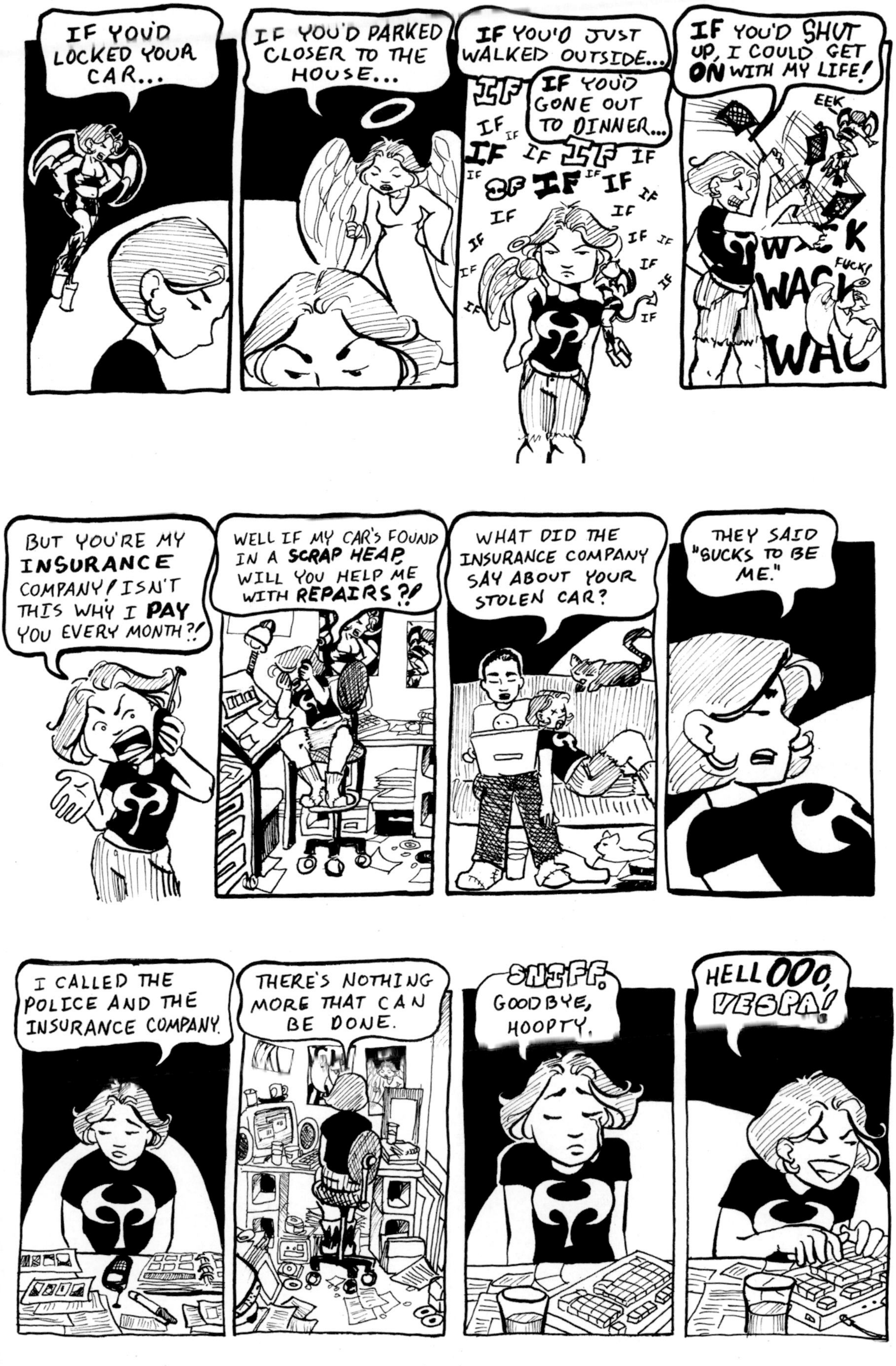

IF YOU'D LOCKED YOUR CAR...
IF YOU'D PARKED CLOSER TO THE HOUSE...
IF YOU'D JUST WALKED OUTSIDE...
IF YOU'D GONE OUT TO DINNER...
IF IF IF IF IF IF IF IF IF IF IF IF IF IF IF IF IF IF IF
IF YOU'D SHUT UP, I COULD GET ON WITH MY LIFE!
EEK
WACK WACK WAC
FUCK!
BUT YOU'RE MY INSURANCE COMPANY! ISN'T THIS WHY I PAY YOU EVERY MONTH?!
WELL IF MY CAR'S FOUND IN A SCRAP HEAP, WILL YOU HELP ME WITH REPAIRS?!
WHAT DID THE INSURANCE COMPANY SAY ABOUT YOUR STOLEN CAR?
THEY SAID "SUCKS TO BE ME."
I CALLED THE POLICE AND THE INSURANCE COMPANY.
THERE'S NOTHING MORE THAT CAN BE DONE.
SNIFF. GOODBYE, HOOPTY.
HELLOOO, VESPA!

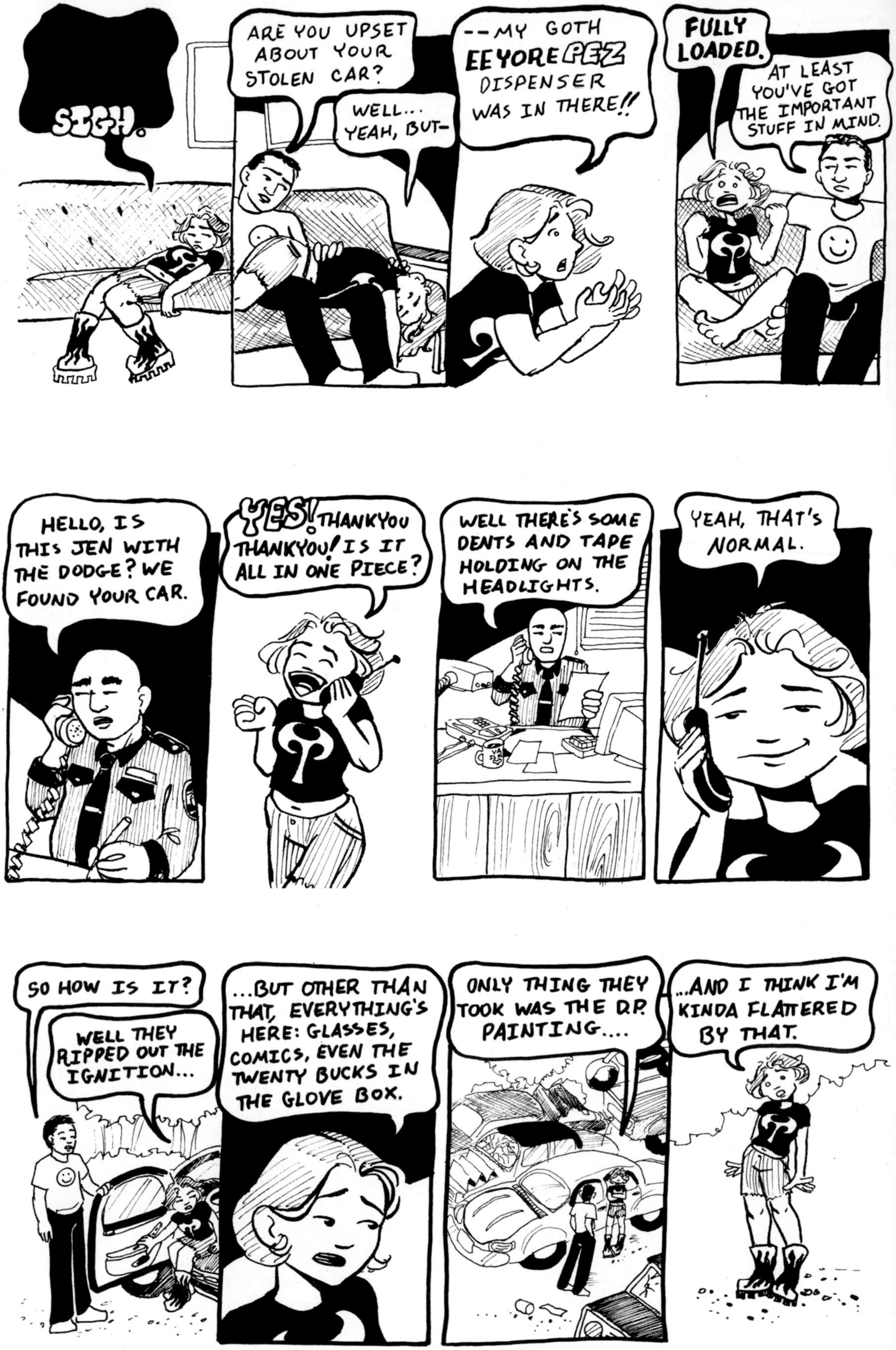
SIGH.
ARE YOU UPSET ABOUT YOUR STOLEN CAR?
WELL... YEAH, BUT-
--MY GOTH EEYORE PEZ DISPENSER WAS IN THERE!!
FULLY LOADED.
AT LEAST YOU'VE GOT THE IMPORTANT STUFF IN MIND.
HELLO, IS THIS JEN WITH THE DODGE? WE FOUND YOUR CAR.
YES! THANKYOU THANKYOU! IS IT ALL IN ONE PIECE?
WELL THERE'S SOME DENTS AND TAPE HOLDING ON THE HEADLIGHTS.
YEAH, THAT'S NORMAL.
SO HOW IS IT?
WELL THEY RIPPED OUT THE IGNITION...
...BUT OTHER THAN THAT, EVERYTHING'S HERE: GLASSES, COMICS, EVEN THE TWENTY BUCKS IN THE GLOVE BOX.
ONLY THING THEY TOOK WAS THE D.P. PAINTING....
...AND I THINK I'M KINDA FLATTERED BY THAT.

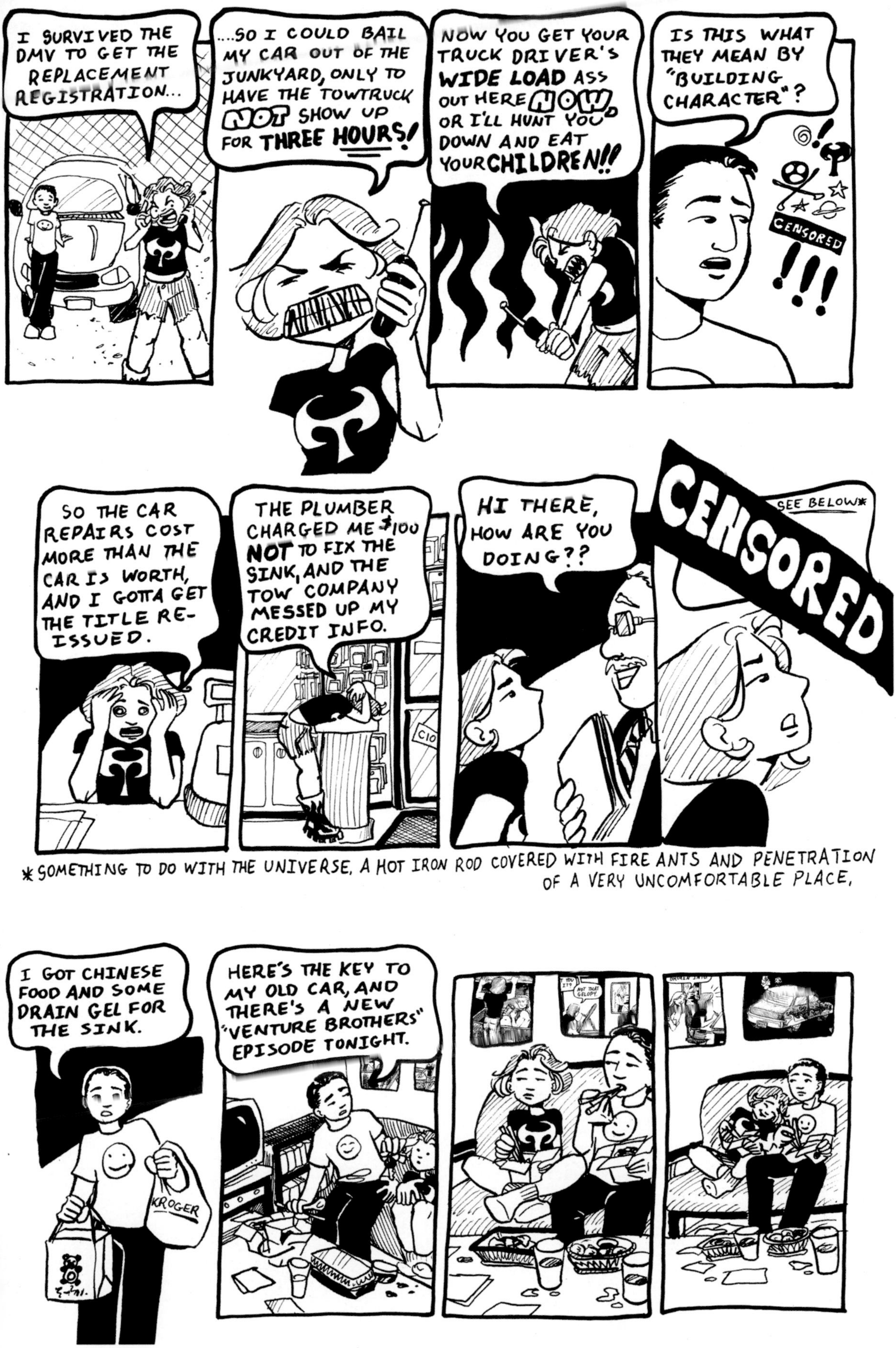
I SURVIVED THE DMV TO GET THE REPLACEMENT REGISTRATION...
....SO I COULD BAIL MY CAR OUT OF THE JUNKYARD, ONLY TO HAVE THE TOWTRUCK NOT SHOW UP FOR THREE HOURS!
NOW YOU GET YOUR TRUCK DRIVER'S WIDE LOAD ASS OUT HERE NOW, OR I'LL HUNT YOU DOWN AND EAT YOUR CHILDREN!!
IS THIS WHAT THEY MEAN BY "BUILDING CHARACTER"?
CENSORED
!!!
SO THE CAR REPAIRS COST MORE THAN THE CAR IS WORTH, AND I GOTTA GET THE TITLE RE-ISSUED.
THE PLUMBER CHARGED ME $100 NOT TO FIX THE SINK, AND THE TOW COMPANY MESSED UP MY CREDIT INFO.
HI THERE, HOW ARE YOU DOING??
CENSORED
SEE BELOW*
* SOMETHING TO DO WITH THE UNIVERSE, A HOT IRON ROD COVERED WITH FIRE ANTS AND PENETRATION OF A VERY UNCOMFORTABLE PLACE,
I GOT CHINESE FOOD AND SOME DRAIN GEL FOR THE SINK.
KROGER
HERE'S THE KEY TO MY OLD CAR, AND THERE'S A NEW "VENTURE BROTHERS" EPISODE TONIGHT.

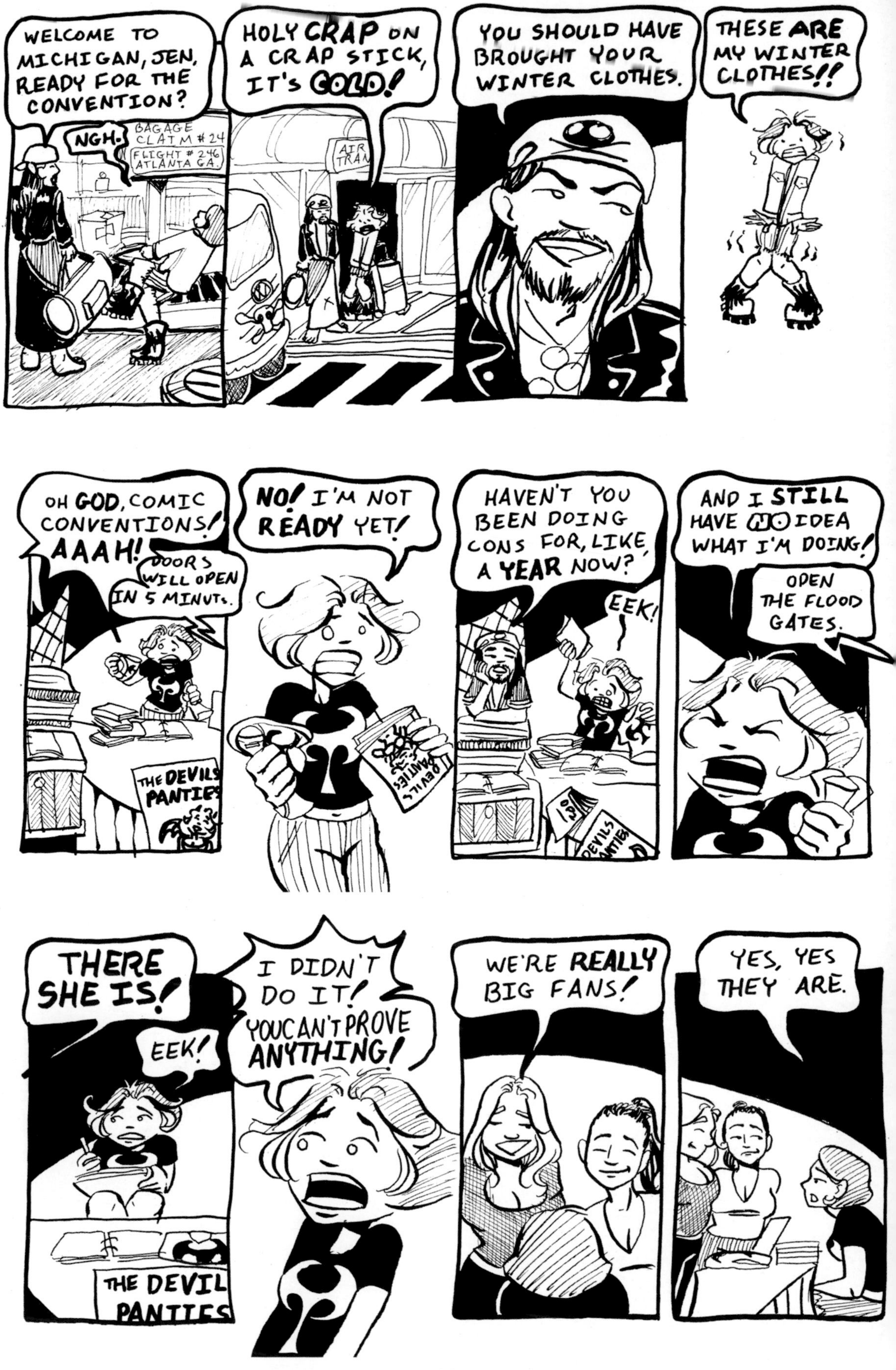
WELCOME TO MICHIGAN, JEN, READY FOR THE CONVENTION?
NGH.
BAGAGE CLAIM # 24
FLIGHT # 246 ATLANTA GA.
HOLY CRAP ON A CRAP STICK, IT'S COLD!
YOU SHOULD HAVE BROUGHT YOUR WINTER CLOTHES.
THESE ARE MY WINTER CLOTHES!!
OH GOD, COMIC CONVENTIONS! AAAH!
DOORS WILL OPEN IN 5 MINUTs.
THE DEVILS PANTIES
NO! I'M NOT READY YET!
DEVILS PANTIES
HAVEN'T YOU BEEN DOING CONS FOR, LIKE, A YEAR NOW?
EEK!
AND I STILL HAVE NO IDEA WHAT I'M DOING!
OPEN THE FLOOD GATES.
THERE SHE IS!
EEK!
THE DEVIL PANTIES
I DIDN'T DO IT! YOU CAN'T PROVE ANYTHING!
WE'RE REALLY BIG FANS!
YES, YES THEY ARE.

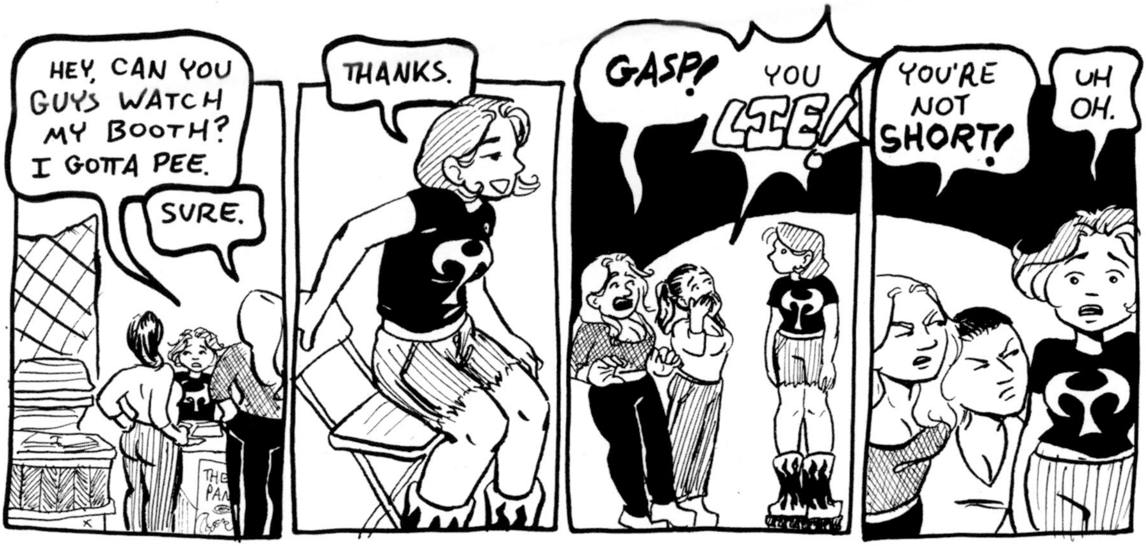
HEY, CAN YOU GUYS WATCH MY BOOTH? I GOTTA PEE.
SURE.
THANKS.
GASP!
YOU LIE!
YOU'RE NOT SHORT!
UH OH.

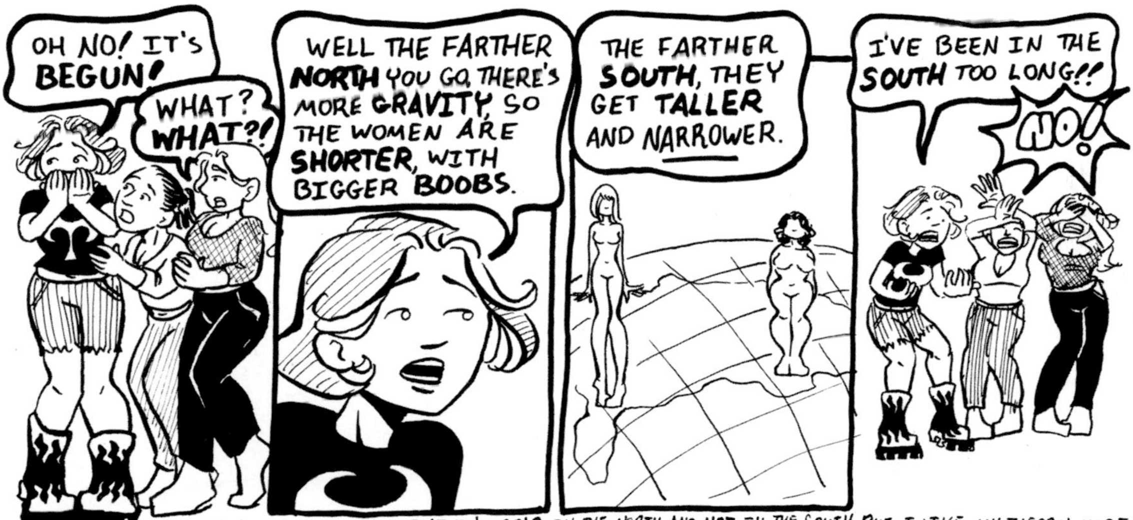
OH NO! IT'S BEGUN!
WHAT? WHAT?!
WELL THE FARTHER NORTH YOU GO, THERE'S MORE GRAVITY, SO THE WOMEN ARE SHORTER, WITH BIGGER BOOBS.
THE FARTHER SOUTH, THEY GET TALLER AND NARROWER.
I'VE BEEN IN THE SOUTH TOO LONG!!
NO!

OK, SO IT MIGHT HAVE TO DO WITH THE FACT THAT IT'S COLD IN THE NORTH AND HOT IN THE SOUTH, BUT I LIKE MY THEORY MORE.

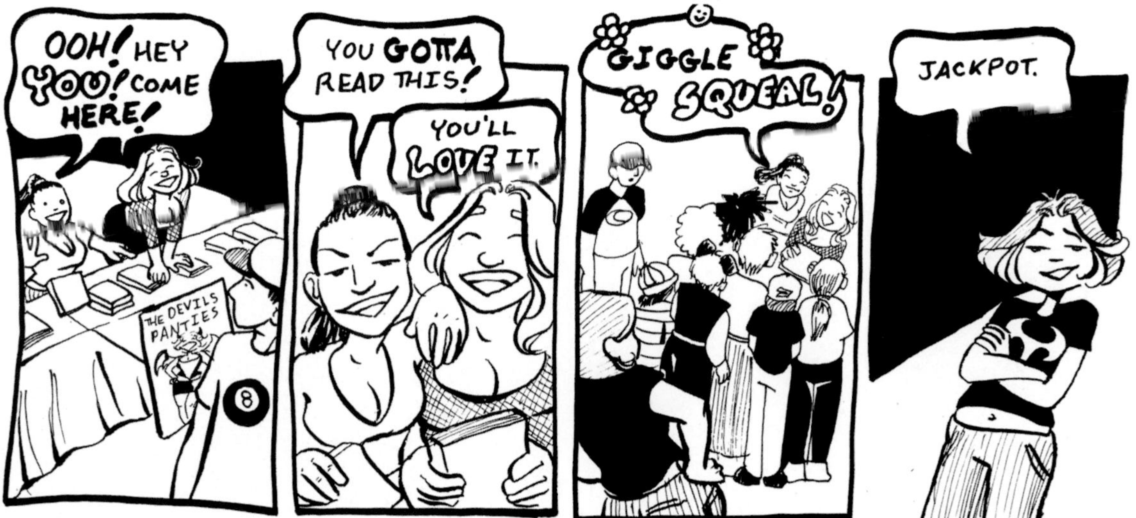
OOH! HEY YOU! COME HERE!
THE DEVILS PANTIES
YOU GOTTA READ THIS!
YOU'LL LOVE IT.
GIGGLE SQUEAL!
JACKPOT.

Panel 1: NIGEL! NIGEL! / WHAT?! WHAT?!

Panel 2: I'VE GOT MINIONS! / WELL DONE! / BOOZ FUND

Panel 3: NO TOUCH! THEY'RE MINE!

Panel 4: MWA HA HA

Panel 5: EEK?

THANKS FOR WATCHING MY TABLE. HERE. / CAFFEINE! / THE DEVIL'S PANTIES

YAY! IT'S POP. / NO, IT'S COLA.

BUT IT TASTES LIKE PEPSI. / POP. COLA. / POP COLA.

HICK. / YANKEE.

LET US TAKE YOU OUT TO DINNER. WHERE ARE YOU STAYING? / THE DEVILS PANTIES

OUT BACK. / WHAT HOTEL?

NO, I MEAN I'M SLEEPING IN A VAN IN THE PARKING LOT.

THE COMIC ARTIST LIFE JUST OOZES GLAMOUR, DOESN'T IT?

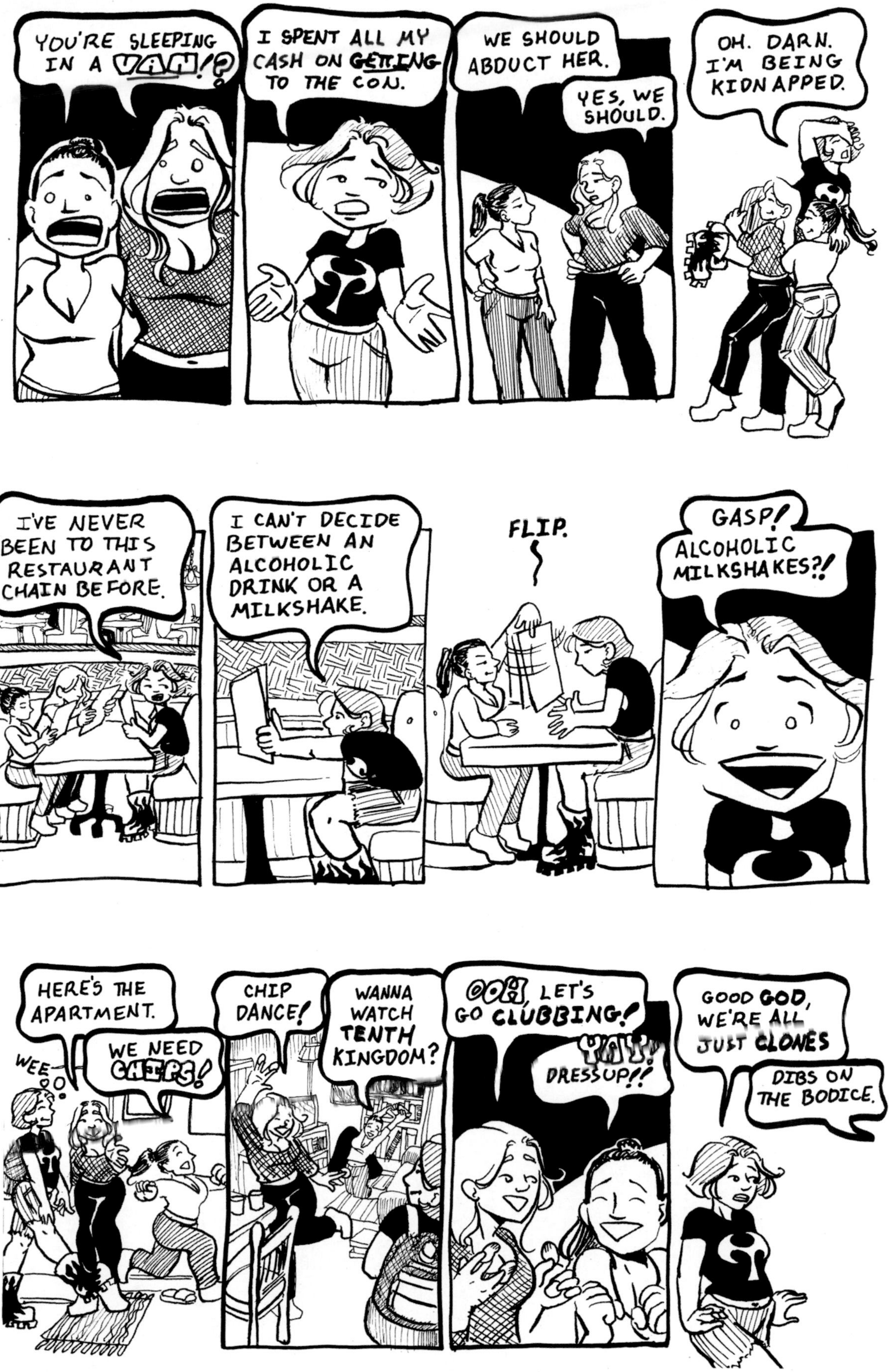
YOU'RE SLEEPING IN A VAN!?
I SPENT ALL MY CASH ON GETTING TO THE CON.
WE SHOULD ABDUCT HER.
YES, WE SHOULD.
OH. DARN. I'M BEING KIDNAPPED.
I'VE NEVER BEEN TO THIS RESTAURANT CHAIN BEFORE.
I CAN'T DECIDE BETWEEN AN ALCOHOLIC DRINK OR A MILKSHAKE.
FLIP.
GASP! ALCOHOLIC MILKSHAKES?!
HERE'S THE APARTMENT.
WEE
WE NEED CHIPS!
CHIP DANCE!
WANNA WATCH TENTH KINGDOM?
OOH, LET'S GO CLUBBING!
YAY! DRESSUP!!
GOOD GOD, WE'RE ALL JUST CLONES
DIBS ON THE BODICE.

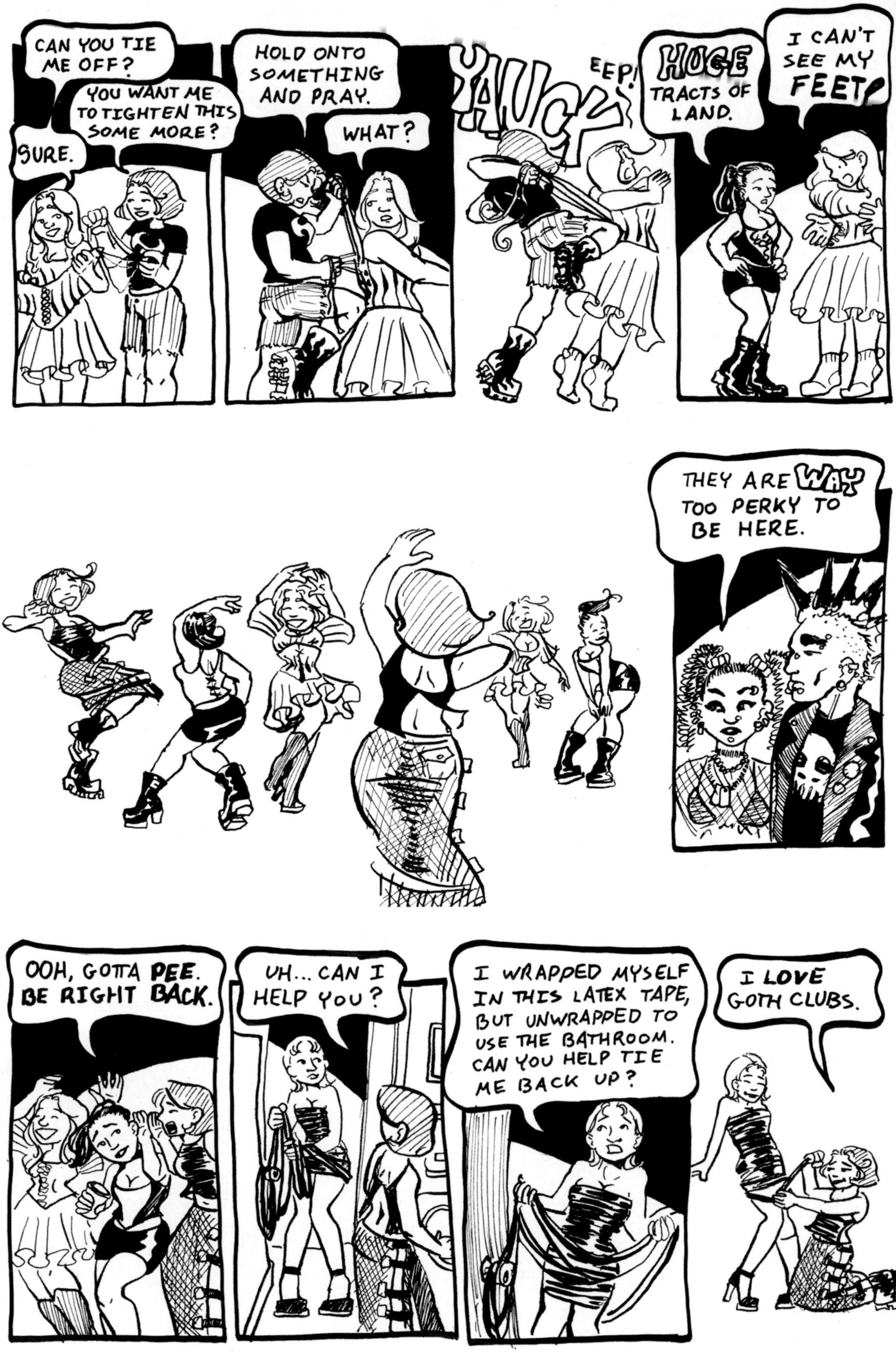
CAN YOU TIE ME OFF?
SURE.
YOU WANT ME TO TIGHTEN THIS SOME MORE?
HOLD ONTO SOMETHING AND PRAY.
WHAT?
YAUCK!
EEP!
HUGE TRACTS OF LAND.
I CAN'T SEE MY FEET!
THEY ARE WAY TOO PERKY TO BE HERE.
OOH, GOTTA PEE. BE RIGHT BACK.
UH... CAN I HELP YOU?
I WRAPPED MYSELF IN THIS LATEX TAPE, BUT UNWRAPPED TO USE THE BATHROOM. CAN YOU HELP TIE ME BACK UP?
I LOVE GOTH CLUBS.

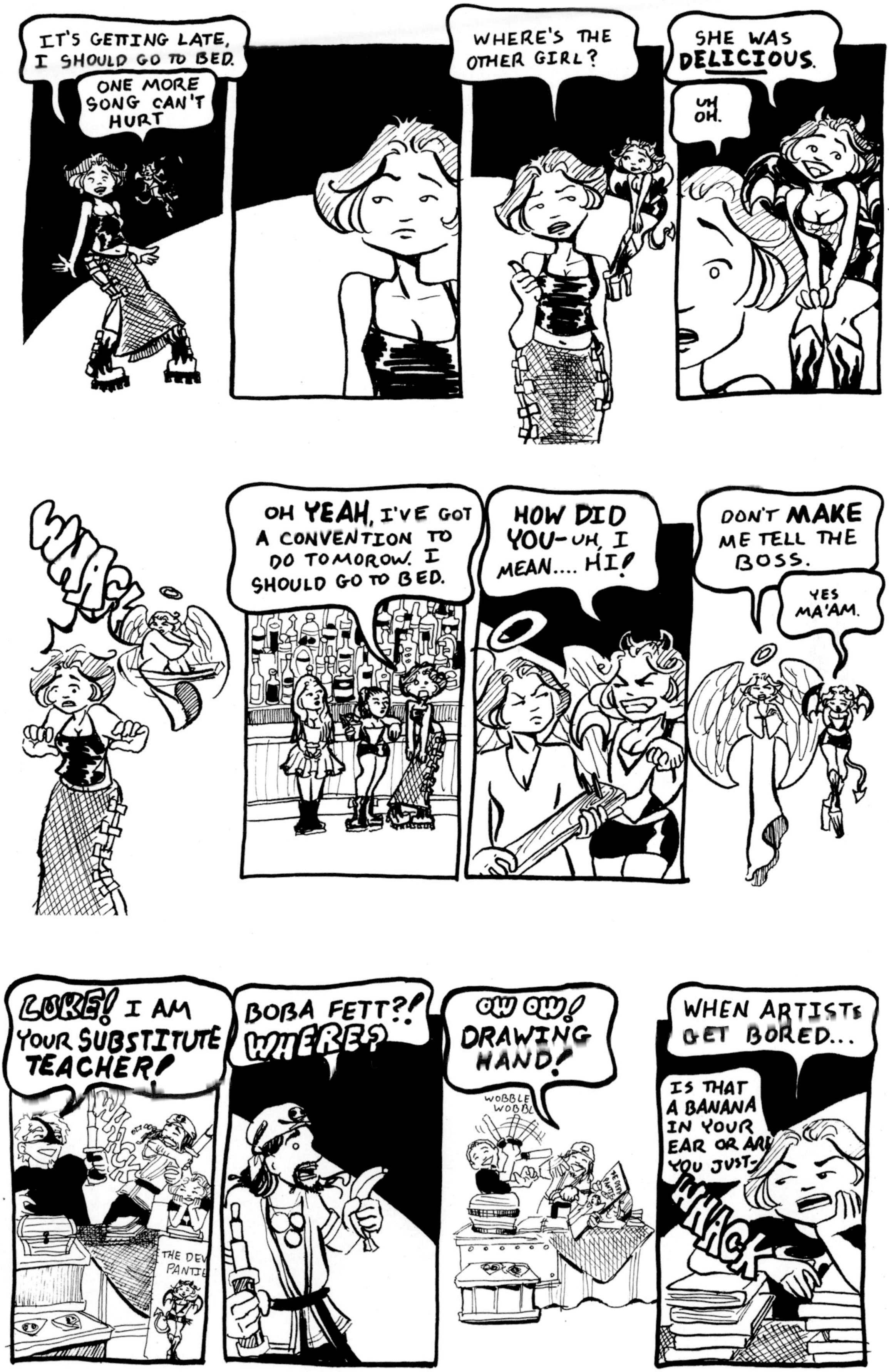
IT'S GETTING LATE, I SHOULD GO TO BED.
ONE MORE SONG CAN'T HURT
WHERE'S THE OTHER GIRL?
SHE WAS DELICIOUS.
UH OH.
WHACK
OH YEAH, I'VE GOT A CONVENTION TO DO TOMOROW. I SHOULD GO TO BED.
HOW DID YOU- UH, I MEAN.... HI!
DON'T MAKE ME TELL THE BOSS.
YES MA'AM.
LUKE! I AM YOUR SUBSTITUTE TEACHER!
THE DEV PANTIE
BOBA FETT?! WHERE?
OW OW! DRAWING HAND!
WOBBLE WOBBL
WHEN ARTISTS GET BORED...
IS THAT A BANANA IN YOUR EAR OR ARE YOU JUST-
WHACK

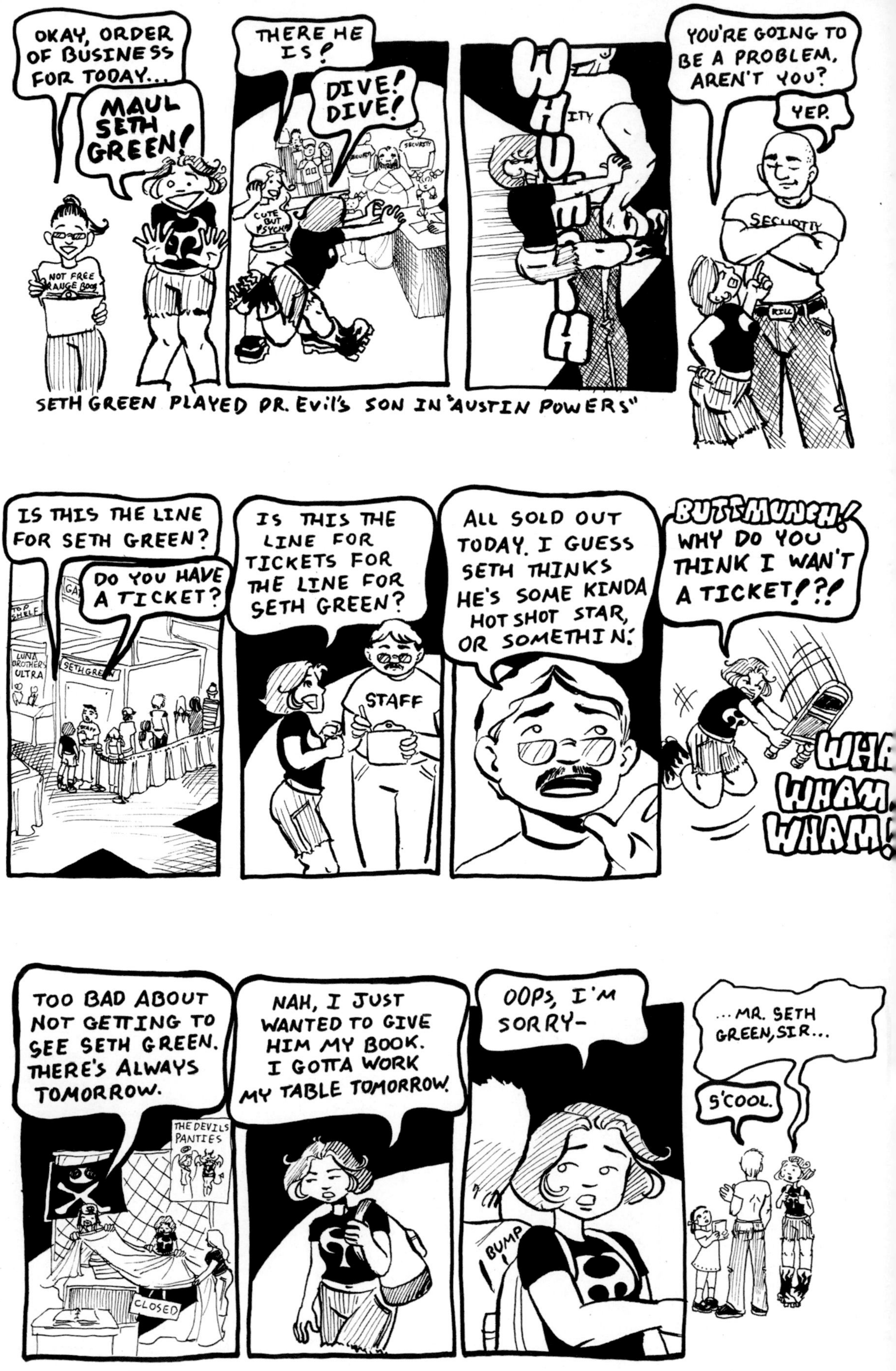
OKAY, ORDER OF BUSINESS FOR TODAY...
MAUL SETH GREEN!
NOT FREE RANGE BOOB
THERE HE IS!
DIVE! DIVE!
CUTE BUT PSYCHO
WHUMPH
YOU'RE GOING TO BE A PROBLEM, AREN'T YOU?
YEP.
SECURITY
SETH GREEN PLAYED DR. EVIL'S SON IN "AUSTIN POWERS"
IS THIS THE LINE FOR SETH GREEN?
DO YOU HAVE A TICKET?
IS THIS THE LINE FOR TICKETS FOR THE LINE FOR SETH GREEN?
STAFF
ALL SOLD OUT TODAY. I GUESS SETH THINKS HE'S SOME KINDA HOT SHOT STAR, OR SOMETHIN'.
BUTTMUNCH! WHY DO YOU THINK I WAN'T A TICKET!?!
WHAM, WHAM! WHAM!
TOO BAD ABOUT NOT GETTING TO SEE SETH GREEN. THERE'S ALWAYS TOMORROW.
THE DEVILS PANTIES
CLOSED
NAH, I JUST WANTED TO GIVE HIM MY BOOK. I GOTTA WORK MY TABLE TOMORROW.
OOPS, I'M SORRY-
BUMP
...MR. SETH GREEN, SIR...
S'COOL.

WOULD YOU LIKE ME TO SIGN THIS?

MKAY.

PARDON ME, MR. GREEN, I'D LIKE YOU TO HAVE THIS.

OH, HEY DID YOU DRAW THIS?

YEAH, HOPE YOU LIKE IT.

THANKS!

THAT WAS VERY PROFESSIONAL OF YOU, JEN.

OHMYGOD OHMYGOD OHMYGOD OHMYGOD

SHE APPROACHED SETH GREEN IN A VERY PROFESSIONAL MANNER.

I ESPECIALLY LIKED THE PART WHERE SHE TRAMPLED THREE FIVE YEAR OLDS TO GET TO HIM.

BE AFRAID

I MET SETH GREEN I MET SETH GREEN I MET SETH GREEN I MET SETH GREEN I MET SETH GREEN I MET SETH GREEN I MET SETH GREEN I MET SETH GREEN

YOU DO REALIZE HE'S STILL BEHIND US, RIGHT?

YUP!

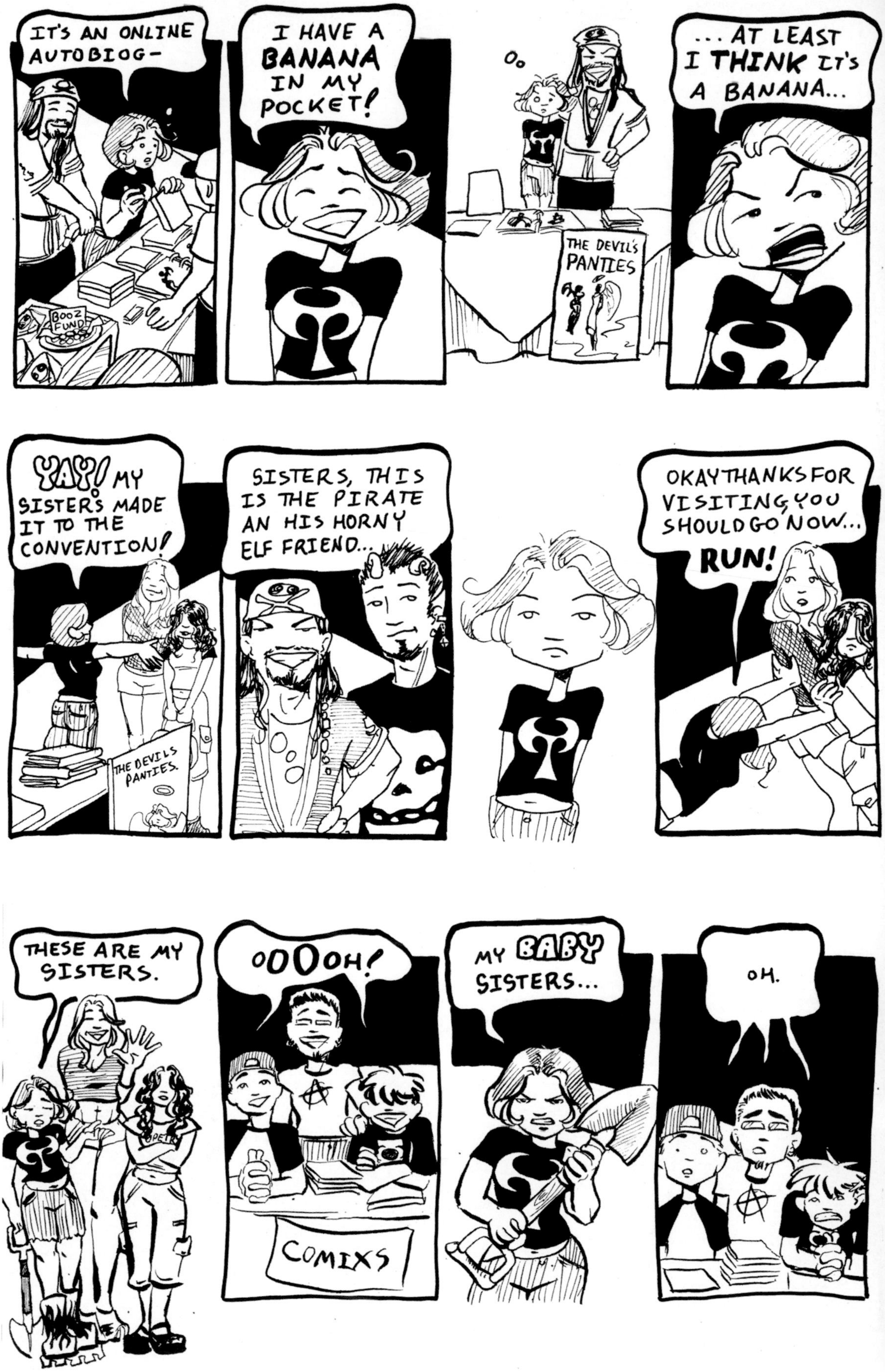
IT'S AN ONLINE AUTOBIOG-
BOOZ FUND
I HAVE A BANANA IN MY POCKET!
Oo
THE DEVIL'S PANTIES
... AT LEAST I THINK IT'S A BANANA...
YAY! MY SISTERS MADE IT TO THE CONVENTION!
THE DEVILS PANTIES
SISTERS, THIS IS THE PIRATE AN HIS HORNY ELF FRIEND...
OKAYTHANKSFOR VISITING,YOU SHOULDGO NOW...
RUN!
THESE ARE MY SISTERS.
OOOOH!
COMIXS
MY BABY SISTERS...
OH.

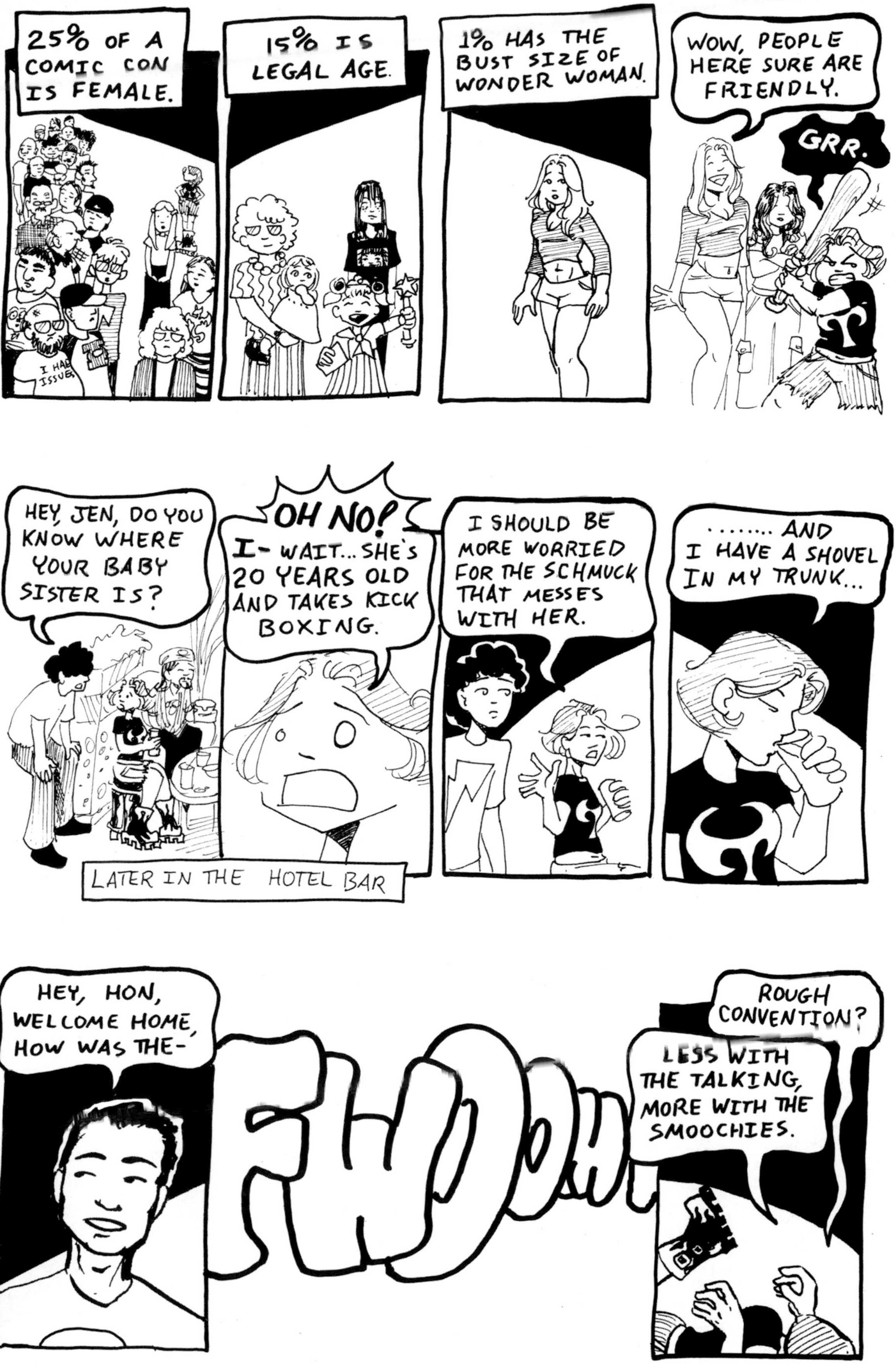
25% OF A COMIC CON IS FEMALE.
15% IS LEGAL AGE.
1% HAS THE BUST SIZE OF WONDER WOMAN.
WOW, PEOPLE HERE SURE ARE FRIENDLY.
GRR.
HEY, JEN, DO YOU KNOW WHERE YOUR BABY SISTER IS?
OH NO!
I- WAIT... SHE'S 20 YEARS OLD AND TAKES KICK BOXING.
I SHOULD BE MORE WORRIED FOR THE SCHMUCK THAT MESSES WITH HER.
.... AND I HAVE A SHOVEL IN MY TRUNK...
LATER IN THE HOTEL BAR
HEY, HON, WELCOME HOME, HOW WAS THE-
FWOOSH
ROUGH CONVENTION?
LESS WITH THE TALKING, MORE WITH THE SMOOCHIES.

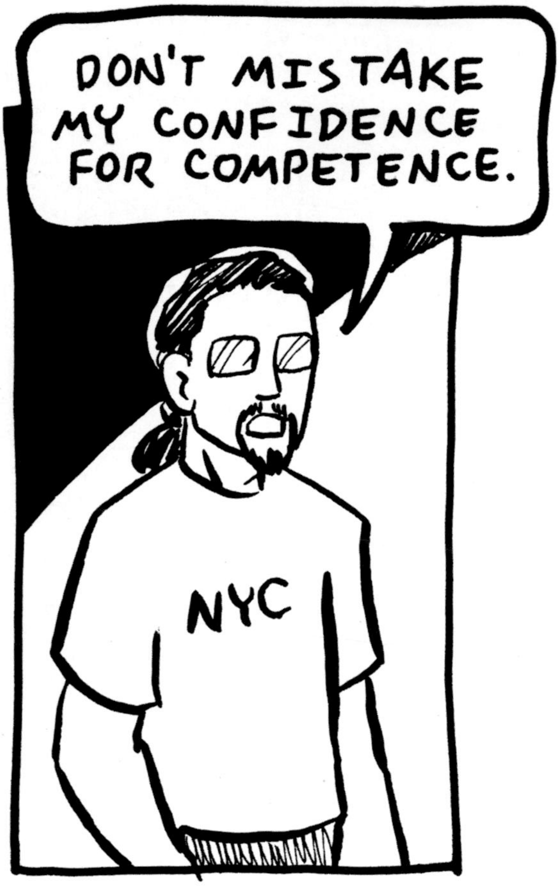
DON'T MISTAKE MY CONFIDENCE FOR COMPETENCE.
NYC

-CHRIS

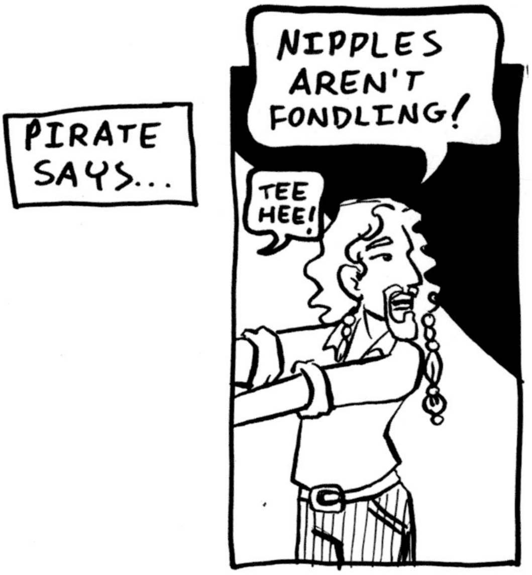
PIRATE SAYS...
NIPPLES AREN'T FONDLING!
TEE HEE!

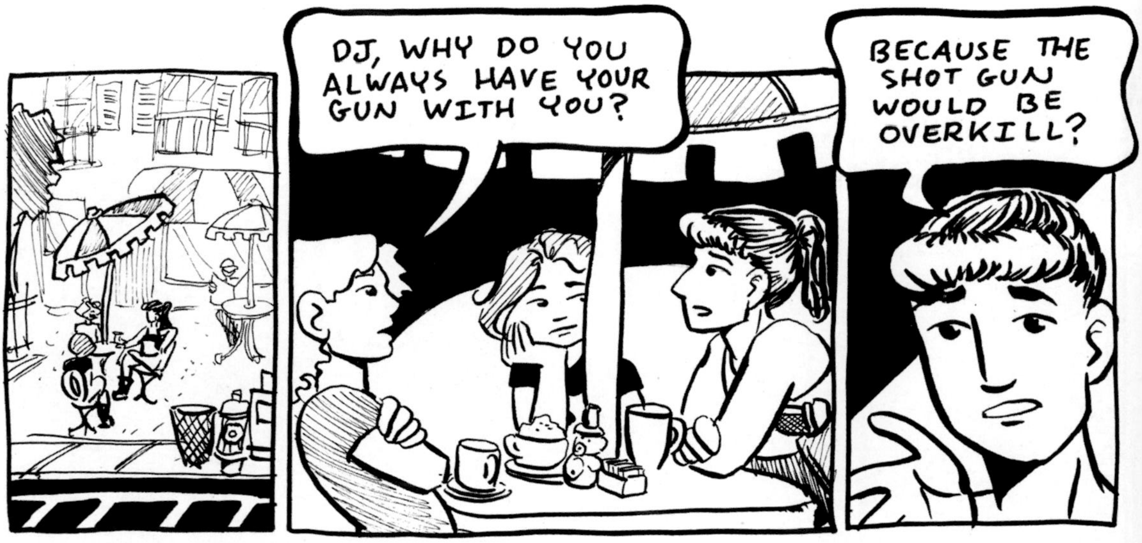
DJ, WHY DO YOU ALWAYS HAVE YOUR GUN WITH YOU?
BECAUSE THE SHOT GUN WOULD BE OVERKILL?

HEY, JEN, READY TO GET A PEDICURE?

YEAH, ONE MORE MINUTE.

WHAT ARE YOU DOING IN THERE?

SHAVING MY TOES.

THEY HAVE THE BEST CHAIRS FOR YOUR PEDICURE.

PRESS THAT BUTTON.

OH!..... OH MY. WRRRR

THIS CHAIR HAS TOUCHED ME IN WAYS I'VE NEVER BEEN TOUCHED BEFORE.

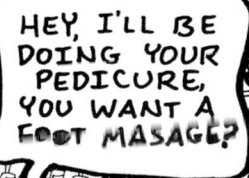

HEY, I'LL BE DOING YOUR PEDICURE, YOU WANT A FOOT MASAGE?

UM...NO, THAT'S OKAY... THANKS.

LIFE'S "TO DO" LIST.

☑ Dance on a bar
☑ Go Go Boots
☑ Publish Comic
☑ Quit Day Job
☑ Get Flying MONKEY
☑ Cabana Boy
☐ Go to England
☐ MO... COUNTRY
☐ WO... ...tion
☐ Ch...

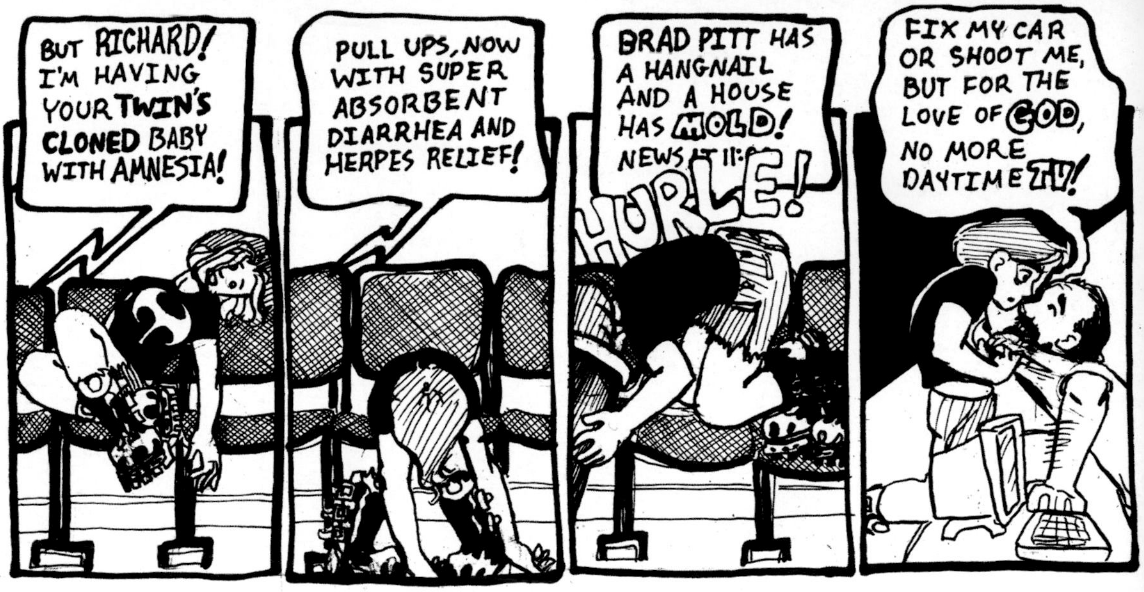
BUT RICHARD! I'M HAVING YOUR TWIN'S CLONED BABY WITH AMNESIA!
PULL UPS, NOW WITH SUPER ABSORBENT DIARRHEA AND HERPES RELIEF!
BRAD PITT HAS A HANGNAIL AND A HOUSE HAS MOLD!
HURLE!
FIX MY CAR OR SHOOT ME, BUT FOR THE LOVE OF GOD, NO MORE DAYTIME TV!

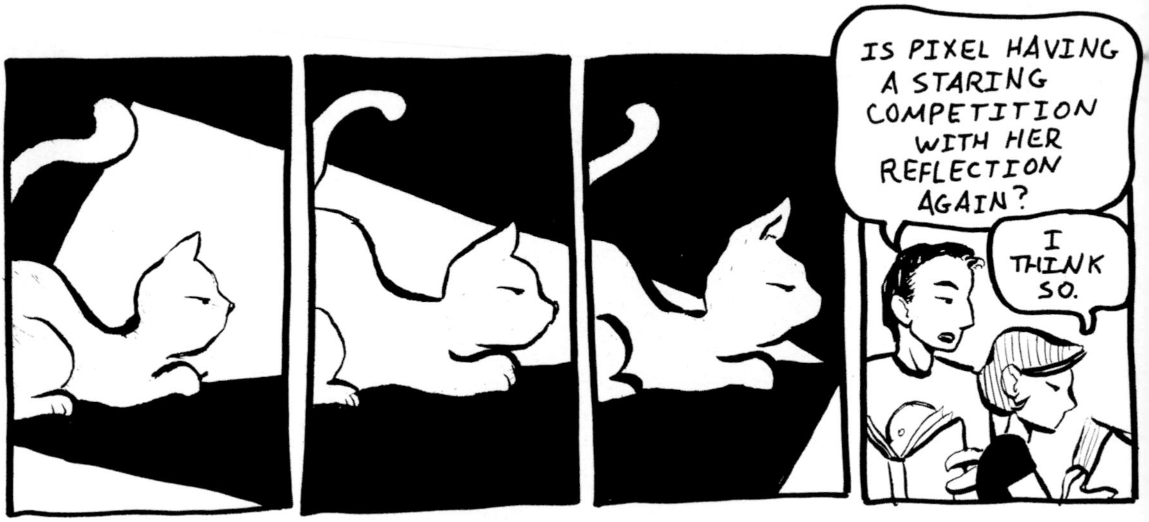
IS PIXEL HAVING A STARING COMPETITION WITH HER REFLECTION AGAIN?
I THINK SO.

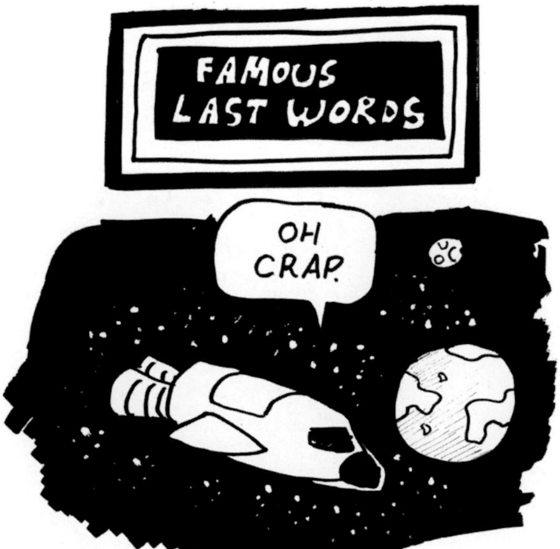
FAMOUS LAST WORDS
OH CRAP.

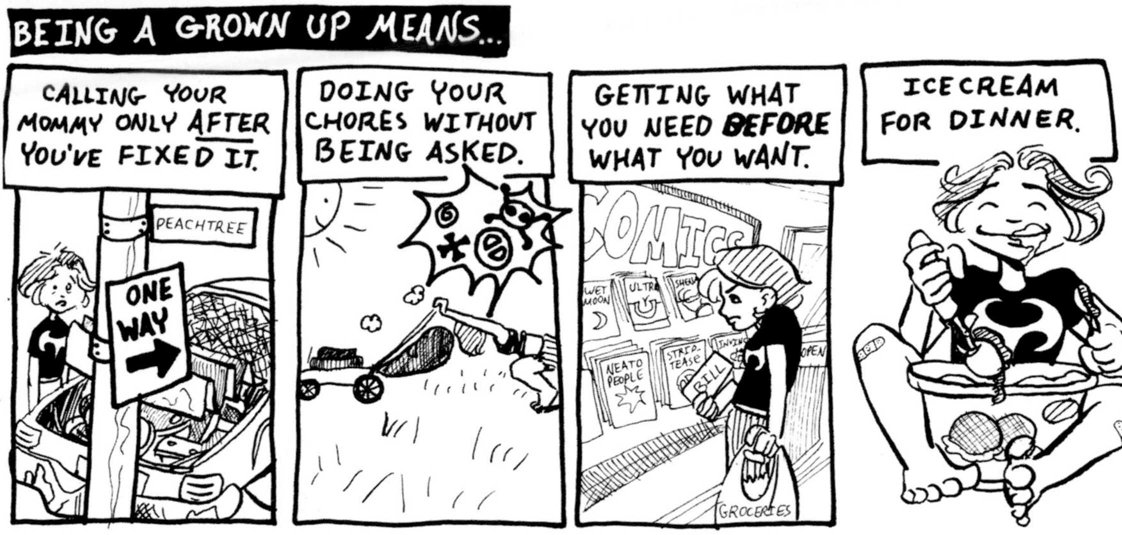
BEING A GROWN UP MEANS...
CALLING YOUR MOMMY ONLY AFTER YOU'VE FIXED IT.
PEACHTREE
ONE WAY
DOING YOUR CHORES WITHOUT BEING ASKED.
GETTING WHAT YOU NEED BEFORE WHAT YOU WANT.
COMICS
NEATO PEOPLE
BILL
OPEN
GROCERIES
ICECREAM FOR DINNER.

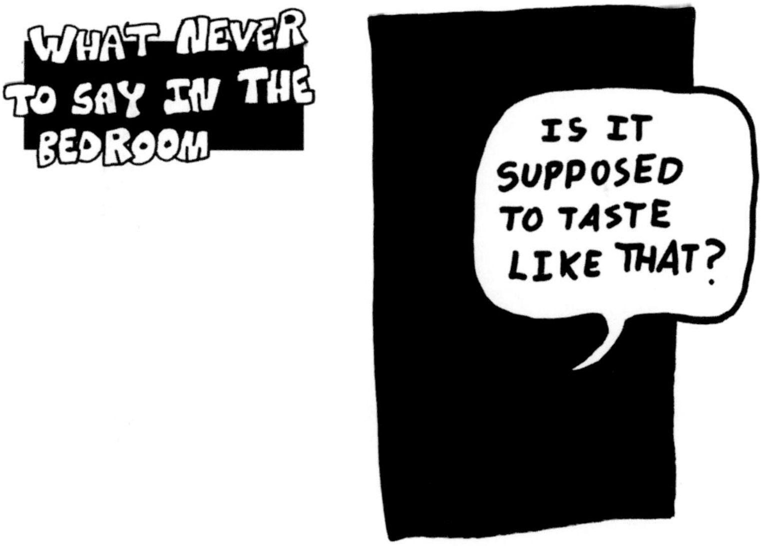
WHAT NEVER TO SAY IN THE BEDROOM
IS IT SUPPOSED TO TASTE LIKE THAT?

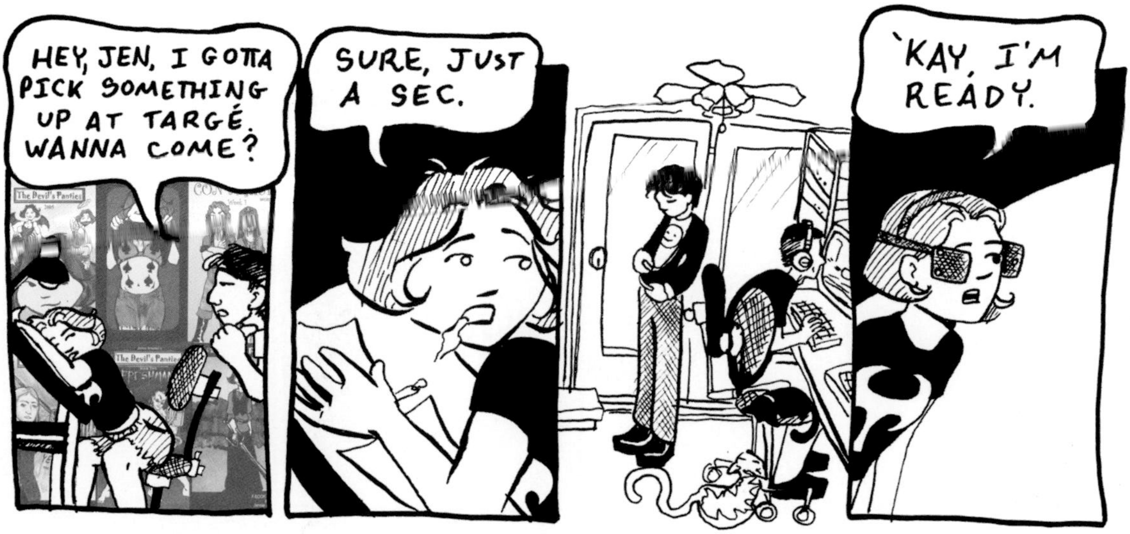
HEY, JEN, I GOTTA PICK SOMETHING UP AT TARGÉ. WANNA COME?
The Devil's Panties
SURE, JUST A SEC.
`KAY, I'M READY.

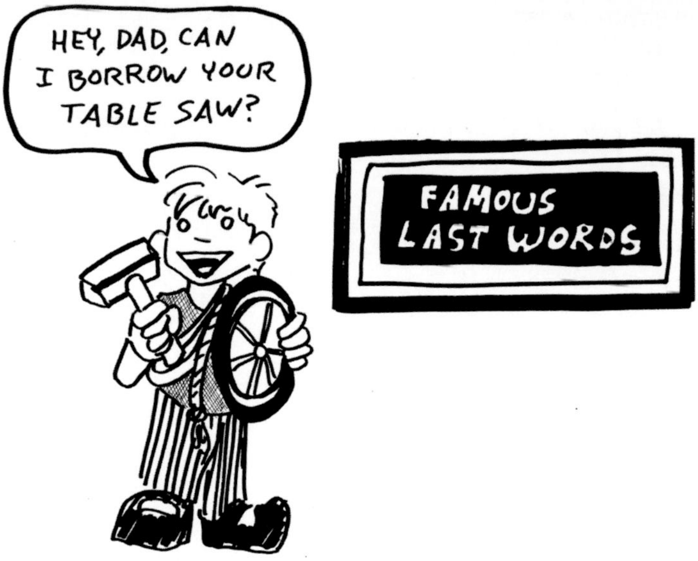
HEY, DAD, CAN I BORROW YOUR TABLE SAW?
FAMOUS LAST WORDS

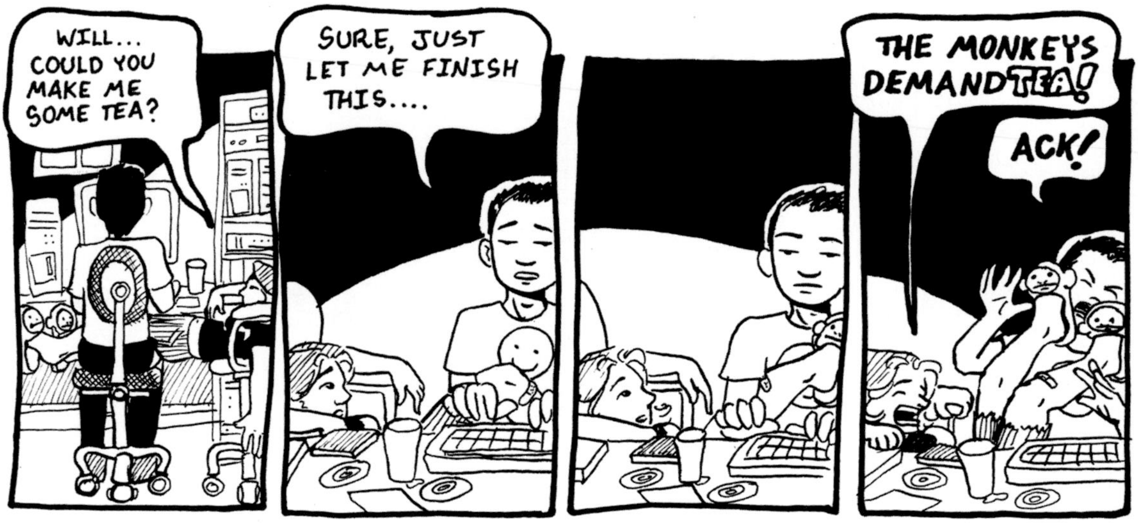
WILL... COULD YOU MAKE ME SOME TEA?
SURE, JUST LET ME FINISH THIS....
THE MONKEYS DEMAND TEA!
ACK!

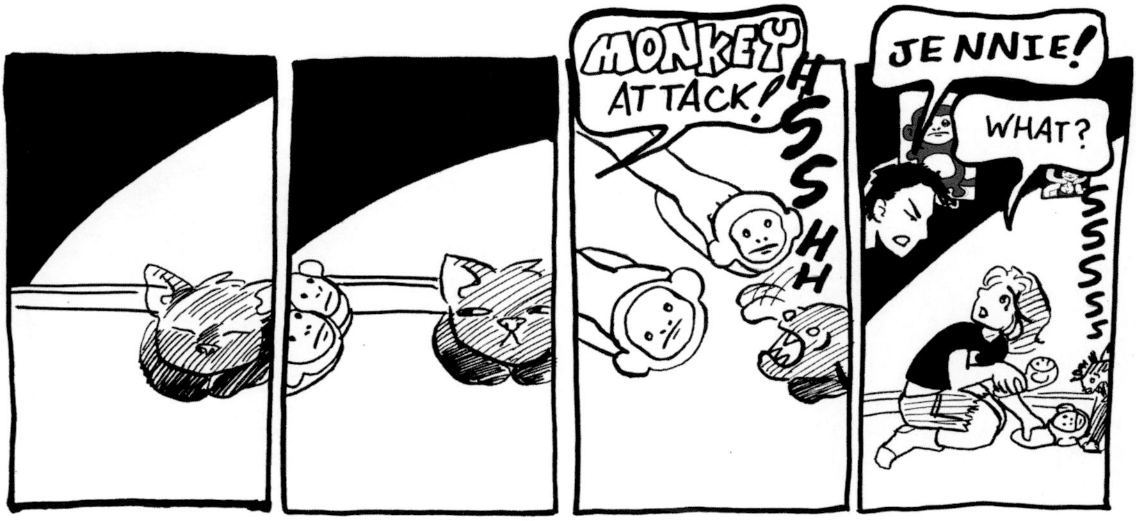
MONKEY ATTACK!
JENNIE!
WHAT?

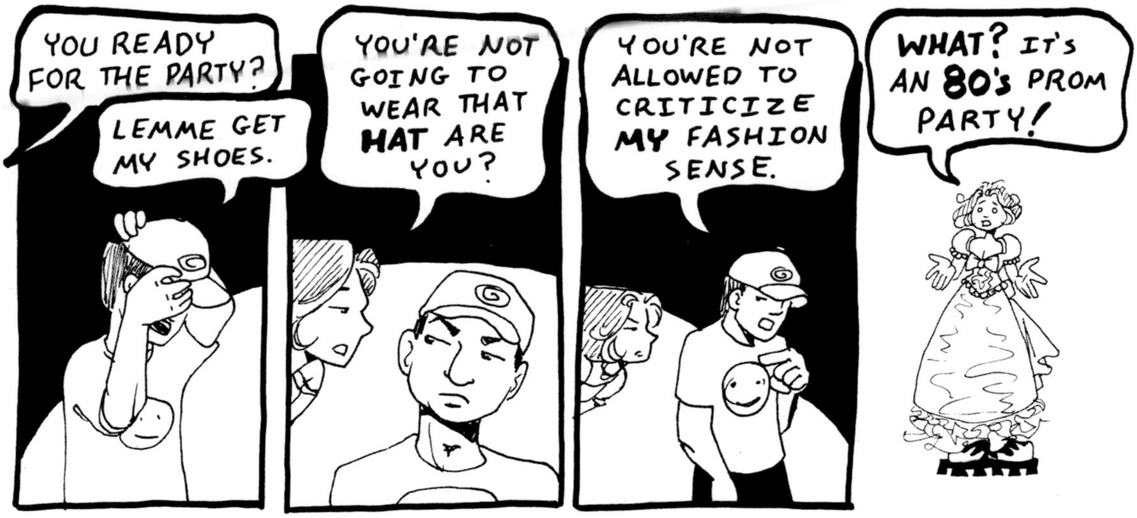
YOU READY FOR THE PARTY?
LEMME GET MY SHOES.
YOU'RE NOT GOING TO WEAR THAT HAT ARE YOU?
YOU'RE NOT ALLOWED TO CRITICIZE MY FASHION SENSE.
WHAT? IT'S AN 80's PROM PARTY!

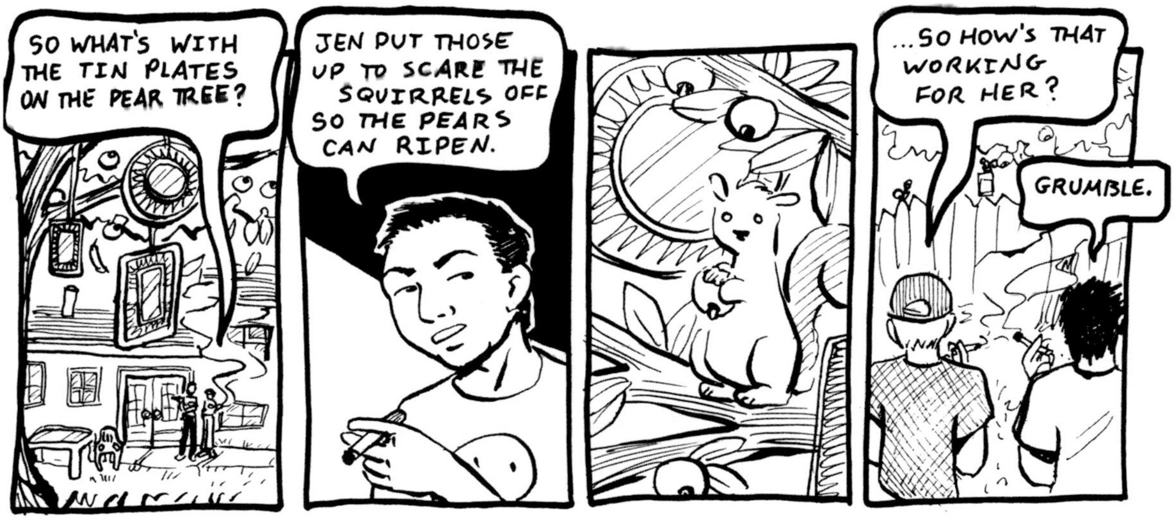
SO WHAT'S WITH THE TIN PLATES ON THE PEAR TREE?
JEN PUT THOSE UP TO SCARE THE SQUIRRELS OFF SO THE PEARS CAN RIPEN.
...SO HOW'S THAT WORKING FOR HER?
GRUMBLE.

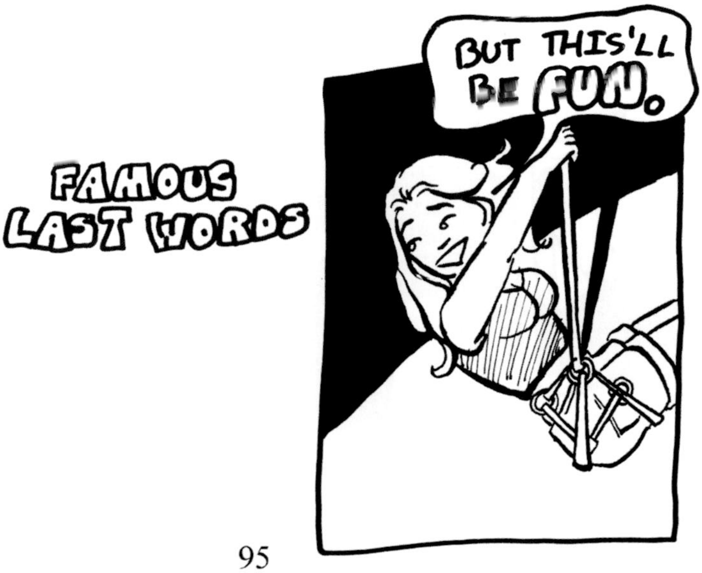
FAMOUS LAST WORDS
BUT THIS'LL BE FUN.

HEY, JEN, GOT A NEW WORKER.

THIS IS BETTY.

HI!

ESTROGEN!!

I MEAN, HI.

SO THIS IS A STRESSFUL JOB?

NOT REALLY, YOU JUST— AH SHIT.

HEY SWEET CHEEKS, YOU EATIN' THAT CHOCOLATE HUH?

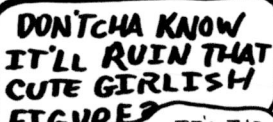
DON'TCHA KNOW IT'LL RUIN THAT CUTE GIRLISH FIGURE?

IT'S THE ONLY THING THAT'S KEEPING YOU ALIVE, MR. GOBS.

YOU JUST HAVE TO HAVE A HIGH TOLERANCE TO TESTOSTERONE.

SO WHAT'S A NICE GIRL LIKE YOU DO WHEN YOU'RE NOT WAITING ON GUYS LIKE ME?

WELL, I PLAY TROMBONE IN A BAND.

HEH HEH, I GOTTA TROMBONE YOU CAN PLAY.

GEE WHIZ SIR, I DON'T KNOW IF I SHOULD OVER-CHARGE YOU OR KICK YOU IN THE MOUTH.

HEY, BETTY, WHATCHA DOING?

OH, I GOT THE LICENSE PLATE # OF THAT ASS WHO JUST LEFT.

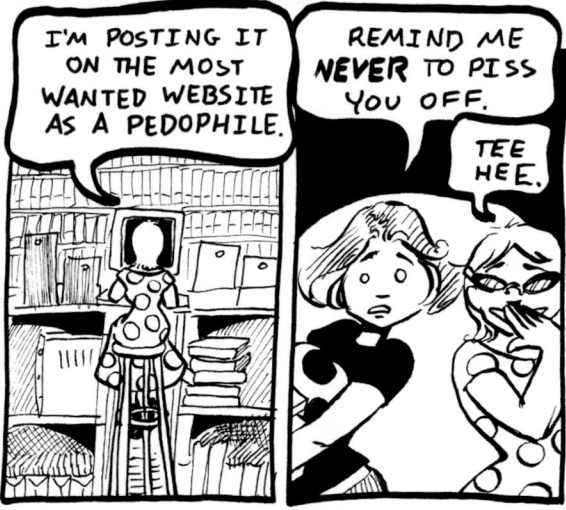

I'M POSTING IT ON THE MOST WANTED WEBSITE AS A PEDOPHILE.

REMIND ME **NEVER** TO PISS YOU OFF.

TEE HEE.

KYACKITY YACK Y YACK YACKITY YA KYACK YACK YAC YACKITY YACK Y ACK YACK YACKIT CK YACK YACK Y KY YACK A YACK YA YACK

OOOH I REALLY NEEDED THAT.

WHAT, CAFFEINE FIX?

NO, ESTROGEN FIX.

IT'S PAPER, IT **MUST** BE SAT UPON.

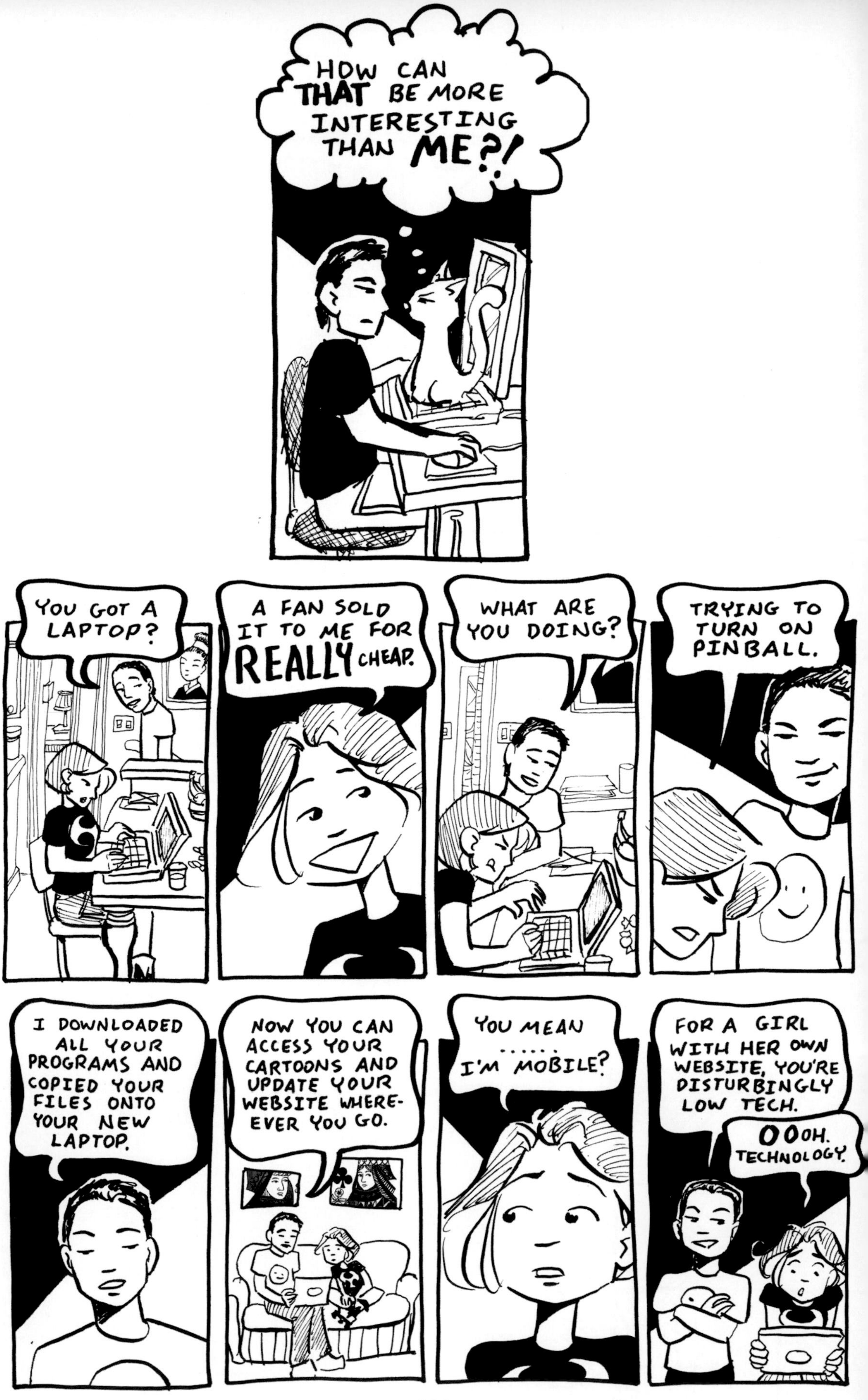
HOW CAN THAT BE MORE INTERESTING THAN ME?!
YOU GOT A LAPTOP?
A FAN SOLD IT TO ME FOR REALLY CHEAP.
WHAT ARE YOU DOING?
TRYING TO TURN ON PINBALL.
I DOWNLOADED ALL YOUR PROGRAMS AND COPIED YOUR FILES ONTO YOUR NEW LAPTOP.
NOW YOU CAN ACCESS YOUR CARTOONS AND UPDATE YOUR WEBSITE WHERE-EVER YOU GO.
YOU MEAN ...... I'M MOBILE?
FOR A GIRL WITH HER OWN WEBSITE, YOU'RE DISTURBINGLY LOW TECH.
OOOH. TECHNOLOGY.

HEY, ARIE, YOU ON YOUR WAY TO CHICAGO CON?

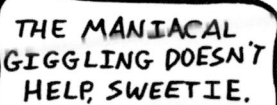

THE MANIACAL GIGGLING DOESN'T HELP, SWEETIE.

OR THE HYPERVENTILATING.

WHERE ARE YOU IN ILLINOIS?!

YAY! ARIE'S HERE!

LEMME GET MY OVERNIGHT STUFF...

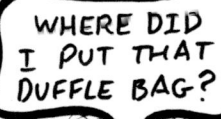

WHERE DID I PUT THAT DUFFLE BAG?

(EEK!)

IS THAT **ARMOR?**

JUST IN CASE.

OH GOD, I GOT **SO** LOST.

I'VE GOT THE NAVIGATIONAL SENSE OF A STONED SQUIRREL.

SORRY, I'M TRYING TO PICTURE THAT.

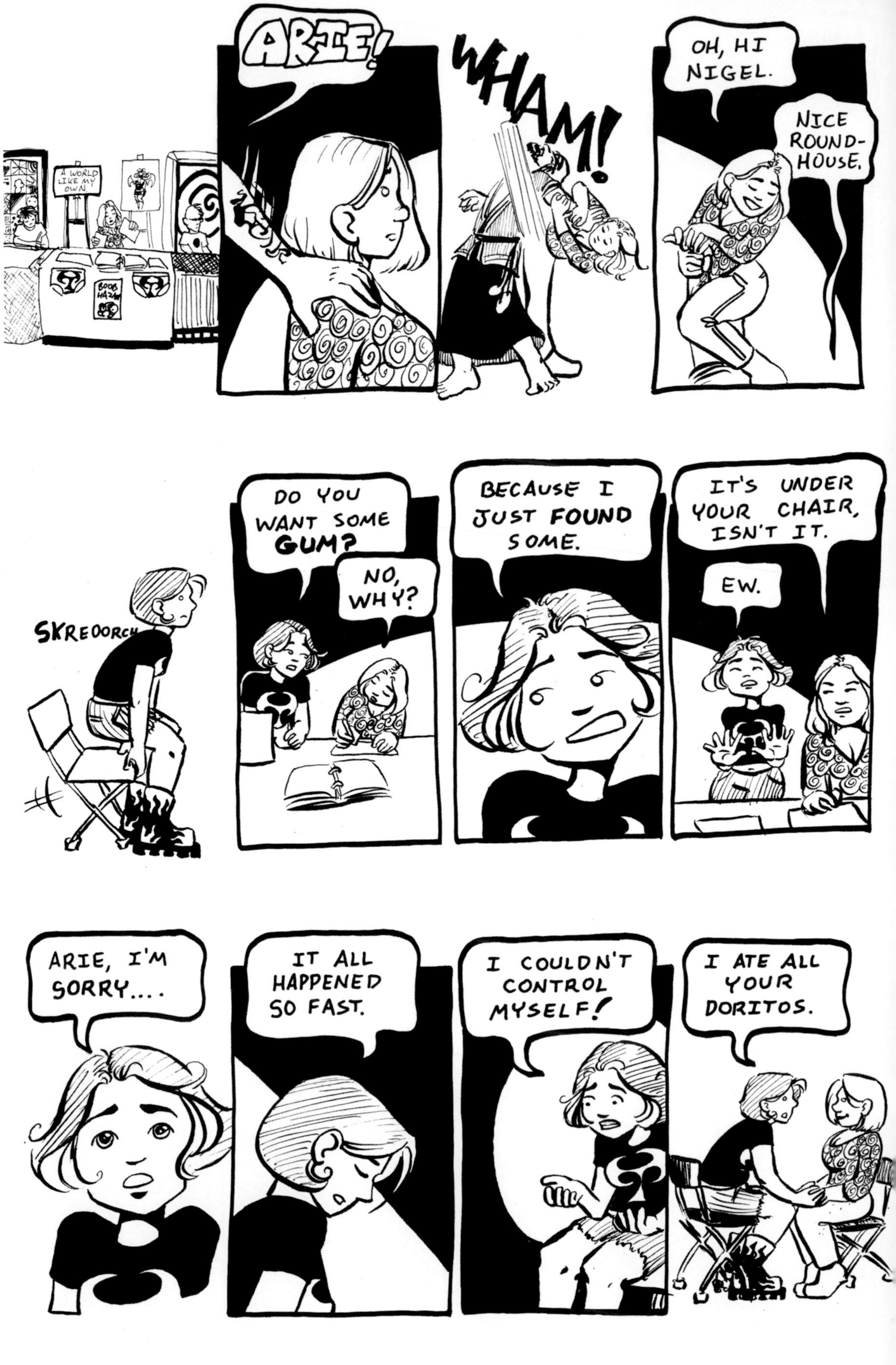
A WORLD LIKE MY OWN
ARIE!
WHAM!
OH, HI NIGEL.
NICE ROUND-HOUSE.
SKREOORCH
DO YOU WANT SOME GUM?
NO, WHY?
BECAUSE I JUST FOUND SOME.
IT'S UNDER YOUR CHAIR, ISN'T IT.
EW.
ARIE, I'M SORRY....
IT ALL HAPPENED SO FAST.
I COULDN'T CONTROL MYSELF!
I ATE ALL YOUR DORITOS.

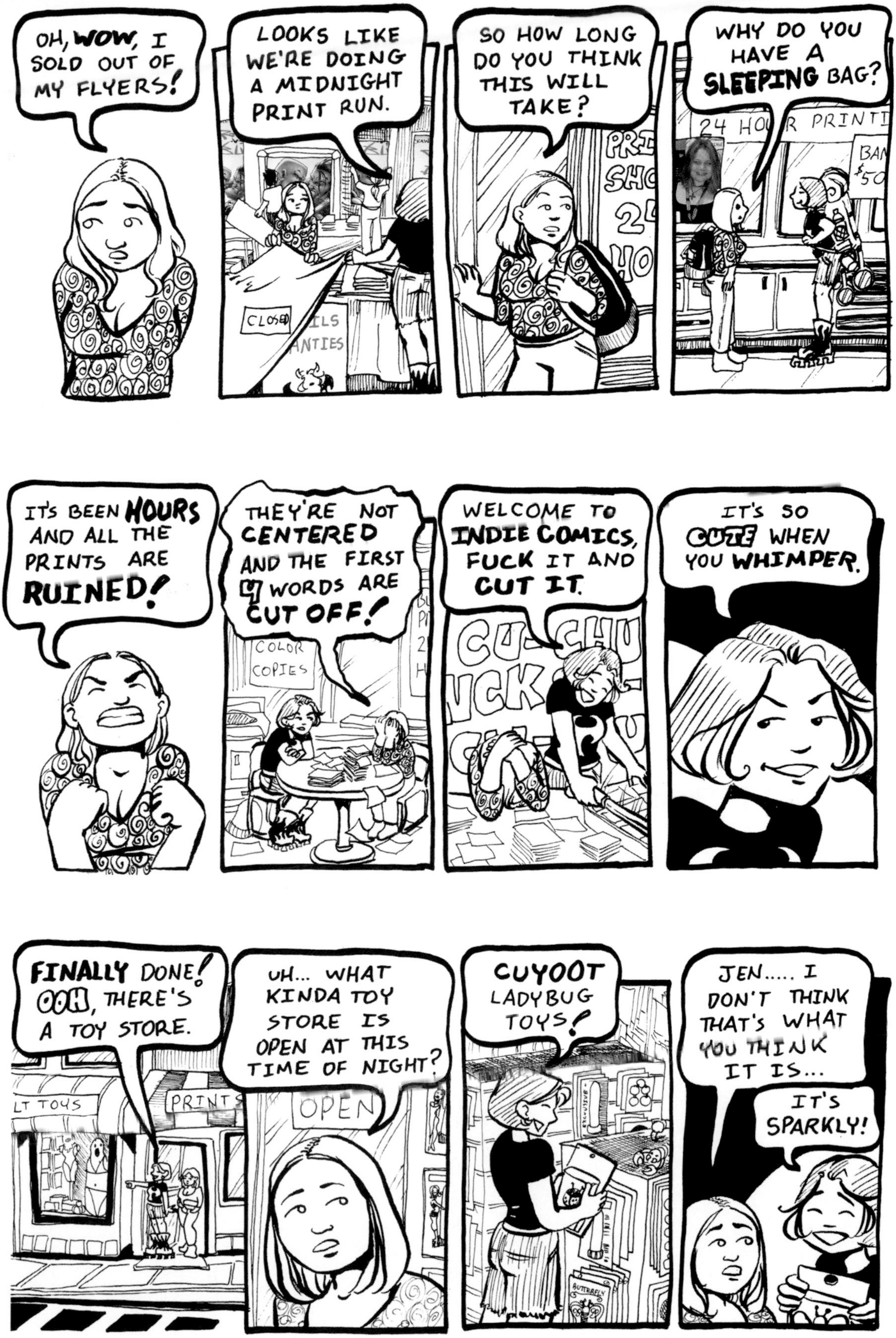
OH, WOW, I SOLD OUT OF MY FLYERS!
LOOKS LIKE WE'RE DOING A MIDNIGHT PRINT RUN.
CLOSED
SO HOW LONG DO YOU THINK THIS WILL TAKE?
WHY DO YOU HAVE A SLEEPING BAG?
IT'S BEEN HOURS AND ALL THE PRINTS ARE RUINED!
THEY'RE NOT CENTERED AND THE FIRST 4 WORDS ARE CUT OFF!
COLOR COPIES
WELCOME TO INDIE COMICS, FUCK IT AND CUT IT.
IT'S SO CUTE WHEN YOU WHIMPER.
FINALLY DONE! OOH, THERE'S A TOY STORE.
PRINTS
UH... WHAT KINDA TOY STORE IS OPEN AT THIS TIME OF NIGHT?
OPEN
CUYOOT LADYBUG TOYS!
JEN..... I DON'T THINK THAT'S WHAT YOU THINK IT IS...
IT'S SPARKLY!

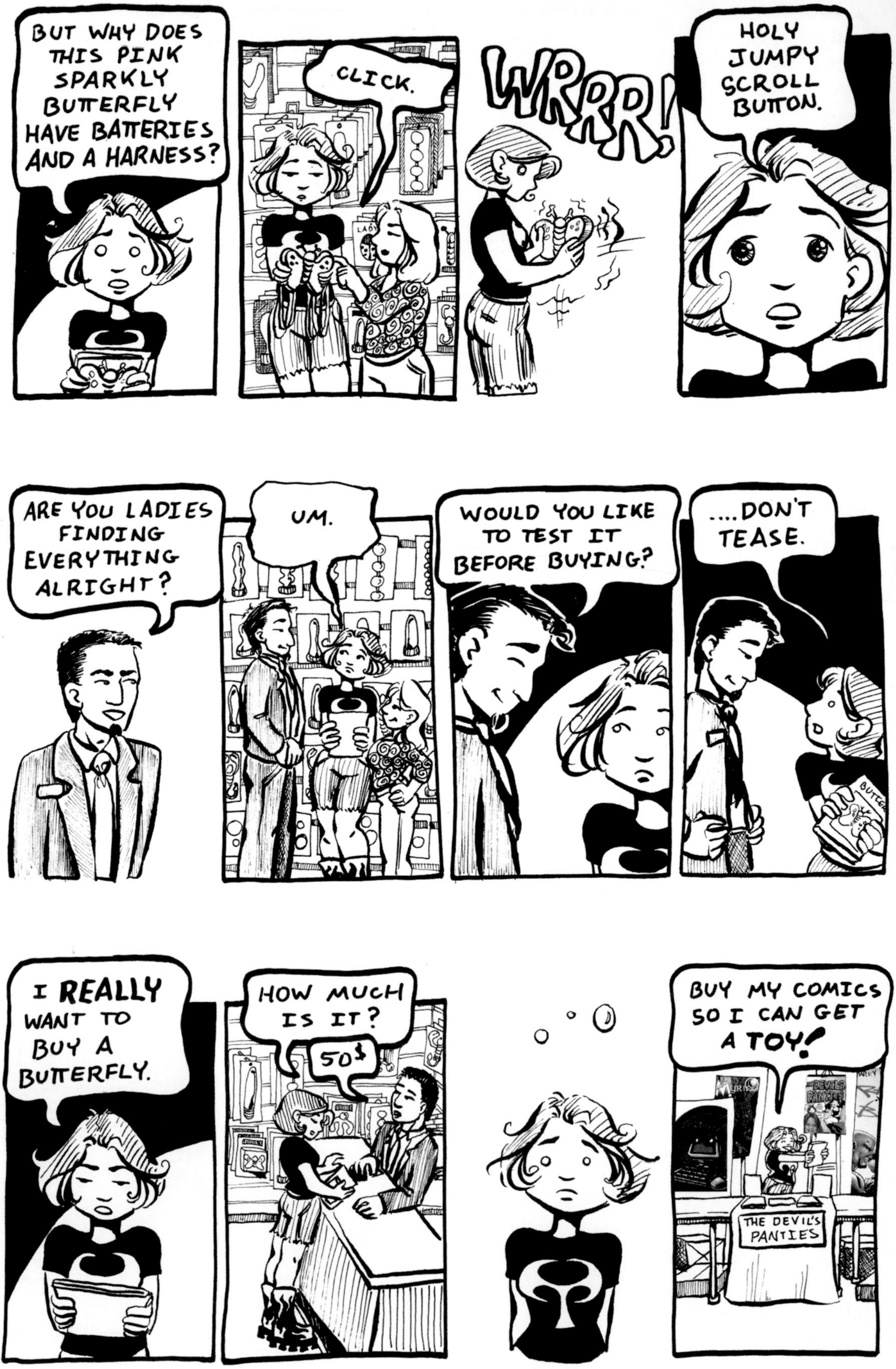
BUT WHY DOES THIS PINK SPARKLY BUTTERFLY HAVE BATTERIES AND A HARNESS?
CLICK.
WRRR!
HOLY JUMPY SCROLL BUTTON.
ARE YOU LADIES FINDING EVERYTHING ALRIGHT?
UM.
WOULD YOU LIKE TO TEST IT BEFORE BUYING?
....DON'T TEASE.
I REALLY WANT TO BUY A BUTTERFLY.
HOW MUCH IS IT?
50$
BUY MY COMICS SO I CAN GET A TOY!
THE DEVIL'S PANTIES

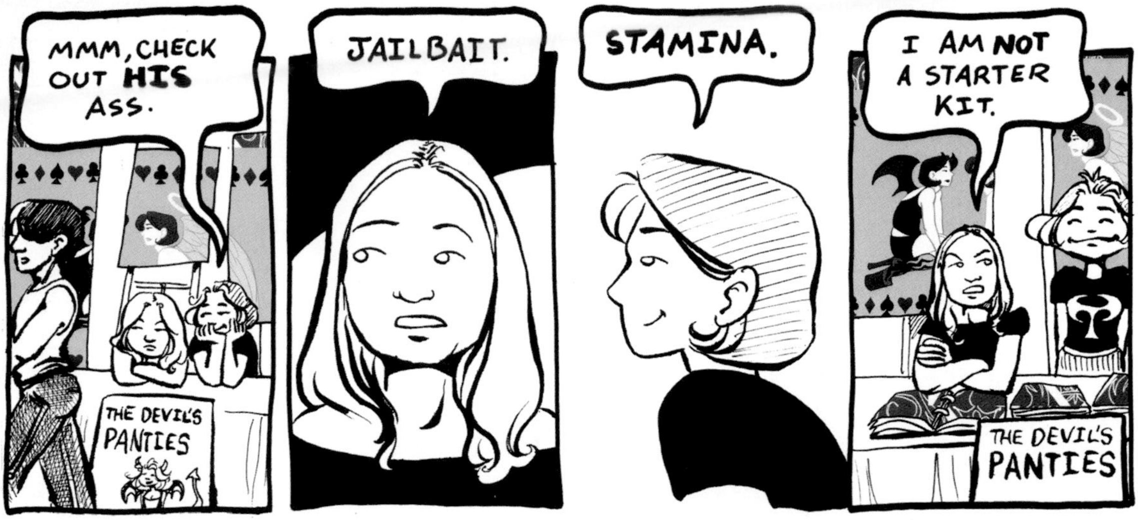
MMM, CHECK OUT HIS ASS.
THE DEVIL'S PANTIES
JAILBAIT.
STAMINA.
I AM NOT A STARTER KIT.
THE DEVIL'S PANTIES

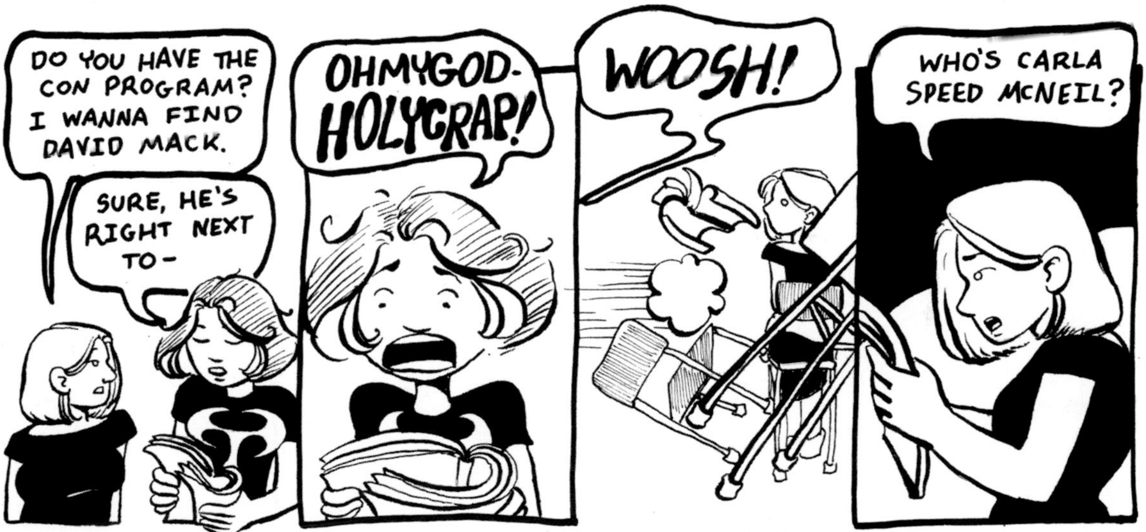
DO YOU HAVE THE CON PROGRAM? I WANNA FIND DAVID MACK.
SURE, HE'S RIGHT NEXT TO-
OHMYGOD-HOLYCRAP!
WOOSH!
WHO'S CARLA SPEED McNEIL?

www.lightspeedpress.com

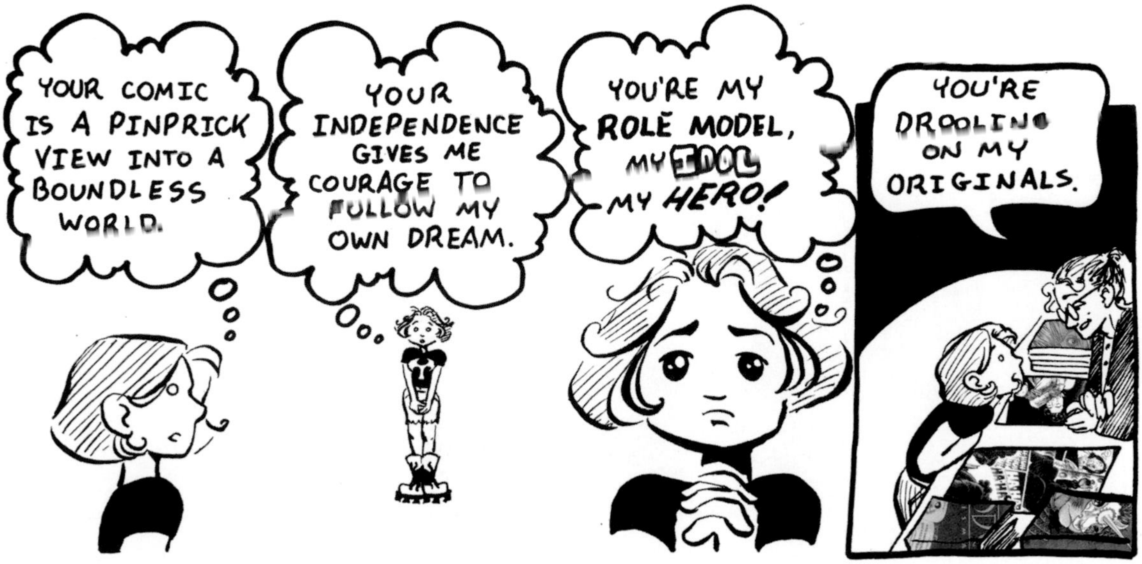
YOUR COMIC IS A PINPRICK VIEW INTO A BOUNDLESS WORLD.
YOUR INDEPENDENCE GIVES ME COURAGE TO FOLLOW MY OWN DREAM.
YOU'RE MY ROLE MODEL, MY IDOL MY HERO!
YOU'RE DROOLING ON MY ORIGINALS.

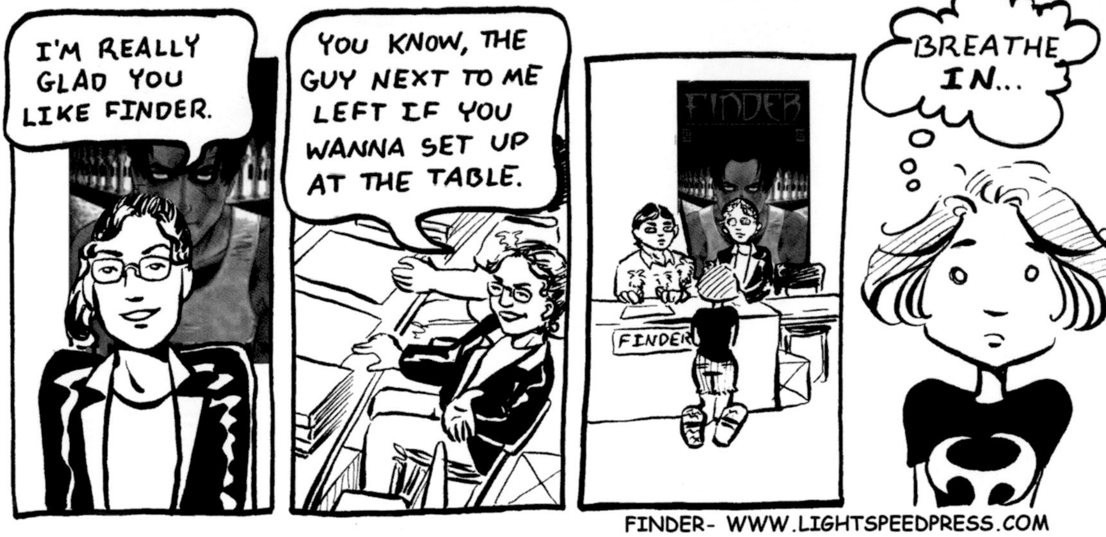
I'M REALLY GLAD YOU LIKE FINDER.
YOU KNOW, THE GUY NEXT TO ME LEFT IF YOU WANNA SET UP AT THE TABLE.
FINDER
FINDER
BREATHE IN...

FINDER- WWW.LIGHTSPEEDPRESS.COM

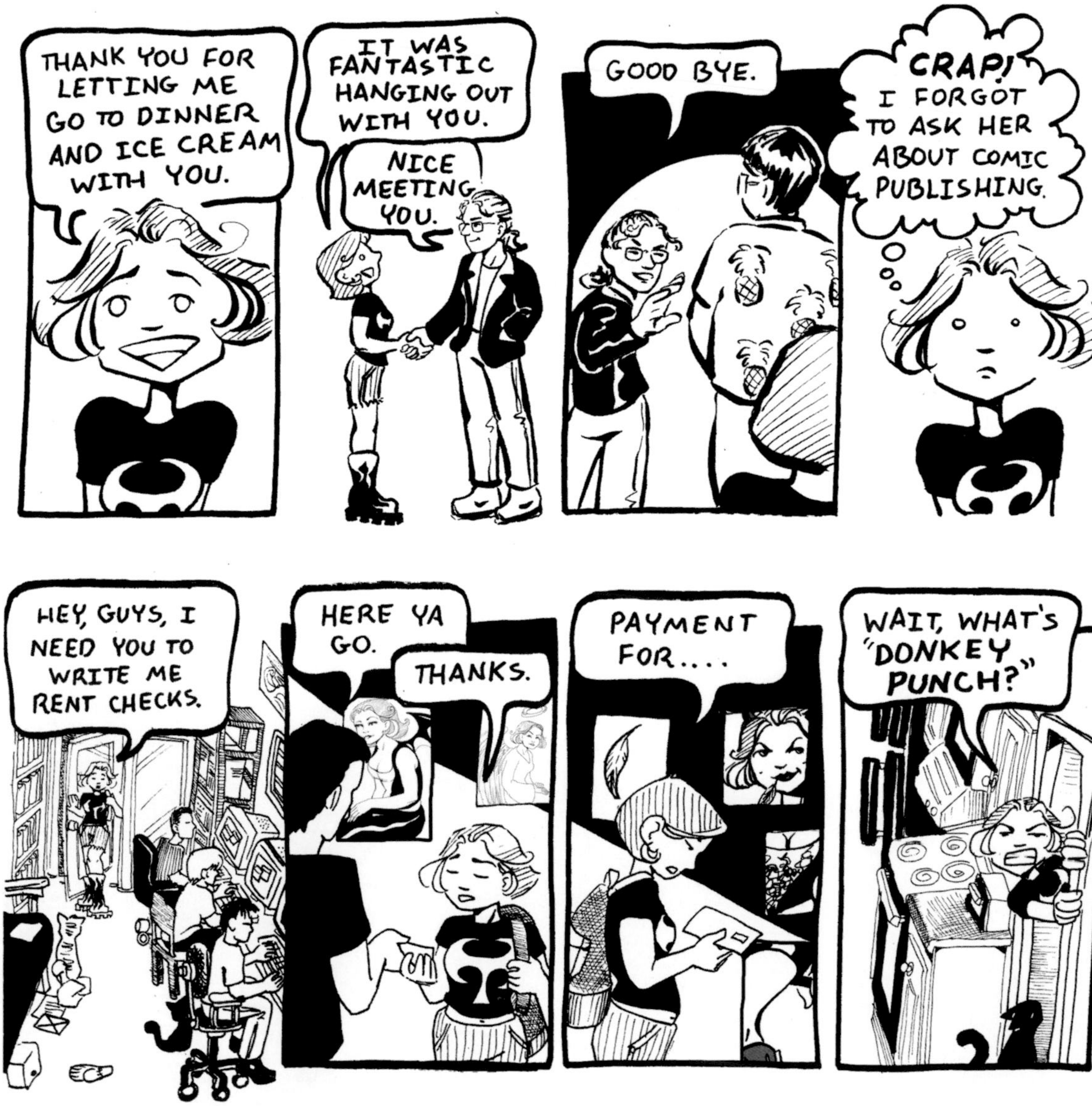
THANK YOU FOR LETTING ME GO TO DINNER AND ICE CREAM WITH YOU.
IT WAS FANTASTIC HANGING OUT WITH YOU.
NICE MEETING YOU.
GOOD BYE.
CRAP! I FORGOT TO ASK HER ABOUT COMIC PUBLISHING.
HEY, GUYS, I NEED YOU TO WRITE ME RENT CHECKS.
HERE YA GO.
THANKS.
PAYMENT FOR....
WAIT, WHAT'S "DONKEY PUNCH?"

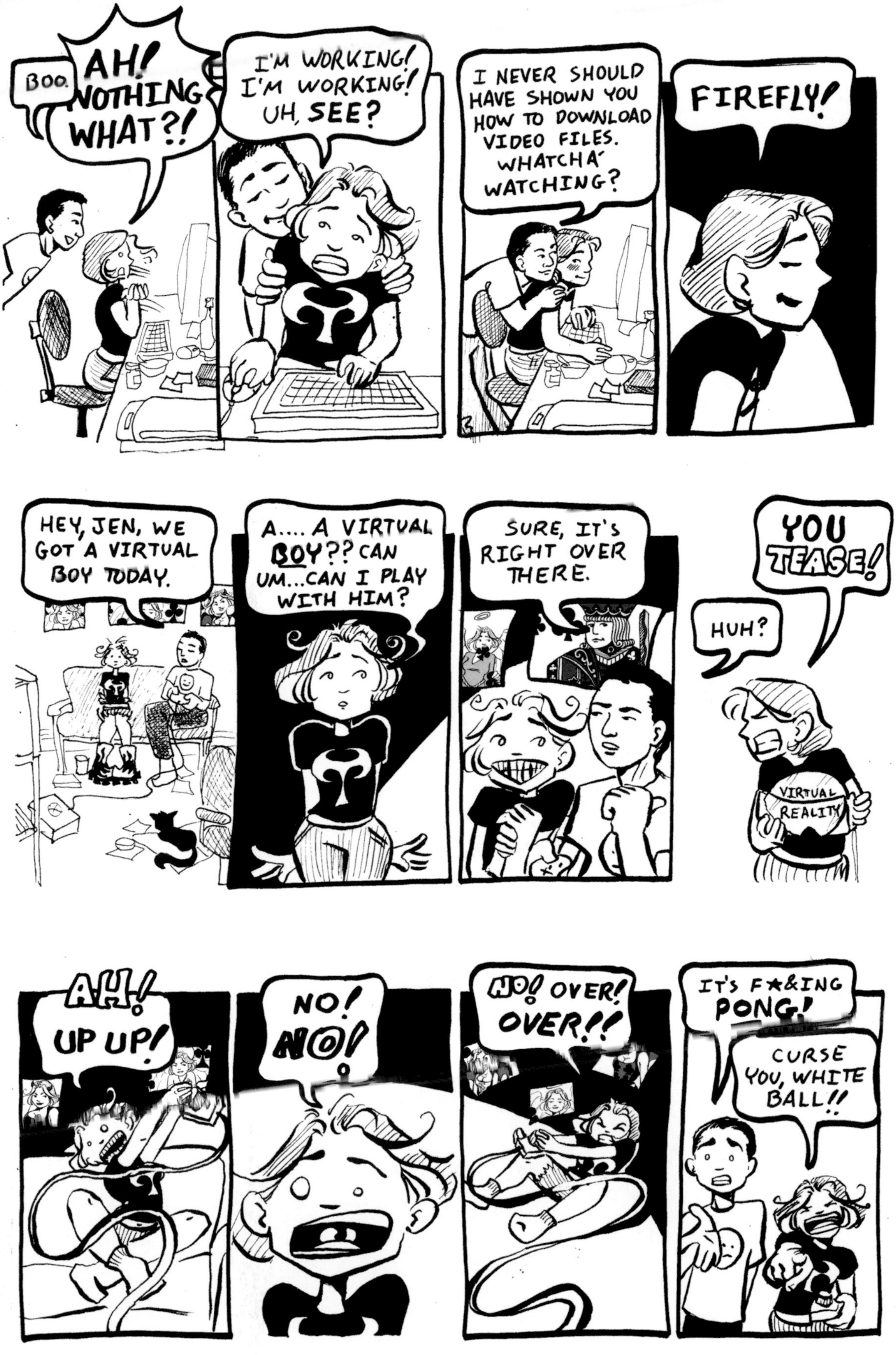
BOO.
AH! NOTHING WHAT?!
I'M WORKING! I'M WORKING! UH, SEE?
I NEVER SHOULD HAVE SHOWN YOU HOW TO DOWNLOAD VIDEO FILES. WHATCHA' WATCHING?
FIREFLY!
HEY, JEN, WE GOT A VIRTUAL BOY TODAY.
A.... A VIRTUAL BOY?? CAN UM...CAN I PLAY WITH HIM?
SURE, IT'S RIGHT OVER THERE.
HUH?
YOU TEASE!
VIRTUAL REALITY
AH! UP UP!
NO! NO!
NO! OVER! OVER!!
IT'S F★&ING PONG!
CURSE YOU, WHITE BALL!!

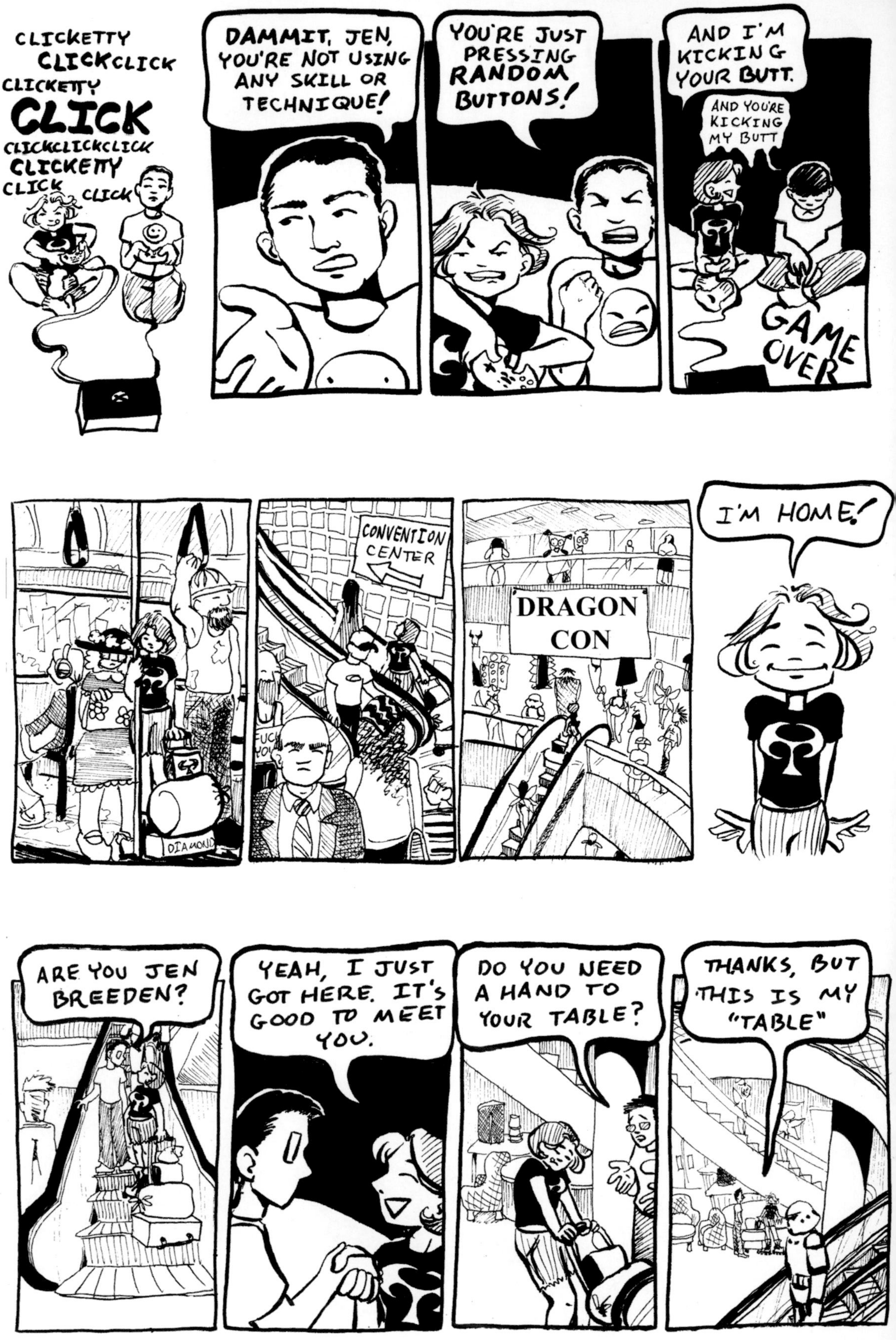
CLICKETTY
CLICKCLICK
CLICKETTY
CLICK
CLICKCLICKCLICK
CLICKETTY
CLICK CLICK
DAMMIT, JEN, YOU'RE NOT USING ANY SKILL OR TECHNIQUE!
YOU'RE JUST PRESSING RANDOM BUTTONS!
AND I'M KICKING YOUR BUTT.
AND YOU'RE KICKING MY BUTT
GAME OVER
DIAMOND
CONVENTION CENTER
DRAGON CON
I'M HOME!
ARE YOU JEN BREEDEN?
YEAH, I JUST GOT HERE. IT'S GOOD TO MEET YOU.
DO YOU NEED A HAND TO YOUR TABLE?
THANKS, BUT THIS IS MY "TABLE"

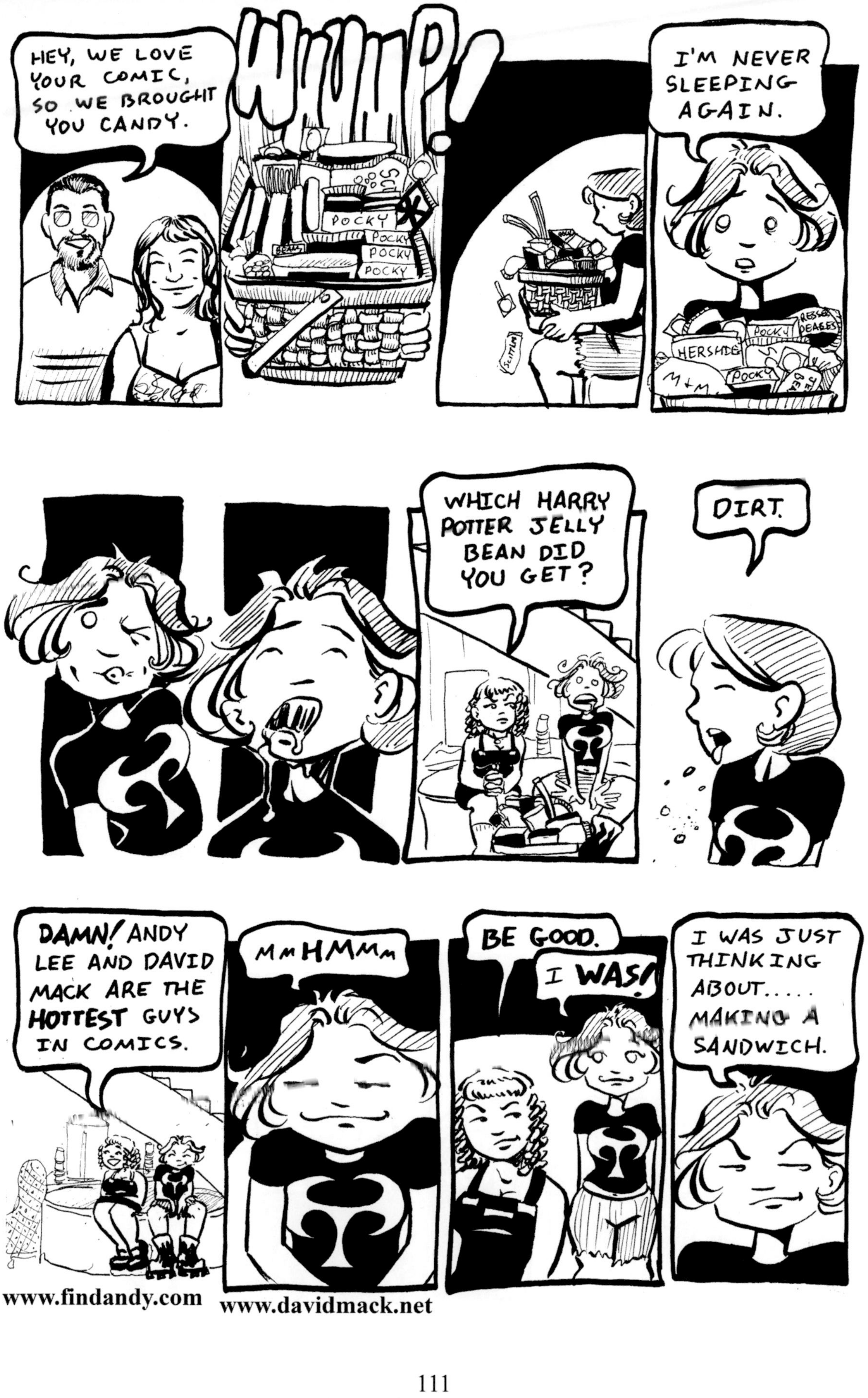
HEY, WE LOVE YOUR COMIC, SO WE BROUGHT YOU CANDY.
WHUMP!
I'M NEVER SLEEPING AGAIN.
WHICH HARRY POTTER JELLY BEAN DID YOU GET?
DIRT.
DAMN! ANDY LEE AND DAVID MACK ARE THE HOTTEST GUYS IN COMICS.
MmHMMm
BE GOOD.
I WAS!
I WAS JUST THINKING ABOUT..... MAKING A SANDWICH.

www.findandy.com www.davidmack.net

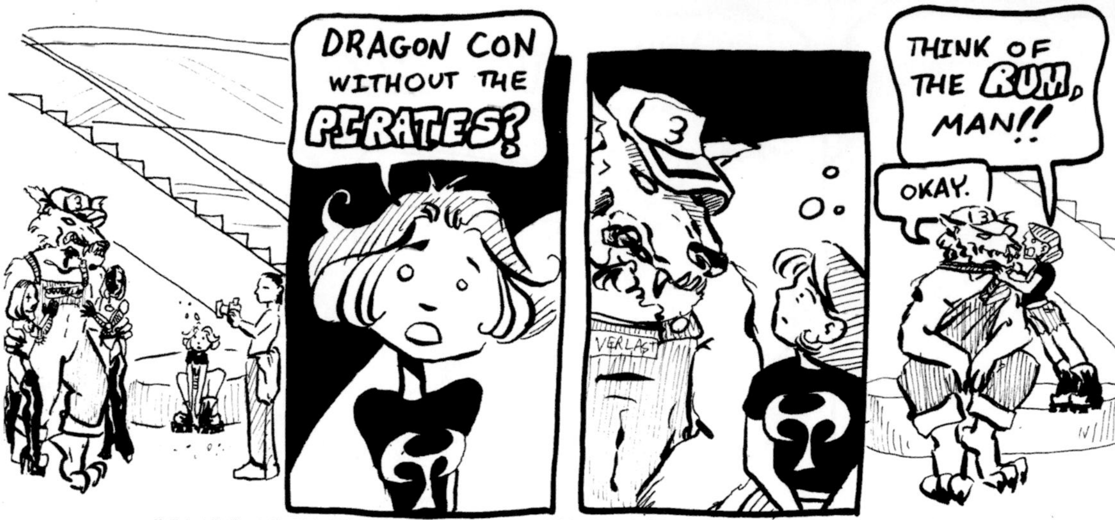
DRAGON CON WITHOUT THE PIRATES?
THINK OF THE RUM, MAN!!
OKAY.

"BUBBA" THE REDNECK WEREWOLF BY MITCH HYMAN

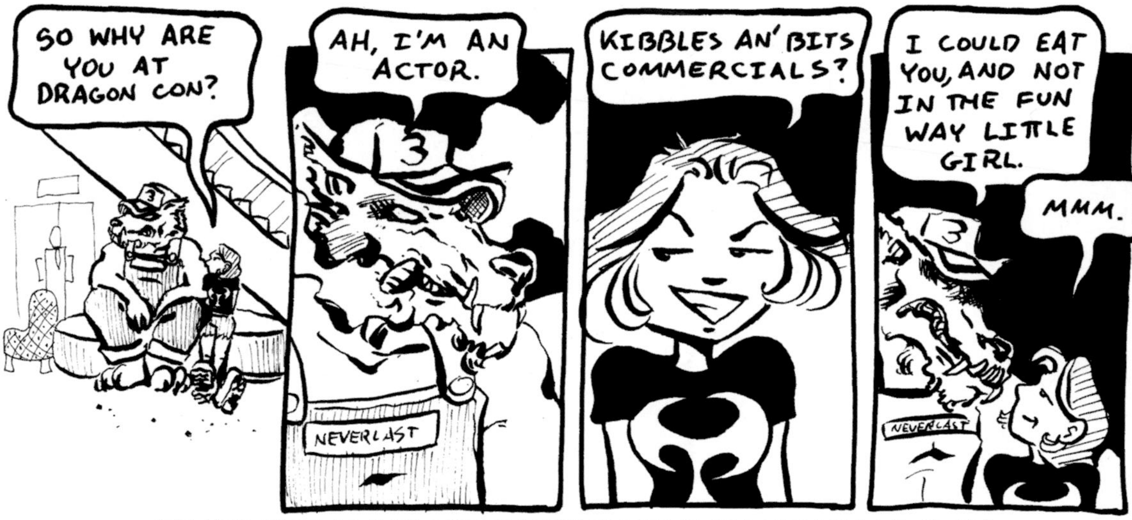
SO WHY ARE YOU AT DRAGON CON?
AH, I'M AN ACTOR.
KIBBLES AN' BITS COMMERCIALS?
I COULD EAT YOU, AND NOT IN THE FUN WAY LITTLE GIRL.
MMM.

"BUBBA" THE REDNECK WEREWOLF BY MITCH HYMAN

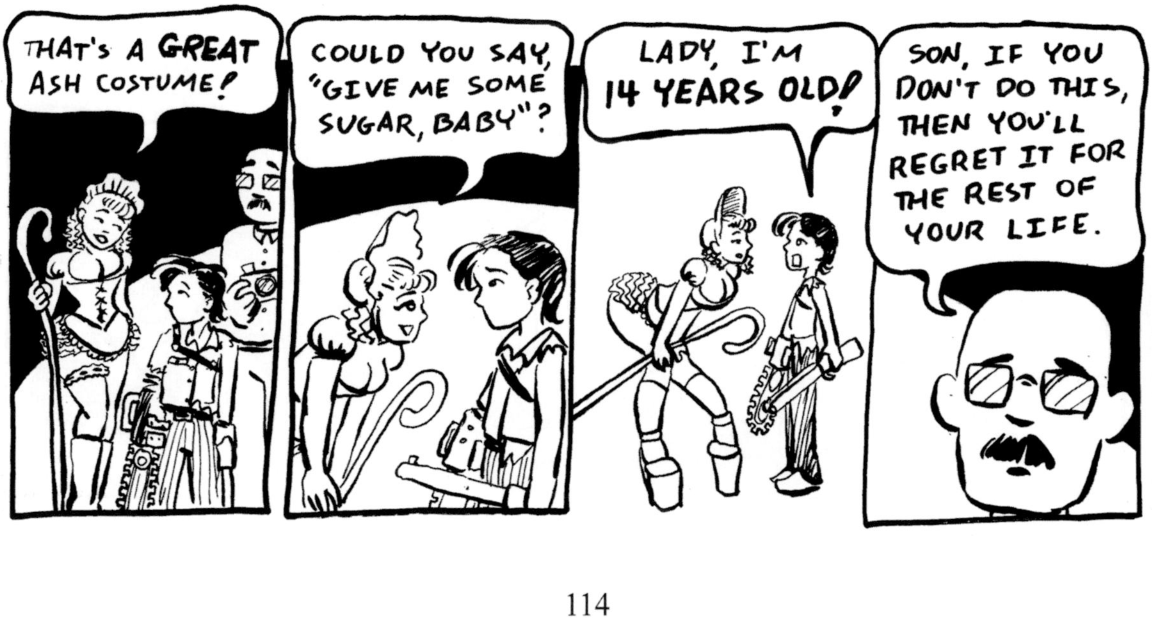
THAT'S A GREAT ASH COSTUME!
COULD YOU SAY, "GIVE ME SOME SUGAR, BABY"?
LADY, I'M 14 YEARS OLD!
SON, IF YOU DON'T DO THIS, THEN YOU'LL REGRET IT FOR THE REST OF YOUR LIFE.

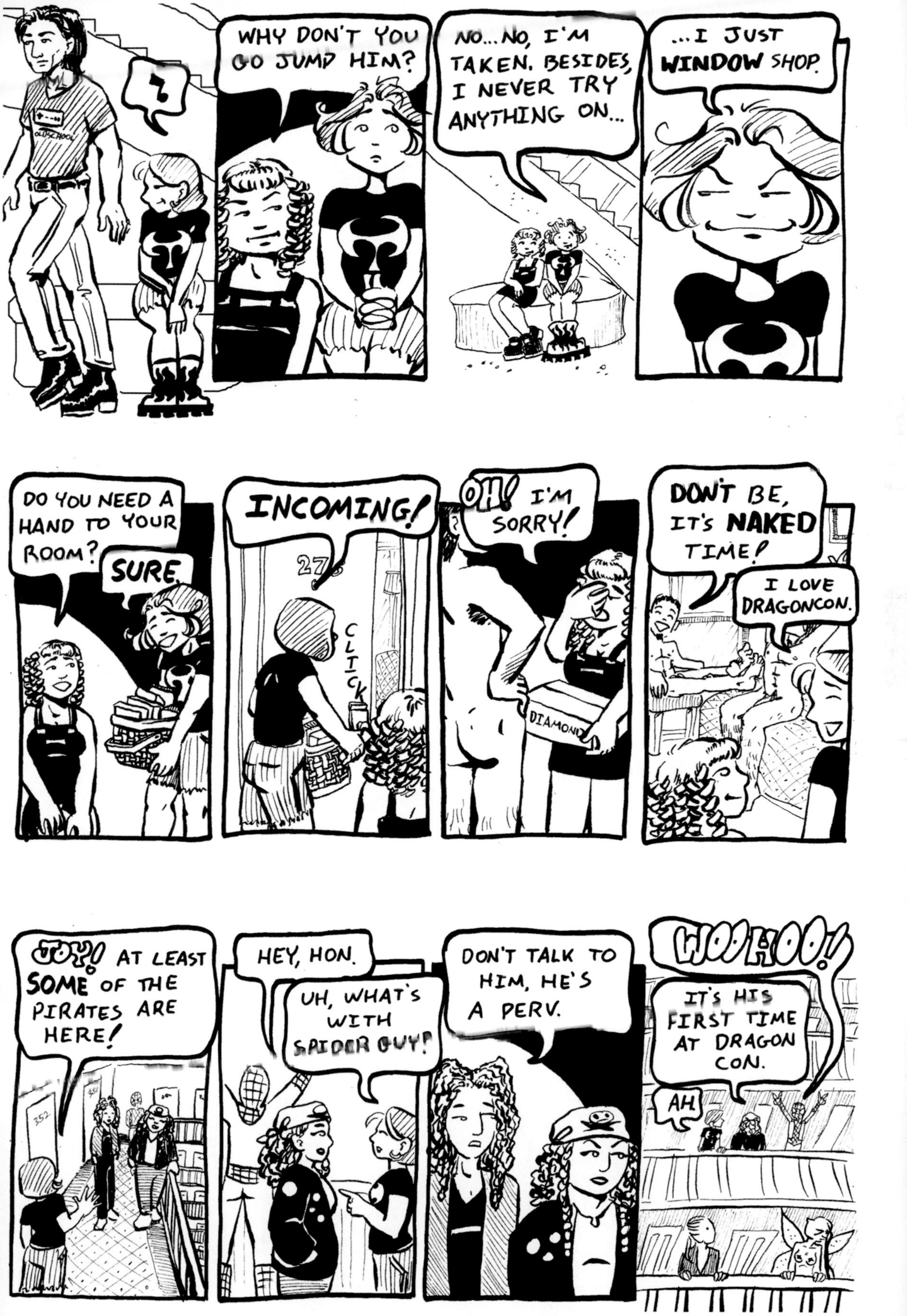
WHY DON'T YOU GO JUMP HIM?
NO... NO, I'M TAKEN. BESIDES, I NEVER TRY ANYTHING ON...
...I JUST WINDOW SHOP.
DO YOU NEED A HAND TO YOUR ROOM?
SURE.
INCOMING!
27
CLICK
OH! I'M SORRY!
DIAMOND
DON'T BE, IT'S NAKED TIME!
I LOVE DRAGONCON.
JOY! AT LEAST SOME OF THE PIRATES ARE HERE!
352
HEY, HON.
UH, WHAT'S WITH SPIDER GUY?
DON'T TALK TO HIM, HE'S A PERV.
WOO-HOO!
IT'S HIS FIRST TIME AT DRAGON CON.
AH.

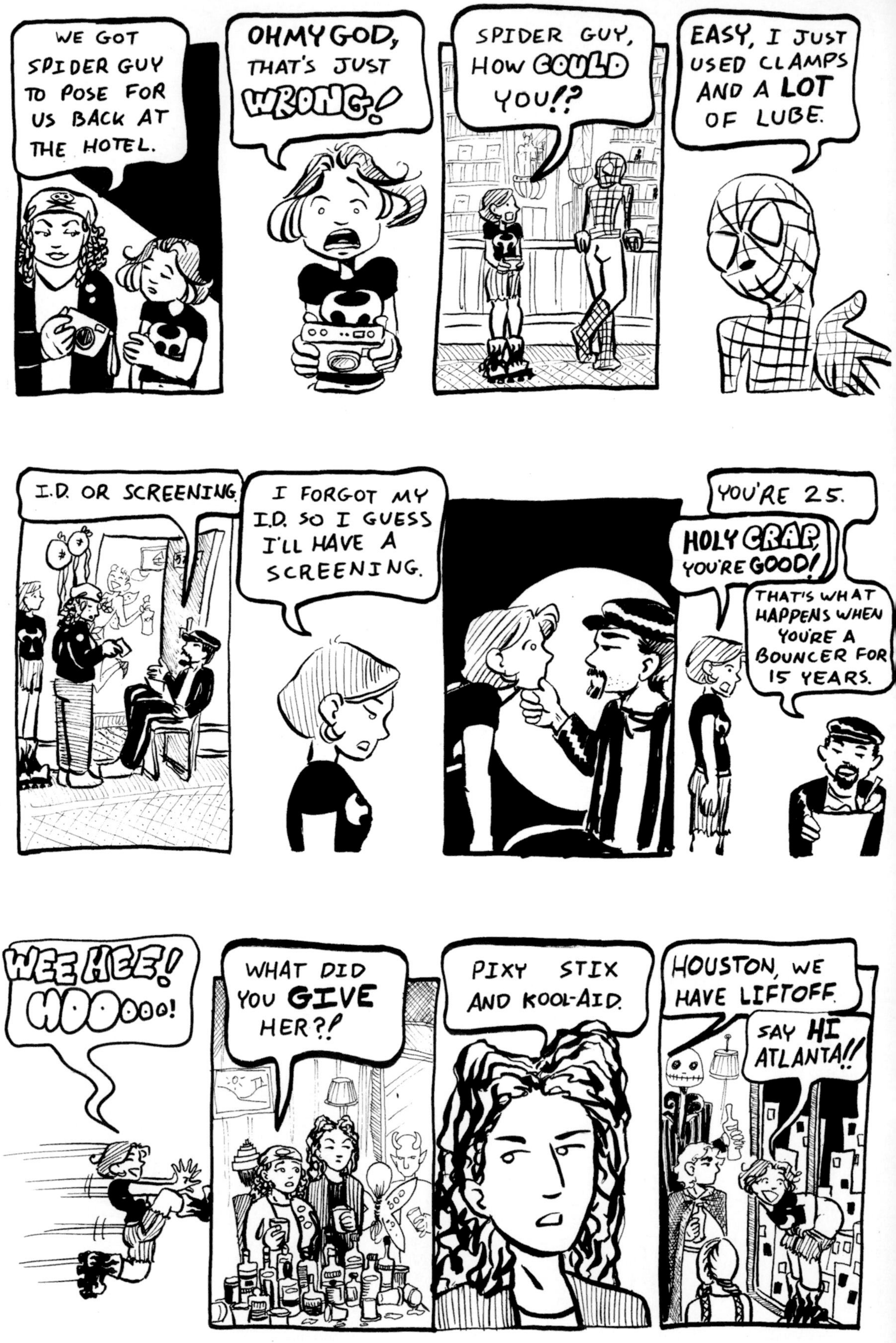
WE GOT SPIDER GUY TO POSE FOR US BACK AT THE HOTEL.
OHMYGOD, THAT'S JUST WRONG!
SPIDER GUY, HOW COULD YOU!?
EASY, I JUST USED CLAMPS AND A LOT OF LUBE.
I.D. OR SCREENING.
I FORGOT MY I.D. SO I GUESS I'LL HAVE A SCREENING.
YOU'RE 25.
HOLY CRAP, YOU'RE GOOD!
THAT'S WHAT HAPPENS WHEN YOU'RE A BOUNCER FOR 15 YEARS.
WEE HEE! HOOOooo!
WHAT DID YOU GIVE HER?!
PIXY STIX AND KOOL-AID.
HOUSTON, WE HAVE LIFTOFF.
SAY HI ATLANTA!!

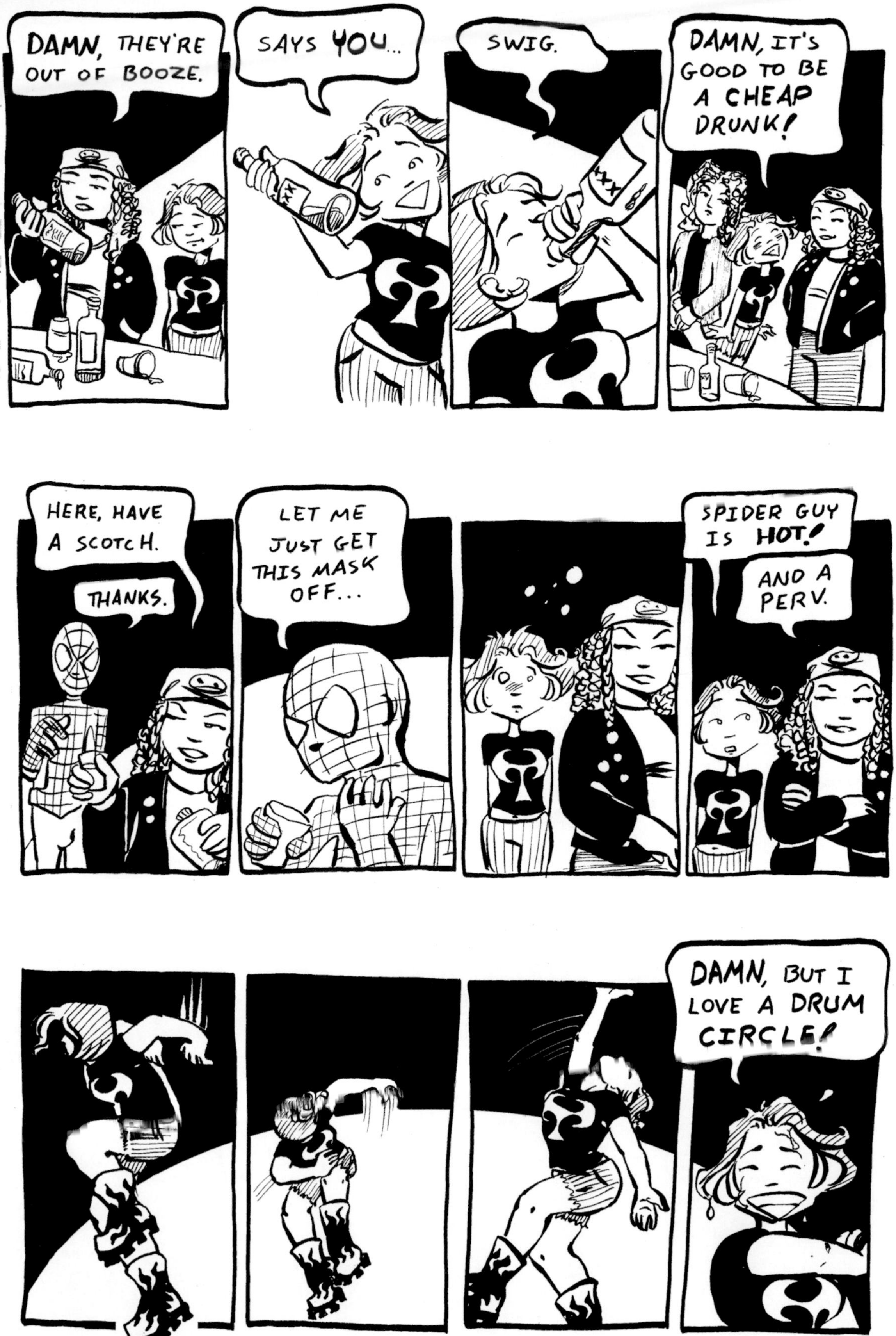
DAMN, THEY'RE OUT OF BOOZE.
SAYS YOU...
SWIG.
DAMN, IT'S GOOD TO BE A CHEAP DRUNK!
HERE, HAVE A SCOTCH.
THANKS.
LET ME JUST GET THIS MASK OFF...
SPIDER GUY IS HOT!
AND A PERV.
DAMN, BUT I LOVE A DRUM CIRCLE!

WHAT ARE YOU WATCHING?

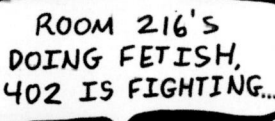

ROOM 216'S DOING FETISH, 402 IS FIGHTING...

YOU DON'T KNOW ME

...AND 621 IS DOING SOMETHING WIH CLOWNS.

WHO NEEDS TELEVISION WHEN YOU HAVE DRAGON CON?

IT WAS **GREAT** MEETING YOU! SEE YOU NEXT YEAR!

THANKS FOR LETTING ME USE YOUR **HUSBAND!**

HE'S A PROFESSIONAL **MASSEUR!**

SURE HE IS.

OH MY GOD. DRAGON CON WAS **SO** MUCH **FUN.** PEOPLE GAVE ME **CANDY** AND **BOOZE.**

AND PRETTY GIRLS WANTED TO GET THEIR **PICTURES** TAKEN WITH ME AND AND AND

HON. GO TO BED. YOU'RE WIGGING OUT.

OH, I'VE BEEN LIKE THIS AAAALLL WEEKEND!

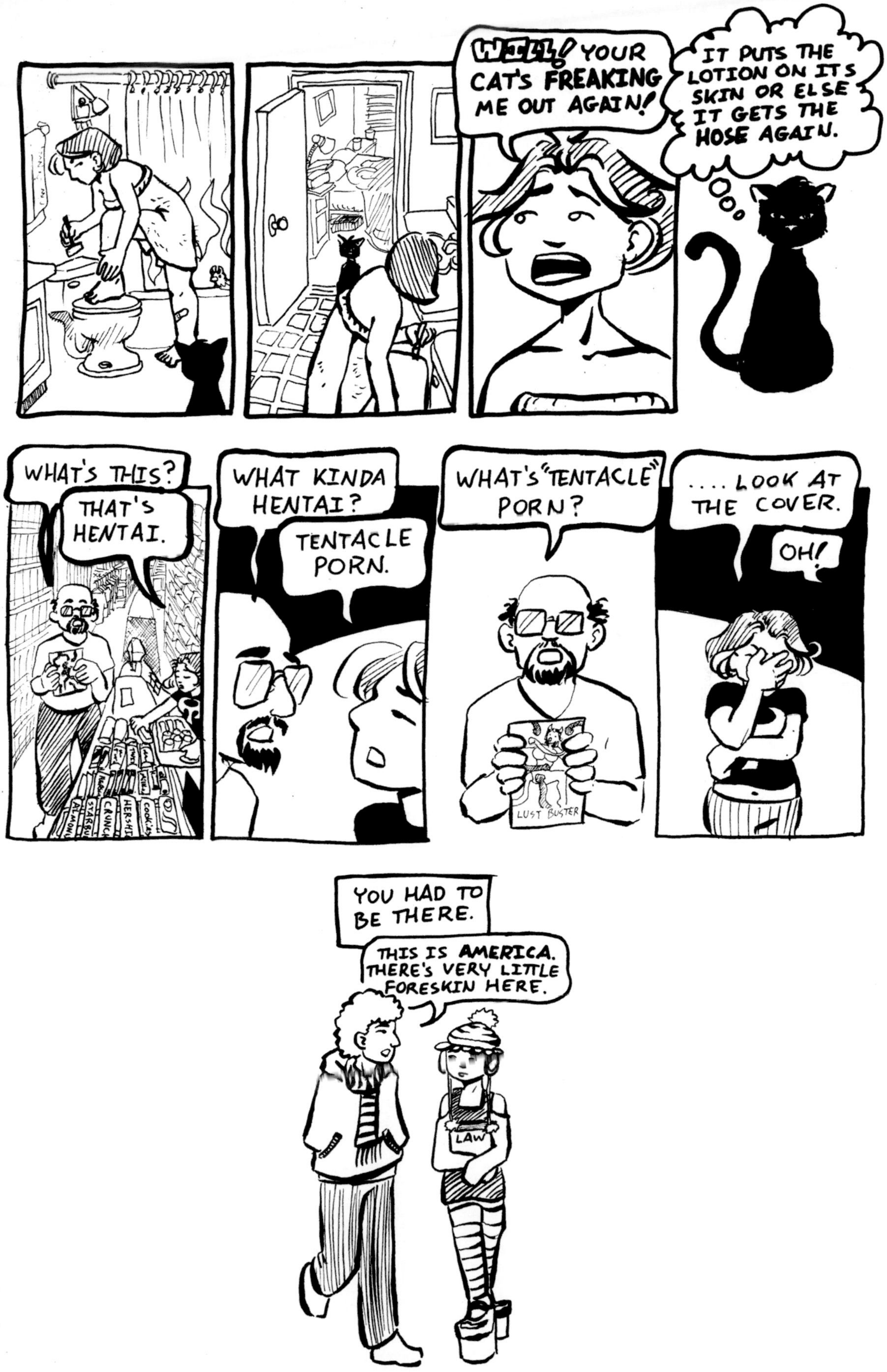
WELL! YOUR CAT'S FREAKING ME OUT AGAIN!
IT PUTS THE LOTION ON ITS SKIN OR ELSE IT GETS THE HOSE AGAIN.
WHAT'S THIS?
THAT'S HENTAI.
WHAT KINDA HENTAI?
TENTACLE PORN.
WHAT'S "TENTACLE" PORN?
LUST BUSTER
.... LOOK AT THE COVER.
OH!
YOU HAD TO BE THERE.
THIS IS AMERICA. THERE'S VERY LITTLE FORESKIN HERE.
LAW

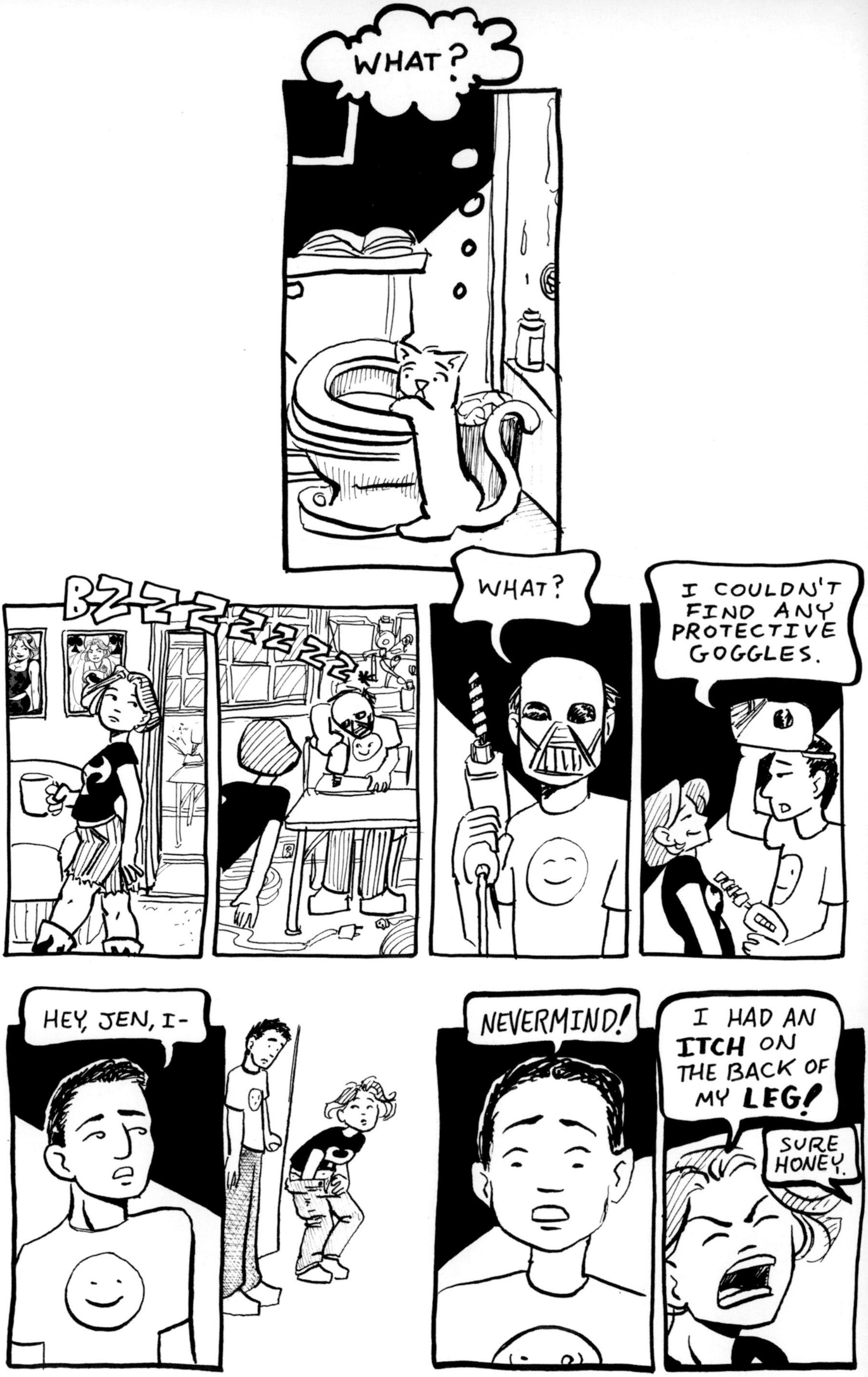
WHAT?
BZZZZZZZZZZ
WHAT?
I COULDN'T FIND ANY PROTECTIVE GOGGLES.
HEY, JEN, I-
NEVERMIND!
I HAD AN ITCH ON THE BACK OF MY LEG!
SURE HONEY.

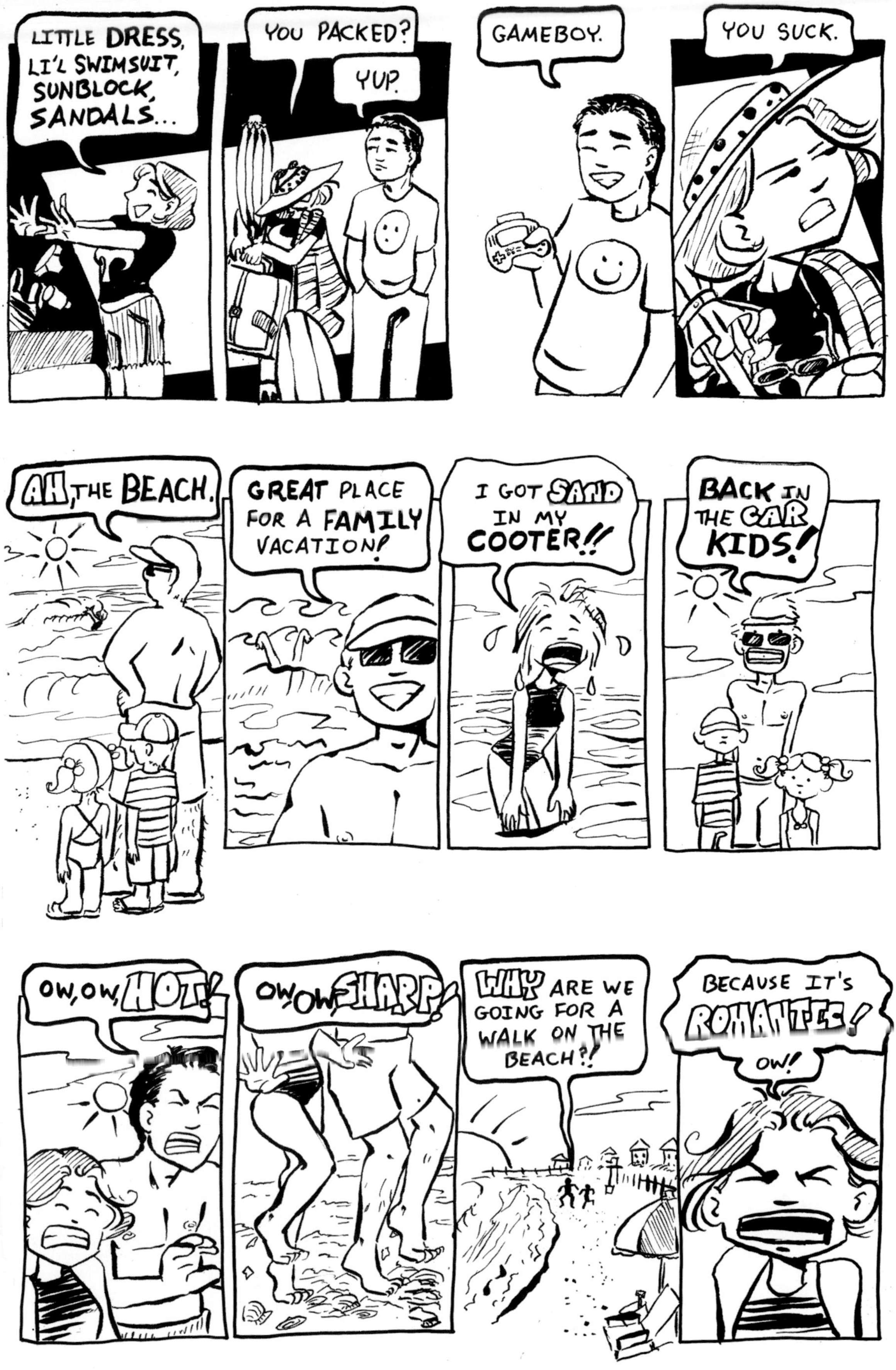
LITTLE DRESS, LI'L SWIMSUIT, SUNBLOCK, SANDALS...
YOU PACKED?
YUP.
GAMEBOY.
YOU SUCK.
AH, THE BEACH.
GREAT PLACE FOR A FAMILY VACATION!
I GOT SAND IN MY COOTER!!
BACK IN THE CAR KIDS!
OW, OW, HOT!
OW, OW, SHARP!
WHY ARE WE GOING FOR A WALK ON THE BEACH?!
BECAUSE IT'S ROMANTIC!
OW!

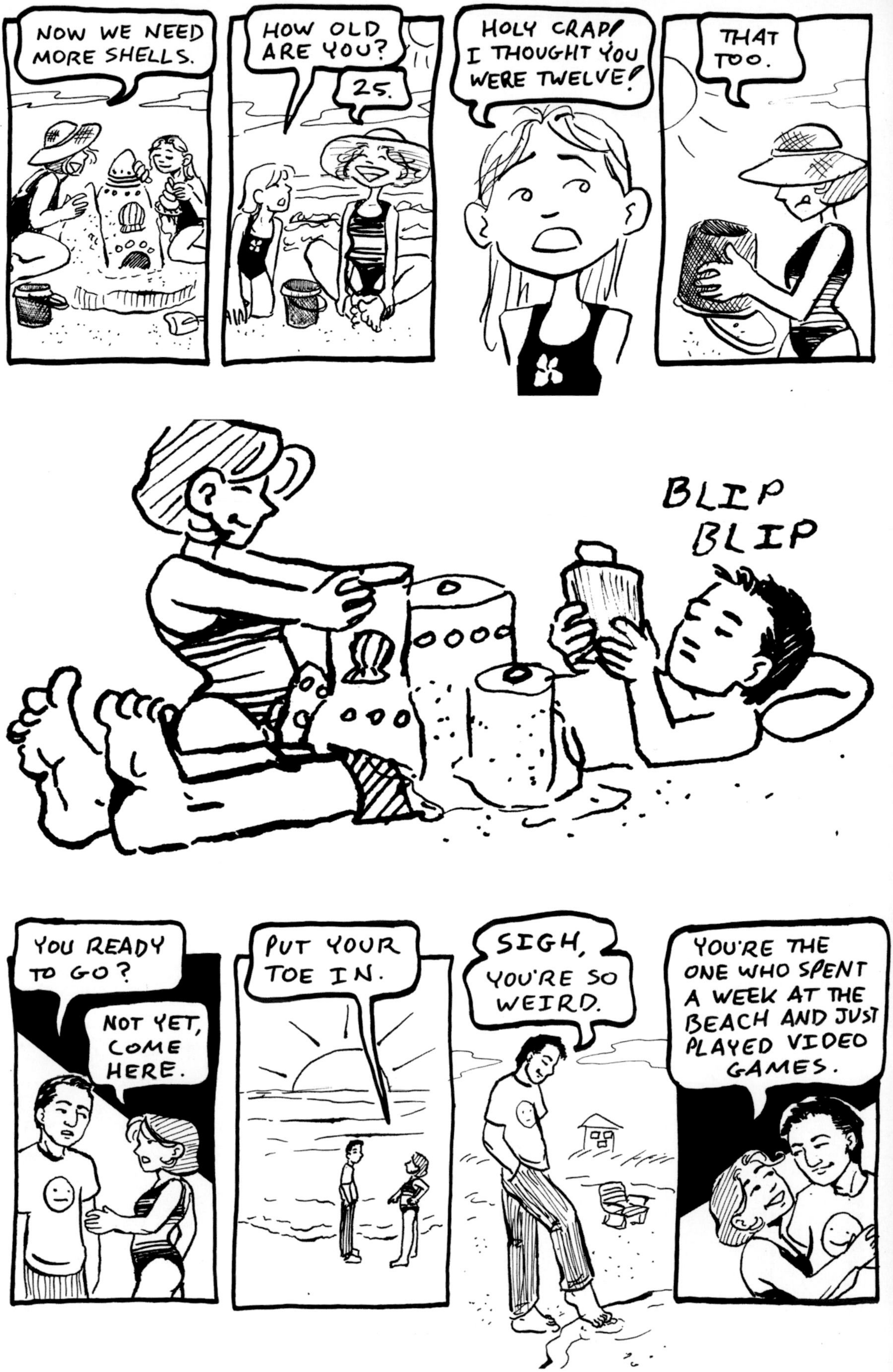
NOW WE NEED MORE SHELLS.
HOW OLD ARE YOU?
25.
HOLY CRAP! I THOUGHT YOU WERE TWELVE!
THAT TOO.
BLIP BLIP
YOU READY TO GO?
NOT YET, COME HERE.
PUT YOUR TOE IN.
SIGH, YOU'RE SO WEIRD.
YOU'RE THE ONE WHO SPENT A WEEK AT THE BEACH AND JUST PLAYED VIDEO GAMES.

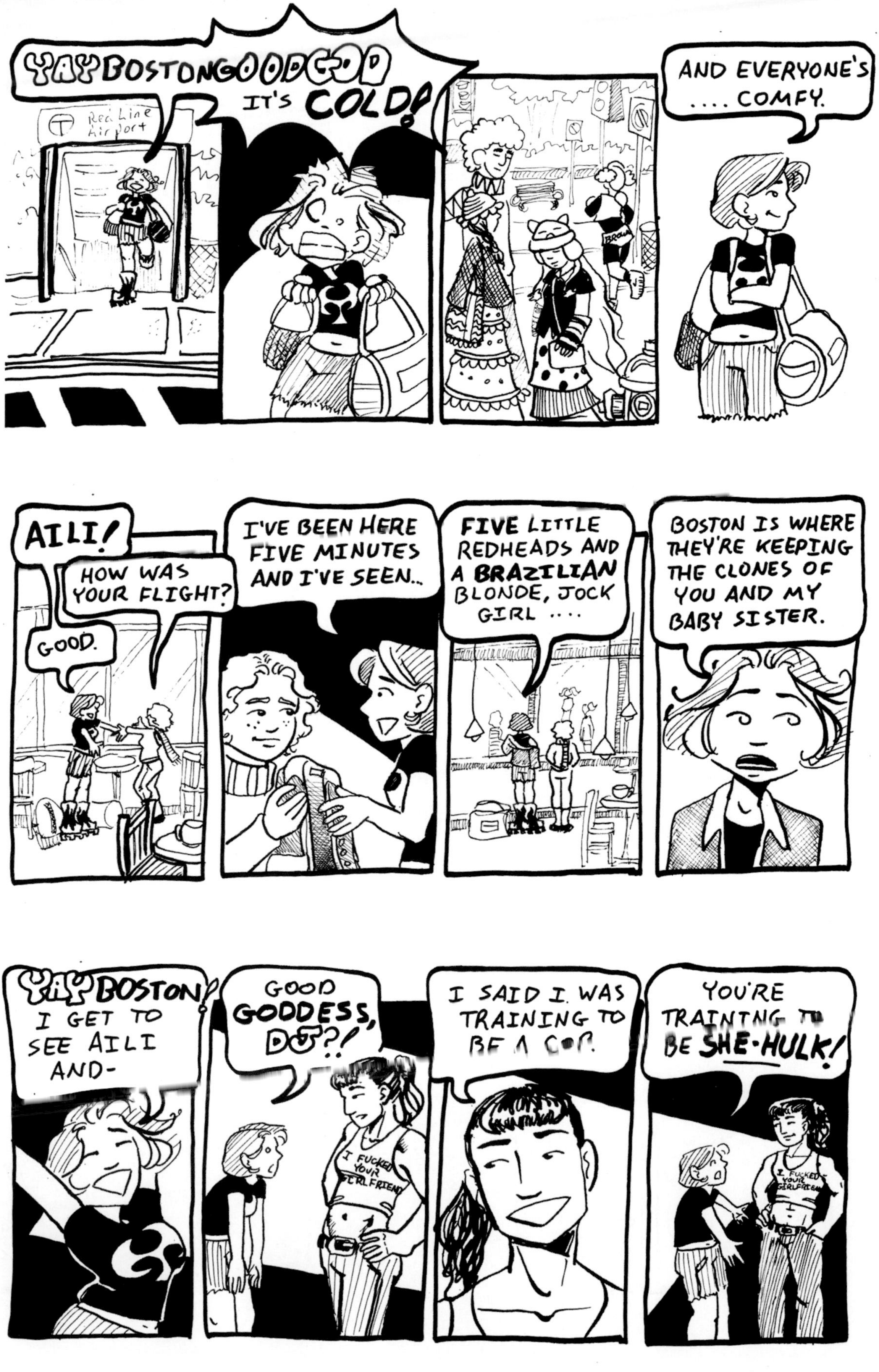
YAY BOSTON GOOD GOD IT'S COLD!
Red Line Airport
AND EVERYONE'S .... COMFY.
AILI!
HOW WAS YOUR FLIGHT?
GOOD.
I'VE BEEN HERE FIVE MINUTES AND I'VE SEEN..
FIVE LITTLE REDHEADS AND A BRAZILIAN BLONDE, JOCK GIRL ....
BOSTON IS WHERE THEY'RE KEEPING THE CLONES OF YOU AND MY BABY SISTER.
YAY BOSTON! I GET TO SEE AILI AND-
GOOD GODDESS, DJ?!
I FUCKED YOUR GIRLFRIEND
I SAID I WAS TRAINING TO BE A COP.
YOU'RE TRAINING TO BE SHE-HULK!

WHAT NEVER TO SAY IN THE BEDROOM.

WHAT'S FOREPLAY?

GIRL COP PEZ DISPENSER

YOUR BOOBS GOT SMALL.

GIRL RULE

OOH! OOH!

DO MINE! DO MINE!

BREST INSPECTOR

WHY ARE THE BOOBS GONE?!

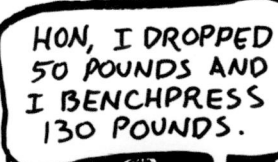

HON, I DROPPED 50 POUNDS AND I BENCHPRESS 130 POUNDS.

I FUCKED YOUR GIRLFRIEN

BUT WHY ARE THE BOOBS GONE?!

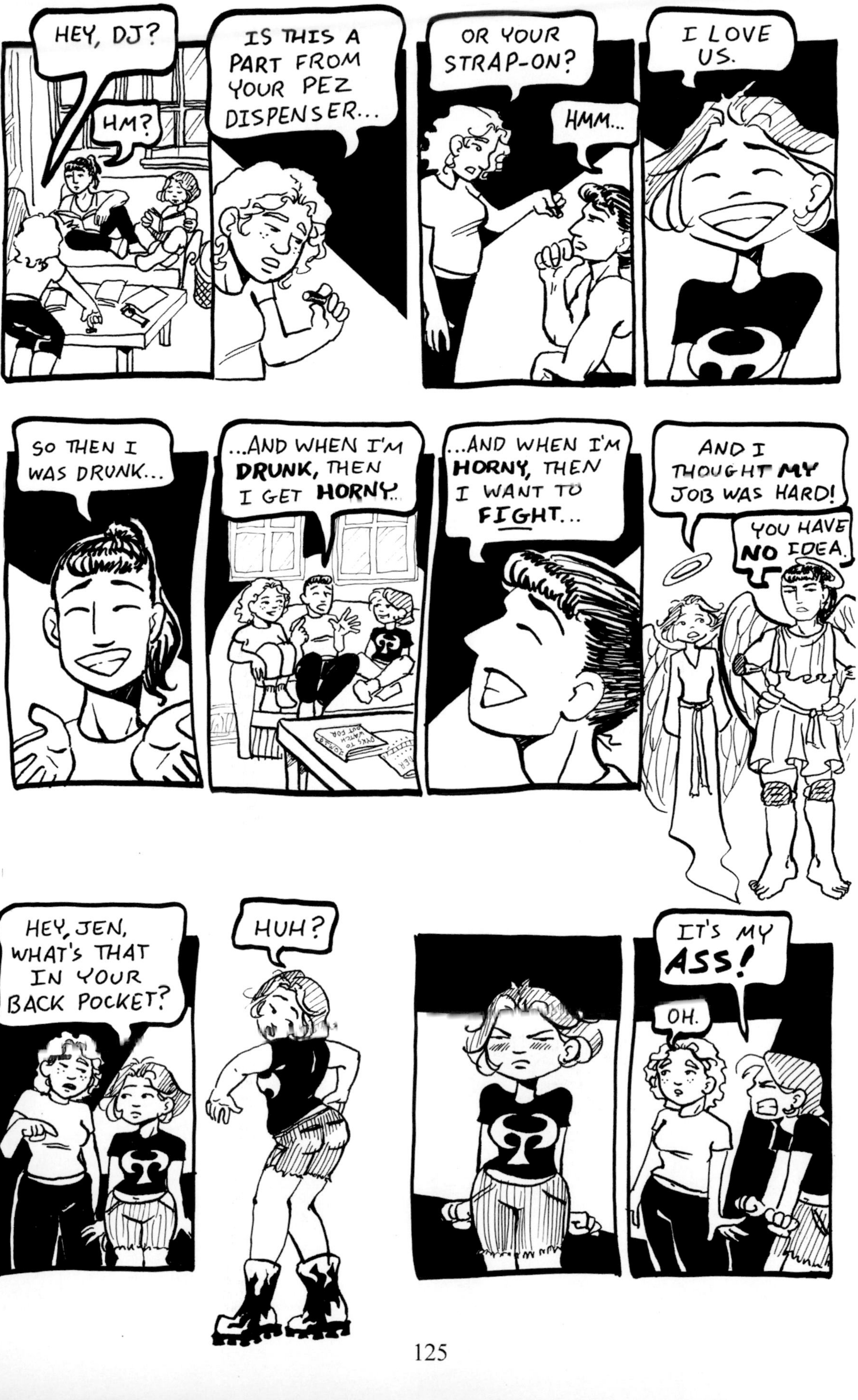
HEY, DJ?
HM?
IS THIS A PART FROM YOUR PEZ DISPENSER...
OR YOUR STRAP-ON?
HMM...
I LOVE US.
SO THEN I WAS DRUNK...
...AND WHEN I'M DRUNK, THEN I GET HORNY...
...AND WHEN I'M HORNY, THEN I WANT TO FIGHT...
AND I THOUGHT MY JOB WAS HARD!
YOU HAVE NO IDEA.
HEY, JEN, WHAT'S THAT IN YOUR BACK POCKET?
HUH?
IT'S MY ASS!
OH.

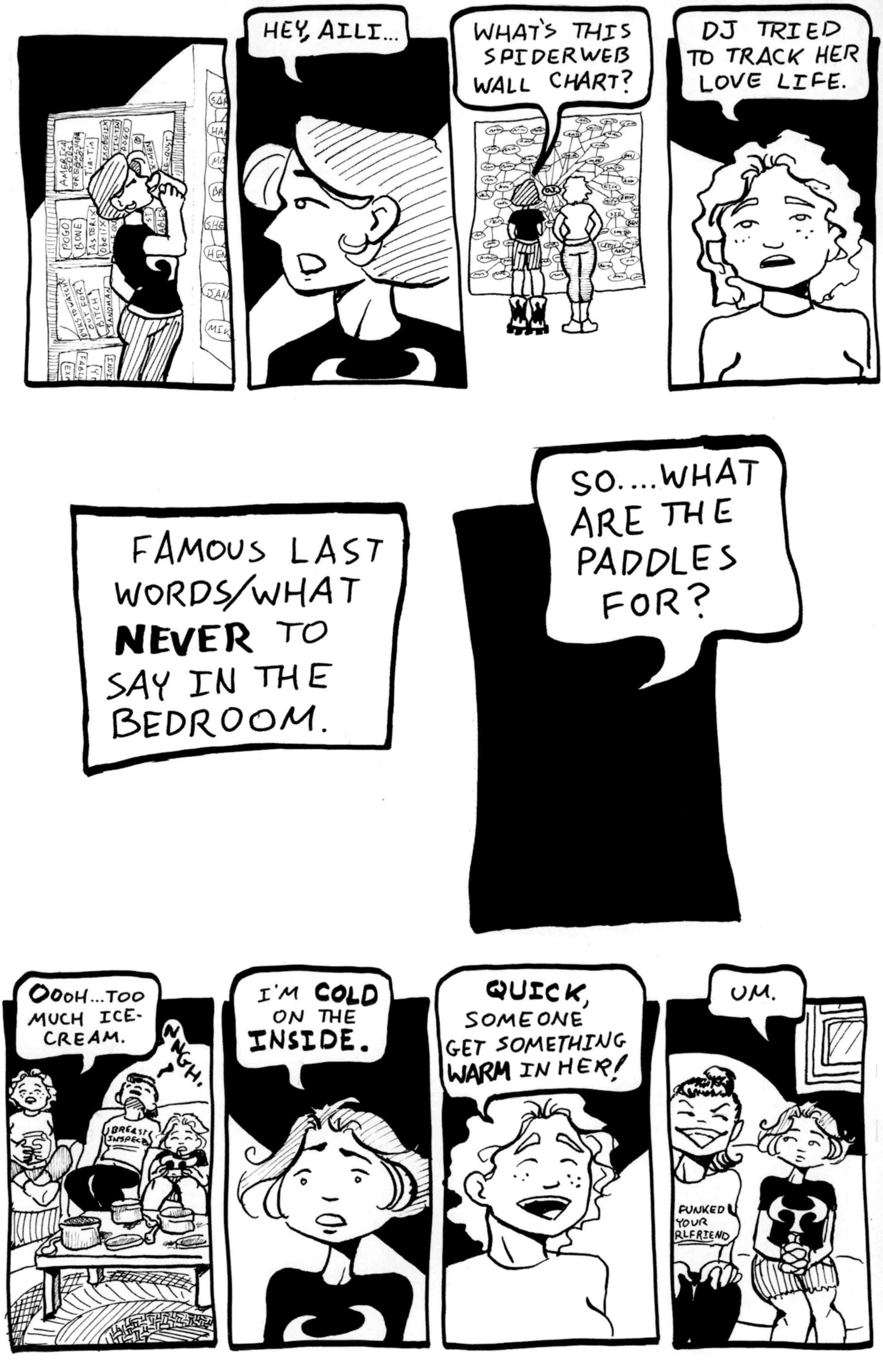
HEY, AILI...
WHAT'S THIS SPIDERWEB WALL CHART?
DJ TRIED TO TRACK HER LOVE LIFE.
FAMOUS LAST WORDS/WHAT NEVER TO SAY IN THE BEDROOM.
SO....WHAT ARE THE PADDLES FOR?
OOOH...TOO MUCH ICE-CREAM.
NNGH.
I'M COLD ON THE INSIDE.
QUICK, SOMEONE GET SOMETHING WARM IN HER!
UM.

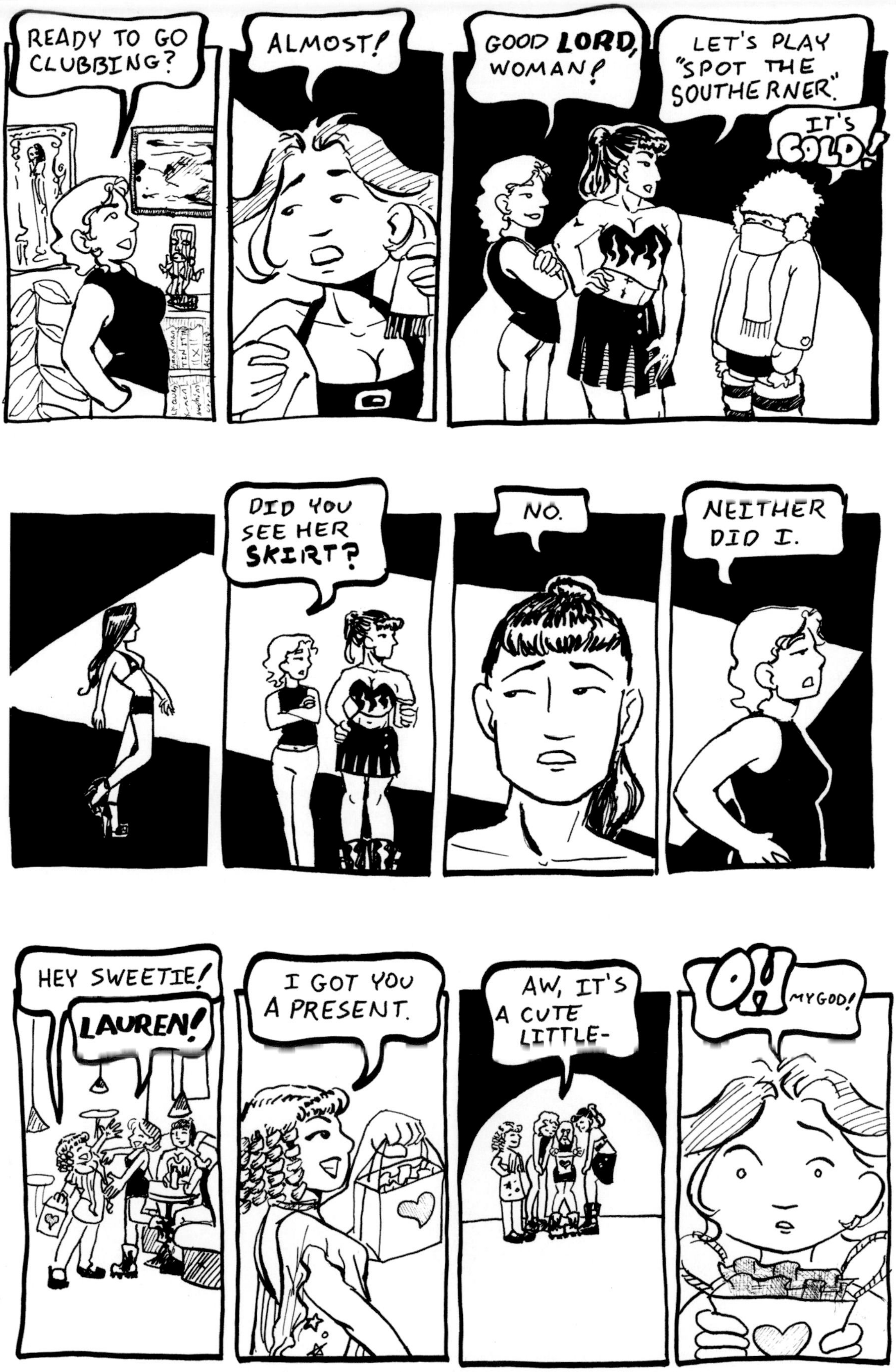
READY TO GO CLUBBING?
ALMOST!
GOOD LORD, WOMAN!
LET'S PLAY "SPOT THE SOUTHERNER".
IT'S COLD!
DID YOU SEE HER SKIRT?
NO.
NEITHER DID I.
HEY SWEETIE!
LAUREN!
I GOT YOU A PRESENT.
AW, IT'S A CUTE LITTLE-
OH MY GOD!

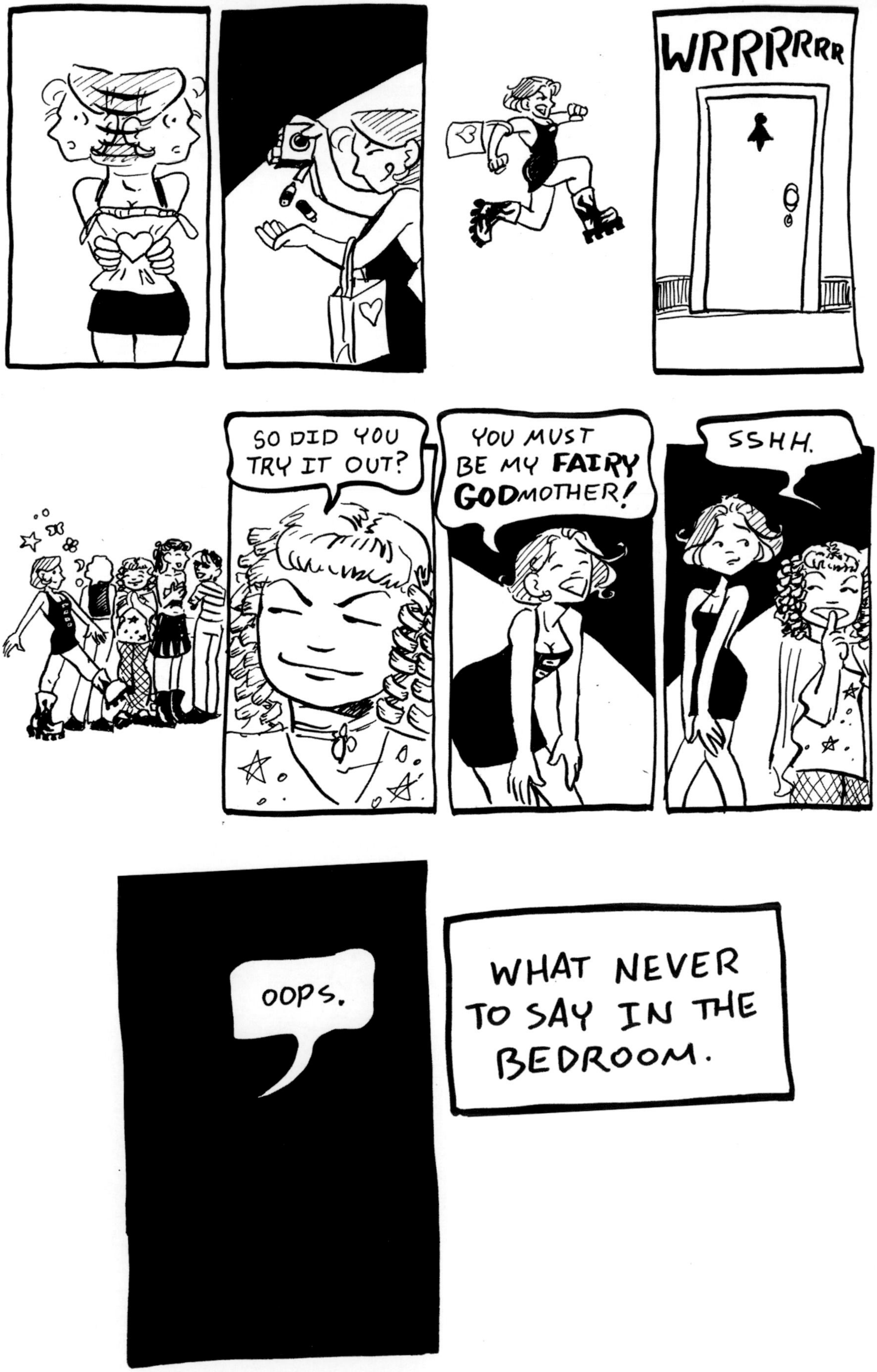
WRRRRRR
SO DID YOU TRY IT OUT?
YOU MUST BE MY FAIRY GODMOTHER!
SSHH.
OOPS.
WHAT NEVER TO SAY IN THE BEDROOM.

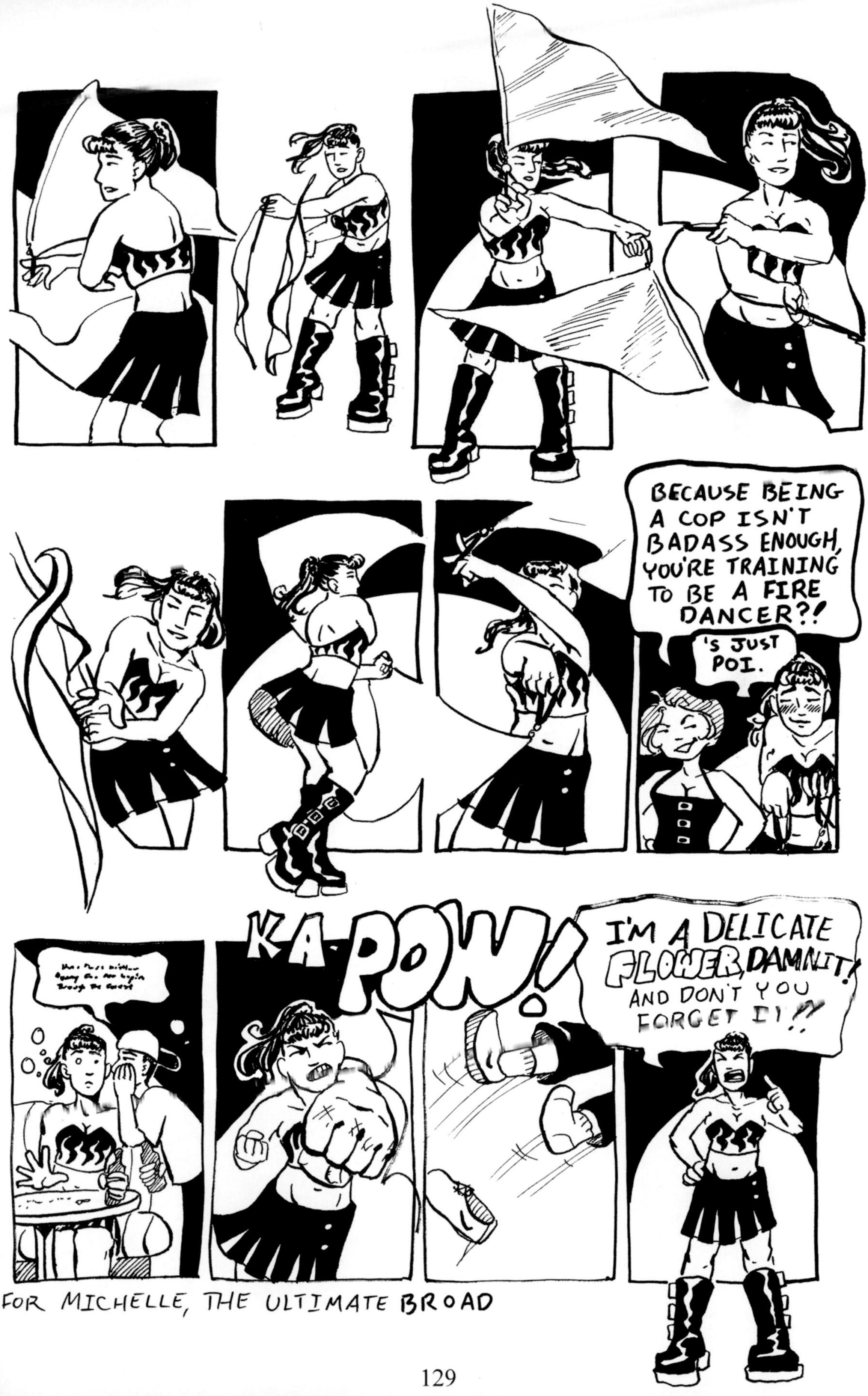
BECAUSE BEING A COP ISN'T BADASS ENOUGH, YOU'RE TRAINING TO BE A FIRE DANCER?!
'S JUST POI.
KA-POW!
I'M A DELICATE FLOWER, DAMNIT! AND DON'T YOU FORGET IT!!
FOR MICHELLE, THE ULTIMATE BROAD

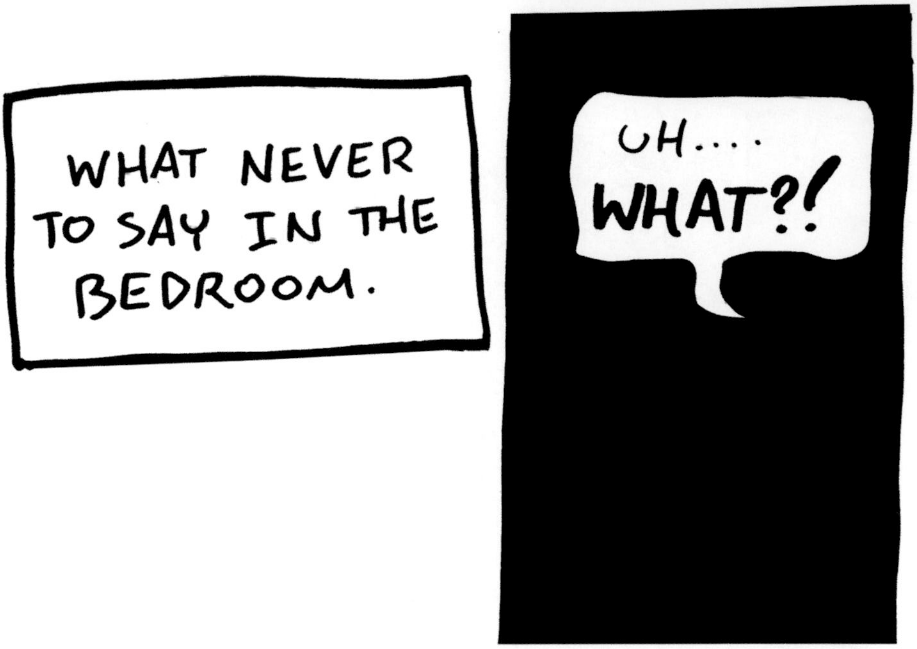
WHAT NEVER TO SAY IN THE BEDROOM.
UH.... WHAT?!

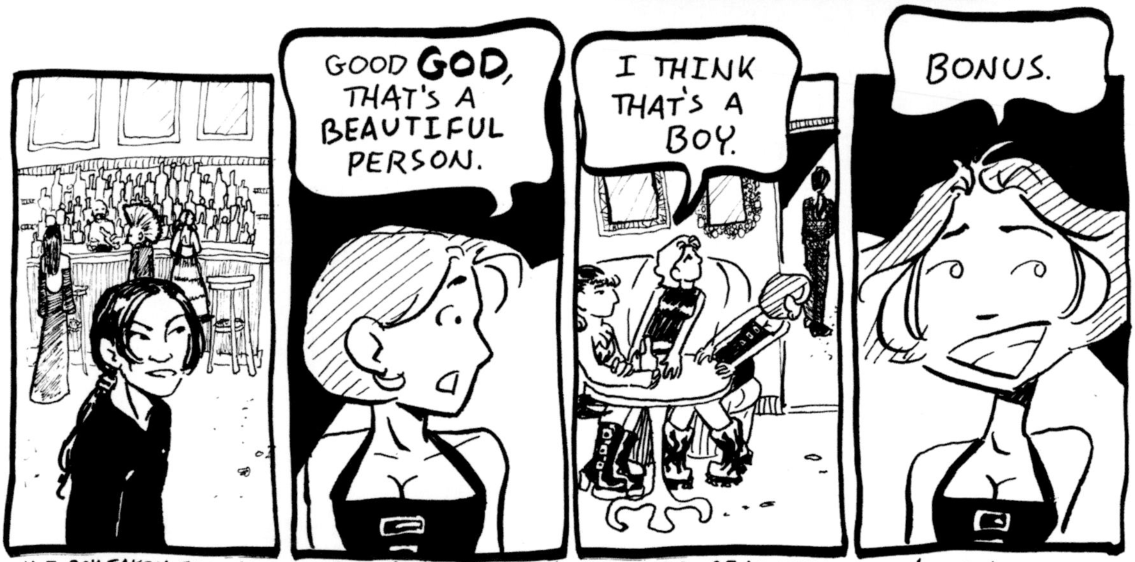
GOOD GOD, THAT'S A BEAUTIFUL PERSON.
I THINK THAT'S A BOY.
BONUS.

HOT BOY TAKEN FROM "POLLY and the PIRATES" By Ted Naifeh. GO READ IT! www.tednaifeh.com

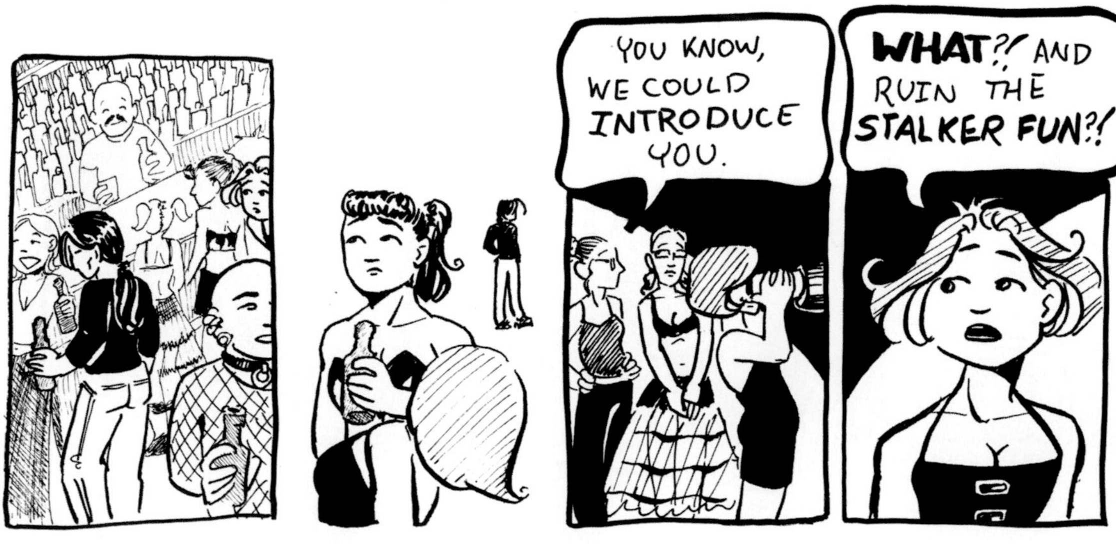
YOU KNOW, WE COULD INTRODUCE YOU.
WHAT?! AND RUIN THE STALKER FUN?!

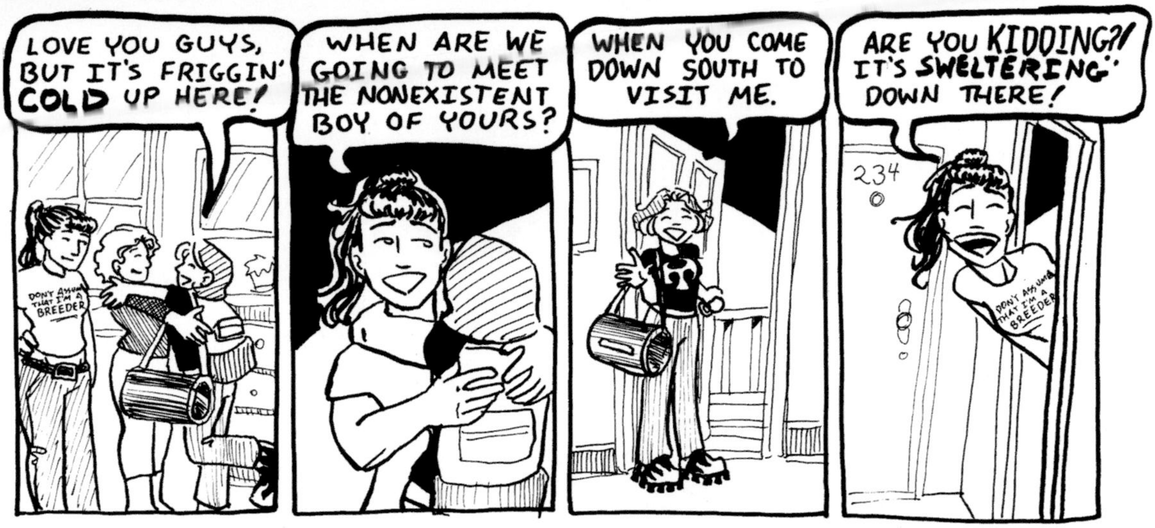
LOVE YOU GUYS, BUT IT'S FRIGGIN' COLD UP HERE!
DON'T ASSUME THAT I'M A BREEDER
WHEN ARE WE GOING TO MEET THE NONEXISTENT BOY OF YOURS?
WHEN YOU COME DOWN SOUTH TO VISIT ME.
ARE YOU KIDDING?! IT'S SWELTERING DOWN THERE!
234
DON'T ASSUME THAT I'M A BREEDER

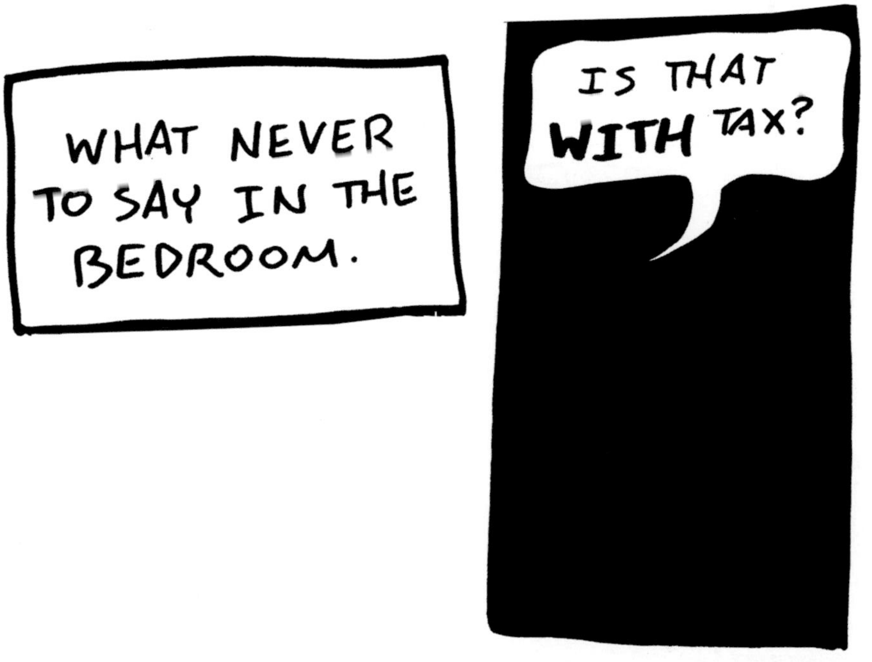
WHAT NEVER TO SAY IN THE BEDROOM.
IS THAT WITH TAX?

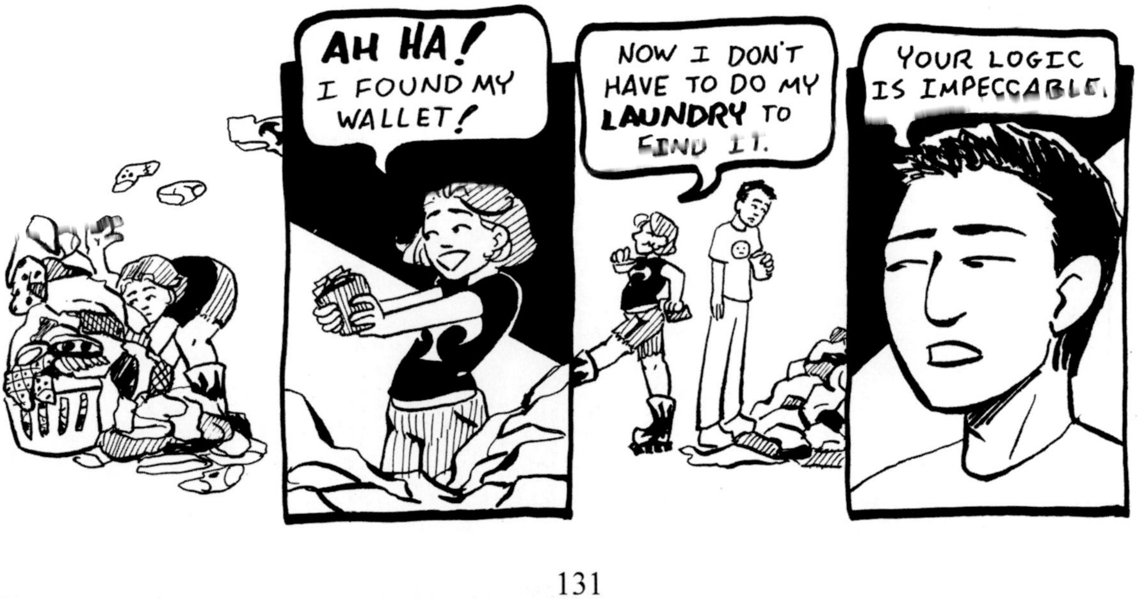
AH HA! I FOUND MY WALLET!
NOW I DON'T HAVE TO DO MY LAUNDRY TO FIND IT.
YOUR LOGIC IS IMPECCABLE.

Panel 1: KNOCK! KNOCK!

Panel 2: I'M HERE FOR YOUR **CHILDREN!**

Panel 3: READY TO GO RAVAGE THE NEIGHBORHOOD FOR CANDY?

YAY!

Panel 4: WORRIED?

NOPE. THEY'VE HAD THEIR SHOTS

FLY MY PRETTIES! FLY!!

Panel 5: AUNT JEN, CAN WE GO HOME NOW?

Panel 6: TWO MORE HOUSES!

Panel 7: I WILL **NOT** BE THE AUNT THAT TOOK YOU KIDS ON A CRAPPY HAUL!

Panel 8: BUT I **AM** THE AUNT WHO FORGOT WHERE YOU LIVE.

NO 'ES BUENO

Panel 9: OKAY KIDS, WHAT KIND OF HALLOWEEN CANDY DID YOU GET?

Panel 10: I GOT A CANDY CANE?

Panel 11: I GOT A HEART LOLLYPOP...

Panel 12: WELL NOW WE KNOW WHICH HOUSES TO EGG.

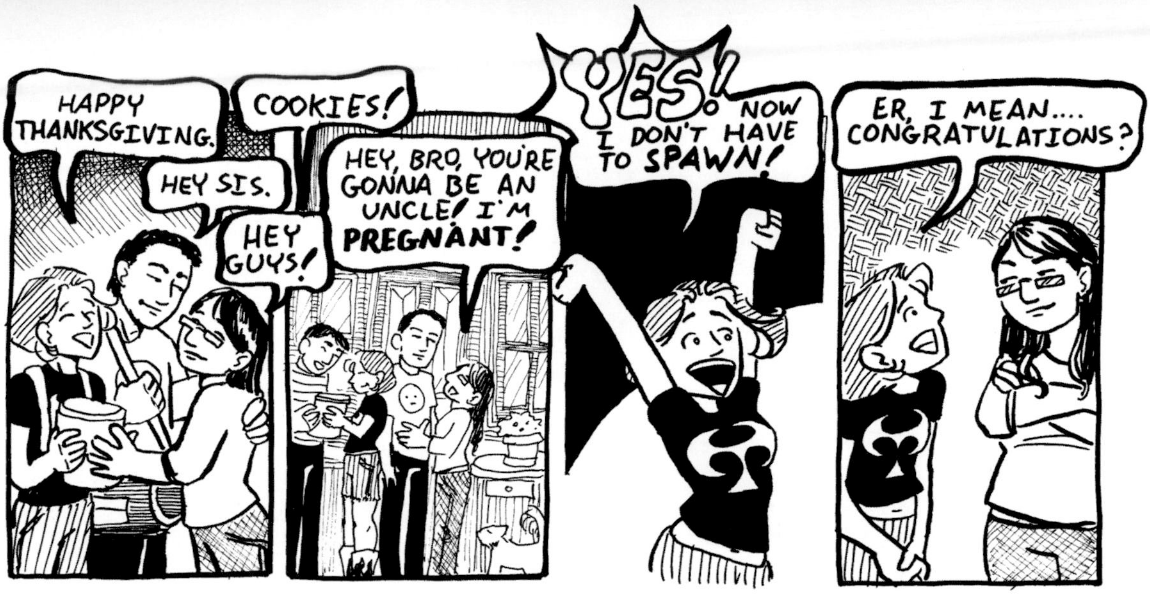
HAPPY THANKSGIVING.
COOKIES!
HEY SIS.
HEY GUYS!
HEY, BRO, YOU'RE GONNA BE AN UNCLE! I'M PREGNANT!
YES! NOW I DON'T HAVE TO SPAWN!
ER, I MEAN.... CONGRATULATIONS?

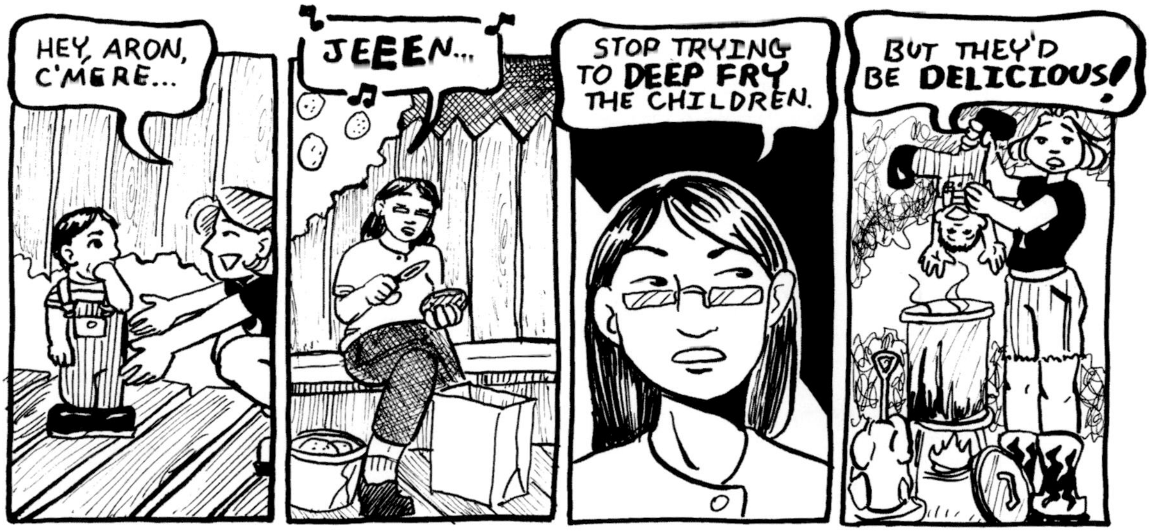
HEY, ARON, C'MERE...
JEEEN...
STOP TRYING TO DEEP FRY THE CHILDREN.
BUT THEY'D BE DELICIOUS!

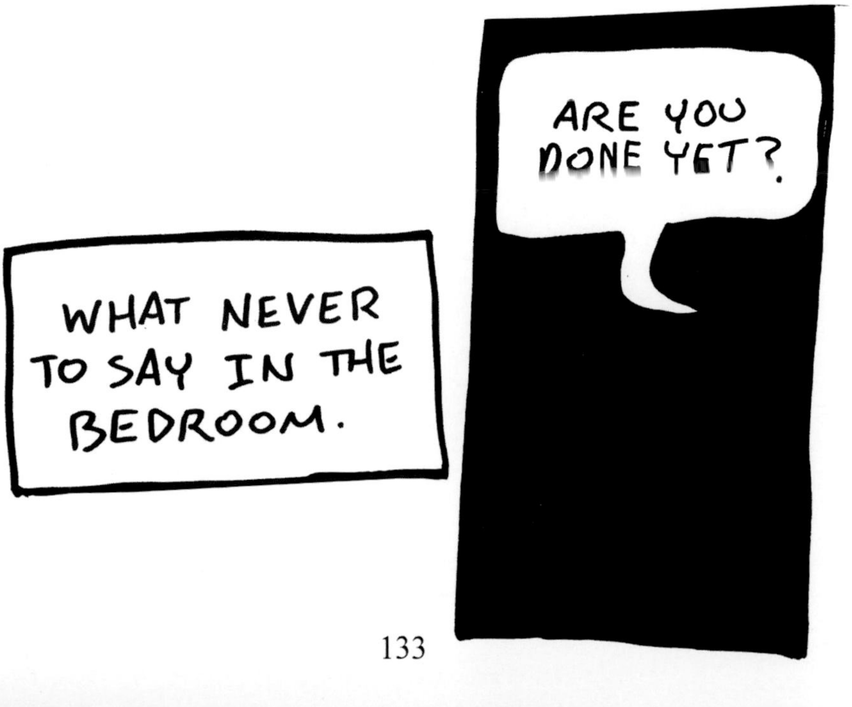
WHAT NEVER TO SAY IN THE BEDROOM.
ARE YOU DONE YET?

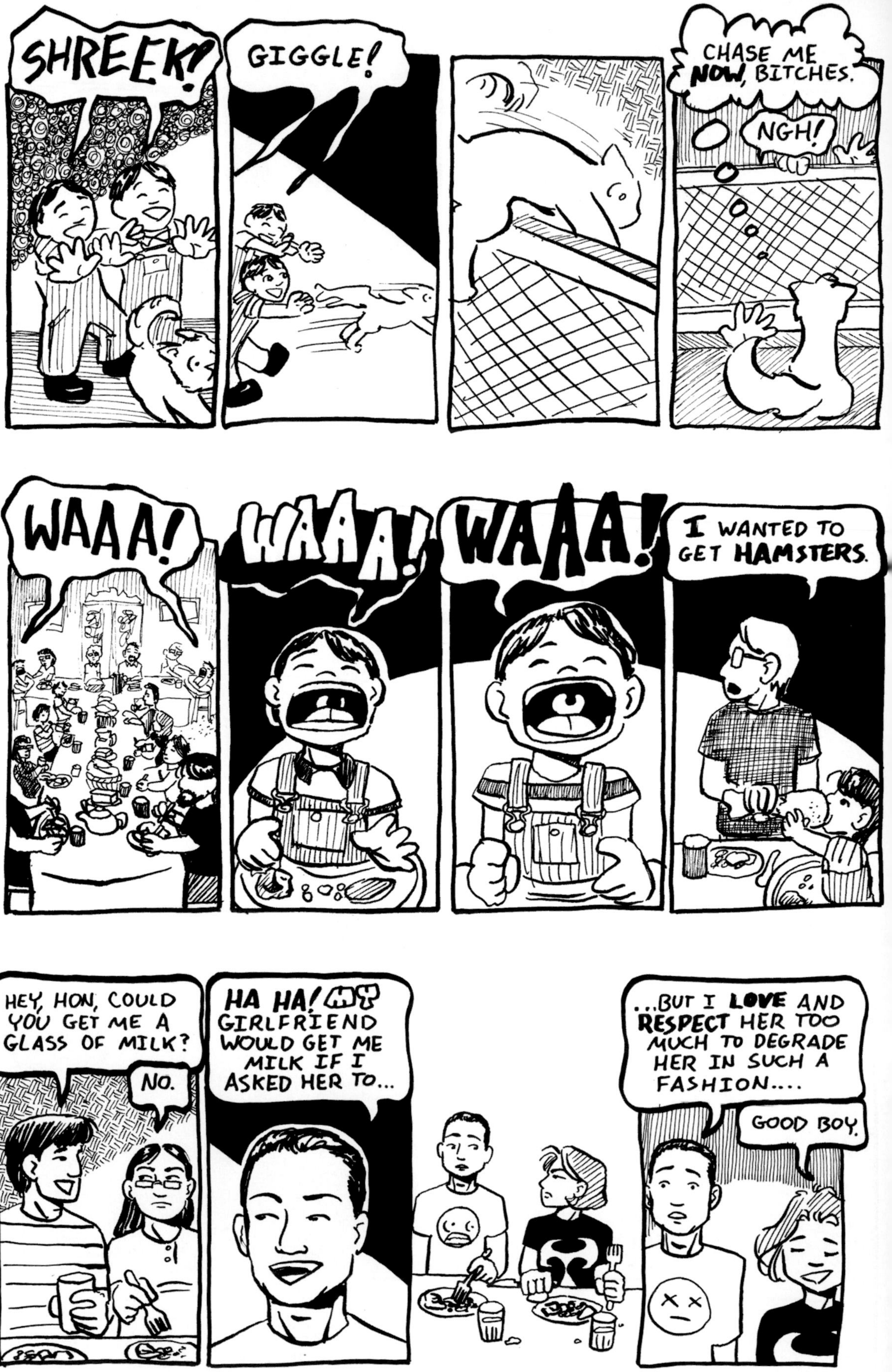
SHREEK!
GIGGLE!
CHASE ME NOW, BITCHES.
NGH!
WAAA!
WAAA!
WAAA!
I WANTED TO GET HAMSTERS.
HEY, HON, COULD YOU GET ME A GLASS OF MILK?
NO.
HA HA! MY GIRLFRIEND WOULD GET ME MILK IF I ASKED HER TO...
...BUT I LOVE AND RESPECT HER TOO MUCH TO DEGRADE HER IN SUCH A FASHION....
GOOD BOY.

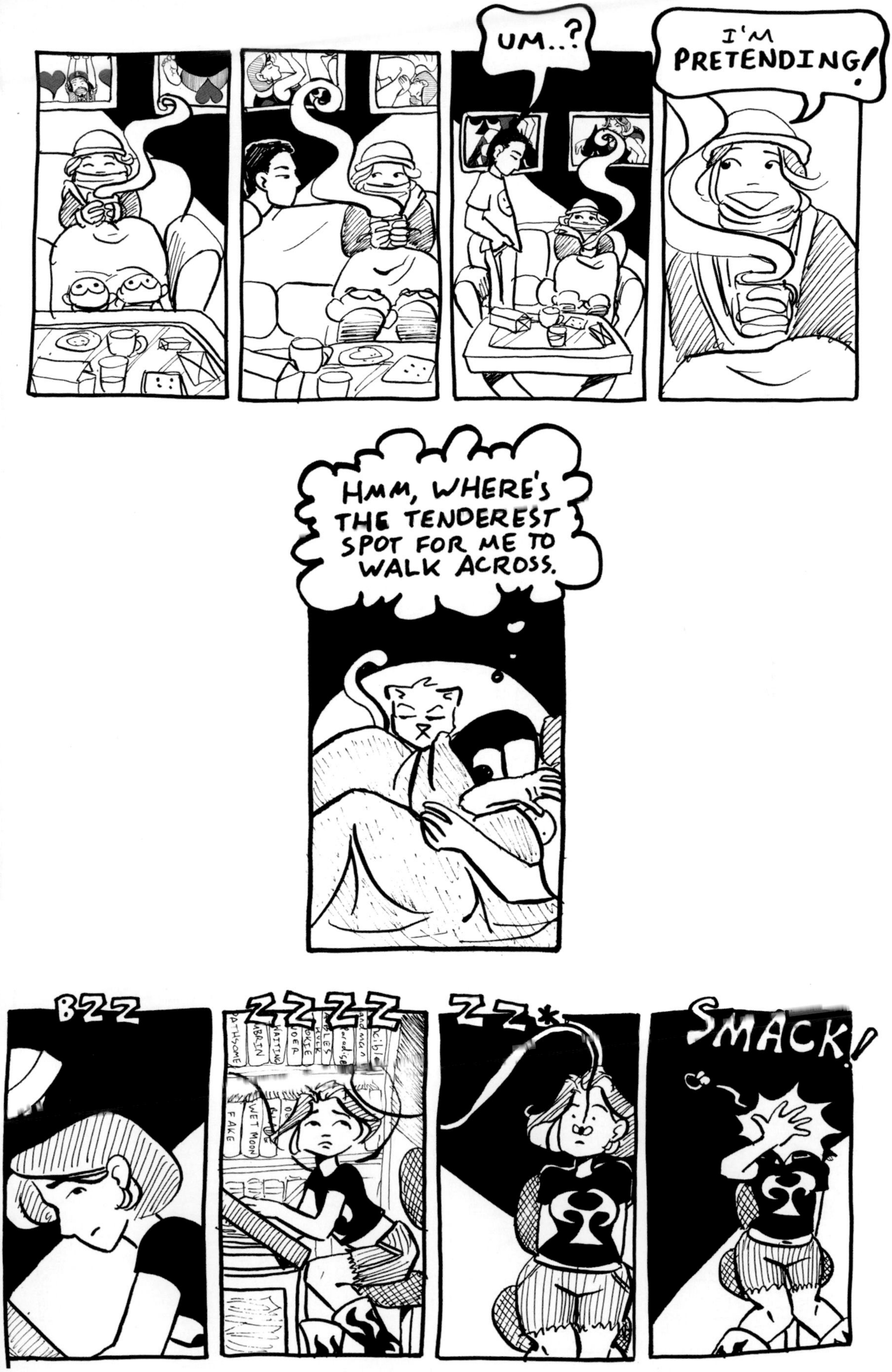
UM..?
I'M PRETENDING!
HMM, WHERE'S THE TENDEREST SPOT FOR ME TO WALK ACROSS.
BZZ
ZZZZ
ZZ*
SMACK!

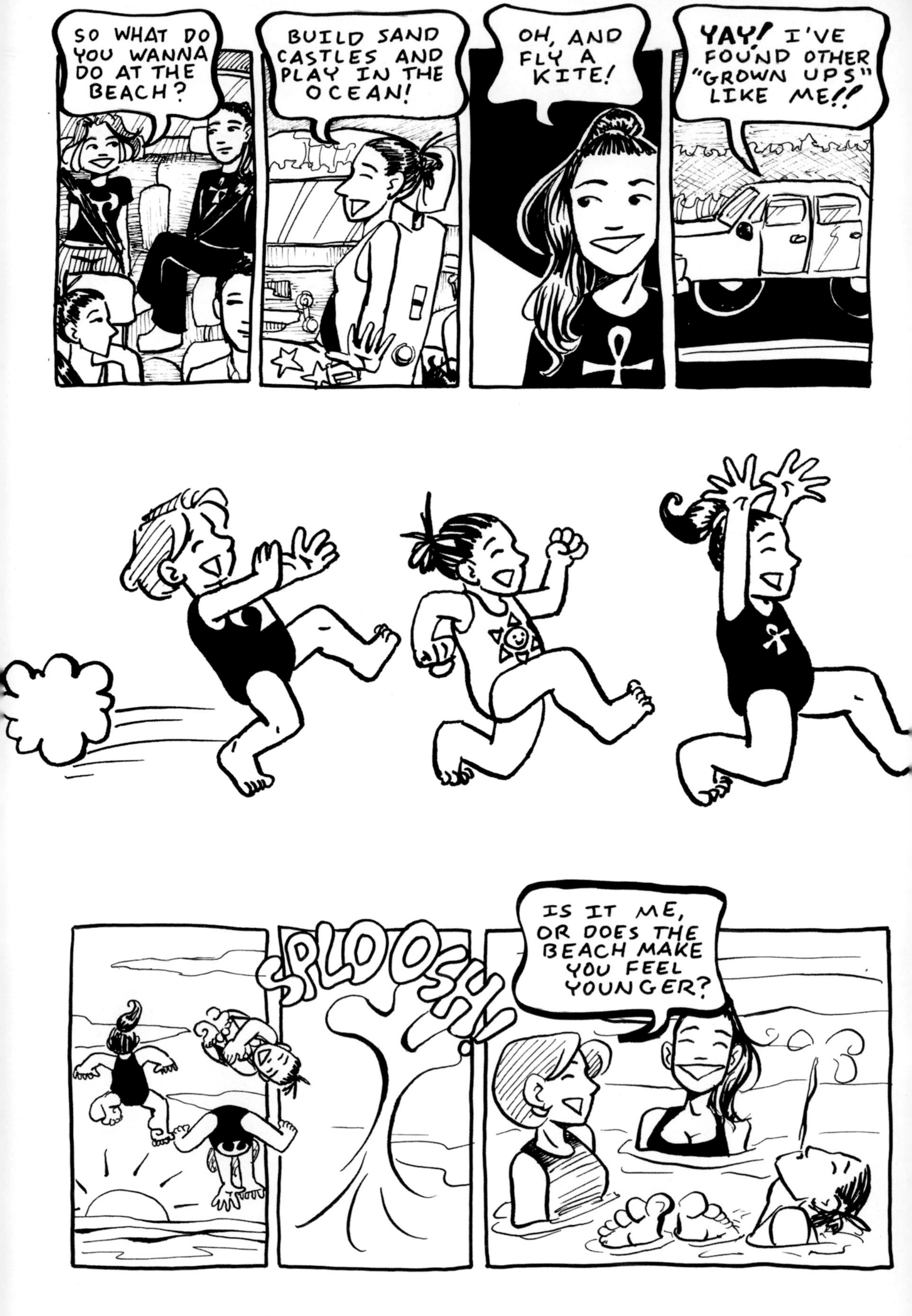

SO WHAT DO YOU WANNA DO AT THE BEACH?
BUILD SAND CASTLES AND PLAY IN THE OCEAN!
OH, AND FLY A KITE!
YAY! I'VE FOUND OTHER "GROWN UPS" LIKE ME!!
SPLOOSH!!
IS IT ME, OR DOES THE BEACH MAKE YOU FEEL YOUNGER?

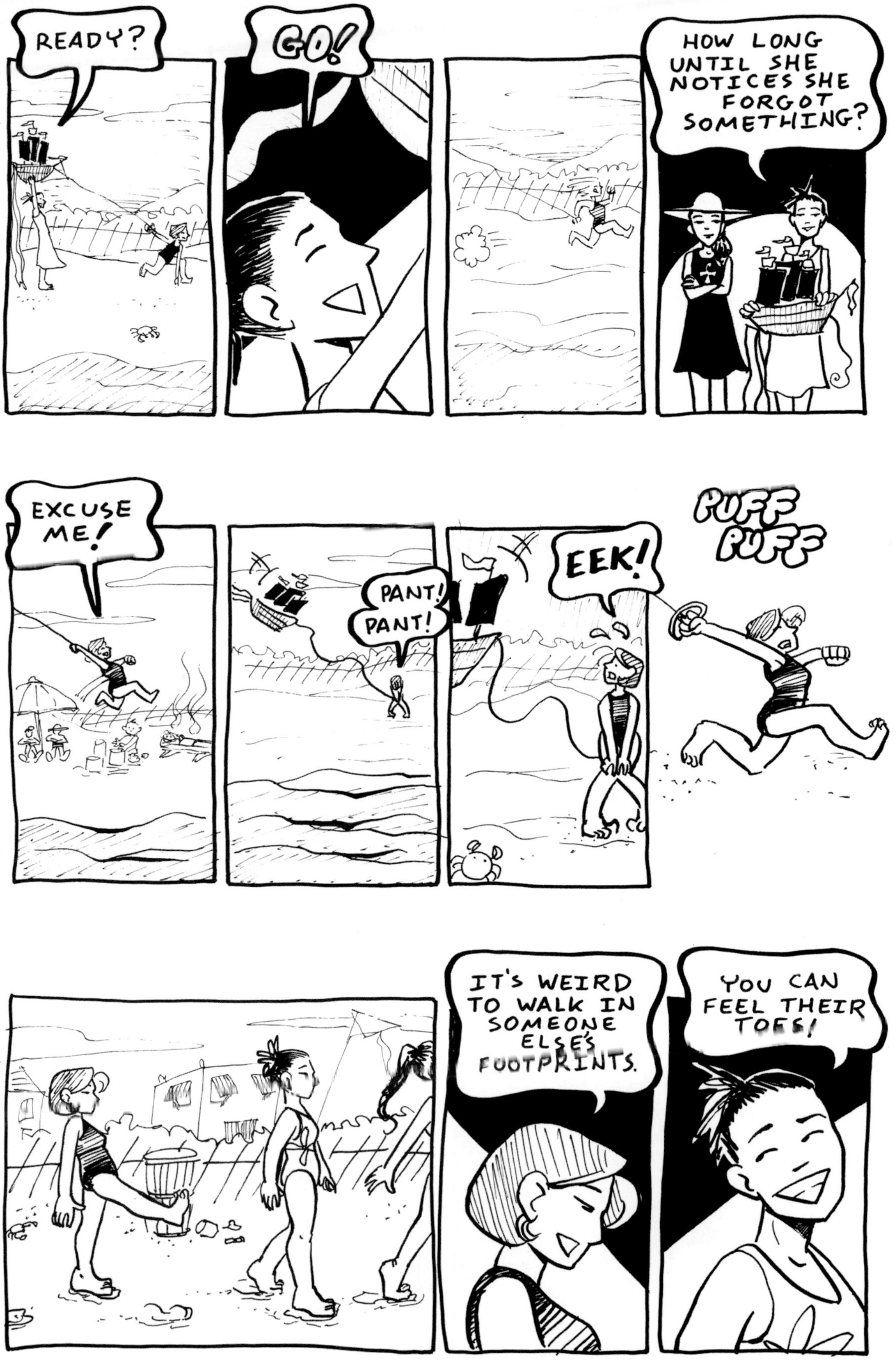
READY?
GO!
HOW LONG UNTIL SHE NOTICES SHE FORGOT SOMETHING?
EXCUSE ME!
PANT! PANT!
EEK!
PUFF PUFF
IT'S WEIRD TO WALK IN SOMEONE ELSE'S FOOTPRINTS.
YOU CAN FEEL THEIR TOES!

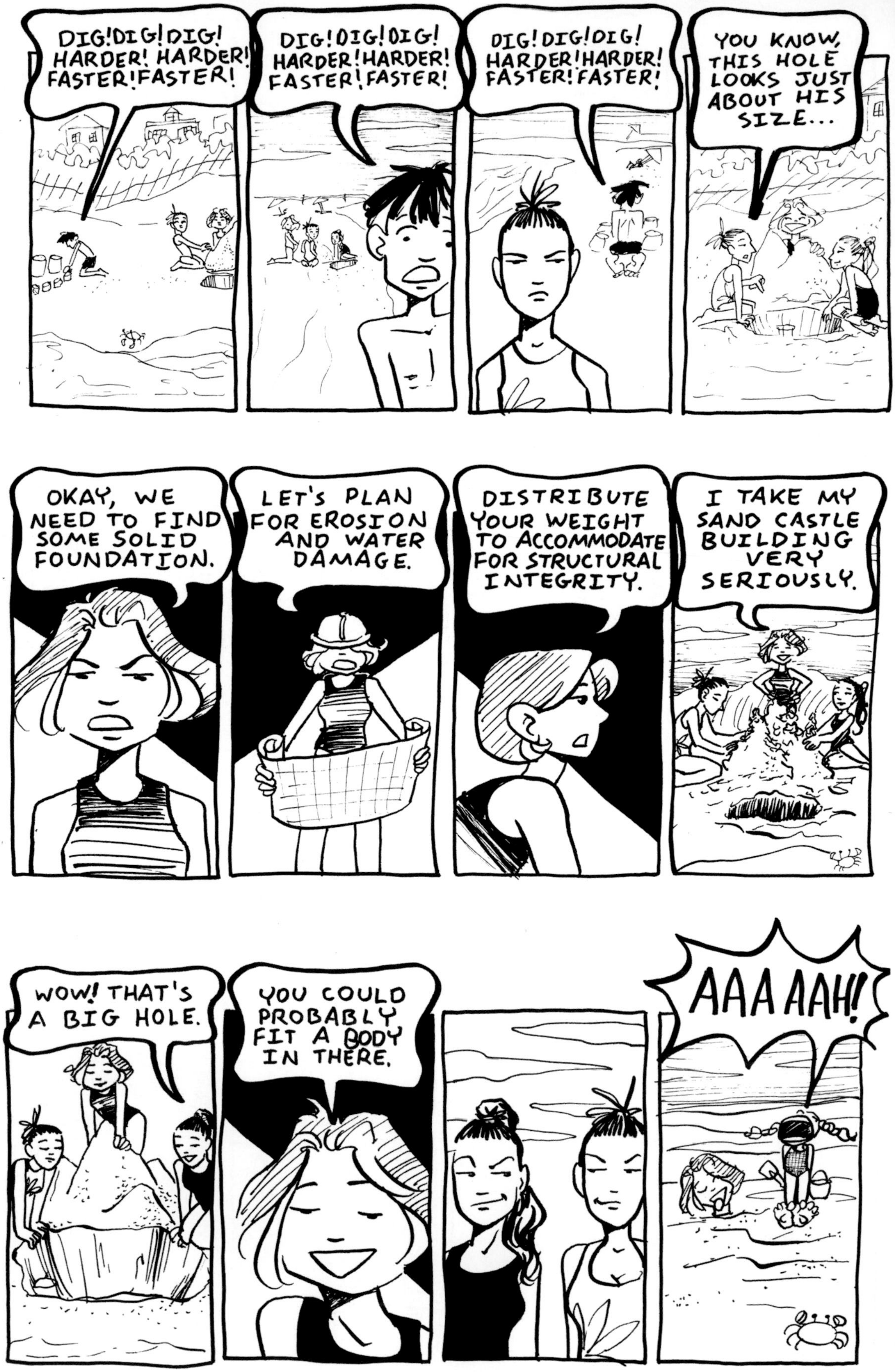
DIG! DIG! DIG! HARDER! HARDER! FASTER! FASTER!
DIG! DIG! DIG! HARDER! HARDER! FASTER! FASTER!
DIG! DIG! DIG! HARDER! HARDER! FASTER! FASTER!
YOU KNOW, THIS HOLE LOOKS JUST ABOUT HIS SIZE...
OKAY, WE NEED TO FIND SOME SOLID FOUNDATION.
LET'S PLAN FOR EROSION AND WATER DAMAGE.
DISTRIBUTE YOUR WEIGHT TO ACCOMMODATE FOR STRUCTURAL INTEGRITY.
I TAKE MY SAND CASTLE BUILDING VERY SERIOUSLY.
WOW! THAT'S A BIG HOLE.
YOU COULD PROBABLY FIT A BODY IN THERE.
AAAAAH!

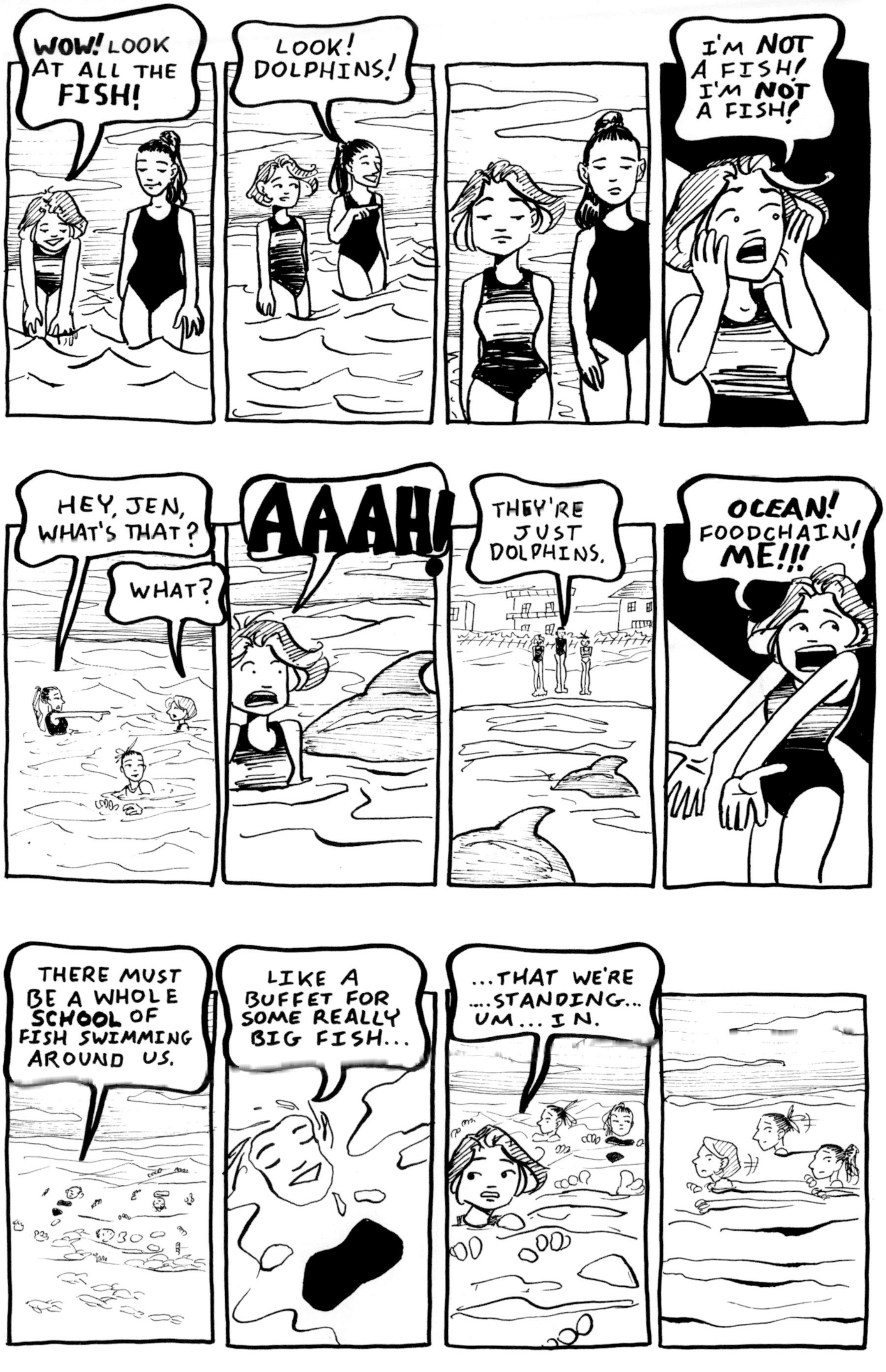
WOW! LOOK AT ALL THE FISH!
LOOK! DOLPHINS!
I'M NOT A FISH! I'M NOT A FISH!
HEY, JEN, WHAT'S THAT?
WHAT?
AAAH!
THEY'RE JUST DOLPHINS.
OCEAN! FOODCHAIN! ME!!!
THERE MUST BE A WHOLE SCHOOL OF FISH SWIMMING AROUND US.
LIKE A BUFFET FOR SOME REALLY BIG FISH...
...THAT WE'RE ....STANDING... UM... IN.

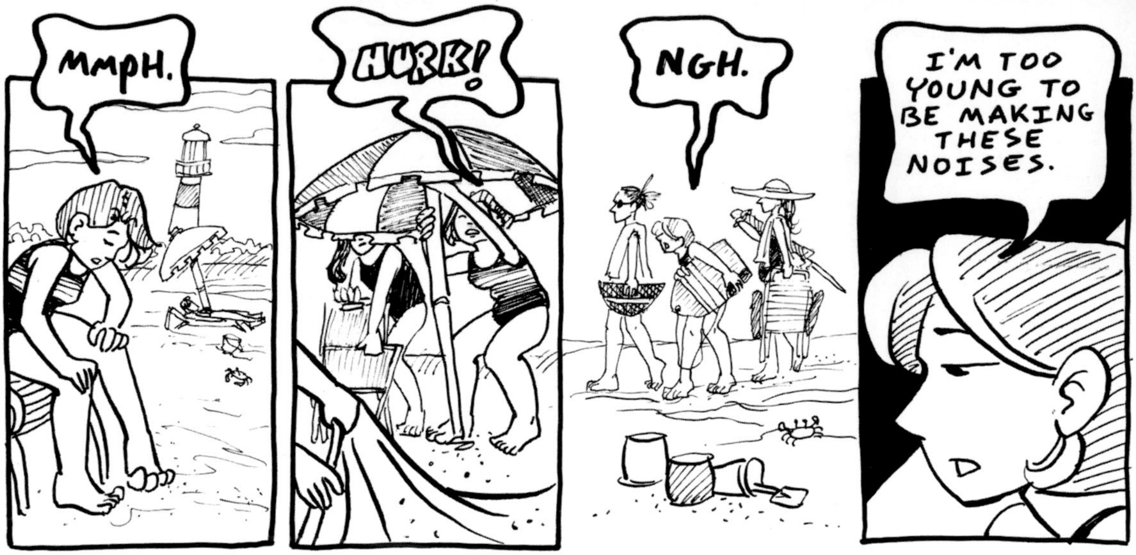
MMPH.
HURK!
NGH.
I'M TOO YOUNG TO BE MAKING THESE NOISES.

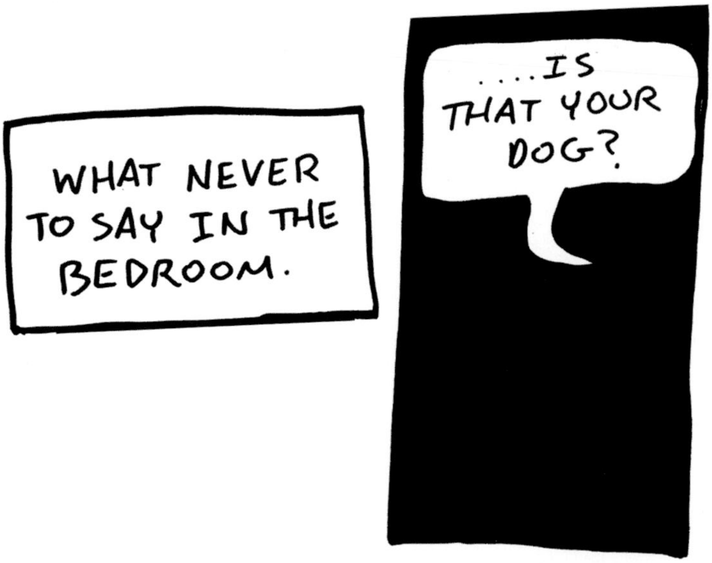
WHAT NEVER TO SAY IN THE BEDROOM.
....IS THAT YOUR DOG?

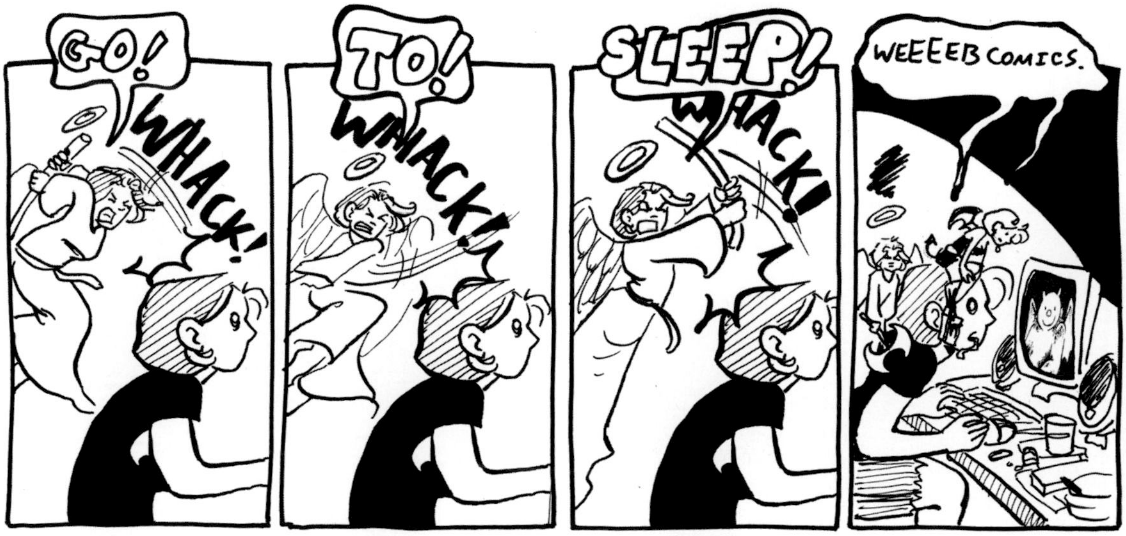
GO!
WHACK!
TO!
WHACK!
SLEEP!
WHACK!
WEEEEB COMICS.

HOW OWNING A DOG PREPARES A MAN FOR DATING A WOMAN.

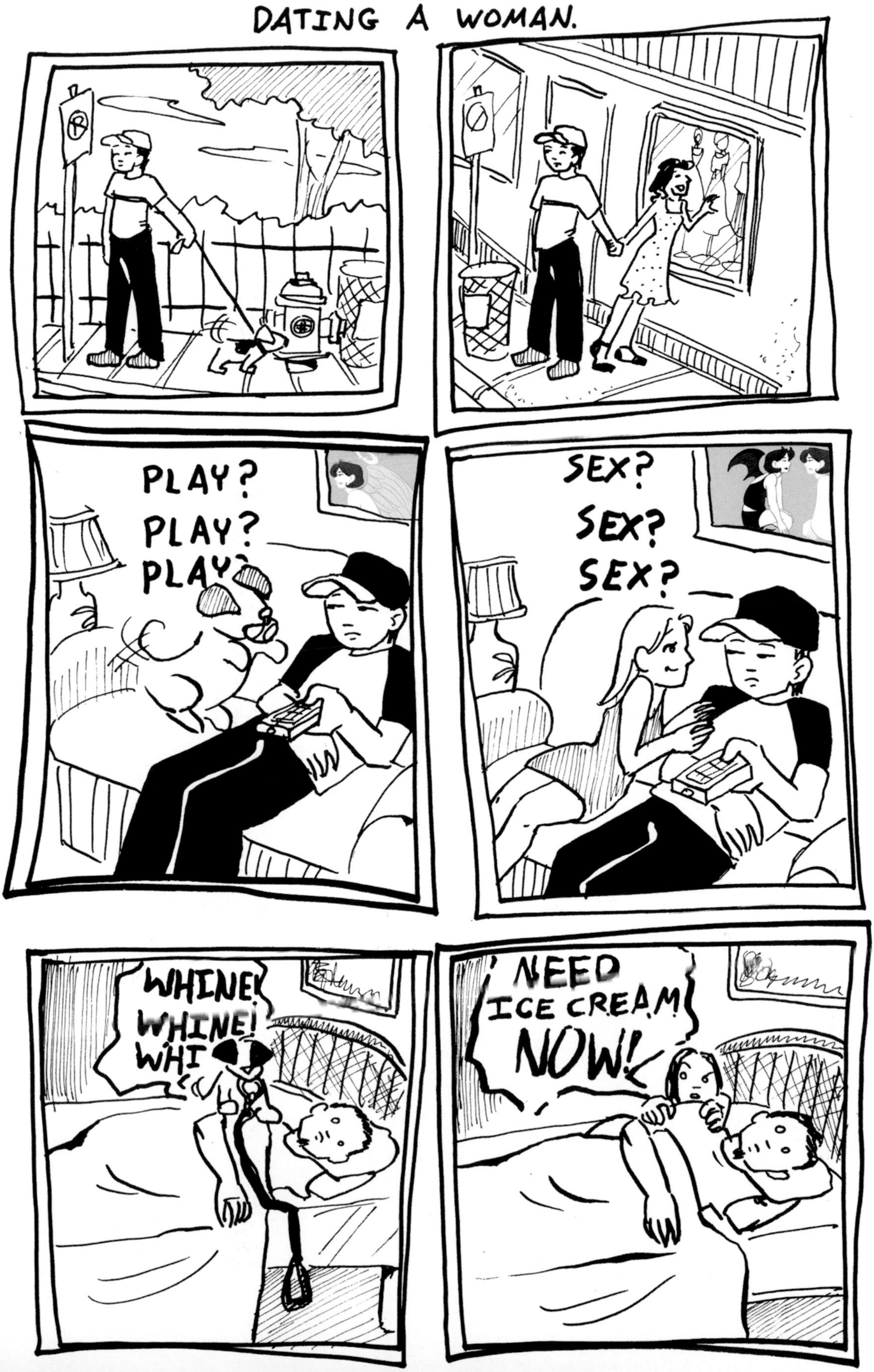
PLAY? PLAY? PLAY?
SEX? SEX? SEX?
WHINE! WHINE! WHI
NEED ICE CREAM NOW!

HOW OWNING A DOG PREPARES A MAN FOR DATING A WOMAN.

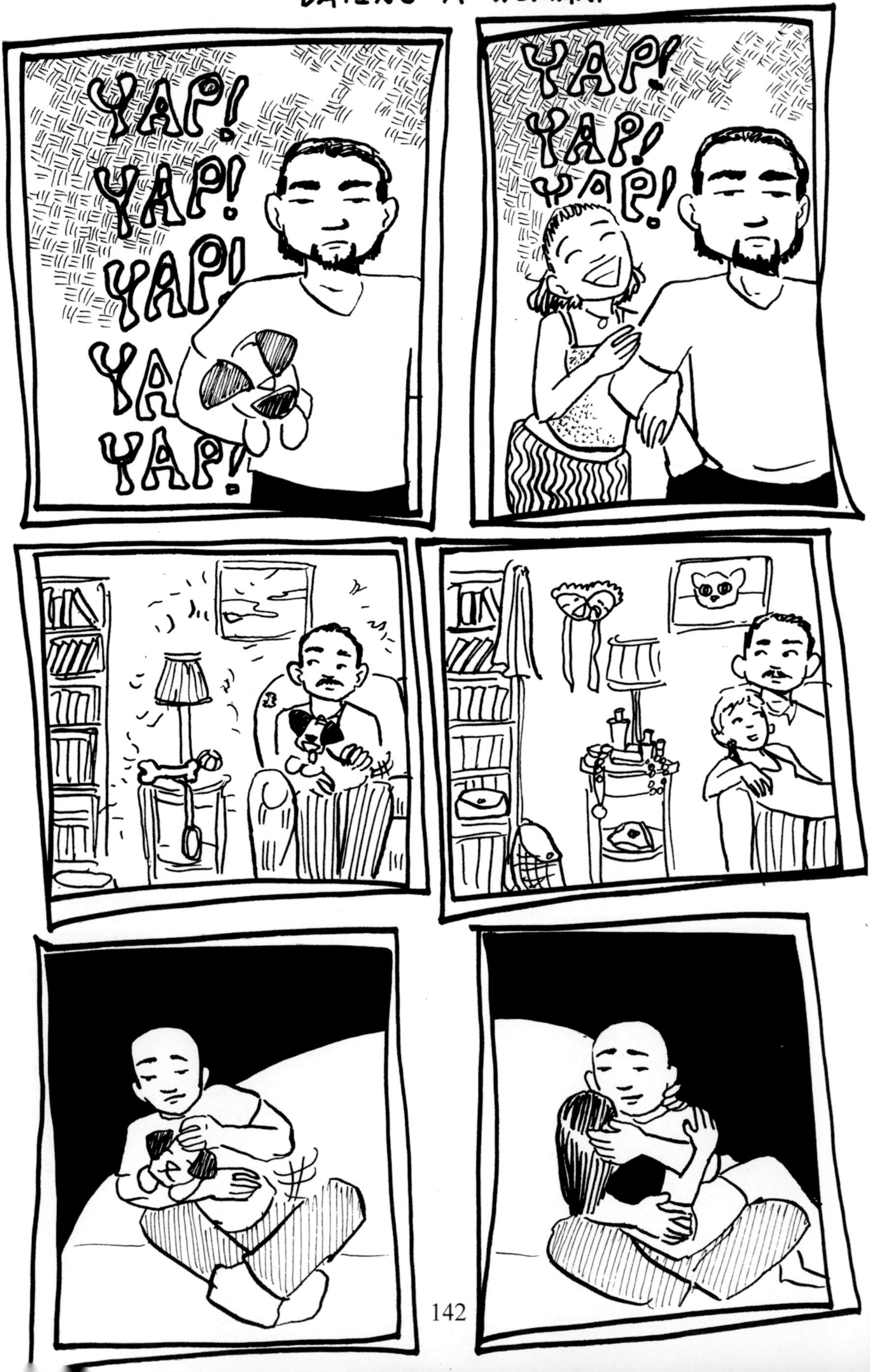
YAP!
YAP!
YAP!
YA
YAP!
YAP!
YAP!
YAP!

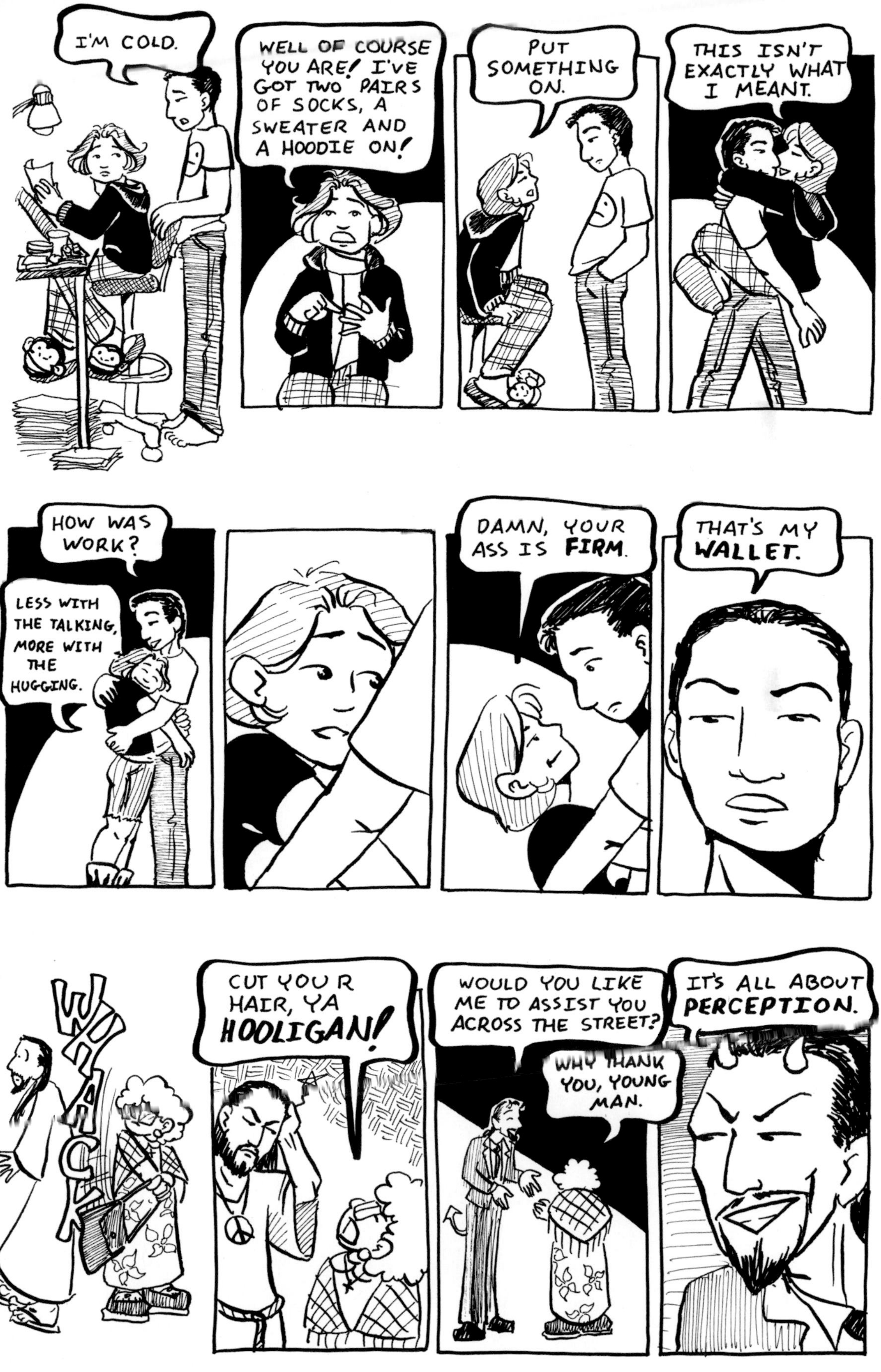
I'M COLD.
WELL OF COURSE YOU ARE! I'VE GOT TWO PAIRS OF SOCKS, A SWEATER AND A HOODIE ON!
PUT SOMETHING ON.
THIS ISN'T EXACTLY WHAT I MEANT.
HOW WAS WORK?
LESS WITH THE TALKING, MORE WITH THE HUGGING.
DAMN, YOUR ASS IS FIRM.
THAT'S MY WALLET.
WHACK
CUT YOUR HAIR, YA HOOLIGAN!
WOULD YOU LIKE ME TO ASSIST YOU ACROSS THE STREET?
WHY THANK YOU, YOUNG MAN.
IT'S ALL ABOUT PERCEPTION.

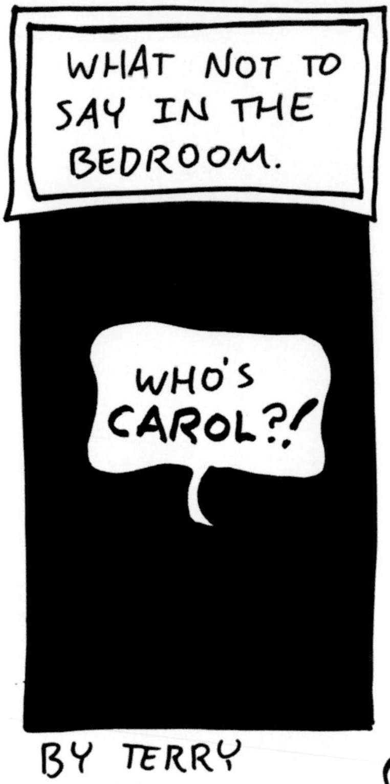
WHAT NOT TO SAY IN THE BEDROOM.
WHO'S CAROL?!
BY TERRY

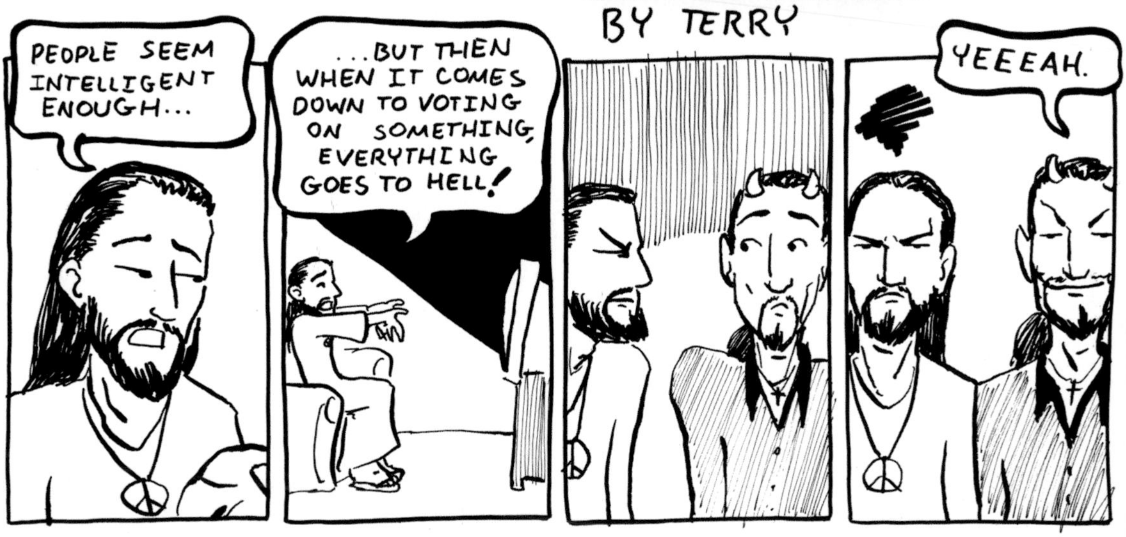
PEOPLE SEEM INTELLIGENT ENOUGH...
...BUT THEN WHEN IT COMES DOWN TO VOTING ON SOMETHING, EVERYTHING GOES TO HELL!
YEEEAH.

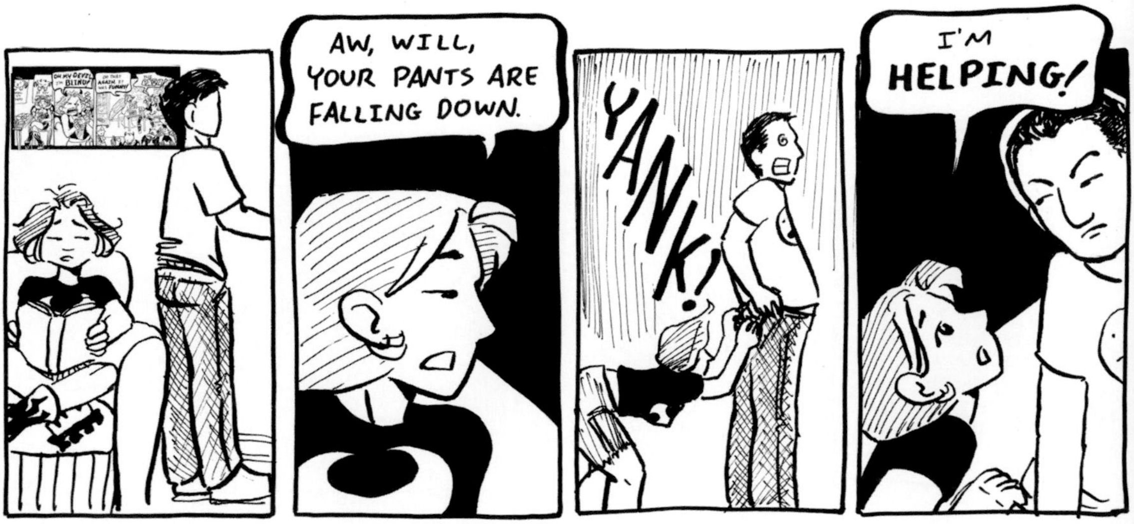
AW, WILL, YOUR PANTS ARE FALLING DOWN.
YANK!
I'M HELPING!

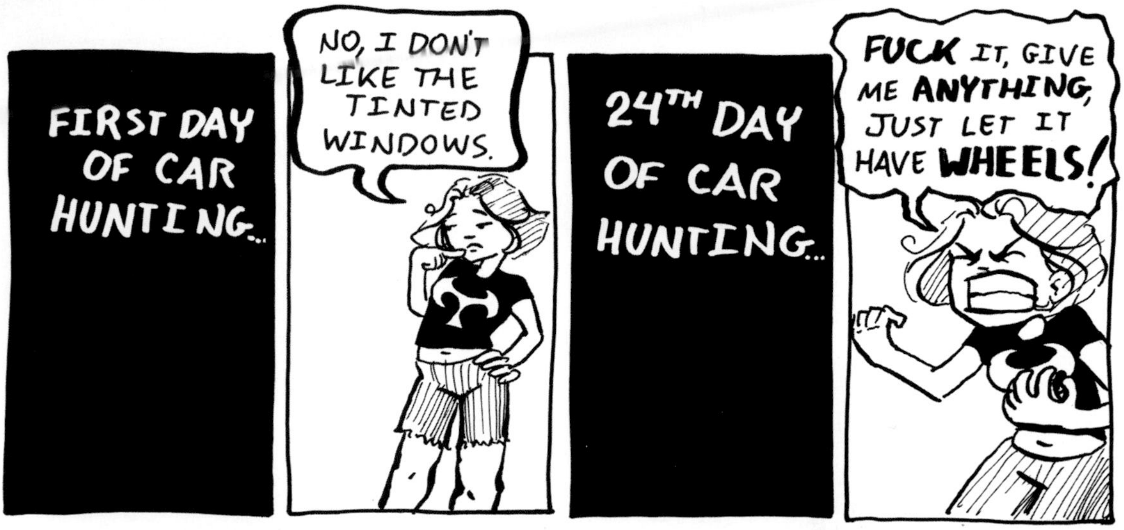
FIRST DAY OF CAR HUNTING...
NO, I DON'T LIKE THE TINTED WINDOWS.
24TH DAY OF CAR HUNTING...
FUCK IT, GIVE ME ANYTHING, JUST LET IT HAVE WHEELS!

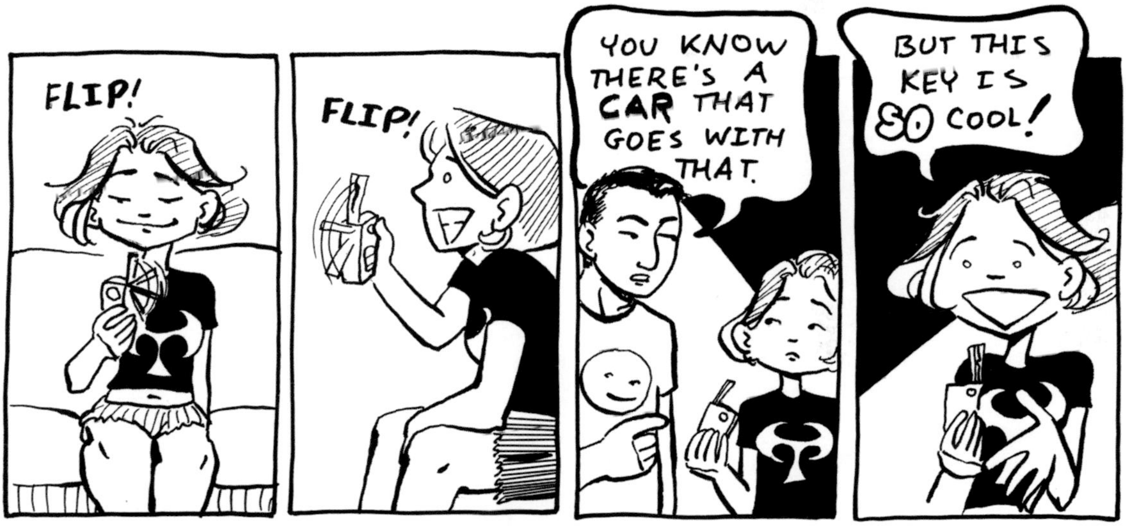
FLIP!
FLIP!
YOU KNOW THERE'S A CAR THAT GOES WITH THAT.
BUT THIS KEY IS SO COOL!

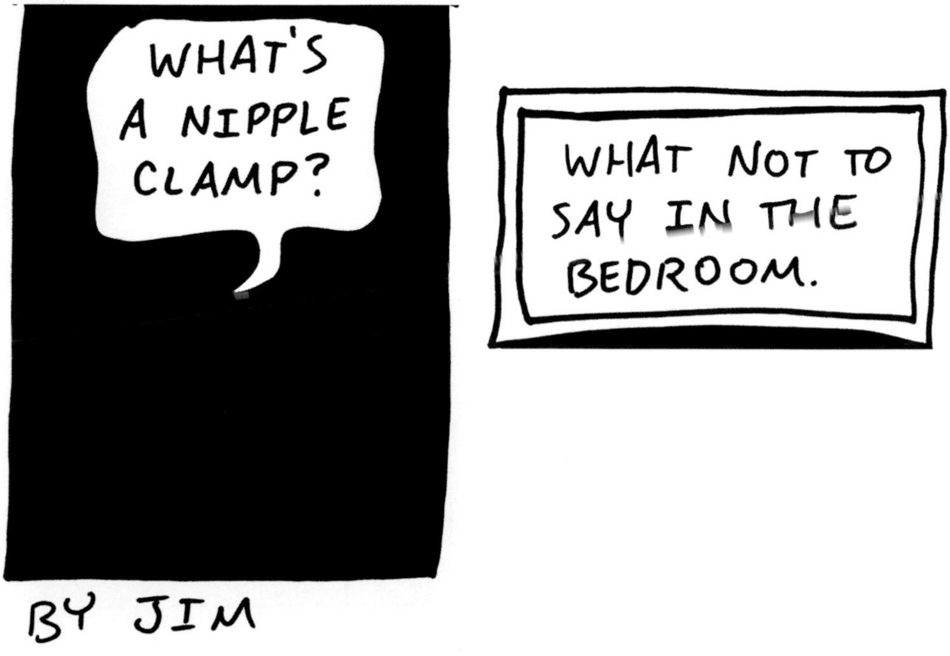
WHAT'S A NIPPLE CLAMP?
WHAT NOT TO SAY IN THE BEDROOM.
BY JIM

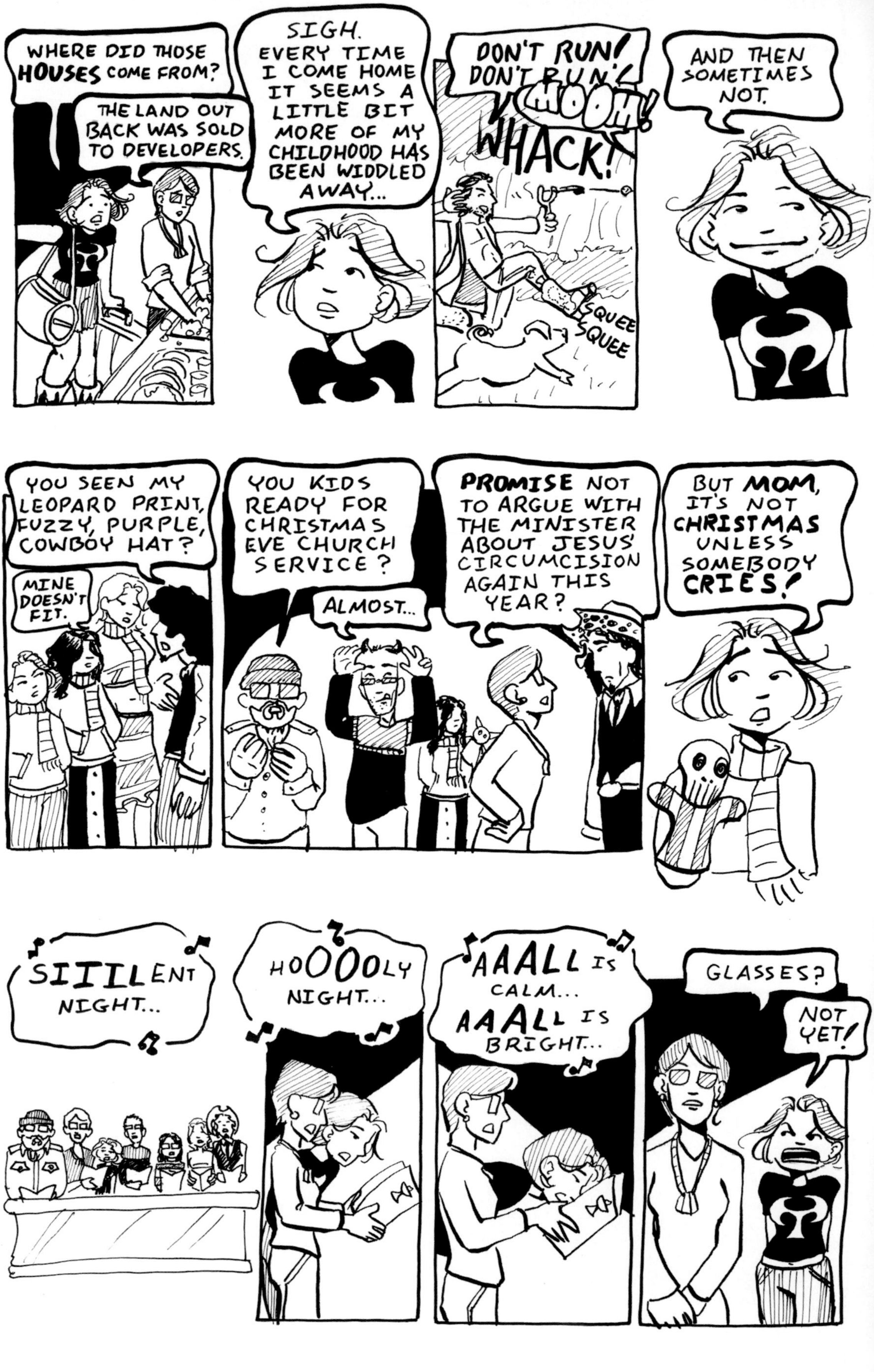
WHERE DID THOSE HOUSES COME FROM?
THE LAND OUT BACK WAS SOLD TO DEVELOPERS.
SIGH. EVERY TIME I COME HOME IT SEEMS A LITTLE BIT MORE OF MY CHILDHOOD HAS BEEN WIDDLED AWAY...
DON'T RUN! DON'T RUN!
MOOH!
WHACK!
SQUEE SQUEE
AND THEN SOMETIMES NOT.
YOU SEEN MY LEOPARD PRINT, FUZZY, PURPLE, COWBOY HAT?
MINE DOESN'T FIT.
YOU KIDS READY FOR CHRISTMAS EVE CHURCH SERVICE?
ALMOST...
PROMISE NOT TO ARGUE WITH THE MINISTER ABOUT JESUS' CIRCUMCISION AGAIN THIS YEAR?
BUT MOM, IT'S NOT CHRISTMAS UNLESS SOMEBODY CRIES!
SIIILENT NIGHT...
HOOOOOLY NIGHT...
AAALL IS CALM... AAALL IS BRIGHT...
GLASSES?
NOT YET!

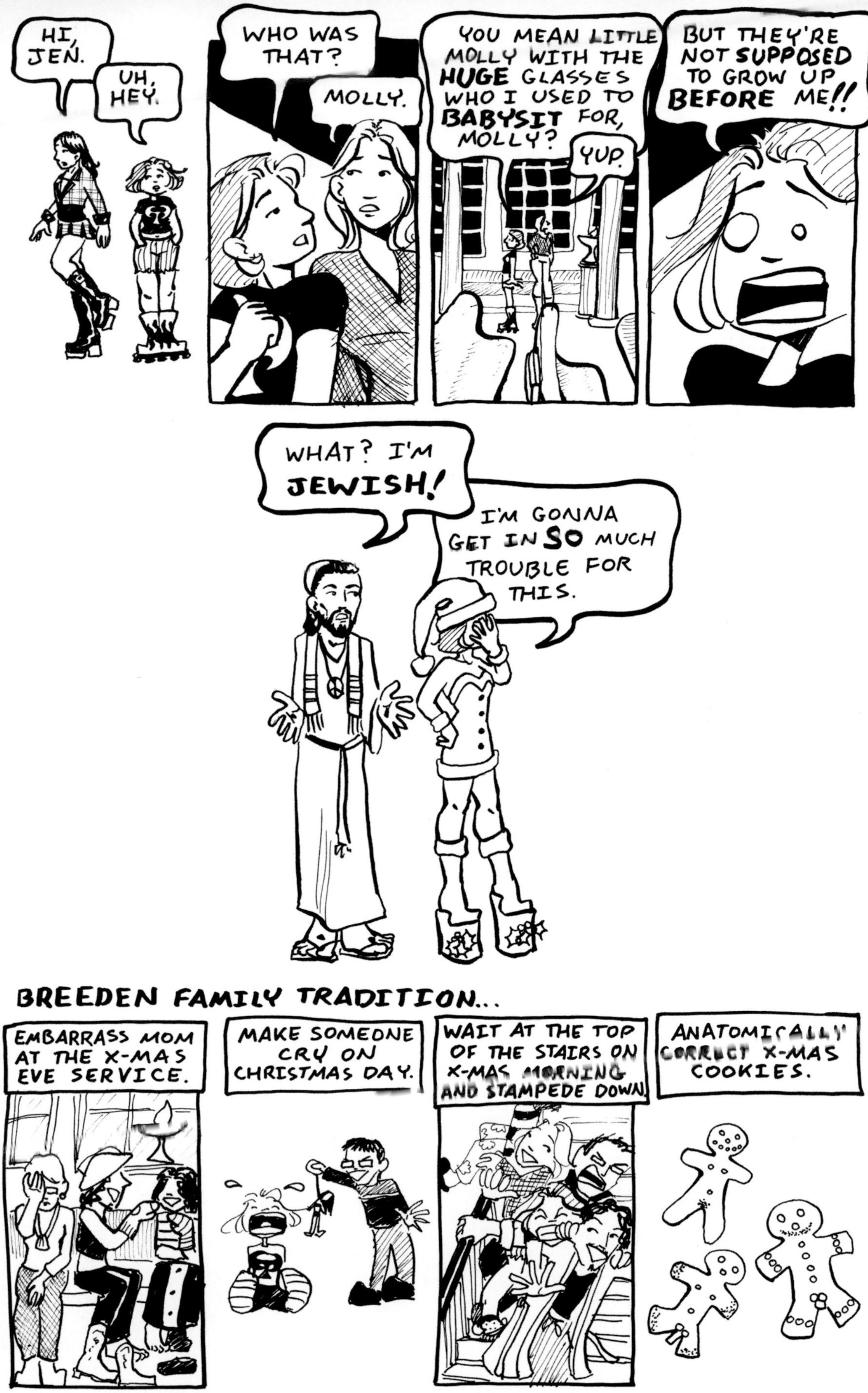
HI, JEN.
UH, HEY.
WHO WAS THAT?
MOLLY.
YOU MEAN LITTLE MOLLY WITH THE HUGE GLASSES WHO I USED TO BABYSIT FOR, MOLLY?
YUP.
BUT THEY'RE NOT SUPPOSED TO GROW UP BEFORE ME!!
WHAT? I'M JEWISH!
I'M GONNA GET IN SO MUCH TROUBLE FOR THIS.
BREEDEN FAMILY TRADITION...
EMBARRASS MOM AT THE X-MAS EVE SERVICE.
MAKE SOMEONE CRY ON CHRISTMAS DAY.
WAIT AT THE TOP OF THE STAIRS ON X-MAS MORNING AND STAMPEDE DOWN.
ANATOMICALLY CORRECT X-MAS COOKIES.

HERE, JEN, MERRY X-MAS.

CLANG

I MADE YOU A **SHIELD** FOR WHEN YOU RUN AROUND IN THE WOODS AND HIT PEOPLE WITH PADDED STICKS.

PADDED IS THE OPERATIVE WORD HERE.

SO HOW'S LITTLE PRINCESS PORCELAIN?

FOOD?

FOOD!

WELL, SHE'S ALRIGHT...

BUT AFTER SHE STARTED PEEING OUT OF HER NAVEL...

FOOD! FOOD!

YOU REALIZED HE WAS A **PRINCE** PORCELAIN?

YUP.

FOOD! YOU WILL BE.

SO YOUR PIG'S A BOY. YOU GOING TO CHANGE HIS NAME?

WELL WE WERE THINKING ABOUT NAMING HIM—

CRASH

LITTLE **FUCKER!** GET OUT OF THERE!

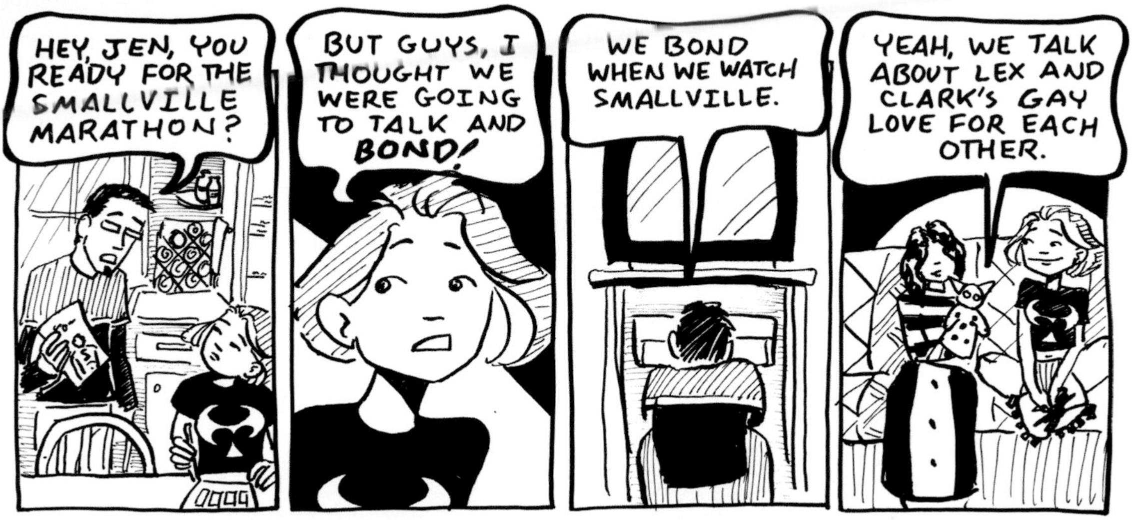
HEY, JEN, YOU READY FOR THE SMALLVILLE MARATHON?
BUT GUYS, I THOUGHT WE WERE GOING TO TALK AND BOND!
WE BOND WHEN WE WATCH SMALLVILLE.
YEAH, WE TALK ABOUT LEX AND CLARK'S GAY LOVE FOR EACH OTHER.

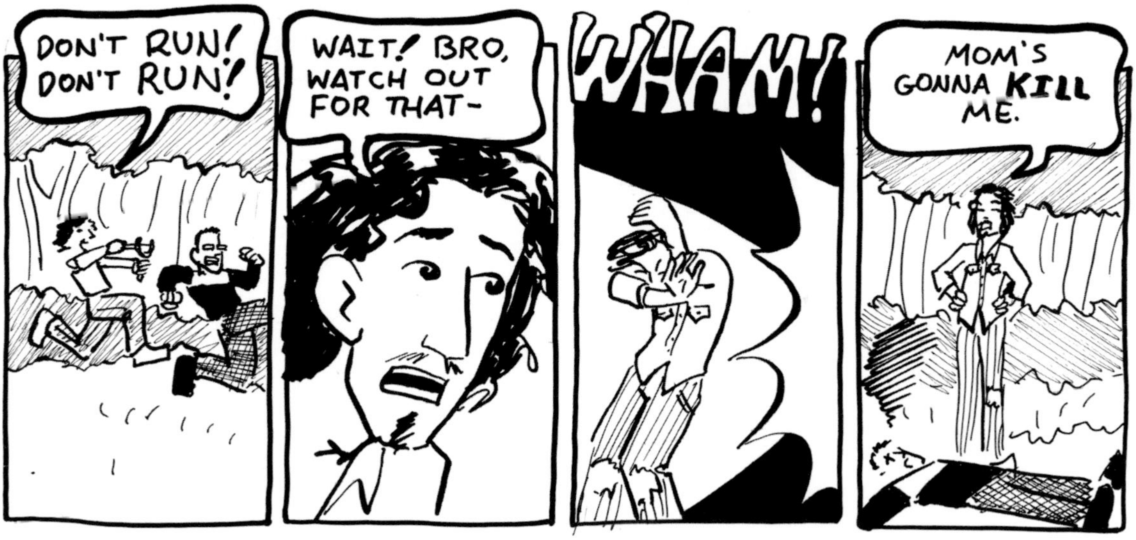
DON'T RUN! DON'T RUN!
WAIT! BRO, WATCH OUT FOR THAT-
WHAM!
MOM'S GONNA KILL ME.

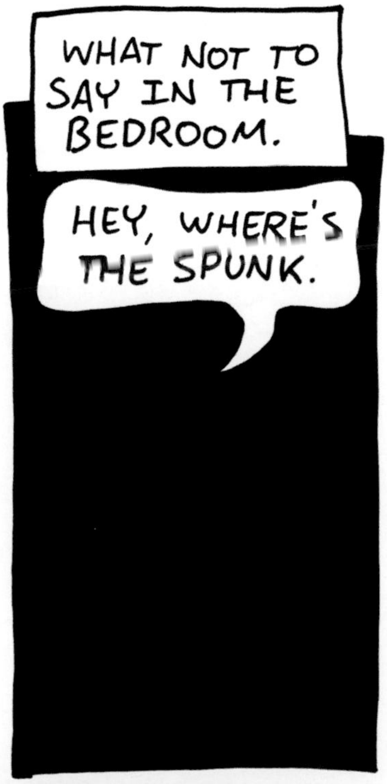
WHAT NOT TO SAY IN THE BEDROOM.
HEY, WHERE'S THE SPUNK.

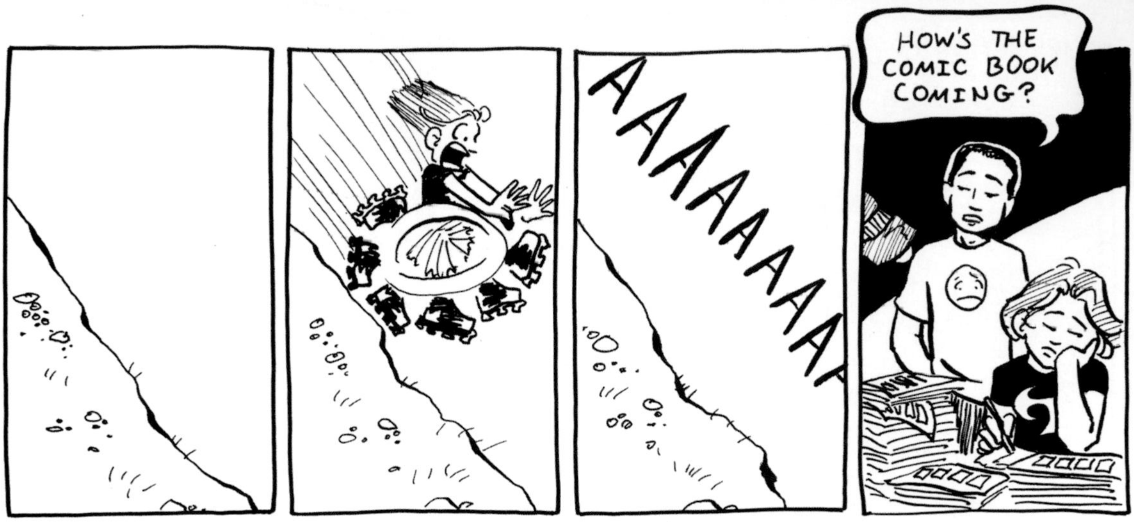
AAAAAAAAA
HOW'S THE COMIC BOOK COMING?

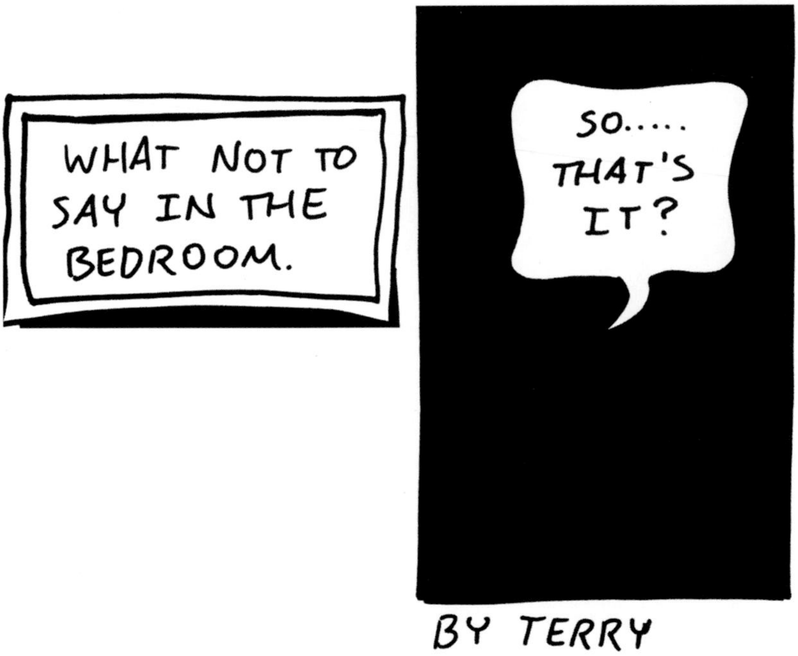
WHAT NOT TO SAY IN THE BEDROOM.
SO..... THAT'S IT?
BY TERRY

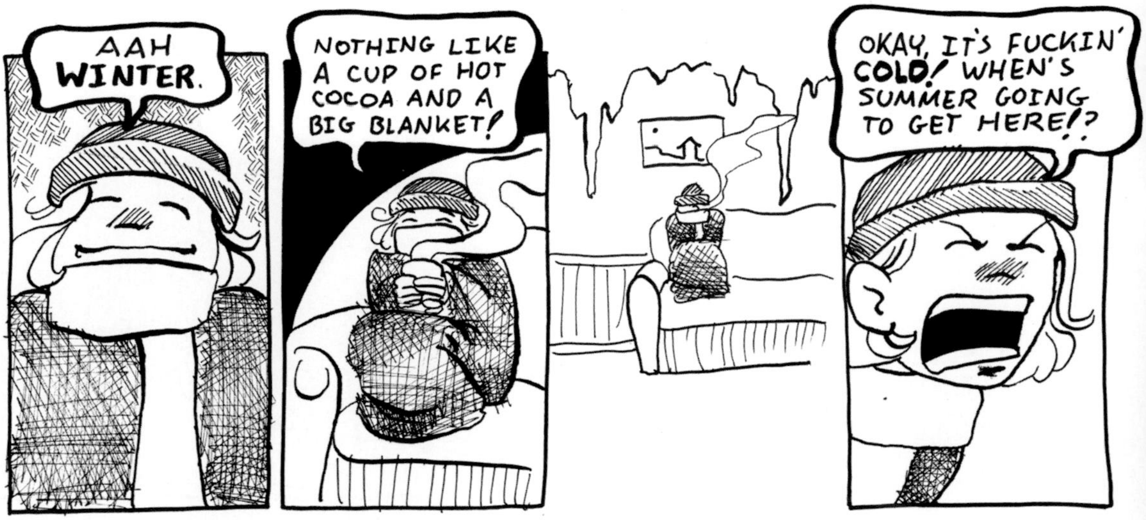
AAH WINTER.
NOTHING LIKE A CUP OF HOT COCOA AND A BIG BLANKET!
OKAY, IT'S FUCKIN' COLD! WHEN'S SUMMER GOING TO GET HERE!?

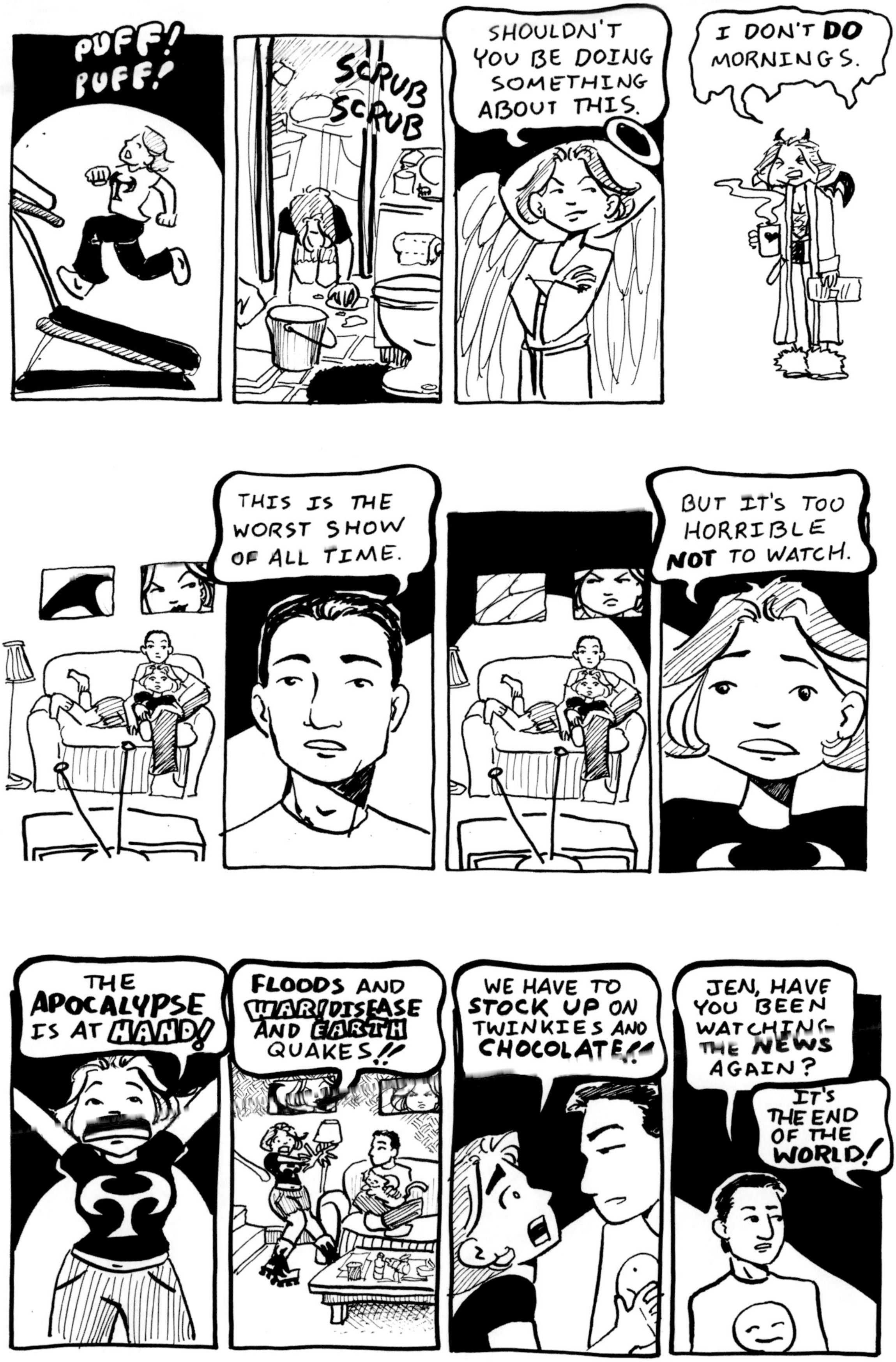
PUFF! PUFF!
SCRUB SCRUB
SHOULDN'T YOU BE DOING SOMETHING ABOUT THIS.
I DON'T DO MORNINGS.
THIS IS THE WORST SHOW OF ALL TIME.
BUT IT'S TOO HORRIBLE NOT TO WATCH.
THE APOCALYPSE IS AT HAND!
FLOODS AND WAR! DISEASE AND EARTH QUAKES!!
WE HAVE TO STOCK UP ON TWINKIES AND CHOCOLATE!!
JEN, HAVE YOU BEEN WATCHING THE NEWS AGAIN?
IT'S THE END OF THE WORLD!

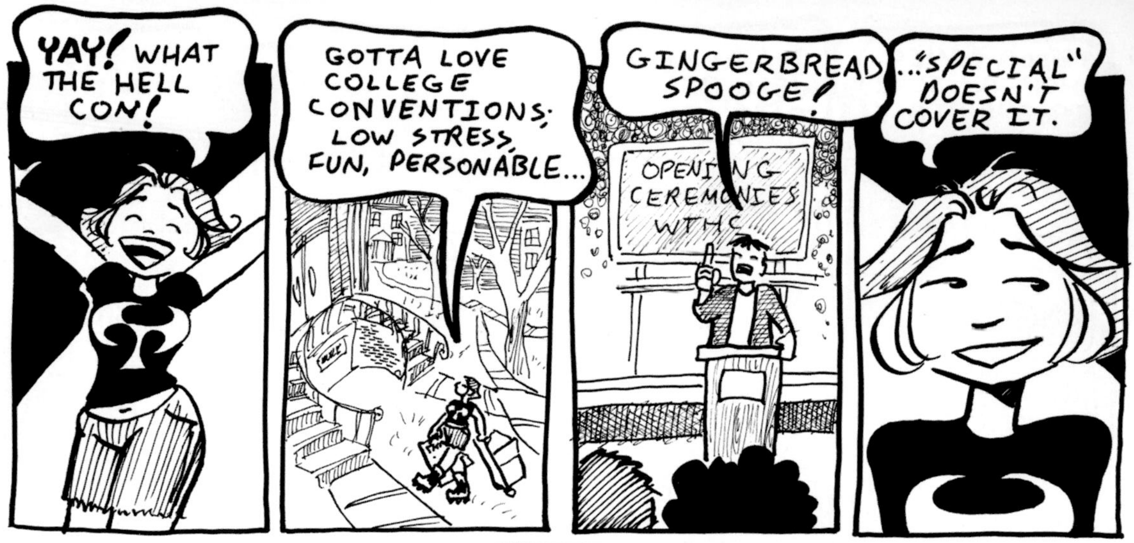
YAY! WHAT THE HELL CON!
GOTTA LOVE COLLEGE CONVENTIONS: LOW STRESS, FUN, PERSONABLE...
OPENING CEREMONIES WTHC
GINGERBREAD SPOOGE!
..."SPECIAL" DOESN'T COVER IT.

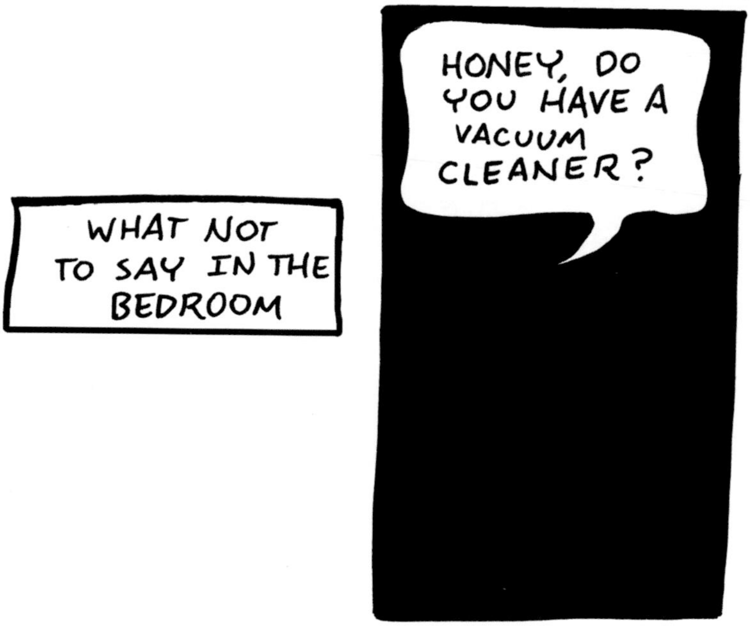
WHAT NOT TO SAY IN THE BEDROOM
HONEY, DO YOU HAVE A VACUUM CLEANER?

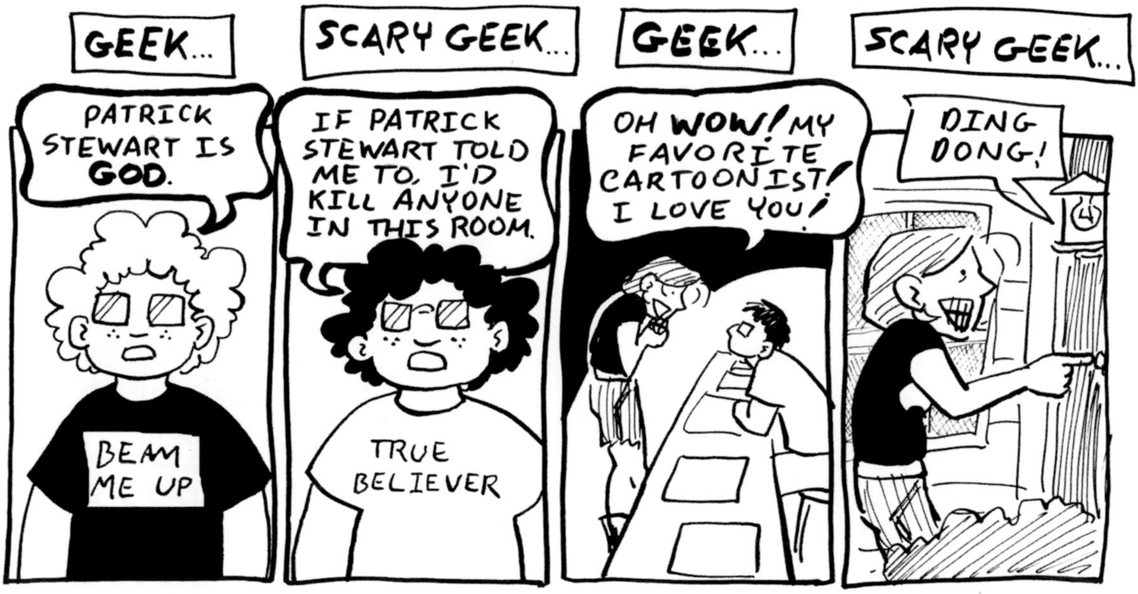
GEEK...
PATRICK STEWART IS GOD.
BEAM ME UP
SCARY GEEK...
IF PATRICK STEWART TOLD ME TO, I'D KILL ANYONE IN THIS ROOM.
TRUE BELIEVER
GEEK...
OH WOW! MY FAVORITE CARTOONIST! I LOVE YOU!
SCARY GEEK...
DING DONG!

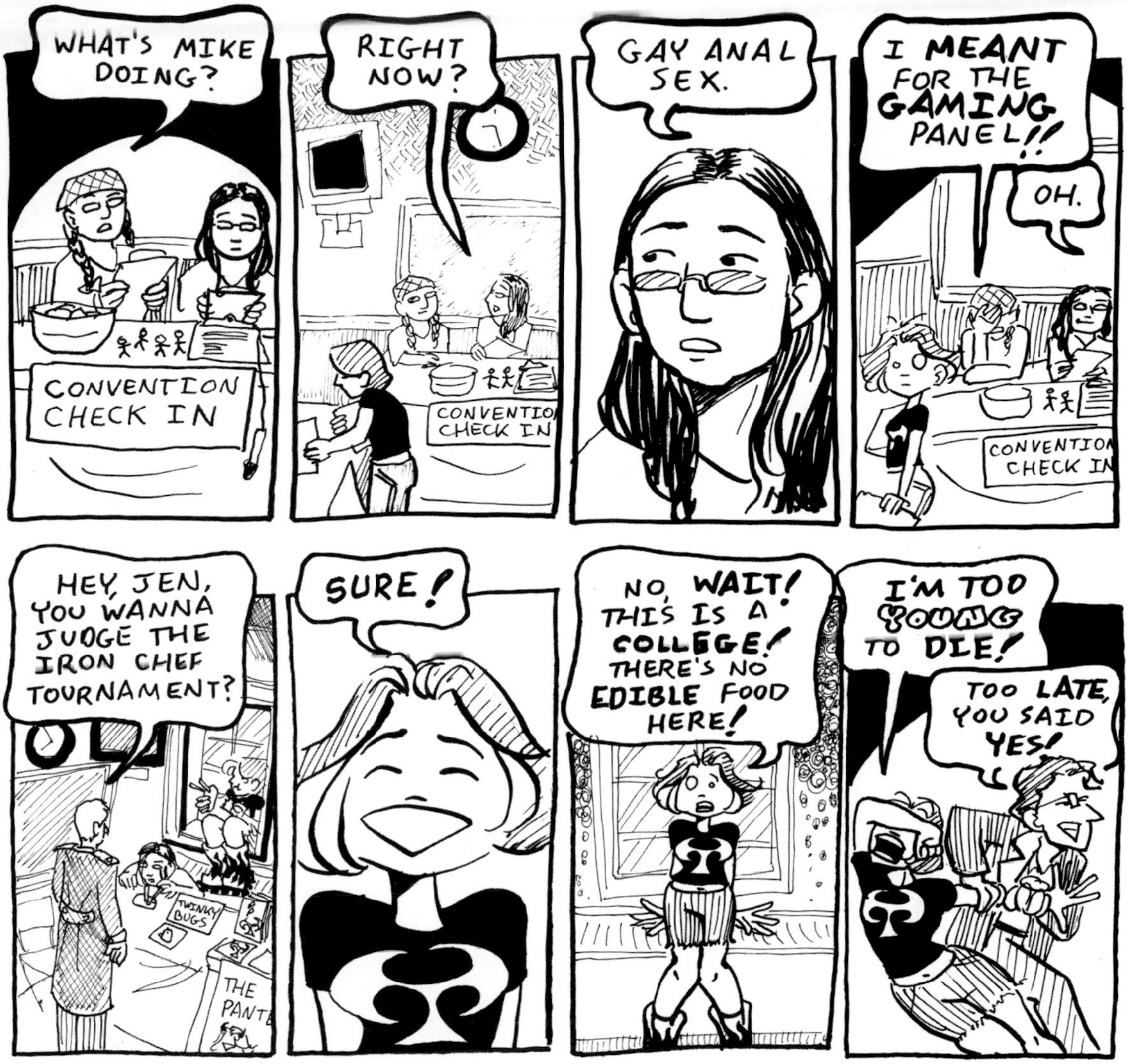
WHAT'S MIKE DOING?
CONVENTION CHECK IN
RIGHT NOW?
CONVENTION CHECK IN
GAY ANAL SEX.
I MEANT FOR THE GAMING PANEL!!
OH.
CONVENTION CHECK IN
HEY, JEN, YOU WANNA JUDGE THE IRON CHEF TOURNAMENT?
TWINKY BUGS
THE PANT
SURE!
NO, WAIT! THIS IS A COLLEGE! THERE'S NO EDIBLE FOOD HERE!
I'M TOO YOUNG TO DIE!
TOO LATE, YOU SAID YES!

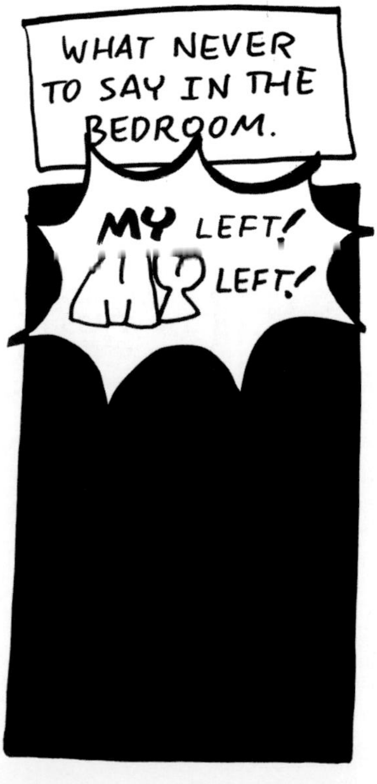
WHAT NEVER TO SAY IN THE BEDROOM.
MY LEFT!
LEFT!

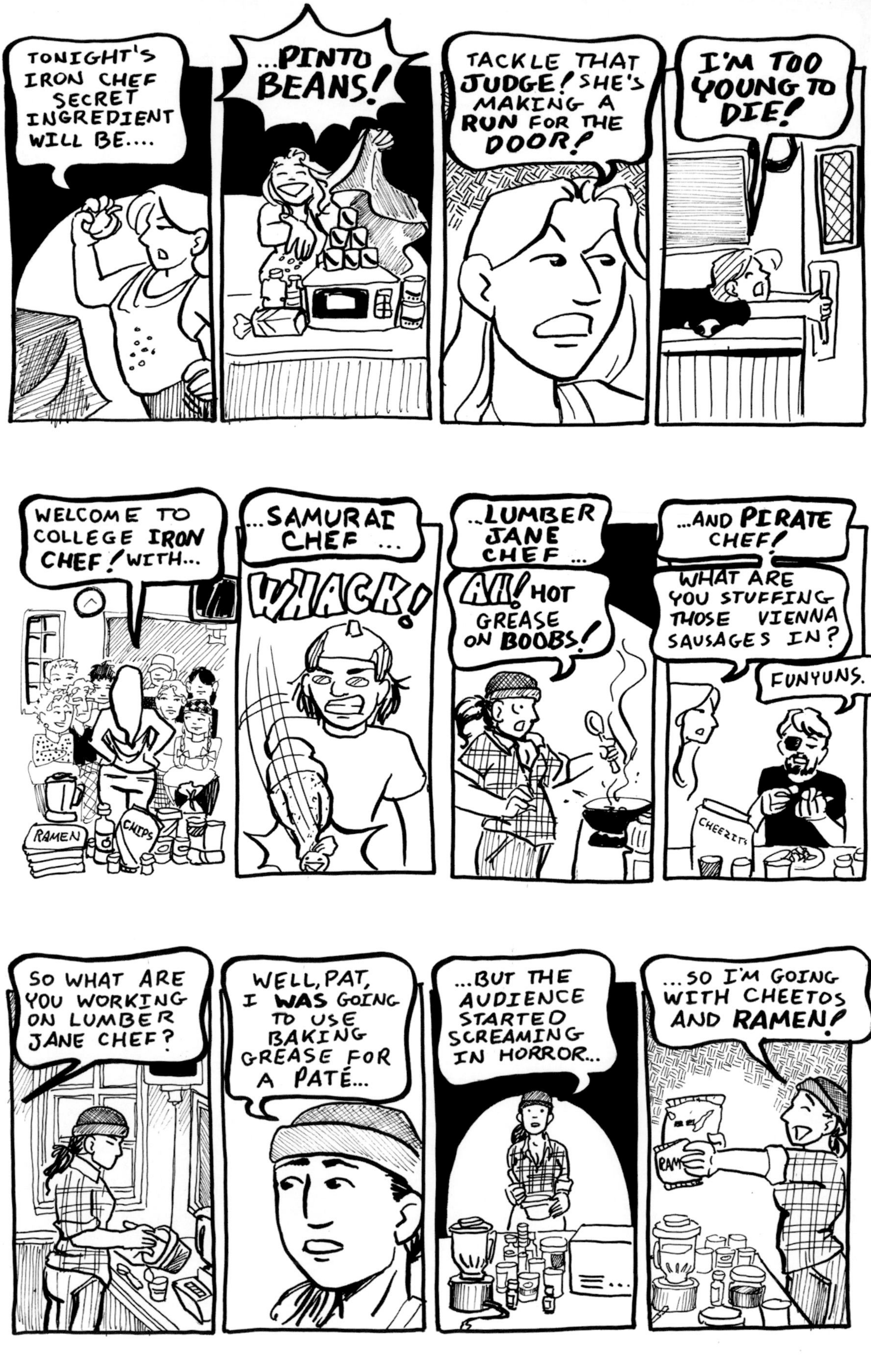
TONIGHT'S IRON CHEF SECRET INGREDIENT WILL BE....
...PINTO BEANS!
TACKLE THAT JUDGE! SHE'S MAKING A RUN FOR THE DOOR!
I'M TOO YOUNG TO DIE!
WELCOME TO COLLEGE IRON CHEF! WITH...
RAMEN
CHIPS
...SAMURAI CHEF ...
WHACK!
..LUMBER JANE CHEF ...
AII! HOT GREASE ON BOOBS!
...AND PIRATE CHEF!
WHAT ARE YOU STUFFING THOSE VIENNA SAUSAGES IN?
FUNYUNS.
CHEEZITS
SO WHAT ARE YOU WORKING ON LUMBER JANE CHEF?
WELL, PAT, I WAS GOING TO USE BAKING GREASE FOR A PATÉ...
...BUT THE AUDIENCE STARTED SCREAMING IN HORROR...
...SO I'M GOING WITH CHEETOS AND RAMEN!

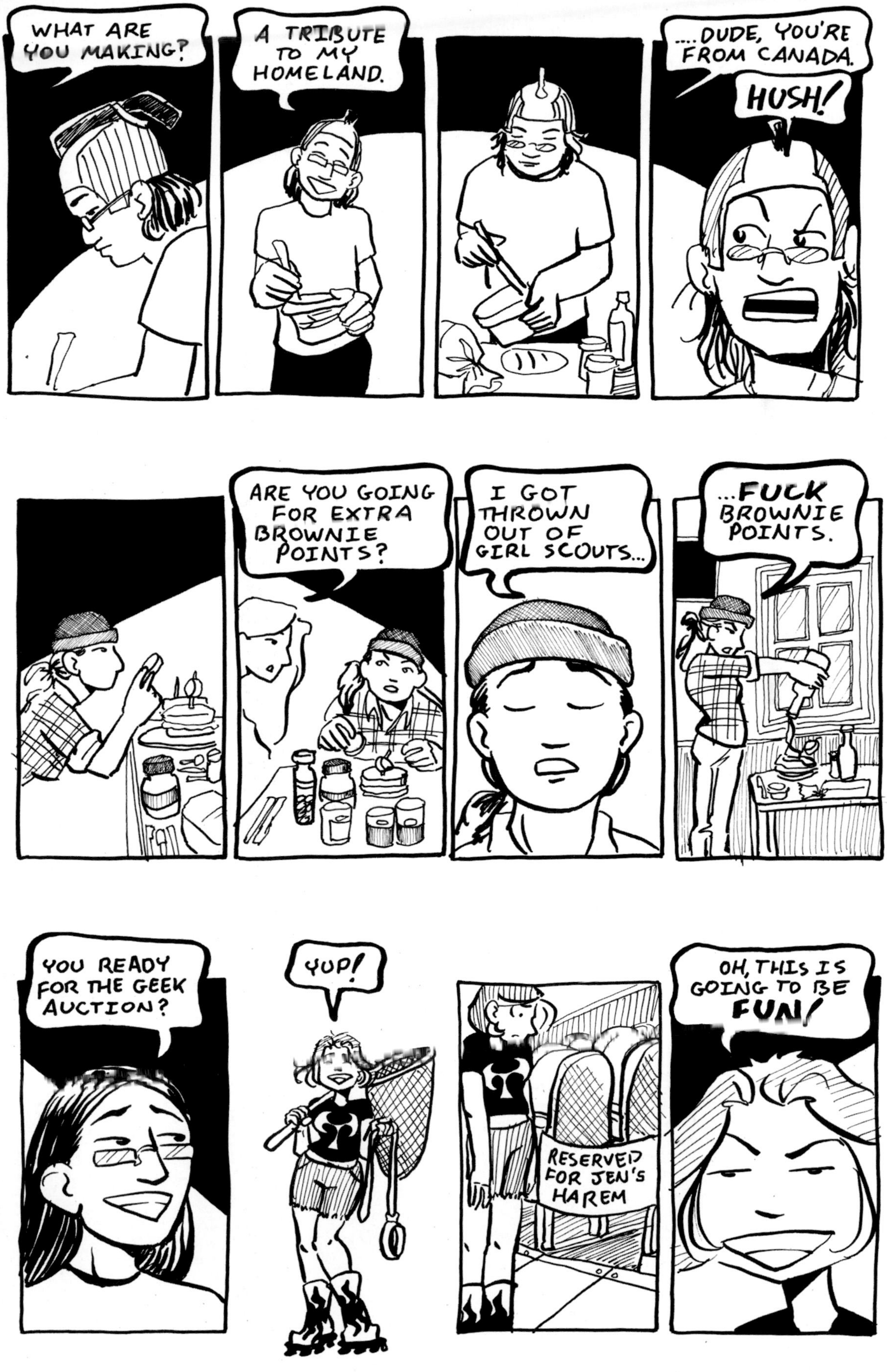
WHAT ARE YOU MAKING?
A TRIBUTE TO MY HOMELAND.
....DUDE, YOU'RE FROM CANADA.
HUSH!
ARE YOU GOING FOR EXTRA BROWNIE POINTS?
I GOT THROWN OUT OF GIRL SCOUTS...
...FUCK BROWNIE POINTS.
YOU READY FOR THE GEEK AUCTION?
YUP!
RESERVED FOR JEN'S HAREM
OH, THIS IS GOING TO BE FUN!

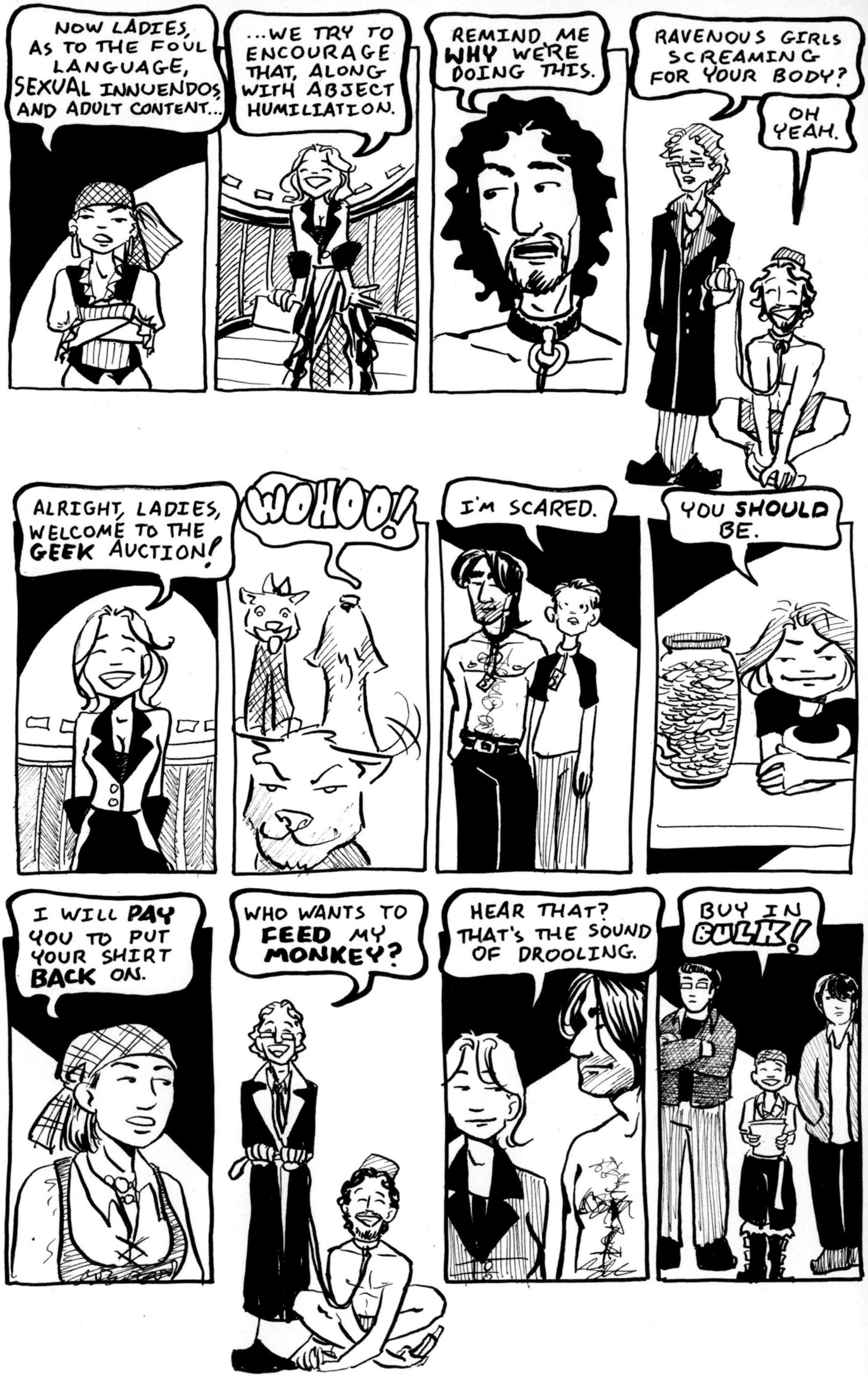
NOW LADIES, AS TO THE FOUL LANGUAGE, SEXUAL INNUENDOS AND ADULT CONTENT...
...WE TRY TO ENCOURAGE THAT, ALONG WITH ABJECT HUMILIATION.
REMIND ME WHY WE'RE DOING THIS.
RAVENOUS GIRLS SCREAMING FOR YOUR BODY?
OH YEAH.
ALRIGHT, LADIES, WELCOME TO THE GEEK AUCTION!
WOHOO!
I'M SCARED.
YOU SHOULD BE.
I WILL PAY YOU TO PUT YOUR SHIRT BACK ON.
WHO WANTS TO FEED MY MONKEY?
HEAR THAT? THAT'S THE SOUND OF DROOLING.
BUY IN BULK!

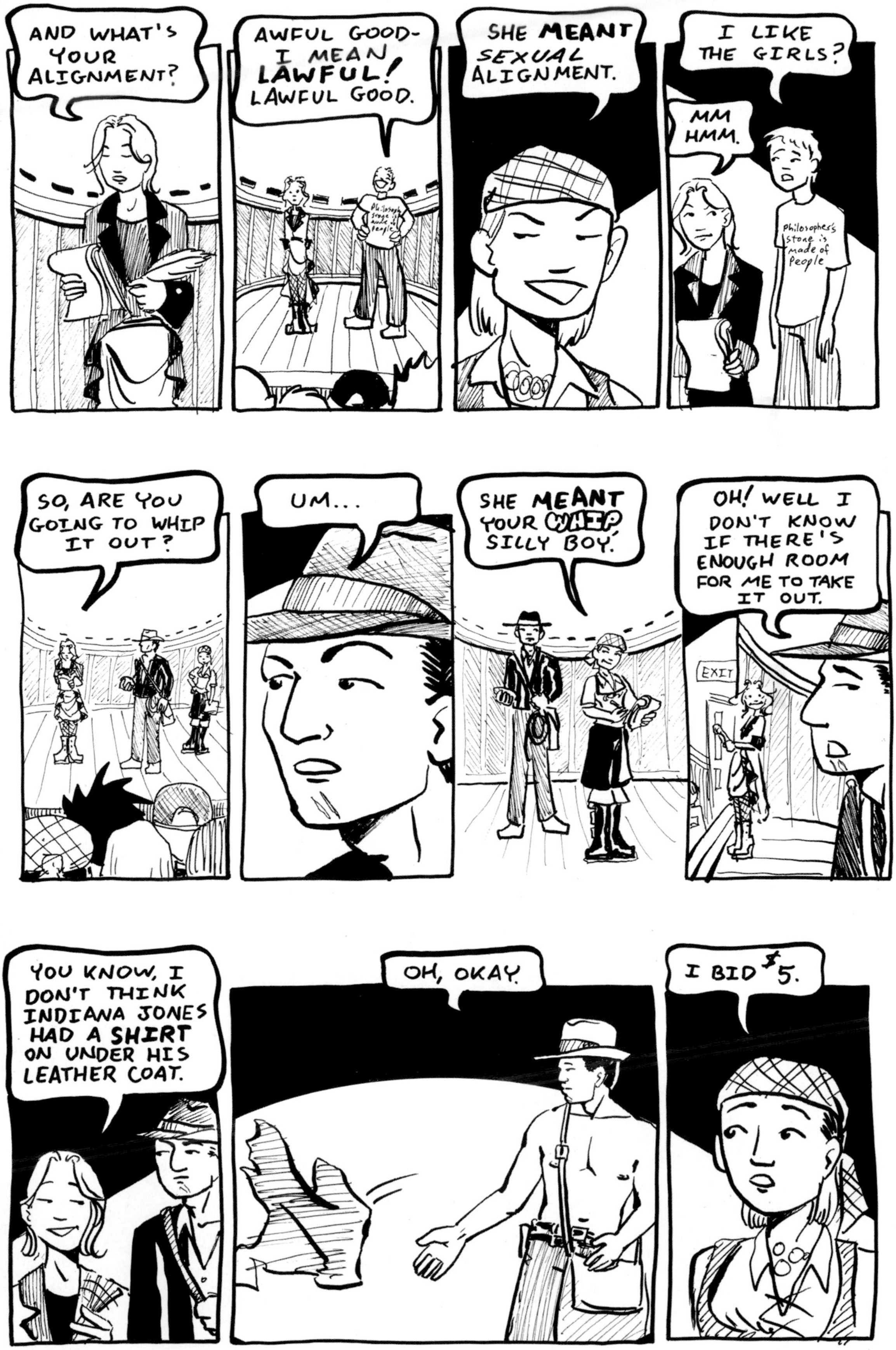
AND WHAT'S YOUR ALIGNMENT?
AWFUL GOOD- I MEAN LAWFUL! LAWFUL GOOD.
Philosopher's stone is made of people
SHE MEANT SEXUAL ALIGNMENT.
I LIKE THE GIRLS?
MM HMM.
Philosopher's stone is made of people
SO, ARE YOU GOING TO WHIP IT OUT?
UM...
SHE MEANT YOUR WHIP SILLY BOY.
OH! WELL I DON'T KNOW IF THERE'S ENOUGH ROOM FOR ME TO TAKE IT OUT.
EXIT
YOU KNOW, I DON'T THINK INDIANA JONES HAD A SHIRT ON UNDER HIS LEATHER COAT.
OH, OKAY.
I BID $5.

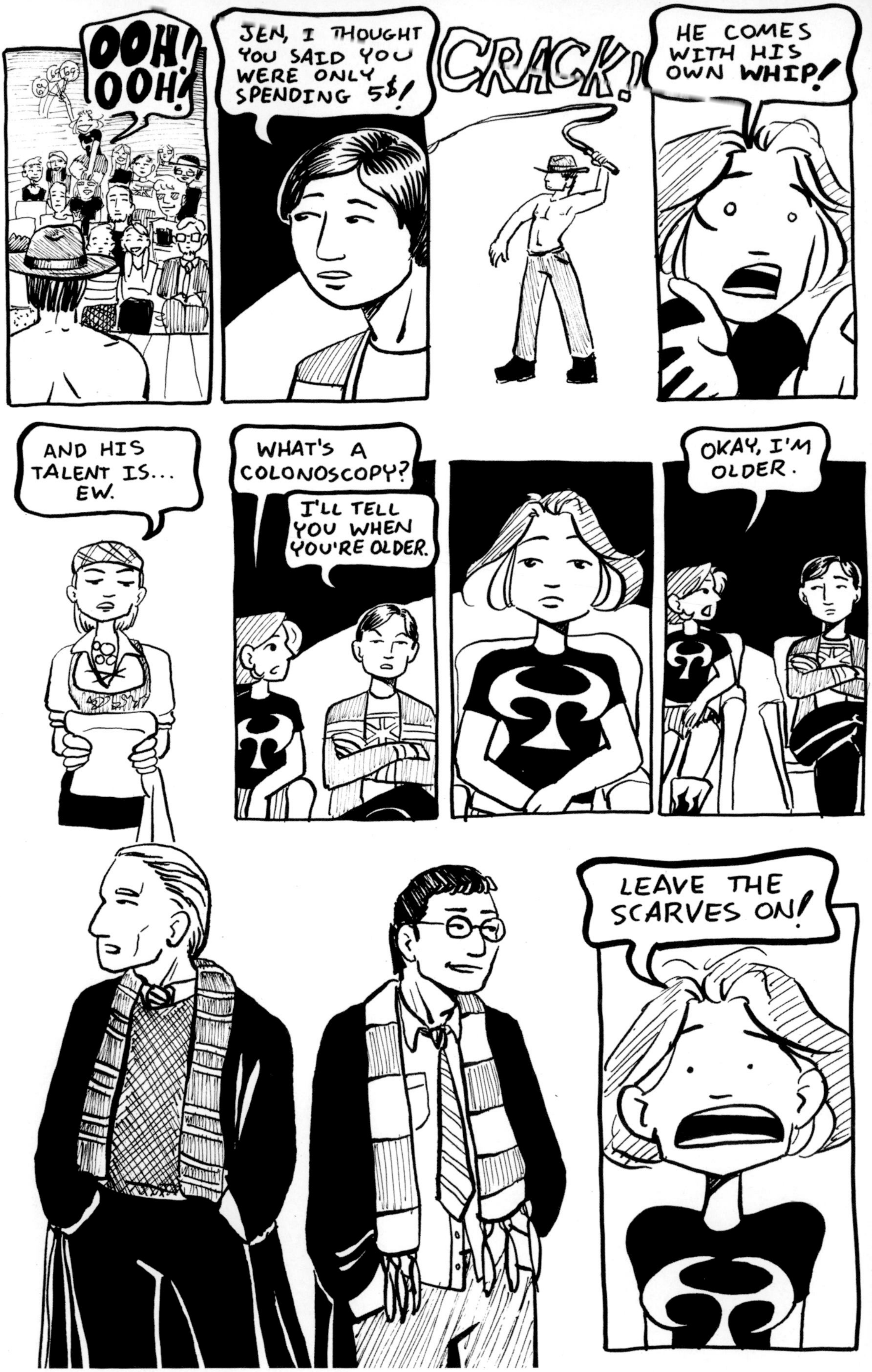
OOH! OOH!
JEN, I THOUGHT YOU SAID YOU WERE ONLY SPENDING 5$!
CRACK!
HE COMES WITH HIS OWN WHIP!
AND HIS TALENT IS... EW.
WHAT'S A COLONOSCOPY?
I'LL TELL YOU WHEN YOU'RE OLDER.
OKAY, I'M OLDER.
LEAVE THE SCARVES ON!

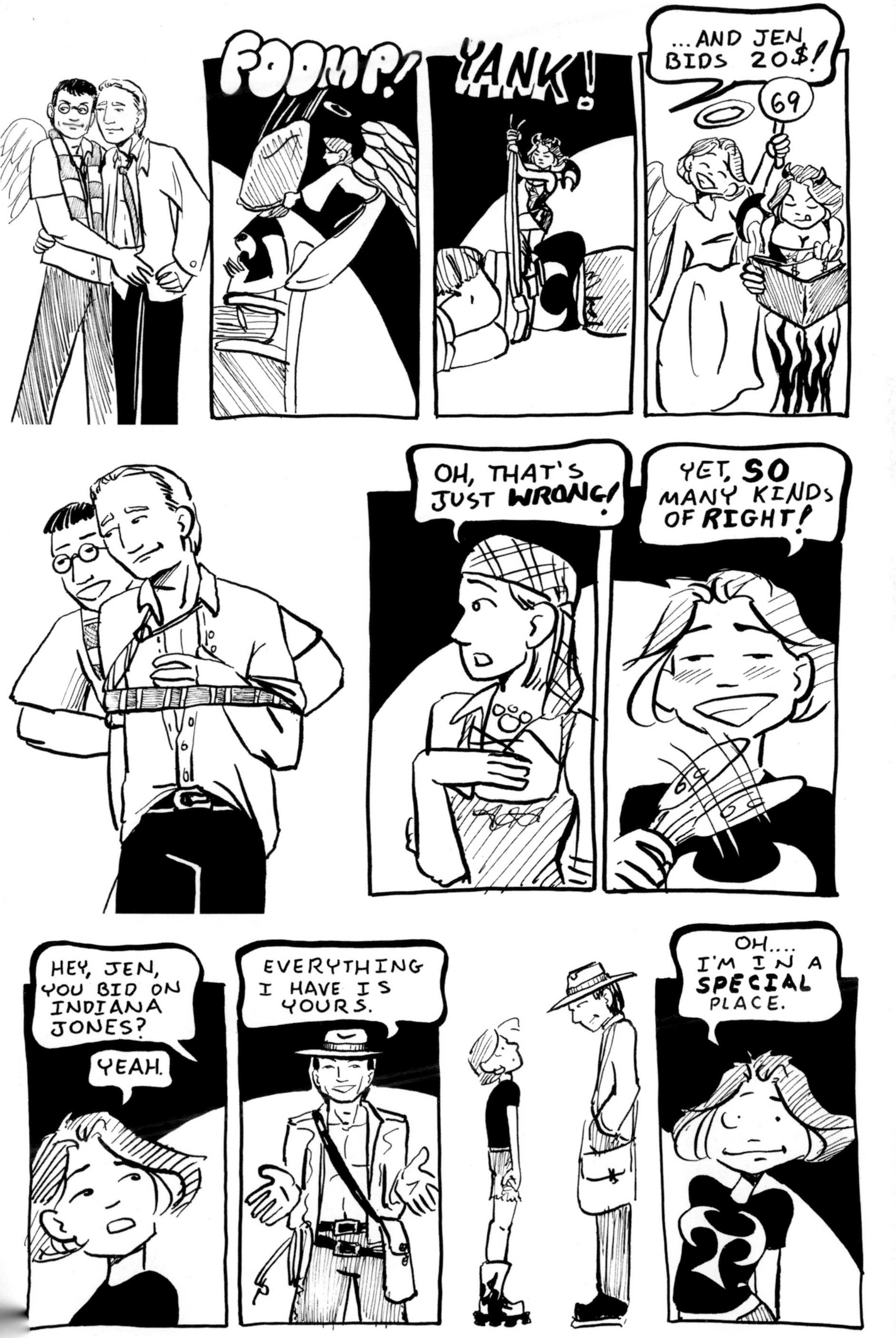
FOOMP!
YANK!
...AND JEN BIDS 20$!
69
OH, THAT'S JUST WRONG!
YET, SO MANY KINDS OF RIGHT!
HEY, JEN, YOU BID ON INDIANA JONES?
YEAH.
EVERYTHING I HAVE IS YOURS.
OH.... I'M IN A SPECIAL PLACE.

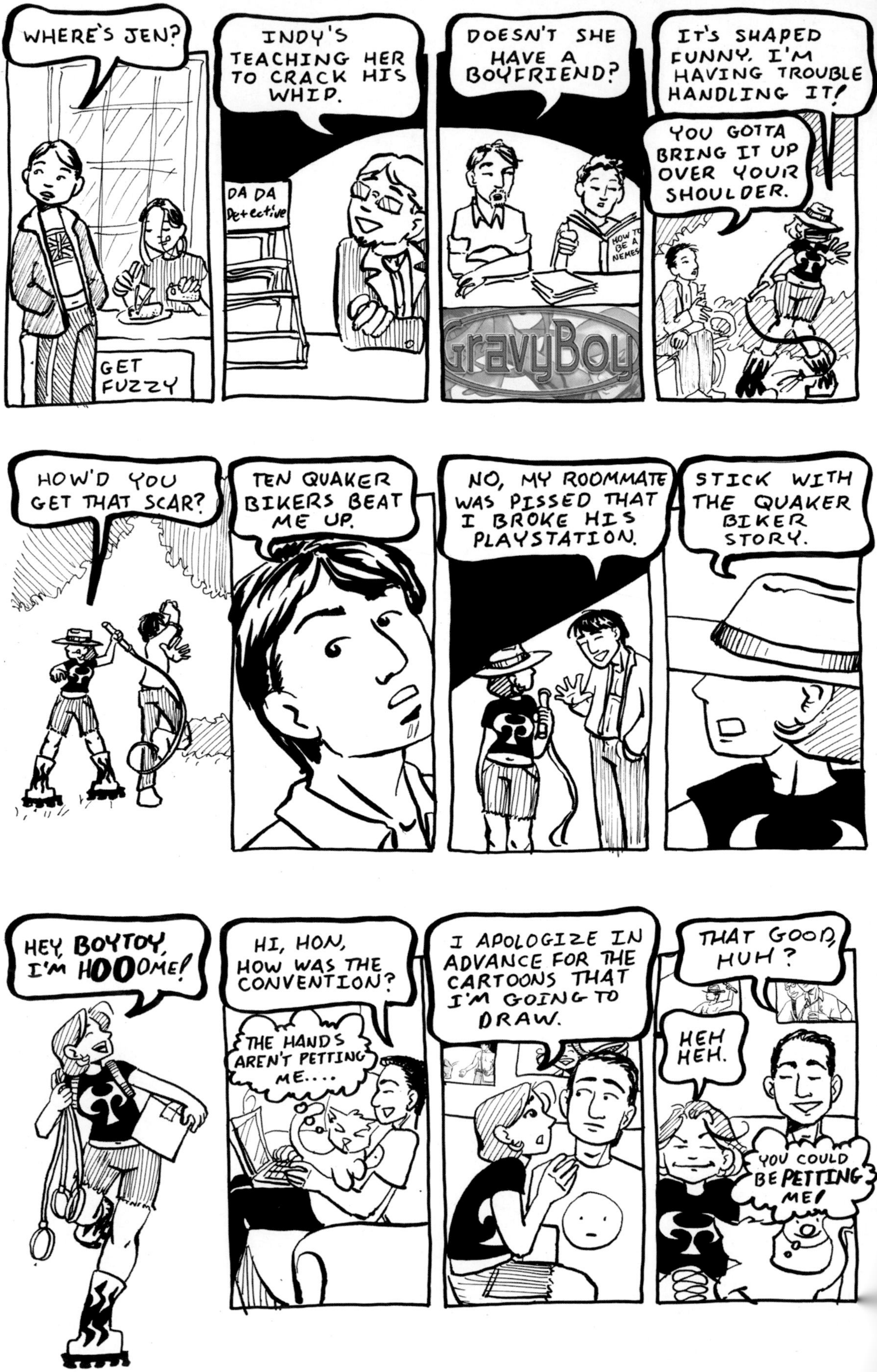
WHERE'S JEN?
GET FUZZY
INDY'S TEACHING HER TO CRACK HIS WHIP.
DA DA Detective
DOESN'T SHE HAVE A BOYFRIEND?
HOW TO BE A NEMES
GravyBoy
IT'S SHAPED FUNNY. I'M HAVING TROUBLE HANDLING IT!
YOU GOTTA BRING IT UP OVER YOUR SHOULDER.
HOW'D YOU GET THAT SCAR?
TEN QUAKER BIKERS BEAT ME UP.
NO, MY ROOMMATE WAS PISSED THAT I BROKE HIS PLAYSTATION.
STICK WITH THE QUAKER BIKER STORY.
HEY, BOYTOY, I'M HOOOme!
HI, HON, HOW WAS THE CONVENTION?
THE HANDS AREN'T PETTING ME....
I APOLOGIZE IN ADVANCE FOR THE CARTOONS THAT I'M GOING TO DRAW.
THAT GOOD, HUH?
HEH HEH.
YOU COULD BE PETTING ME!

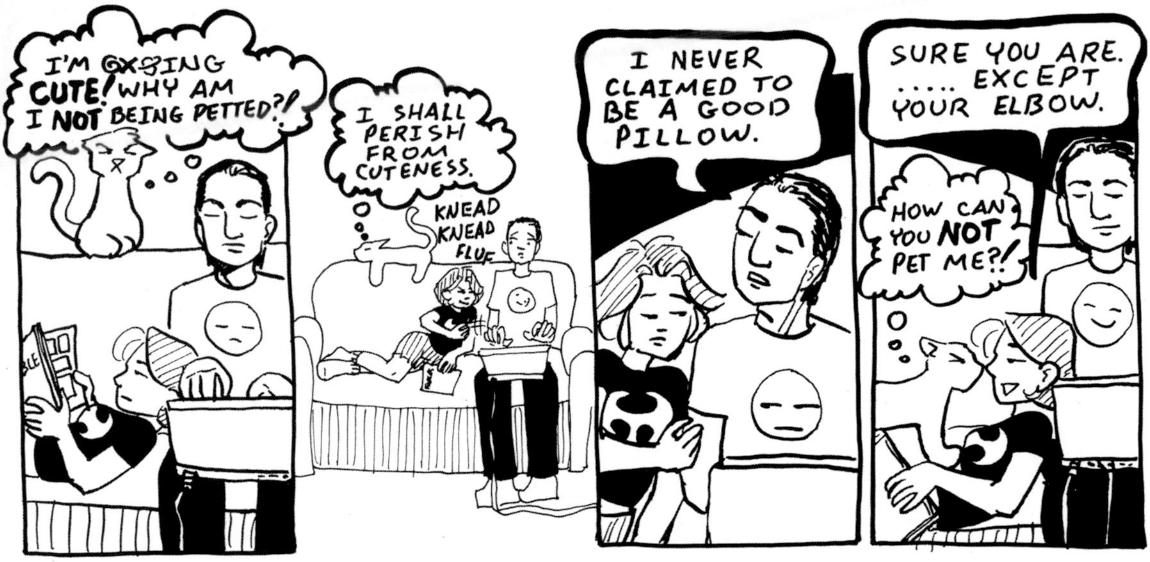
I'M @X$ING CUTE! WHY AM I NOT BEING PETTED?!
I SHALL PERISH FROM CUTENESS.
KNEAD KNEAD FLUF
I NEVER CLAIMED TO BE A GOOD PILLOW.
SURE YOU ARE. ..... EXCEPT YOUR ELBOW.
HOW CAN YOU NOT PET ME?!

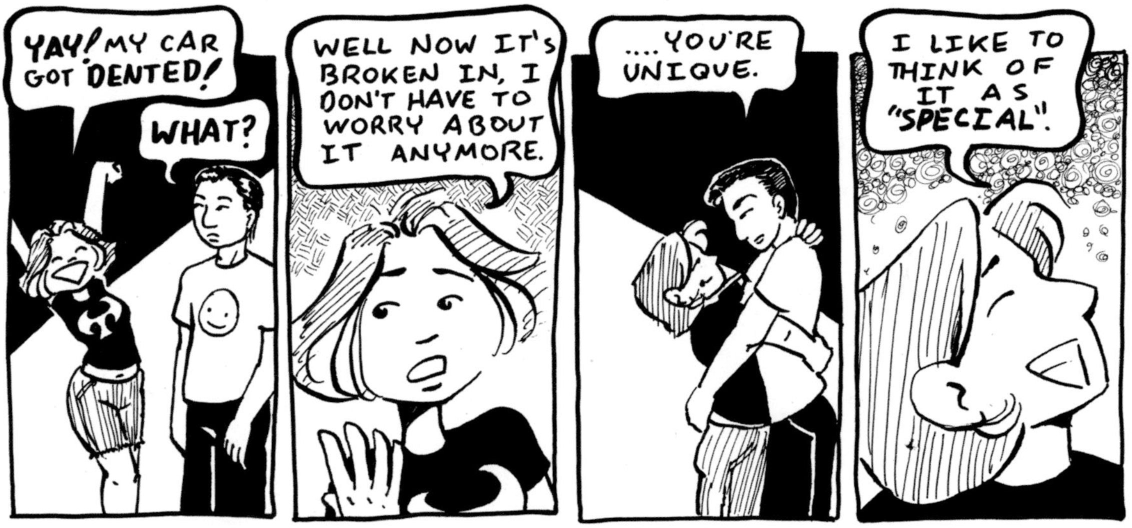
YAY! MY CAR GOT DENTED!
WHAT?
WELL NOW IT'S BROKEN IN, I DON'T HAVE TO WORRY ABOUT IT ANYMORE.
....YOU'RE UNIQUE.
I LIKE TO THINK OF IT AS "SPECIAL".

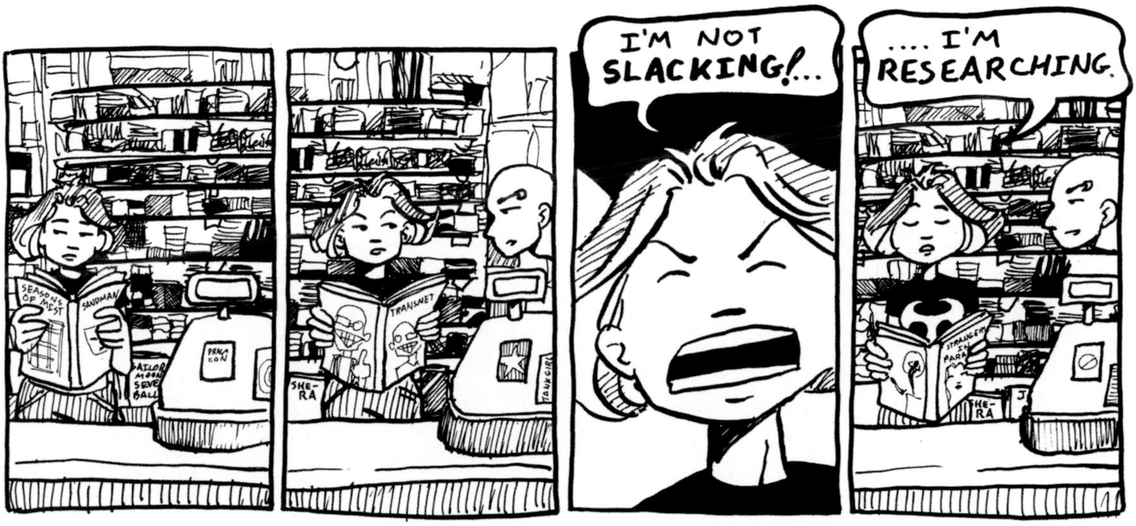
SANDMAN
SHE-RA
TRANSMET
I'M NOT SLACKING!...
....I'M RESEARCHING.

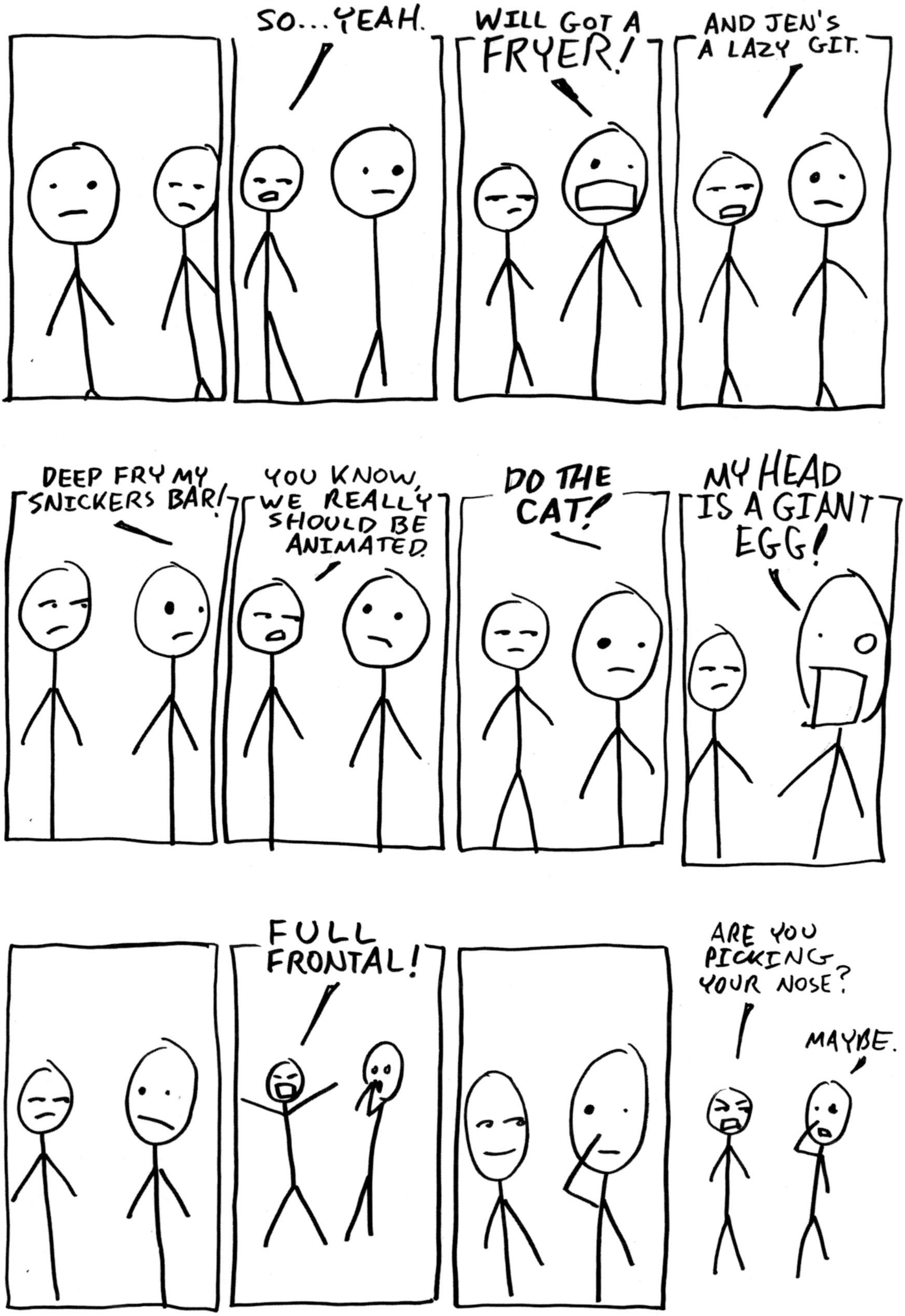
SO... YEAH.
WILL GOT A FRYER!
AND JEN'S A LAZY GIT.
DEEP FRY MY SNICKERS BAR!
YOU KNOW, WE REALLY SHOULD BE ANIMATED.
DO THE CAT!
MY HEAD IS A GIANT EGG!
FULL FRONTAL!
ARE YOU PICKING YOUR NOSE?
MAYBE.

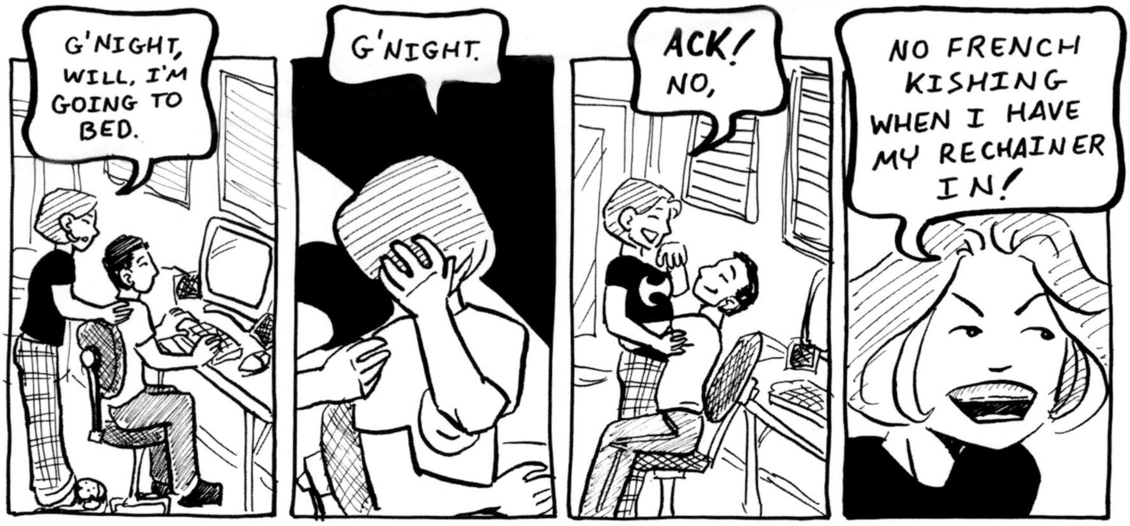
G'NIGHT, WILL, I'M GOING TO BED.
G'NIGHT.
ACK! NO,
NO FRENCH KISHING WHEN I HAVE MY RECHAINER IN!

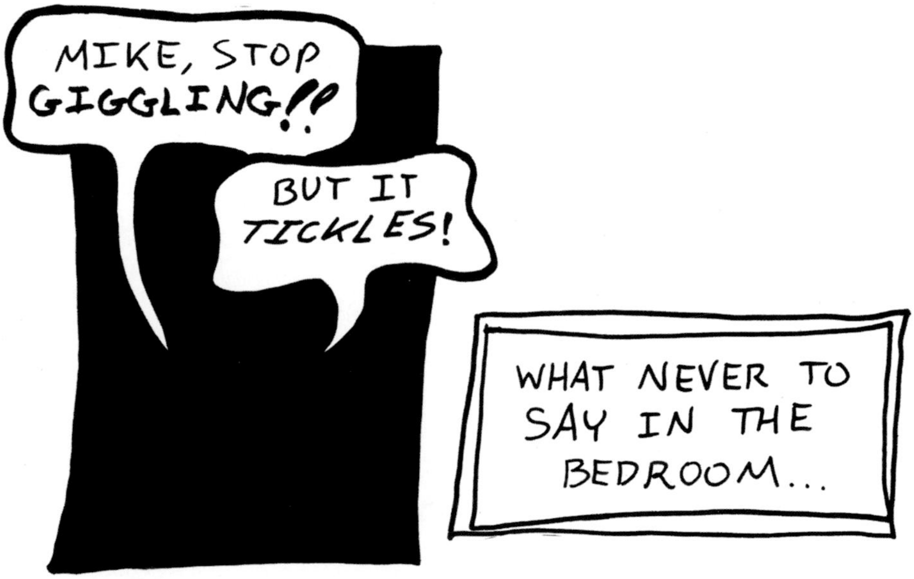
MIKE, STOP GIGGLING!!
BUT IT TICKLES!
WHAT NEVER TO SAY IN THE BEDROOM...

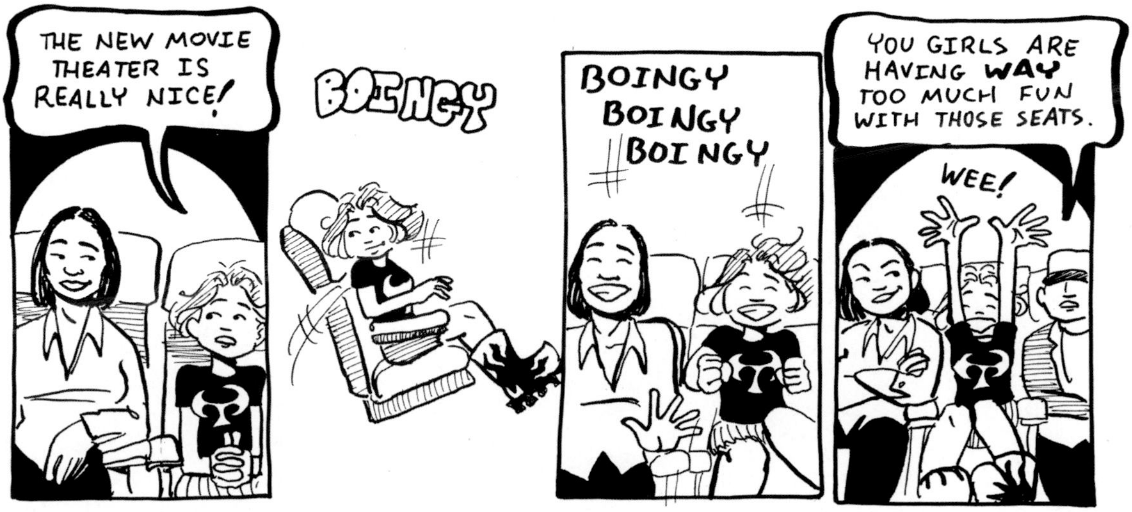
THE NEW MOVIE THEATER IS REALLY NICE!
BOINGY
BOINGY BOINGY BOINGY
YOU GIRLS ARE HAVING WAY TOO MUCH FUN WITH THOSE SEATS.
WEE!

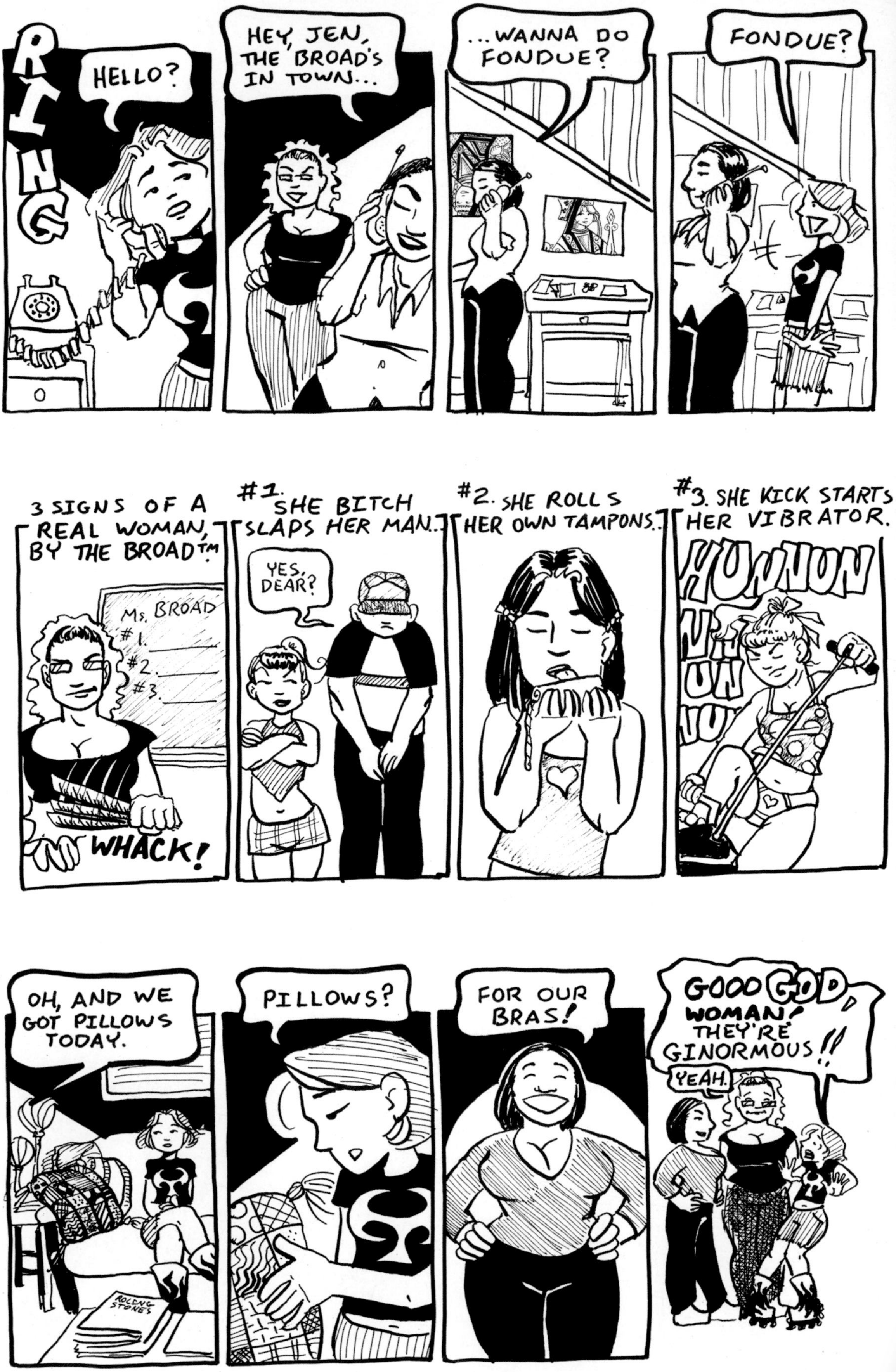
RING
HELLO?
HEY, JEN, THE BROAD'S IN TOWN...
...WANNA DO FONDUE?
FONDUE?
3 SIGNS OF A REAL WOMAN, BY THE BROAD™
MS. BROAD
#1.
#2.
#3.
WHACK!
#1. SHE BITCH SLAPS HER MAN...
YES, DEAR?
#2. SHE ROLLS HER OWN TAMPONS...
#3. SHE KICK STARTS HER VIBRATOR.
OH, AND WE GOT PILLOWS TODAY.
ROLLING STONES
PILLOWS?
FOR OUR BRAS!
GOOD GOD, WOMAN! THEY'RE GINORMOUS!!
YEAH.

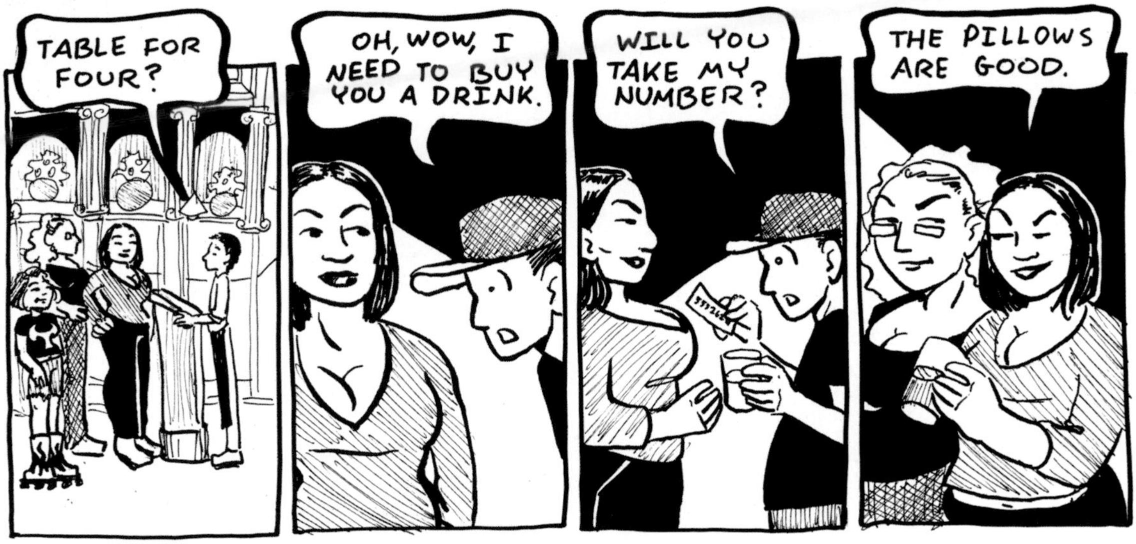
TABLE FOR FOUR?
OH, WOW, I NEED TO BUY YOU A DRINK.
WILL YOU TAKE MY NUMBER?
THE PILLOWS ARE GOOD.

You had to be there...

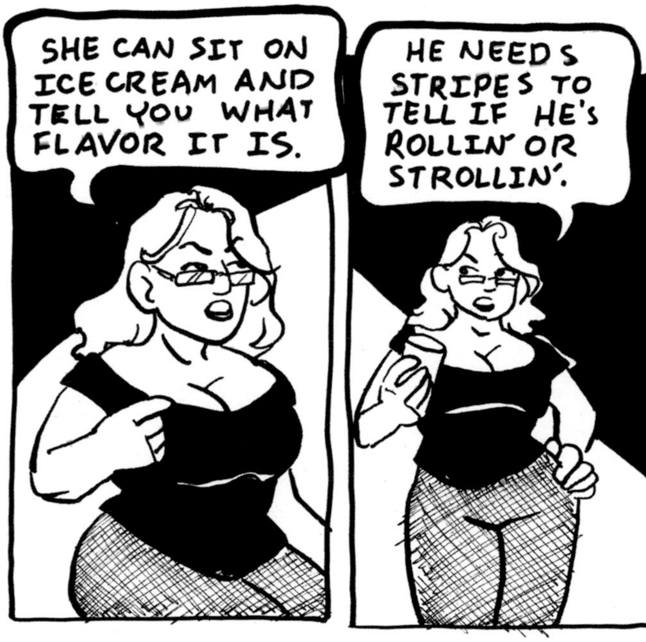
SHE CAN SIT ON ICE CREAM AND TELL YOU WHAT FLAVOR IT IS.
HE NEEDS STRIPES TO TELL IF HE'S ROLLIN' OR STROLLIN'.

DAME VS. BROAD.

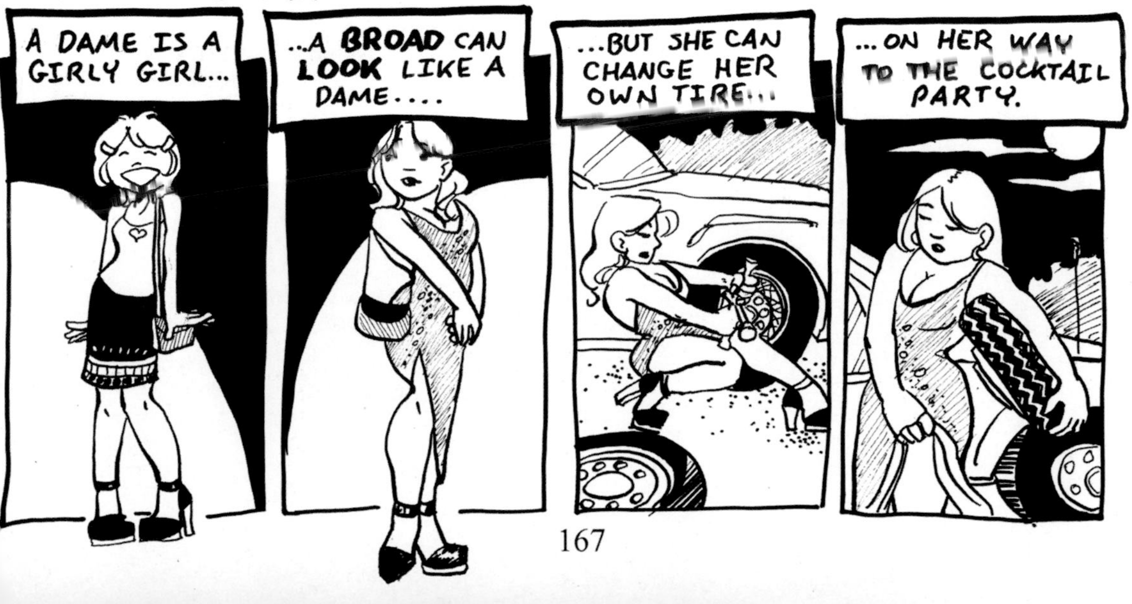
A DAME IS A GIRLY GIRL...
...A BROAD CAN LOOK LIKE A DAME....
...BUT SHE CAN CHANGE HER OWN TIRE...
...ON HER WAY TO THE COCKTAIL PARTY.

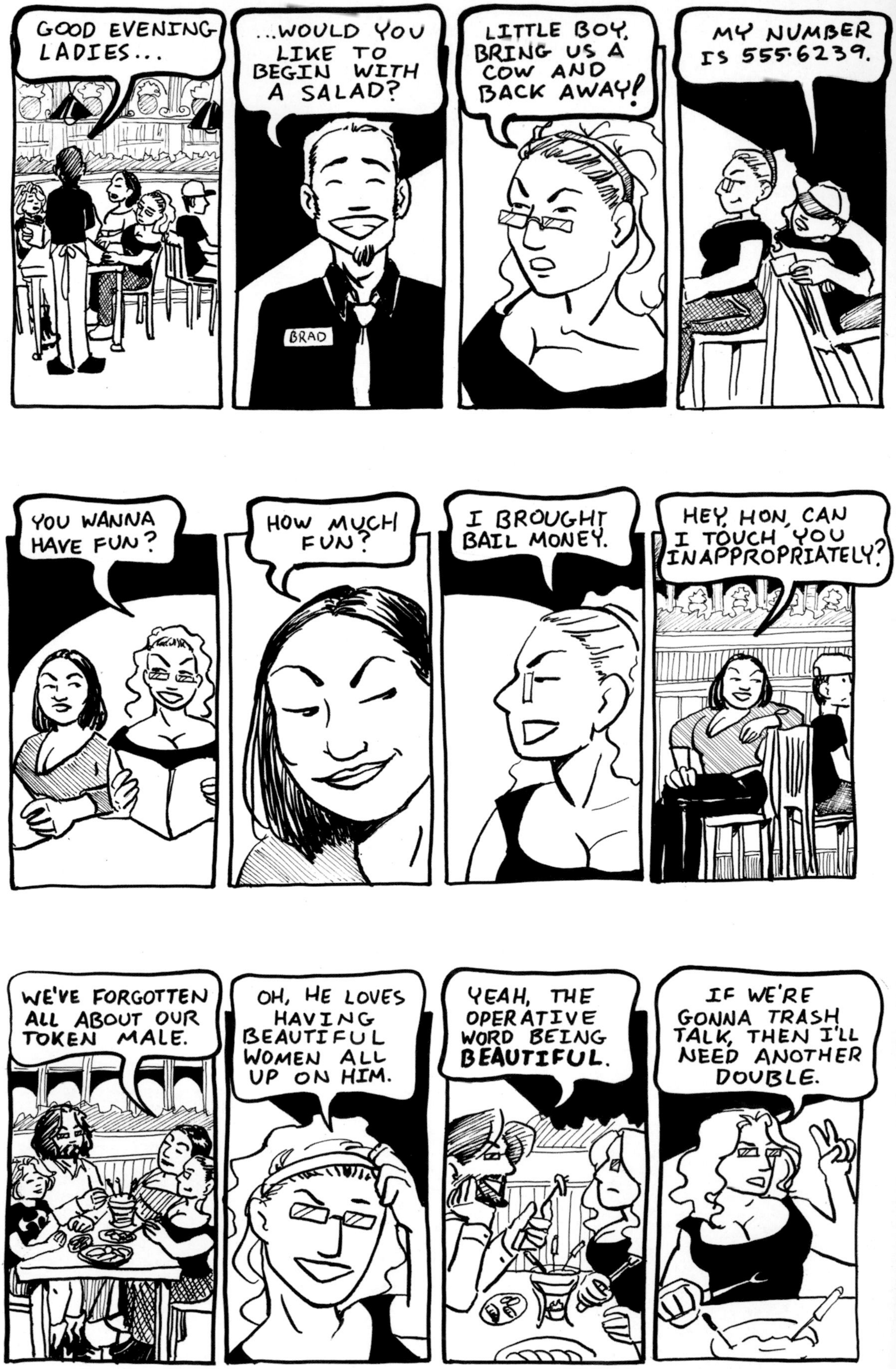
GOOD EVENING LADIES...
...WOULD YOU LIKE TO BEGIN WITH A SALAD?
BRAD
LITTLE BOY, BRING US A COW AND BACK AWAY!
MY NUMBER IS 555-6239.
YOU WANNA HAVE FUN?
HOW MUCH FUN?
I BROUGHT BAIL MONEY.
HEY, HON, CAN I TOUCH YOU INAPPROPRIATELY?
WE'VE FORGOTTEN ALL ABOUT OUR TOKEN MALE.
OH, HE LOVES HAVING BEAUTIFUL WOMEN ALL UP ON HIM.
YEAH, THE OPERATIVE WORD BEING **BEAUTIFUL**.
IF WE'RE GONNA TRASH TALK, THEN I'LL NEED ANOTHER DOUBLE.

THE BROAD

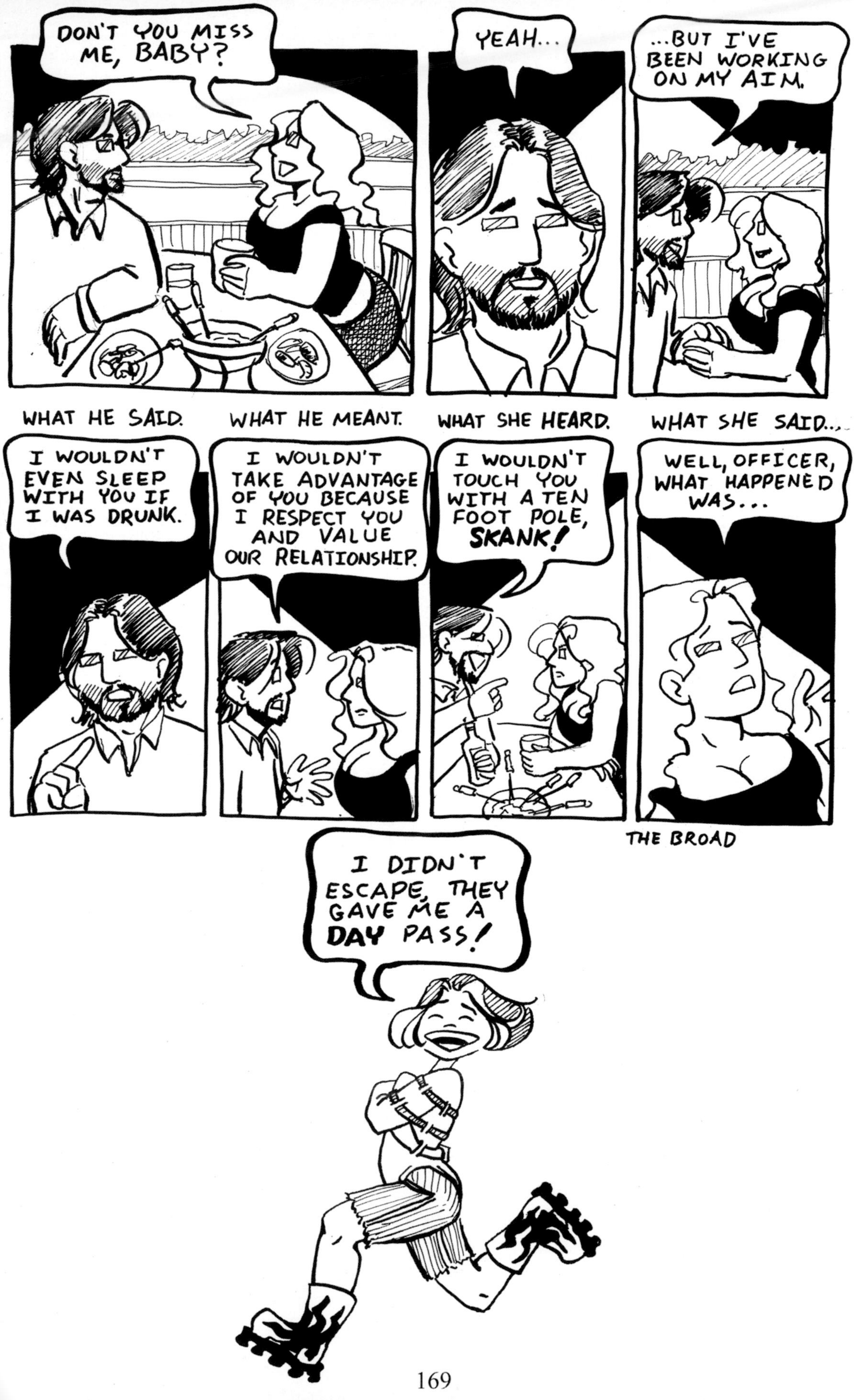
DON'T YOU MISS ME, BABY?
YEAH...
...BUT I'VE BEEN WORKING ON MY AIM.
WHAT HE SAID.
I WOULDN'T EVEN SLEEP WITH YOU IF I WAS DRUNK.
WHAT HE MEANT.
I WOULDN'T TAKE ADVANTAGE OF YOU BECAUSE I RESPECT YOU AND VALUE OUR RELATIONSHIP.
WHAT SHE HEARD.
I WOULDN'T TOUCH YOU WITH A TEN FOOT POLE, SKANK!
WHAT SHE SAID...
WELL, OFFICER, WHAT HAPPENED WAS...
THE BROAD
I DIDN'T ESCAPE, THEY GAVE ME A DAY PASS!

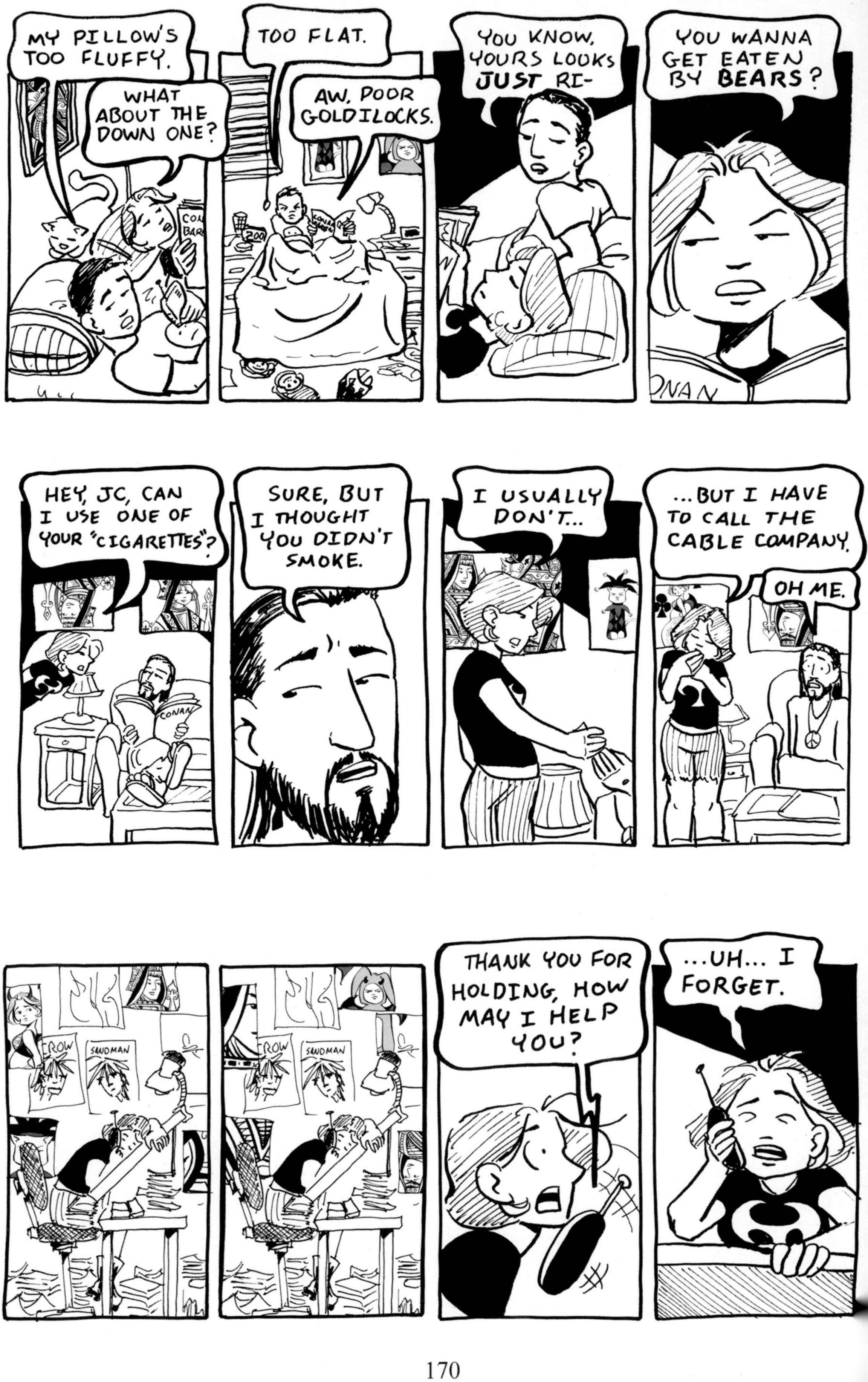
MY PILLOW'S TOO FLUFFY.
WHAT ABOUT THE DOWN ONE?
TOO FLAT.
AW, POOR GOLDILOCKS.
YOU KNOW, YOURS LOOKS JUST RI-
YOU WANNA GET EATEN BY BEARS?
HEY, JC, CAN I USE ONE OF YOUR "CIGARETTES"?
SURE, BUT I THOUGHT YOU DIDN'T SMOKE.
I USUALLY DON'T...
...BUT I HAVE TO CALL THE CABLE COMPANY.
OH ME.
CROW
SANDMAN
THANK YOU FOR HOLDING, HOW MAY I HELP YOU?
...UH... I FORGET.

MA'AM, WOULD YOU PLEASE HOLD?

SURE...

...AS LONG AS YOU KNOW THAT I'M DOING A TEQUILA SHOT FOR EVERY MINUTE I'M ON HOLD.

UH OH.

CAN'T SLEEP...

...CABLE GUY MIGHT CALL...

RING

HELLO!?

THIS IS THE CABLE COMPANY. HOW WAS THE SERVICE YOU RECEIVED?

WHAT SERVICE!?

FUCKING CABLE BULL IT LL TEAR RD IR RIPG IR INTE AND PUT ASH SEV ELLS AND GR AT MY FEE THE DEV R THE GO OUT EY HE ON EARTH.

WHAM! CRASH! WHUMP CRINKLE

I FOUND MY CHOCOLATE STASH...

...THE UNIVERSE MAY LIVE.

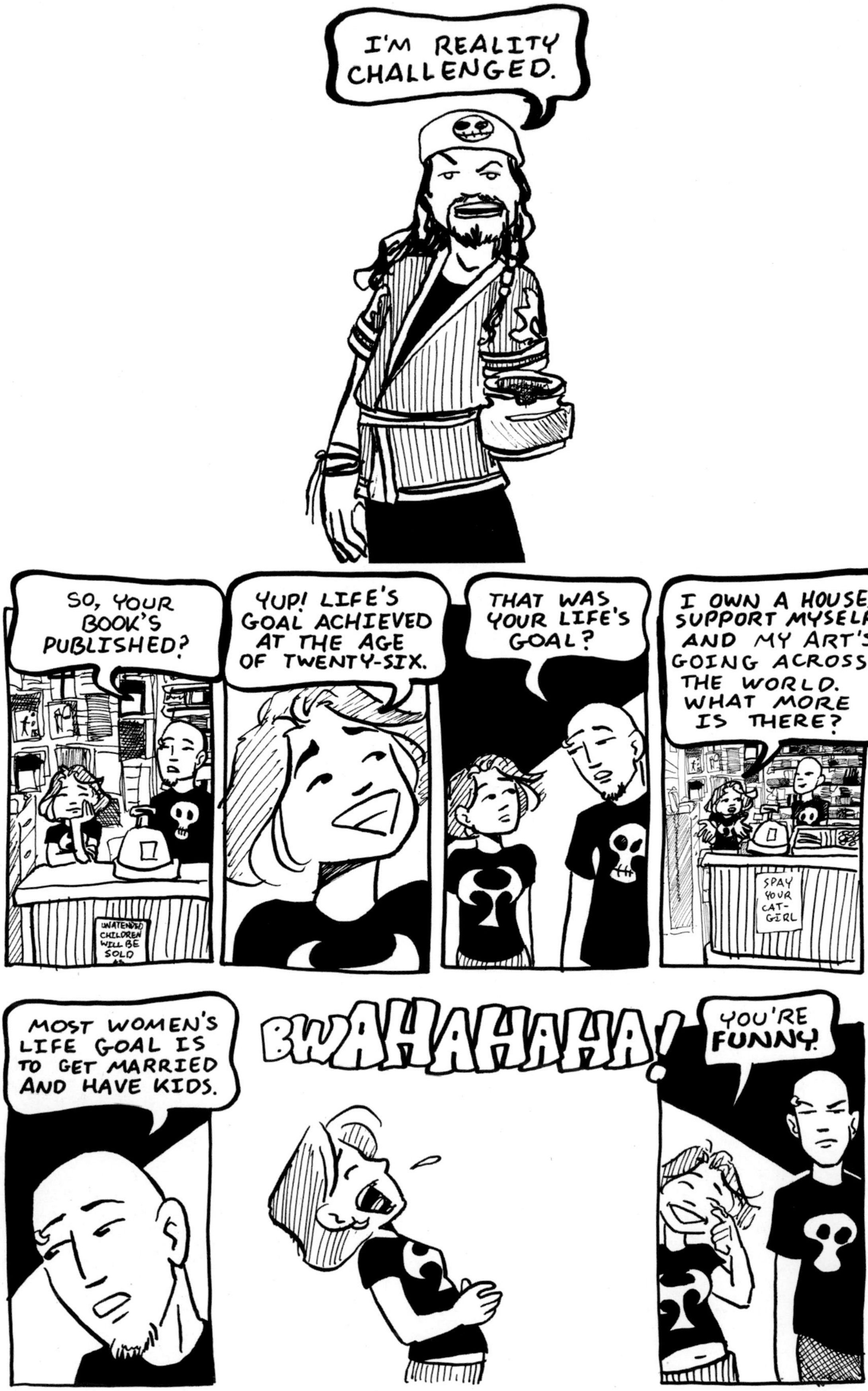
I'M REALITY CHALLENGED.
SO, YOUR BOOK'S PUBLISHED?
UNATTENDED CHILDREN WILL BE SOLD
YUP! LIFE'S GOAL ACHIEVED AT THE AGE OF TWENTY-SIX.
THAT WAS YOUR LIFE'S GOAL?
I OWN A HOUSE, SUPPORT MYSELF, AND MY ART'S GOING ACROSS THE WORLD. WHAT MORE IS THERE?
SPAY YOUR CAT-GIRL
MOST WOMEN'S LIFE GOAL IS TO GET MARRIED AND HAVE KIDS.
BWAHAHAHAHA!
YOU'RE FUNNY.

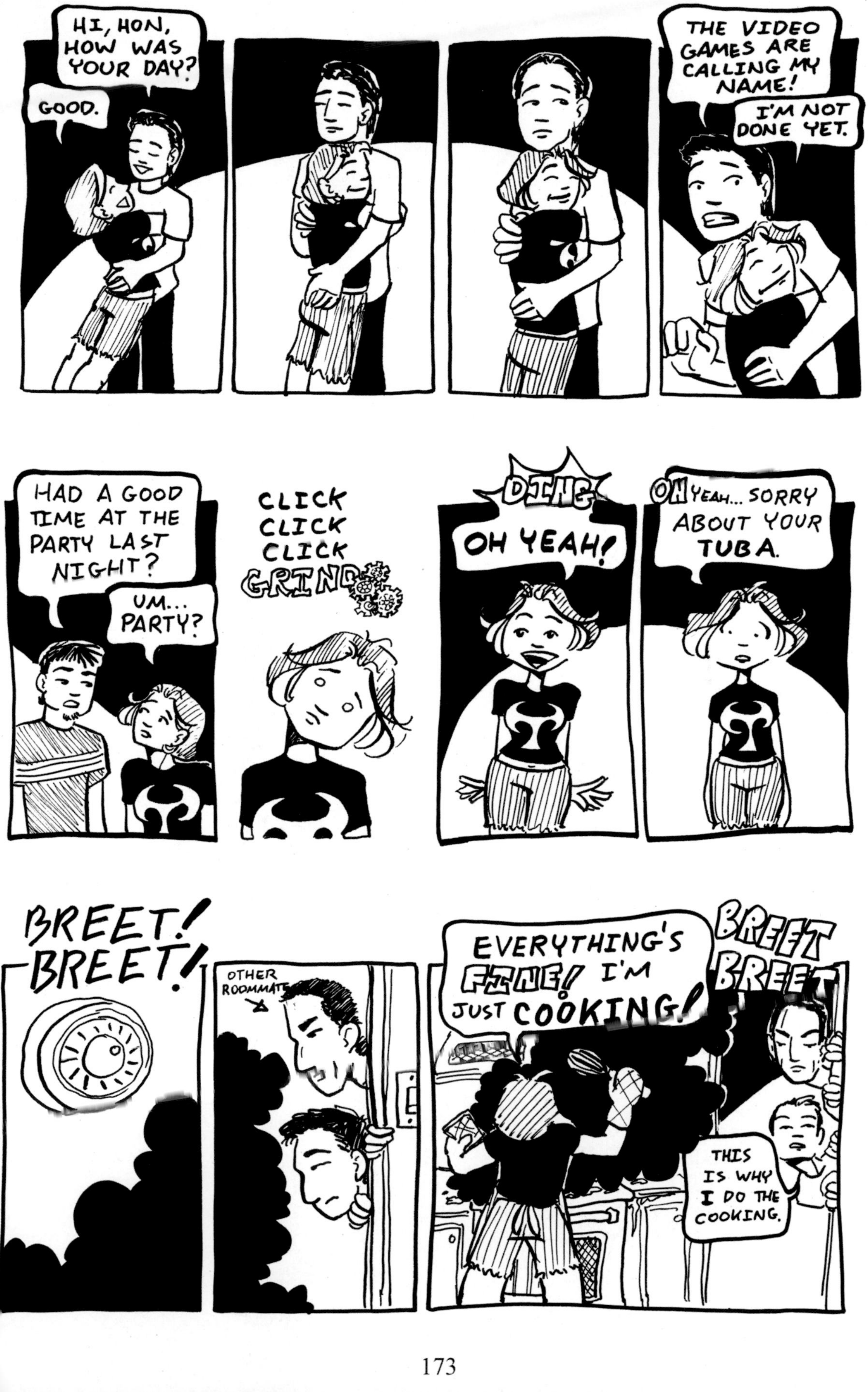
HI, HON, HOW WAS YOUR DAY?
GOOD.
THE VIDEO GAMES ARE CALLING MY NAME!
I'M NOT DONE YET.
HAD A GOOD TIME AT THE PARTY LAST NIGHT?
UM... PARTY?
CLICK CLICK CLICK GRIND
DING
OH YEAH!
OH YEAH... SORRY ABOUT YOUR TUBA.
BREET! BREET!
OTHER ROOMMATE
EVERYTHING'S FINE! I'M JUST COOKING!
BREET BREET
THIS IS WHY I DO THE COOKING.

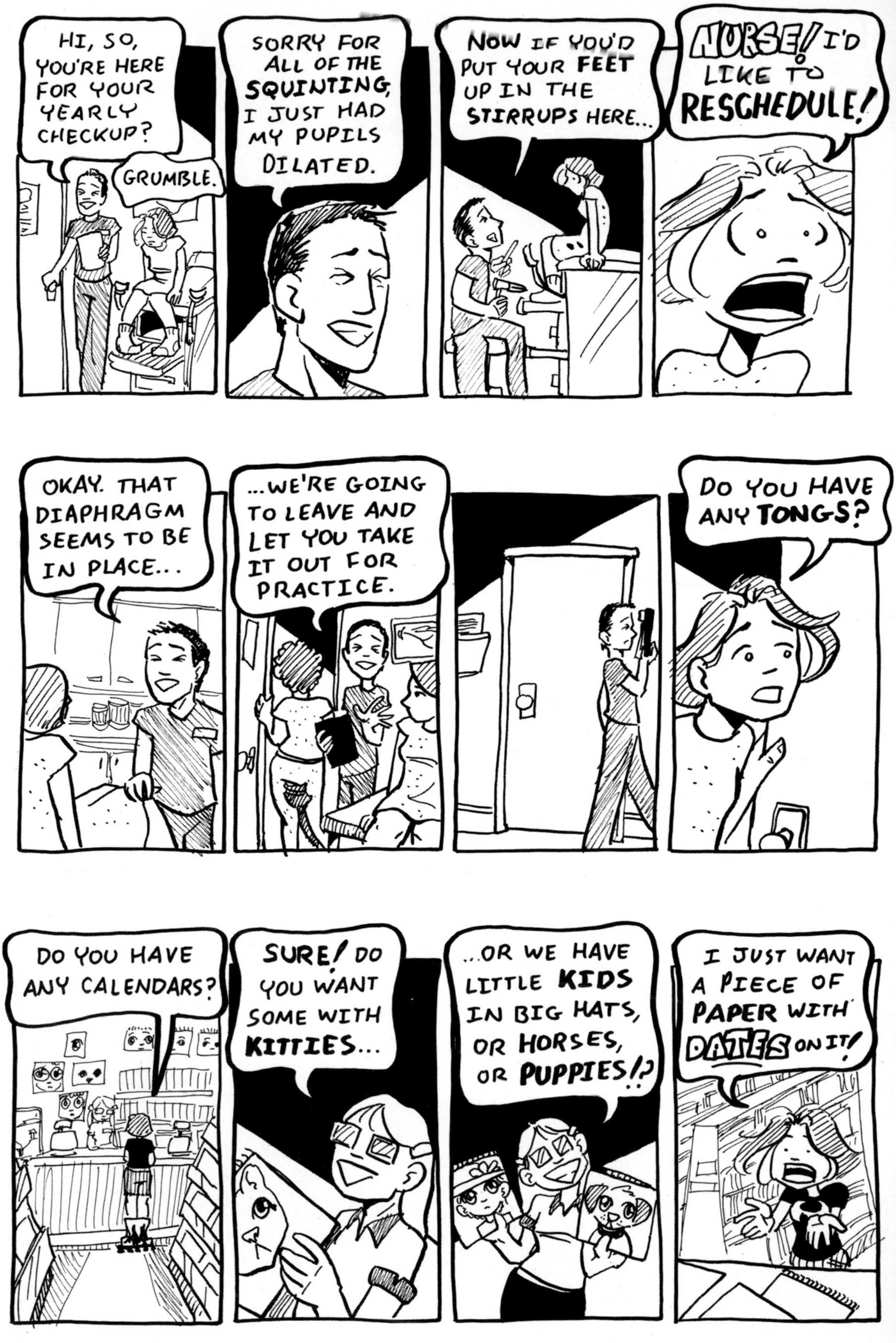
HI, SO, YOU'RE HERE FOR YOUR YEARLY CHECKUP?
GRUMBLE.
SORRY FOR ALL OF THE SQUINTING, I JUST HAD MY PUPILS DILATED.
NOW IF YOU'D PUT YOUR FEET UP IN THE STIRRUPS HERE...
NURSE! I'D LIKE TO RESCHEDULE!
OKAY. THAT DIAPHRAGM SEEMS TO BE IN PLACE...
...WE'RE GOING TO LEAVE AND LET YOU TAKE IT OUT FOR PRACTICE.
DO YOU HAVE ANY TONGS?
DO YOU HAVE ANY CALENDARS?
SURE! DO YOU WANT SOME WITH KITTIES...
...OR WE HAVE LITTLE KIDS IN BIG HATS, OR HORSES, OR PUPPIES!?
I JUST WANT A PIECE OF PAPER WITH DATES ON IT!

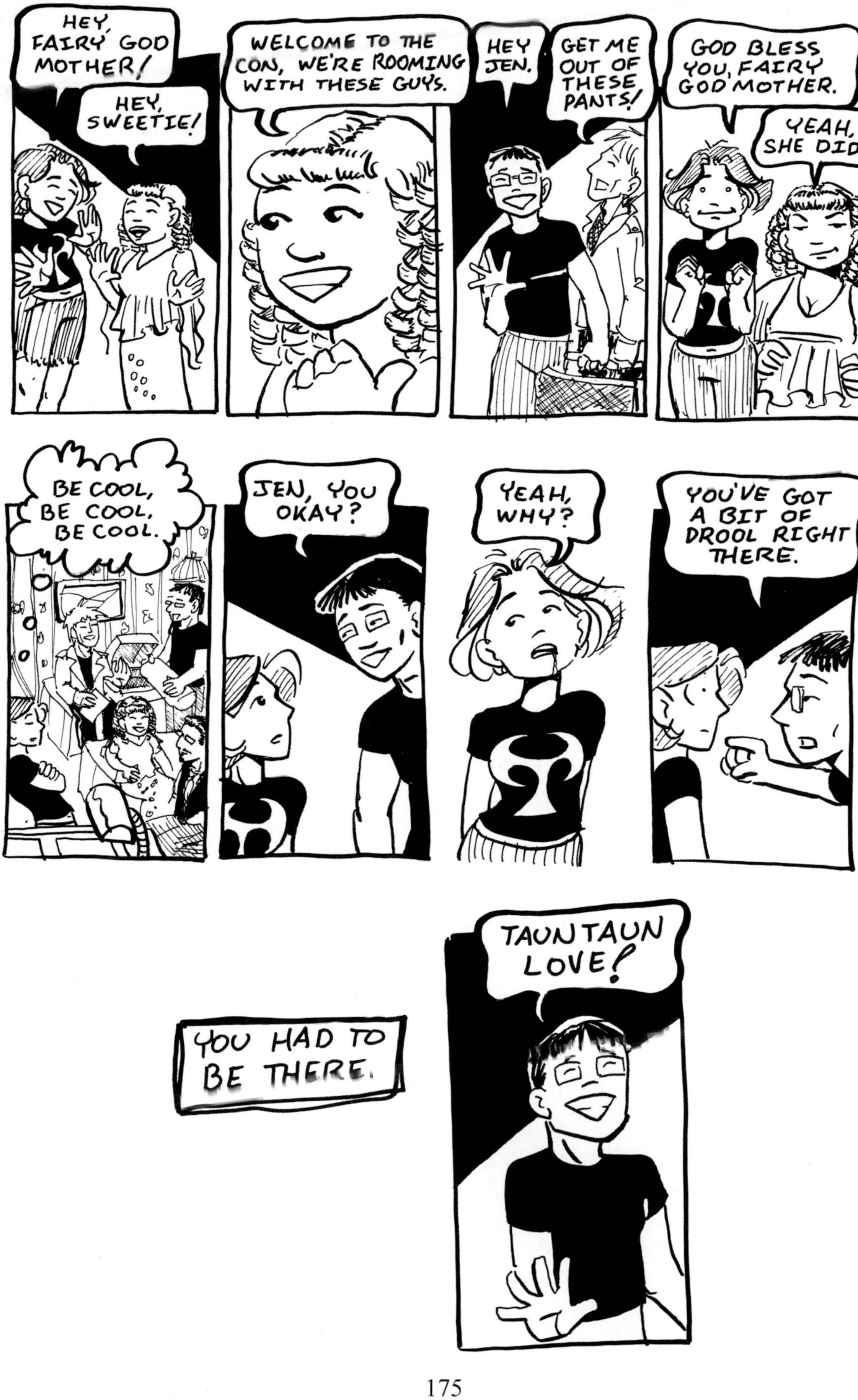
HEY, FAIRY GOD MOTHER!
HEY, SWEETIE!
WELCOME TO THE CON, WE'RE ROOMING WITH THESE GUYS.
HEY JEN.
GET ME OUT OF THESE PANTS!
GOD BLESS YOU, FAIRY GOD MOTHER.
YEAH, SHE DID.
BE COOL, BE COOL, BE COOL.
JEN, YOU OKAY?
YEAH, WHY?
YOU'VE GOT A BIT OF DROOL RIGHT THERE.
YOU HAD TO BE THERE.
TAUNTAUN LOVE!

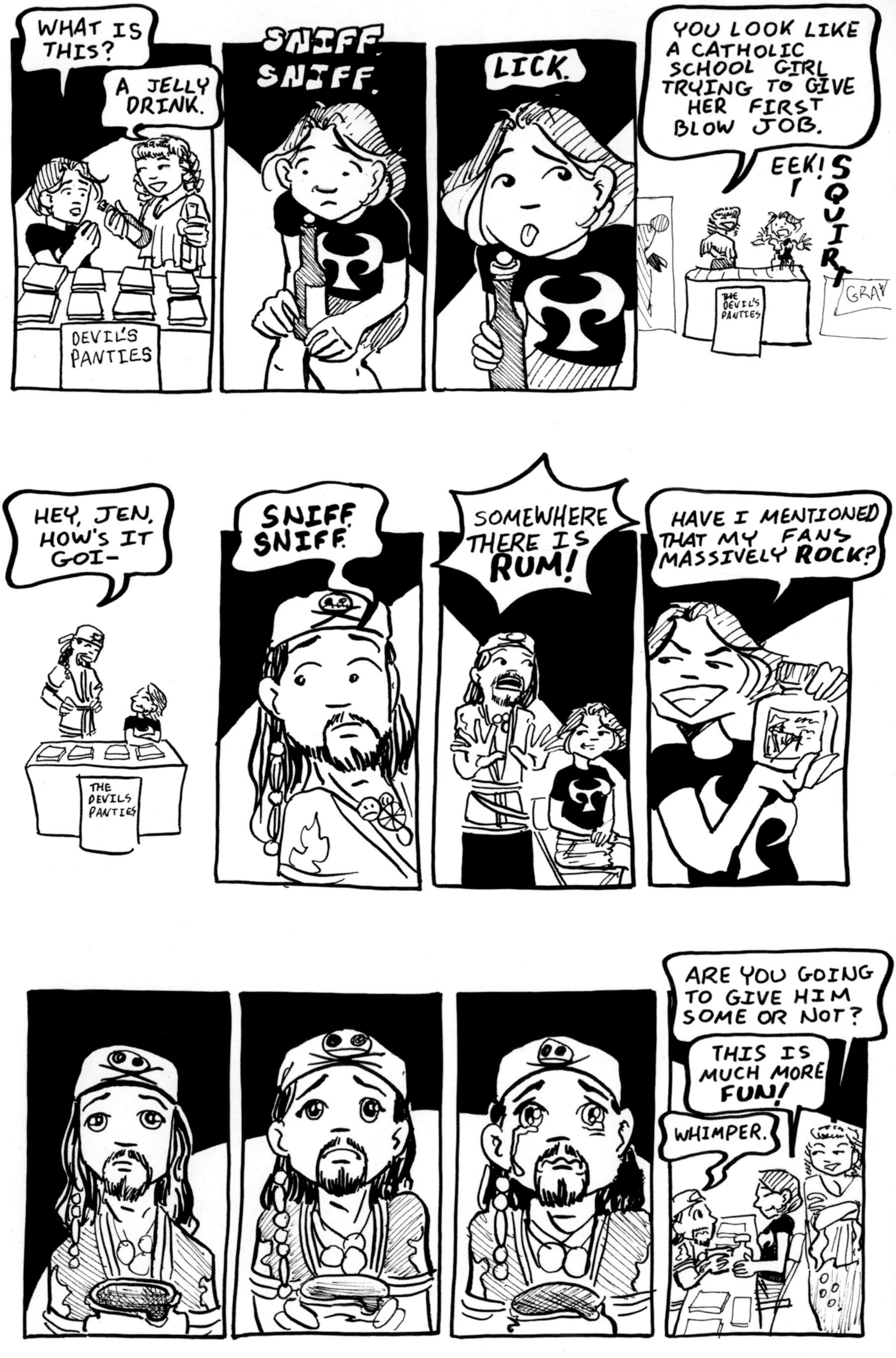
WHAT IS THIS?
A JELLY DRINK.
DEVIL'S PANTIES
SNIFF SNIFF.
LICK.
YOU LOOK LIKE A CATHOLIC SCHOOL GIRL TRYING TO GIVE HER FIRST BLOW JOB.
EEK!
SQUIRT
THE DEVIL'S PANTIES
HEY, JEN, HOW'S IT GOI-
THE DEVILS PANTIES
SNIFF. SNIFF.
SOMEWHERE THERE IS RUM!
HAVE I MENTIONED THAT MY FANS MASSIVELY ROCK?
ARE YOU GOING TO GIVE HIM SOME OR NOT?
THIS IS MUCH MORE FUN!
WHIMPER.

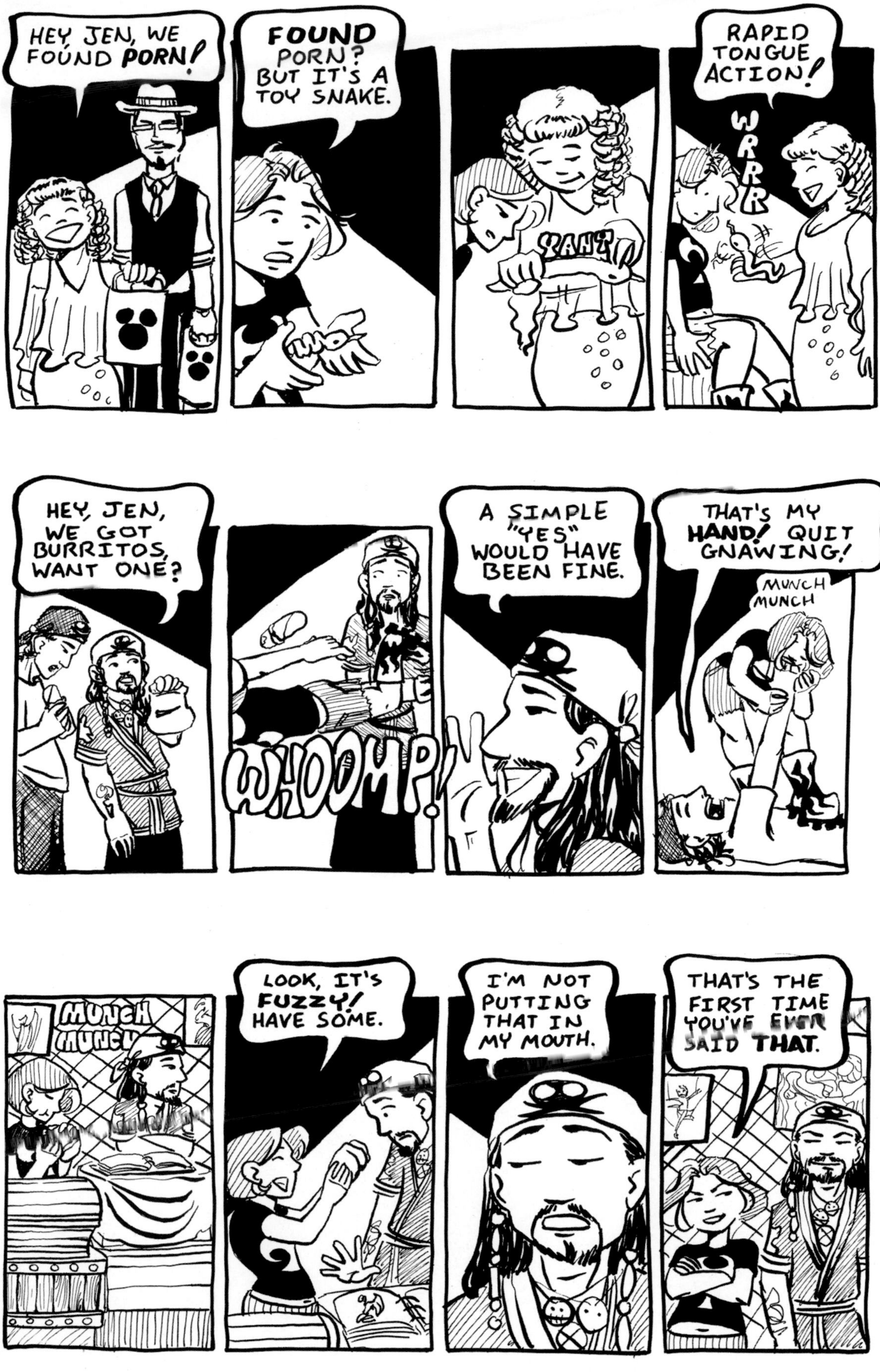
HEY, JEN, WE FOUND PORN!
FOUND PORN? BUT IT'S A TOY SNAKE.
RAPID TONGUE ACTION!
WRRR
HEY, JEN, WE GOT BURRITOS, WANT ONE?
WHOOMP!
A SIMPLE "YES" WOULD HAVE BEEN FINE.
THAT'S MY HAND! QUIT GNAWING!
MUNCH MUNCH
MUNCH MUNCH
LOOK, IT'S FUZZY! HAVE SOME.
I'M NOT PUTTING THAT IN MY MOUTH.
THAT'S THE FIRST TIME YOU'VE EVER SAID THAT.

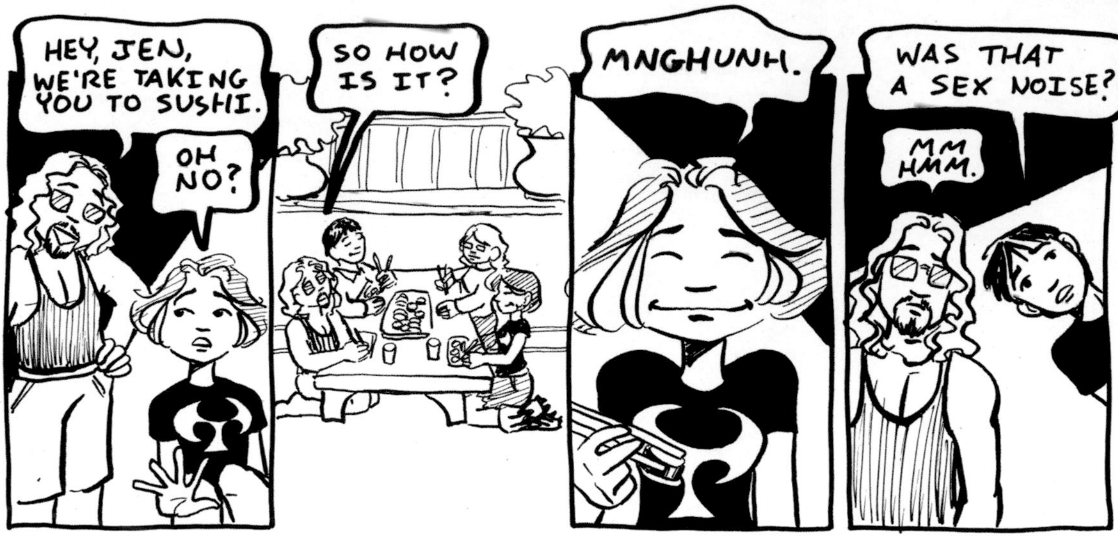
HEY, JEN, WE'RE TAKING YOU TO SUSHI.
OH NO?
SO HOW IS IT?
MNGHUNH.
WAS THAT A SEX NOISE?
MM HMM.

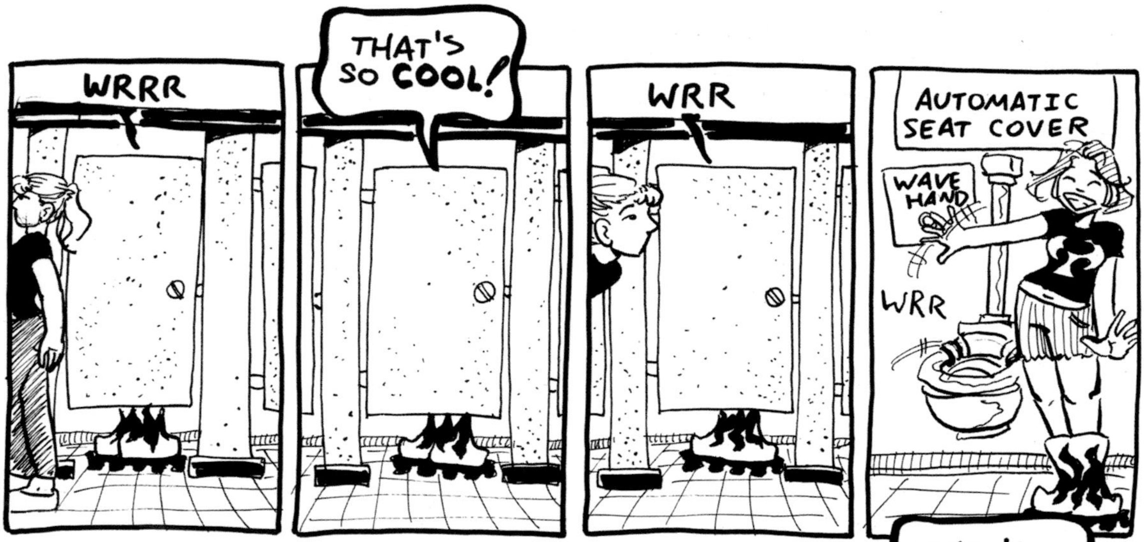
WRRR
THAT'S SO COOL!
WRR
AUTOMATIC SEAT COVER
WAVE HAND
WRR

I couldn't decide which cartoon aptly described my delight and the other bathroom attendants bewilderment.

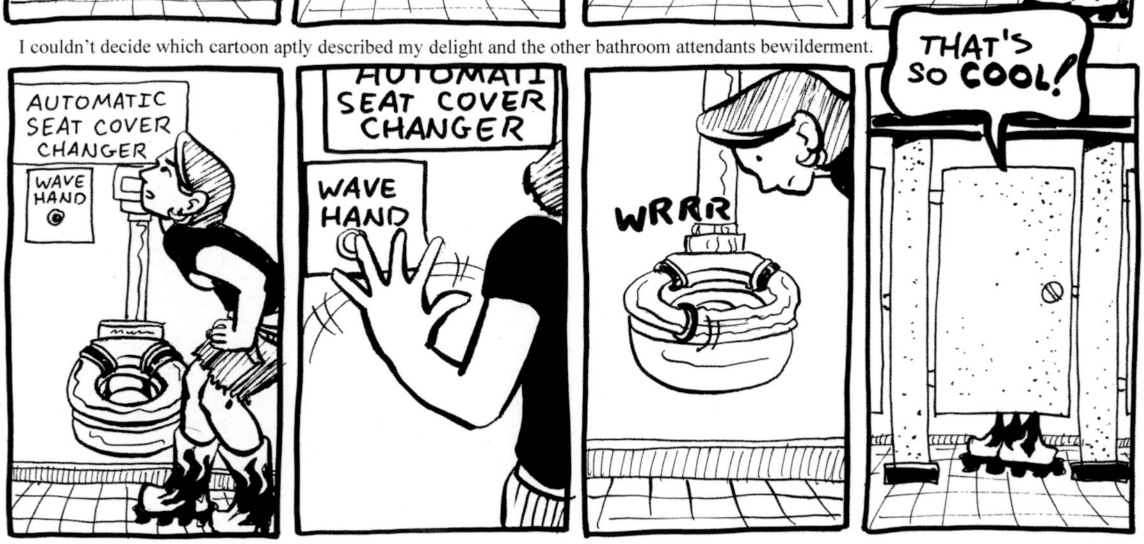
AUTOMATIC SEAT COVER CHANGER
WAVE HAND
SEAT COVER CHANGER
WAVE HAND
WRRR
THAT'S SO COOL!

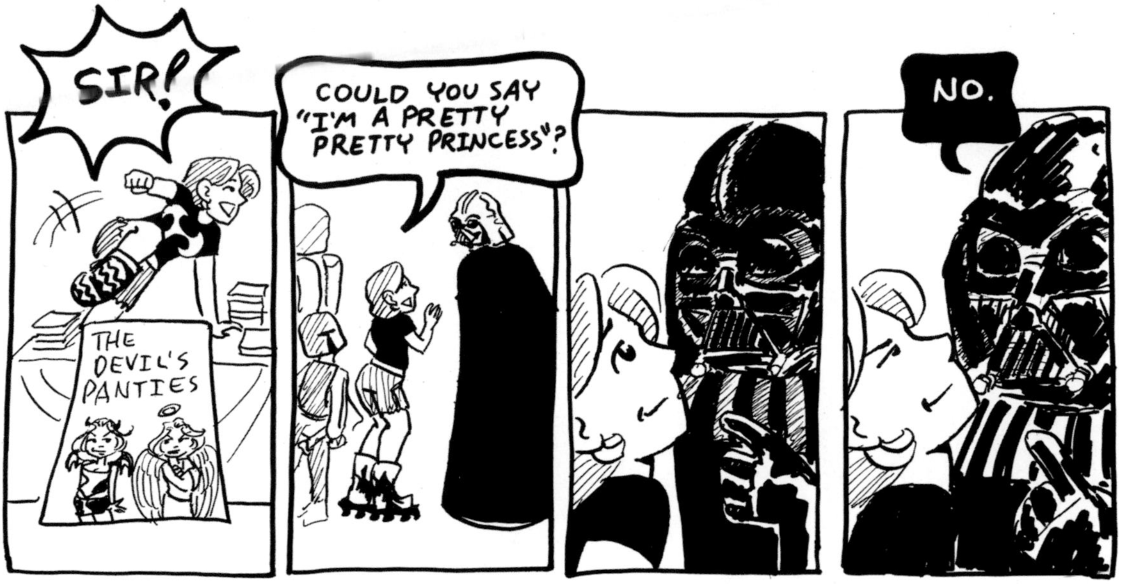
SIR?
THE DEVIL'S PANTIES
COULD YOU SAY "I'M A PRETTY PRETTY PRINCESS"?
NO.

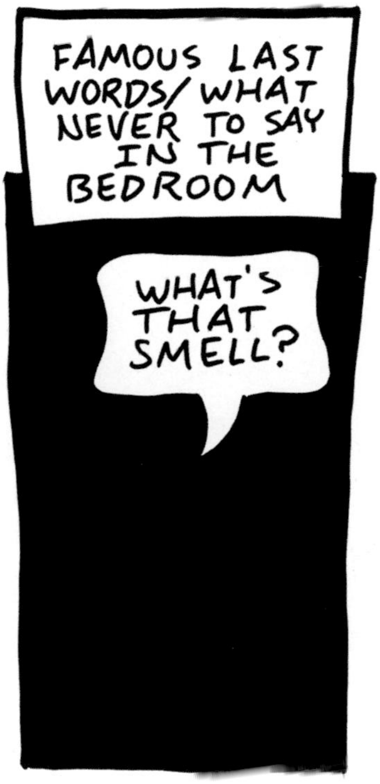
FAMOUS LAST WORDS/ WHAT NEVER TO SAY IN THE BEDROOM
WHAT'S THAT SMELL?

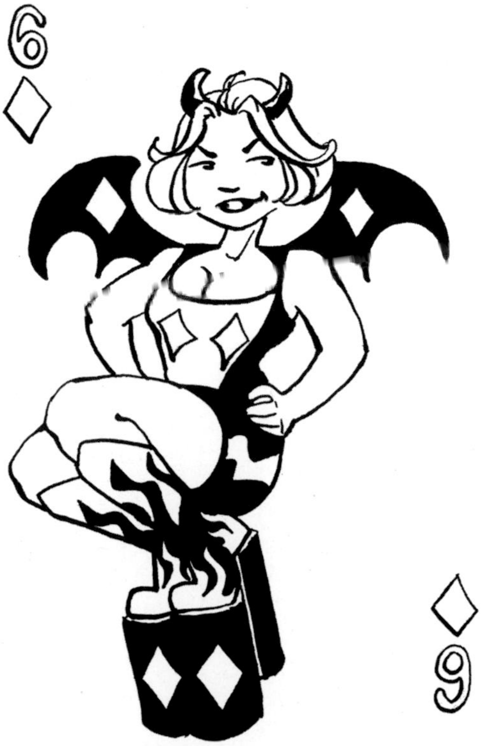
6
9

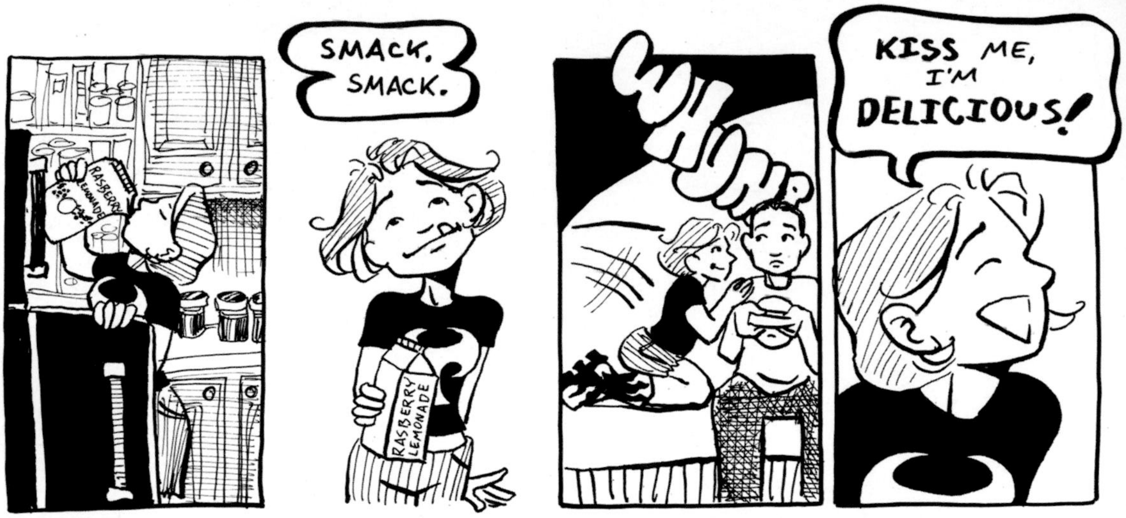
RASBERRY LEMONADE
SMACK. SMACK.
RASBERRY LEMONADE
KISS ME, I'M DELICIOUS!

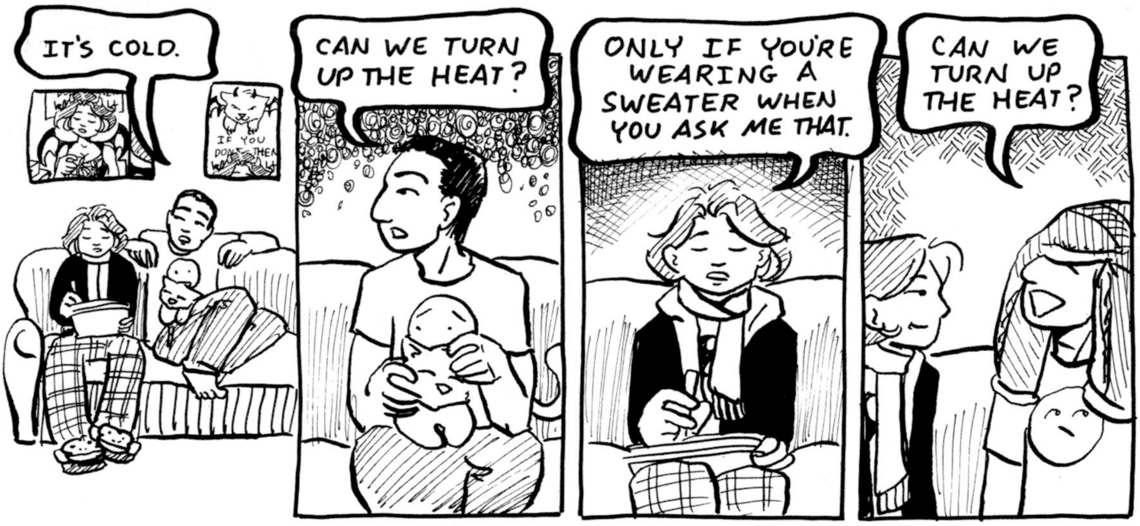
IT'S COLD.
CAN WE TURN UP THE HEAT?
ONLY IF YOU'RE WEARING A SWEATER WHEN YOU ASK ME THAT.
CAN WE TURN UP THE HEAT?

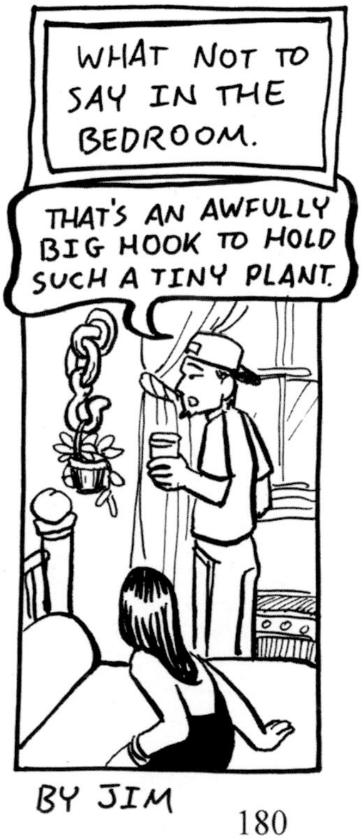
WHAT NOT TO SAY IN THE BEDROOM.
THAT'S AN AWFULLY BIG HOOK TO HOLD SUCH A TINY PLANT.
BY JIM

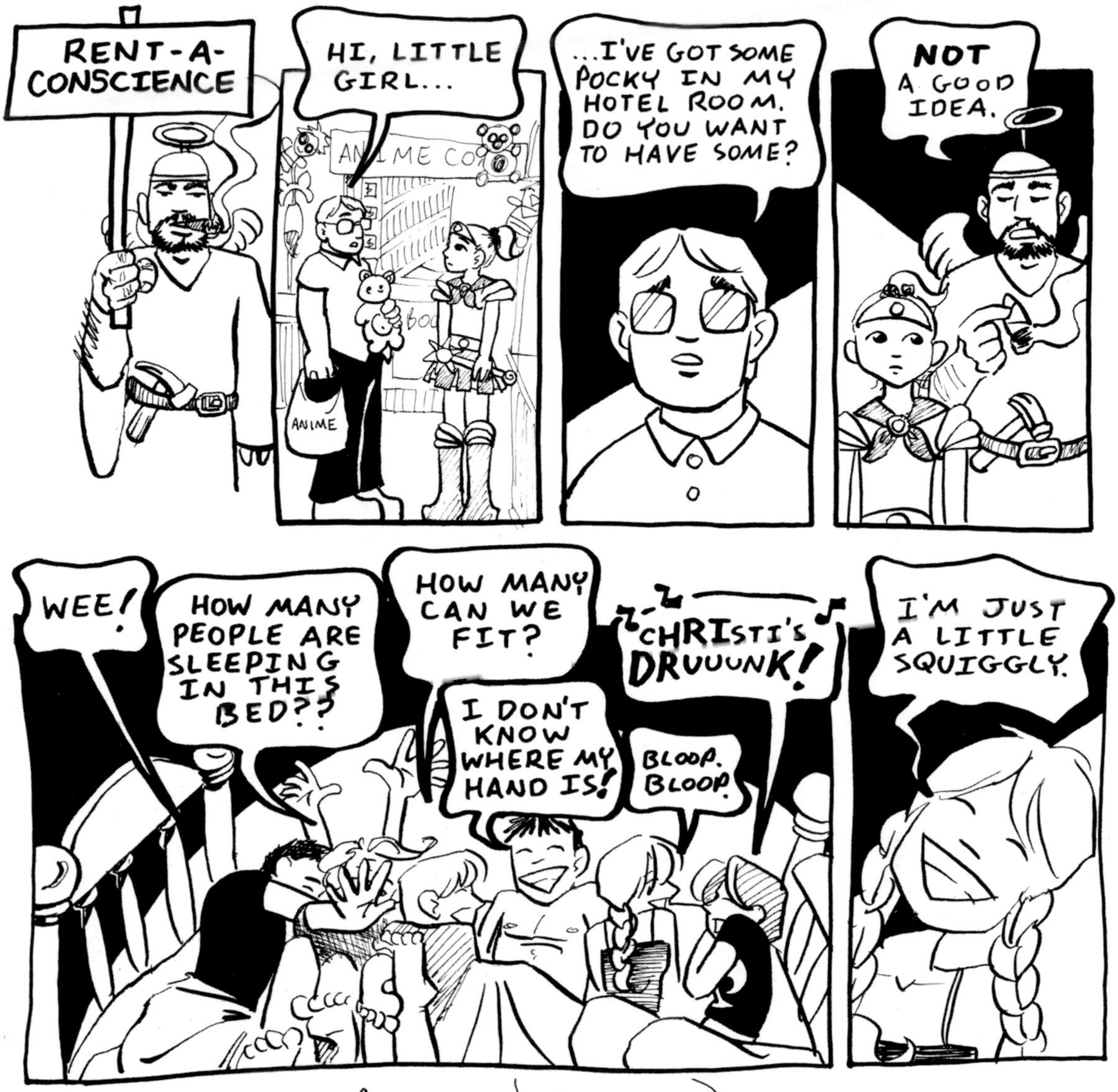
RENT-A-CONSCIENCE
HI, LITTLE GIRL...
ANIME CO
ANIME
...I'VE GOT SOME POCKY IN MY HOTEL ROOM. DO YOU WANT TO HAVE SOME?
NOT A GOOD IDEA.
WEE!
HOW MANY PEOPLE ARE SLEEPING IN THIS BED??
HOW MANY CAN WE FIT?
I DON'T KNOW WHERE MY HAND IS!
BLOOP. BLOOP.
CHRISTI'S DRUUUNK!
I'M JUST A LITTLE SQUIGGLY.

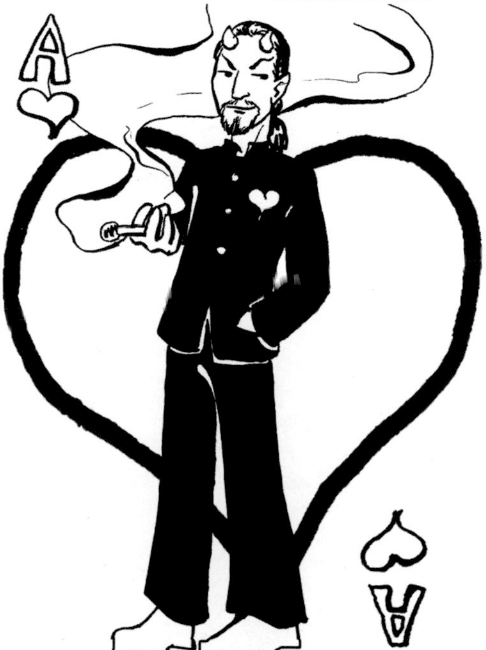
A
A

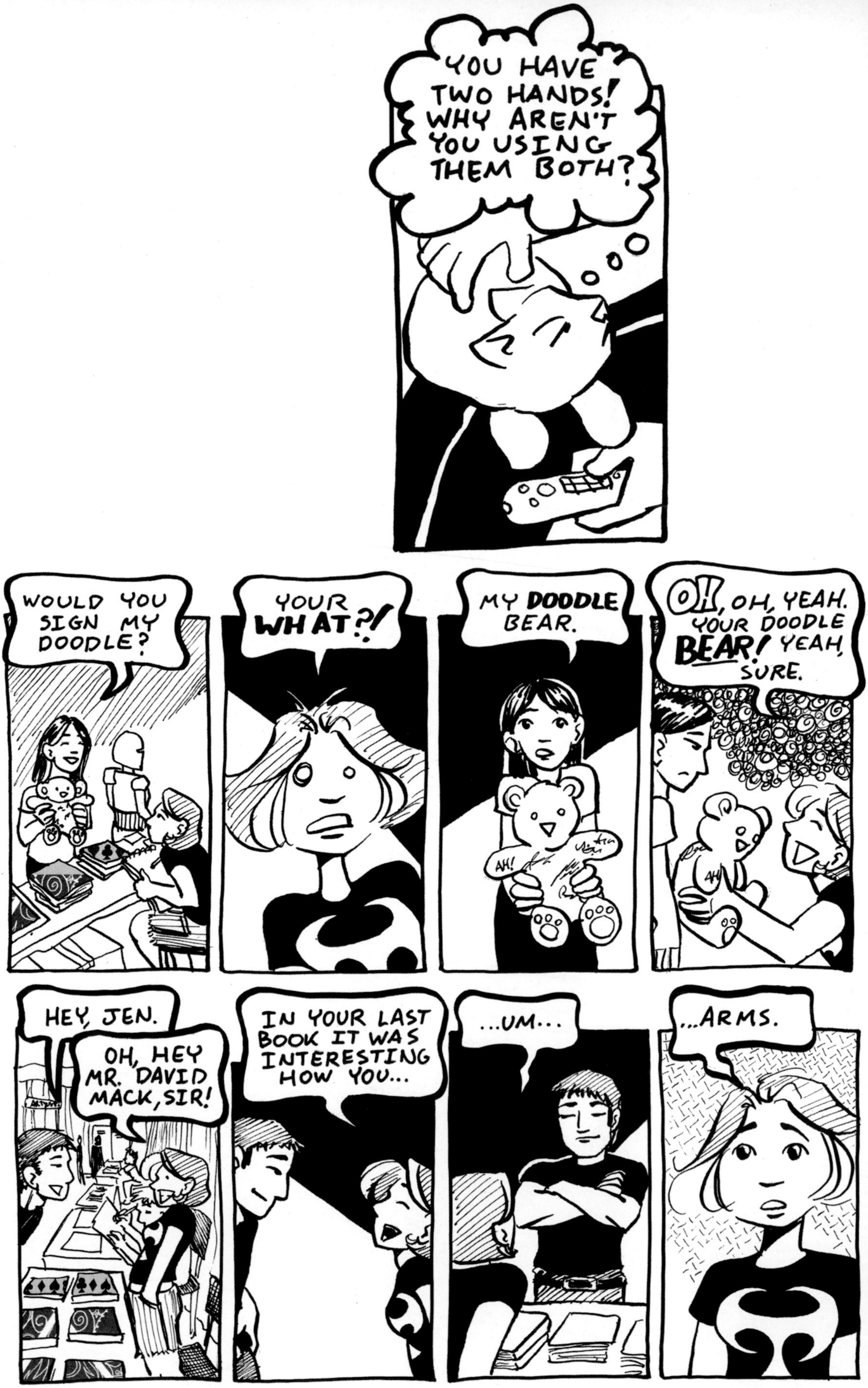
YOU HAVE TWO HANDS! WHY AREN'T YOU USING THEM BOTH?
WOULD YOU SIGN MY DOODLE?
YOUR WHAT?!
MY DOODLE BEAR.
OH, OH, YEAH. YOUR DOODLE BEAR! YEAH, SURE.
HEY, JEN.
OH, HEY MR. DAVID MACK, SIR!
IN YOUR LAST BOOK IT WAS INTERESTING HOW YOU...
...UM...
...ARMS.

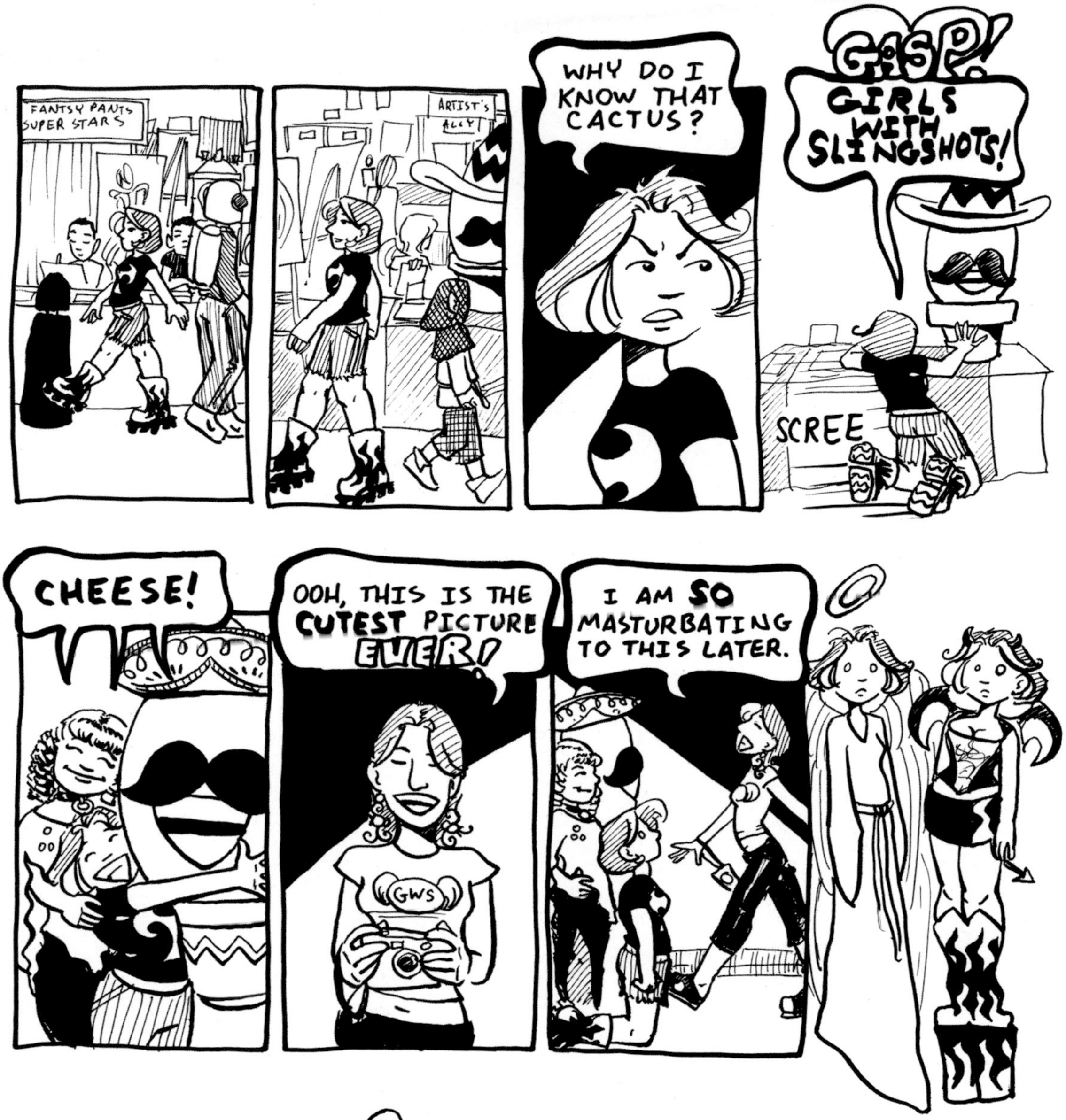
FANTSY PANTS SUPER STARS
ARTIST'S ALLY
WHY DO I KNOW THAT CACTUS?
GASP!
GIRLS WITH SLINGSHOTS!
SCREE
CHEESE!
OOH, THIS IS THE CUTEST PICTURE EVER!
GWS
I AM SO MASTURBATING TO THIS LATER.

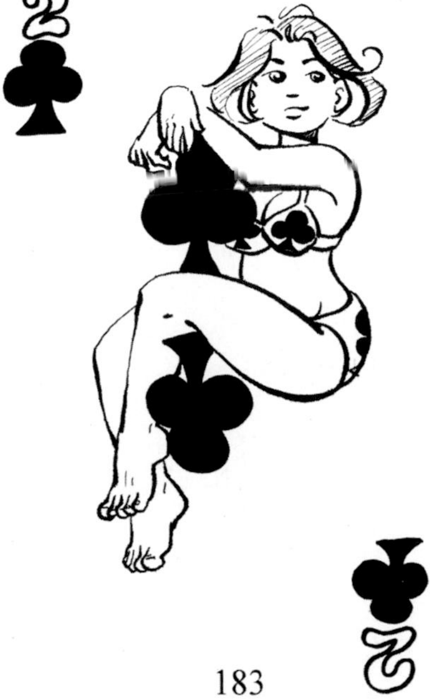
2
2

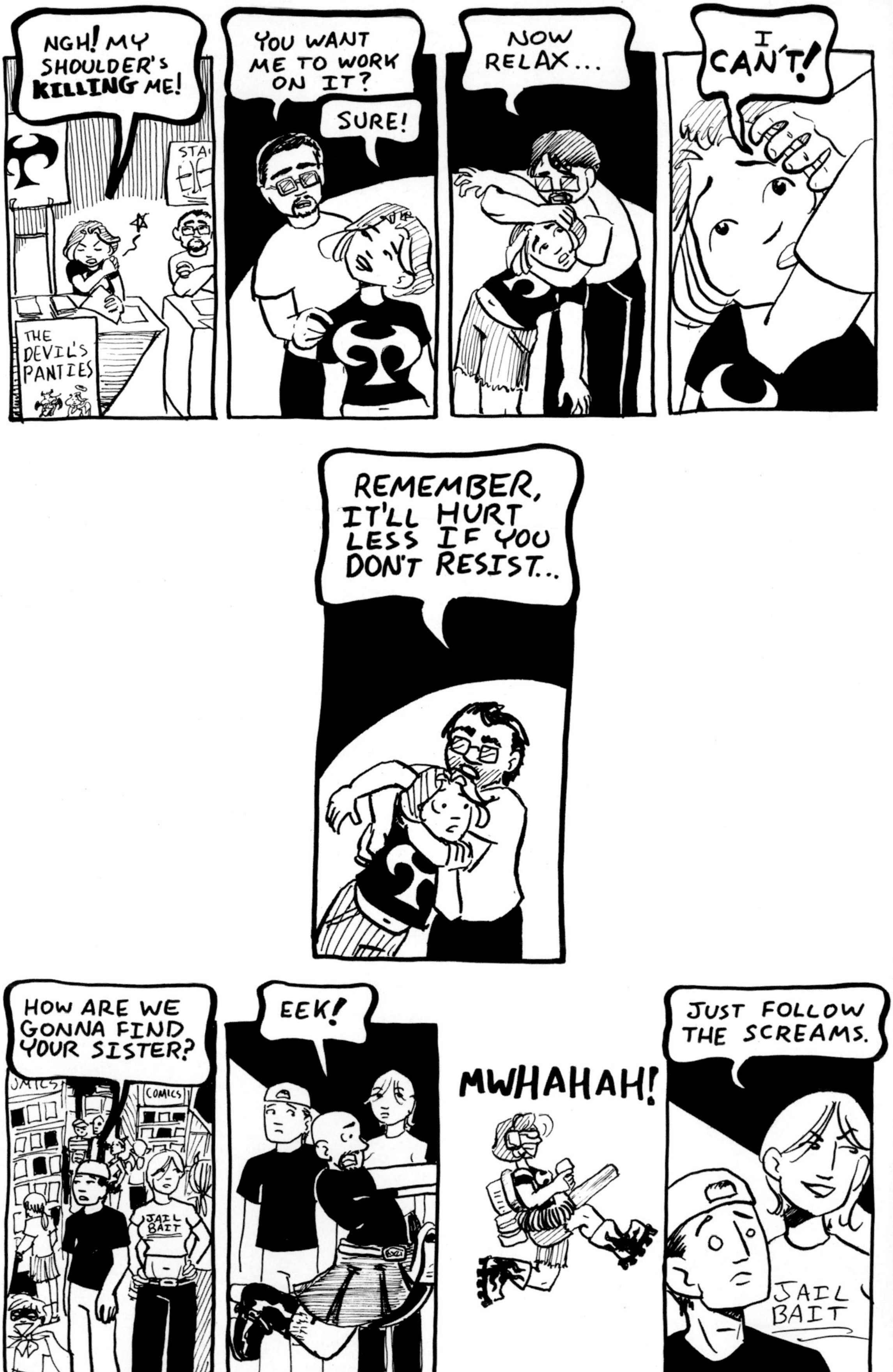
NGH! MY SHOULDER'S KILLING ME!
THE DEVIL'S PANTIES
YOU WANT ME TO WORK ON IT?
SURE!
NOW RELAX...
I CAN'T!
REMEMBER, IT'LL HURT LESS IF YOU DON'T RESIST...
HOW ARE WE GONNA FIND YOUR SISTER?
COMICS
JAIL BAIT
EEK!
MWHAHAH!
JUST FOLLOW THE SCREAMS.
JAIL BAIT

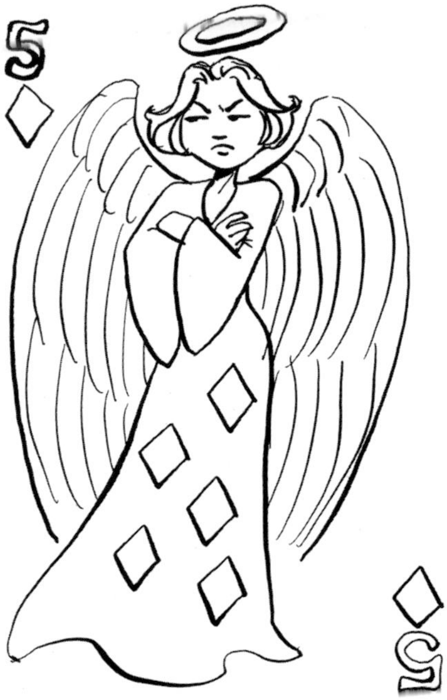
5
5

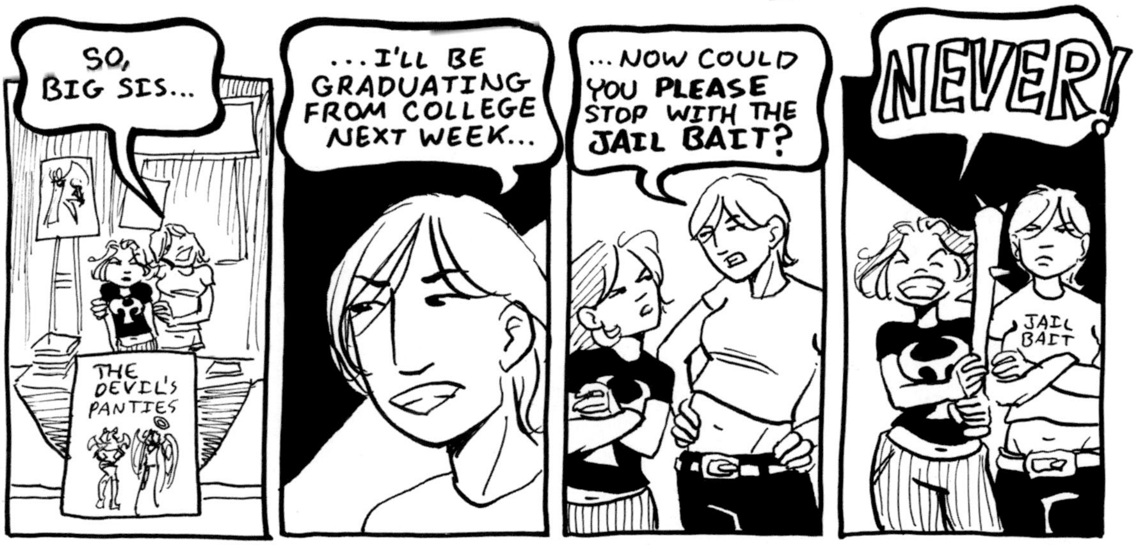
SO, BIG SIS...
THE DEVIL'S PANTIES
...I'LL BE GRADUATING FROM COLLEGE NEXT WEEK...
...NOW COULD YOU **PLEASE** STOP WITH THE **JAIL BAIT**?
NEVER!
JAIL BAIT

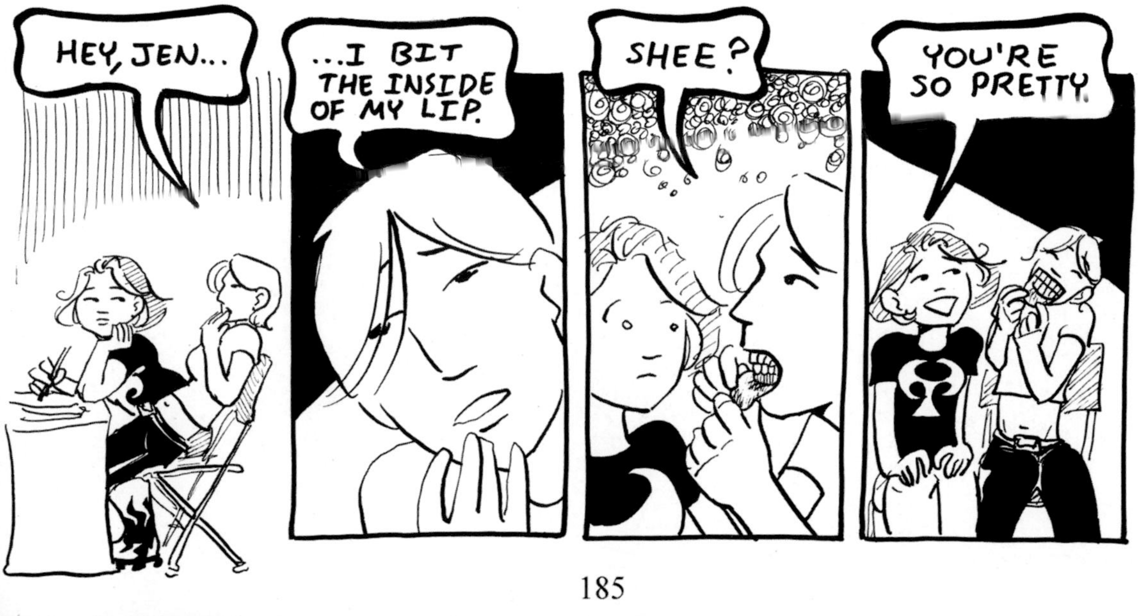
HEY, JEN...
...I BIT THE INSIDE OF MY LIP.
SHEE?
YOU'RE SO PRETTY.

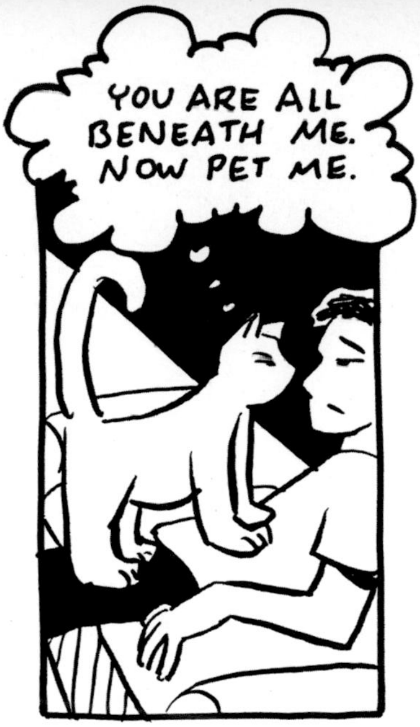
YOU ARE ALL BENEATH ME. NOW PET ME.

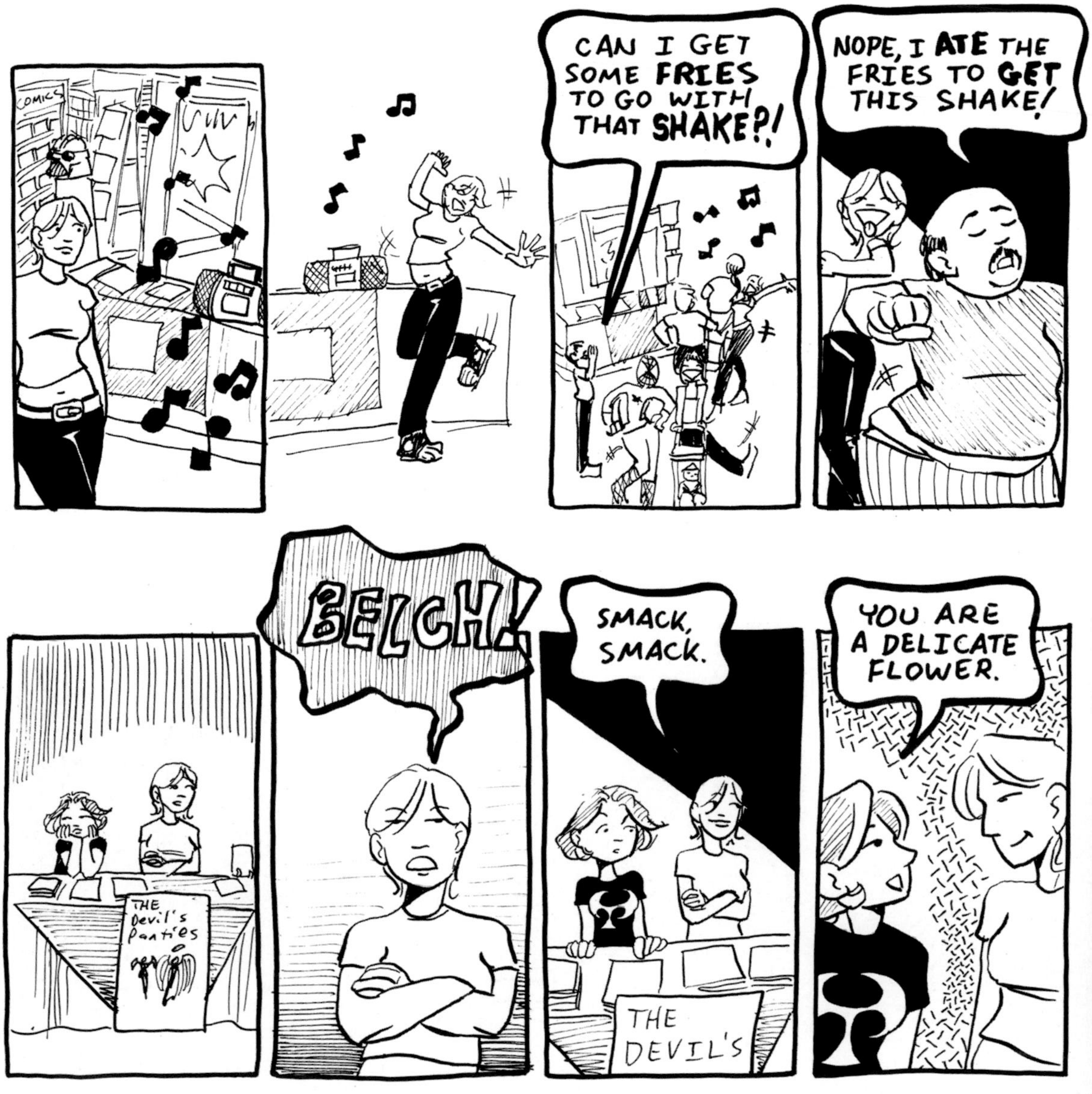
COMICS
CAN I GET SOME FRIES TO GO WITH THAT SHAKE?!
NOPE, I ATE THE FRIES TO GET THIS SHAKE!
THE Devil's Panties
BELCH!
SMACK, SMACK.
THE DEVIL'S
YOU ARE A DELICATE FLOWER.

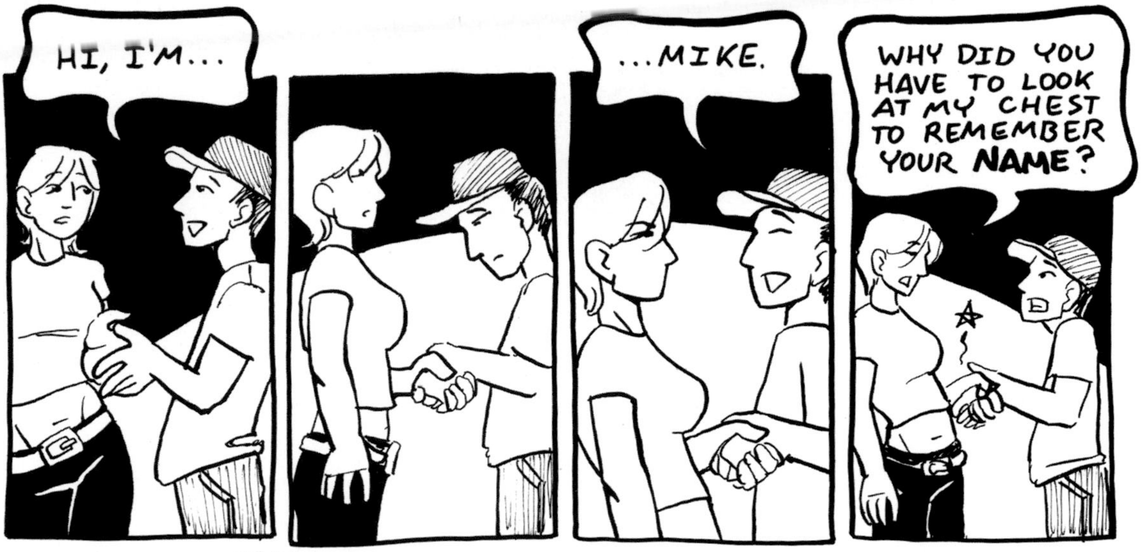
HI, I'M...
...MIKE.
WHY DID YOU HAVE TO LOOK AT MY CHEST TO REMEMBER YOUR NAME?

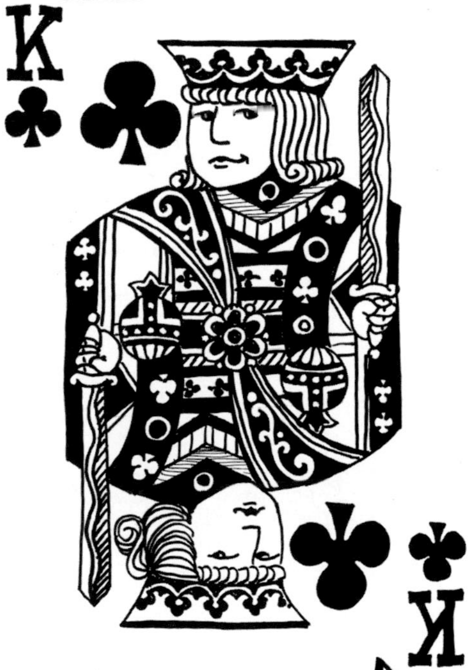
K
K

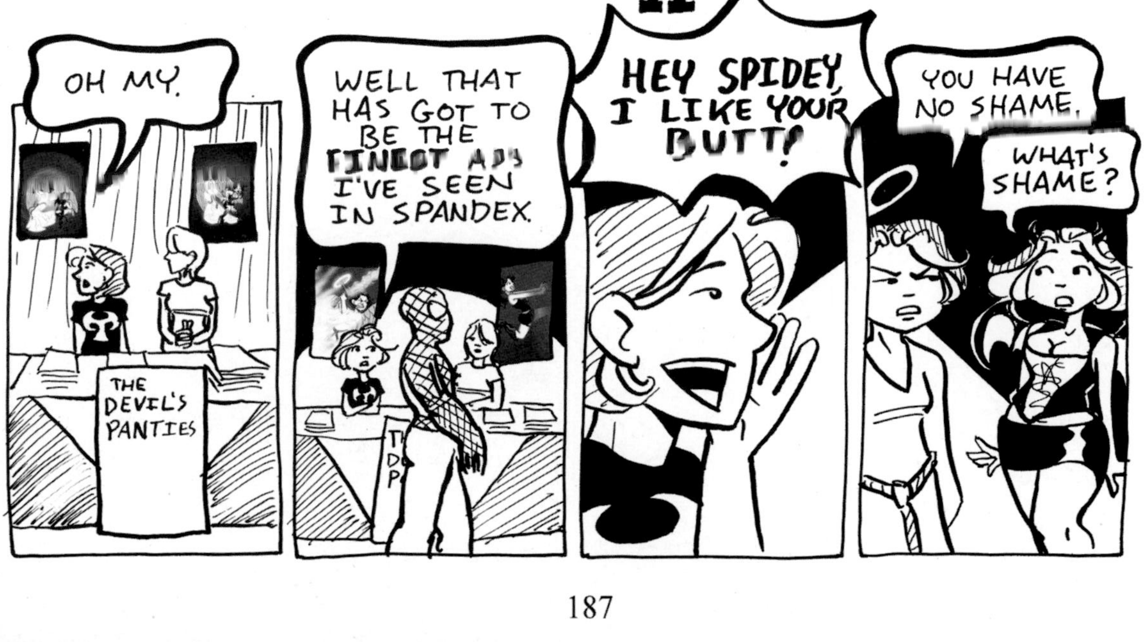
OH MY.
THE DEVIL'S PANTIES
WELL THAT HAS GOT TO BE THE FINEST ASS I'VE SEEN IN SPANDEX.
HEY SPIDEY, I LIKE YOUR BUTT!
YOU HAVE NO SHAME.
WHAT'S SHAME?

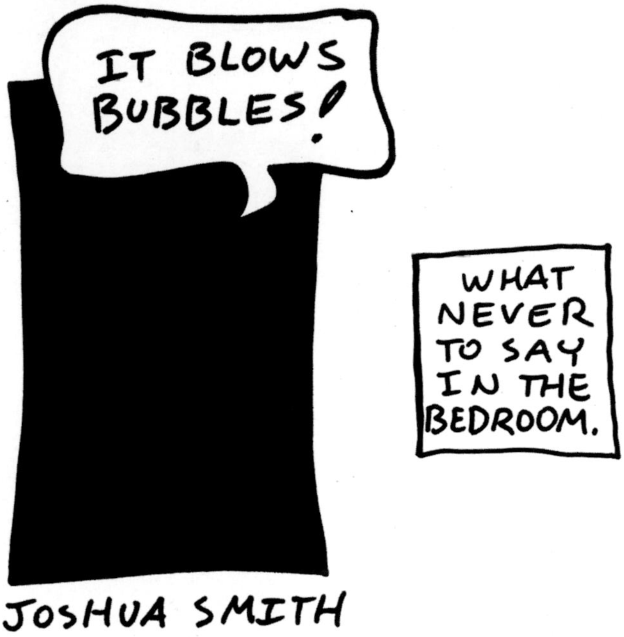
IT BLOWS BUBBLES!
WHAT NEVER TO SAY IN THE BEDROOM.
JOSHUA SMITH

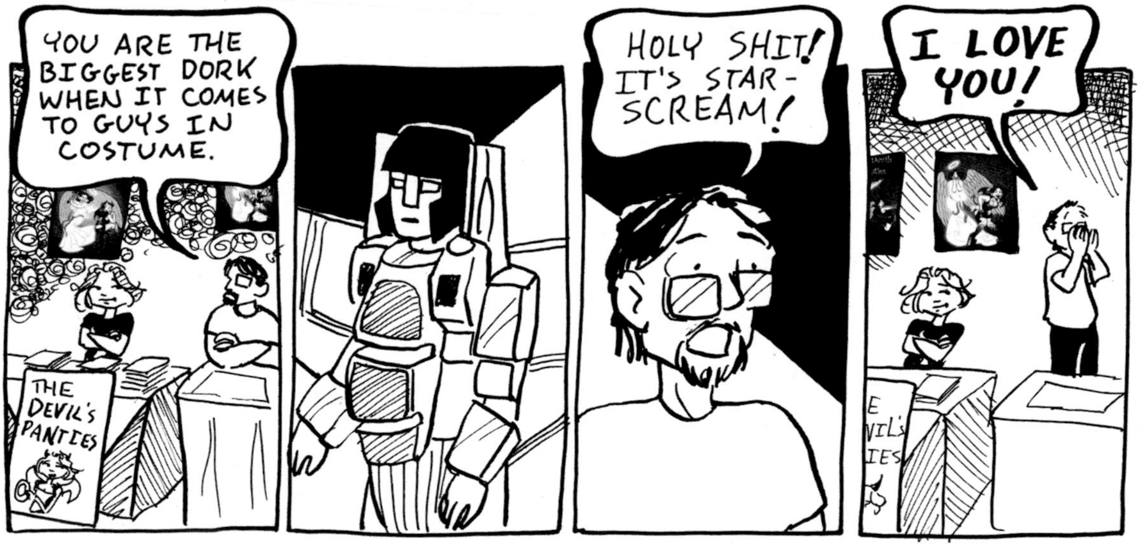
YOU ARE THE BIGGEST DORK WHEN IT COMES TO GUYS IN COSTUME.
THE DEVIL'S PANTIES
HOLY SHIT! IT'S STAR-SCREAM!
I LOVE YOU!

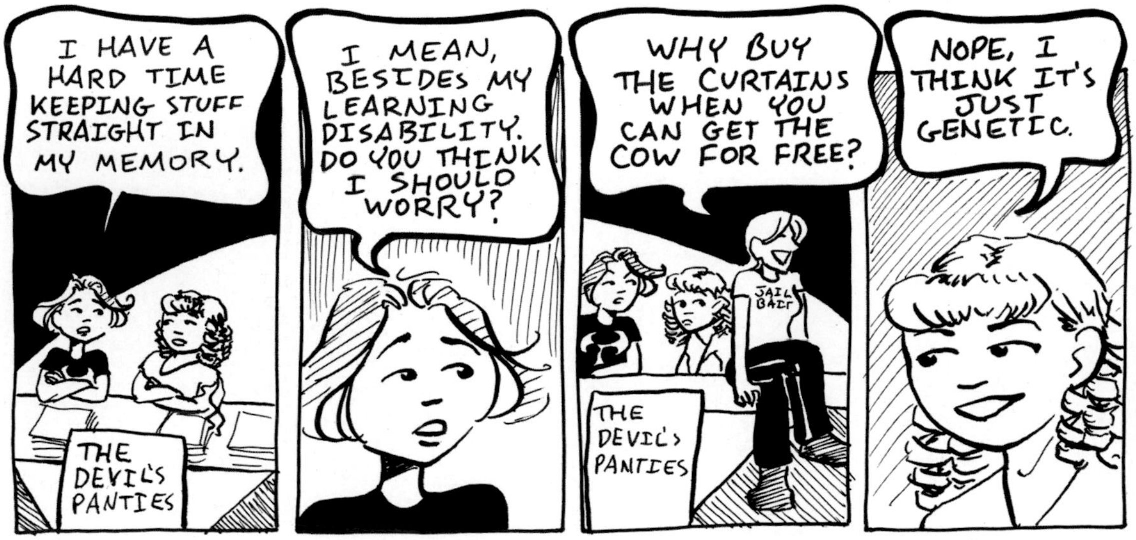
I HAVE A HARD TIME KEEPING STUFF STRAIGHT IN MY MEMORY.
THE DEVIL'S PANTIES
I MEAN, BESIDES MY LEARNING DISABILITY. DO YOU THINK I SHOULD WORRY?
WHY BUY THE CURTAINS WHEN YOU CAN GET THE COW FOR FREE?
JAIL BAIT
THE DEVIL'S PANTIES
NOPE, I THINK IT'S JUST GENETIC.

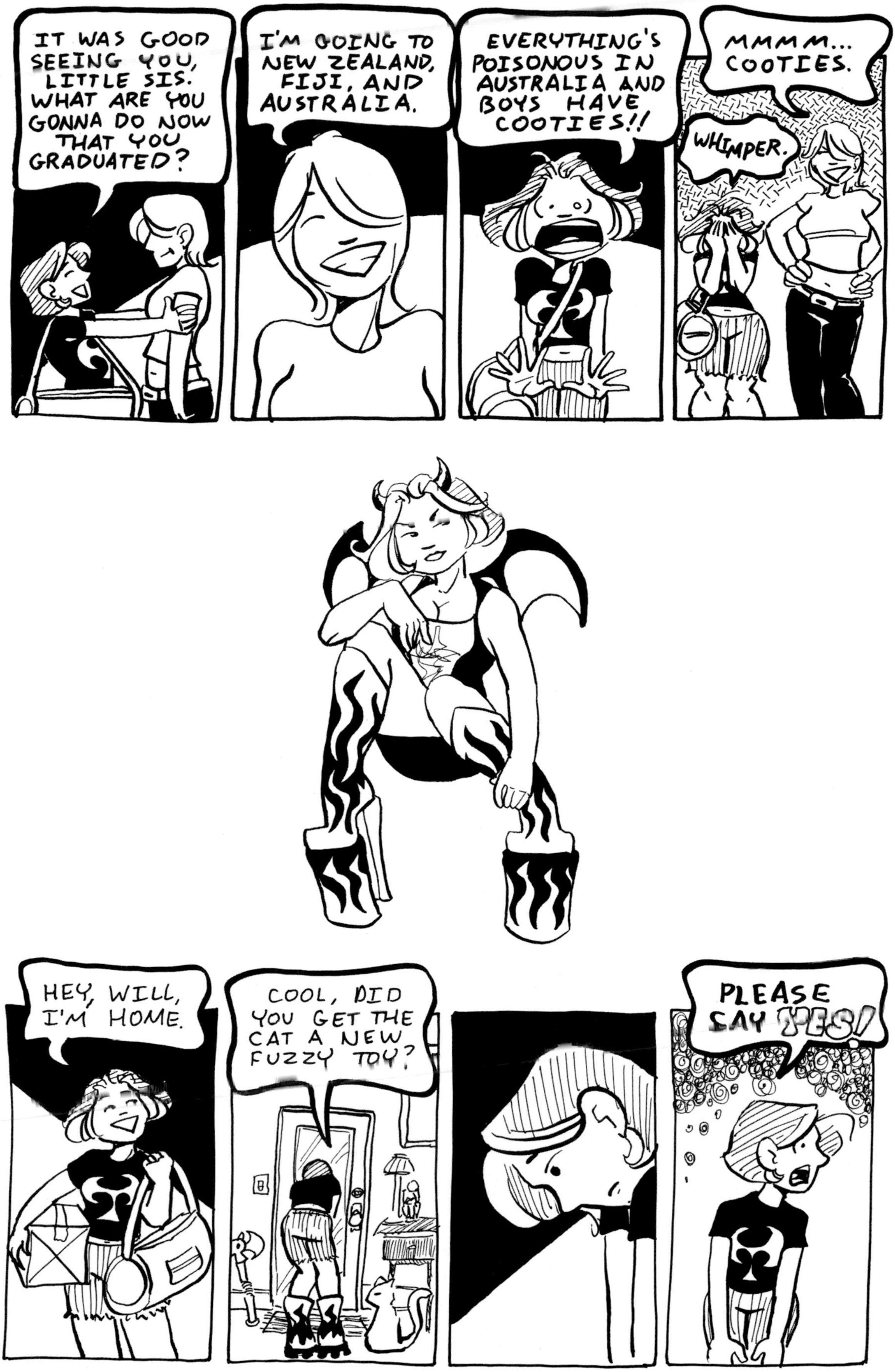
IT WAS GOOD SEEING YOU, LITTLE SIS. WHAT ARE YOU GONNA DO NOW THAT YOU GRADUATED?
I'M GOING TO NEW ZEALAND, FIJI, AND AUSTRALIA.
EVERYTHING'S POISONOUS IN AUSTRALIA AND BOYS HAVE COOTIES!!
MMMMM... COOTIES.
WHIMPER.
HEY, WILL, I'M HOME.
COOL, DID YOU GET THE CAT A NEW FUZZY TOY?
PLEASE SAY YES!

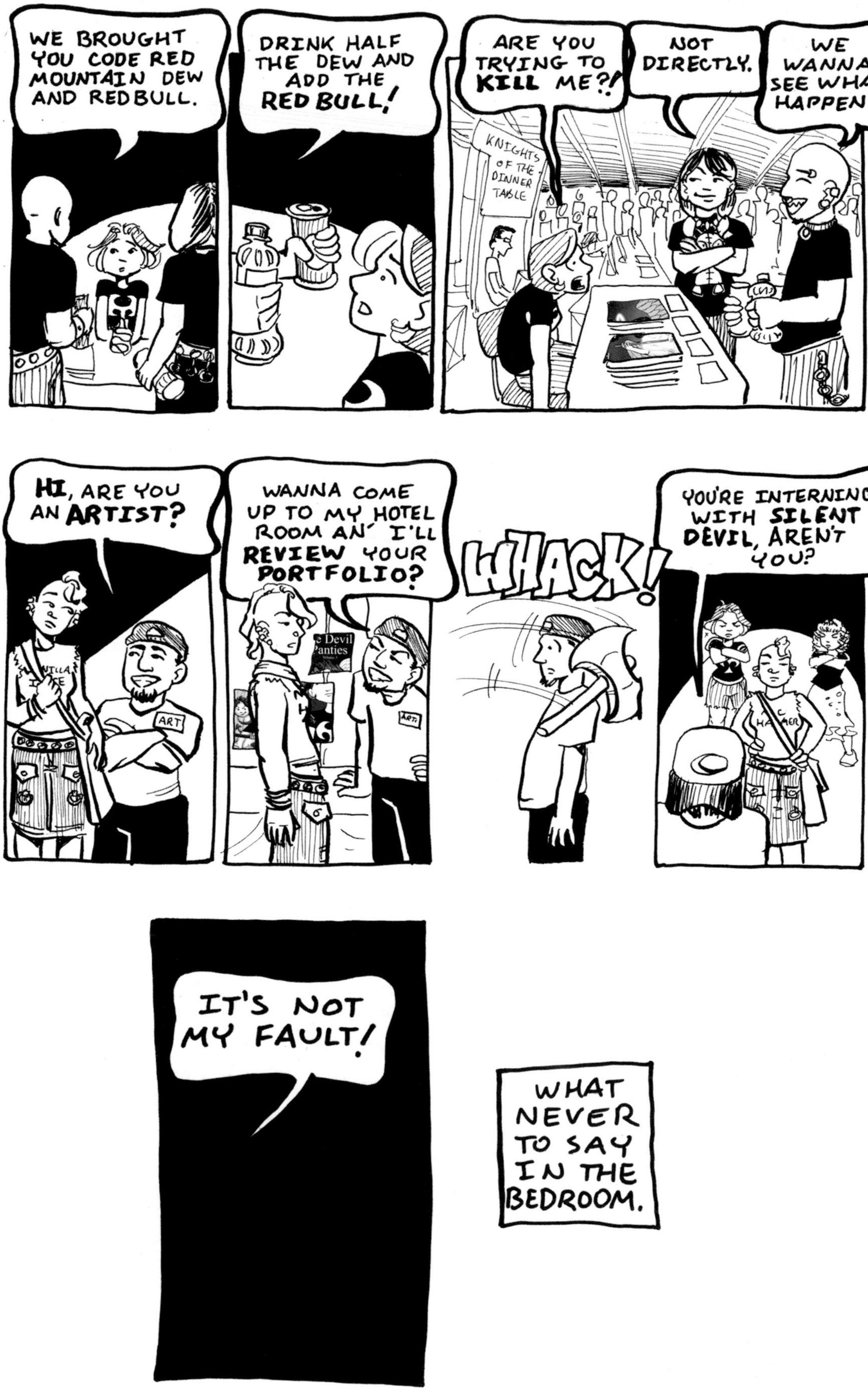
WE BROUGHT YOU CODE RED MOUNTAIN DEW AND REDBULL.
DRINK HALF THE DEW AND ADD THE RED BULL!
ARE YOU TRYING TO KILL ME?!
KNIGHTS OF THE DINNER TABLE
NOT DIRECTLY.
WE WANNA SEE WHAT HAPPENS.
HI, ARE YOU AN ARTIST?
ART
WANNA COME UP TO MY HOTEL ROOM AN' I'LL REVIEW YOUR PORTFOLIO?
ART
WHACK!
YOU'RE INTERNING WITH SILENT DEVIL, AREN'T YOU?
IT'S NOT MY FAULT!
WHAT NEVER TO SAY IN THE BEDROOM.

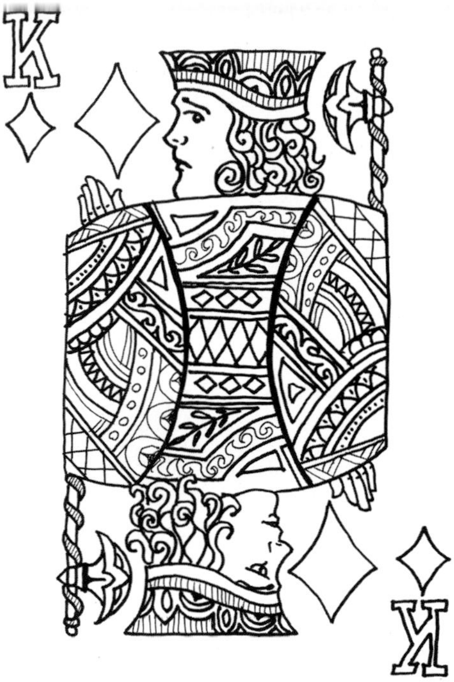

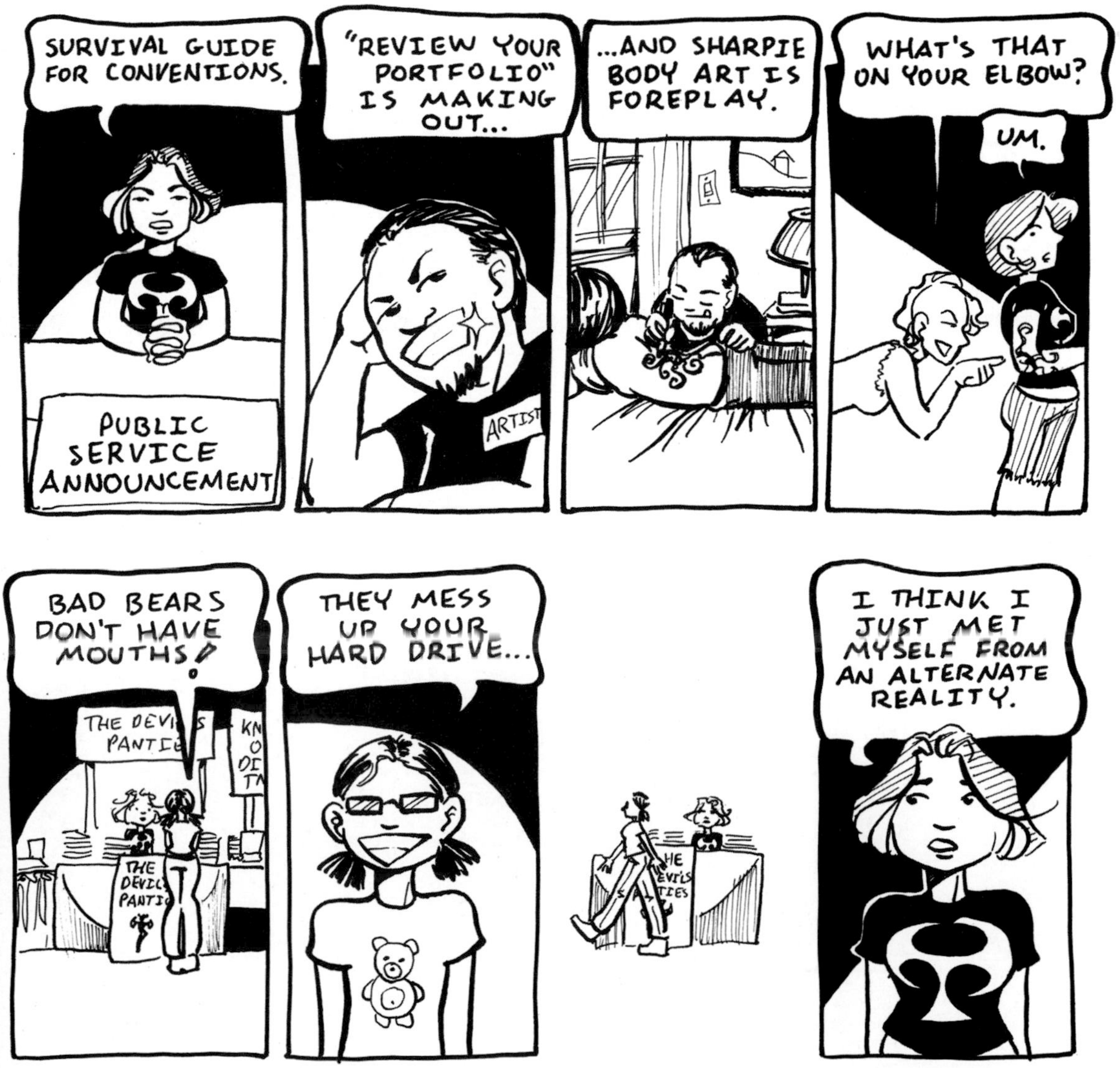
SURVIVAL GUIDE FOR CONVENTIONS.
PUBLIC SERVICE ANNOUNCEMENT
"REVIEW YOUR PORTFOLIO" IS MAKING OUT...
ARTIST
...AND SHARPIE BODY ART IS FOREPLAY.
WHAT'S THAT ON YOUR ELBOW?
UM.
BAD BEARS DON'T HAVE MOUTHS!
THE DEVILS PANTIES
THEY MESS UP YOUR HARD DRIVE...
I THINK I JUST MET MYSELF FROM AN ALTERNATE REALITY.

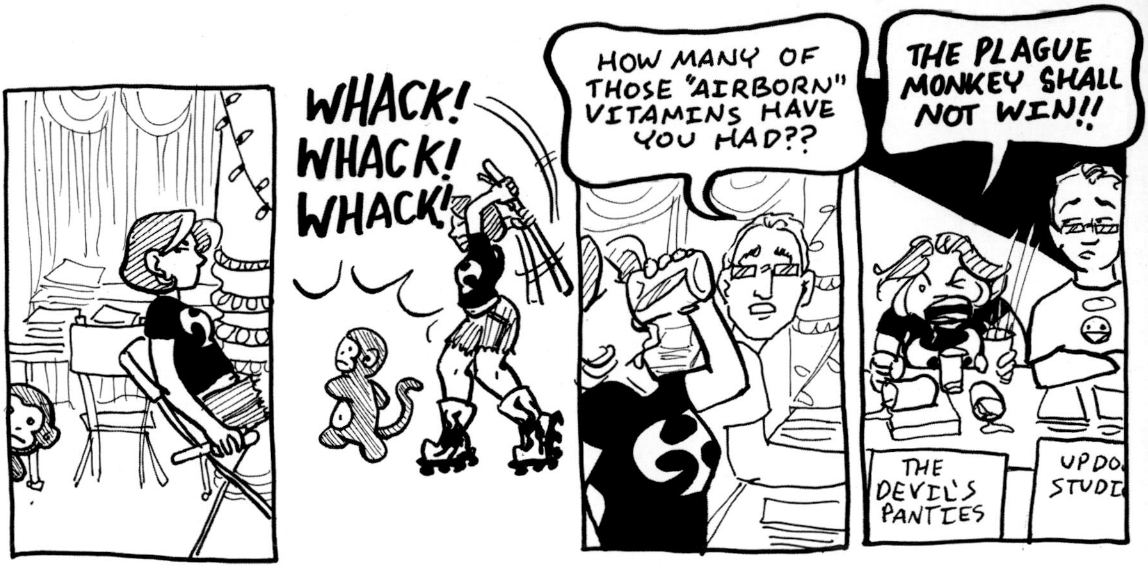
WHACK! WHACK! WHACK!
HOW MANY OF THOSE "AIRBORN" VITAMINS HAVE YOU HAD??
THE PLAGUE MONKEY SHALL NOT WIN!!
THE DEVIL'S PANTIES

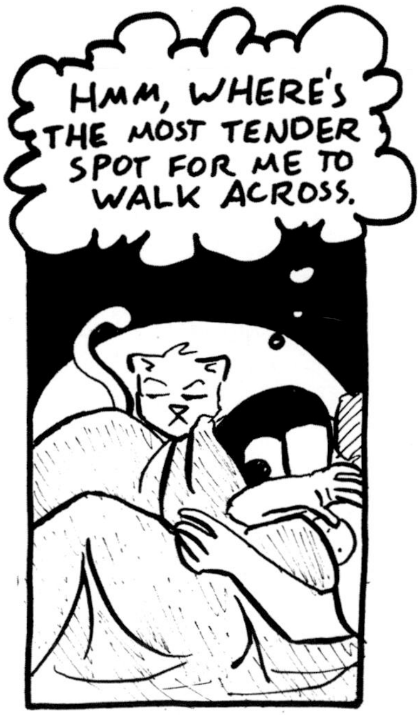
HMM, WHERE'S THE MOST TENDER SPOT FOR ME TO WALK ACROSS.

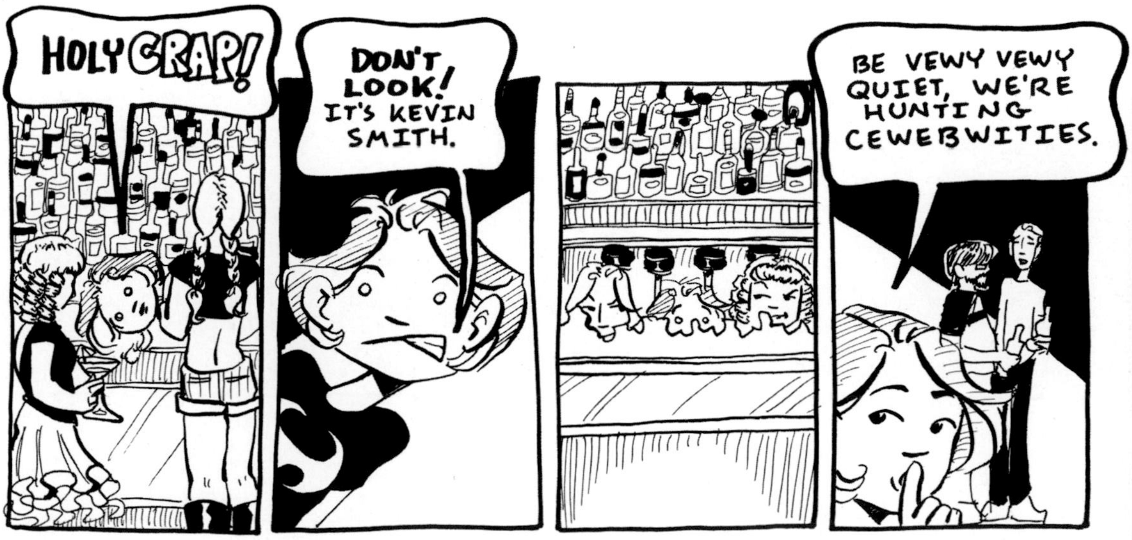
HOLY CRAP!
DON'T LOOK! IT'S KEVIN SMITH.
BE VEWY VEWY QUIET, WE'RE HUNTING CEWEBWITIES.

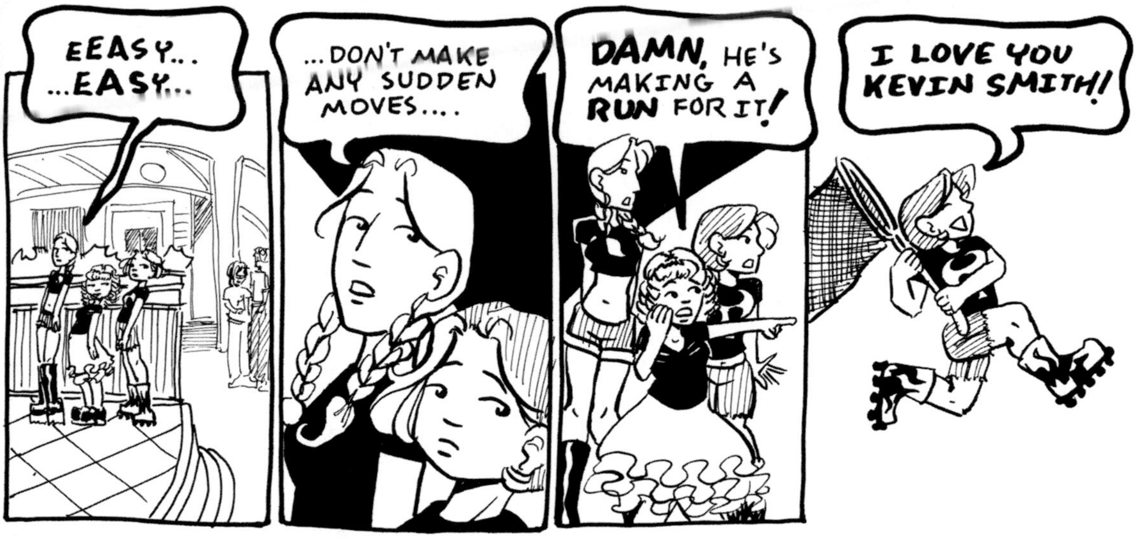
EEASY...
...EASY...
...DON'T MAKE ANY SUDDEN MOVES....
DAMN, HE'S MAKING A RUN FOR IT!
I LOVE YOU KEVIN SMITH!

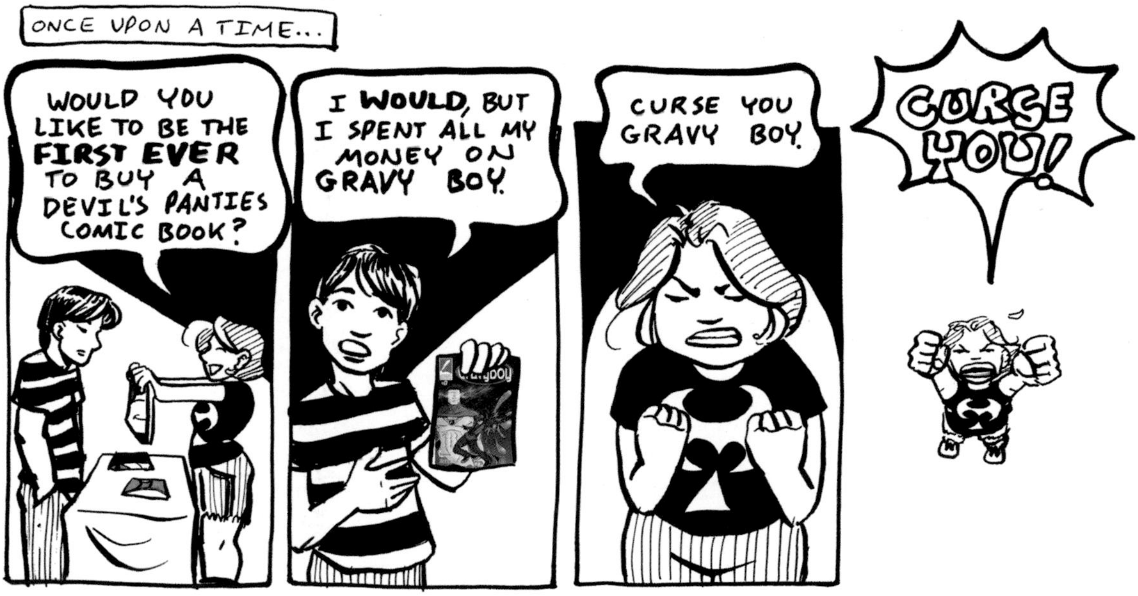
ONCE UPON A TIME...
WOULD YOU LIKE TO BE THE FIRST EVER TO BUY A DEVIL'S PANTIES COMIC BOOK?
I WOULD, BUT I SPENT ALL MY MONEY ON GRAVY BOY.
CURSE YOU GRAVY BOY.
CURSE YOU!

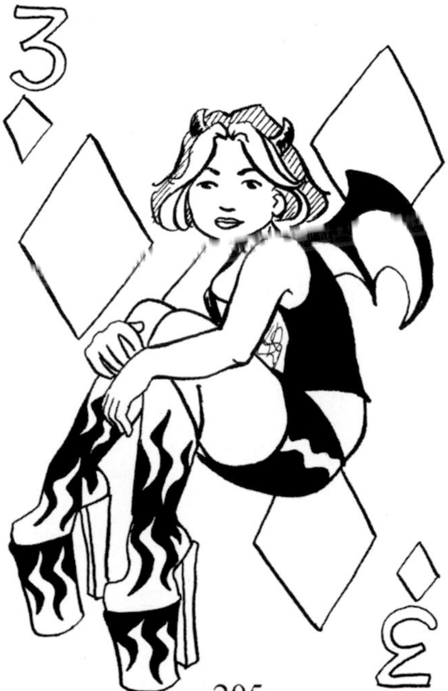
3
3

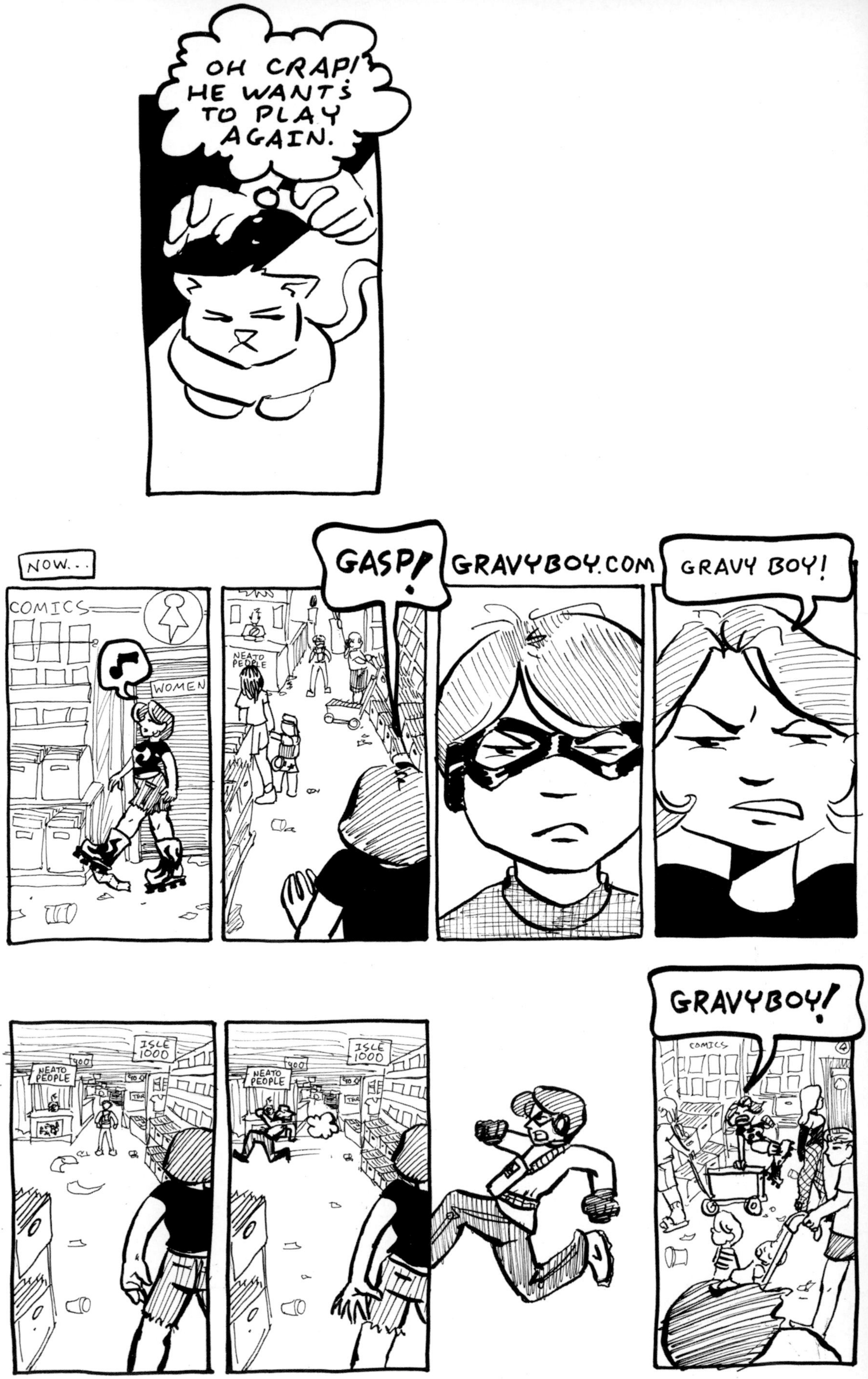
OH CRAP! HE WANTS TO PLAY AGAIN.
NOW...
COMICS
WOMEN
NEATO PEOPLE
GASP!
GRAVYBOY.COM
GRAVY BOY!
NEATO PEOPLE
ISLE 1000
NEATO PEOPLE
ISLE 1000
GRAVYBOY!
COMICS

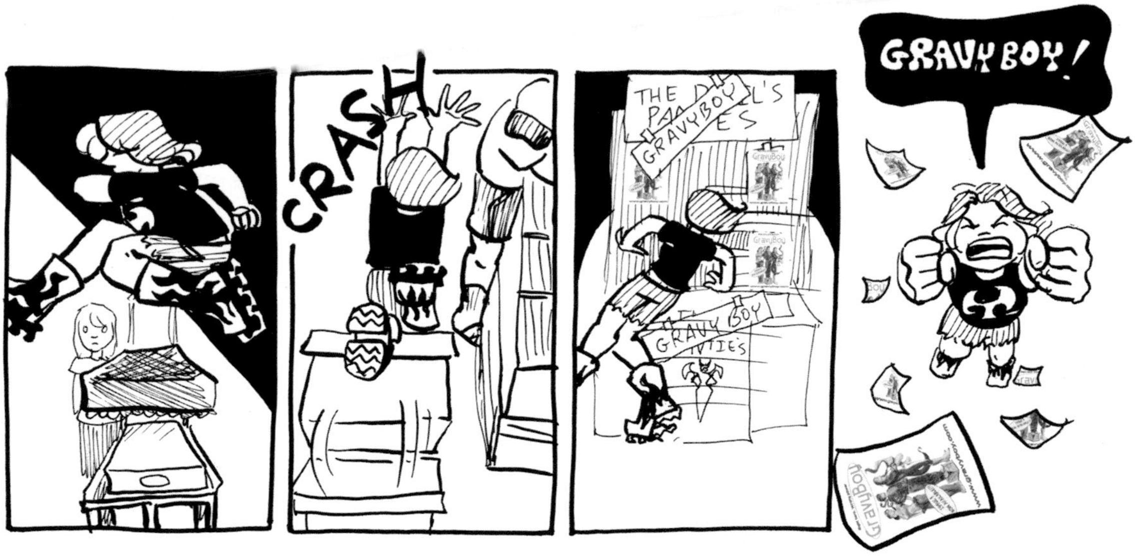
CRASH
GRAVYBOY
GRAVYBOY!

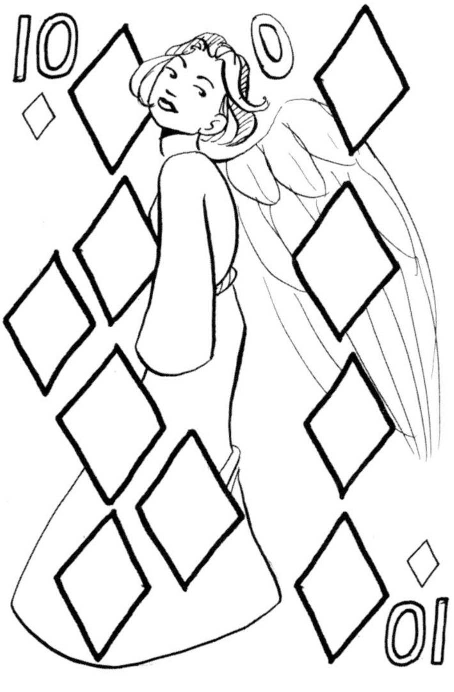
10

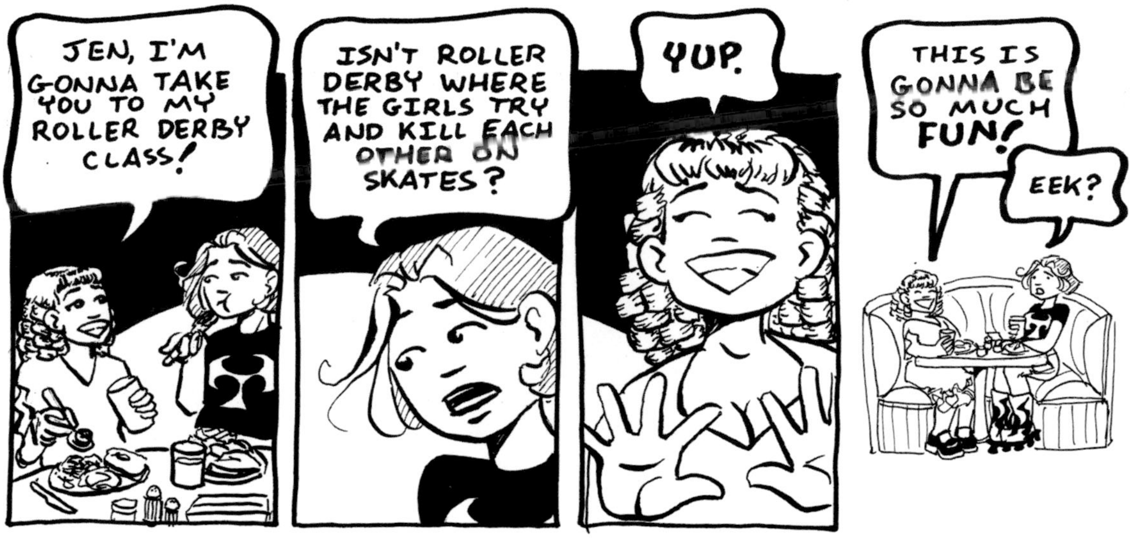
JEN, I'M GONNA TAKE YOU TO MY ROLLER DERBY CLASS!
ISN'T ROLLER DERBY WHERE THE GIRLS TRY AND KILL EACH OTHER ON SKATES?
YUP.
THIS IS GONNA BE SO MUCH FUN!
EEK?

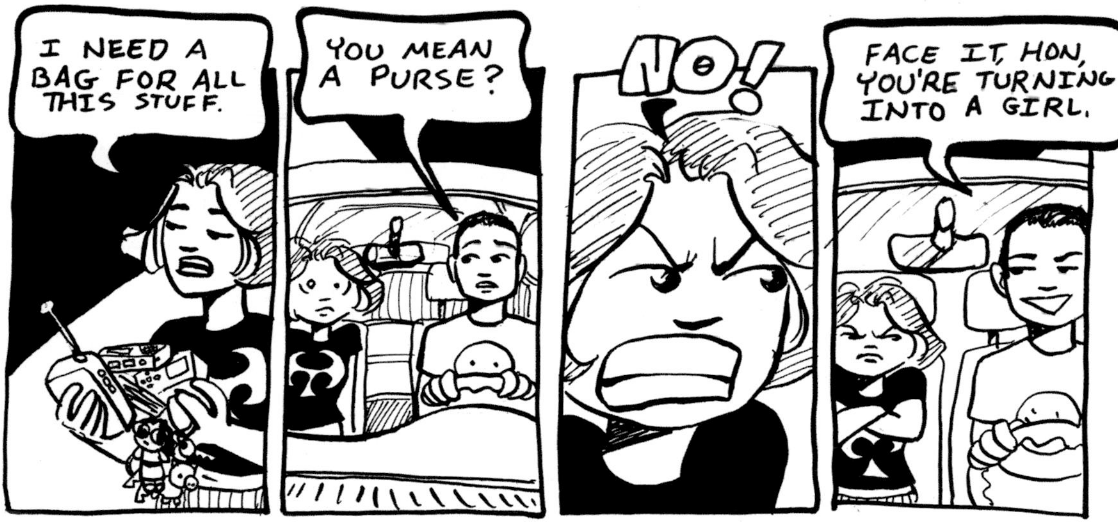
I NEED A BAG FOR ALL THIS STUFF.
YOU MEAN A PURSE?
NO!
FACE IT, HON, YOU'RE TURNING INTO A GIRL.

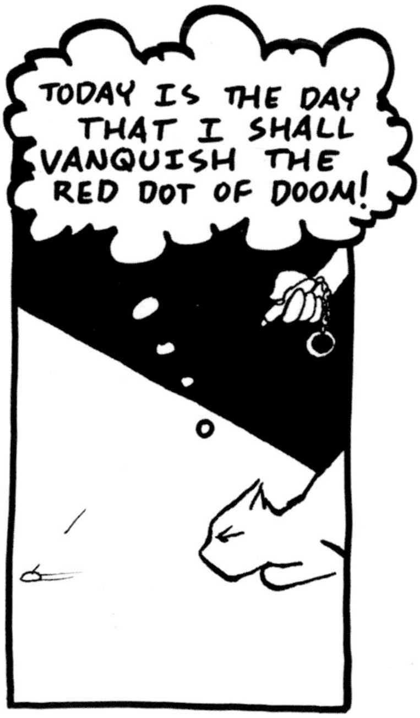
TODAY IS THE DAY THAT I SHALL VANQUISH THE RED DOT OF DOOM!

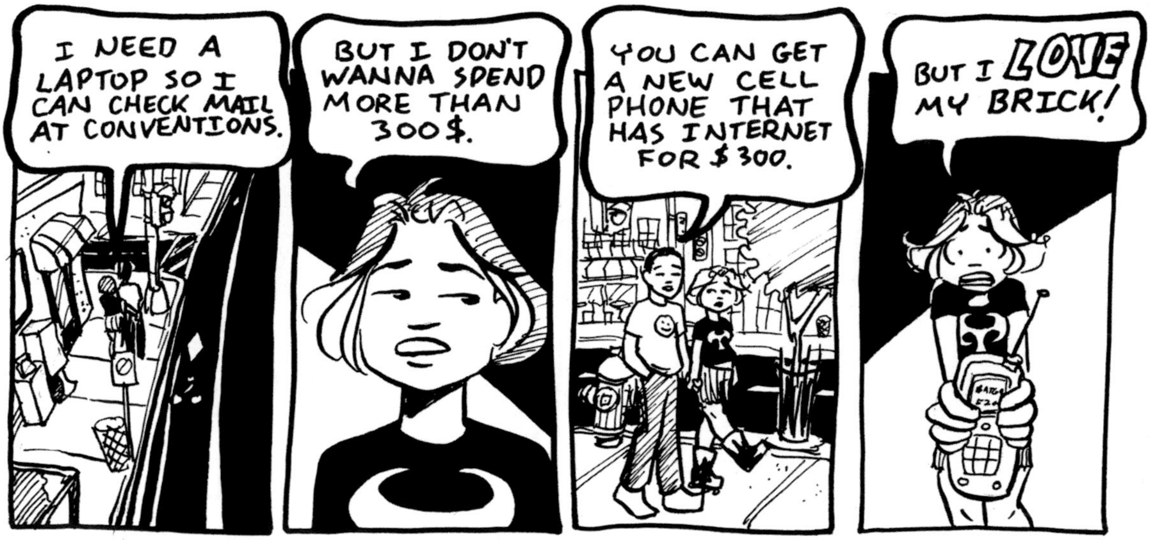
I NEED A LAPTOP SO I CAN CHECK MAIL AT CONVENTIONS.
BUT I DON'T WANNA SPEND MORE THAN 300$.
YOU CAN GET A NEW CELL PHONE THAT HAS INTERNET FOR $300.
BUT I LOVE MY BRICK!

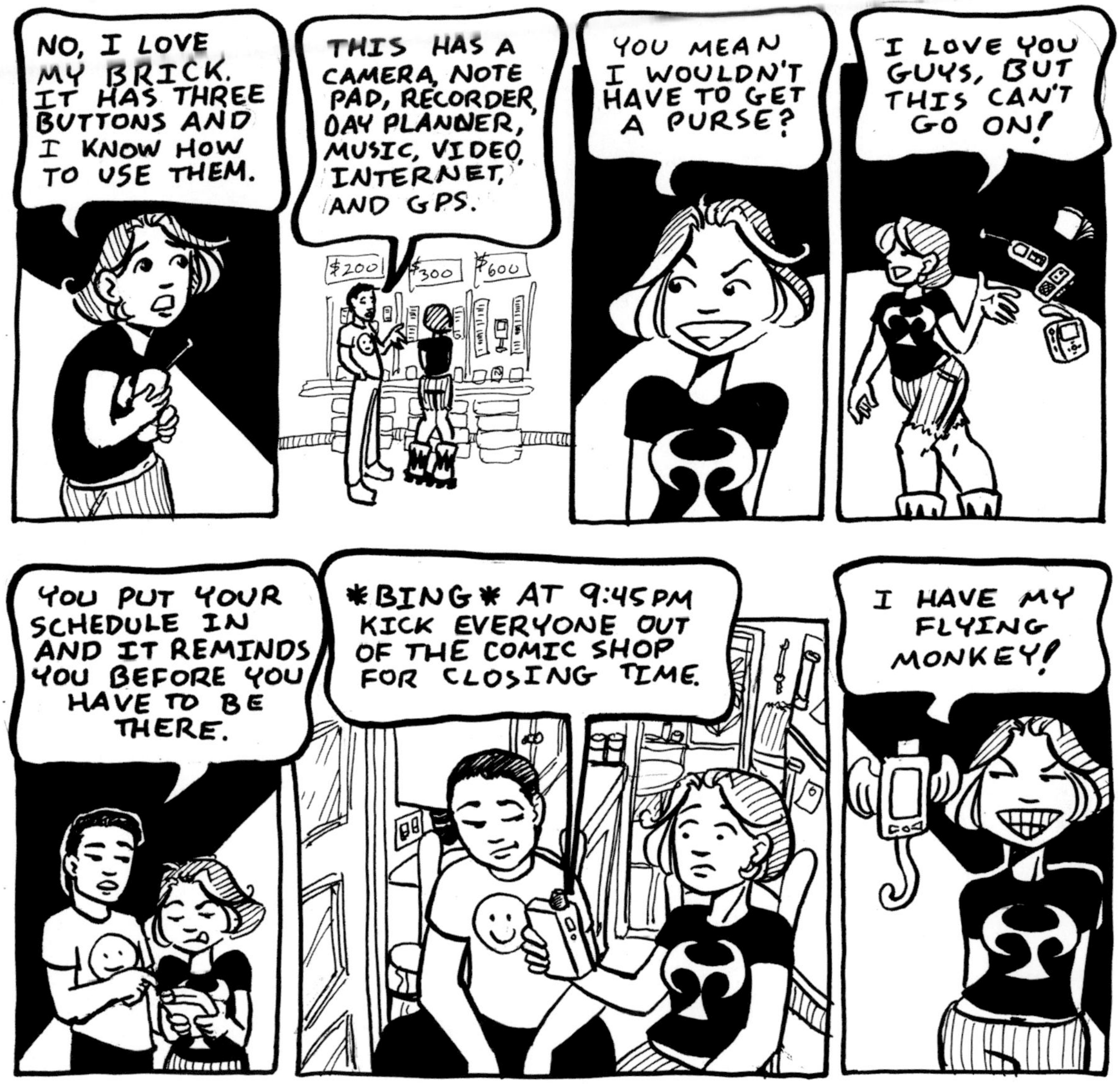
NO, I LOVE MY BRICK. IT HAS THREE BUTTONS AND I KNOW HOW TO USE THEM.
THIS HAS A CAMERA, NOTE PAD, RECORDER, DAY PLANNER, MUSIC, VIDEO, INTERNET, AND GPS.
$200
$300
$600
YOU MEAN I WOULDN'T HAVE TO GET A PURSE?
I LOVE YOU GUYS, BUT THIS CAN'T GO ON!
YOU PUT YOUR SCHEDULE IN AND IT REMINDS YOU BEFORE YOU HAVE TO BE THERE.
BING AT 9:45 PM KICK EVERYONE OUT OF THE COMIC SHOP FOR CLOSING TIME.
I HAVE MY FLYING MONKEY!

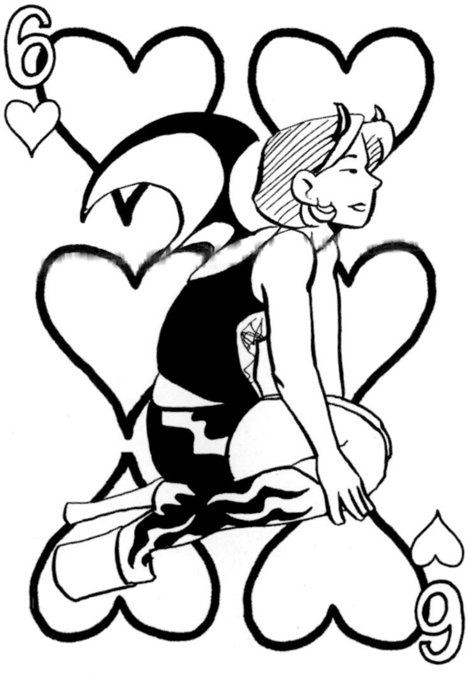
6
9

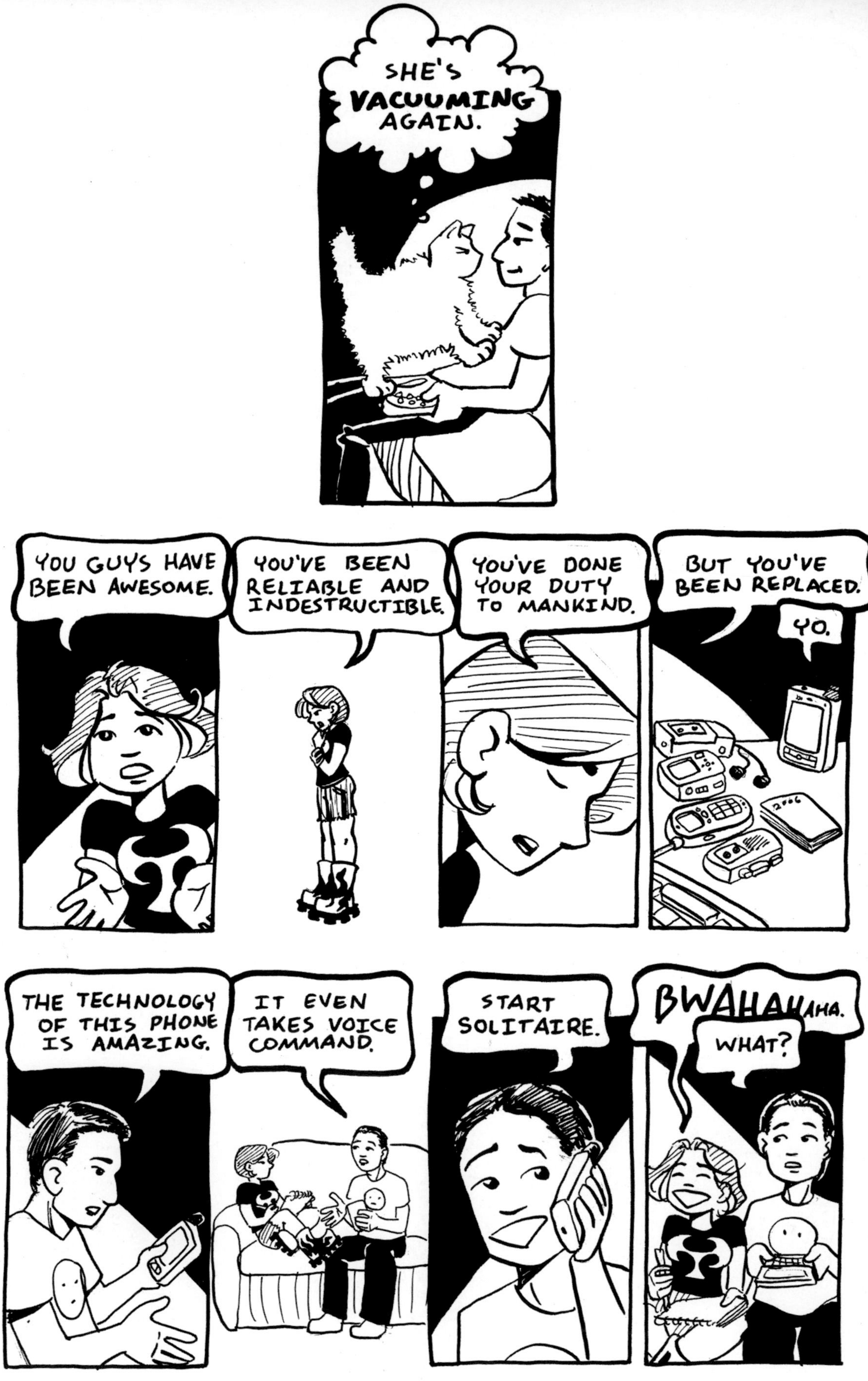
SHE'S VACUUMING AGAIN.
YOU GUYS HAVE BEEN AWESOME.
YOU'VE BEEN RELIABLE AND INDESTRUCTIBLE.
YOU'VE DONE YOUR DUTY TO MANKIND.
BUT YOU'VE BEEN REPLACED.
YO.
THE TECHNOLOGY OF THIS PHONE IS AMAZING.
IT EVEN TAKES VOICE COMMAND.
START SOLITAIRE.
BWAHAHAHA.
WHAT?

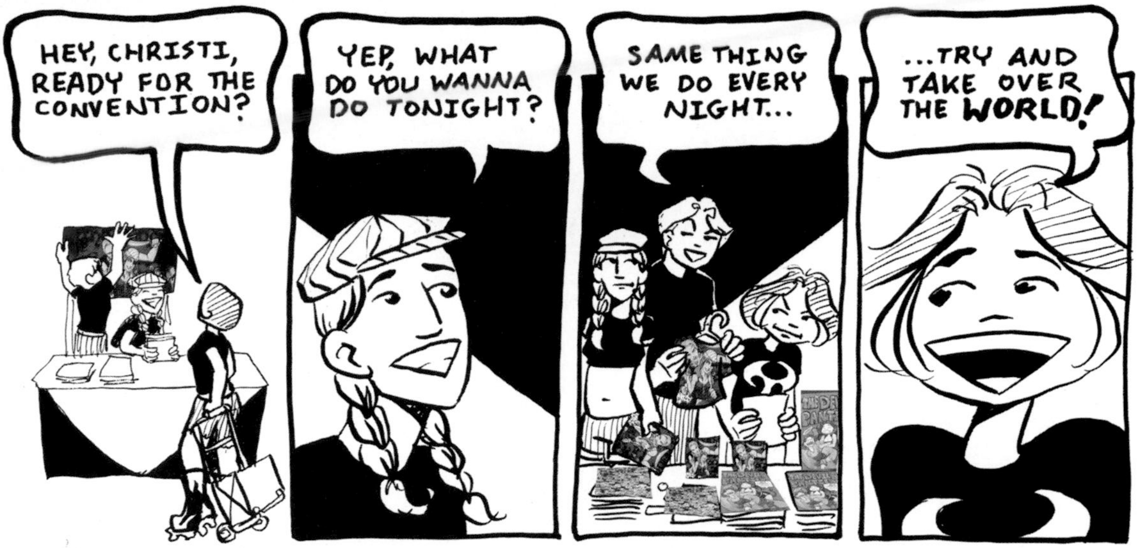
HEY, CHRISTI, READY FOR THE CONVENTION?
YEP, WHAT DO YOU WANNA DO TONIGHT?
SAME THING WE DO EVERY NIGHT...
...TRY AND TAKE OVER THE WORLD!

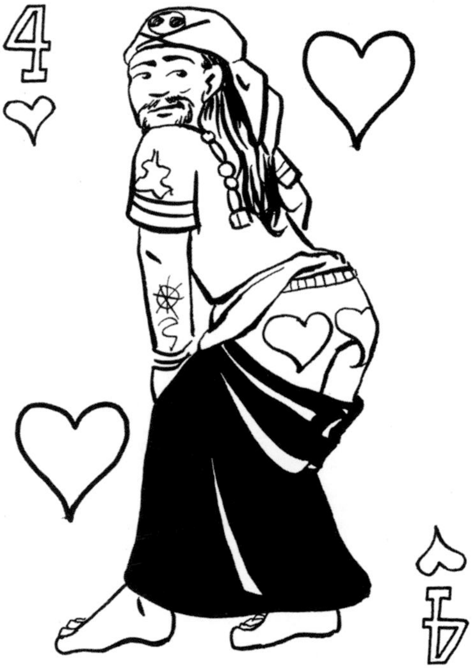

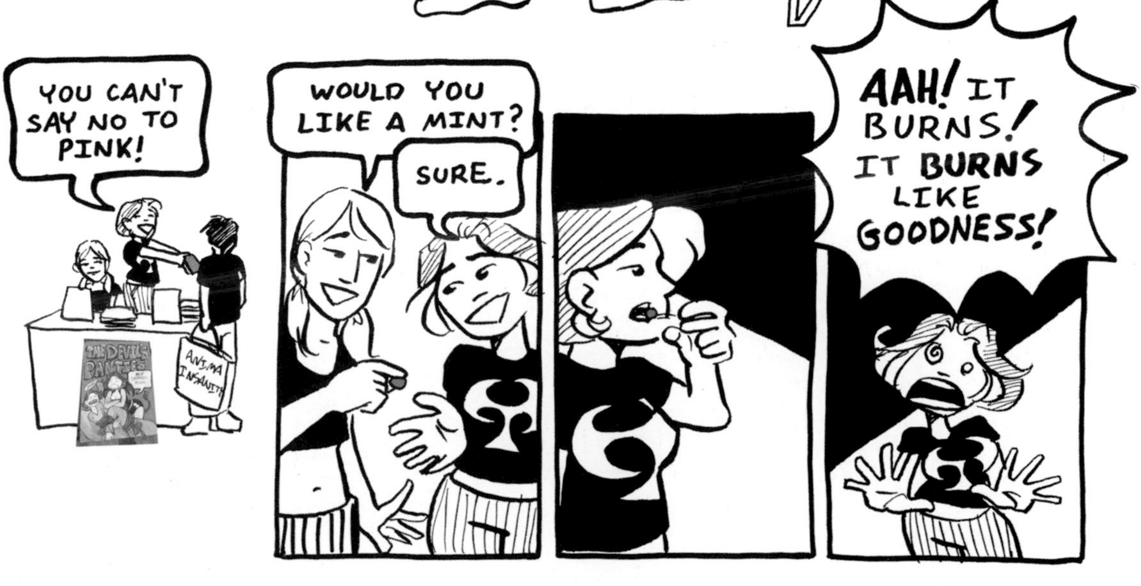
YOU CAN'T SAY NO TO PINK!
WOULD YOU LIKE A MINT?
SURE.
AAH! IT BURNS! IT BURNS LIKE GOODNESS!

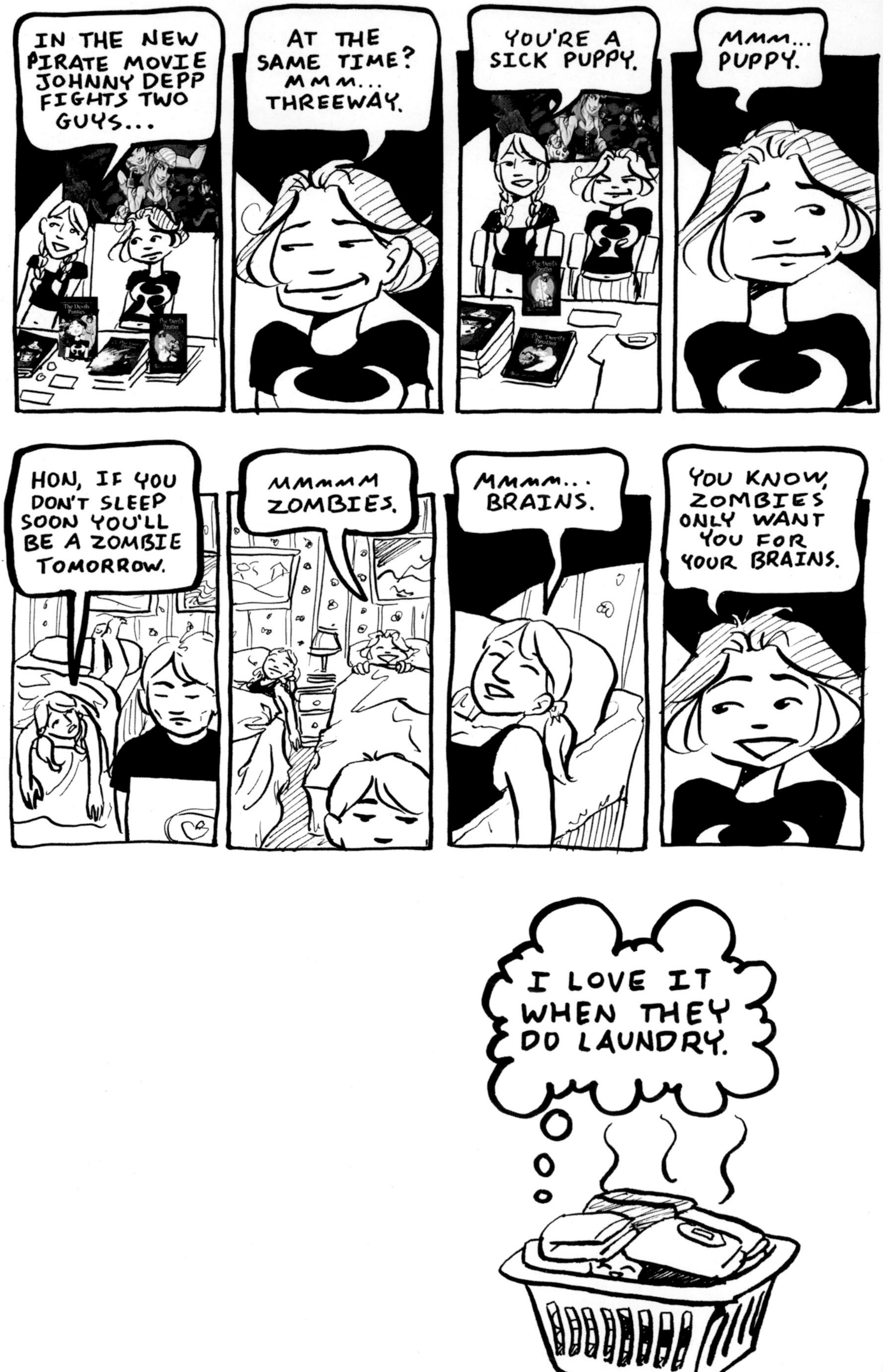

IN THE NEW PIRATE MOVIE JOHNNY DEPP FIGHTS TWO GUYS...
AT THE SAME TIME? MMM... THREEWAY.
YOU'RE A SICK PUPPY.
MMM... PUPPY.
HON, IF YOU DON'T SLEEP SOON YOU'LL BE A ZOMBIE TOMORROW.
MMMMM ZOMBIES.
MMMM... BRAINS.
YOU KNOW, ZOMBIES ONLY WANT YOU FOR YOUR BRAINS.
I LOVE IT WHEN THEY DO LAUNDRY.

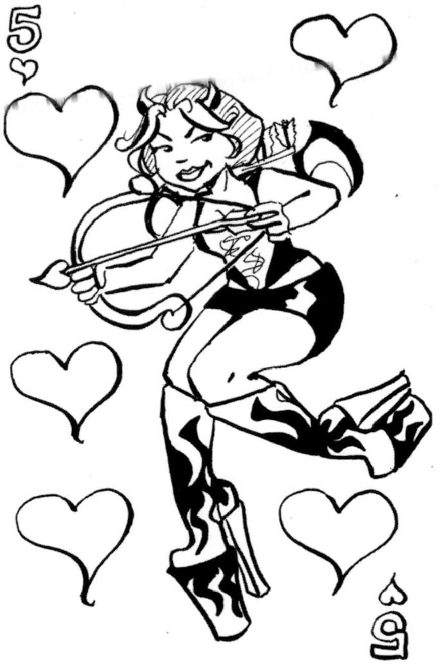
5
5

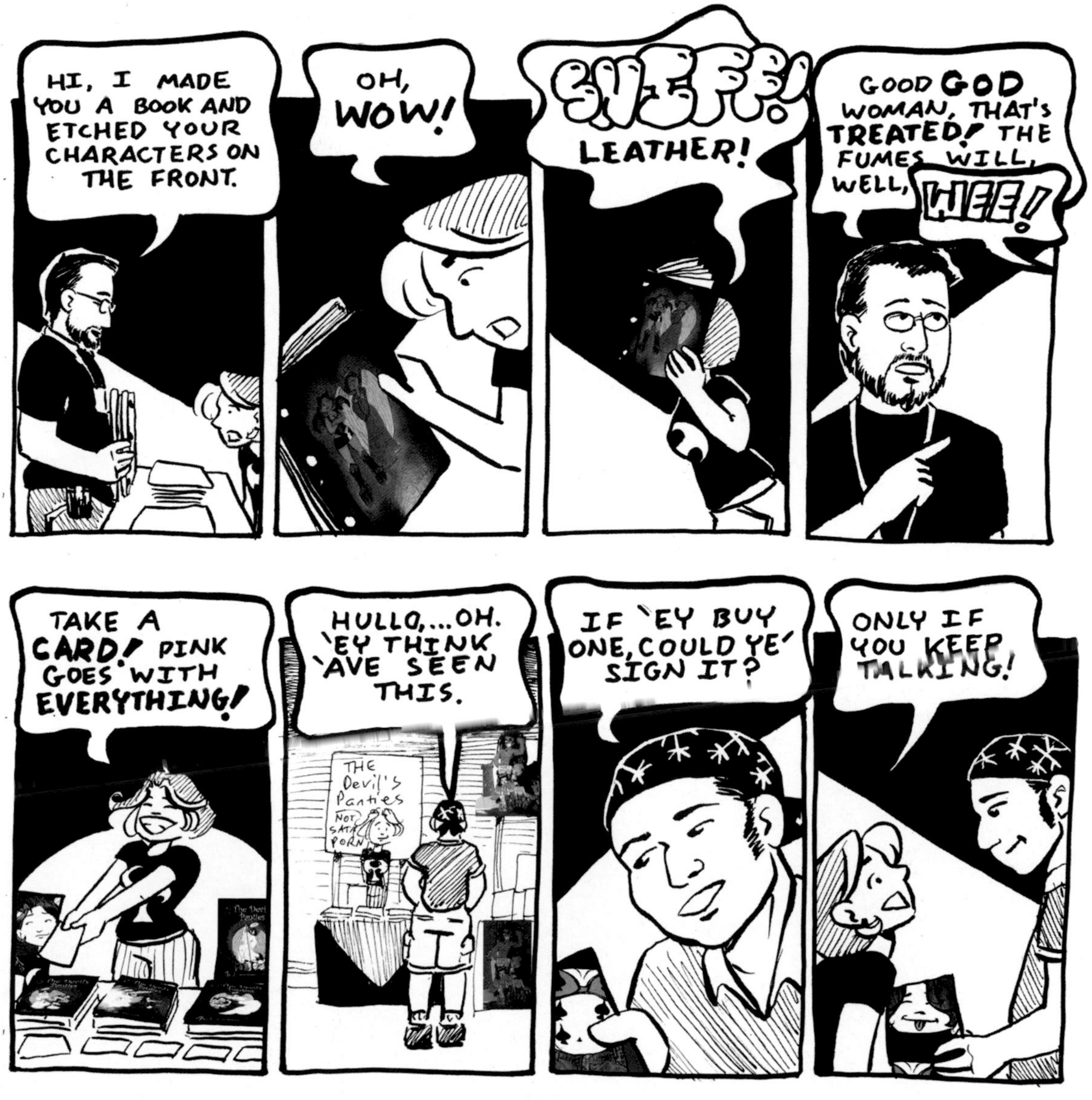
HI, I MADE YOU A BOOK AND ETCHED YOUR CHARACTERS ON THE FRONT.
OH, WOW!
SNIFF! LEATHER!
GOOD GOD WOMAN, THAT'S TREATED! THE FUMES WILL, WELL,
WHEE!
TAKE A CARD! PINK GOES WITH EVERYTHING!
The Devil's Panties
HULLO,...OH. `EY THINK `AVE SEEN THIS.
THE Devil's Panties
IF `EY BUY ONE, COULD YE' SIGN IT?
ONLY IF YOU KEEP TALKING!

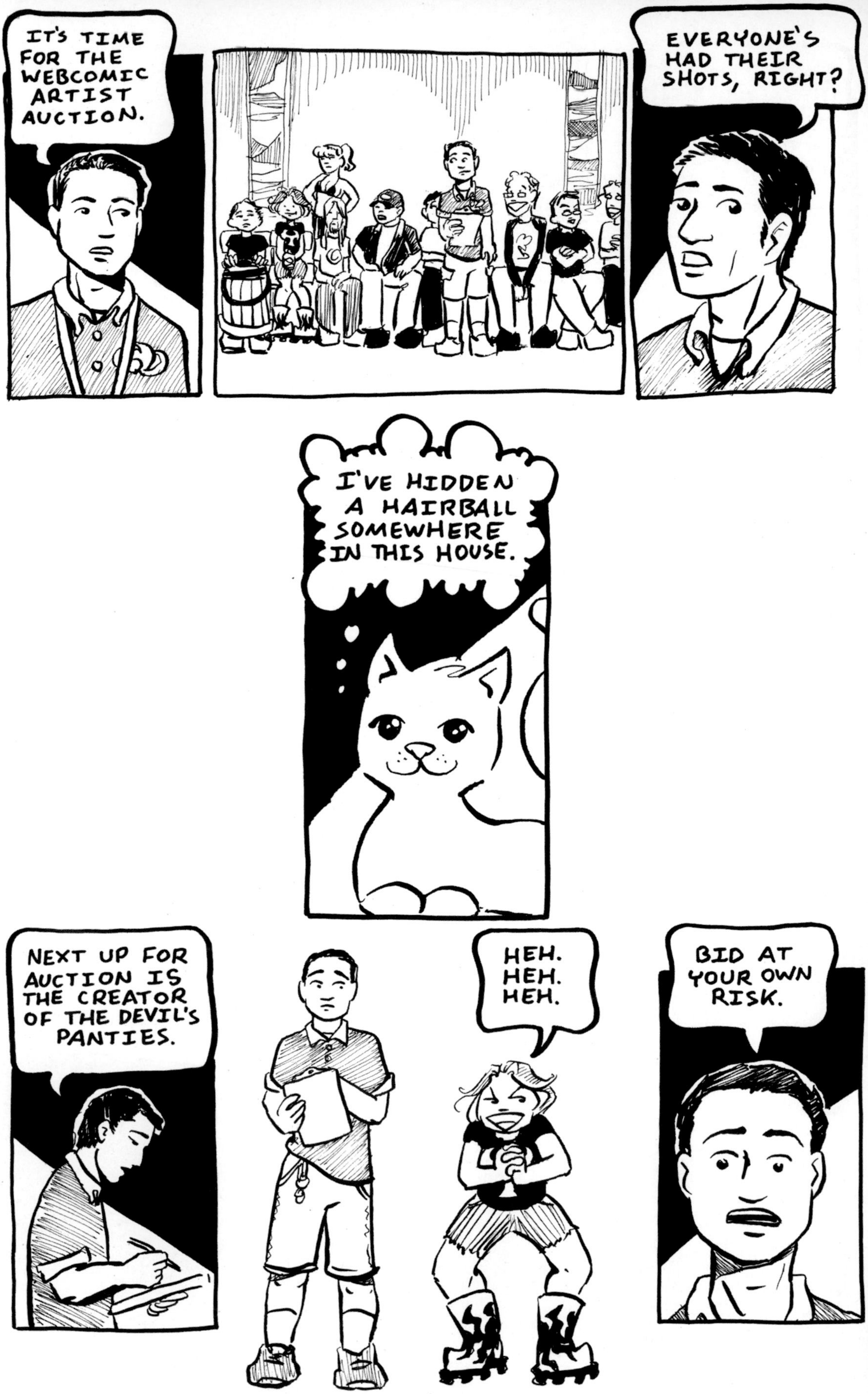
IT'S TIME FOR THE WEBCOMIC ARTIST AUCTION.
EVERYONE'S HAD THEIR SHOTS, RIGHT?
I'VE HIDDEN A HAIRBALL SOMEWHERE IN THIS HOUSE.
NEXT UP FOR AUCTION IS THE CREATOR OF THE DEVIL'S PANTIES.
HEH. HEH. HEH.
BID AT YOUR OWN RISK.

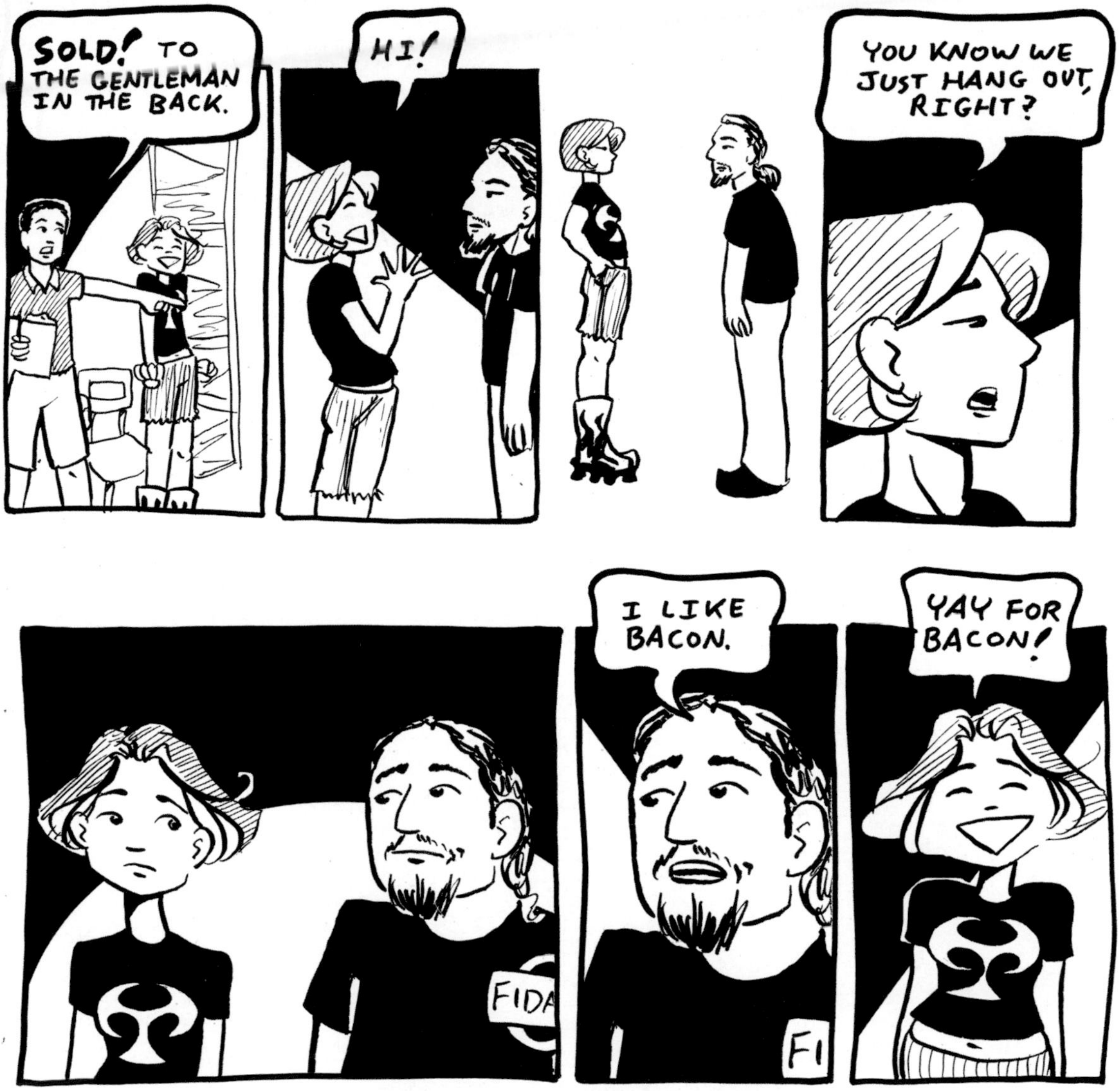
SOLD! TO THE GENTLEMAN IN THE BACK.
HI!
YOU KNOW WE JUST HANG OUT, RIGHT?
FIDA
I LIKE BACON.
FI
YAY FOR BACON!

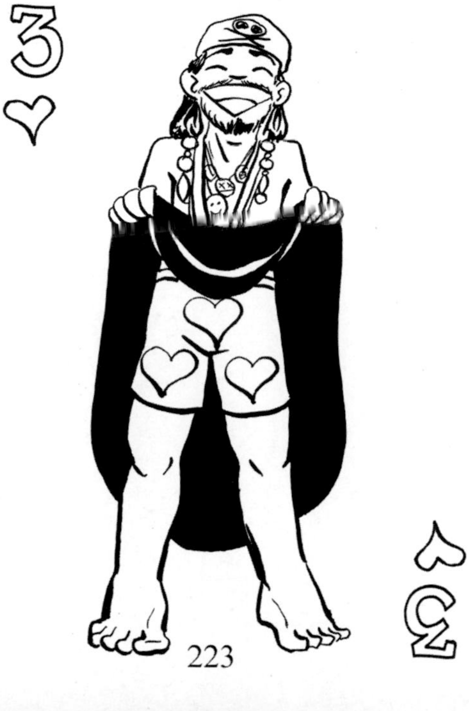
3
3

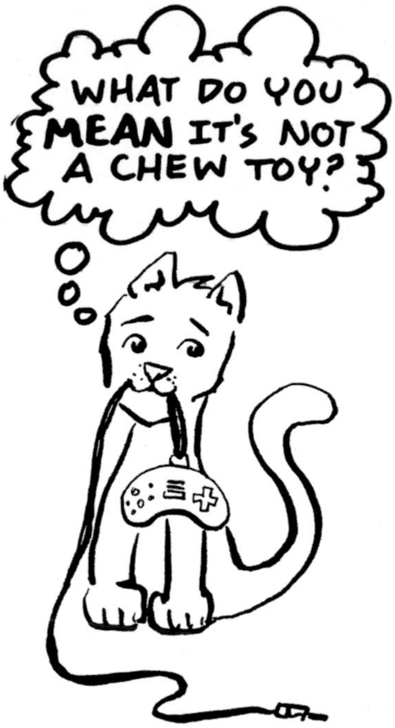
WHAT DO YOU MEAN IT'S NOT A CHEW TOY?

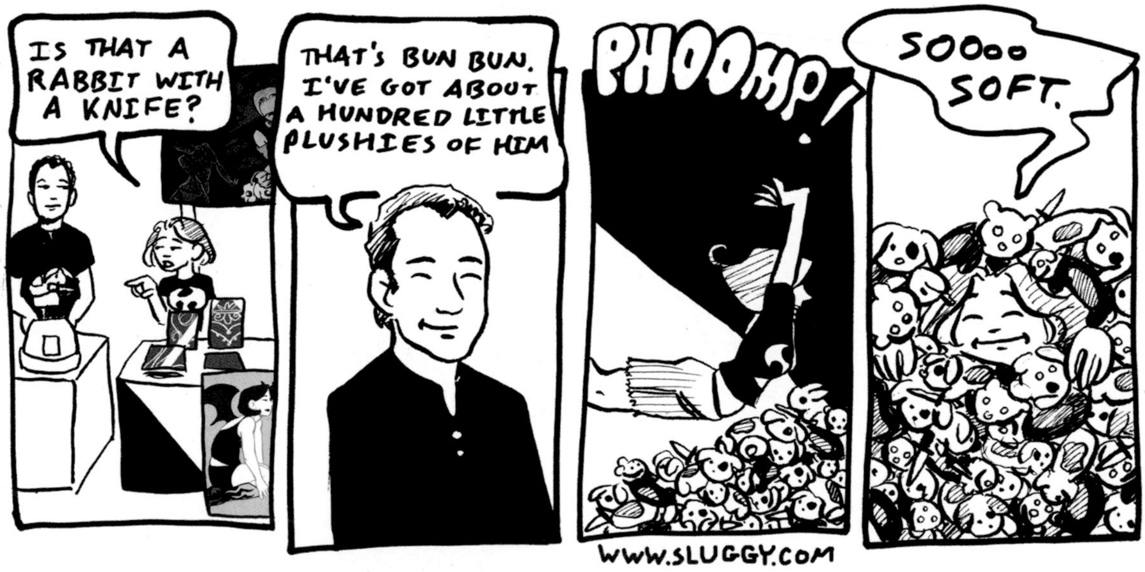
IS THAT A RABBIT WITH A KNIFE?
THAT'S BUN BUN. I'VE GOT ABOUT A HUNDRED LITTLE PLUSHIES OF HIM
PHOOMP!
SOOooo SOFT.
WWW.SLUGGY.COM

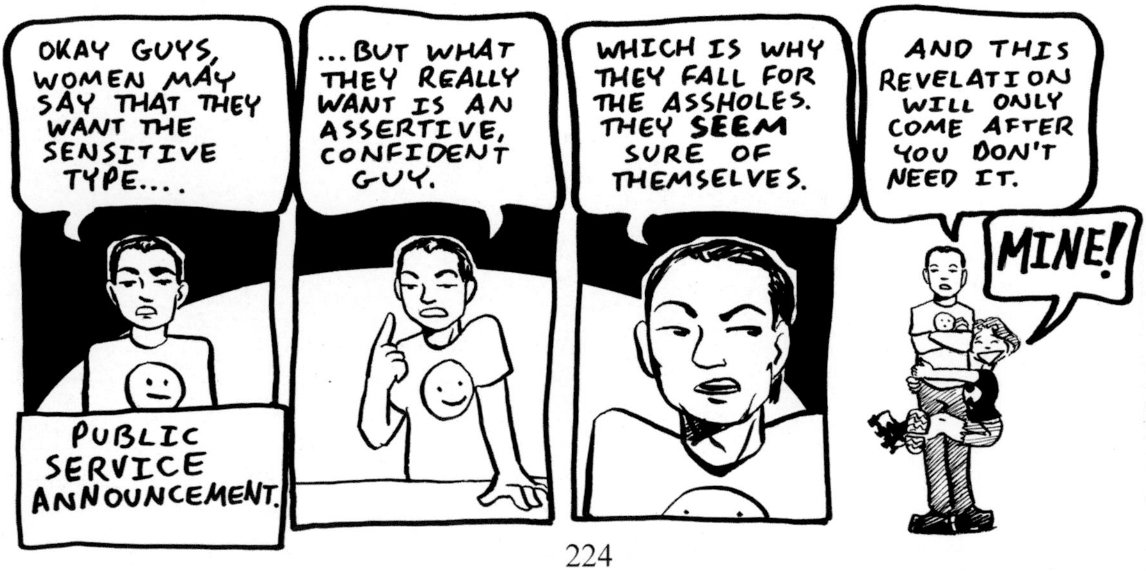
OKAY GUYS, WOMEN MAY SAY THAT THEY WANT THE SENSITIVE TYPE....
PUBLIC SERVICE ANNOUNCEMENT.
...BUT WHAT THEY REALLY WANT IS AN ASSERTIVE, CONFIDENT GUY.
WHICH IS WHY THEY FALL FOR THE ASSHOLES. THEY SEEM SURE OF THEMSELVES.
AND THIS REVELATION WILL ONLY COME AFTER YOU DON'T NEED IT.
MINE!

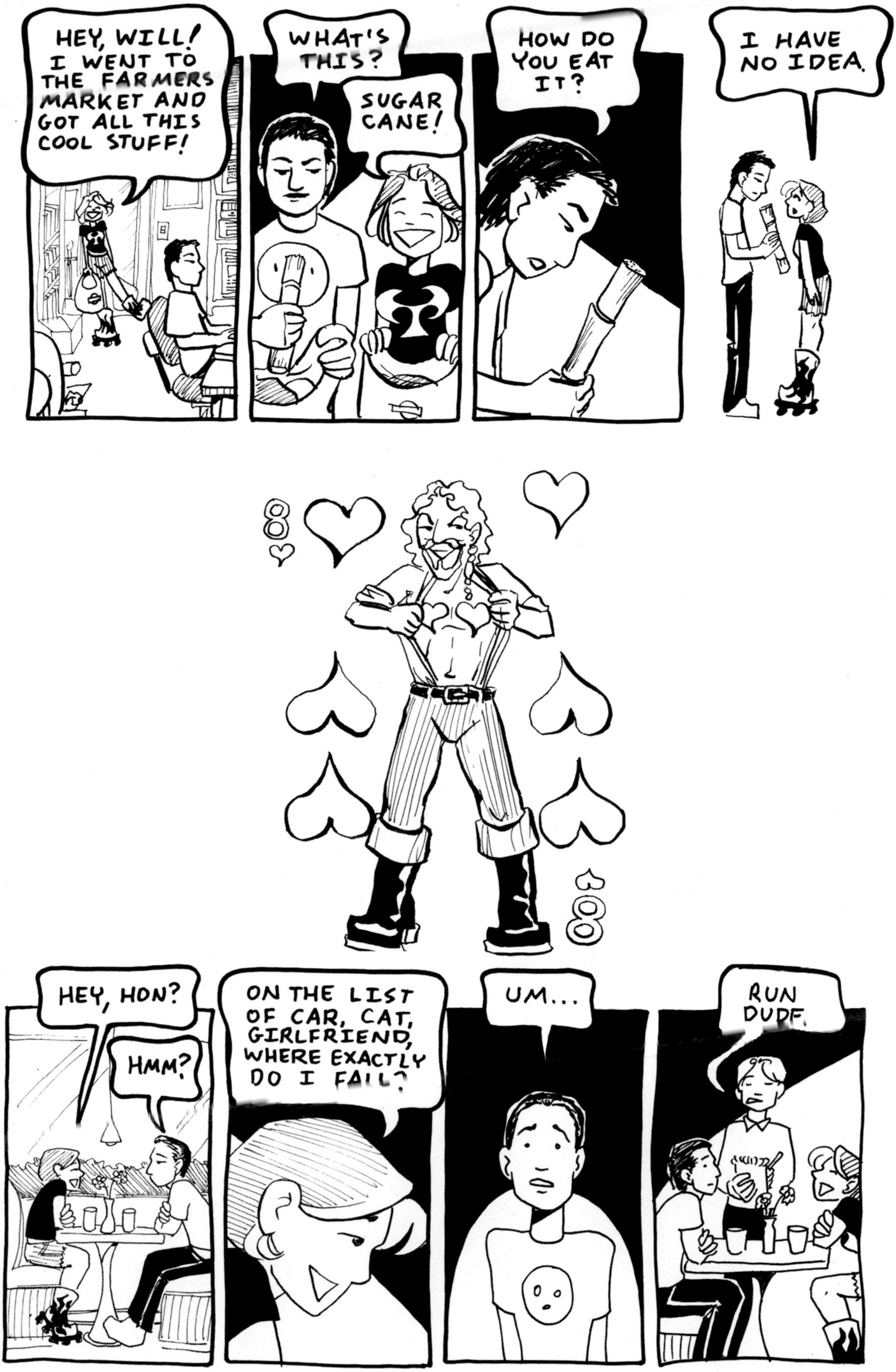
HEY, WILL! I WENT TO THE FARMERS MARKET AND GOT ALL THIS COOL STUFF!
WHAT'S THIS?
SUGAR CANE!
HOW DO YOU EAT IT?
I HAVE NO IDEA.
8
8
HEY, HON?
HMM?
ON THE LIST OF CAR, CAT, GIRLFRIEND, WHERE EXACTLY DO I FALL?
UM...
RUN DUDE.

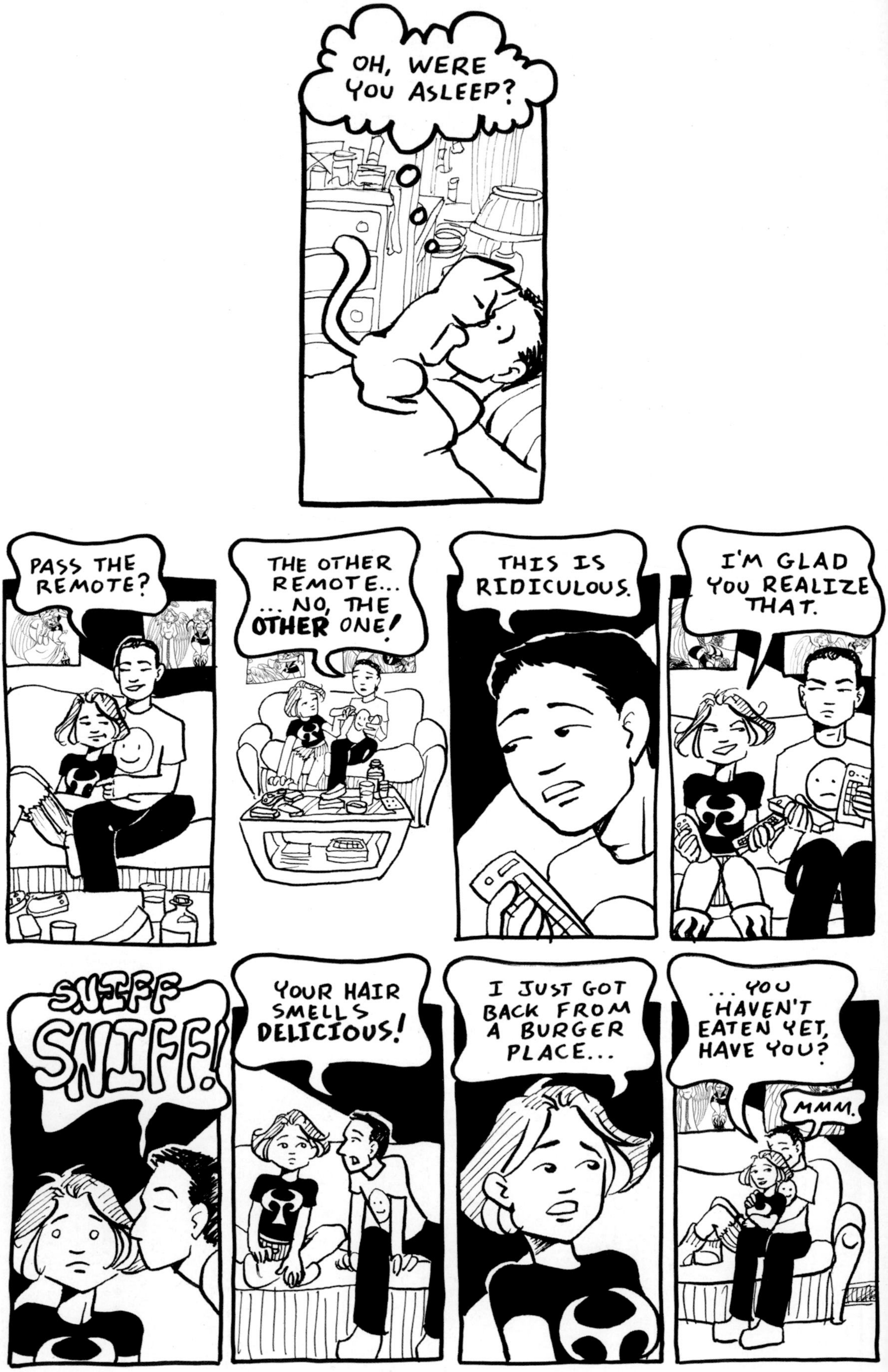
OH, WERE YOU ASLEEP?
PASS THE REMOTE?
THE OTHER REMOTE... ...NO, THE OTHER ONE!
THIS IS RIDICULOUS.
I'M GLAD YOU REALIZE THAT.
SNIFF SNIFF!
YOUR HAIR SMELLS DELICIOUS!
I JUST GOT BACK FROM A BURGER PLACE...
...YOU HAVEN'T EATEN YET, HAVE YOU?
MMM.

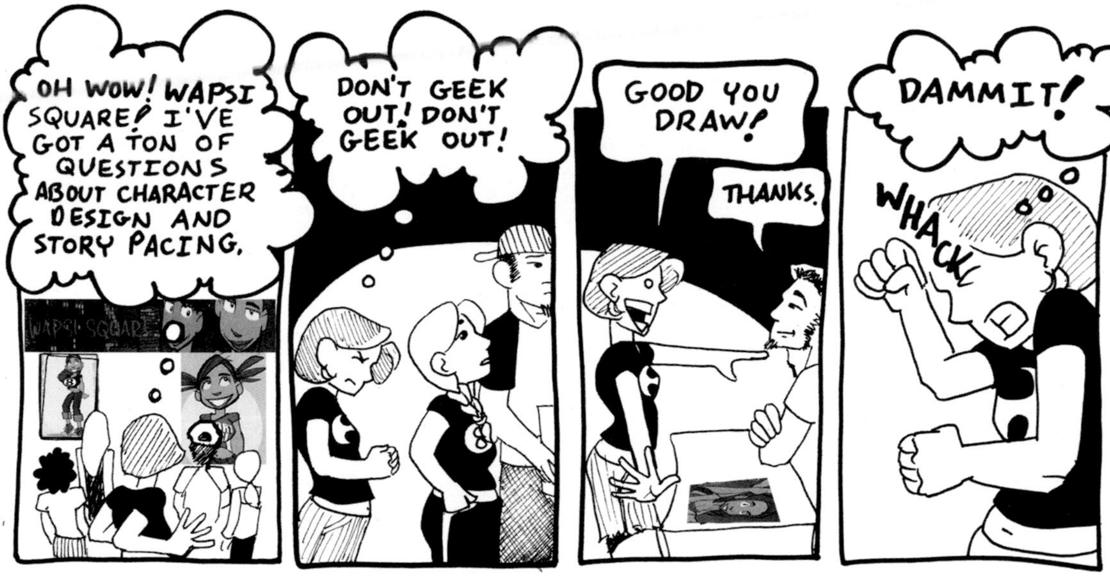
OH WOW! WAPSI SQUARE! I'VE GOT A TON OF QUESTIONS ABOUT CHARACTER DESIGN AND STORY PACING.
WAPSI SQUARE
DON'T GEEK OUT! DON'T GEEK OUT!
GOOD YOU DRAW!
THANKS.
DAMMIT!
WHACK!

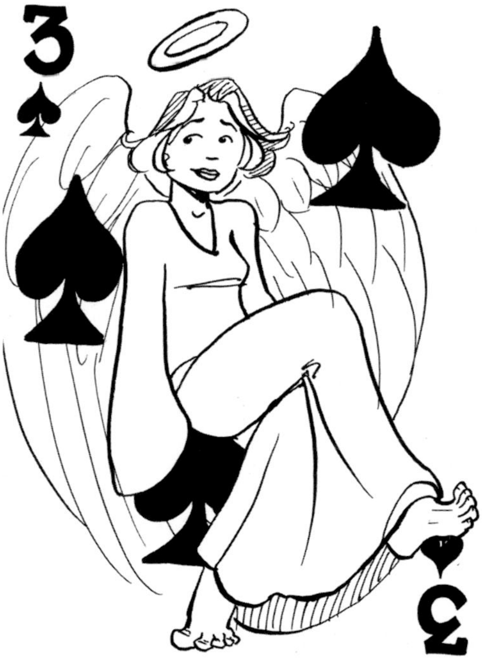
3
3

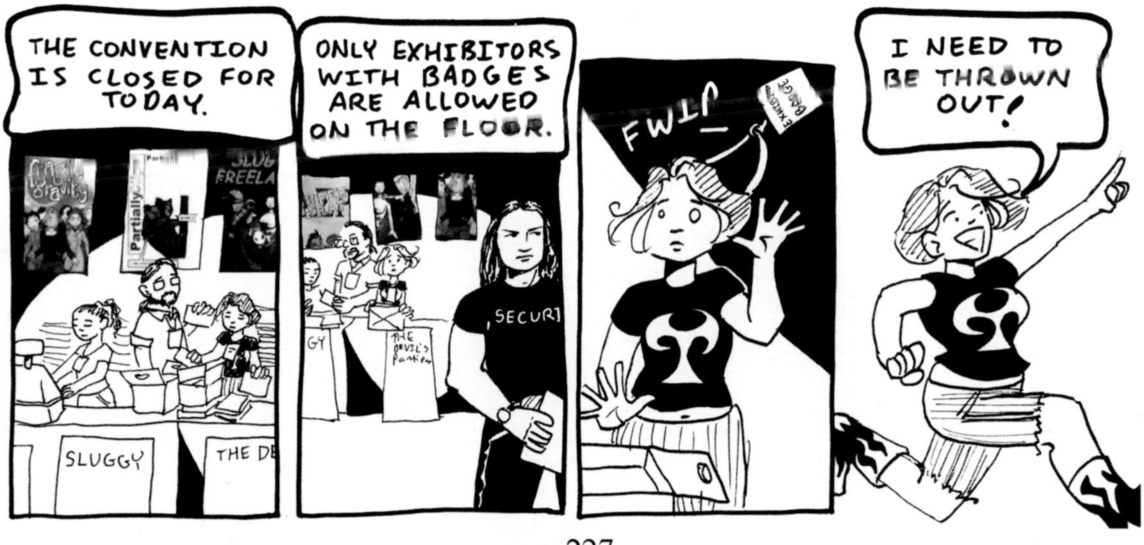
THE CONVENTION IS CLOSED FOR TODAY.
SLUGGY
THE DE
ONLY EXHIBITORS WITH BADGES ARE ALLOWED ON THE FLOOR.
SECURI
FWIP
I NEED TO BE THROWN OUT!

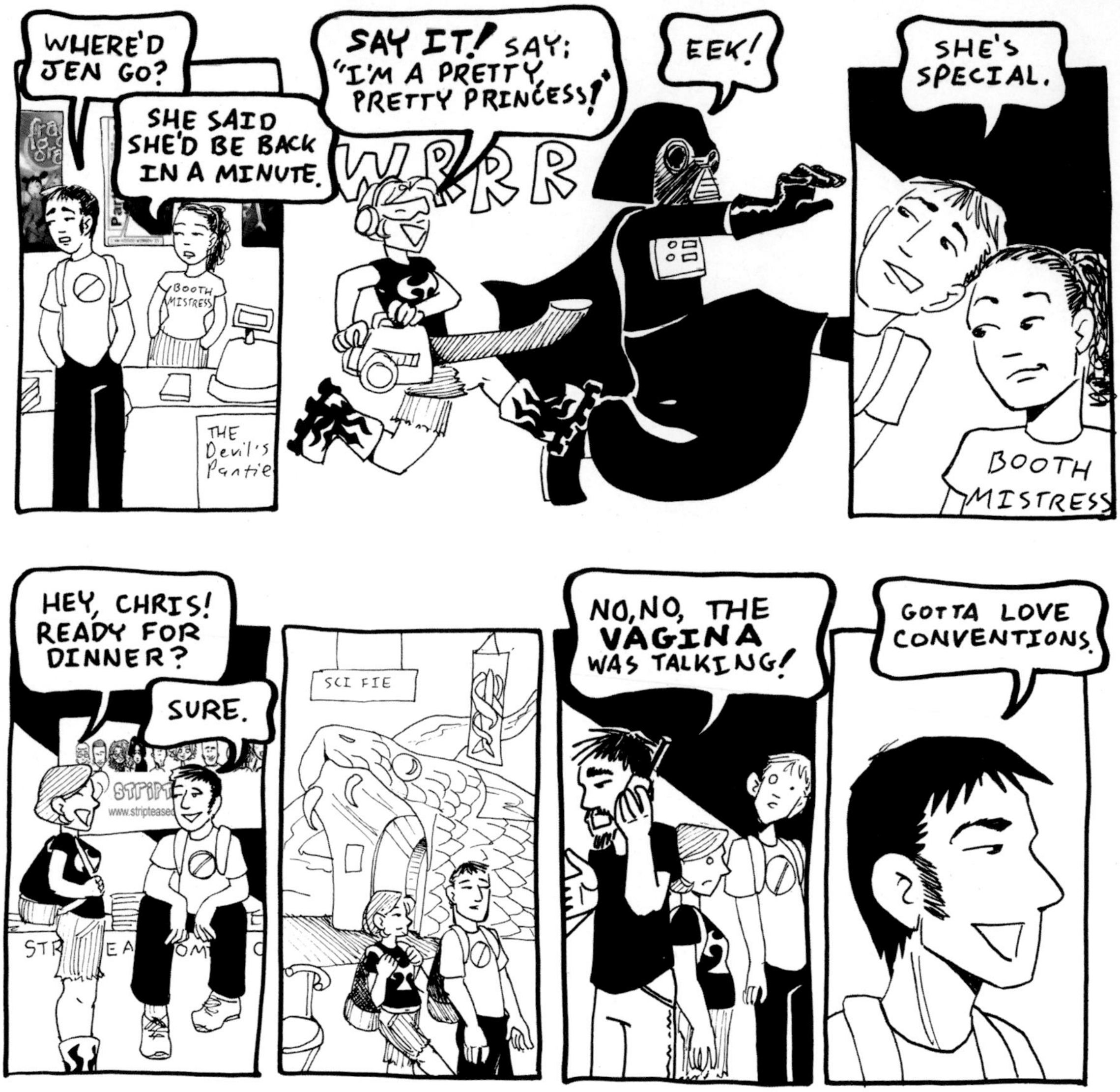
WHERE'D JEN GO?
SHE SAID SHE'D BE BACK IN A MINUTE.
BOOTH MISTRESS
THE Devil's Pantie
SAY IT! SAY: "I'M A PRETTY, PRETTY PRINCESS!"
WRRR
EEK!
SHE'S SPECIAL.
BOOTH MISTRESS
HEY, CHRIS! READY FOR DINNER?
SURE.
SCI FIE
NO, NO, THE VAGINA WAS TALKING!
GOTTA LOVE CONVENTIONS.

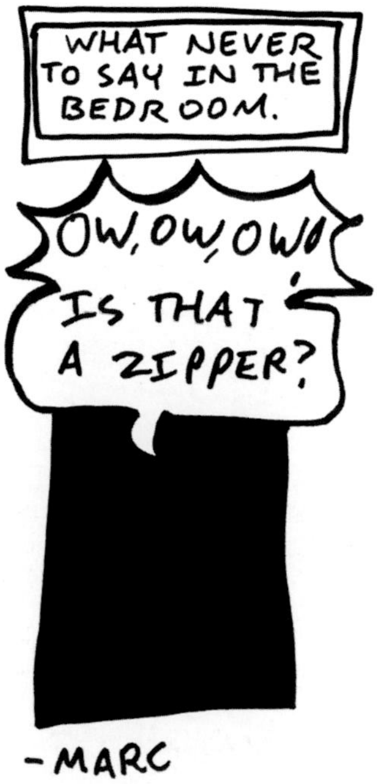
WHAT NEVER TO SAY IN THE BEDROOM.
OW, OW, OW!
IS THAT A ZIPPER?
-MARC

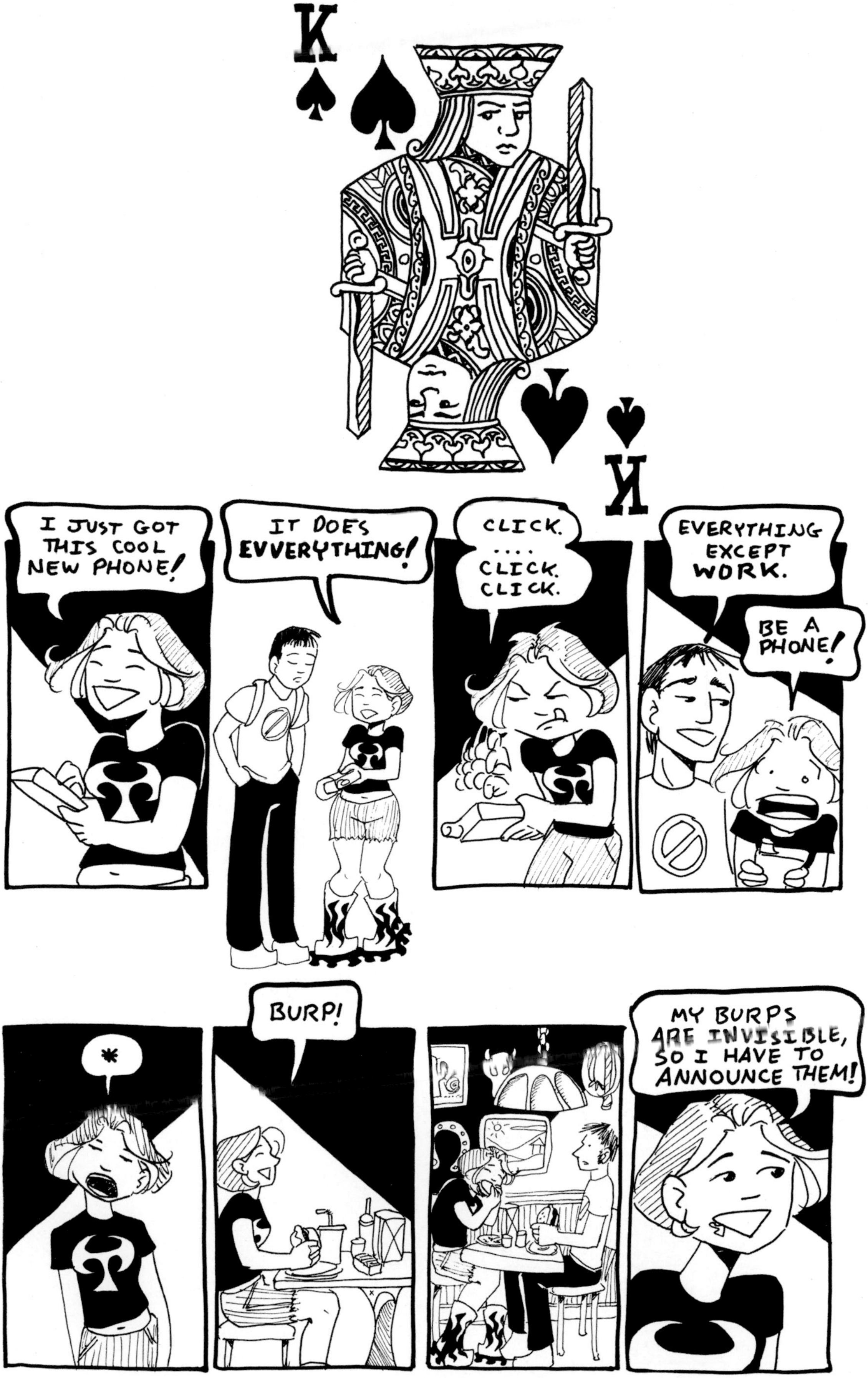
K
K
I JUST GOT THIS COOL NEW PHONE!
IT DOES EVVERYTHING!
CLICK. .... CLICK. CLICK.
EVERYTHING EXCEPT WORK.
BE A PHONE!
*
BURP!
MY BURPS ARE INVISIBLE, SO I HAVE TO ANNOUNCE THEM!

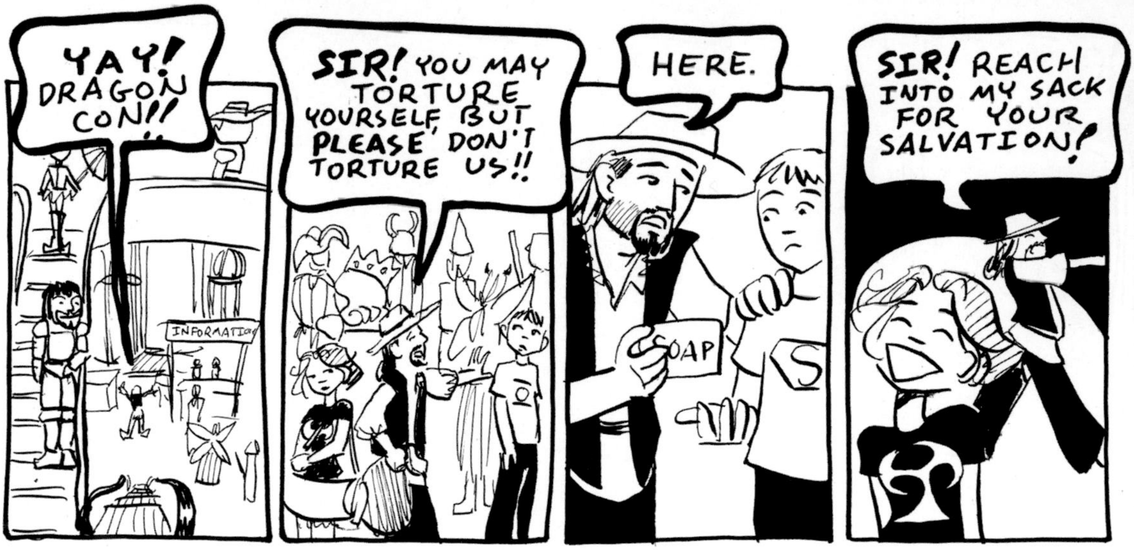
YAY! DRAGON CON!!
SIR! YOU MAY TORTURE YOURSELF, BUT PLEASE DON'T TORTURE US!!
HERE.
SOAP
SIR! REACH INTO MY SACK FOR YOUR SALVATION!

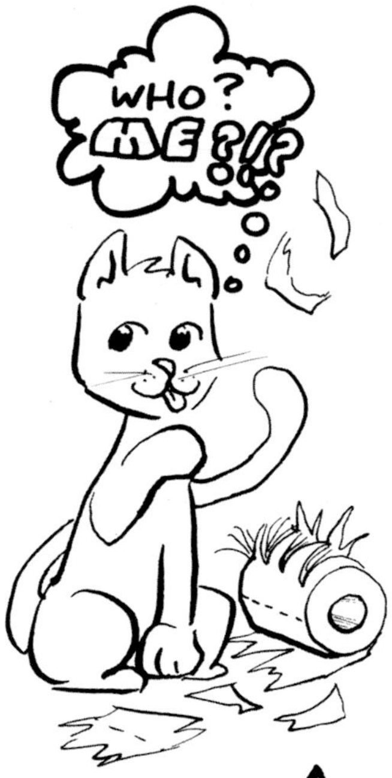
WHO? ME?!?

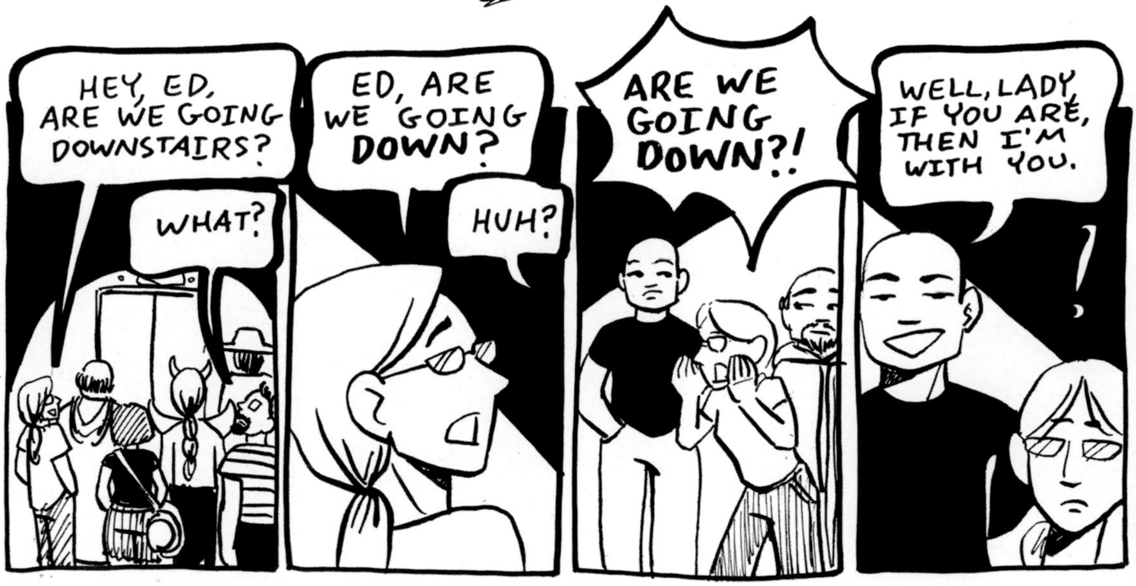
HEY, ED, ARE WE GOING DOWNSTAIRS?
WHAT?
ED, ARE WE GOING DOWN?
HUH?
ARE WE GOING DOWN?!
WELL, LADY, IF YOU ARE, THEN I'M WITH YOU.
!

WOOO!

SORRY, THAT'S JUST MY CANE.

BUT YES, I **AM** HAPPY TO SEE YOU.

THAT'S THE NICEST THING THAT'S HAPPENED TO ME SINCE DARTH MAUL **GOOSED** ME.

WANT SOME COFFEE AND BAILEYS?

SURE!

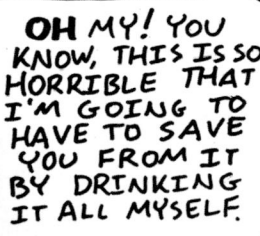
OH MY! YOU KNOW, THIS IS SO HORRIBLE THAT I'M GOING TO HAVE TO SAVE YOU FROM IT BY DRINKING IT ALL MYSELF.

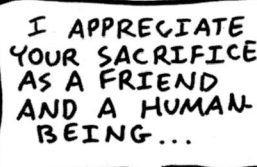
I APPRECIATE YOUR SACRIFICE AS A FRIEND AND A HUMAN BEING...

... BUT FUCK OFF.

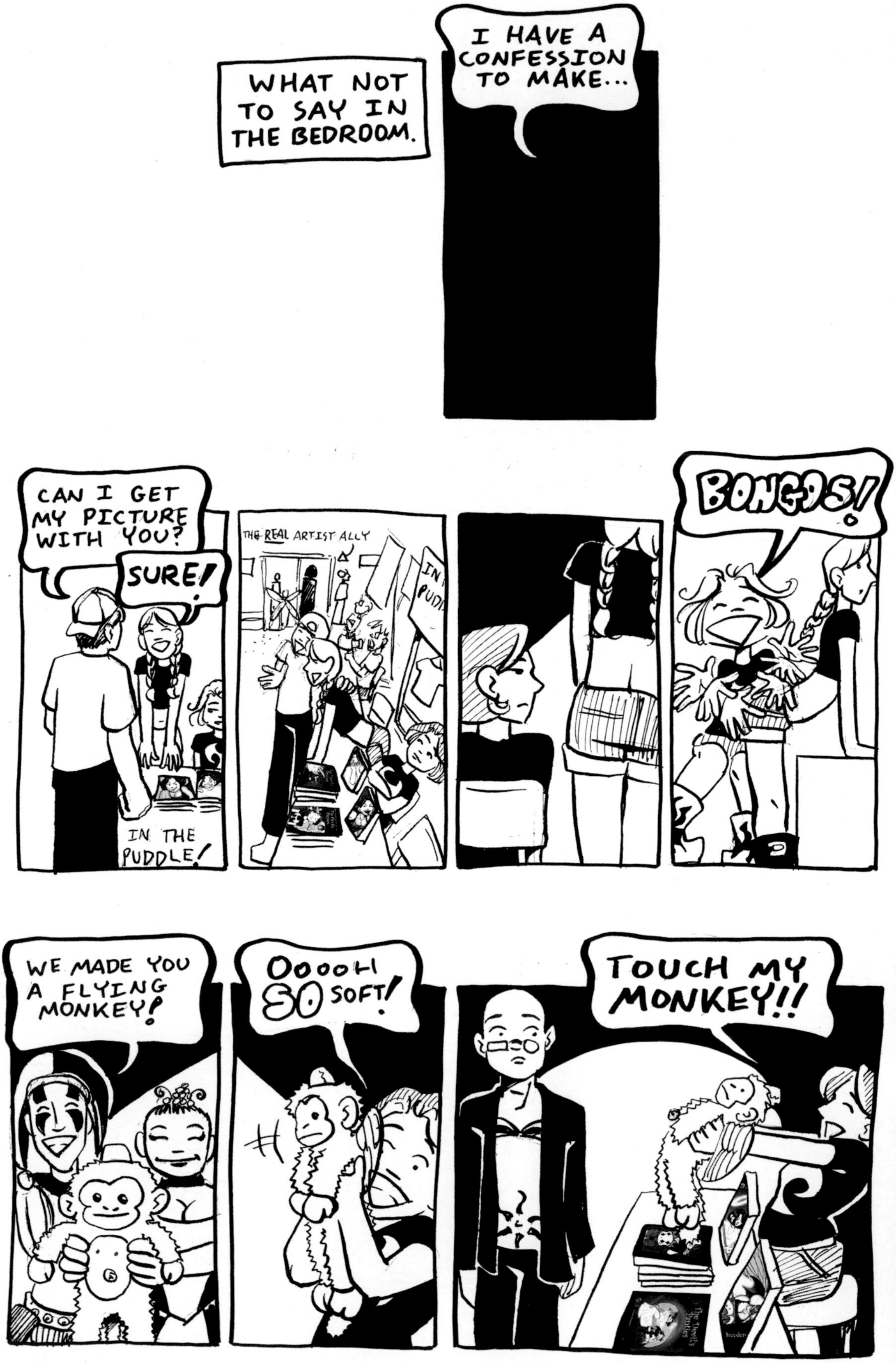
WHAT NOT TO SAY IN THE BEDROOM.
I HAVE A CONFESSION TO MAKE...
CAN I GET MY PICTURE WITH YOU?
SURE!
IN THE PUDDLE!
THE REAL ARTIST ALLY
BONGOS!
WE MADE YOU A FLYING MONKEY!
OOOOH SO SOFT!
TOUCH MY MONKEY!!

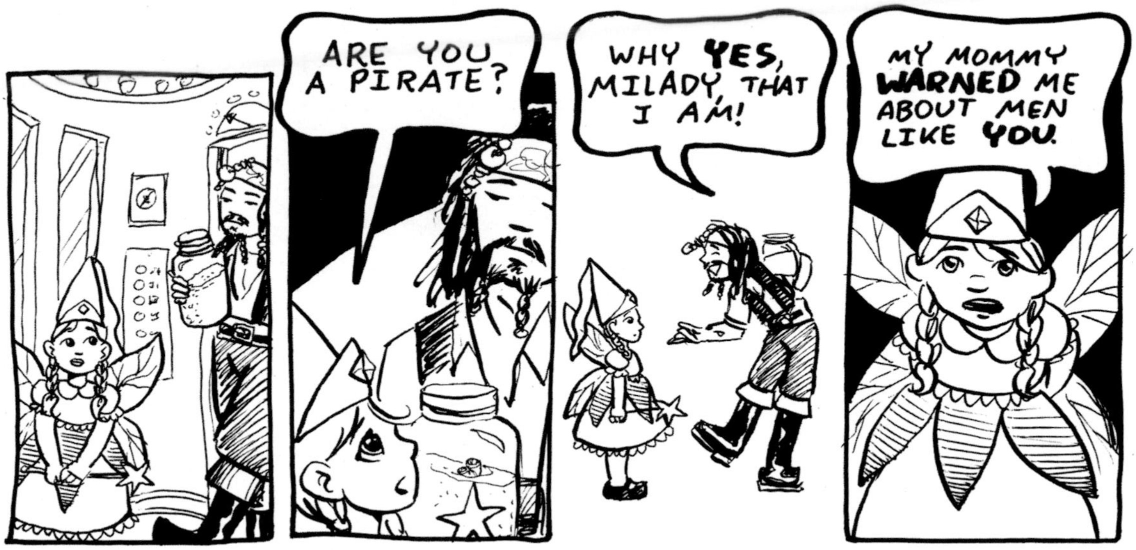

ARE YOU A PIRATE?
WHY YES, MILADY, THAT I AM!
MY MOMMY WARNED ME ABOUT MEN LIKE YOU.

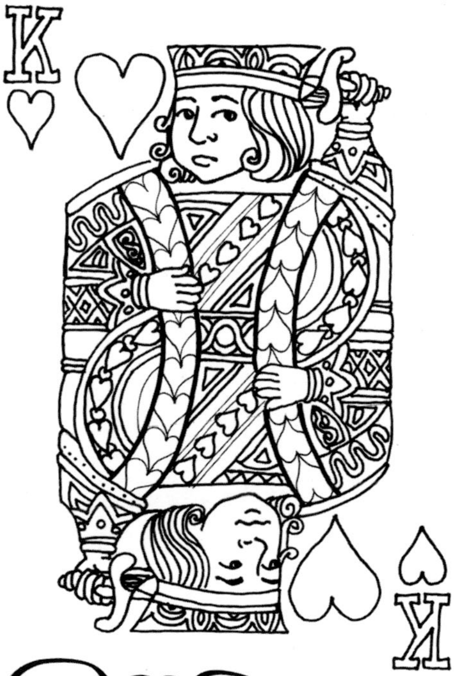

K
K

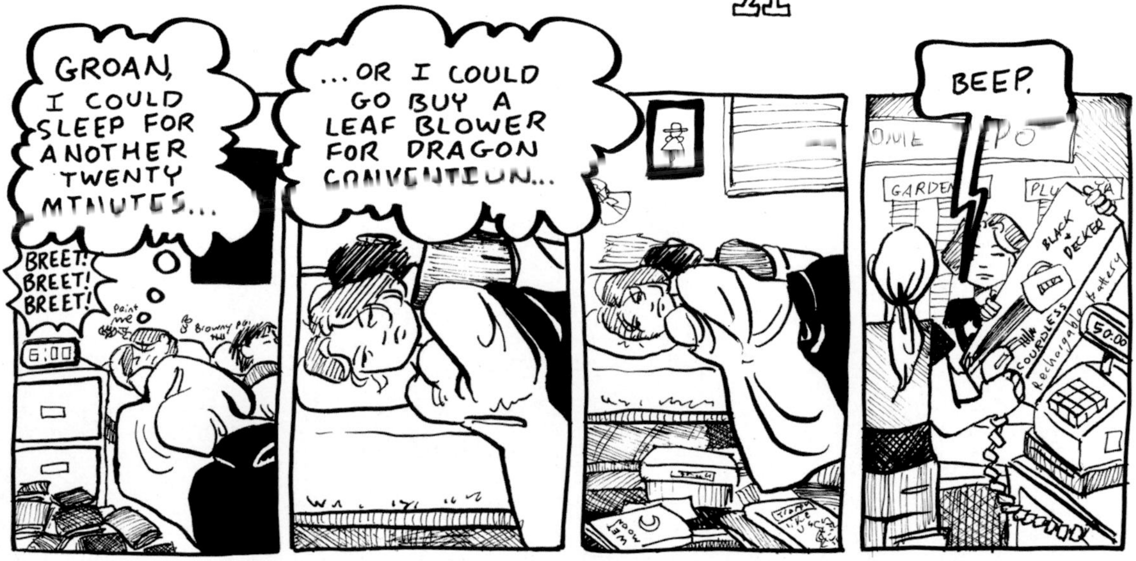

GROAN, I COULD SLEEP FOR ANOTHER TWENTY MINUTES...
BREET! BREET! BREET!
6:00
...OR I COULD GO BUY A LEAF BLOWER FOR DRAGON CONVENTION...
BEEP.
GARDEN
BLACK + DECKER
CORDLESS
Rechargable battery
50.00

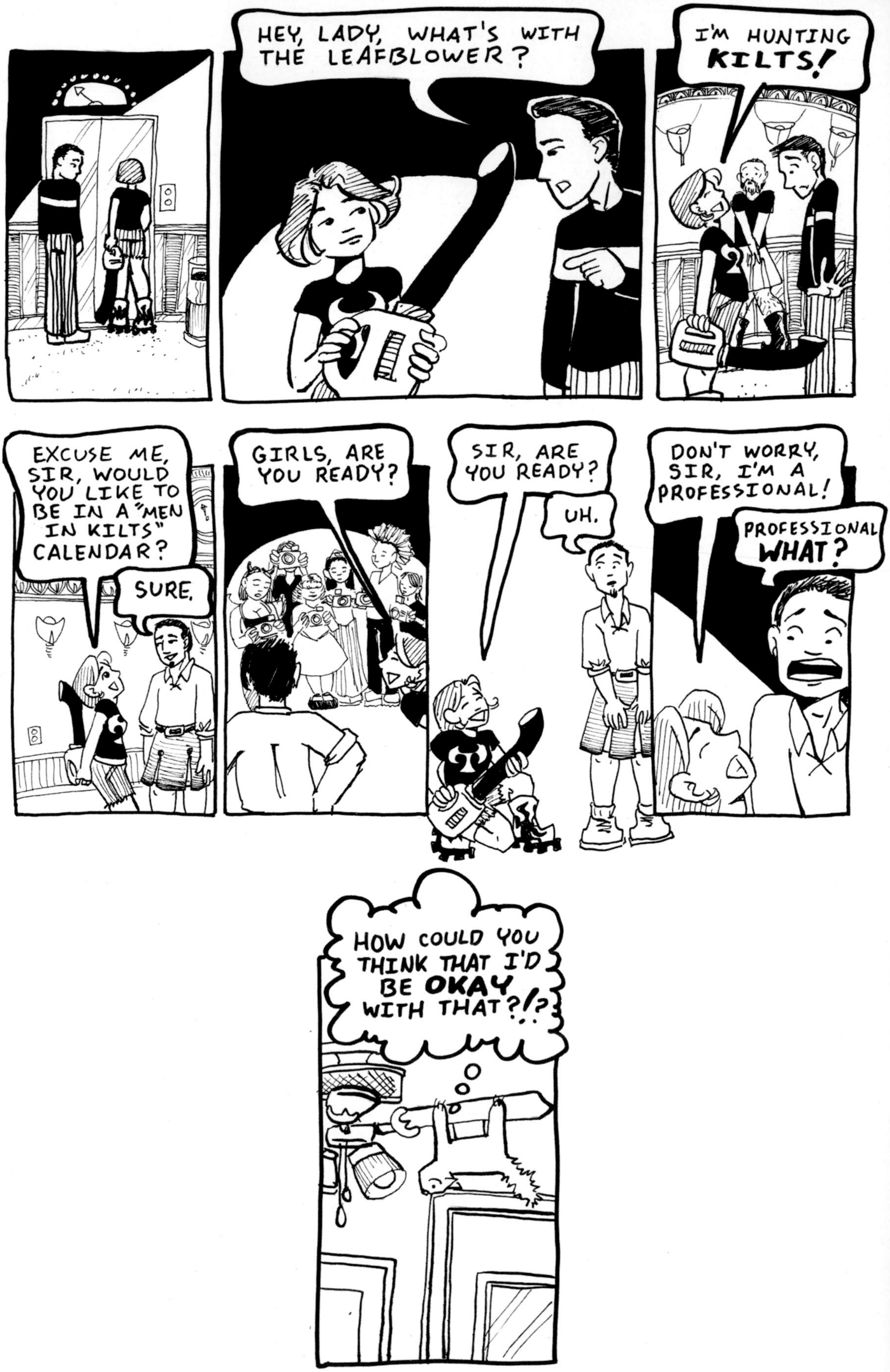
HEY, LADY, WHAT'S WITH THE LEAFBLOWER?
I'M HUNTING KILTS!
EXCUSE ME, SIR, WOULD YOU LIKE TO BE IN A "MEN IN KILTS" CALENDAR?
SURE.
GIRLS, ARE YOU READY?
SIR, ARE YOU READY?
UH.
DON'T WORRY, SIR, I'M A PROFESSIONAL!
PROFESSIONAL WHAT?
HOW COULD YOU THINK THAT I'D BE OKAY WITH THAT?!?

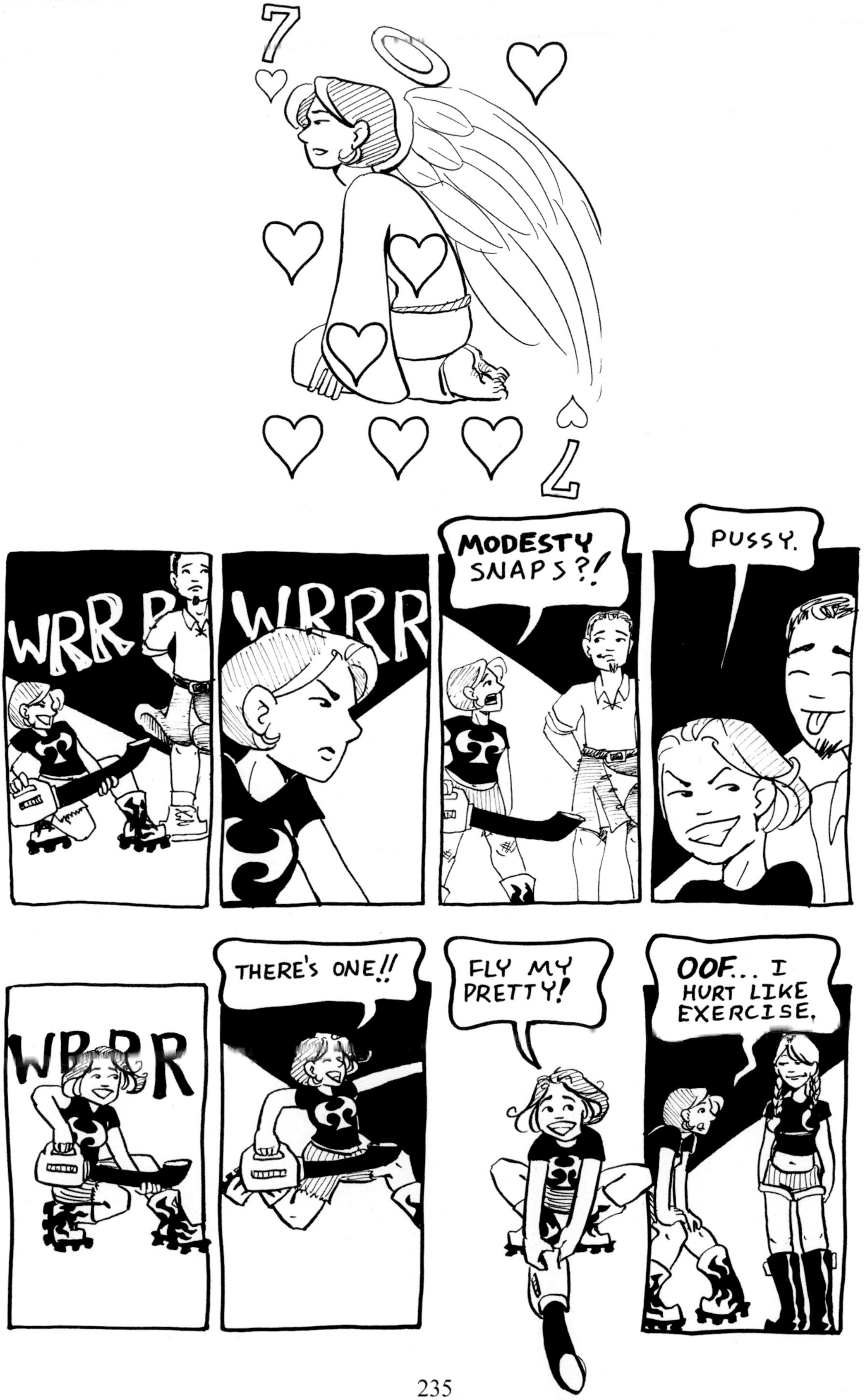
7
7
WRRR
WRRR
MODESTY SNAPS?!
PUSSY.
WRRR
THERE'S ONE!!
FLY MY PRETTY!
OOF... I HURT LIKE EXERCISE.

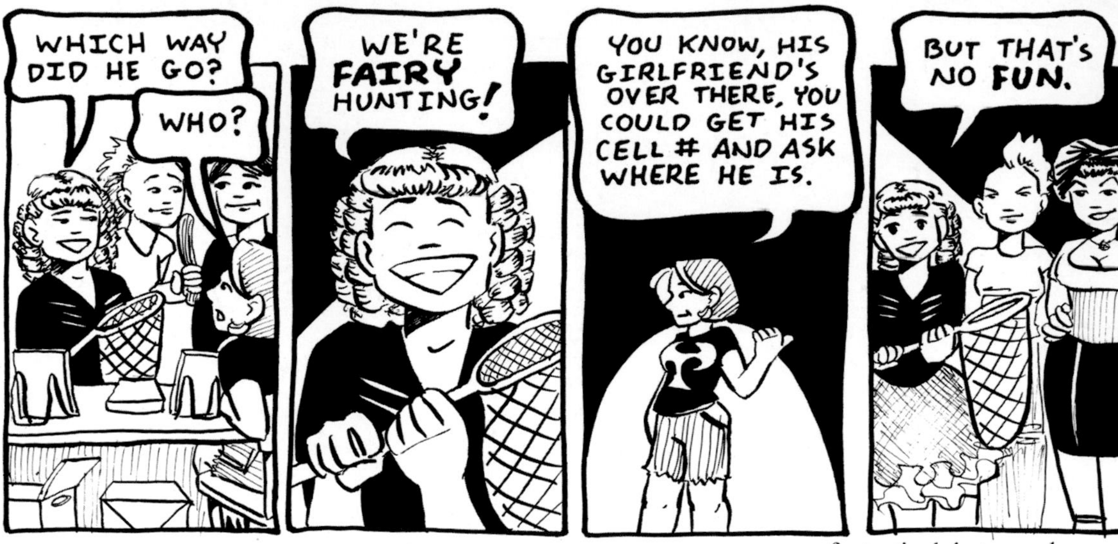
WHICH WAY DID HE GO?
WHO?
WE'RE FAIRY HUNTING!
YOU KNOW, HIS GIRLFRIEND'S OVER THERE, YOU COULD GET HIS CELL # AND ASK WHERE HE IS.
BUT THAT'S NO FUN.

www.fantasticalphotography.com

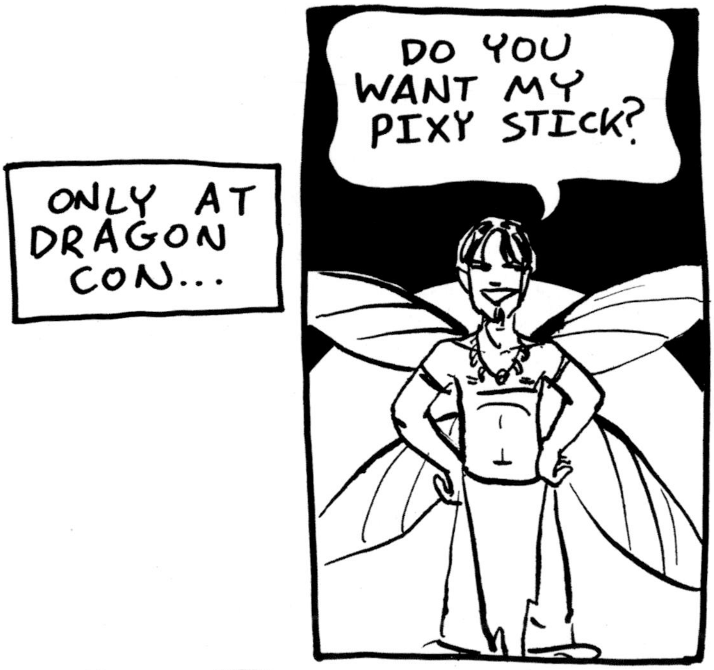
ONLY AT DRAGON CON...
DO YOU WANT MY PIXY STICK?

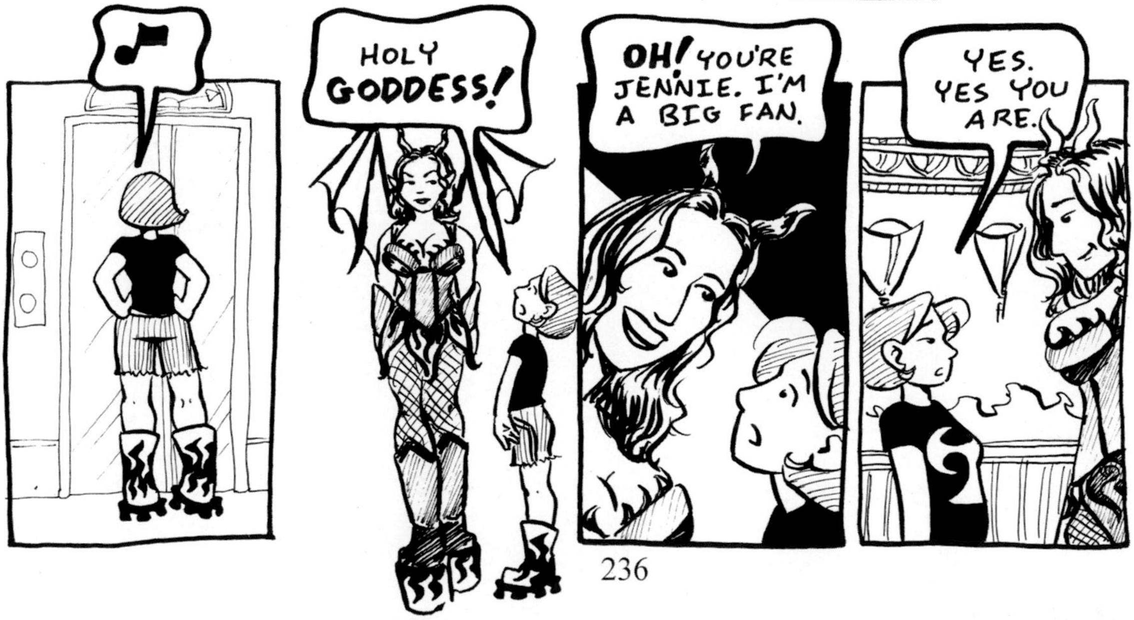
♪
HOLY GODDESS!
OH! YOU'RE JENNIE. I'M A BIG FAN.
YES. YES YOU ARE.

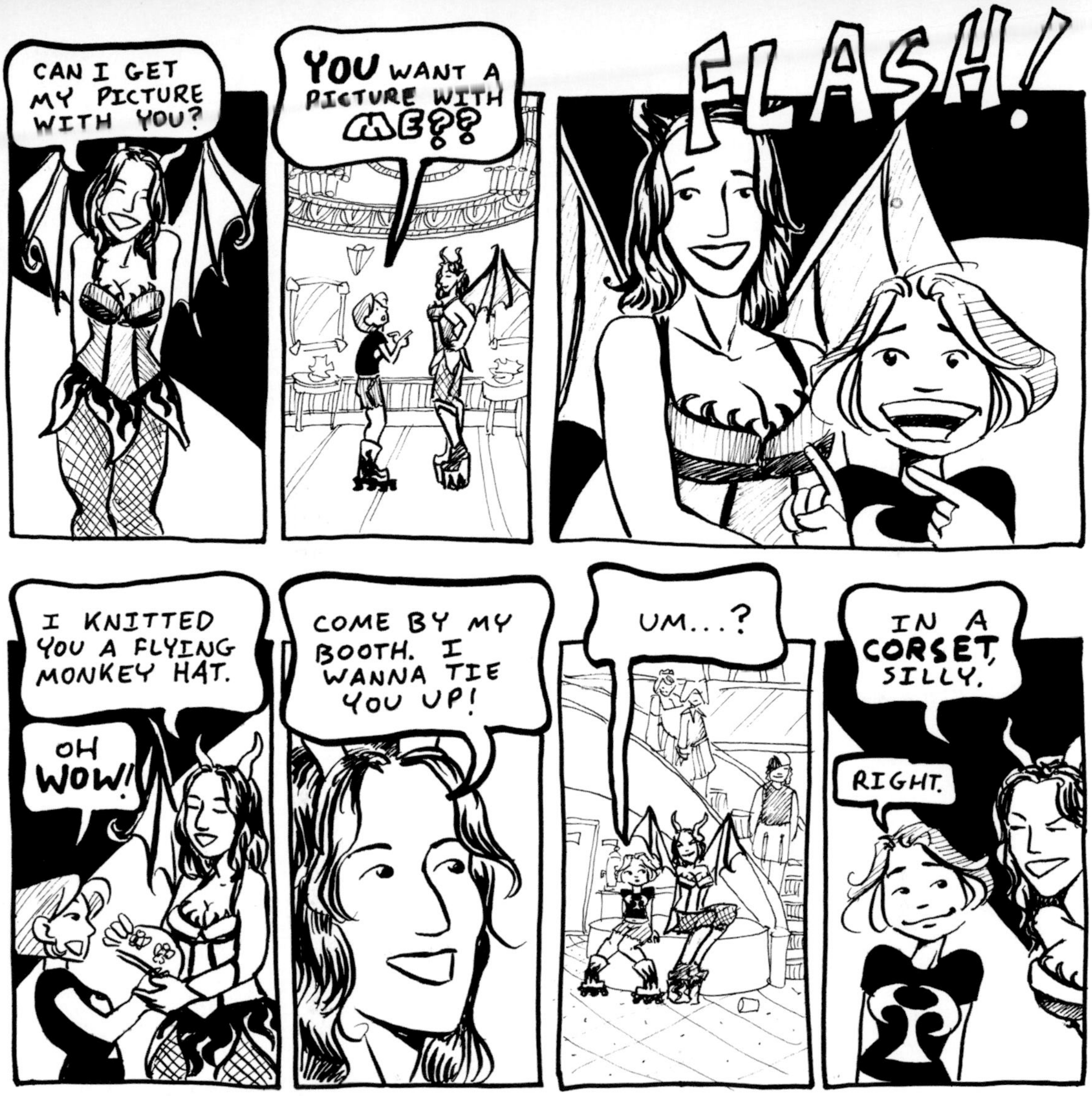
CAN I GET MY PICTURE WITH YOU?
YOU WANT A PICTURE WITH ME??
FLASH!
I KNITTED YOU A FLYING MONKEY HAT.
OH WOW!
COME BY MY BOOTH. I WANNA TIE YOU UP!
UM...?
IN A CORSET, SILLY.
RIGHT.

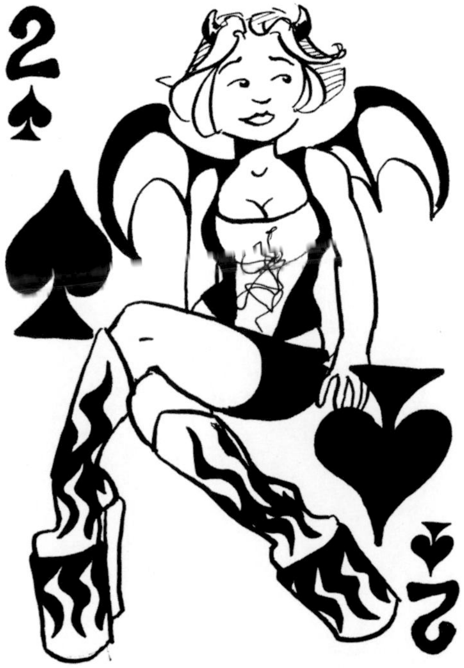
2
2

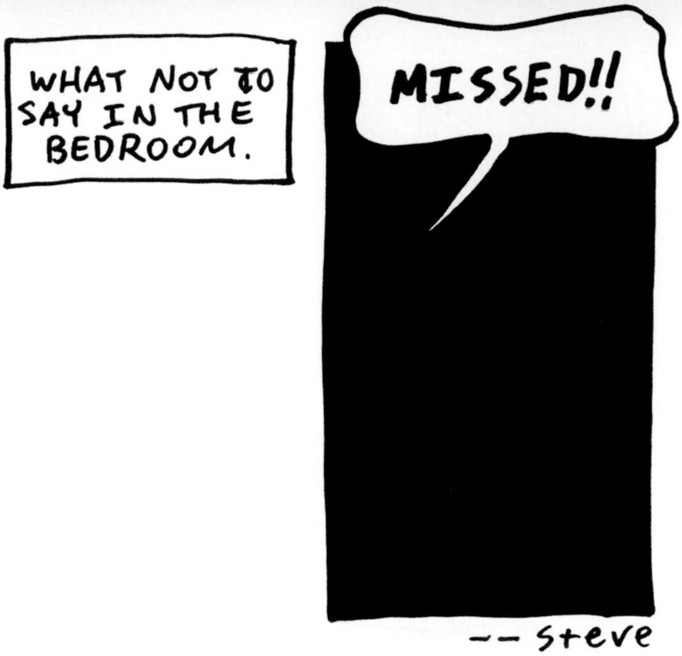
WHAT NOT TO SAY IN THE BEDROOM.
MISSED!!
-- steve

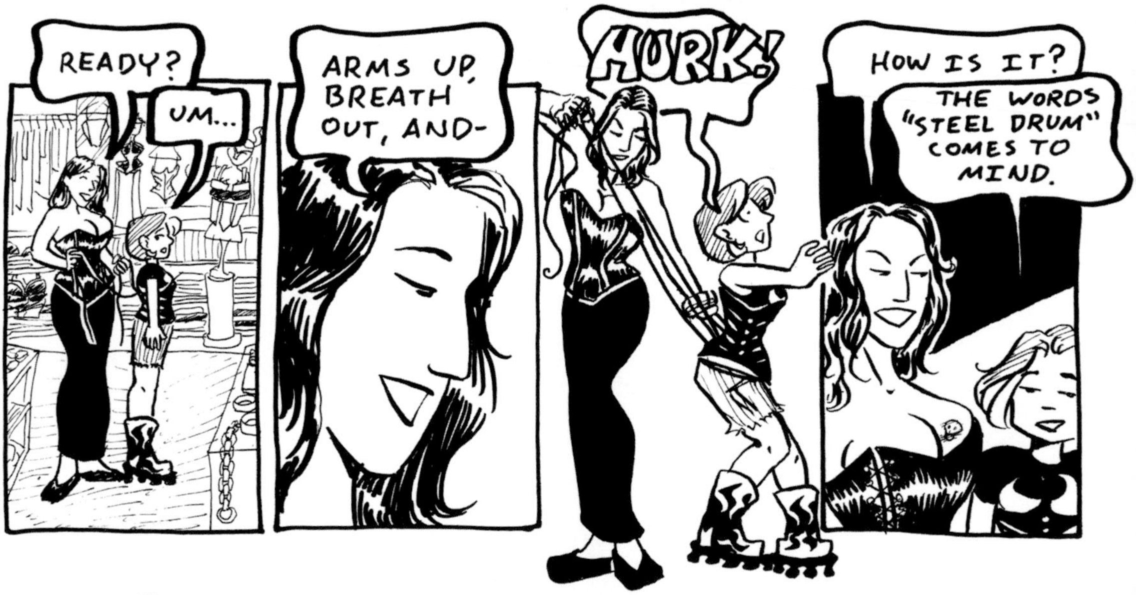
READY?
UM...
ARMS UP, BREATH OUT, AND-
HURK!
HOW IS IT?
THE WORDS "STEEL DRUM" COMES TO MIND.

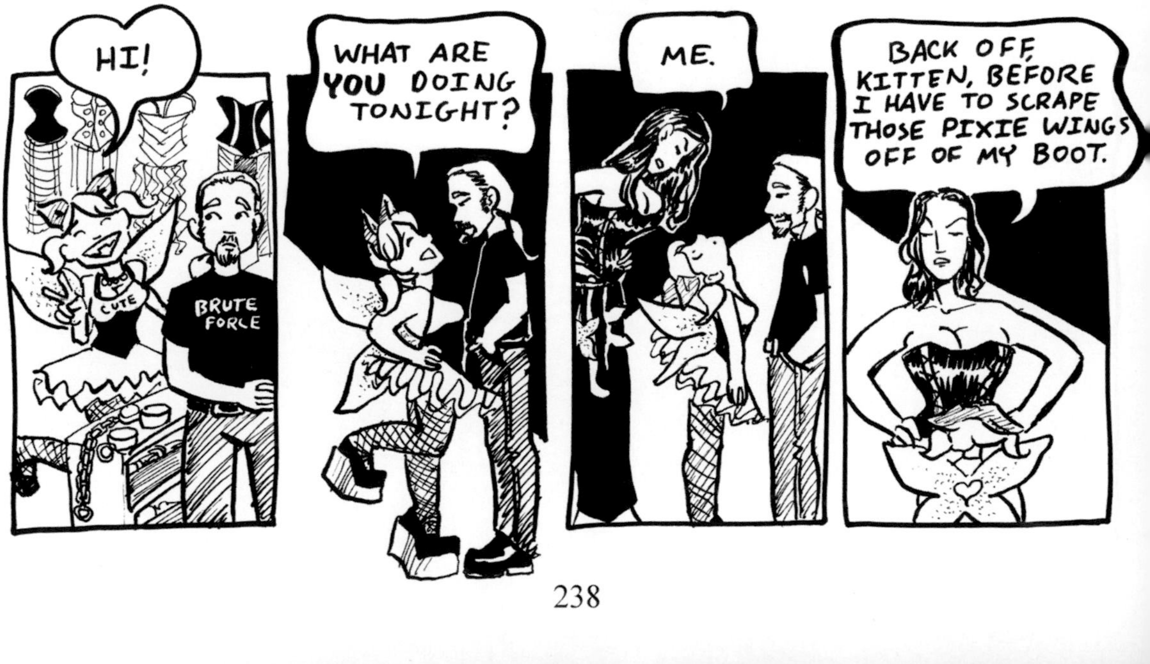
HI!
CUTE
BRUTE FORCE
WHAT ARE YOU DOING TONIGHT?
ME.
BACK OFF, KITTEN, BEFORE I HAVE TO SCRAPE THOSE PIXIE WINGS OFF OF MY BOOT.

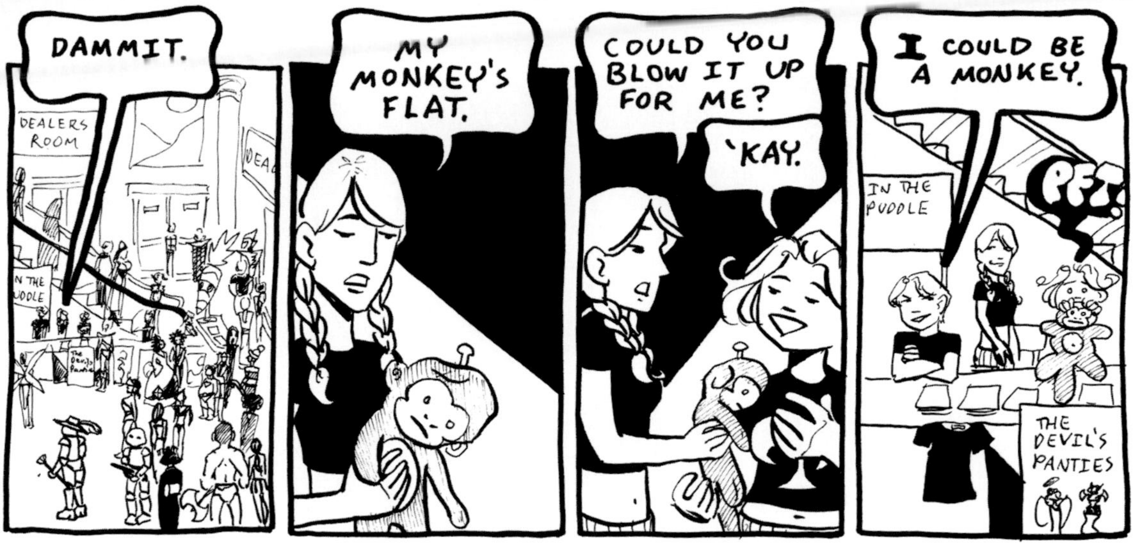
DAMMIT.
DEALERS ROOM
IN THE PUDDLE
MY MONKEY'S FLAT.
COULD YOU BLOW IT UP FOR ME?
'KAY.
I COULD BE A MONKEY.
IN THE PUDDLE
PFFT!
THE DEVIL'S PANTIES

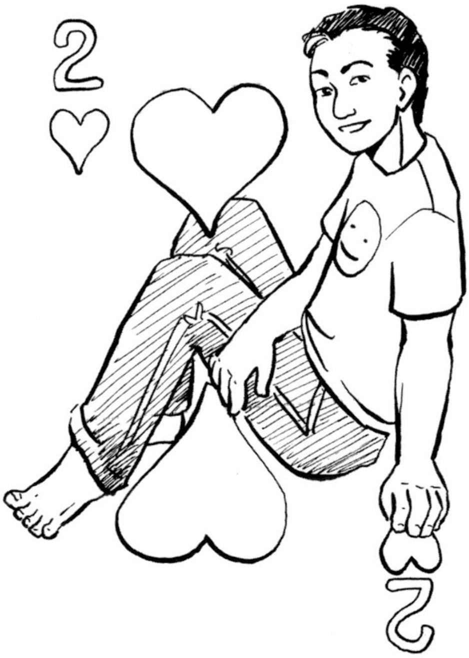
2
2

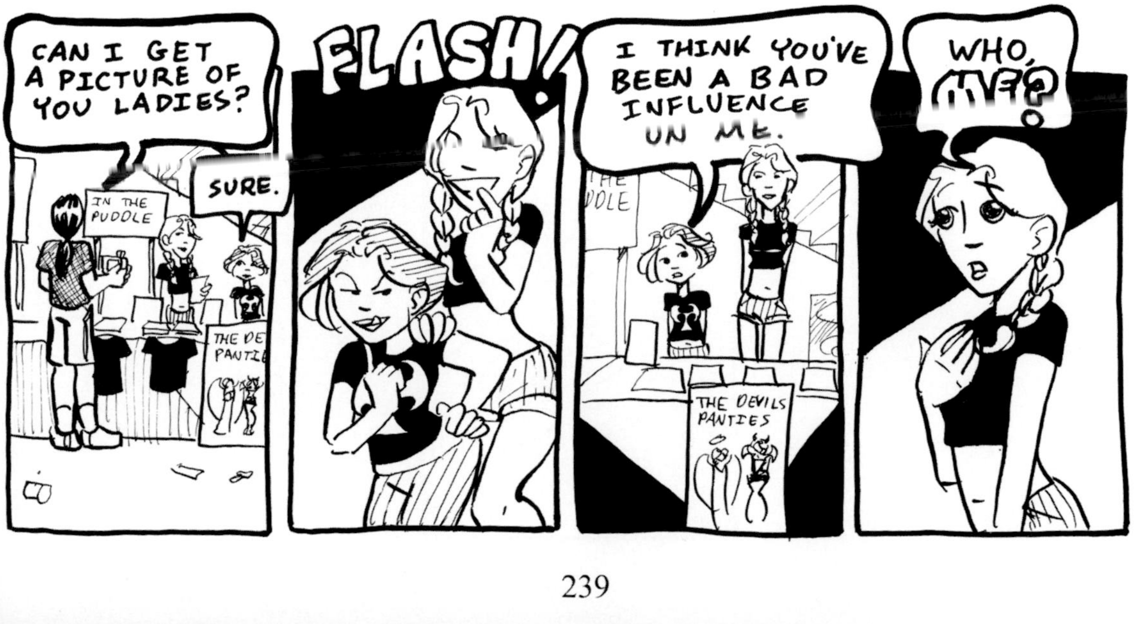
CAN I GET A PICTURE OF YOU LADIES?
IN THE PUDDLE
SURE.
FLASH!
I THINK YOU'VE BEEN A BAD INFLUENCE ON ME.
THE DEVILS PANTIES
WHO,

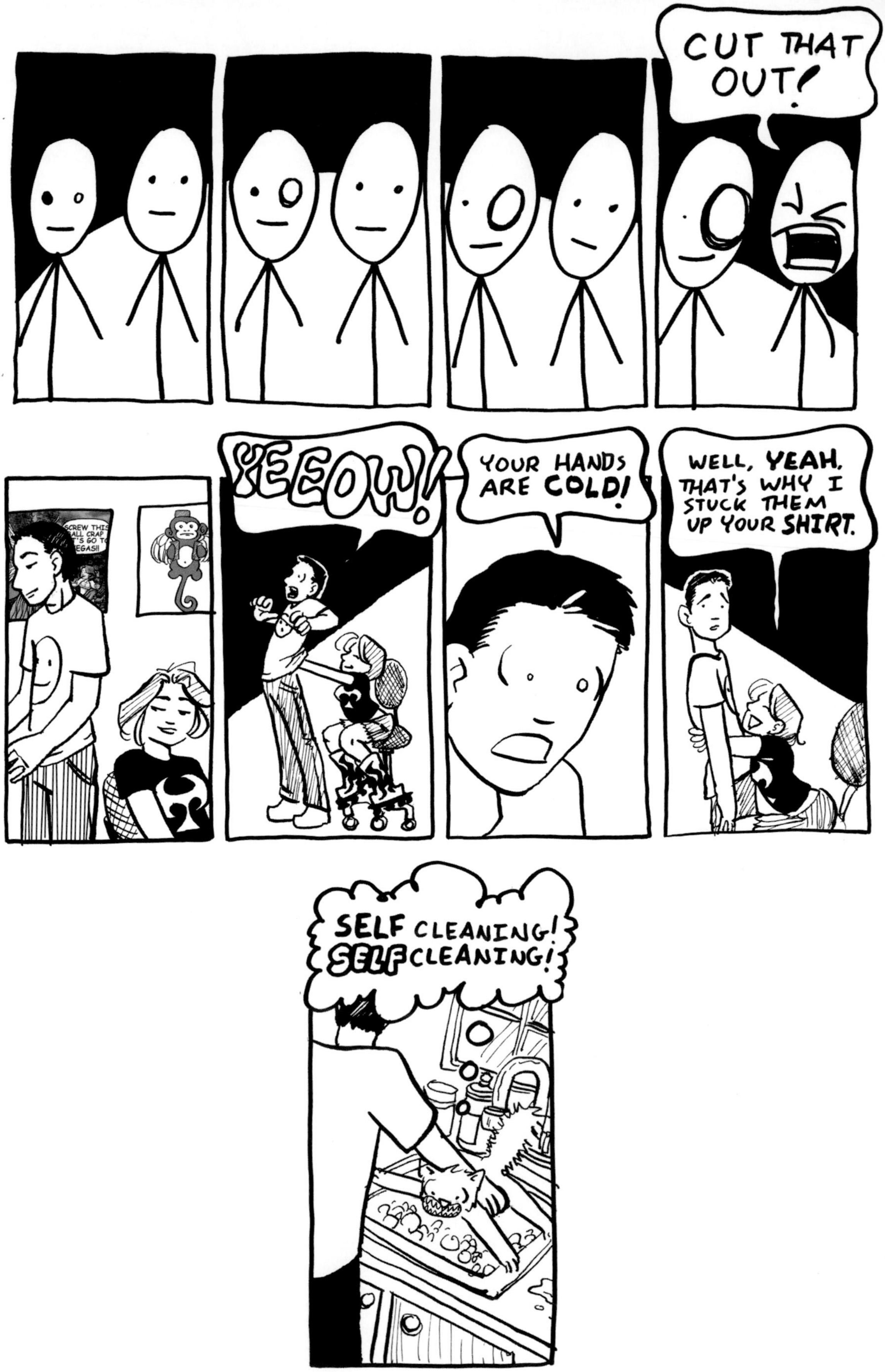
CUT THAT OUT!
YEEOW!!
YOUR HANDS ARE COLD!
WELL, YEAH. THAT'S WHY I STUCK THEM UP YOUR SHIRT.
SELF CLEANING! SELF CLEANING!

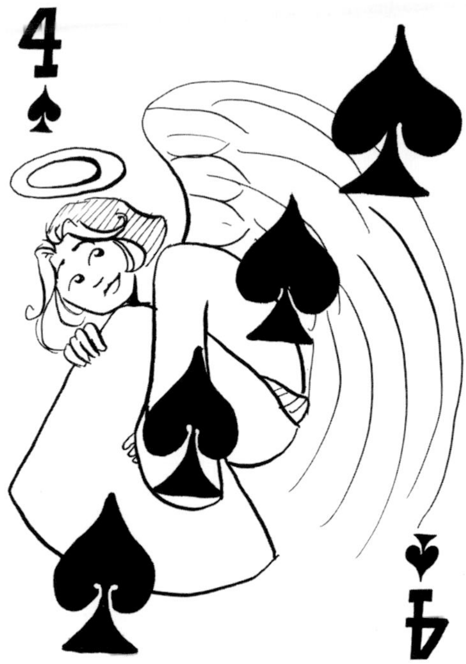
4
4

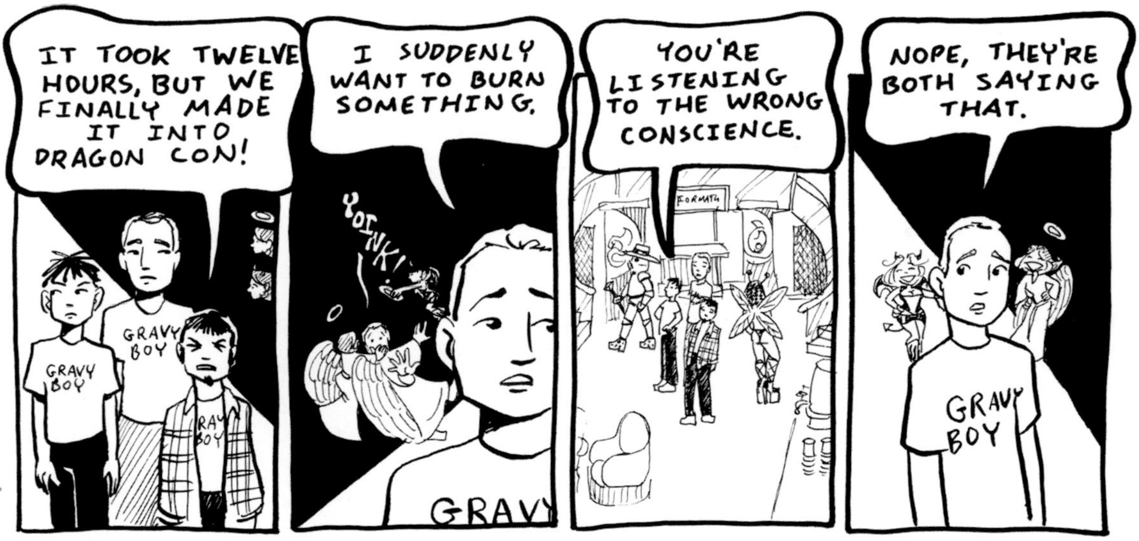
IT TOOK TWELVE HOURS, BUT WE FINALLY MADE IT INTO DRAGON CON!
GRAVY BOY
GRAVY BOY
I SUDDENLY WANT TO BURN SOMETHING.
YOINK!
GRAVY
YOU'RE LISTENING TO THE WRONG CONSCIENCE.
NOPE, THEY'RE BOTH SAYING THAT.
GRAVY BOY

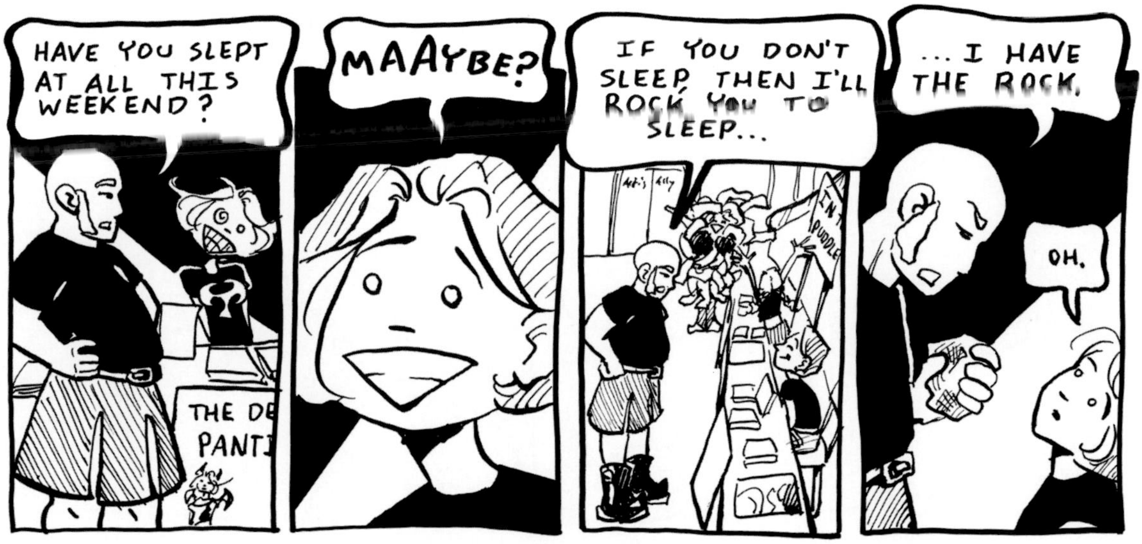
HAVE YOU SLEPT AT ALL THIS WEEKEND?
MAAYBE?
IF YOU DON'T SLEEP, THEN I'LL ROCK YOU TO SLEEP...
...I HAVE THE ROCK.
OH.

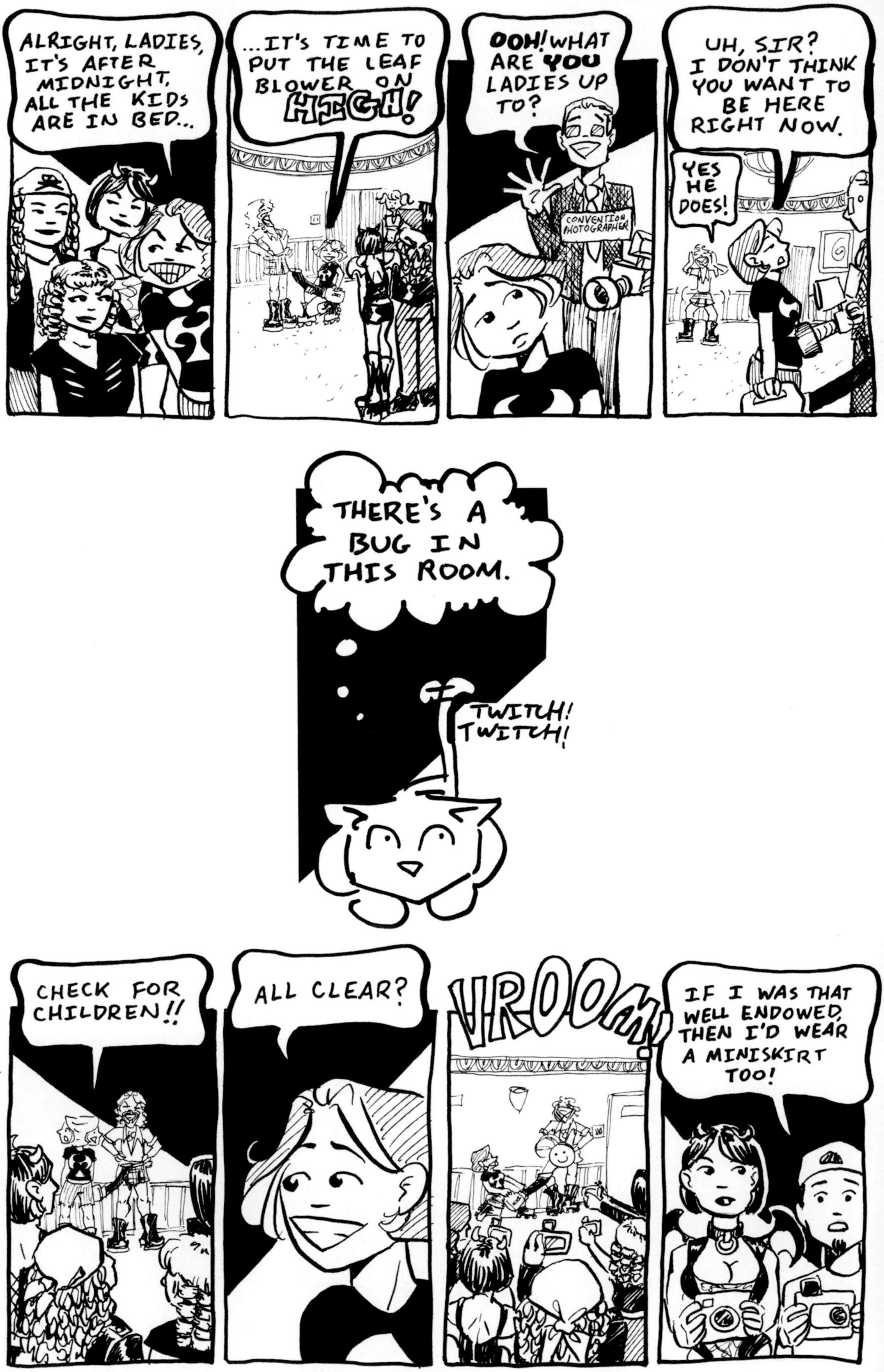
ALRIGHT, LADIES, IT'S AFTER MIDNIGHT, ALL THE KIDS ARE IN BED...
...IT'S TIME TO PUT THE LEAF BLOWER ON HIGH!
OOH! WHAT ARE YOU LADIES UP TO?
CONVENTION PHOTOGRAPHER
UH, SIR? I DON'T THINK YOU WANT TO BE HERE RIGHT NOW.
YES HE DOES!
THERE'S A BUG IN THIS ROOM.
TWITCH! TWITCH!
CHECK FOR CHILDREN!!
ALL CLEAR?
VROOOM!
IF I WAS THAT WELL ENDOWED, THEN I'D WEAR A MINISKIRT TOO!

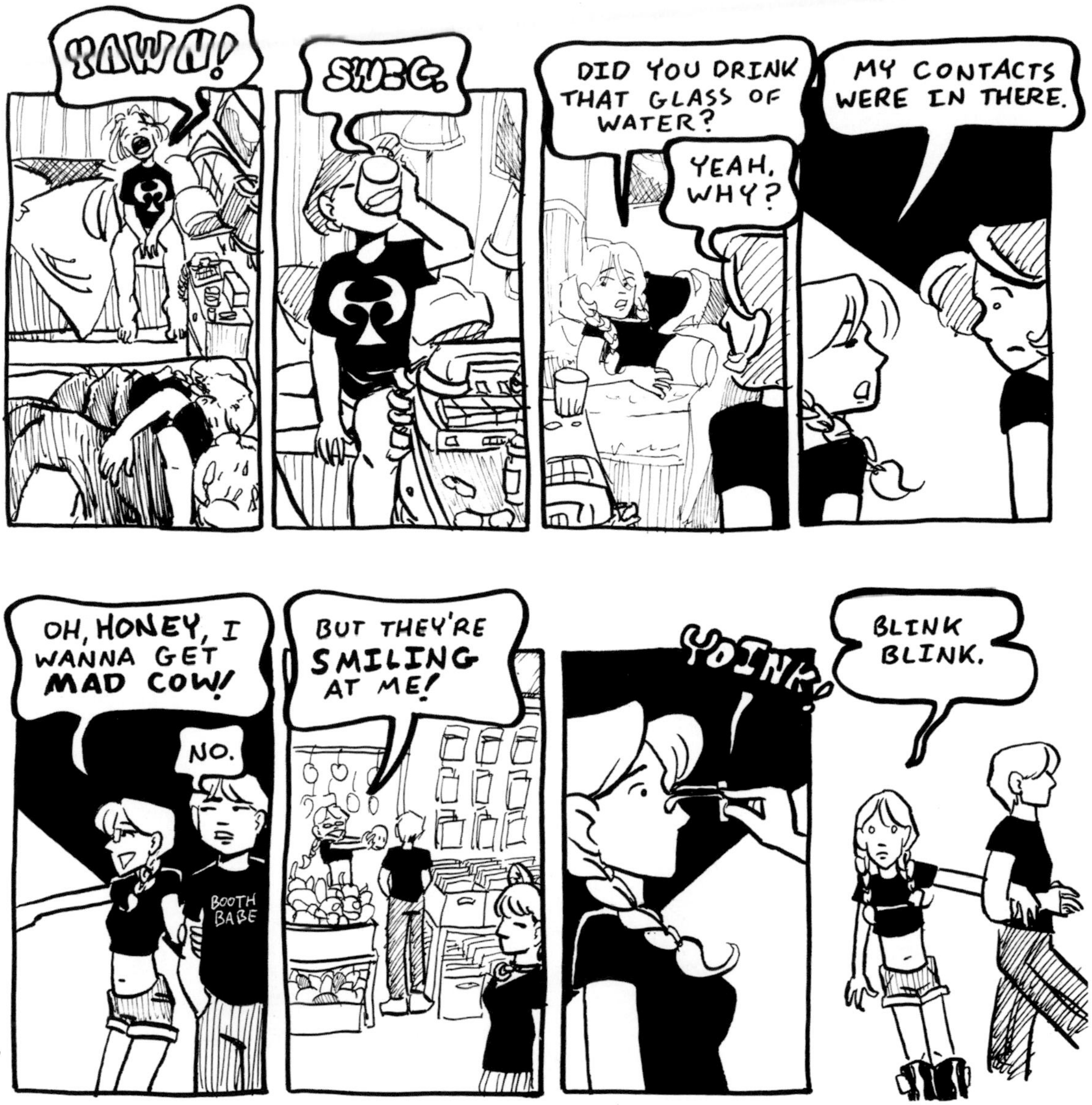
YAWN!
SWIG.
DID YOU DRINK THAT GLASS OF WATER?
YEAH, WHY?
MY CONTACTS WERE IN THERE.
OH, HONEY, I WANNA GET MAD COW!
NO.
BOOTH BABE
BUT THEY'RE SMILING AT ME!
YOINK!
BLINK BLINK.

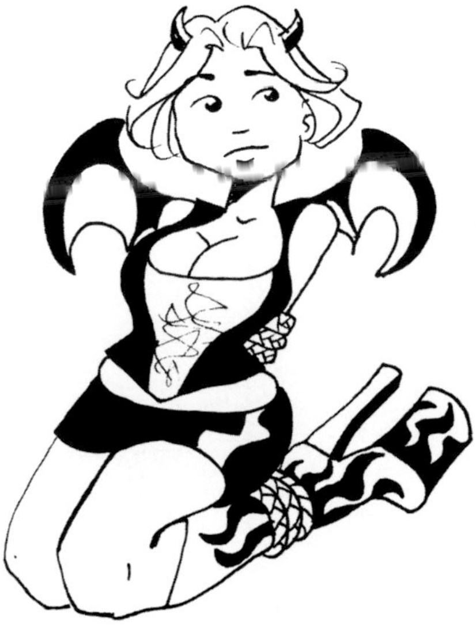

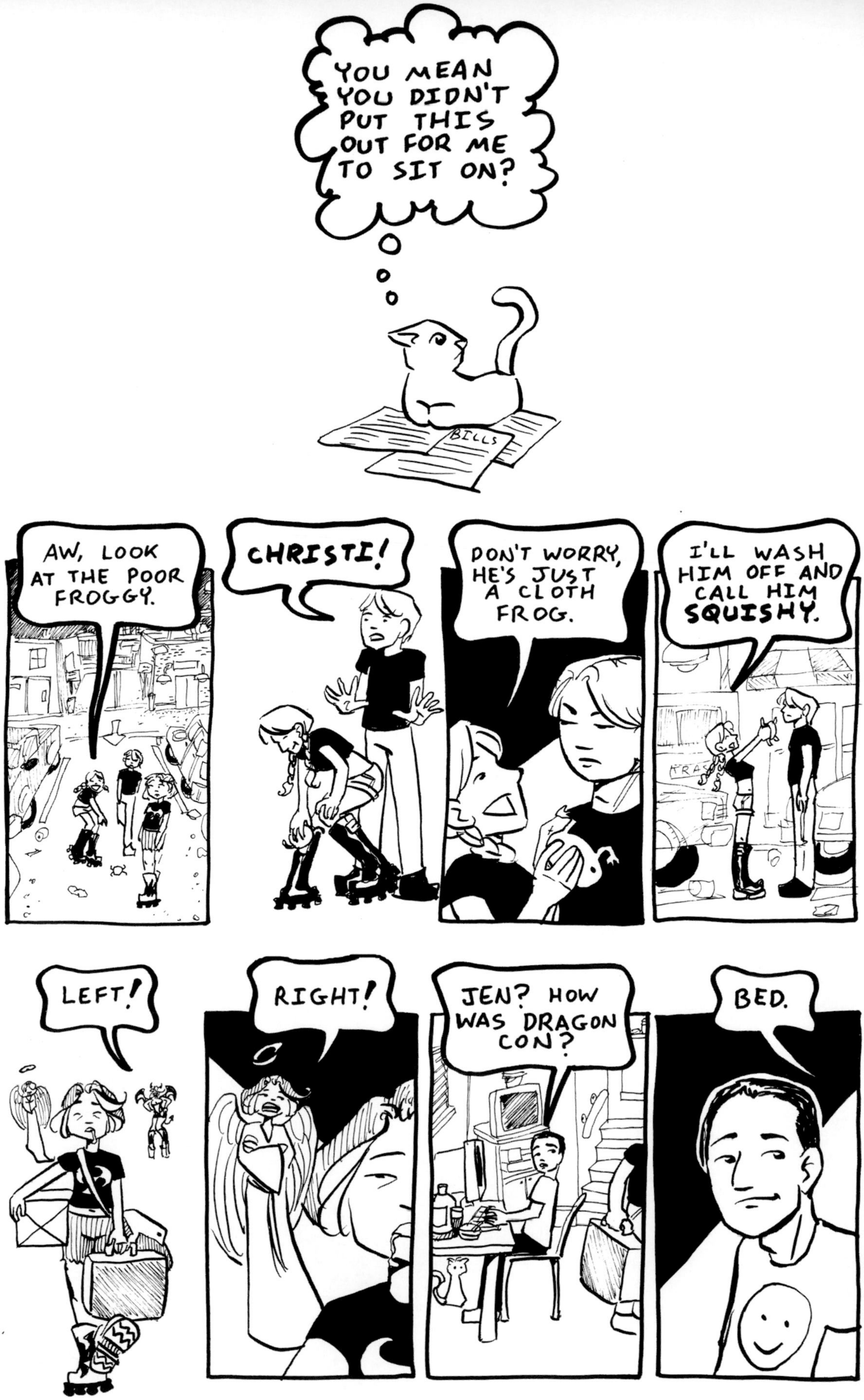
YOU MEAN YOU DIDN'T PUT THIS OUT FOR ME TO SIT ON?
BILLS
AW, LOOK AT THE POOR FROGGY.
CHRISTI!
DON'T WORRY, HE'S JUST A CLOTH FROG.
I'LL WASH HIM OFF AND CALL HIM SQUISHY.
LEFT!
RIGHT!
JEN? HOW WAS DRAGON CON?
BED.

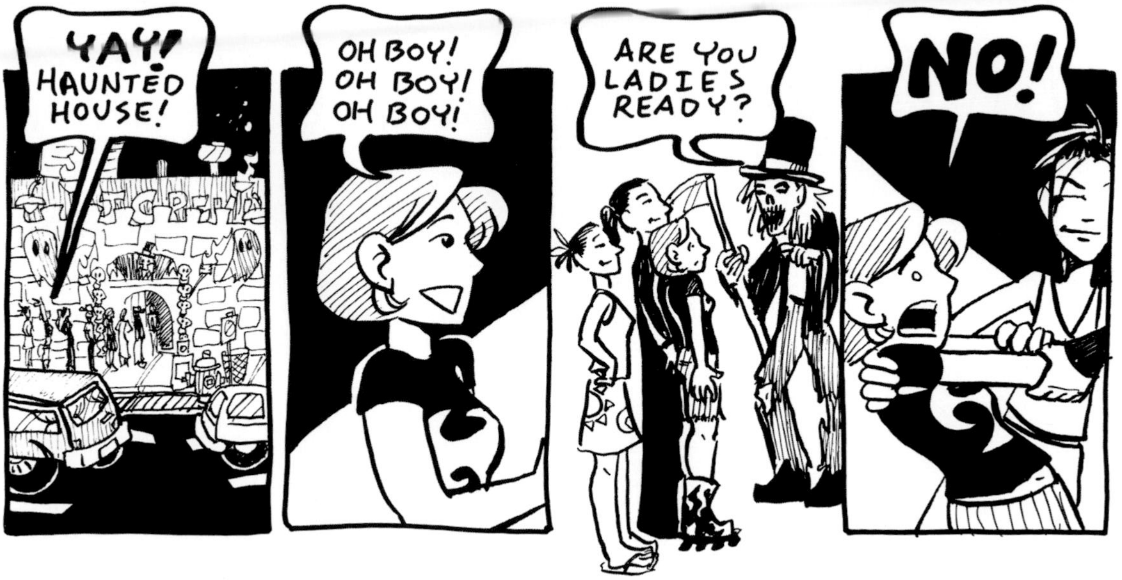
YAY! HAUNTED HOUSE!
OH BOY! OH BOY! OH BOY!
ARE YOU LADIES READY?
NO!

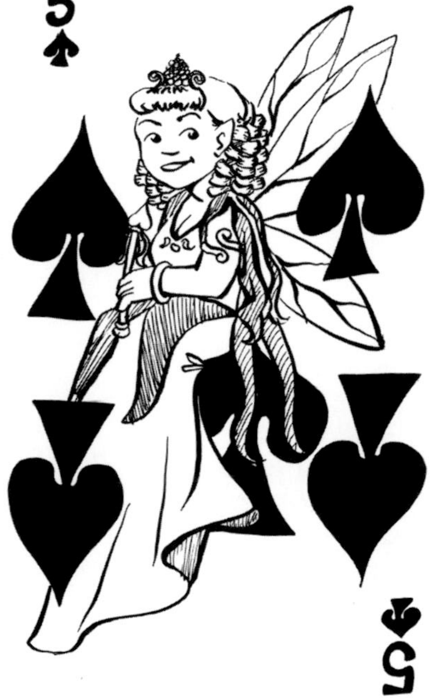
5
5

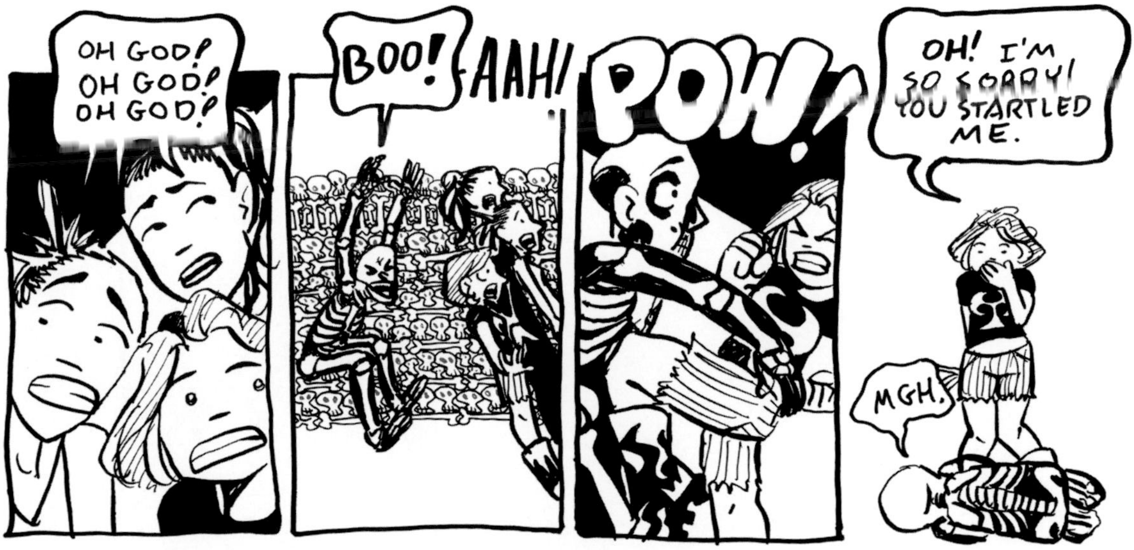
OH GOD! OH GOD! OH GOD!
BOO!
AAH!
POW!
OH! I'M SO SORRY! YOU STARTLED ME.
MGH.

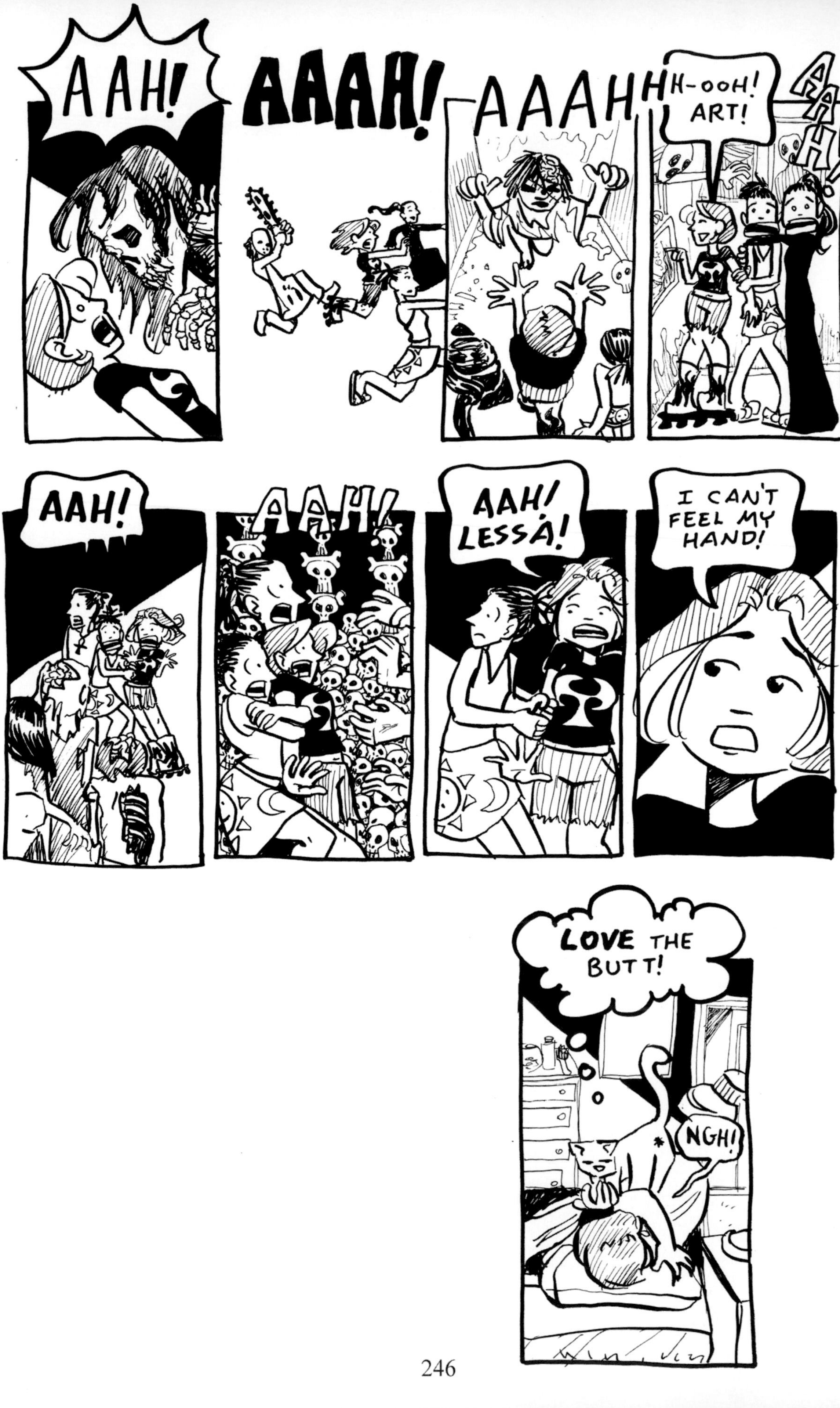
AAH!
AAAAH!
AAAAHH-OOH! ART!
AAH!
AAH!
AAH!
AAH! LESSA!
I CAN'T FEEL MY HAND!
LOVE THE BUTT!
NGH!

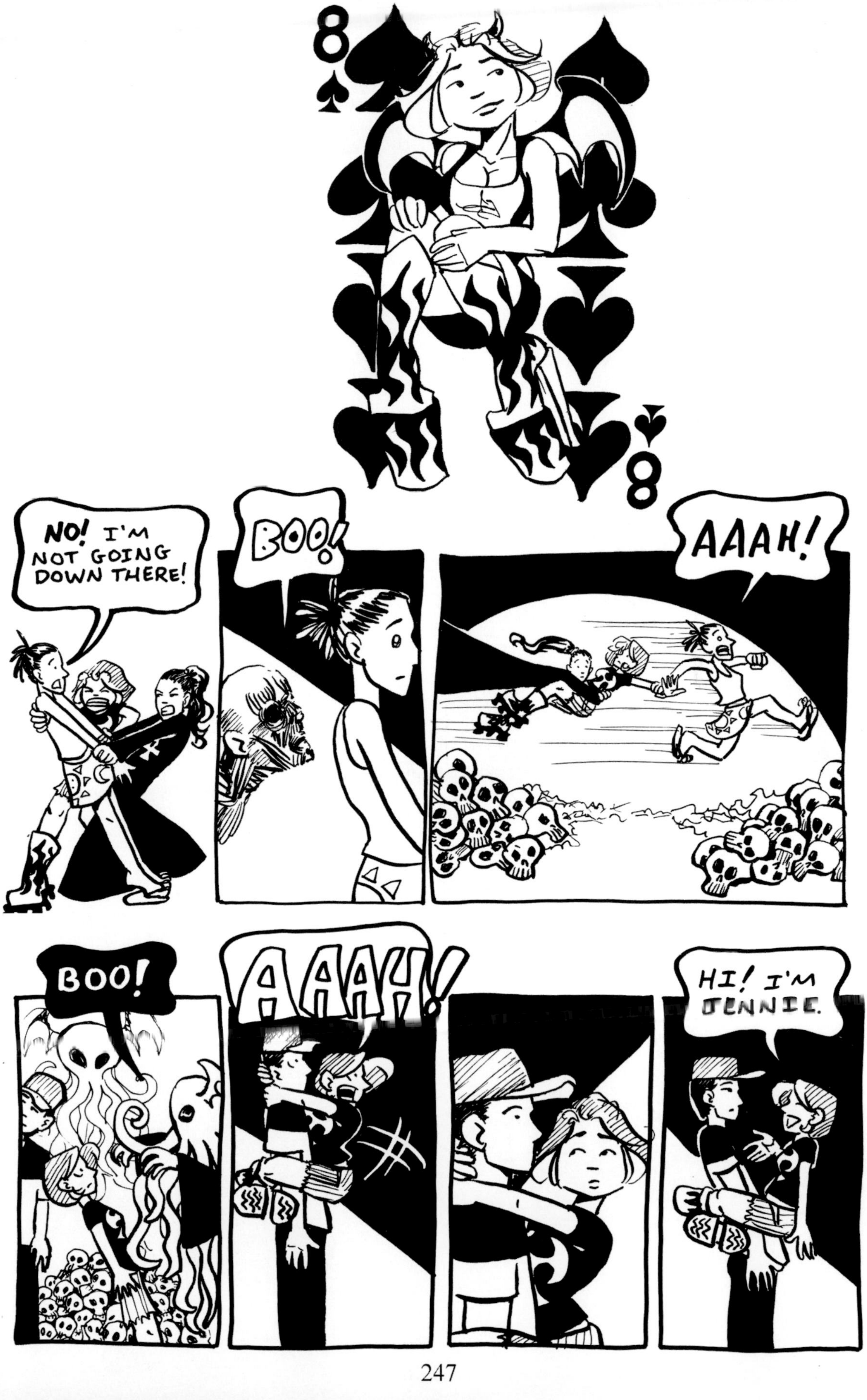
8
8
NO! I'M NOT GOING DOWN THERE!
BOO!
AAAH!
BOO!
AAAH!
HI! I'M JENNIE.

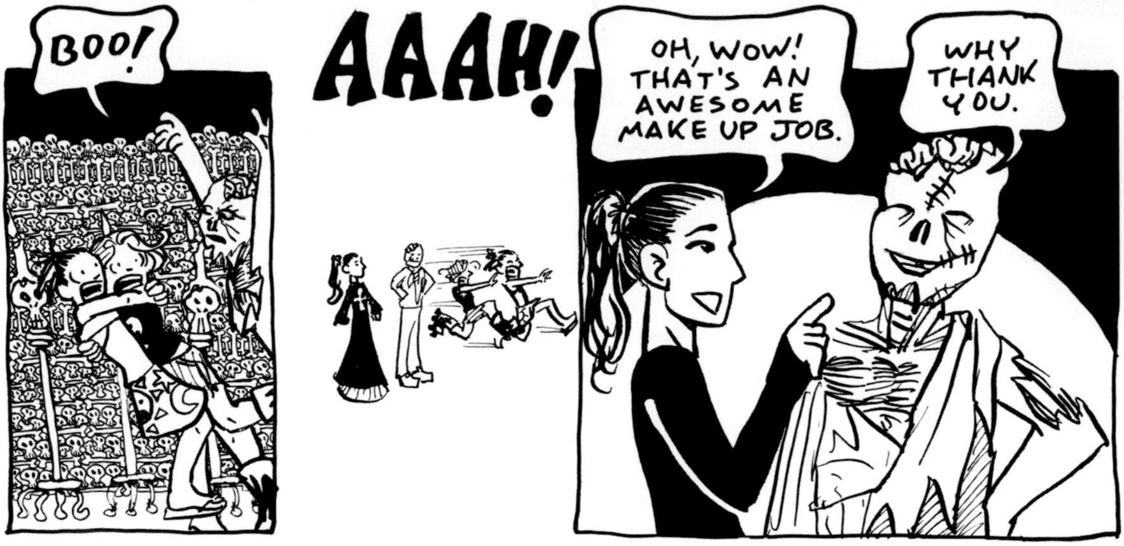
BOO!
AAAH!
OH, WOW! THAT'S AN AWESOME MAKE UP JOB.
WHY THANK YOU.

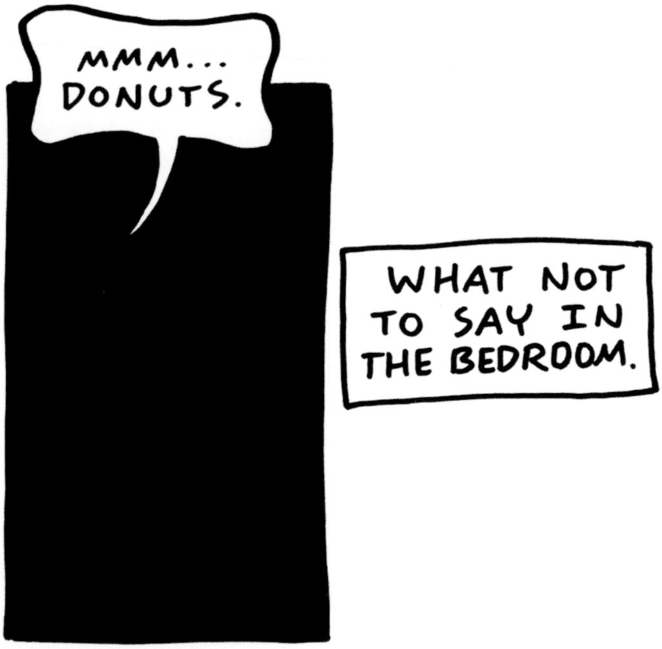
MMM... DONUTS.
WHAT NOT TO SAY IN THE BEDROOM.

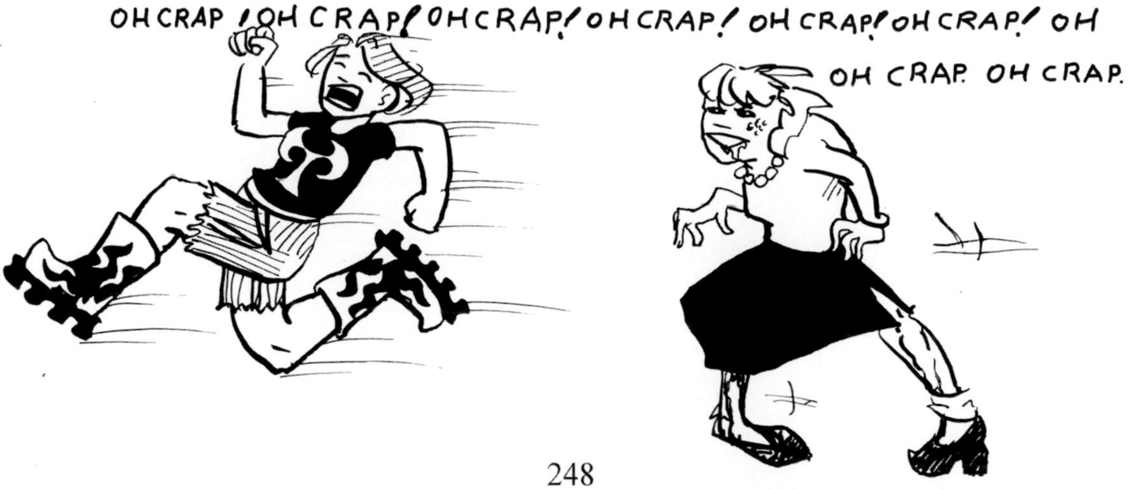
OH CRAP! OH CRAP! OH CRAP! OH CRAP! OH CRAP! OH CRAP! OH
OH CRAP. OH CRAP.

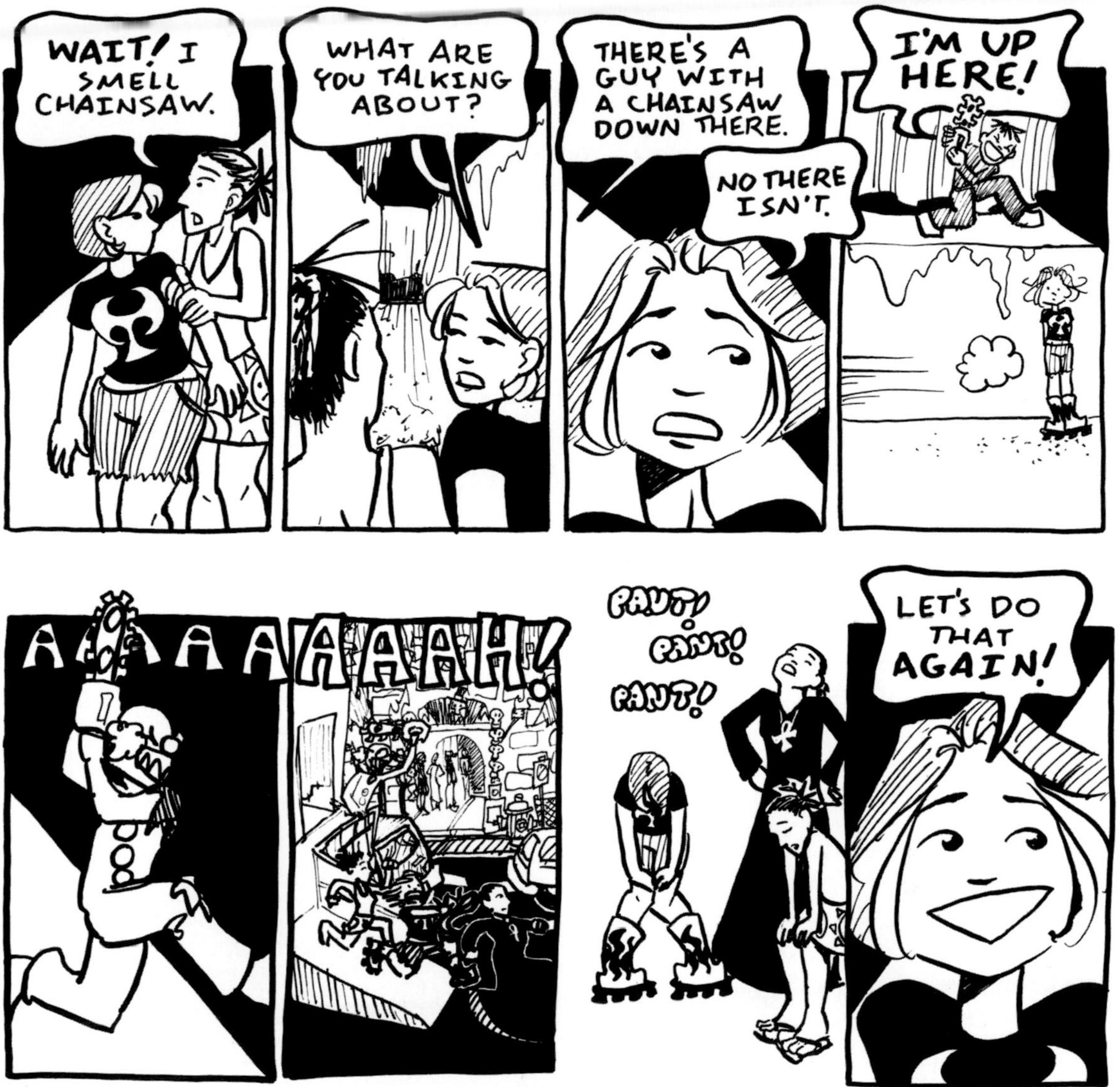
WAIT! I SMELL CHAINSAW.
WHAT ARE YOU TALKING ABOUT?
THERE'S A GUY WITH A CHAINSAW DOWN THERE.
NO THERE ISN'T.
I'M UP HERE!
AAAAAAAAAH!
PANT! PANT! PANT!
LET'S DO THAT AGAIN!

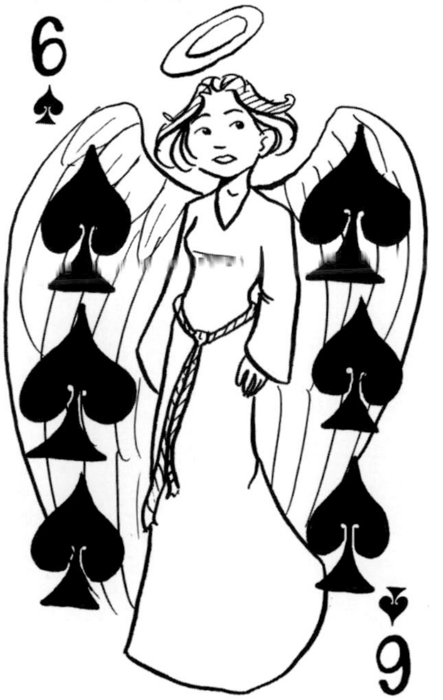
6

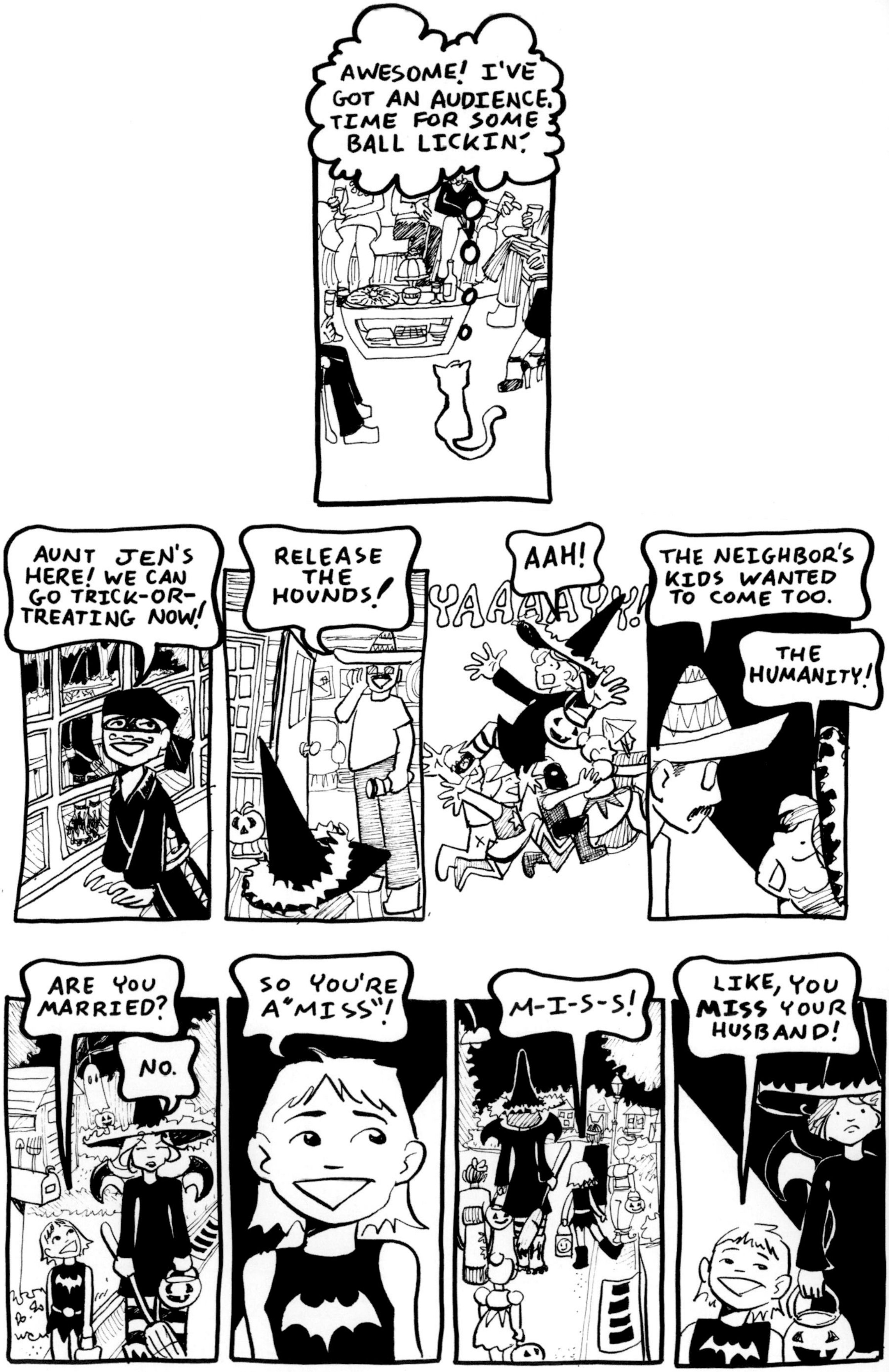
AWESOME! I'VE GOT AN AUDIENCE. TIME FOR SOME BALL LICKIN'.
AUNT JEN'S HERE! WE CAN GO TRICK-OR-TREATING NOW!
RELEASE THE HOUNDS!
AAH!
YAAAAAYY!
THE NEIGHBOR'S KIDS WANTED TO COME TOO.
THE HUMANITY!
ARE YOU MARRIED?
NO.
SO YOU'RE A "MISS"!
M-I-S-S!
LIKE, YOU MISS YOUR HUSBAND!

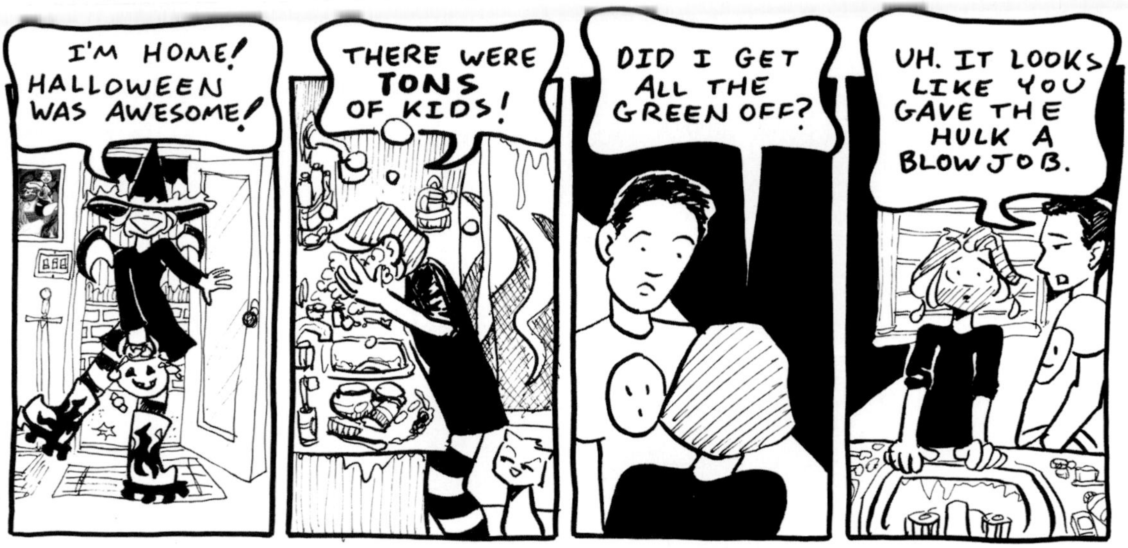
I'M HOME! HALLOWEEN WAS AWESOME!
THERE WERE TONS OF KIDS!
DID I GET ALL THE GREEN OFF?
UH. IT LOOKS LIKE YOU GAVE THE HULK A BLOWJOB.

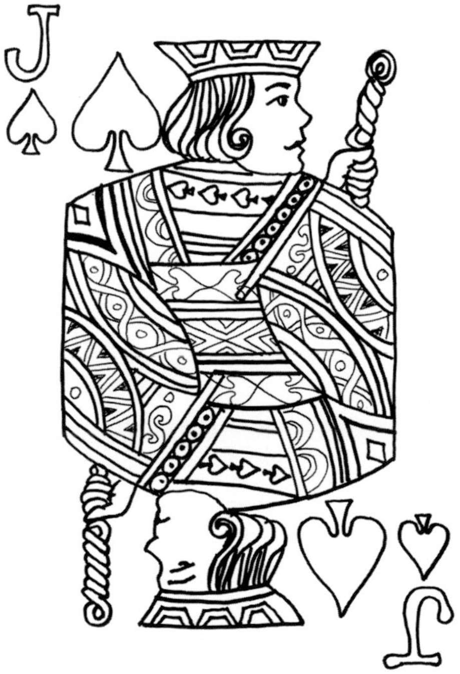
J
J

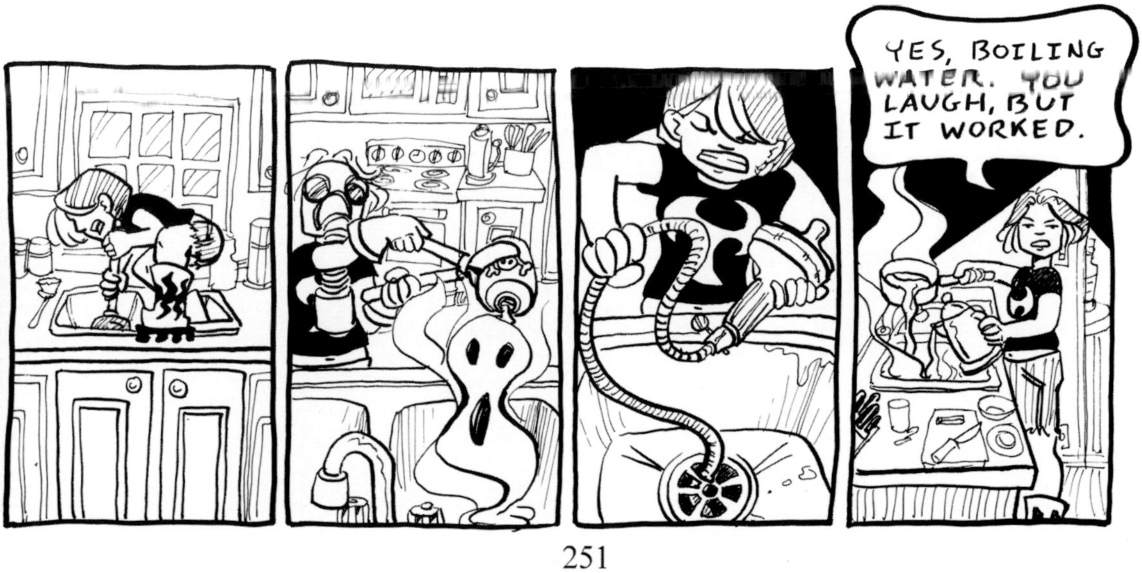
YES, BOILING WATER. YOU LAUGH, BUT IT WORKED.

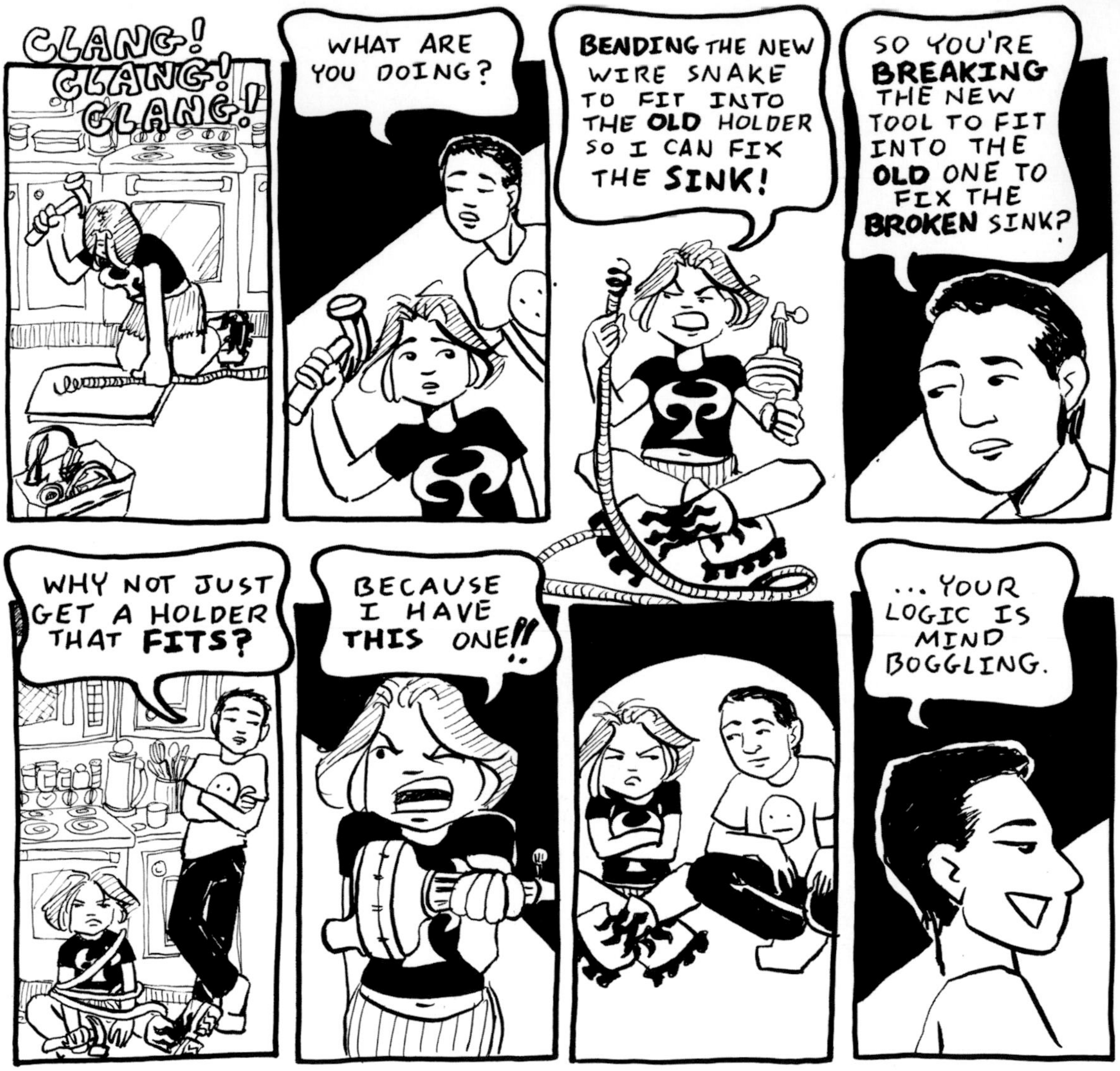
CLANG! CLANG! CLANG!
WHAT ARE YOU DOING?
BENDING THE NEW WIRE SNAKE TO FIT INTO THE OLD HOLDER SO I CAN FIX THE SINK!
SO YOU'RE BREAKING THE NEW TOOL TO FIT INTO THE OLD ONE TO FIX THE BROKEN SINK?
WHY NOT JUST GET A HOLDER THAT FITS?
BECAUSE I HAVE THIS ONE!!
... YOUR LOGIC IS MIND BOGGLING.

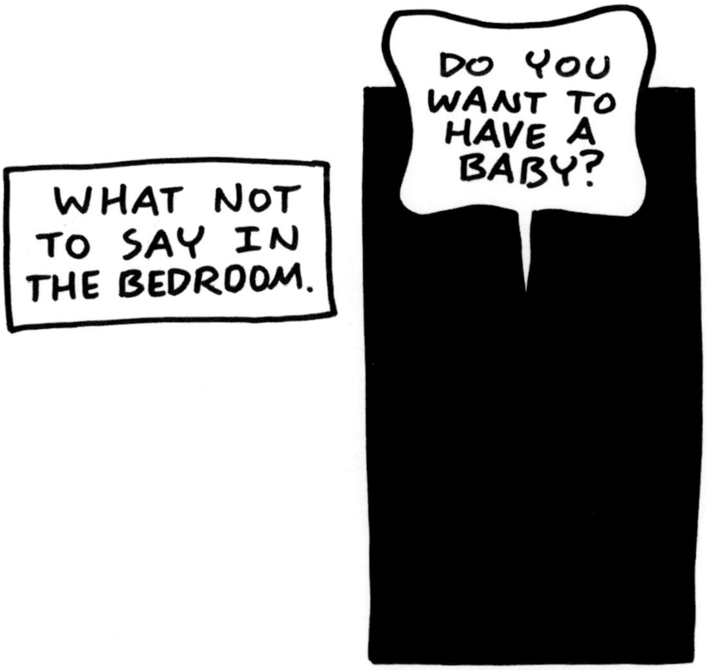
WHAT NOT TO SAY IN THE BEDROOM.
DO YOU WANT TO HAVE A BABY?

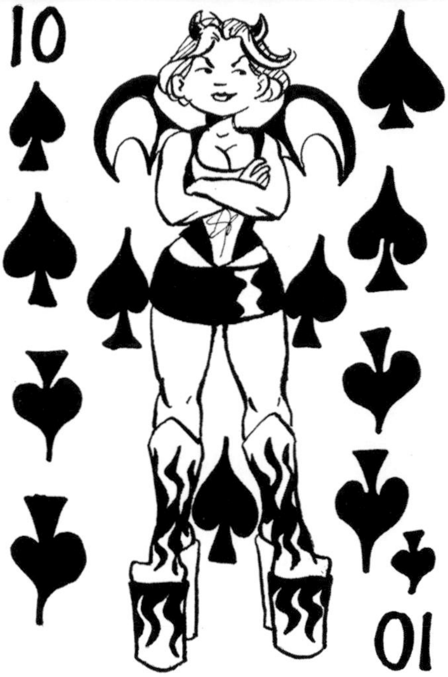
10
01

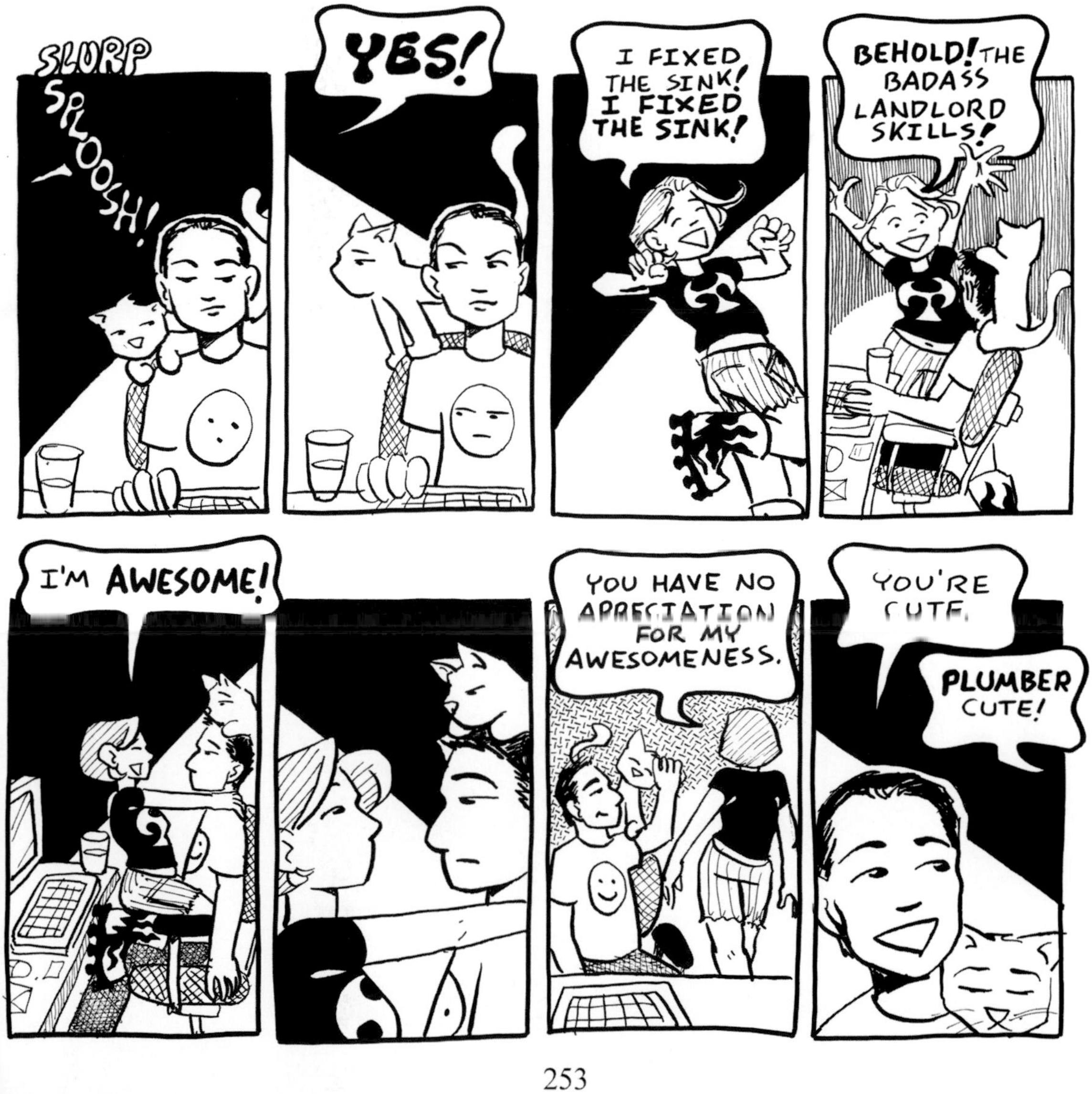
SLURP
SPLOOSH!
YES!
I FIXED THE SINK! I FIXED THE SINK!
BEHOLD! THE BADASS LANDLORD SKILLS!
I'M AWESOME!
YOU HAVE NO APPRECIATION FOR MY AWESOMENESS.
YOU'RE CUTE.
PLUMBER CUTE!

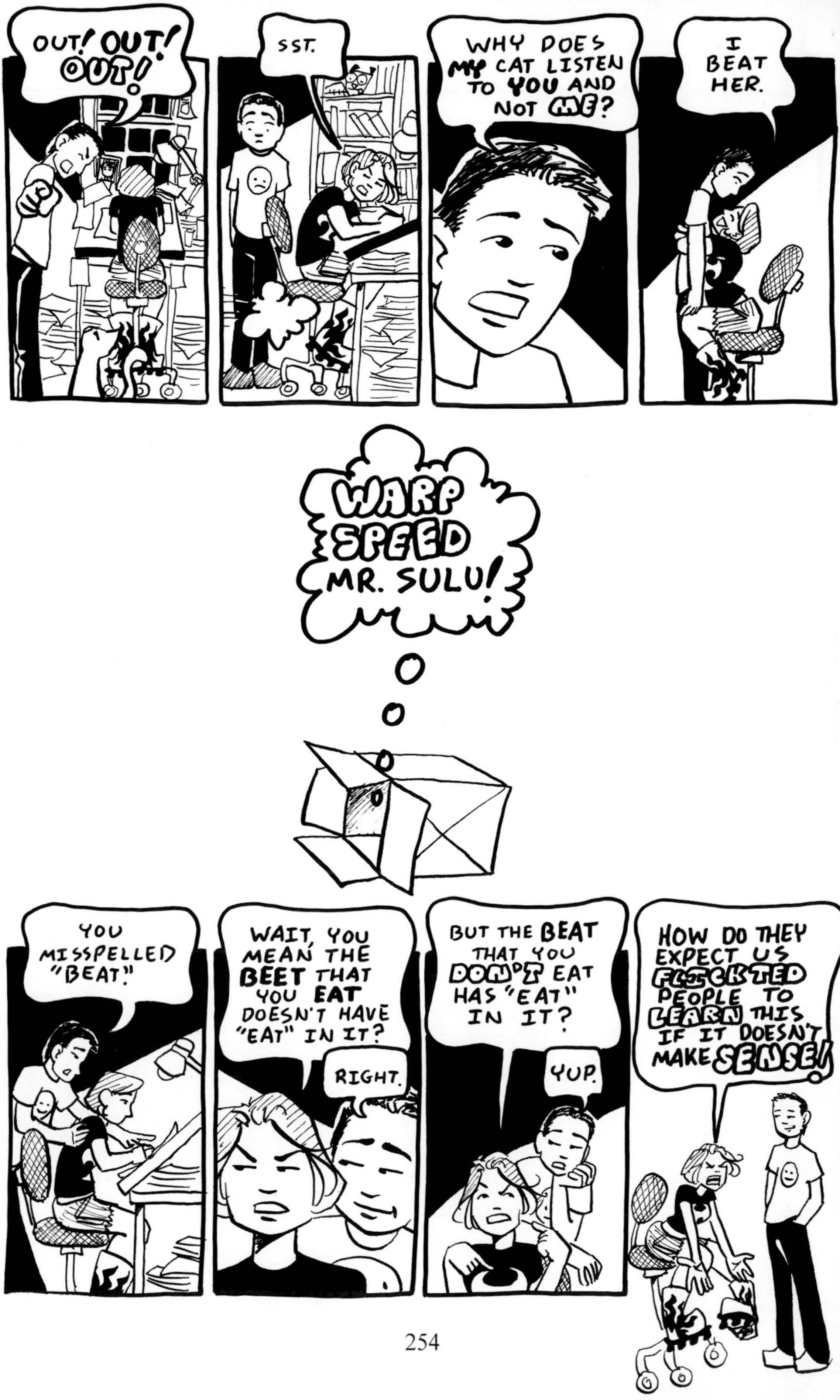
OUT! OUT! OUT!
SST.
WHY DOES MY CAT LISTEN TO YOU AND NOT ME?
I BEAT HER.
WARP SPEED MR. SULU!
YOU MISSPELLED "BEAT."
WAIT, YOU MEAN THE BEET THAT YOU EAT DOESN'T HAVE "EAT" IN IT?
RIGHT.
BUT THE BEAT THAT YOU DON'T EAT HAS "EAT" IN IT?
YUP.
HOW DO THEY EXPECT US FLICKTED PEOPLE TO LEARN THIS IF IT DOESN'T MAKE SENSE!

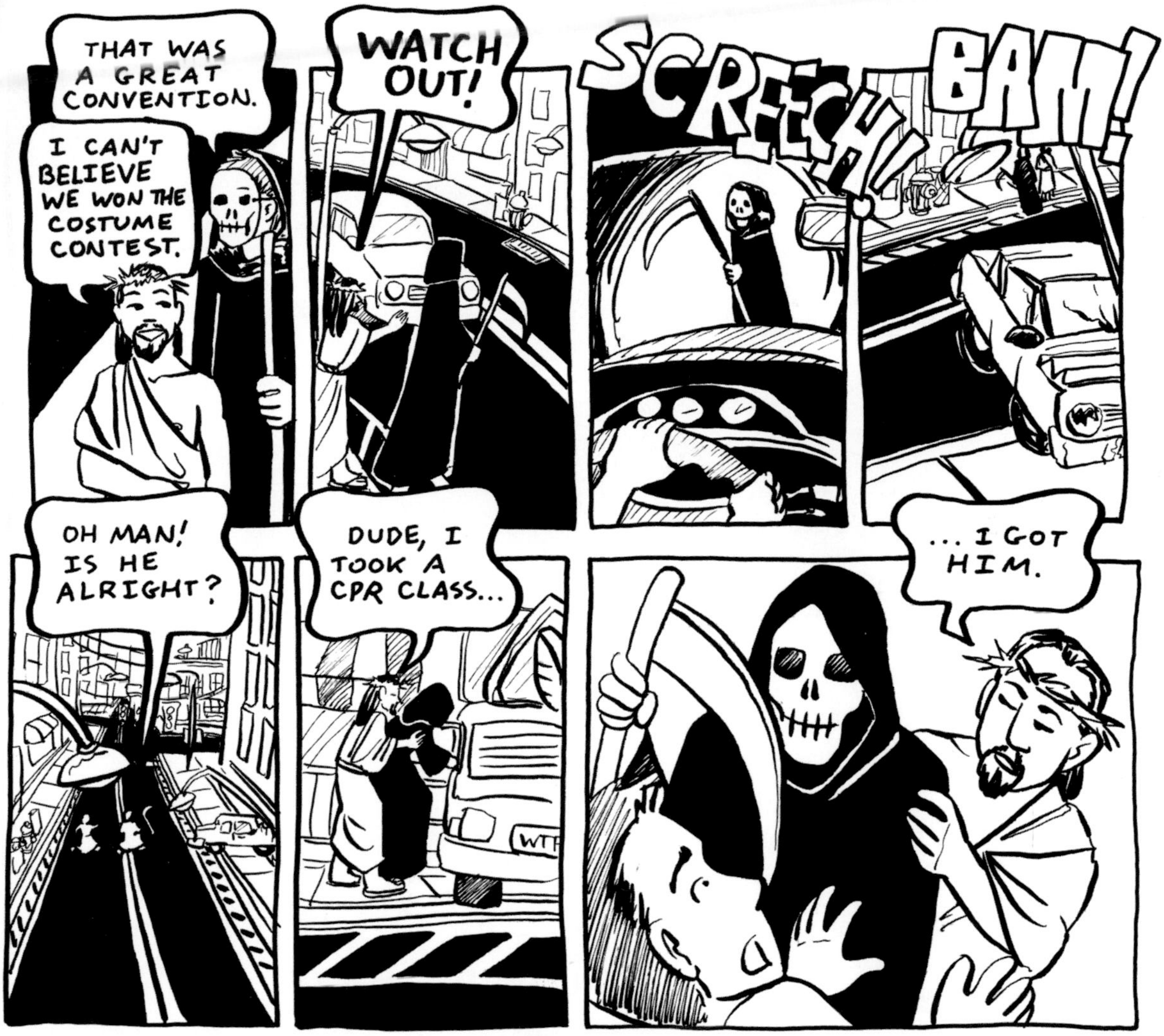
THAT WAS A GREAT CONVENTION.
I CAN'T BELIEVE WE WON THE COSTUME CONTEST.
WATCH OUT!
SCREECH!
BAM!
OH MAN! IS HE ALRIGHT?
DUDE, I TOOK A CPR CLASS...
WTF
... I GOT HIM.

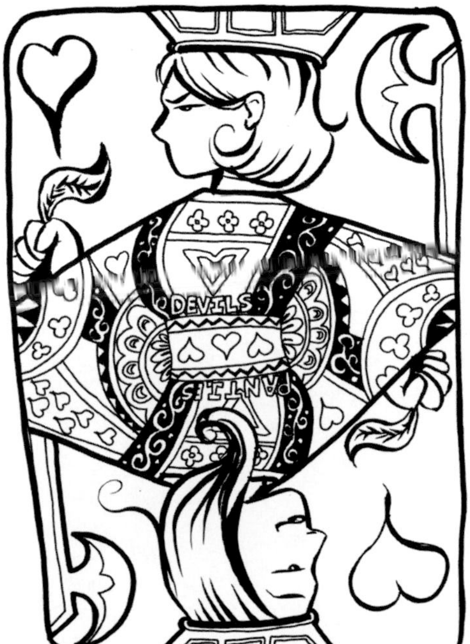
DEVILS

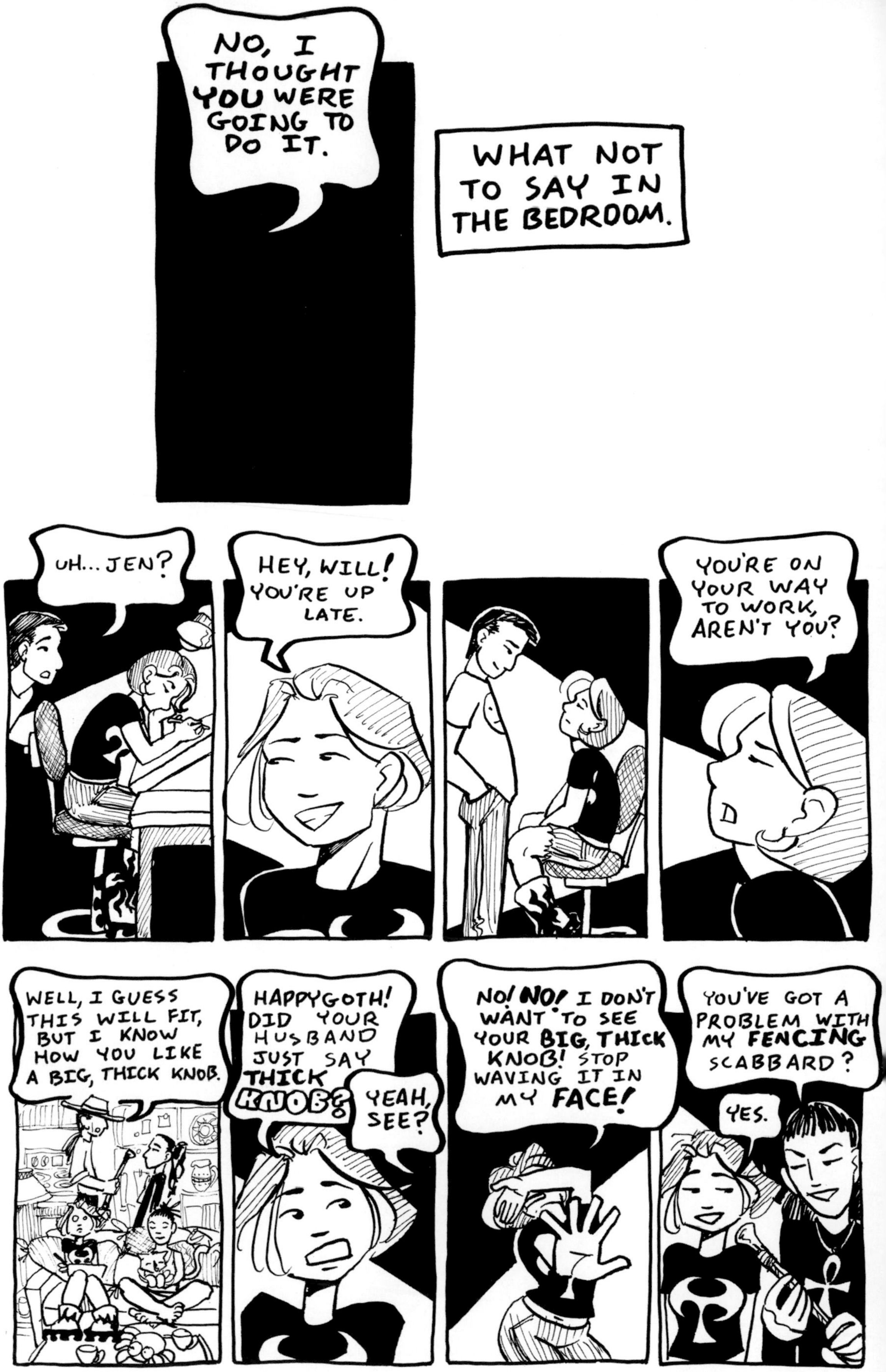

NO, I THOUGHT YOU WERE GOING TO DO IT.
WHAT NOT TO SAY IN THE BEDROOM.
UH... JEN?
HEY, WILL! YOU'RE UP LATE.
YOU'RE ON YOUR WAY TO WORK, AREN'T YOU?
WELL, I GUESS THIS WILL FIT, BUT I KNOW HOW YOU LIKE A BIG, THICK KNOB.
HAPPYGOTH! DID YOUR HUSBAND JUST SAY THICK KNOB?
YEAH, SEE?
NO! NO! I DON'T WANT TO SEE YOUR BIG, THICK KNOB! STOP WAVING IT IN MY FACE!
YOU'VE GOT A PROBLEM WITH MY FENCING SCABBARD?
YES.

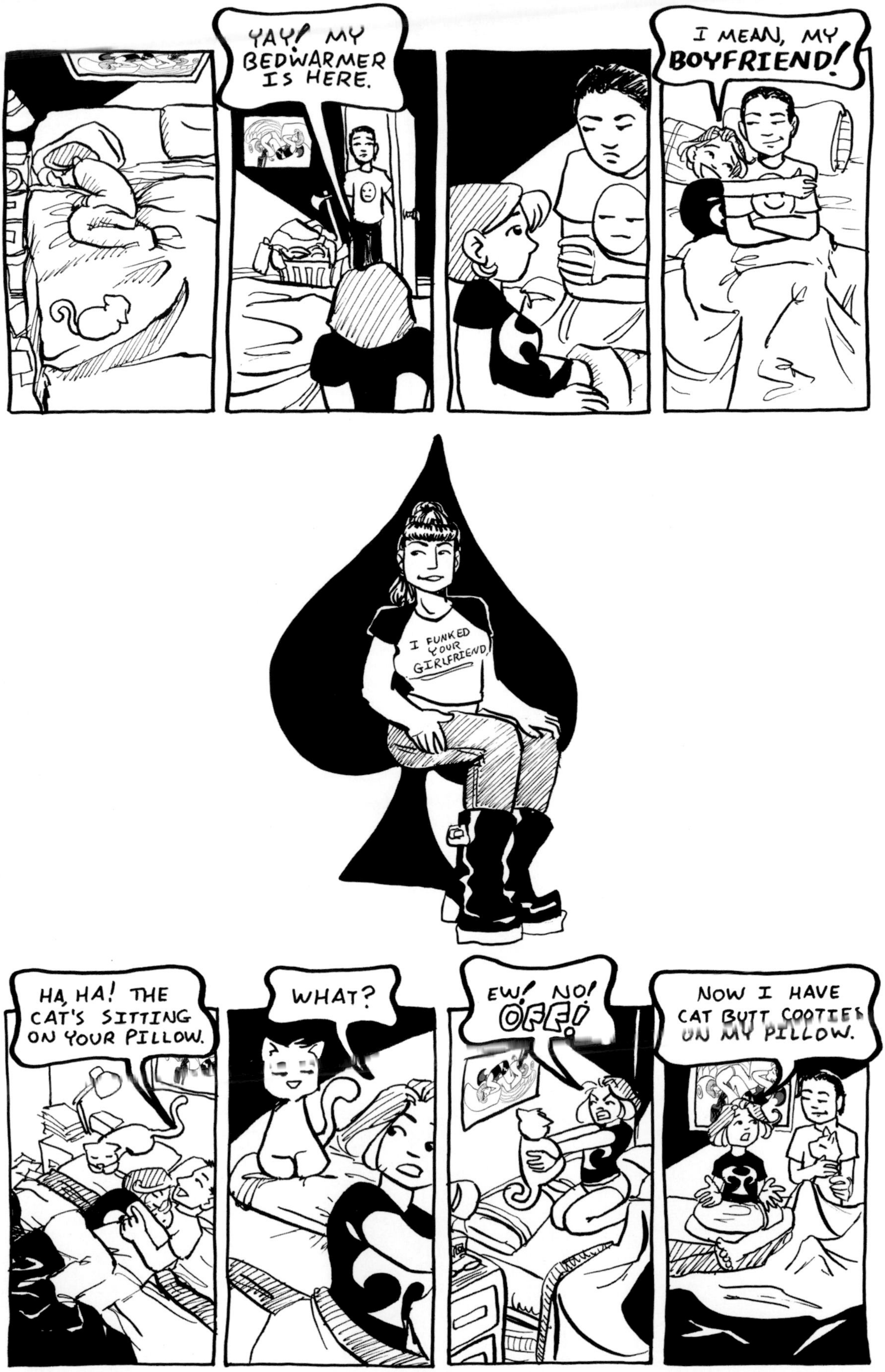
YAY! MY BEDWARMER IS HERE.
I MEAN, MY BOYFRIEND!
I FUNKED YOUR GIRLFRIEND
HA, HA! THE CAT'S SITTING ON YOUR PILLOW.
WHAT?
EW! NO! OFF!
NOW I HAVE CAT BUTT COOTIES ON MY PILLOW.

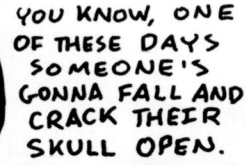

YOU KNOW, ONE OF THESE DAYS SOMEONE'S GONNA FALL AND CRACK THEIR SKULL OPEN.

I'LL JUST HAVE TO FIGURE OUT WHAT TO TELL THE COPS AFTER I COLLECT YOUR LIFE INSURANCE.

LOVE YOU TOO.

YOU KNOW WHAT'S WRONG WITH THIS?

WHAT'S THAT?

YOU TRUST ME.

JUST BECAUSE I GOT MYSELF UP HERE, DOESN'T MEAN I KNOW HOW TO GET DOWN.

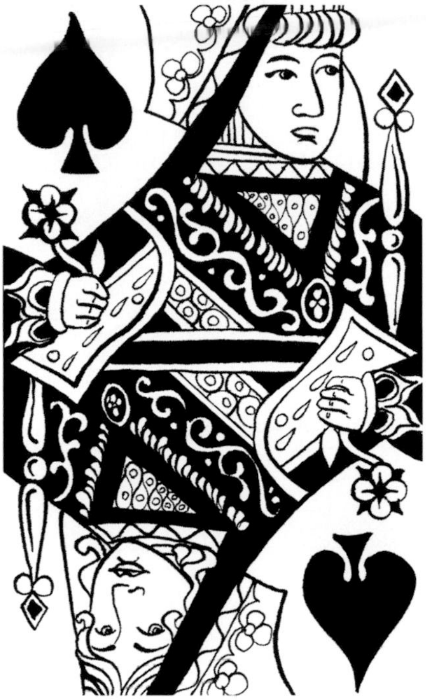

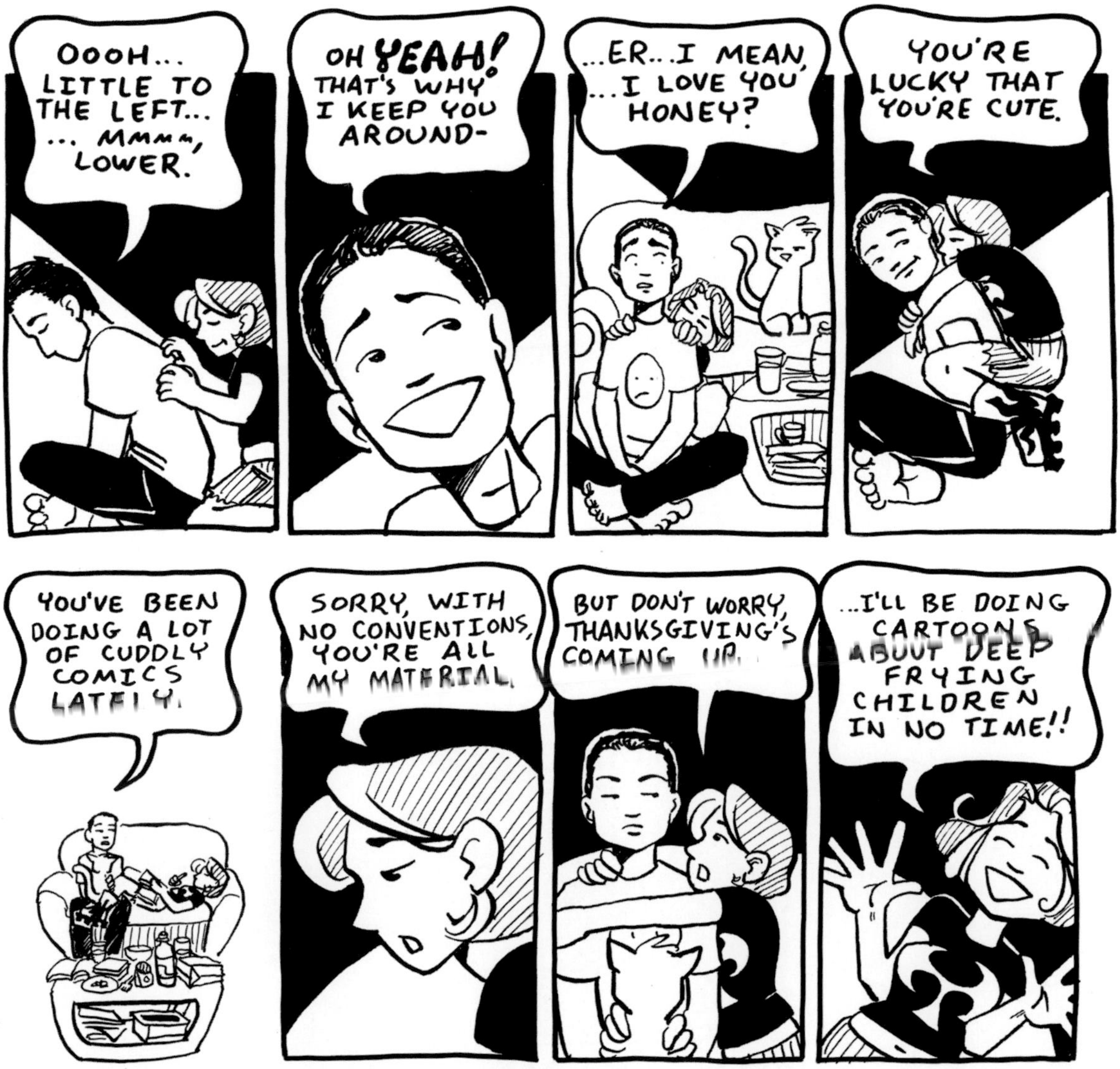
OOOH... LITTLE TO THE LEFT... ... MMMM, LOWER.
OH YEAH! THAT'S WHY I KEEP YOU AROUND-
...ER...I MEAN, ...I LOVE YOU HONEY?
YOU'RE LUCKY THAT YOU'RE CUTE.
YOU'VE BEEN DOING A LOT OF CUDDLY COMICS LATELY.
SORRY, WITH NO CONVENTIONS, YOU'RE ALL MY MATERIAL.
BUT DON'T WORRY, THANKSGIVING'S COMING UP.
...I'LL BE DOING CARTOONS ABOUT DEEP FRYING CHILDREN IN NO TIME!!

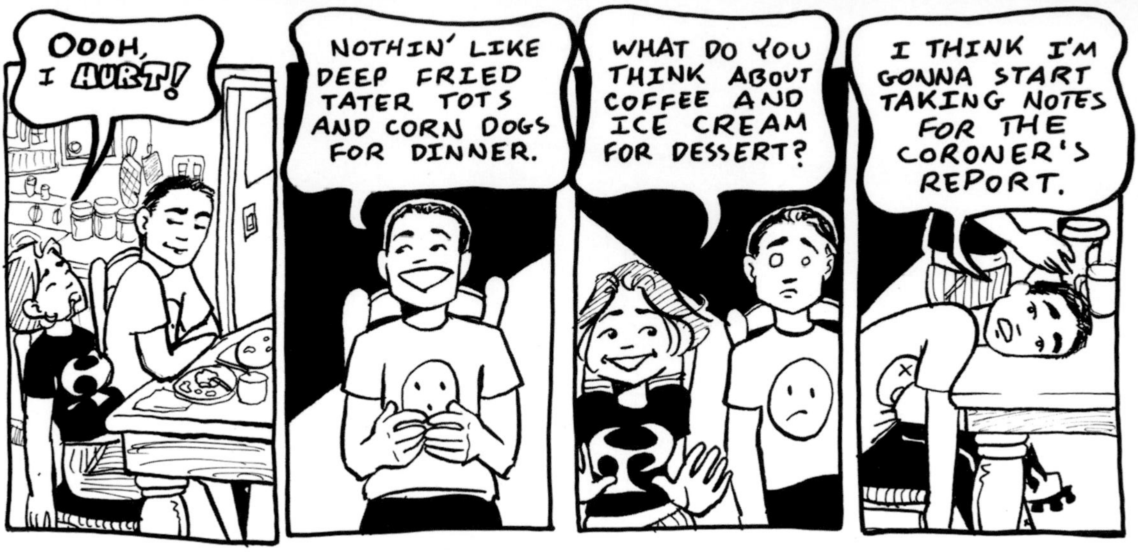
OOOH, I HURT!
NOTHIN' LIKE DEEP FRIED TATER TOTS AND CORN DOGS FOR DINNER.
WHAT DO YOU THINK ABOUT COFFEE AND ICE CREAM FOR DESSERT?
I THINK I'M GONNA START TAKING NOTES FOR THE CORONER'S REPORT.

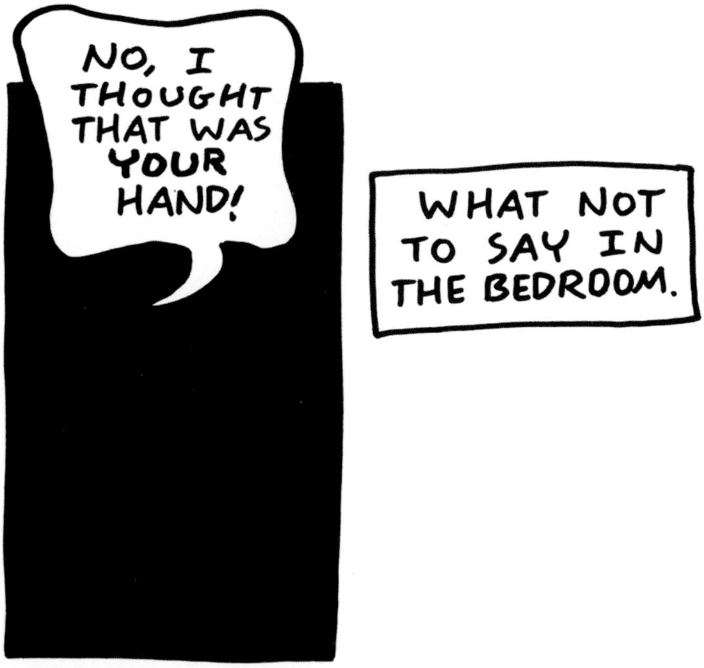
NO, I THOUGHT THAT WAS YOUR HAND!
WHAT NOT TO SAY IN THE BEDROOM.

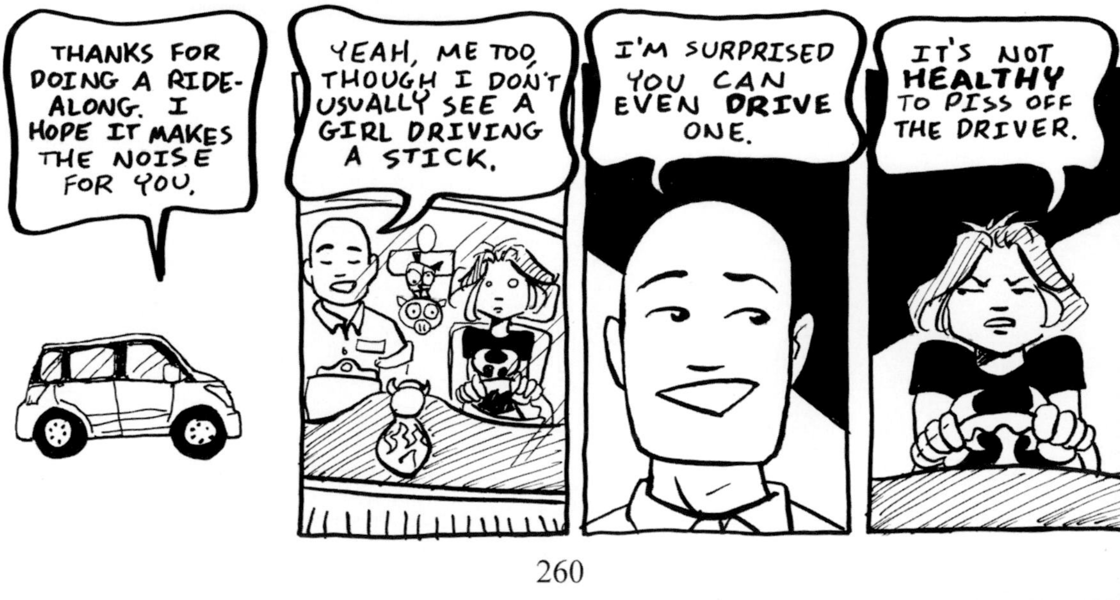
THANKS FOR DOING A RIDE-ALONG. I HOPE IT MAKES THE NOISE FOR YOU.
YEAH, ME TOO, THOUGH I DON'T USUALLY SEE A GIRL DRIVING A STICK.
I'M SURPRISED YOU CAN EVEN DRIVE ONE.
IT'S NOT HEALTHY TO PISS OFF THE DRIVER.

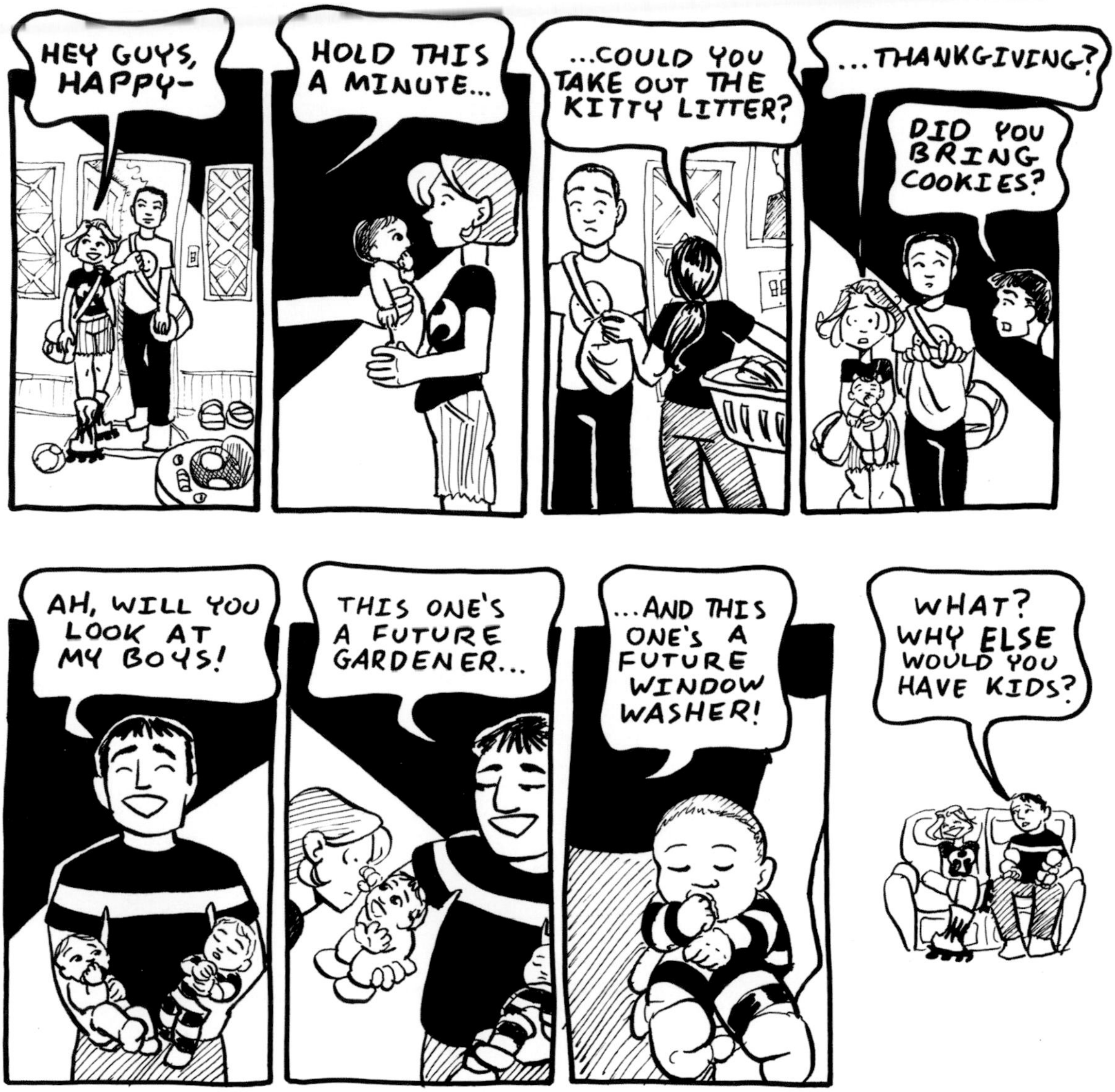
HEY GUYS, HAPPY-
HOLD THIS A MINUTE...
...COULD YOU TAKE OUT THE KITTY LITTER?
...THANKGIVING?
DID YOU BRING COOKIES?
AH, WILL YOU LOOK AT MY BOYS!
THIS ONE'S A FUTURE GARDENER...
...AND THIS ONE'S A FUTURE WINDOW WASHER!
WHAT? WHY ELSE WOULD YOU HAVE KIDS?

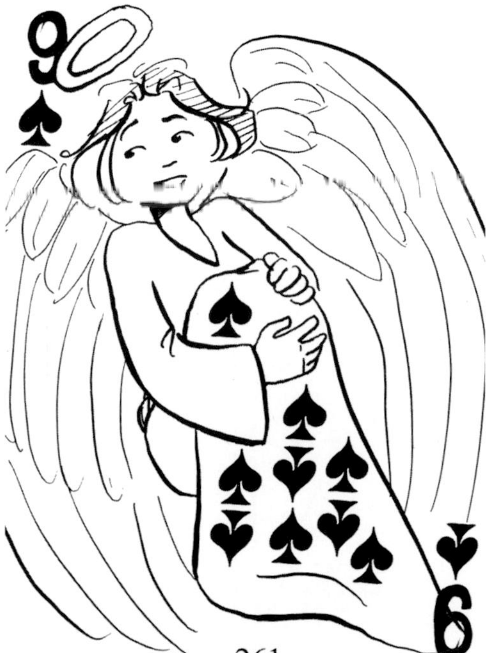
9
6

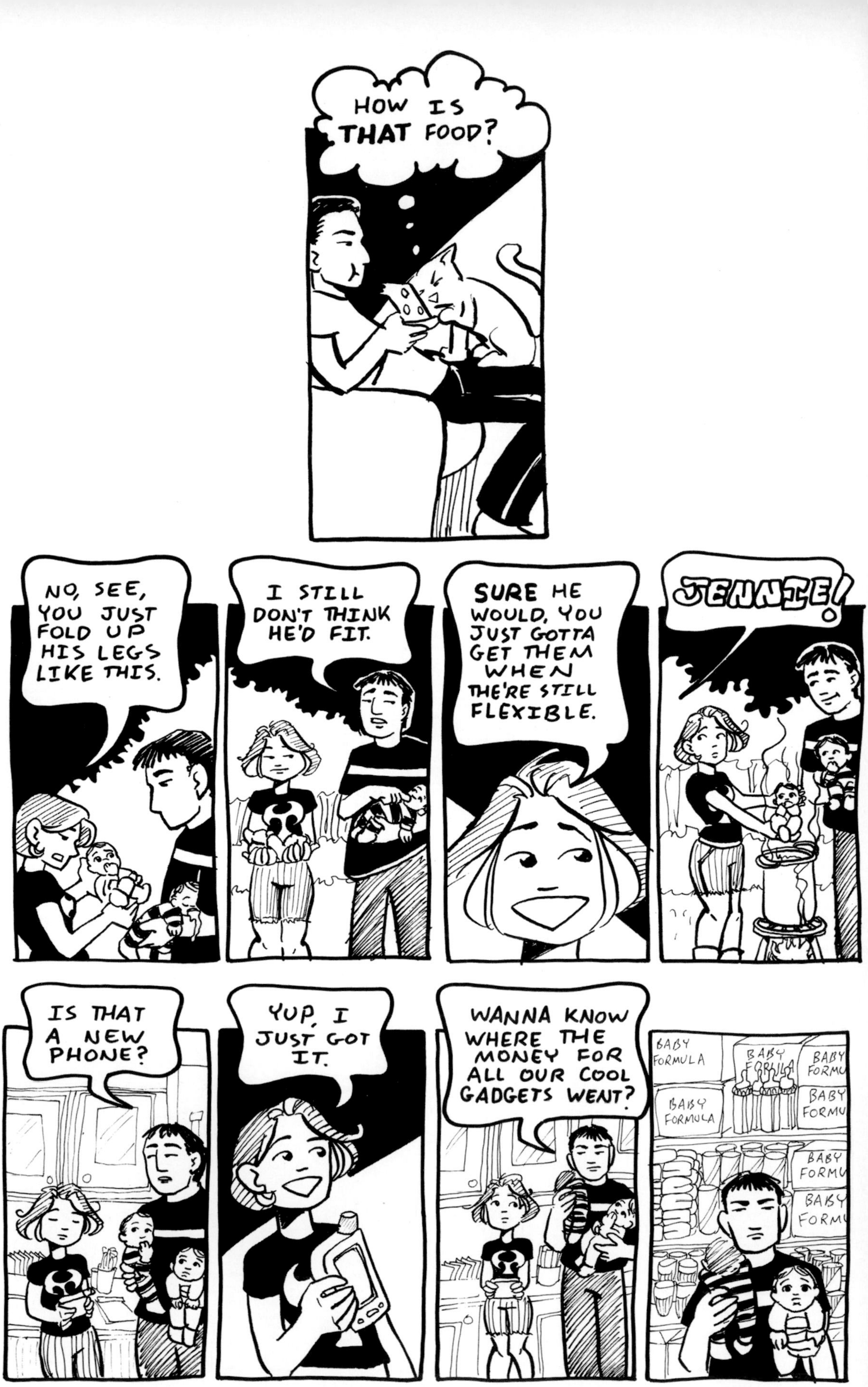
HOW IS THAT FOOD?
NO, SEE, YOU JUST FOLD UP HIS LEGS LIKE THIS.
I STILL DON'T THINK HE'D FIT.
SURE HE WOULD, YOU JUST GOTTA GET THEM WHEN THE'RE STILL FLEXIBLE.
JENNIE!
IS THAT A NEW PHONE?
YUP, I JUST GOT IT.
WANNA KNOW WHERE THE MONEY FOR ALL OUR COOL GADGETS WENT?
BABY FORMULA
BABY FORMULA
BABY FORMULA
BABY FORMULA

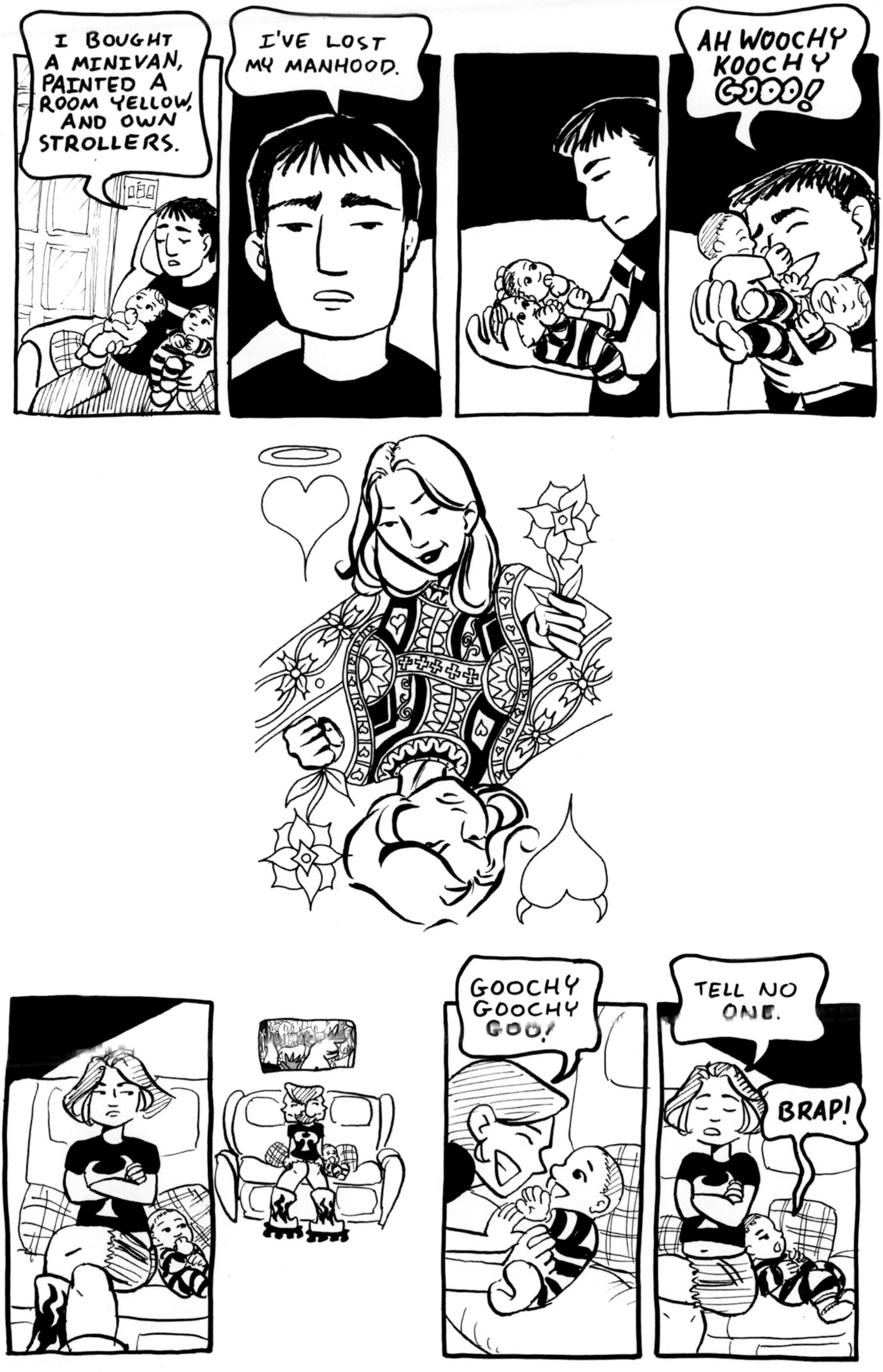

I BOUGHT A MINIVAN, PAINTED A ROOM YELLOW, AND OWN STROLLERS.
I'VE LOST MY MANHOOD.
AH WOOCHY KOOCHY GOOO!
GOOCHY GOOCHY GOO!
TELL NO ONE.
BRAP!

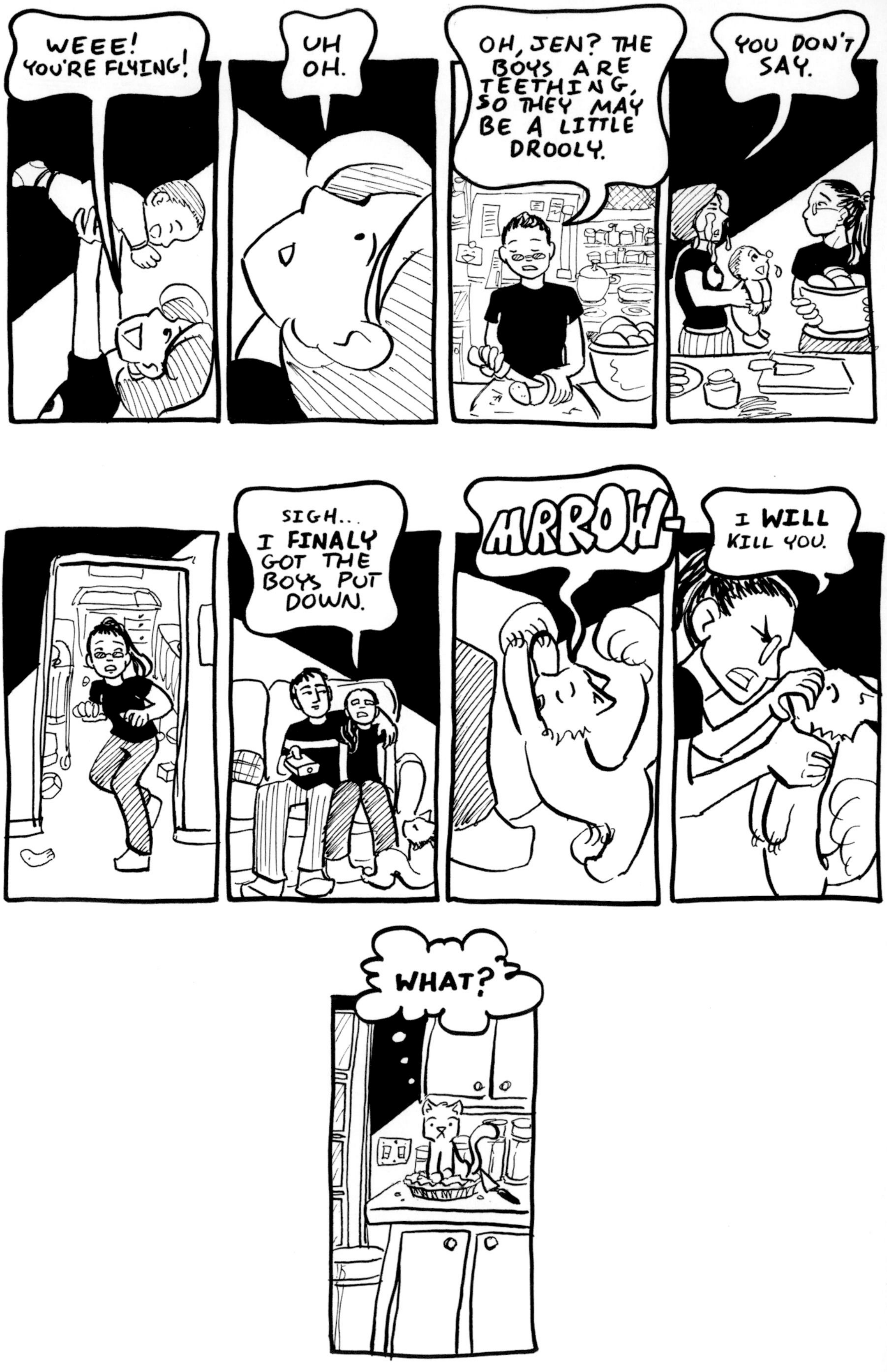
WEEE! YOU'RE FLYING!
UH OH.
OH, JEN? THE BOYS ARE TEETHING, SO THEY MAY BE A LITTLE DROOLY.
YOU DON'T SAY.
SIGH... I FINALY GOT THE BOYS PUT DOWN.
MRROW-
I WILL KILL YOU.
WHAT?

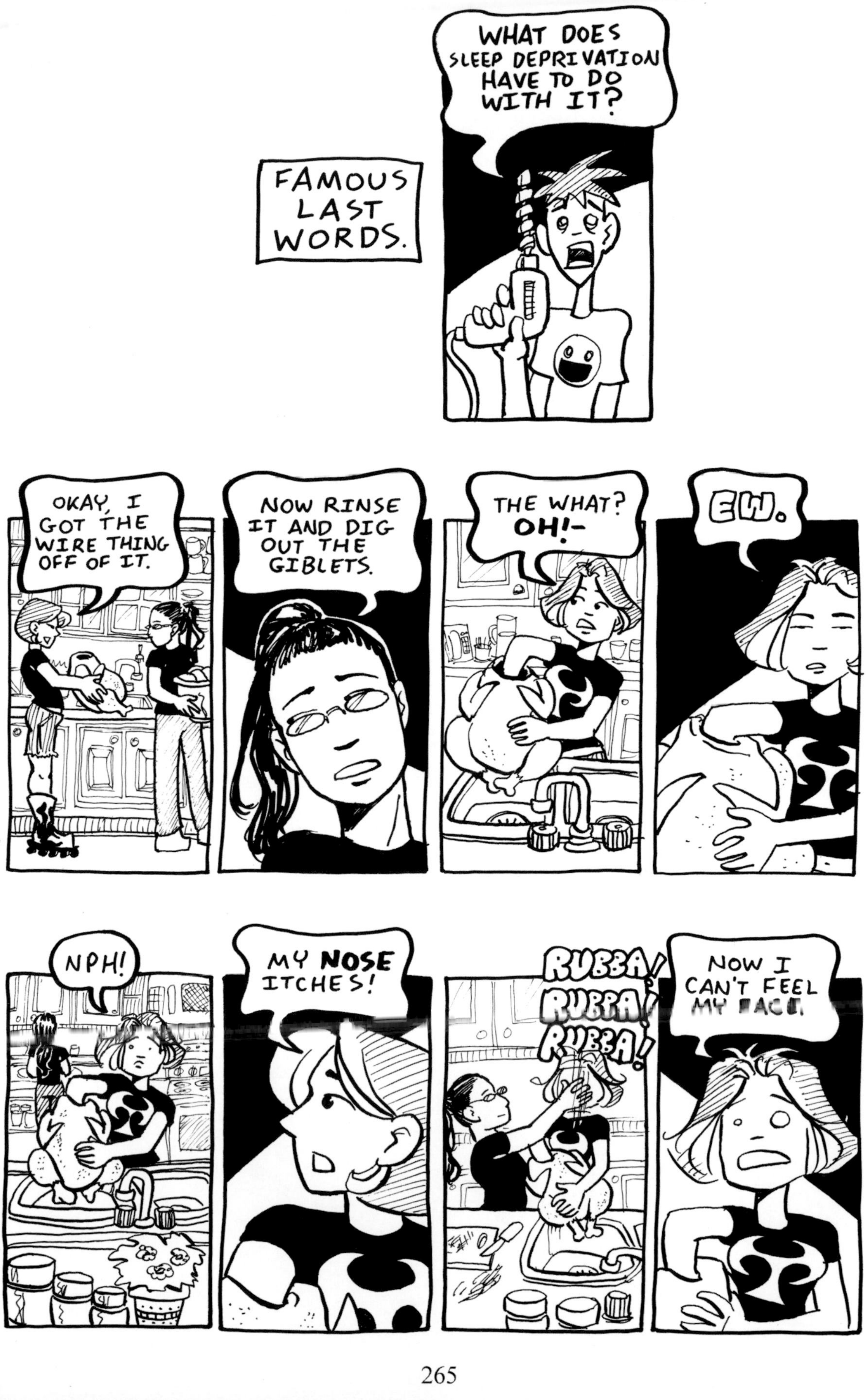
WHAT DOES SLEEP DEPRIVATION HAVE TO DO WITH IT?
FAMOUS LAST WORDS.
OKAY, I GOT THE WIRE THING OFF OF IT.
NOW RINSE IT AND DIG OUT THE GIBLETS.
THE WHAT? OH!-
EW.
NPH!
MY NOSE ITCHES!
RUBBA! RUBBA! RUBBA!
NOW I CAN'T FEEL MY FACE.

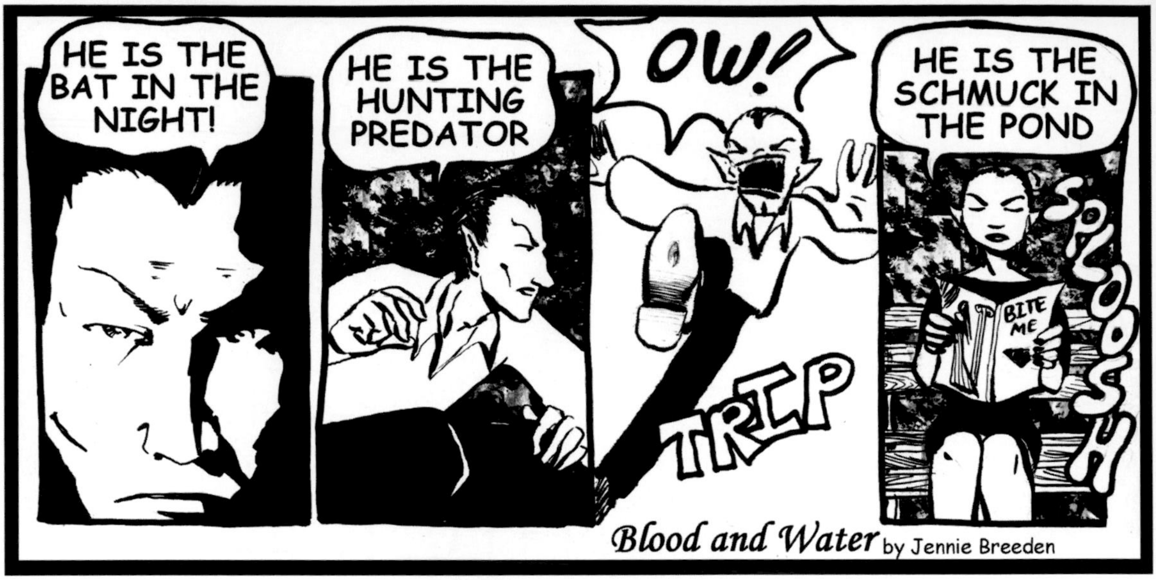
HE IS THE BAT IN THE NIGHT!
HE IS THE HUNTING PREDATOR
OW!
TRIP
HE IS THE SCHMUCK IN THE POND
BITE ME
SPLOOOSH
Blood and Water by Jennie Breeden

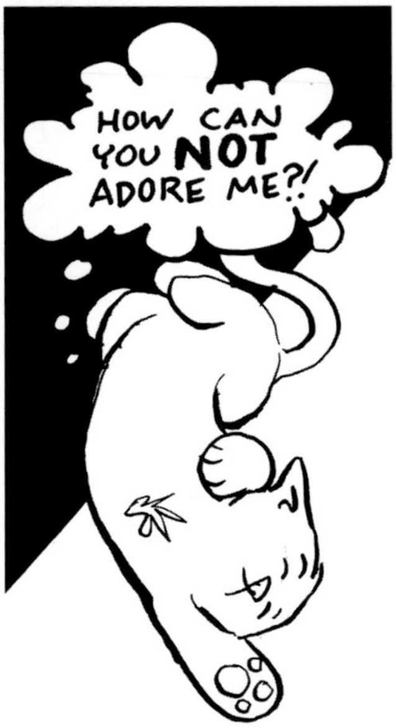
HOW CAN YOU NOT ADORE ME?!

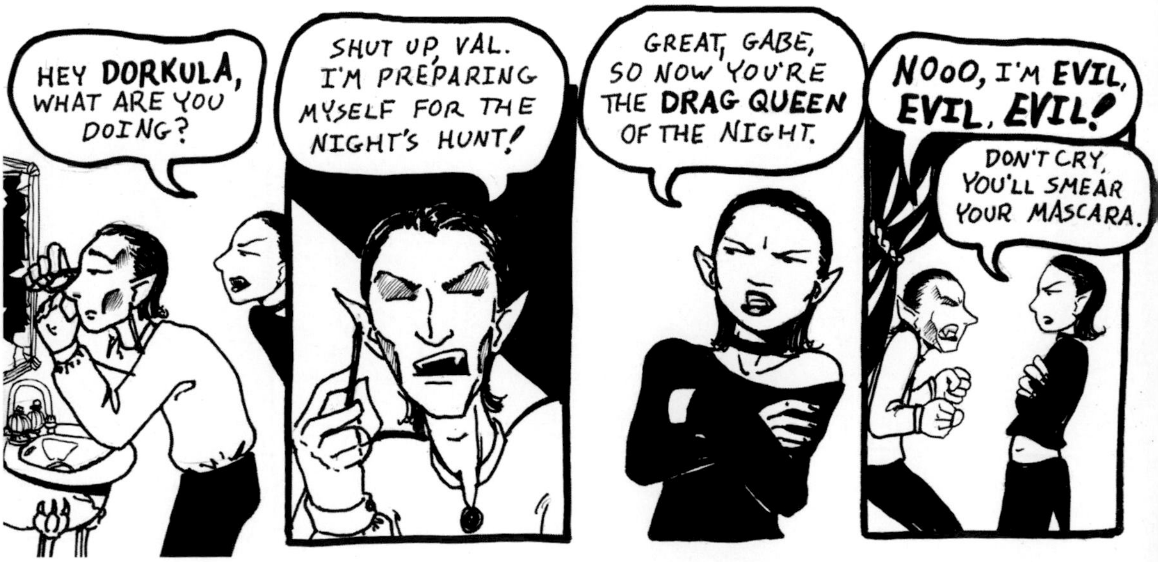
HEY DORKULA, WHAT ARE YOU DOING?
SHUT UP, VAL. I'M PREPARING MYSELF FOR THE NIGHT'S HUNT!
GREAT, GABE, SO NOW YOU'RE THE DRAG QUEEN OF THE NIGHT.
NOoO, I'M EVIL, EVIL, EVIL!
DON'T CRY, YOU'LL SMEAR YOUR MASCARA.

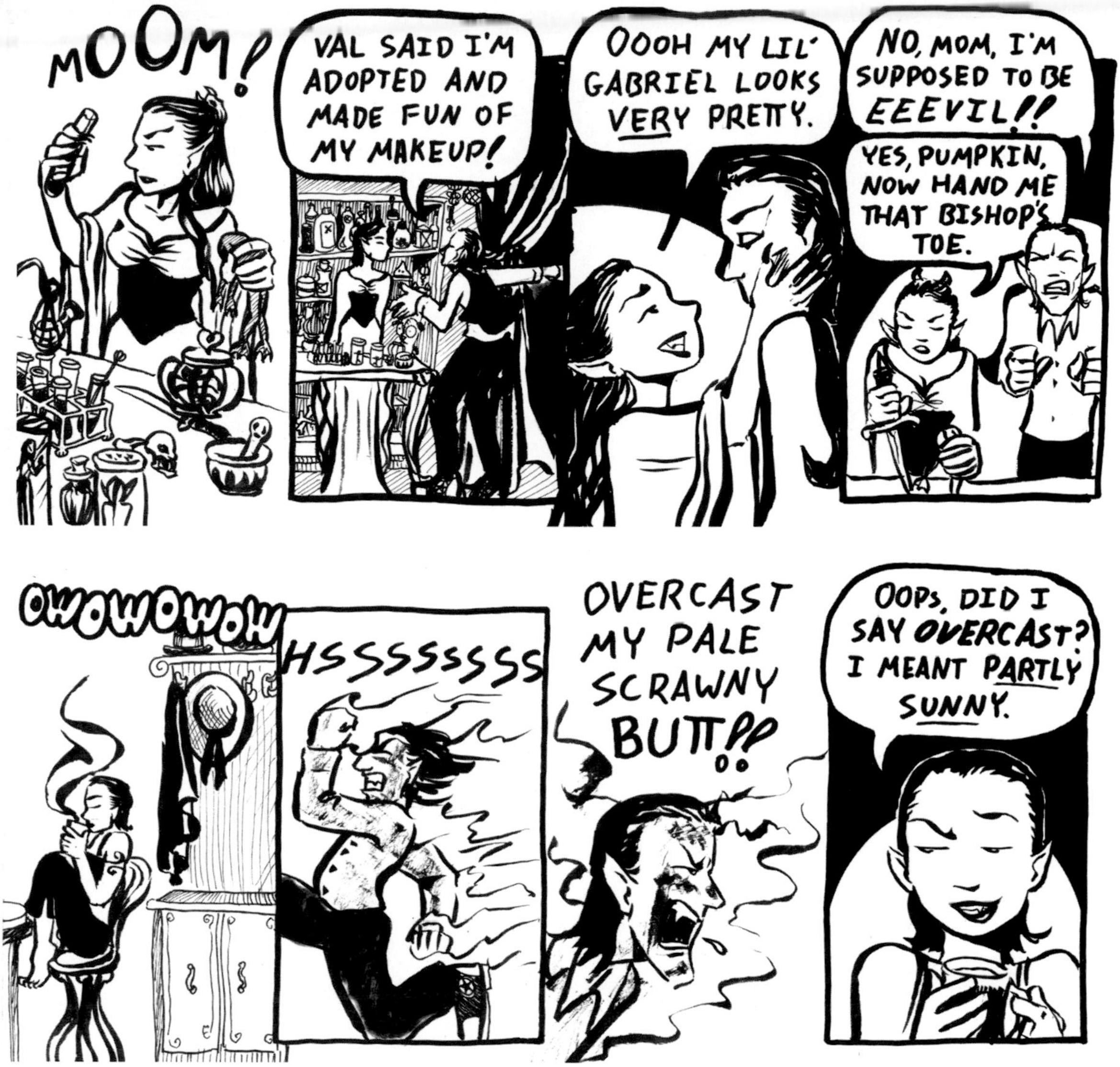
MOOM!
VAL SAID I'M ADOPTED AND MADE FUN OF MY MAKEUP!
OOOH MY LIL' GABRIEL LOOKS VERY PRETTY.
NO, MOM, I'M SUPPOSED TO BE EEEVIL!!
YES, PUMPKIN, NOW HAND ME THAT BISHOP'S TOE.
OWOWOWOW
HSSSSSSSS
OVERCAST MY PALE SCRAWNY BUTT!!
OOPS, DID I SAY OVERCAST? I MEANT PARTLY SUNNY.

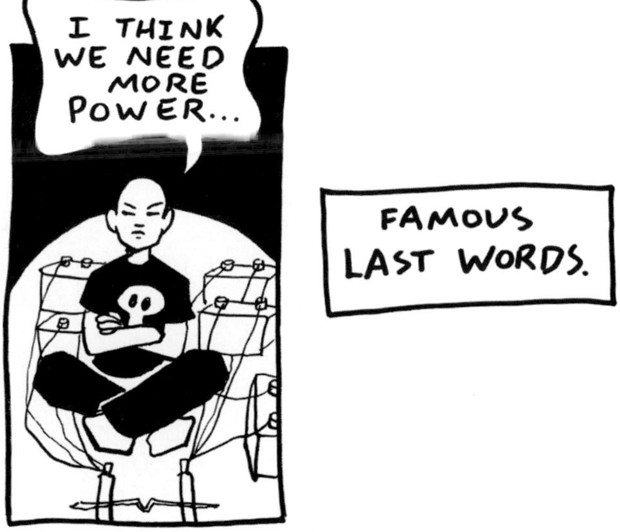
I THINK WE NEED MORE POWER...
FAMOUS LAST WORDS.

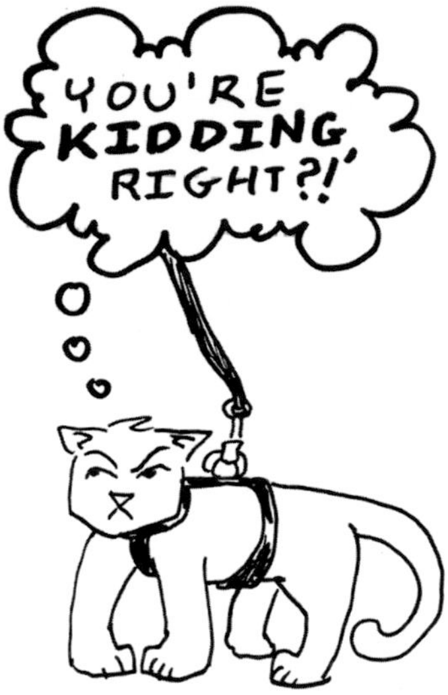
YOU'RE KIDDING, RIGHT?!

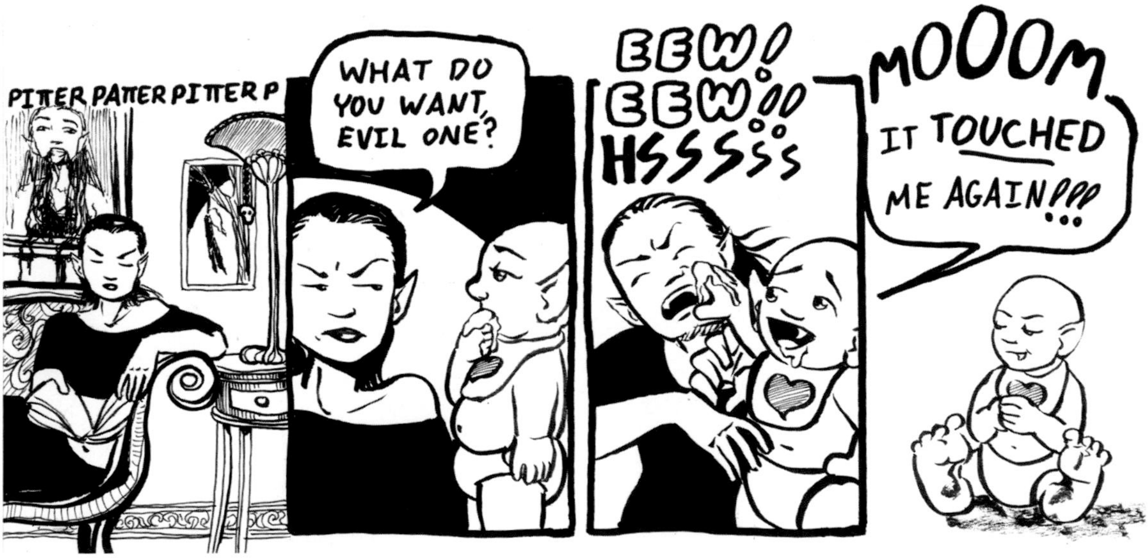
PITTER PATTER PITTER P
WHAT DO YOU WANT, EVIL ONE?
EEW! EEW!! HSSSSS
MOOOM
IT TOUCHED ME AGAIN!!!

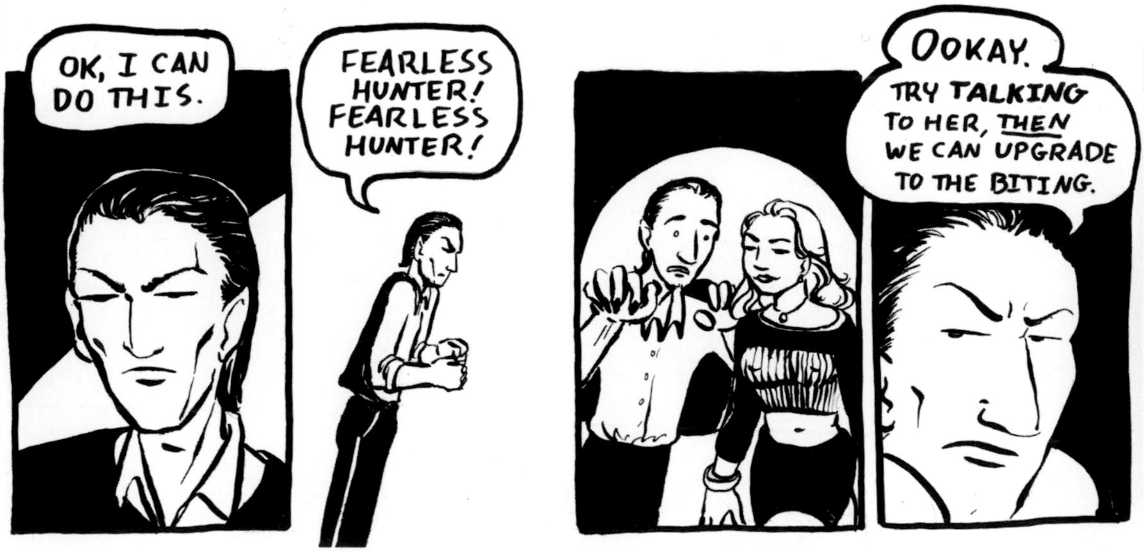
OK, I CAN DO THIS.
FEARLESS HUNTER! FEARLESS HUNTER!
OOKAY.
TRY TALKING TO HER, THEN WE CAN UPGRADE TO THE BITING.

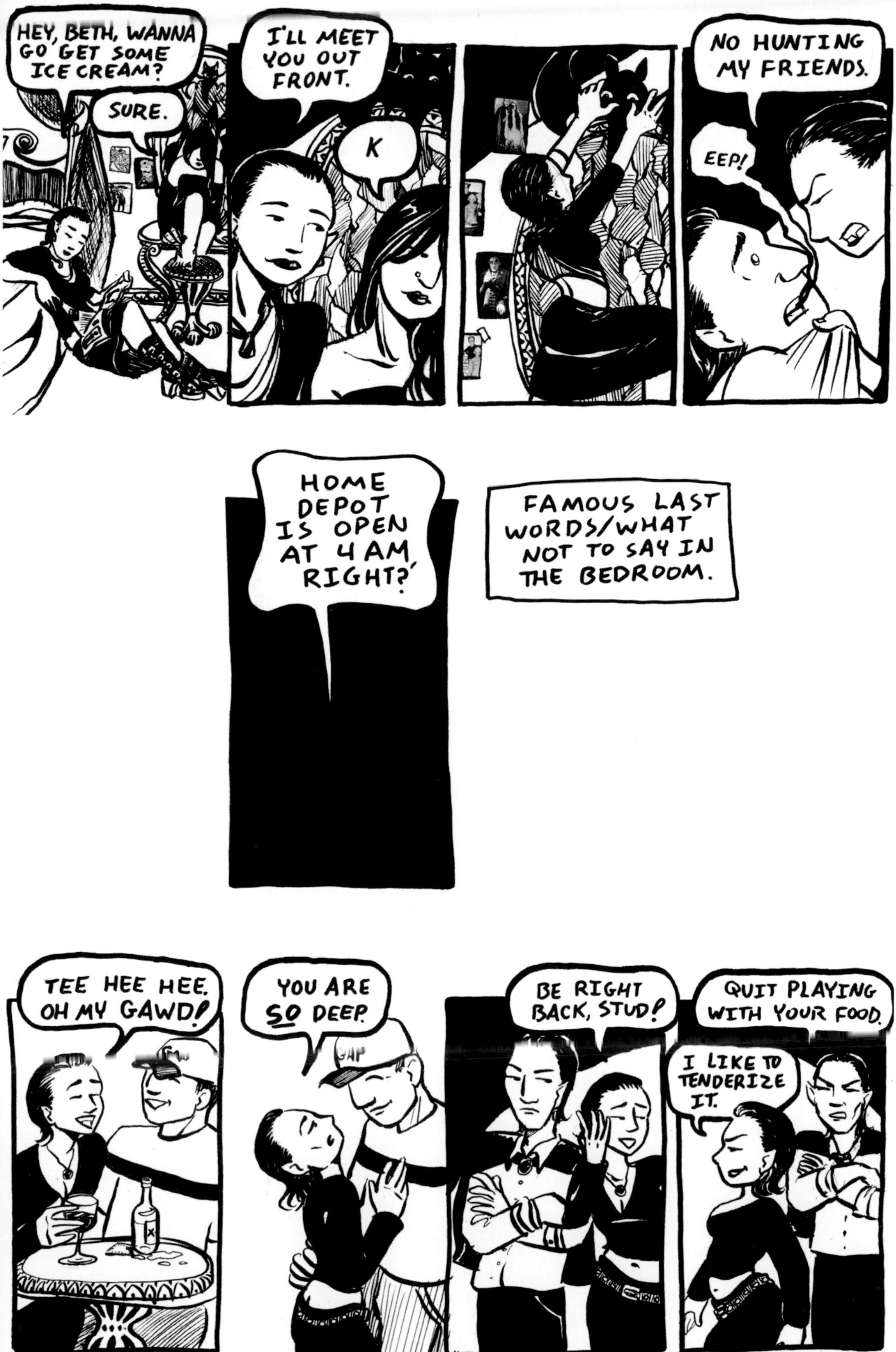
HEY, BETH, WANNA GO GET SOME ICE CREAM?
SURE.
I'LL MEET YOU OUT FRONT.
K
NO HUNTING MY FRIENDS.
EEP!
HOME DEPOT IS OPEN AT 4 AM, RIGHT?
FAMOUS LAST WORDS/WHAT NOT TO SAY IN THE BEDROOM.
TEE HEE HEE. OH MY GAWD!
YOU ARE SO DEEP.
GAP
BE RIGHT BACK, STUD!
QUIT PLAYING WITH YOUR FOOD.
I LIKE TO TENDERIZE IT.

VAL, HONEY, YOUR MOM AND I ARE GOING OUT TONIGHT.

SO YOU'RE RESPONSIBLE FOR THINGS HERE...

WHICH INCLUDES **THIS.**

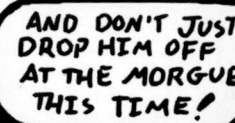

AND DON'T JUST DROP HIM OFF AT THE MORGUE THIS TIME!

HSSS.

SNIFF SNIFF?

YOU HAVEN'T BEEN STASHING CORPSE'S FINGERS IN THERE **AGAIN,** HAVE YOU?!

BLURBLE

OH FOR THE LOVE OF ALL THINGS**EVIL!**

HOW LONG HAS THAT **TWINKIE** BEEN IN THERE!?

I'M COMFORTABLE. HOW CAN YOU NOT BE?

Page 1

LAN parties are creepy because you have 15 guys in your garage and an empty house.

Page 2

Yes, I LARP (live action role playing). I hunt down my friends in the woods with a padded stick. Sometimes nature gets in the way.

Page 3

I crap you not, he asked about hypnotists.

Page 4

I'm in the south. Once a month I get a guy in the comic shop who calls me "sugar" or "sweet heart" and I don't know why, but my stomach convulses. I want to yell at him, "Do you even KNOW me? How the hell do YOU know if I'm SWEET!?!"

Page 5

I usually have one-week stints where I exercise and then I'm over it for about eight months.

Page 6

The last panel the guy has his horseshoe upside-down, which is actually bad luck.

Page 7

I didn't actually get to say the storm trooper thing to the little brats.

Page 8

At Heroes Con, when I met the Pirate, I found out that there was a rumor that I was sleeping around. Suddenly I wanted to put a bag over my head and cut off any possibility of mistaken flirtation. I drove myself nuts until I realized that it's not my fault that a$$ holes can't tell the difference between being polite and flirting.

Page 9

I didn't actually hand out soap and sandwiches, but sometimes I wish someone would.

Page 10

My friend, Karl, shuffled through the con gnawing on raw meat and anyone who interacted with him. Later, he said that a couple girls hit on him when he was in the zombie makeup, which creeped him out. The girl is from a vampire comic that I did for Acrimony.org

Page 11

Pictures of the "Panties sale to Superman" can be found at devilspanties.keenspot.com/ Dragoncon.html. There's also a picture of the two little grim reaper boys from the last panel.

Page 12

No matter how articulate I try to be, it just degenerates into "boobies". The evil Willow was a girl in a really good costume.

Page 13

I don't make this kind of stuff up. The pirate lady created the best Dragon Con drinking game ever!

Page 14

Agwa is florescent green.

Page 15

The pirates covered me in pink Sharpie. Some of it was hard to explain to Will.

Page 16

It wasn't until Ddragon con 2006 that I actually get the leaf blower, though.

Page 17

Clothes are replaceable. The books are my babies.

Page 18

Every time I see my sister she asks if I'm gay yet.

Page 19

The baby of the family has omnipotent guilt power.

Page 20

Yup, we went to Pegasus.

Page 21

I showed up a day early to visit my sister and found out after the class that the professor had planned a class around my visit to talk about webcomics.

Page 22

My sister pointed out that I had the comic equivalent of a reality show.

Page 23

It was weird. The parking garage was closed, but when I touched the gate it opened. I don't question good luck.

Page 24

Those one-dollar, vintage He-Man figures were awesome!

Page 25

I dressed up as Scary Godmother **www.jillthompsonart.com**

Page 26

Watercolors make the BEST makeup.

Page 27

I used an orange, plastic pom-pom for my hair, and it came in handy.

Page 28
This holiday can't truly be appreciated without children.
Page 29
I got the breaking boarders idea from 9 Chickweed Lane.
Page 30
The only sport I've ever gone to watch…
Well, there was that one hockey game.
Page 31
My boyfriend's sister's husband's sister had twin boys, and we see them every Thanksgiving.
Page 32
I like to mess with babies, but I LOVE to give them back to their parents.
Page 33
When the grandmother saw that I had put the baby in the soup pot she ran to get her camera.
Page 34
Black Friday always weirds me out.
Page 35
They never make fun shoes in adult sizes.
Page 36
You know you're stuck when they make you be in the family Christmas photo.
Page 37
I swear, that's what she said; "you have baby now."
Page 38
Pixel has "cute" down to an art.
Page 39
I take no responsibility for the "mao" cartoon.
Page 40
My dad never did anything half way.
Page 41
Okay, they didn't put us in muzzles, but my brother did have a Klingon death match with stockings and turkey prongs. That's exactly what we wore to church too. The oldest boy is in red satin shirt and leopard print gloves.
Page 42
This is my mom's favorite Christmas cartoon. And that's exactly what I said when David Mack showed up.
Page 43
Okay, so I didn't actually lift my shirt, but I was thinking about it.
Page 44
Going salsa dancing with my siblings is a little

out of context, but I couldn't work it into a story ark so here it is out of left field.
Page 45
I had used my glasses from fifth grade for driving and only updated the prescription in 2006. Now I'm addicted to being able to see the leaves on the trees. But I'm not going to change my character design. Hell, I've got long hair, 5'6" and now wear glasses. I was never being very accurate anyway.
Page 46
I'm not talking about a mouse. My mom loved this cartoon, but my sister just said, "Ew."
I got Jehovah's Witnesses at the door and realized the fastest way to get rid of them was to simply say, "Yes".
Page 47
I went to What The Hell Convention at Goucher College. Four of the girls were wearing t-shirts that I had brought; Invader Zim, Labyrinth, and Batman. I almost thought they had raided my luggage.
Page 48
My favorite part of this convention is the Geek Auction. You buy one dance with the boy you're bidding on, and the guys sometimes get dressed up as themes. It's a lot of fun.
Page 49
I ended up buying a lot of guys.
Page 50
The girl at my knee is actually a guy.
Page 51
I got a lung infection after the con. I still drew the comic strip, but I used Sharpie. This was the birth of the Plague Monkey.
Page 52
I have a thing for Asian guys. The background images in the third strip are all covers to the mini comics that I did about high school and college, all of which are available on my website.
Page 53
Some sneezes are just orgasmic. The background pictures are snapshots of the magnets that I made with glass beads.
Page 54
Never ask an EMS guy how his day was. These cartoons were drawn about two years ago. I know McDonalds defeats the purpose of exercising, but it's really the only reason for

exercising in the first place.

Page 55

They were $30 Hot Topic boots. The soles fell off of them. My mom asked me what I wanted for my birthday and I told her New Rock boots. They're very expensive, but I figure it's about time to invest.

Page 56

It took two months to soften the leather enough to get my foot in, and a solid year before they stopped hurting, but they're worth it.

Page 57

Yeah, I'm not good at sports and don't pretend to be.

Page 58

Nigel just wanted someone to drive with him, but I slept through the drive. Later, Nigel told me just how close to death we came.

Page 59

It was a really slow convention.

Page 60

Yeah, I'm a total letch at conventions.

Page 61

The guys who don't have their toys anymore are the ones who enjoyed them the most.

Page 62

I'm not exaggerating, fourteen cats. The smell was pretty extreme.

Page 63

They had fourteen cats, two ferrets, a rabbit, and a horny toad.

Page 64

A friend of mine has one of these giant rabbits. They're terrifying. The's at least three feet long. She could eat my face!

Page 65

I believe cats have very deep, philosophical thoughts like the answer to life, the universe, and everything.

Page 66

It's a very odd moment when you realize that someone in a comic shop is actually wearing deodorant. You think I'm exaggerating.

Page 67

I swear, a sushi place had a "Little Nemo Special". I almost didn't get the cartoon done that day because "Dragon's Bones" was so damn good. I have a webcomic and yet the computer is a total mystery to me.

Page 68

I mow the lawn. I do a good job. But then I have to do it again the very next week! It's just not fair.

Page 69

LAN parties will always be an oddity to me. So much testosterone.

Page 70

I leave a hickey ONCE in three years and he'll never let me forget it.

Page 71

I wore those boots that one night, and then I had Steph take them, because I knew that some day I'd think it would be a good idea to wear them again, despite barely surviving the first time.

Page 72

It's amazing what we'll do to ourselves for a cat call.

Page 73

I love renting kids out so you have an excuse to do all the fun kid things.

Page 74

I can only have one bite of those deep fried Snickers bars. They're good, but just so damn sweet. I don't know how my sister can do it—those kids wear me out.

Page 75

I swear those instruments were rusty.

Page 76

Okay, I left the door unlocked ONCE! But good GOD, it had electrical tape holding on the headlights!

Page 77

I didn't actually get a Vespa, but I looked into it. I decided that the neighborhood between my home and work was just a little too sketchy for me to be driving a scooter through it at 11pm.

Page 78

Seriously, $20 was still in the glove box, but the painting on cardboard was gone. That was just too cool.

Page 79

It's amazing what Chinese takeout can do for a bad week. Actually, the car was stolen the week before the convention. They found it, but it was in the car prison for the weekend of the convention. Needles to say, I was a very stressed puppy during my weekend of sleeping in a parking lot with some pirates.

Page 80
I didn't realize I was going to Michigan. That's kinda north of Georgia.

Page 81
These were the girls from aworldlikemyown. com They saved me. And they're seriously that short!

Page 82
I found out that they were local and dropped hints that I wanted to sleep on their couch. Little hints like, "Can I sleep on your couch?"

Page 83
I had never been to a Red Robin before. You have no idea how much I needed that Bailey's milkshake.

Page 84
This clubbing adventure actually took place in Philly at the next convention. I seriously had to unwrap a girl in the bathroom.

Page 85
The guys were being so silly I had to do a cartoon about it… wait, was this at Heroes Con? It might have been. I combine a lot of the cons, so I don't have to do cartoons saying "I'm home," "Now I'm gone!"

Page 86
That's really how I met Seth Green. I gave up on trying to get on the signing list and on my way out the door, I literally ran into him. I then mowed down three five-year-olds to give him my book.

Page 87
Yes, I danced like a monkey the whole way out of the convention and he was walking right behind me as I did so. I have no shame.

Page 88
My sisters came to Heroes Con.

Page 89
I finally came to terms with my Amazonian baby sister being hot…Sorta.

Page 90
I didn't go to Vermont to have lunch with my two best friends. If I did, though, we had this virtual conversation. Apparently DJ is inseparable from her sidearm now.

Page 91
Yes, of course I shaved my toes. I don't want the pedicure people handling my hobbit feet. I'd much rather have them handle stubbly feet. I didn't let him give me a foot massage

because then he'd touch my legs, and those were stubbly. Yes, I'm a freak in many different ways.

Page 92
I catch up on all my daytime television when I'm at the mechanics. My car also breaks down a lot.

Page 93
The comics in the window are Wet Moon and Ultra, which were done by classmates of mine from Savannah College of Art and Design; Striip Tease, which is a web comic done by my old roommate; and Neato People, which is the comic that the characters from Strip Tease work on. The other two are Sheena and Invincible. I just threw those two in because I love Invincible and Sheena has boobies.

Page 94
Yes, I assault my boyfriend and his cat with my monkey slippers.

Page 95
I had to go to the party because I had a blue satin 1980's prom dress covered in bows and lace. Yes, the squirrels were using the pans as mirrors, and it turns out that the pears aren't the kind that you can eat anyway.

Page 96
Breaking the panels in the third strip is something that I saw done in 9 chickweed lane.

Page 97
I've got my own webpage and I still think writing code is like trying to hammer a square into a circle. The monkey ninja pirate was inevitable.

Page 98
I never draw Will reading a book, (because he doesn't) but reading his phone, instead. He has a whole library on the thing. It's weird. In college my housemate, Chris, would stay up all night working on his web comic, Stripteasecomic.com, and I'd ask him if he was just up or still up.

Page 99
Yes, I tried it once. Just once.

Page 100
Betty would really wear outfits like that. She could do the voice of Bobby's mom (Minnesota) on cue. It was creepy. The second strip was actually another co-worker

who made the chocolate comment. The third strip happened word for word.

Page 101
Be afraid, be very afraid.

Page 102
Will got upset because the laptop that the fan sold me is better than his. I know next to nothing about technology and he's a tech geek.

Page 103
Arie's the artist of **www.aworldlikemyown. com.** She plays SCA and is just as bad with directions as I am.

Page 104
She also takes self defense.

Page 105
Most indie artists are very familiar with the midnight print run. Poor Arie was waaay too hung up on little things like cropping and having all the words on the flyer. I honestly thought it was a normal toy store that happened to be open at 1 AM

Page 106
It was my first time in a porn store. Dildos are illegal in Georgia, so our shops are kinda nasty. The ones up north are so pretty! The clerk had on a suit and showed me the Calvin and Hobbs tattoo he had on his arm.

Page 107
Carla Speed McNeil is my role model. She writes, draws, produces, prints, distributes, and advertises her own comic book; Finder. **www.lightspeedpress.com**

Page 108
I sat next to her for an hour before the guy came to take back his table, but not before I was interviewed by the Chicago Tribune.

Page 109
I don't know how to play video games. I'm pretty good at the first Mario Brothers. I played it when it first came out, and that's about it.

Page 110
I sat on a bench under the stairs at Dragon con handing out my card for three years. In 2006 the convention gave me a table… under the stairs.

Page 111
We played jelly bean Russian Roulette. Everyone takes one and we figure out who got the snot flavor by the look on their face.

Page 112
Characters found on this page are; Jessica Rabbit, Waldo, the Photo Gnome (he's an Atlanta thing). The Conan guy is a regular at Dragon con and the brunette is the husband who gave me the back rub. It wasn't until Dragon con 2006 that I actually got a leaf blower for the men in kilts.

Page 113
Bubba was supposed to have his own movie coming out, which is why he's wearing sun glasses; and the Pirate was supposed to have a part in the movie, which is why Bubba is standing in for him in these comics. I don't know what ever happened to the movie.

Page 114
Bubba's posing with two girls dressed as David Mack's Siamese twins from Kabuki.

Page 115
I don't make this stuff up.

Page 116
He was in standard porn positions; I just made up the part about the clamps and lube. IT's just the most random thing I could think of and I leave it up to the reader to make up the rest.

Page 117
There's a drum circle each night at Dragon con.

Page 118
That's Andy Lee in a David Mack "you don't know me" t-shirt. We never did find out if the couple in room 352 was arguing or having sex.

Page 119
The cat in all the strips is Pixel. She's a black cat, but that's a pain to draw, so she's usually just white. The customer seriously asked me this. I overheard the foreskin thing in Boston. I've blocked the rest of it out.

Page 120
I have a blurry camera phone picture of Darth Vader in my garage drilling.

Pages 121, 122
Will spent the whole week sitting in the beach house playing on his game boy.

Page 123
Aili's my redhead friend from first grade who got me into comics and drawing. DJ I met in middle school and she just gets more buff every time I see her.

Page 124
It took me three days to get used to DJ's boob size. She'd been a double D cup since middle school.

Page 125
I didn't make any of this up. Except the "what's in your pocket" happened in college when Lessa had me lay on the floor for a photo project.

Page 126
DJ's t-shirt says "breast inspector" and "I funked your girlfriend".

Page 127
We went to Toast in Boston and Christian Beranek from Silent Devil met us there and offered me a publishing contract.

Page 128
This was also the night that Lauren gave me my first sex toy. She was also the one who brought Christian to me, so she MUST be my fairy godmother.

Page 129
I took photos of DJ doing the Poi at the club for reference for these cartoons.

Page 130
I have a thing for effeminate, Asian men.

Page 131
DJ can only visit me in the winter so she doesn't get heat stroke, and I can only visit her in the summer so I don't freeze to death.

Page 132
I dress as Jill Thompson's Scary Godmother for Halloween each year: **www. jillthompsonart.com.**

Page 133
I only bake cookies once a year and that's for Thanksgiving. That's a lemon tree in their backyard that we make lemonade from for dinner. Gotta love Savannah.

Page 134
This was all word for word. Except the cat, I don't know what he was thinking.

Page 135
It was actually kind of hot that day, but I got so into wearing the scarf and hat and drinking hot chocolate that I forgot it wasn't cold.

Page 136
Lessa and Happy Goth went to the beach with me. We had fun being silly, They buried me in the sand and built boobs in the sand.

Page 137
Happy Goth had a kite shaped like a pirate ship. The only way to keep it up was to keep running.

Page 138
There was a kid next to us who wouldn't shut up. The girls gave me a mermaid body after we scared the kids with the "decapitated head on the beach" routine.

Page 139
Dolphins are great and all, but when you're in the "wilds" of the ocean and they get THAT close, then it's a bit creepy.

Page 140
The web comics cartoon was inevitable. We've all done it. Just one more strip and then bed, just one more, just…

Page 141
These strips were thought up while hiking with a friend and his dog.

Page 142
I'm not a big animal person and some of the girls I've met are psycho. I don't know how anyone can put up with some of us girls.

Page 143
All too often we overlook the meaning or nature of something because it's all dressed up.

Page 144
This is as close to politics as I'll get with my comic strips. I just don't understand how people can still be prejudiced to gays and women and… nope, I'm not getting political.

Page 145
I got a Jetta (it broke down three months later, and so I traded it in for my boyfriend's Scion). The flip key was the best part.

Page 146
It seems that everyone who grew up in the woods now have subdivisions over the next hill. My brother wore a leopard print, fuzzy, cowboy hat and matching gloves to Christmas Eve church service. We're Unitarians.

Page 147
My mom started the tradition of anatomically correct Christmas cookies. You should see her sand castles.

Page 148
After these strips, I got a sticker in the mail. It said "pigs are friends, not food". I grew up with pigs, they're fantastic pets. They're insanely smart. They're also delicious.

Page 149
When my brothers were 13 and 15 they were in Jamaica, and a bus hit the younger brother. As he lay there unconscious, my other brothers thoughts were "mom's gonna kill me." He came home with a band-aid on his chin and a great story. Later in life, this same brother broke his neck, flipped his truck twice, and likes to jump out of planes.

Page 150
Ever run down a hill and realize that you're just falling and barely keeping your feet under you? You know that you're an inch away from falling on your face. That's what doing a monthly comic book feels like.

Page 151
I'm industrious in the morning, but tend to slack off in the afternoon. Any time I go on a plane trip I end up watching CNN in the airport terminal. It's all apocalyptic news.

Page 152
Coffee makes me crazy.

Page 153
It drives me mad when people use "god bless" as a way of saying goodbye. They assume that you're the same relition. They'd go ape shit if someone told them to accept the goddess as their creator and savior.

Page 154
All these were conversations at What the Hell con in Guilford College… well, except for the vacuum thing.

Page 155
The fifth panel is Twinkie Bugs. Phillip, from Furmentation xodin.comicgenesis.com, makes them out of pez, pixie stixs, and a Twinkie.

Page 156
I was scared at first, but those college kids did amazing things with pinto beans and a microwave.

Page 157
He really is from Canada and they really had a section taped off for me.

Page 158
In the second comic strip the girls were howling like wolves (yes, those are supposed to be wolves) and I've got a jar of money with me. The monkey boy was so cute!

Page 159
I'm not making any of those conversations up.

Page 160
I honestly didn't know what a colonoscopy was, and I wish I never did find out. Apparently it's big in Japan. Without the scarves, then it's just not Harry Potter.

Page 161
That morning we were just talking about how gross it was that people were counting down until the Harry Potter girl was of age. Then these two guys, who were over 21, showed up dressed like that. Yes, I'm ashamed, but they were hot!

Page 162
The girl in the first panel talking does the comic agirlsandherfed.com The story of how indy got his scars was really good, but very long. I did ask Will before I did the hot Indy comics, and the guy's girlfriend e-mailed me to tell me she really liked them.

Page 163
Poor Will puts up with so much. Okay, so I drew one very big, detailed comic shop background and now, every time I draw the comic shop, I just paste in different parts of that background. It saves huge amounts of time.

Page 164
Yes, I was too tired to do a comic, so I did stick figures. This is one of my favorite comics that I've ever done. "My head is a giant egg" is a line from "The Animation Show".

Page 165
Yes, I still wear a retainer every other night. The guy beside us was really freaked out by how much fun we were having in those chairs.

Page 166
The Broad is an ex-girlfriend of Karl, who showed up as a zombie one dragon con.

Page 167
I had tape recorded the conversations at dinner that night to use for these comics, but couldn't for the life of me figure out what we were talkinga bout when The Broad delivered the two "you had to be there" lines.

Page 168
To this day, I will always rate the level of a night according to how much bail money is needed.

Page 169
I don't remember where I heard the "day pass" quote.
Page 170
Calling the cable company was one of the more infuriating twelve hours of my life.
Page 171
The tequila really did help.
Page 172
A co-worker really asked me this.
Page 173
I had forgotten all about going to the guy's party. I honestly couldn't remember being there. The sad thing is, I don't drink. I don't cook either. The smoke alarm goes off before the oven timer. Our third housemate has shown up in the comic all of two times in the three years that he's lived with us. He's quiet.
Page 174
This one might be a bit too much information, but my gynecologist had his eyes dilated. How can I NOT do a comic about that? And I was frustrated over calendar choices.
Page 175
My Fairy Godmother/editor hangs out with the hottest comic guys in the industry. I've also been meaning to do a comic for a long time where she takes that wig off. She never wears it anymore. Plus, it's a pain in the butt to draw. Somehow, during that weekend, Andy Lee mentioned that the ultimate love was tauntaun love. A tauntaun is that thing in Star Wars that Hans shoves Luke into to keep him warm. Andy's a strange, strange man.
Page 176
I got that jelly stuff all over my lap too. There's a picture of Nigel begging for the rum devilspanties.keenspot.com/mega06.html
Page 177
Found porn is when you find a toy that was not meant to be pornographic, but is very much so. Just like the vibrating teletubbies.
Page 178
The guy that bought me sushi was also at Dragon con lamenting the lack of Parfait with the Conan looking dude.
Page 179
To this day, I have yet to get someone who is dressed as Darth Vader to say, "I'm a pretty, pretty princes".
Page 180
Strawberry lemonade is the tastiest stuff ever.
Page 181
Anime cons are usually packed with little girls in very skimpy costumes. As a result, there are also some creepy guys lurking about. Some friends and I decided there should be a "conscience rental service". The Conscience would be a big burly man who would walk around with the little jailbait girls. Most conventions you try and fit as many people as possible in one hotel room (because the glamorous life of a comic artist doesn't pay much) and there's usually beer involved.
Page 182
When my sister saw David Mack she told me that she didn't see why I kept going on about him. Then she went to talk to him and he gave her one of his dazzling smiles and crossed his fabulous arms and she couldn't remember what she had meant to say to him.
Page 183
www.girlswithslingshots.com is a fantastic comic. The creator, Danielle Corsetto, can say the most shocking things with the cutest giggle.
Page 184
My neck hurt that entire weekend. A friend did some terrifying contortion things to me, and it did feel better. But mostly I felt fear.
Page 185
My baby sister is fabulously silly.
Page 186
Summer can belch at will. She told me about how she had started dancing to some music one booth was playing. Other people started dancing too. One man yelled to her if fries came with her shake, but it was the rather large gentleman next to her who answered.
Page 187
Mike found me at a later convention and said that he thought this cartoon was funny.
Page 188
My mother DROVE the short bus.
Page 189
Of all the people in my family, the baby is the most outgoing.
Page 190
The first strip is out of an exact conversation.

When one of the babies rolled over you could see part of its leg or arm. Really really creepy.

Page 191
They had a Snoopy theme for the room. The paintings in the comic are pictures of what I did on the wall. The second panel is Starry Night with Snoopy.

Page 192
We take a very leisurely attitude towards out mountain walks.

Page 193
Crowds were forming to watch the deer on the mountain in Georgia, but at my family's house in Virginia, we have to honk at them to get them out of the way on our drive down the driveway.

Page 194
He made deep fried sausage. It was heavenly.

Page 195
The pictures in the background are of our second cat who passed away, my Darth Vader helmet, and the batman utility belt that I got for my birthday.

Page 196
It's fun having your own reality to mess with.

Page 197
Actually, the grandmother said that at the dinner table. The Intern told us about it later.

Page 198
Christi did do her version of this conversation on her webcomic **www.inthedpuddle.com**

Page 199
That's how Nigel and I greet each other. What's a little groping between friends?

Page 200
The dangly bits conversation took place outside of a convention party in Philly.

Page 201
That's how Nigel picked up a long time girlfriend.

Page 202
I thanked them for the Mountain Dew, but saved the Red Bull for later.

Page 203
I honestly have no idea what that girl was talking about.

Page 204
Kevin Smith had stopped by the hotel bar at one of the cons, but had to leave because he was quickly getting mobbed.

Page 205
Heroes con, 2004 was the first convention that I had a table at. I hadn't sold a single comic yet, and that's when I heard of Gravy Boy.

Page 206
At What The Hell con, run by Guilford College in North Carolina, the artists of Gravy Boy and I decided that we should be each other's nemesis. Ever since then, they cover my table with their books every time I leave it unguarded and I throw pixy sticks at them.

Page 207
I did trip over a long box while chasing one of the Gravy Boy creators back to my booth when he saw that I wasn't guarding it.

Page 208
I kept going back to check on the boots.

Page 209
Roller derby is very fun. The girls are tomboys and great friends with each other, but will tear apart other teams of women.

Page 210
That's exactly what the little blond girl said to me.

Page 211
Going to the bathroom in roller skates was the most terrifying experience of my life.

Page 212
I'll wait until Will's done, and then finish his meal. He hates it when I do this because he says it makes him look cheep.

Page 213
I've chased after fire flies all my life. I've never thought of it this way until Will pointed it out.

Pages 214, 215
This is word for word how Will got his car.

Pages 216, 217
I loved my old Neanderthal Cell phone. It was indestructible. But my flying monkey can record cartoon ideas and take reference pictures and keeps my convention schedule. Unfortunately, it also sometimes decides that it doesn't feel like doing what I ask it to.

Page 218
Will really did go on about how technologically advanced the phone was and then began to play solitaire on it.

Page 219
Ironically enough, this comic strip went up the day the Pinky and the Brain DVD came out.

Page 220
The second Pirates of the Caribbean had just come out.

Page 221
His accent was Scottish and made me melt.

Page 222
This was at Connecticon 2006

Page 223
The guy who won the auction asked me to put his brother in the comic strip instead of himself.

Page 224
I got to share a booth with Sluggy at San Diego Con. He had a PILE of plushies. They were soooo soft.

Page 225
Will said that if the house was burning down and it came down to me, the cat, and his car, he said that the car would be outside already, I could get out on my own, and he'd grab the cat.

Page 226
The framed artwork in the background is the cover art to other DP books.

Page 227
I get super stupid when I geek out. These strips are from San Diego con of 2006.. I got to share a booth with Sluggy, Partially clips, Super Frat, and Fragile Gravity.

Page 228
Whenever there's a guy with one of those circle with the bar across it shirts, that's Chris Daily from **www.stripteasecomic. com.** He overheard the conversation of the man on the cell phone and when I posted this cartoon, I got an e-mail saying it was something from a video game. That scares me.

Page 229
Every time I try to show my high tech phone off to someone, it breaks.

Page 230
Based on my "convention humanitarian" strip, someone dressed as a pirate and handed out soap at DragonCon.

Page 231
The women I was sharing a hotel room with introduced me to Bailey's in coffee.

Page 232
We were in the hallway between Artist Alley and the dealer's room at Dragon con. It was a prime traffic spot. In the background of the second strip you can see where the "real" artist alley is.

Page 233
One of the women who I was staying with overheard this on an elevator. No, that's not my pirate. He's just one of many Jack Sparrow costumes at Dragon Con. He even had a jar of sand from the second movie.

Page 234
I've been doing cartoons about it for years, but Dragon con 2006 was the first time that I actually went out and got a cordless, battery operated leaf blower and really did go Kilt Hunting. There's a calendar. It's on my website store.

Page 235
My thighs hurt the next day and I didn't know why. Though, that's not uncommon for Dragon con.

Page 236
One of these days we're going to have a fairy game hunt at Dragon con.

Page 237
I really do fan girl all over my fans.

Page 238
This woman is seriously 6'3" and has an L cup. Her boyfriend is hot. She has trouble with fan girls sniffing around after him, though.

Page 239
In panel one can you find; Storm trooper, storm trooper pimp, barbarian, flaming carrot, overweight trekkie, Waldo, a fairy, and a geisha? There's also Eon Flux, Cowboy Bebop, Cutter, Screamer, Sims girl, and gothic ball couple; but those aren't as recognizable.

Page 240
I just love my stick men. The one guy's eye is getting bigger and bigger.

Page 241
Gravyboy had a really hard time getting into the convention. They're my nemesis. They blamed me. In the background of the second to last panel Christi has found the Spaghetti Monster.

Page 242
It doesn't take much to get Blue Beards kilt up.

Page 243
The contact Drinking didn't happen to me, I was just told the story.

Page 244
Christi did find a squashed toy frog in the parking lot.

Page 245
I didn't punch the Haunted House worker, but I have worked in houses and known people who have gotten hit. I was close though. If you get in my face and scare me, my natural reaction is to defend myself. I got an angry letter from a Haunted House worker saying that it wasn't funny.

Page 246
The house we went to was Nether World in Atlanta. It was SO cool and detailed and so much work went into the decoration. I wanted to go back through with the lights on just so I could admire the art.

Page 247
It was actually Happy Goth who got separated from our group and was clinging to a random guy the whole time.

Page 248
Some of the monsters would chase me and I'd yell, "oh crap, oh crap" and they'd yell it too while they chased me.

Page 249
Lessa really did smell the chainsaw before we saw it. When he jumped down behind us she dragged me down the hall so fast I was bouncing off the walls.

Page 250
This little girl actually said that. And she was in the best Batgirl outfit too. My reply was "Well, I can't say I miss him."

Pages 251-253
I spent a solid week working on that sink.

Page 254
Life makes no sense.

Page 255
This is a story Aaron told me at a convention. The newspaper reporters got to the scene and the headline that printed the next day was "Jesus and Death were walking down the street at 3am".

Page 256
Happy Goth and her husband really do fence.

Page 257
The cat belongs to Will. I'm ambivalent to all animals.

Page 258
We play the leaning game.

Page 259
I think human beings are compelled to have companions so that someone can get those hard to reach places on our backs.

Page 260
Deep fried food sends me into a coma. Will has a deep fryer.

Page 261
Will's sister had twin boys.

Page 262
It's not Thanksgiving without a deep fried critter.

Page 263
I have a confession… I'm a sucker for kids. I just like to give them back too.

Page 264
Will's sister's cat meows really loud.

Page 265
Happy Goth's husband used to do a week long geek scavenger hunt in college. They'd do things like build a working wind mill or solve huge math problems. He'd also played with power tools after four days of no sleep.

Page 266
I did a vampire comic for an online magazine. These are the comics.

Page 267
Another "Famous Last Words" from the geek scavenger hunt. He had five car batteries connected to a wire, and I think he might have touched it at one point.

Page 268
I like putting the vampire family portraits in the background.

Page 269
The pictures on the wall are of literary vampires. One is an actual portrait of Vlad the Impaler and another is a snapshot of the Munsters.

Page 270
I keep a battle axe with my umbrella by the door too. There's a family picture in the background with Val as a preschool dork.

Page 271
I did some sketches for a creepy uncle, but he never showed up.

USE THE GRID TO DRAW THE GIRLS

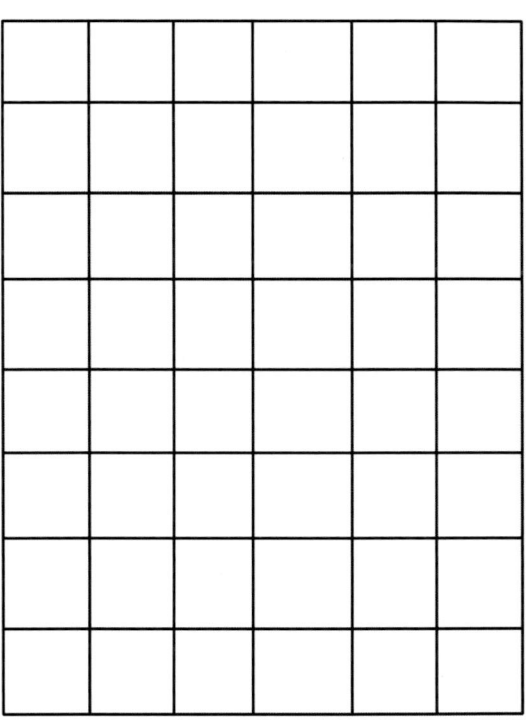

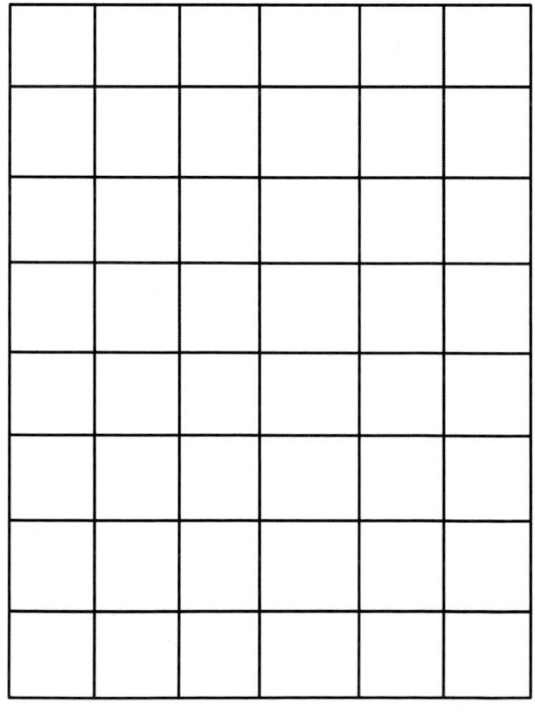

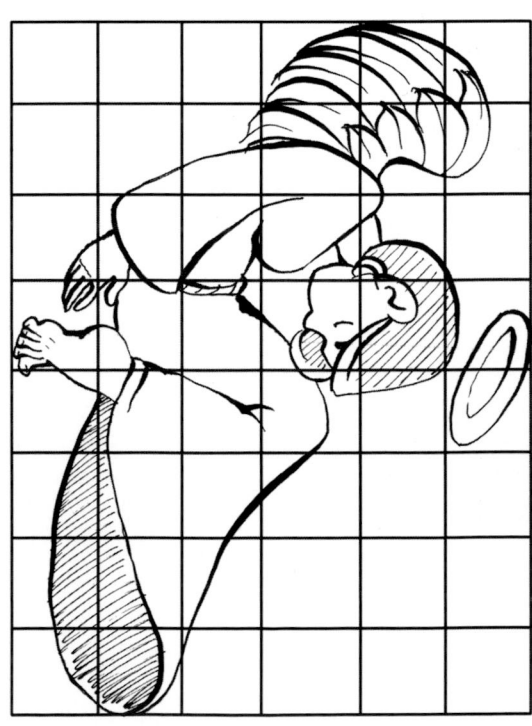

WHO SAID WHAT?

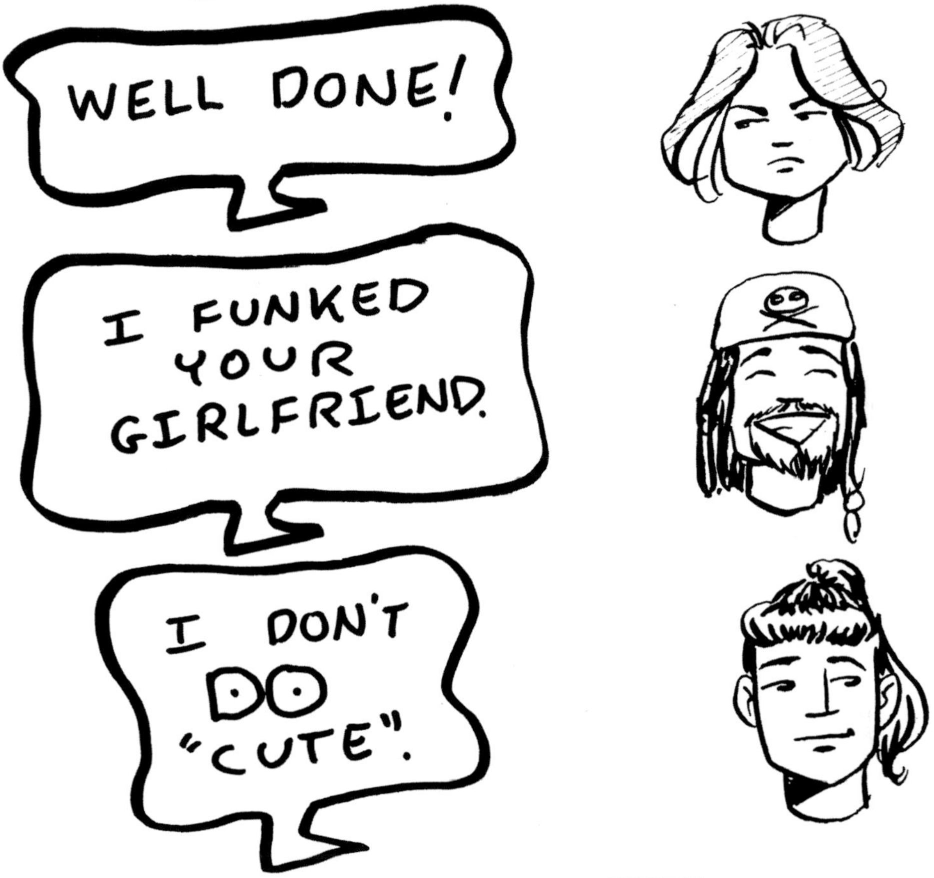
WELL DONE!
I FUNKED YOUR GIRLFRIEND.
I DON'T DO "CUTE".

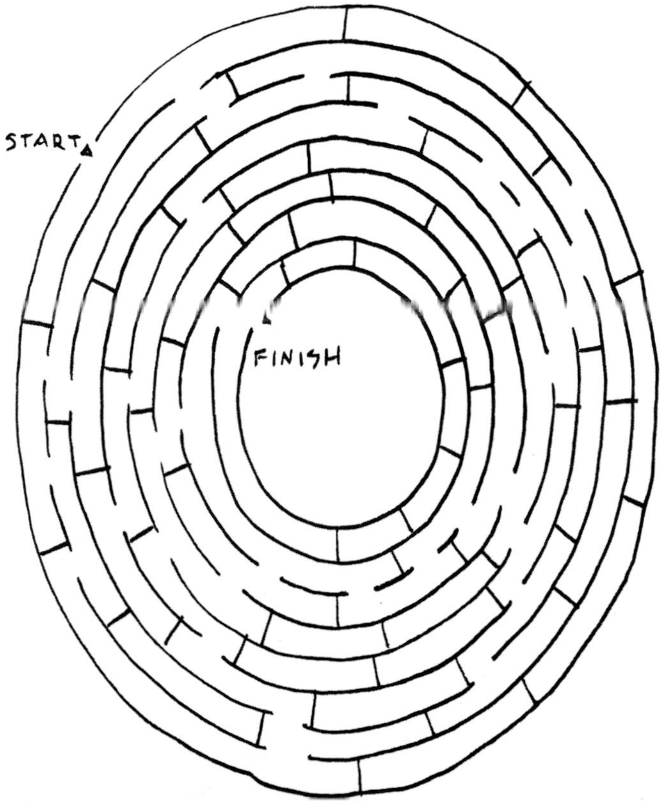
START
FINISH

MLAFE OTBSO _____ _____

OI NOVC NNTE _____

LVEIDS NPAITSE _____ _____

GLUEAP KOYMNE _____ _____

RETIAP _____

MATCH UNSCRAMBLED WORDS WITH IMAGE

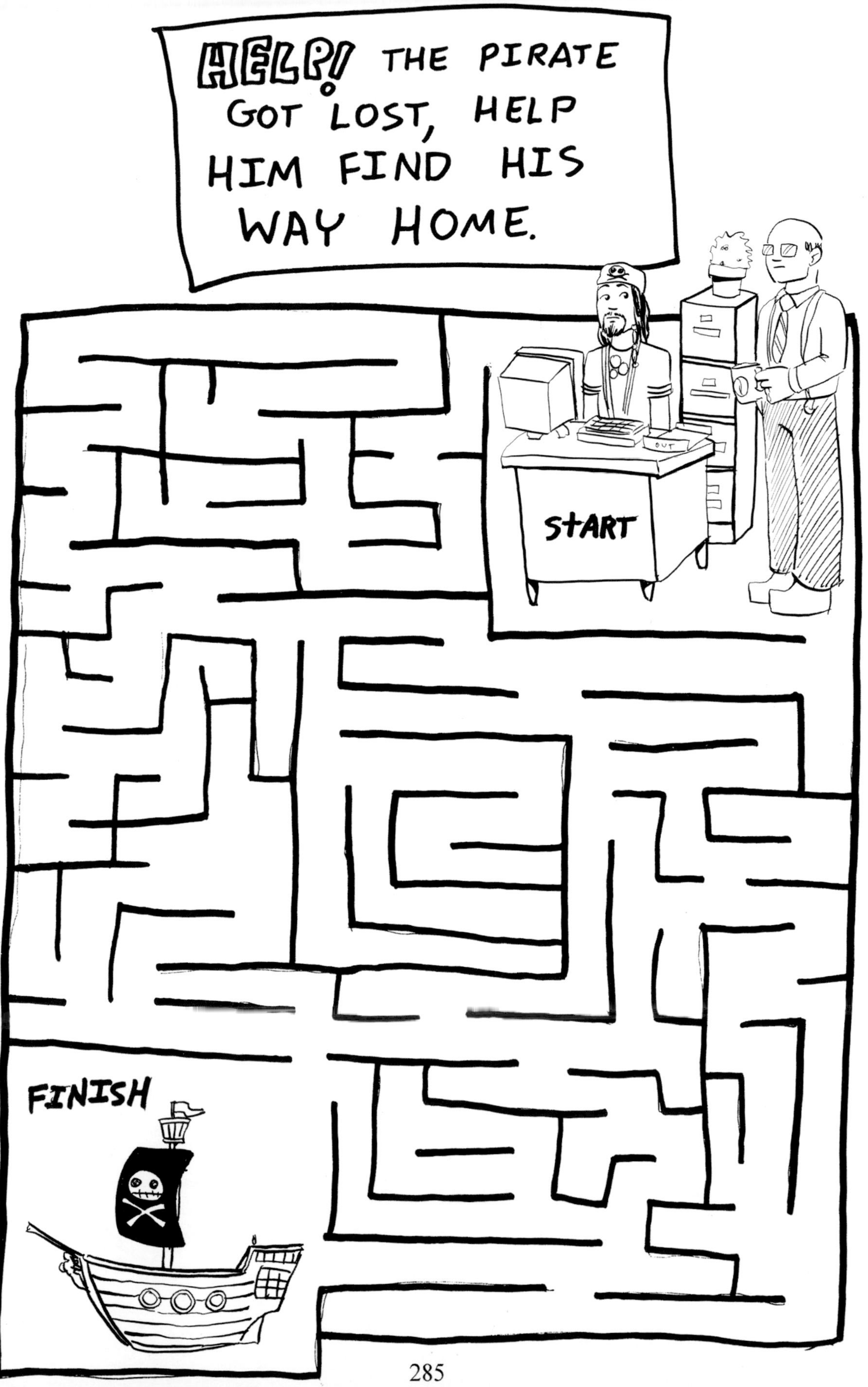
HELP! THE PIRATE GOT LOST, HELP HIM FIND HIS WAY HOME.
START
OUT
FINISH

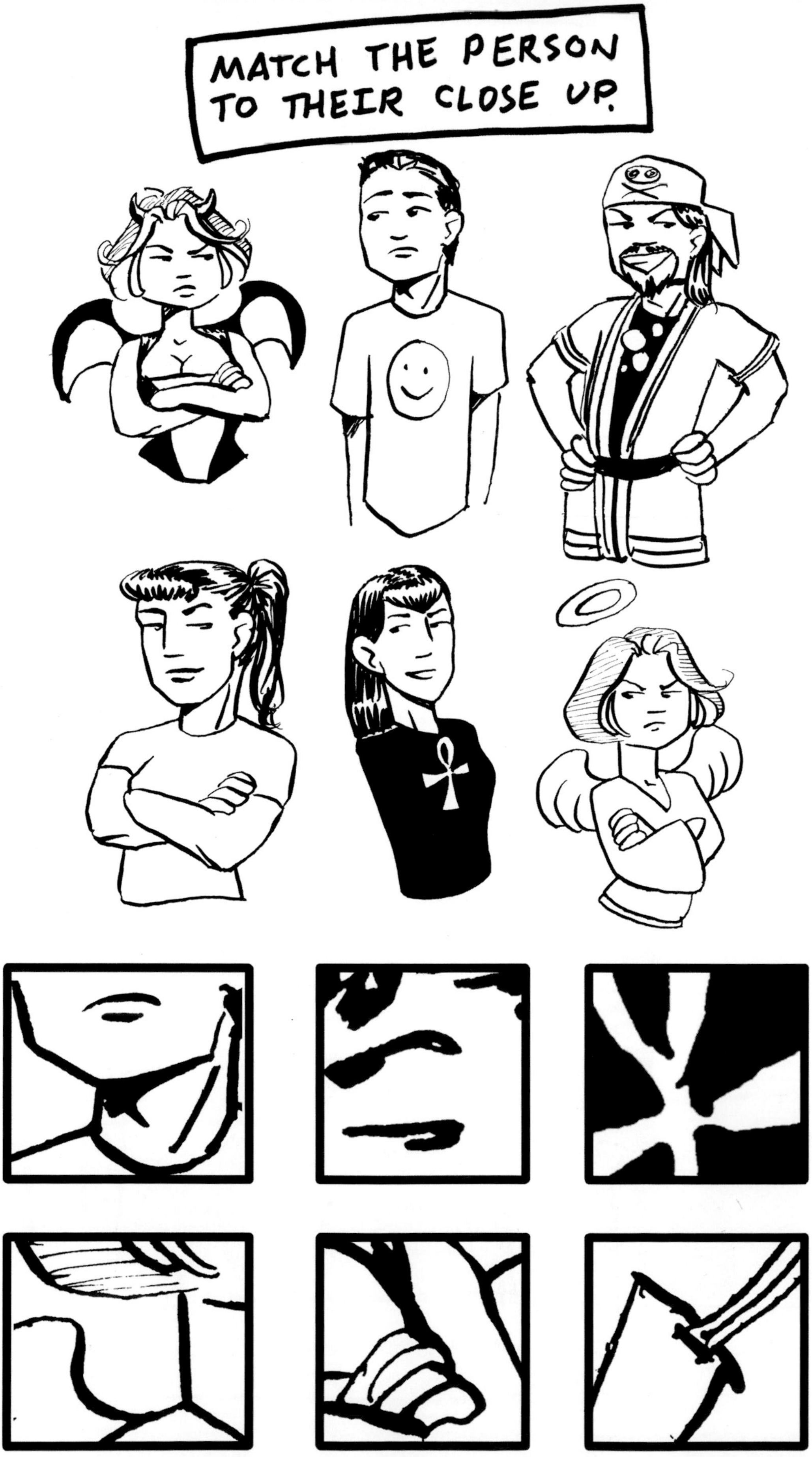
MATCH THE PERSON
TO THEIR CLOSE UP.

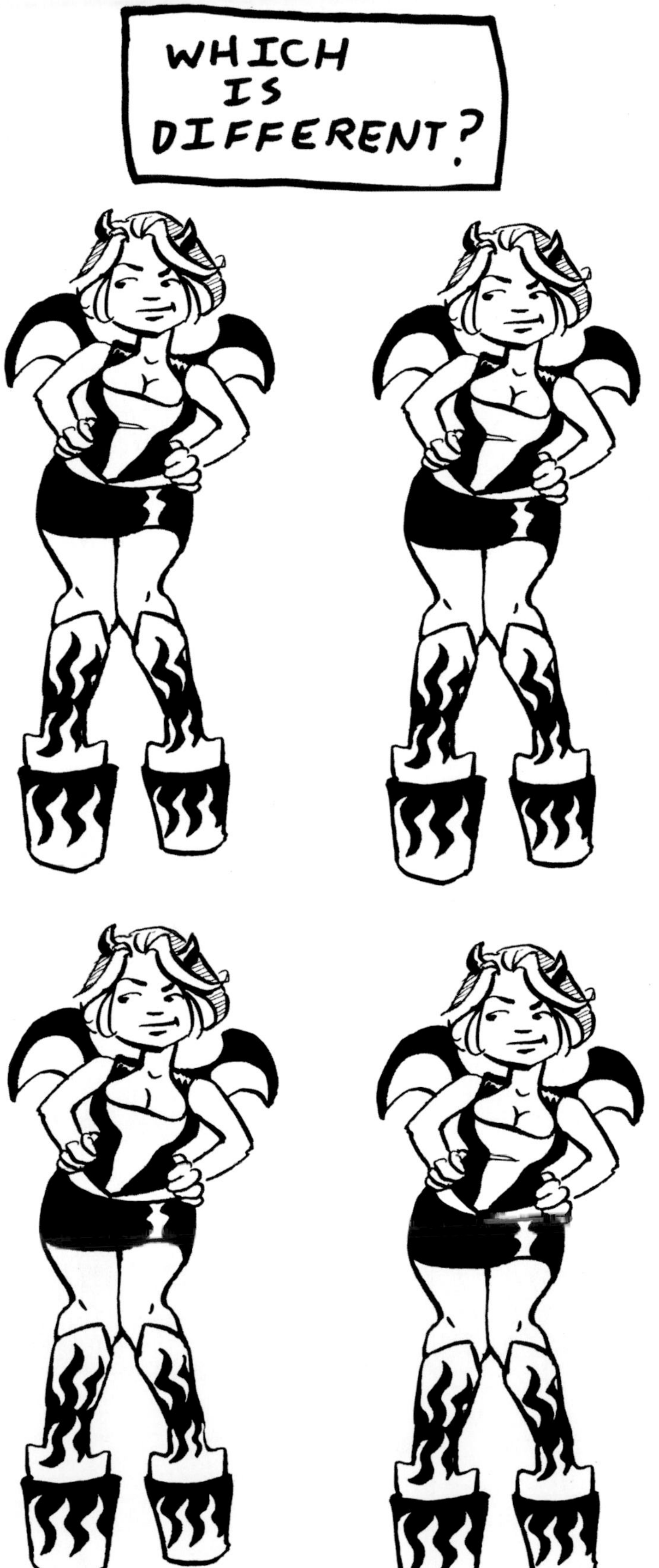
WHICH IS DIFFERENT?

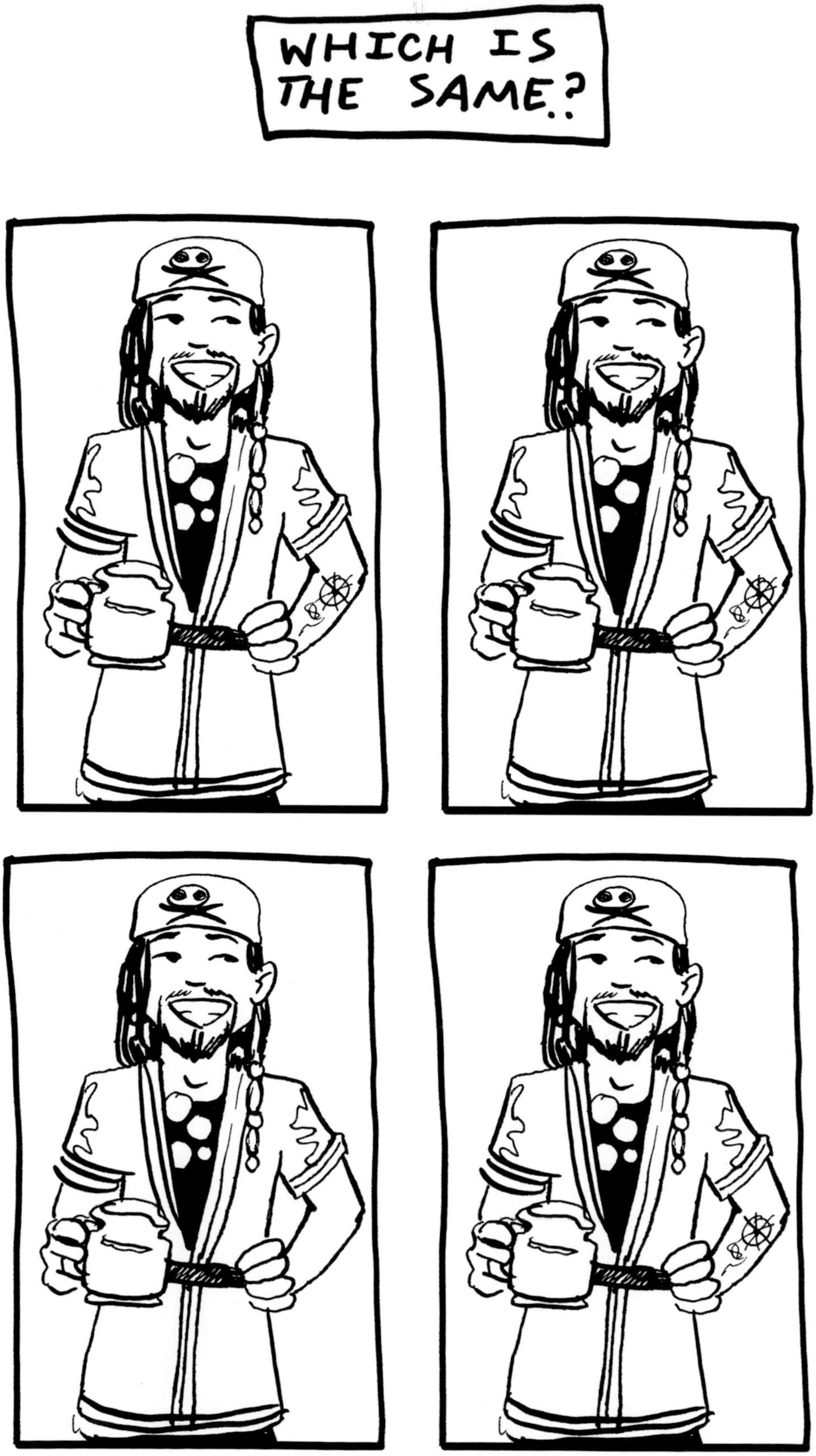
WHICH IS THE SAME.?

UNSCRAMBLE

$\overline{1}\,\overline{2}\,\overline{3}\,\overline{4}\,\overline{5}\,\overline{6}$ $\overline{1}\,\overline{7}\,\overline{8}\,\overline{9}\,\overline{10}\,\overline{11}\,\overline{12}\,\overline{12}$

AHDRT DAVER

$\overline{}\,\overline{}\,\overline{7}\,\overline{}\,\overline{}$ $\overline{}\,\overline{}\,\overline{}\,\overline{}\,\overline{2}$

ELMAF OTBOS

$\overline{}\,\overline{}\,\overline{}\,\overline{}\,\overline{11}$ $\overline{}\,\overline{}\,\overline{}\,\overline{}\,\overline{12}$

LAELBT KRSIT

$\overline{}\,\overline{}\,\overline{}\,\overline{}\,\overline{}\,\overline{}$ $\overline{}\,\overline{}\,\overline{3}\,\overline{4}$

TIUYITL LBTE

$\overline{}\,\overline{}\,\overline{8}\,\overline{}\,\overline{6}$ $\overline{}\,\overline{}\,\overline{5}$

NPKI

$\overline{1}\,\overline{9}$

NEFAICFE

$\overline{}\,\overline{}\,\overline{}\,\overline{}\,\overline{}\,\overline{}\,\overline{}\,\overline{}$
$\overline{10}$

MATCH THE CHARACTER
TO THEIR LOGO

289

ANSWERS

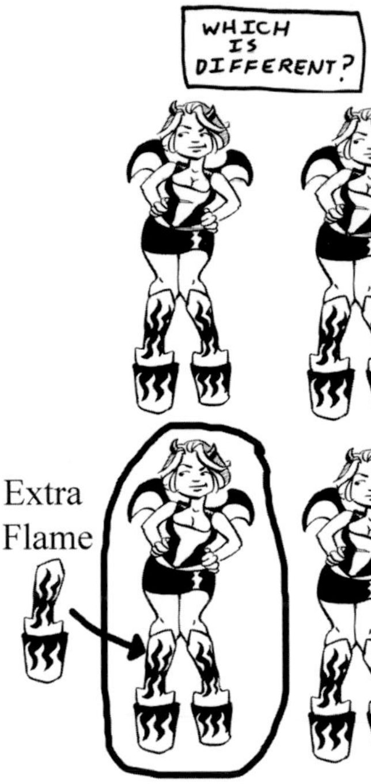
WHICH IS DIFFERENT?
Extra Flame

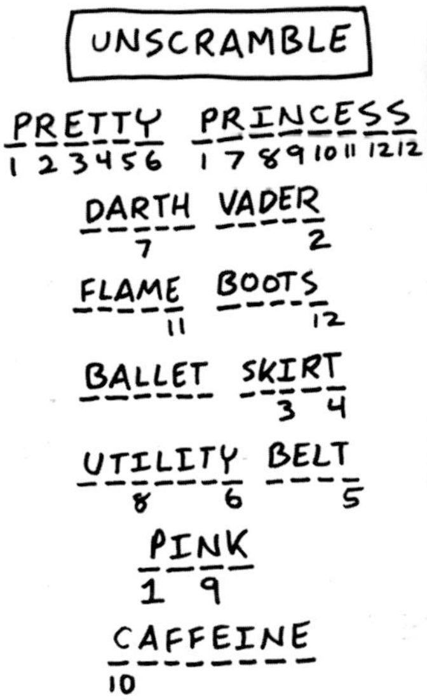
UNSCRAMBLE
PRETTY PRINCESS
1 2 3 4 5 6 1 7 8 9 10 11 12 12
DARTH VADER
7 2
FLAME BOOTS
11 12
BALLET SKIRT
3 4
UTILITY BELT
8 6 5
PINK
1 9
CAFFEINE
10

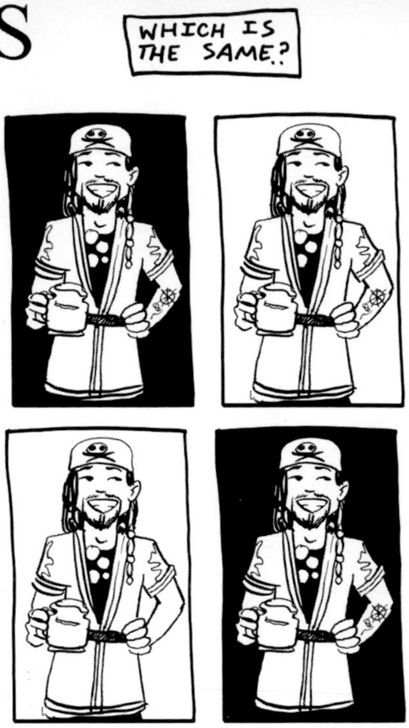
WHICH IS THE SAME?

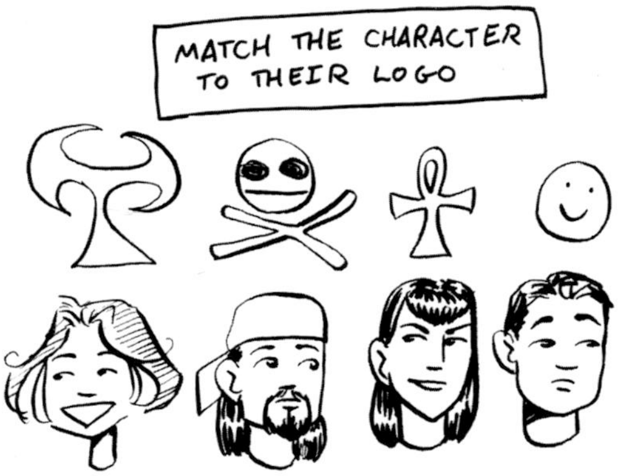
MATCH THE CHARACTER TO THEIR LOGO

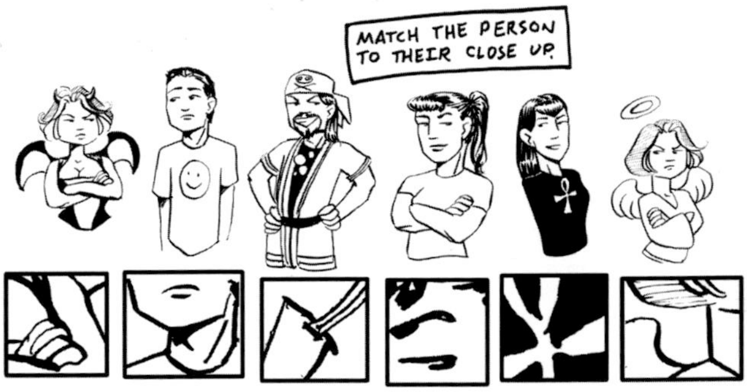
MATCH THE PERSON TO THEIR CLOSE UP

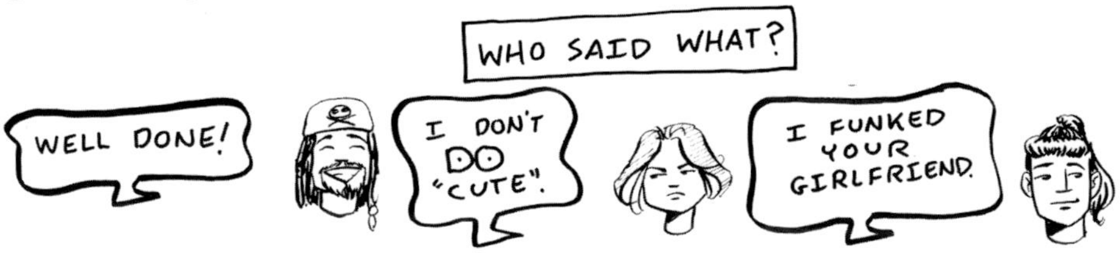
WHO SAID WHAT?
WELL DONE!
I DON'T DO "CUTE".
I FUNKED YOUR GIRLFRIEND.

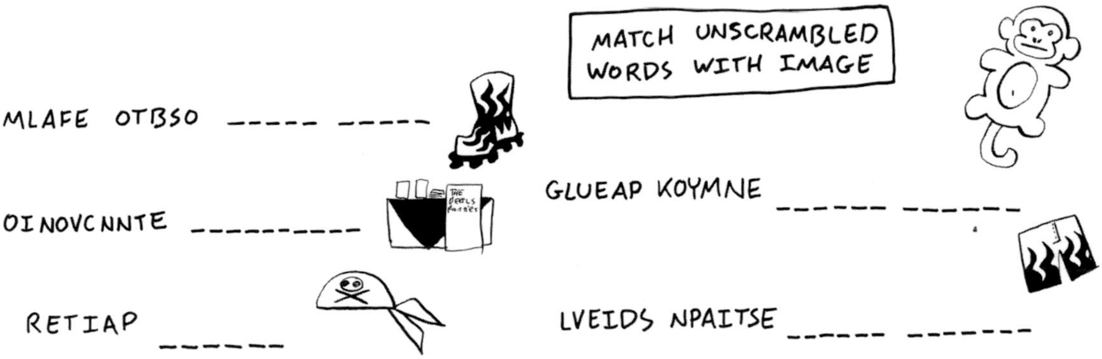
MATCH UNSCRAMBLED WORDS WITH IMAGE
MLAFE OTBSO _____ _____
OINOVCNNTE __________
RETIAP ______
GLUEAP KOYMNE ______ ______
LVEIDS NPAITSE ______ _______

ABOUT THE AUTHOR:

By day, she's a comic shop register monkey and by night she's a raving lunatic with a webcomic. That's what you get when you have a degree from Savannah College of Art and Design in Sequential Art (comic books). Graduates from art college usually begin their careers with food service or retail. Knowing this, Jennie Breeden began a webcomic so that she could retain some shred of art in her daily life (that, and she wanted fanmail). She resides in Atlanta and terrorizes the customers of the local comic shop and schemes her next attack against her rival: her boyfriend's cat.